Broadcasting
Research
Methods

Broadcasting Research Methods

Joseph R. Dominick
The University of Georgia

James E. Fletcher
The University of Georgia

Allyn and Bacon, Inc.
Boston   London   Sidney   Toronto

Library of Congress Cataloging in Publication Data
Main entry under title:

Broadcasting research methods.

Includes bibliographies and indexes.
1. Television broadcasting—Research—Addresses, essays, lectures. I. Dominick, Joseph R. II. Fletcher, James E.
PN1992.45.B76   1984   384.55'4072   84–18404
ISBN   0–205–08307–2

Series editor: Bill Barke
Consulting editor: Robert Avery
Production Administrator: Jane Schulman
Editorial-Production Services: Grace Sheldrick, Wordsworth Associates
Designer: Valerie Ruud
Cover Coordinator: Christy Rosso
Cover Designer: Robert Northrup

Printed in the United States of America.

10 9 8 7 6 5 4 3 2 1   90 89 88 87 86 85

Preface   ix

Introduction   1

Contents

Preface

Broadcasting Research Methods is a collection of original essays intended as an opening argument as to the nature and extent of broadcast research. In preparing this book, we recognized an outstanding body of writing and research directed toward the common purpose of better understanding the social and industrial nature of radio, television, and cable. We have been pleased that throughout the gestation of *Broadcasting Research Methods*, our contributors remained committed to this collection and also to their own contributions to this growing area of scholarly endeavor.

We are grateful to our contributors for their continued support of *Broadcasting Research Methods*. We appreciate the encouragement of our series editor, Bill Barke, and his co-workers at Allyn and Bacon; and of Robert K. Avery of the University of Utah, consulting editor. Our thanks also to Grace Sheldrick of Wordsworth Associates, who served as our managing editor.

We received considerable assistance in manuscript preparation from Barbara Fletcher and Susan Walter.

Through periods of alternating despair and euphoria over the life of this undertaking, we have been sustained by the patience and good humor of our wives, Joan Dominick and Barbara Fletcher.

To all of these people and to the many colleagues and students who acted as sounding boards and advisers, we are most appreciative.

J. R. D.
J. E. F.

Introduction

This collection of original essays deals with research method — procedures frequently used by researchers of the mass media, especially of radio and television. The intended readers are graduate students, advanced undergraduates, and researchers.

The essays fall easily into at least two categories — those dealing with techniques for conducting research and those focusing on particular research problems, enumerating the various ways each problem has been addressed by the research reported in the literature. Within this second group of essays the research problems reviewed include those of primarily theoretical orientation and those oriented to the solution of applied problems. Applied problems are those of communicating organizations, such as an instructional television consortium or a commercial radio network.

Theoretical problems are of a more abstract nature, aimed at deriving guiding principles to explain a variety of specific communication settings or to predict the outcome of communication undertakings.

Neither the theoretical nor applied subcategory is exclusive of the other, since theory enriches applied research, and the study of applied communication settings frequently bears rich theoretical fruit. Many research designs used in studying the electronic media are designs developed especially for theoretical research; the experiment is an instance. At the same time, theories in the communication field either are or will be tied to more general theoretical formulations of human behavior; such connections are inevitable and desirable.

Procedures and Techniques

The first three essays, by Wurtzel, Schreibman, and Carroll, deal with content analysis. Content analysis as a technique is frequently associated with study of the mass media, since the most extensive and dramatic uses of it have been in studies of the media. Wurtzel provides an overview of content analysis, summarizing its history, enumerating the assumptions in which it is rooted, and noting its principal virtues and shortcomings.

Schreibman provides an important service for those who wish to discover an historic basis of comparison in studies of the electronic media. As she notes, there are only a handful of archives in the United States and Canada where a significant number of television programs have been preserved — significant enough to provide the basis for careful study. These archives are currently in a state of foment; many are new; others are now recognizing the value of the television recordings they possess. Few works have yet been published in which the systematic examination of these archived materials has been the research method. Schreibman provides a catalog of the television archives, their principal holdings, and their procedures for accrediting and assisting scholars.

One of the most active areas of content analysis of the electronic media has been the analysis of news — news coverage both of specific events and of particular individuals and countries, and prominent characteristics of the news. Carroll provides both a thorough guide to the present literature and practical advice to the would-be researcher involved in content analysis of news programming.

Following these three essays on content analytic method and procedures are seven essays that connect research procedures developed in related disciplines to the study of particular problems in radio and television. Hocking, for example, provides an excellent synthesis of attitude measurement techniques. Attitude is an important if not preeminent concern in social psychology and also finds broad application in the study of the media. Attitudes are measures in the testing of mass media messages and in the assessment of the effects of a media message on the public.

Lull provides insights into the important contribution of anthropology, with its participant observation methods, to the study of media consumption patterns and to the study of the meaning of the media presence in our homes. Ethnographic studies provide rich data from relatively limited numbers of families,

particularly useful in setting in better perspective other research about the impact of media on our lives. Ethnographic technique is also useful in generating new formulations for study and in establishing generalizations.

Fletcher thoroughly reviews the various physiological variables used to study the mass media. He shatters two heresies about such measurement: that they are impossible to interpret and that they are inevitably connected to emotion. He argues persuasively for interpreting physiological indices as indicators of the state of central nervous processing of communication.

It is an old saw that the economics of the media determine their direction. It is a relatively new idea that the media should be studied with the same tools economists use to study other businesses and institutions. Litman introduces the tools of economics as they might be applied to media industries.

In marketing, segmentation is a first step in developing strategy for selling and distributing a product or service. Applying well-established segmentation procedures to the problems of broadcasting, cable, and satellite communications is relatively new. Gutman provides a balanced and informative view of the state of the art in audience segmentation.

Dominick addresses the thorny issue of establishing proof of causal relationships among a set of measured variables. He discusses at some length path analysis, a process for comparing various possible causal chains to see which is best supported by the data collected in a study.

Wimmer reviews the form and uses of models in developing and understanding research. Too few models in any form are regularly used in broadcasting research, and Wimmer's discussion amounts to a call for action. The benefits that accrue to the judicious use of explanatory and predictive models are well documented here.

Policy research is designed to provide a basis for decisions about the future direction of an institution or of a campaign. Prisuta introduces the policy environment of the United States Federal government, revealing both the interest in and reaction to social science research in particular. He argues strongly for a greater role for the researcher in the evolution of government policies.

Bowes provides insight into a line of research undertaken for its portent for policy. The communication of public institutions should respond to the needs of their constituencies with communication, according to the premise of much of this research. Bowes chronicles the development of this reasoning and its elaboration in research.

Theoretical and Applied Research Families

Seven essays deal with theoretical perspectives on the electronic media. Williams's essay on agenda setting, for example, is an extension of work in anthropological, sociological, and political scientific research into the role or charters of the institutions within a society. Agenda setting maintains that the media's role is to determine the priority of concerns for both public and private discourse. Williams concisely reviews both the procedures and consequences of research into agenda setting.

The uses and gratifications approach provides an extension of the functional perspective currently present in nearly all of the social sciences. A functional definition of some part of our lives says that a thing is best understood by how we use it. Rubin traces the beginnings of this relatively young approach to the analysis of the media, mapping both the principal research procedures involved and the seminal studies in the field.

Gross and Morgan, writing about television and enculturation, are concerned with the ways that television, in particular, helps us to become who we are as members of our own groups and as members of the larger society. According to this perspective, television helps formulate the terms in which we conceive our world.

Signorielli discusses the use of violence indices in television programming. This research provides important inputs to the process of policy formation both for the nation's producers of programs and for the entrepreneurs who bring them into our homes. But it is important also for its stimulation and contribution to theories of individual development and enculturation.

Meyer and Hexamer review research directed at assessing the media's role in children's lives. Much of this work has been undertaken for its potential policy impact on television for children and on television advertising directed toward children. It also has more general benefits in helping to understand the evolving role of nurturing children both by parents and by the institutions that society provides for the young. The special problems of conducting research with child informants and respondents are discussed as well.

Busby expands on one particular concern raised in many discussions of television and children, that the media prescribe sex-roles for both children and adults that are confining and inequitable. Research into sex-role stereotypes in the media has provided important insights into media practices that may unintentionally perpetuate the injustices of unfair distribution of opportunity within society.

Studies of television composition inform the producer and director of the role of various production variables and also contribute to our understanding of the screen's aesthetics. Metallinos provides a thorough review and critique of the available literature and suggests useful research directions for the future.

Bittner and Carroll reveal the application of research to the development and management of media programs with instructional and informational goals. They discuss the systematic development of materials.

It is true that, as with any collection of essays, this collection has not exhausted all possible subjects for essays on research in a burgeoning field of study—the electronic media. On the other hand, it is hoped that these clear and authoritative statements by some of the most productive workers in the field, with enthusiasm and with extensive citations, will incline scholar or student to find the path to other exciting research challenges in this field.

I
Techniques for Conducting Research

Content analysis is one of the most widely used research techniques for understanding and evaluating broadcast messages. A review of mass communication research reveals hundreds of content analysis studies that have been conducted and reported in the literature over the past few years.[1] Yet content analysis is also potentially one of the most misused and misunderstood research techniques. It therefore is important to understand how content analysis is conducted, how to interpret the studies, what the results of content analysis can tell us, and, just as important, what the results *cannot* tell us about communication messages.

What Is Content Analysis?

Bernard Berelson's classic definition of content analysis is: "a research technique for the objective, systematic, and quantitative description of the manifest content of communication."[2] George Gerbner elaborates further, stating: "The purpose of any content analysis is to illuminate or otherwise make apparent possible inferences about something that is not otherwise apparent."[3]

According to Davis, content analysis originally developed from journalism studies conducted on newspapers. Since words or column inches were easily counted, it was not difficult to quantify the way newspapers reported the news. Researchers quickly applied these techniques to a variety of print media and subsequently to investigations of television and radio broadcasts.[4]

As an example of a typical content analysis study, assume a researcher is interested in studying how women are depicted in television commercials. (See the essay by Linda J. Busby in this volume.) Obviously, the enormous number of commercials would make any subjective evaluation unreliable and highly suspect. We can only begin systematically and objectively to understand how women are shown in television commercials by establishing specific criteria for counting and categoriz-

1
Review of Procedures Used in Content Analysis

Alan Wurtzel

ing the various ways they are portrayed. Then we can examine the frequency of occurrence for each category and draw some conclusions from the results.

Content analysis is sometimes called message analysis, because what we are really interested in learning about are the messages received by the audience. Many of these messages are purposive or, to use Berelson's term, *manifest*. In other words, these are messages expressly designed to be communicated to the audience. The issues contained in political speeches broadcast on television, the themes used in dramatic programs, and the daily story count for a local radio station are examples of content analyses that study manifest messages.

Content analysis is also often used to identify another type of message—the *latent* message. Although also communicating to the audience, the latent message is unintended or hidden. For example, Jackson-Beeck and Meadow[5] used content analysis to compare the 1960 Nixon-Kennedy television debates with the 1976 Carter-Ford debates. Since their intention was to analyze the nonpurposive messages rather than to deal solely with spoken (manifest) content, they also analyzed such unintentional (latent) messages as the frequency of speech pauses or a candidate's nonverbal body language. Their study offered a new dimension to our understanding of the ways the total presentation of a candidate during a television debate is an interaction of visual and aural elements. It also added more to our understanding of the role and impact of television in these debates than a single analysis of the issues that were debated.

Sometimes content analysis is used to investigate messages that fall somewhere between the purposive and nonpurposive messages. For example, Dominick, Richman, and Wurtzel[6] were interested in how character problems were solved on children's programs. Since previous research had suggested children frequently model what they see portrayed on television, the study was designed to make visible those trends in the problem-solving strategies to which children were most often exposed.

Content analysis, a useful tool for the social scientist interested in understanding the interaction of television content and the television audience, also has some practical applications for the broadcast executive. For example, a content analysis of competing television news programs within a particular market can provide valuable data for producers and managers in diagnosing problems and in developing improvements. Comparing story frequencies, production methods, and other significant variables of news presentation from an objective distance can give important insights to people who are closely involved in the day-to-day production of news.

Similarly, content analysis techniques can provide programmers and broadcast standards managers with an objective view of their programming. At ABC Television, the Developmental and Social Research unit has worked closely with the network's Broadcast Standards and Practices unit to develop a system for quantifying the depiction of violence on all entertainment programs. The system is used to code every show before broadcast; it quantifies behaviors and also develops a numerical weight for each program based on the type of violence, the victims of violence, and the outcome of violence. This coding enables ABC Broadcast Standards to keep track of the levels of violence that appear on every show. It is a more objective measure than depending solely on individual editor judgments.

Even though content analysis is a flexible and useful research and analytic tool, it is susceptible to many methodological and interpretive pitfalls. Before discussing the techniques used in content analysis, it is important to understand exactly what content analysis can do and what content analysis *cannot* do.

What Content Analysis Can Do

Content analysis is a way to define objectively television or radio content. It is a method by which we make visible and quantifiable, significant behaviors, themes, character portrayals, production variables, and a host of similar elements. Content analysis enables us to separate messages into their component parts. Content analysis is also a means by which we can identify and evaluate underlying relationships among various content elements that may not otherwise be apparent. Finally, content analysis can help us develop hypotheses based on the manifest and latent messages inherent in all broadcast communication, hypotheses that can be researched subsequently through other studies.

What Content Analysis Cannot Do

Content analysis cannot provide information about how the audience perceives, interprets, or comprehends a message. Nor can content analysis, by itself, tell how a message affects an audience's attitudes or behaviors. Simply stating that a news program spends more time on national news than on international news does not automatically mean that viewers know little about foreign events. Stating that some programs contain more violent behavior than others does not necessarily lead to the conclusion that people who watch violent programs will behave more aggressively than those who do not. All that content analysis can do is to tell us what messages exist and how often they appear, and to provide some systematic and objective way to evaluate the individual elements that together comprise a total communication event.

Assessing the impact of messages on audiences requires another research study. Quite often, a content analysis study serves as a preliminary step in conducting further research. For example, in the problem-solving study mentioned earlier, Dominick, Richman, and Wurtzel first identified the three most prevalent types of problem-solving strategies on children's programming and divided them into three categories: aggressive solutions, assertive solutions, and passive nonsolutions. The researchers next measured how these three problem-solving strategies were modeled or imitated by child viewers.[7] The identification

of the problem-solving strategies was determined through content analysis, but the effect of the content messages on the particular audience of interest was investigated through a subsequent experimental research study.

It is important to examine carefully the content and category definitions that are used, since these often will affect the study results. For example, there have been many content analysis studies of how violence is depicted on television programs. Yet, the way the investigator defines violence is a crucial factor in determining the study's outcome. Some researchers believe that violence is any antisocial behavior regardless of context or intention. Thus, they would include the proverbial pie-in-the-face slapstick as well as more aggressive violent behavior. Other researchers believe violence definitions should not include such slapstick horseplay. Obviously, these two different definitions of violence would result in two different analyses of the same program. When comparing content analysis studies, it is crucial to be aware of the various definitions and categories used in each.

Content Analysis Techniques

We can divide content analysis into six basic steps:
1. developing research objectives or hypotheses
2. establishing the unit of analysis
3. determining content categories
4. selecting the sample
5. coding and reliability
6. analyzing data

Developing Research Objectives or Hypotheses

Since content analysis assumes that some content is present, a content study will invariably lead to the collection of some data. Unfortunately, the certainty of results has led some researchers to use content analysis as a fishing expedition in hopes of "teasing out whatever is there." Naturally, studies are bound to uncover findings that are surprising or less than obvious. But a well-designed study, and ultimately a meaningful research project, should begin from a set of carefully developed research objectives or hypotheses.

For example, a researcher is interested in knowing what kinds of programs appeared during the first years of public access on cable TV channels. The researcher's hypothesis was that if the public access channels were to fulfill their potential as a medium of local communication, the types of programming that were broadcast ought to reflect predominantly local issues and concerns. This basic hypothesis, or research objective, gave the study focus and direction in order to answer the researcher's question.[8]

Determining the hypotheses or objectives in advance also offers increased accuracy in developing content categories and in coding the material. In fact, the content categories and the units of analysis (two concepts discussed in detail later in this essay) are developed to address specific questions and objectives, and they can be made more sensitive and discriminating once the study's objectives are clearly outlined.

Unit of Analysis

The unit of analysis (UOA) is whatever the content analysis researcher counts as a specific message or element of communication. The unit of analysis can range in size and complexity from a single word to an entire program. For example, if one were interested in determining the kinds of themes most prevalent in television drama, the unit of analysis most likely would be the individual program. However, if one wishes to see how sex roles interact with major characters on prime-time drama to determine whether heroes, villains, and assertive or aggressive characters were predominantly male or female, the unit of analysis would be each major character appearing in the show or shows under analysis.

Obviously, defining the unit of analysis is a crucial decision that must be made for every study. The UOA determines what is counted and how it is counted; it will also affect the study's accuracy, reliability, and validity.

The more obvious and clear-cut the unit of analysis, the easier the coding and the more reliable the study results. This does not mean that content analysis coding is easy; it is usually time consuming and boring and may be the least interesting part of a content study. But the fewer decisions that a coder must make on judgment or hunch in determining each unit of analysis, the more accurate the study results. For example, using a word as a unit of anaysis is clear-cut and unambiguous, since a word is an "either-it-is-or-it-isn't" situation. On the other hand, coding violent behavior and using a "violent action" or "aggressive incident" as the unit of analysis is less precise and requires more judgment calls by coders. These judgment calls can ultimately affect the study's reliability, since different coders can make different decisions.

Related to the unit of analysis is the way the researcher decides to code each unit. The most common approach is simply to count the frequency of occurrence. For example, in a study comparing television coverage of a presidential campaign, the unit of analysis might be each individual story that dealt with presidential politics.

This approach permits comparison of the frequency with which a Republican or Democratic story appeared over a particular period of time. However, simply counting frequency of occurrence may not always provide the total picture. Assume a one-week count of presidential campaign stories on a television station reveals that fourteen news stories were devoted to Democrats and fifteen stories were devoted to Republicans. At first glance, the coverage appears about even. However, if, instead of counting every story, each story was timed to establish the amount of air-time devoted to the individual stories, a different sort of measure is involved. Adding up the air-time for each story yields a weekly total of air-time. Suppose the totals were thirty-seven minutes devoted to the Republicans and forty-nine minutes devoted to the Democrats. It would thus appear that coverage was not as evenly balanced as the frequency count might have suggested. In fact, although the Republicans had one more story than the Democrats, the Republicans actually had twelve minutes or 25 percent less air-time.

The point is that there is no correct or incorrect variable counting approach. Whenever possible, using more than a single measure is an excellent safeguard against the problems illustrated in this hypothetical example. The unit of analysis should reflect the study objectives or hypotheses, and the method of counting should provide the researcher with data that best reflect the content material under study.

Content Categories

Each unit of analysis ultimately must be pigeon-holed into a particular content category. The development of content categories naturally depends on the study's overall objectives or hypotheses. For example, in Katzman's study of the various themes depicted on daytime serials, he had each content category represent a dramatic theme, such as "social problems," "criminal activities," "medical problems," and "romantic/marital affairs."[9] These broad categories were further subdivided into more specific categories. For instance, the "criminal activity" category was subdivided into murder, theft, blackmail, illegal drug traffic, and so on.

As a rule of thumb, content categories must be mutually exclusive and all inclusive. In other words, each category should be narrowly defined to permit fitting only one type of content within it. Yet when taken as a whole, the content categories together should encompass every possible message, behavior, or whatever other units of analysis exist in the sample population.

Sometimes content categories must be developed based only on an intelligent guess, since, without knowing precisely what the content will be before doing the analysis, one cannot always decide on a precise set of content categories. Problems develop with categories that are either too large and therefore categorize many different kinds of variables in only a few categories, or that are too narrowly defined and thus include only a few variables in many categories.

An example of too large a category would be the use of two categories for analyzing news stories: (1) hard news and (2) soft news. It would not be difficult to categorize all news stories into either category, but the analysis results would be essentially meaningless. Included within the "hard" news category would be stories ranging from international affairs to strictly local issues and events. Obviously, a number of more narrowly defined subcategories under the larger hard news label would provide more insight into the story makeup of the news program.

On the other hand, consider news stories for which so many different categories are developed that once coding is completed the researcher is confronted with dozens of separate categories, each containing only a handful of news stories. Since the purpose of content analysis is to reduce the mass of data into a smaller number of categories so trends or relationships become more apparent, a large number of categories with relatively few items within each does not offer the researcher much help. The point is that the number of content categories developed by the researcher must tread the thin line between too many categories in which such fine distinctions are made that little data reduction is accomplished and too few categories resulting in little or no discrimination of content.

It is not uncommon for a unit of analysis to be categorized into a number of different types of categories. For example, a television news story—which is a study's unit of analysis—may be categorized by story content, by visual presentation (film, videotape, anchorperson only), by aural presentation (voice-over, live sound, wild sound), and by camera shot (long shot, close-up, etc.). Within each content-type, the rules of mutual exclusivity and all inclusivity remain in effect. However, the large number of potential variables can offer a richness of research data for analysis.

Sample Selection

In most content analysis research, the programs, characters, commercials, news stories, or whatever the researcher must count are so numerous that to attempt to analyze each one would be virtually impossible. Consider a researcher interested in evaluating the three nightly network newscasts during a presidential election campaign. Months worth of news programs would have to be gathered and analyzed. This would be extremely difficult and time-consuming. Also, the number of coding errors or other inaccuracies increases with the number of elements that must be analyzed and categorized.

Rather than attempt to cover every newscast in the population, the researcher could select a sample of newscasts that—although fewer than the actual total—accurately represents the large population. If the sample were properly selected, a manageable number of programs would be coded, yet the results would still be generalizable to all newscasts broadcast during the time period from which the sample was drawn.

There are many different types of sampling procedures, each with its own advantages and disadvantages. The researcher must first determine what makes up the overall population. In the case of the news study mentioned above, assume the population includes all network newscasts from the first primary until election day in November. Once the range of the research population is determined, a small sample of programs must be selected that represents the larger whole.

One method is to select at random one day per week for the time period in question and analyze all news shows broadcast that day. An even more sophisticated approach would be to select a sample of shows from the Monday of one week, shows from a Tuesday of the next, a Wednesday next, and so on, to eliminate any possible bias in the sample from differences resulting from various days of the week. Authors of other research studies dealing with larger populations (say prime-time programming) might simply select a two-week period that the researcher believes is representative of the total season's programming and code every program that appeared during prime time for the fourteen days. Of course, it is important for the two weeks to be from a normal time period so the sample does not reflect a bias due to seasonal variations, such as during the Christmas holidays or during the ratings sweep periods.

Another common sampling technique is to choose programs that are most popular among the audience group of interest to the researcher. For example, a researcher concerned with network children's programming could select the top fifteen early evening and top fifteen Saturday morning programs that had the highest Nielsen ratings among children ages six to eleven. A sample of two or three of each of these shows would be recorded and analyzed.

Proper sample selection is of crucial importance to a content analysis study. An unrepresentive sample may have a built-in bias that does not accurately reflect the larger population. Inferences that might be made about such a biased sample will not accurately mirror the larger group and can lead to inaccurate and misleading conclusions.

Coding and Reliability

Once the researcher has developed the unit of analysis and content categories and has selected the sample, he or she is ready to begin pretesting. The easiest way to pretest is to select some randomly chosen materials from the sample group and try out the content analysis system. The pretest will give a good indication of whether the unit of analysis and content category definitions are working and whether the overall system is appropriate for the research objectives.

Generally, a number of individuals are assembled to collect and code the data. The team approach is useful for two reasons. First, content analysis is usually a time-consuming task, and the more people coding simultaneously, the faster the data can be collected. Second, if only one person codes all of the content, any individual biases that might exist (consciously or subconsciously in the mind of the coder) will be reflected in the data and can result in misleading conclusions. However, if a number of individuals each codes the sample material separately, and if a comparison of intercoder reliability is then made, it can be verified that the collected data are the result of the content analysis scheme and not the result of any personal bias. Of course, any intercoder difficulties that do appear must be corrected and resolved before actually conducting the study and collecting real data.

Reliability Coefficients

The easiest way to verify that repeated measures of the same material are being coded similarly by different coders is to conduct a reliability test. This means having two or more coders independently code some sample material and then comparing the results. The formula for the coefficient of reliability given by Holsti[10] is:

$$CR = \frac{2M}{N_1 + N_2}$$

where M = the number of coding decisions on which two judges are in agreement and N_1 and N_2 refer to the number of coding decisions made by judges 1 and 2 respectively. The CR is expressed as a correlation coefficient, where a maximum value of $+1$ equals perfect agreement, a score of zero equals no agreement, and a score of -1 equals perfect inverse agreement where as one score goes up, the other goes down. Generally, CRs will run from zero to $+1$. Usually a correlation of about $+.80$ (or 80 percent agreement) is considered the minimum required to demonstrate that the coding system is sufficiently reliable. However, this figure is arbitrary and depends on a number of factors. For example, if the unit of analysis and content categories are very precise and clear-cut, we would expect much higher CRs, .90 or higher. On the other hand, a researcher using more ambiguous and less obvious UOAs and categories, such as those found in analyses of behaviors or in character portrayals requiring many coder judgments, might consider a

CR of .65 to .70 acceptable. Once the pretest shows an acceptable level of reliability is established, the actual coding begins. However, the researcher should always perform a CR on the final data and report the CR when reporting study results. The coefficient of reliability is an important piece of information to consider in evaluating any content analysis research. It reflects the reliability and stability of the coding procedure on which the entire study is based.[11]

Data Analysis

The data resulting from a content analysis sample are only estimates of the actual content of the larger population from which the sample was selected. In order to determine the reliability of an estimate, some form of inferential statistical analysis should be conducted. The particular type of analysis that is used will depend on the type of data collected. For most studies, data can be divided into two basic types: (1) nominal or frequency data, and (2) score data.

Nominal Data　Nominal data are the classification of elements by name or category into discrete or mutually exclusive units. Sex, race, religion, or political party affiliation are common examples of nominal variables. Obviously, most content analysis studies also use nominal variables by sorting the various content elements into different categories. For example, classifying the types of news stories on a network news program, determining the role characteristics of minority characters in drama, or analyzing the themes of daytime serials are examples of CA studies that use nominal variables.

The most commonly used statistical test for nominal or category data is chi-square (abbreviated with the symbol X^2). Essentially, the chi-square statistic helps the researcher estimate the odds that the frequency distribution across categories observed in the sample occurred strictly by chance. If it can be shown that sheer chance does not seem a likely explanation for the frequency distribution found, then it can be assumed that the results in the sample are also likely to be found in the larger population from which the sample was drawn.

Score Data Score data differ from nominal data in that numerical scores can vary across a continuous range of numbers. The running time of a news story and the number of column inches in a newspaper article are two examples of score variables.

The advantage of using score data is that a large group of figures can be summarized as a numerical average or mean.

The dispersion of scores can also be indexed by using the standard deviation of the responses. This technique permits the measurement and comparison of the amount of score variation from one sample or from one category with another.

As with nominal data, simply reporting different means does not necessarily indicate that the differences will apply to the larger population from which the sample was drawn. In this case, a variety of parametric statistics (such as the t-test or analysis of variance) are used to provide the researcher with information indicating whether the differences found in the sample can be reliably generalized to the larger population.

Additional References

This brief overview of content analysis provides a superficial introduction to the research technique and its application to broadcast research studies. The following references contain more detailed information about content analysis technique and methodology. Also worthwhile are a number of content analysis studies that deal with broadcast-related research topics. Among the research journals in which such articles frequently appear are the *Journal of Broadcasting*, the *Journal of Communication*, and *Journalism Quarterly*.

Adams, William, and Fay Schreibman, eds. *Television Network News: Issues in Content Analysis Research*. Washington, D.C.: George Washington University, 1978.

Berelson, Bernard. *Content Analysis in Communication Research*. Glencoe, Ill.: Free Press, 1952.

Budd, Richard, R. Thorp, and L. Donohew. *Content Analysis of Communications*. New York: Macmillan Co., 1967.

Gerbner, George, *et al.*, eds. *The Analysis of Communication Content*. New York: John Wiley, 1969.

Holsti, Ole R. *Content Analysis for the Social Sciences and Humanities*. Reading, Mass.: Addison-Wesley, 1969.

Krippendorff, Klaus. *Content Analysis: An Introduction to Its Methodology*. Beverly Hills, Ca.: Sage, 1980.

Endnotes

1. Content analysis is an extremely flexible research technique with application extending far beyond the study of radio or television messages. In addition to mass communication research, content analysis is used in such varied disciplines as political science, psycholinguistics, literary analysis and criticism, history, and psychology. However, since the focus of this book is broadcast research, this essay will deal only with content analysis as it relates to this specific research area.
2. Bernard Berelson, *Content Analysis in Communication Research* (Glencoe, Ill.: Free Press, 1952), 18.
3. George Gerbner *et al.*, eds., *The Analysis of Communication Content* (New York): John Wiley, 1969), x.
4. Leslie K. Davis, "Developing a Comprehensive Approach to Video Content Analysis," paper presented to Eastern Communication Association, Boston, March 1978.
5. Marilyn Jackson-Beeck and Robert Meadow, "Content Analysis of Televised Communication Events," *Communication Research* 6 (1979): 321–344.
6. Joseph Dominick, Shanna Richman, and Alan Wurtzel, "Problem Solving in TV Shows Popular with Children: Assertion

vs. Aggression," *Journalism Quarterly* 56 (1979): 455–463.

7. Joseph Dominick, Shanna Richman, and Alan Wurtzel, "The Effects of Television on Children's Problem Solving Behavior: An Experiment," report to the American Broadcasting Company, October 1977.

8. Alan Wurtzel, "Public Access Cable Television: Programming," *Journal of Communication* 25 (1975): 15–21.

9. Nat Katzman, "Television Soap Operas: What's Been Going On Anyway?" *Public Opinion Quarterly* 36 (1972): 200–212.

10. Ole R. Holsti, *Content Analysis for the Social Sciences and Humanities* (Reading, Mass.: Addison-Wesley, 1969), 140.

11. Some critics have suggested that the coefficient of reliability formula for percentage of intercoder agreement tends to overestimate actual reliability because it does not take into account the level of agreement expected by chance alone. A more sophisticated statistic has been reported by Fless. Called the *kappa* statistic, it is designed to measure nominal scale agreement between a fixed pair of raters. Readers interested in the formula and rationale behind the *kappa* statistic should consult J. L. Fless, "Measuring Nominal Scale Agreement Among Many Raters," *Psychological Bulletin* 76 (1971): 378–382.

2

Searching for Television's History

Fay C. Schreibman

Although most people believe that television networks maintain a complete collection of past and current programming, they are mistaken. Most television programs, except for news and public affairs, are owned by production companies independent of the networks. After a television show has been aired in its first run, contracted reruns, and syndication, the program is returned to the production company. The company then has the alternatives of (1) finding another way to make money on the programs through distribution or sale, (2) leaving them on the shelf, (3) donating them to a television archive, or (4) throwing them out. Until recently Option 4 was often the unfortunate choice. Nonetheless, many television programs are available to researchers at various archives throughout the country or through other sources, such as commercial distributors and private collectors.

Identifying exact titles of programs available is not a simple process. Although there are many books on television programs that once existed, there are no comparative books on whether these programs survive and on where they can be found. Until such a resource is created, many scholars in their search for past programs will be duplicating the efforts of earlier researchers.

This essay is a prelude to a comprehensive location listing (union list) of existing television shows. It discusses available reference materials, archives, and organizations with information pertaining to television programming. The reference materials are identified by title and the notation "R-(assigned number)." This refers to the Reference Appendix included as a part of this essay. The Reference Appendix is an annotated listing of these sources, complete with ordering information. Major television archives and information organizations are noted with "A-(assigned number)," referring to the Archive Appendix, which contains descriptions of each institution. The presentation of these data is a step-by-step procedural format outlining the best use of the described resources in accessing desired programs. This approach incorporates a compendium of suggestions from television archivists and scholars of mass media experienced in television research.[1]

The same skills used for research in a library are effective in determining the existence and location of a past television program. It is not unlike locating an out-of-print book. The steps include identifying the exact title and publisher (producer), checking availability in the library or through interlibrary loan, consulting commercial distribution sources, researching special collections in libraries and archives, and contacting the library or archive to use the materials.[2]

Locating a Television Program

There are seven steps in locating a television program. Following these steps in succession will insure a thorough investigation with minimum duplication of effort.

Identify Exact Title of Program Be specific in all research requests. It is worthwhile to note as much information as possible about the program, including the exact and/or original title, program episodes, talent, air dates, production company, production and direction staff, and sponsors.

Several television reference books contain detailed program information: *The Complete Encyclopedia of Television Programs* (R-1), *The New York Times Encyclopedia of Television Programs* (R-2), *The Complete Directory to Prime Time Network TV Shows, 1946-Present* (R-3), and *Total Television: A Comprehensive Guide to Programming from 1948-1980* (R-4). *TV Season* (R-5), an annual publication that began with the 1974-75 season and unfortunately concluded with the 1978-79 season, included all news specials and documentaries as well as entertainment programs. A new reference work, *Universal Television, 1950-1980* (R-6), is the first to survey all television series, telefeatures, pilots, and specials made by a particular production company.

If a program is syndicated currently in the United States or abroad, it will be listed and identified by production company, current distributor, surviving episodes, and past title of series, in source books used by the industry. *Broadcast Information Bureau* (BIB) has published three of these guides annually since 1952: *Series, Serials and Packages: Domestic Edition; Series, Serials and Packages: Foreign Language Edition*; and *TV Feature Film Source Book* (R-7).

For titles of episodes in a series, refer to *Television Drama Series Programming: A Comprehensive Chronicle*, which covers programs from 1947 to 1982 (R-8). A commercial service, *Television Index*, has complete prime-time program information. Since 1949, the weekly publication *Television Index* (R-9) has identified current production facts. Also check past issues of *TV Guide* (R-10) back to April 1953, when it began; and before that time, see *New York Times* television sections.

Several books about particular series identify episode titles: *All in the Family: A Critical Appraisal; Lucy and Ricky and Fred and Ethel: The Story of "I Love Lucy"; Fantastic Television: A Pictorial History of Sci-Fi: the Unusual and the Fantastic from Captain Video to the Star Trek Phenomenon and Beyond . . . The Twilight Zone Companion* (R-11). Reference works about a particular genre of television programming have recently been published. For example: *Children's Television: The First Thirty-Five Years, 1946-81; Television Comedy Series: An Episode Guide to 153 Sitcoms in Syndication*; and *The Serials: Suspense and Drama by Installments* (soap operas) (R-12).

Television newscasts since 1968 are relatively easy to find. Consult *Television News Index and Abstracts* (R-13) for descriptions of network evening newscasts of ABC, CBS, and NBC since August 5, 1968. This valuable resource is published monthly and includes a subject index. An annual index is also distributed. Many major libraries maintain complete sets of the *Abstracts*.

CBS is the only network commercially to distribute transcripts of all their news programs. Since 1963, the network has made available transcripts from *CBS Evening News with Walter Cronkite*, *Face the Nation*, *60 Minutes*, *CBS Reports*, *CBS News Special*, *Magazine*, *30 Minutes*, and other programs. The *CBS News Index* is the finding aid to the *CBS News Television Broadcasts*; it is available only since 1975. *Face the Nation* transcripts and indexes of programs since 1954 are available separately (R–14). Transcripts of NBC's weekly news program, *Meet the Press*, can be purchased (R–15). Since 1981, transcripts of such ABC news programs as *Nightline*, *This Week with David Brinkley*, *20/20*, and *Close-up* documentaries are available (R–16).

PBS's *MacNeil/Lehrer Report* index and transcripts have recently been released under the title of *Broadcast Review and Index* and begin with the 1976 programs (R–17).

Searching for news documentaries is similar to locating titles of entertainment programs. *Documentary in American Television* and its sequel, *The Image Decade: Television Documentary, 1965–1975*, identify a number of programs in discussing the history of this genre (R–18). The encyclopedias previously cited include some documentaries, but only *TV Season* is complete in its listing of documentaries. Again, consult past issues of *TV Guide* and *New York Times* television sections for exact titles of these programs. The *CBS News Index* does not have a distinct section identifying documentaries, but storage of transcripts is by type of news program with one category listing for documentary. Consult the *Index* for the exact codes to identify these programs.

Contact the Local Public Library, College or University Library/Special Collections Division and Media Center, Historical Society, Museum   A number of these institutions own collections of television programs and commercials. If audiovisual resources are not centralized on a campus, then contact academic departments that offer broadcast-related classes.[3] Special divisions at universities that conduct research on mass media might maintain study collections of news and entertainment programs.[4] Local television stations around the country have donated film footage

to area historical societies and museums.[5] Contact these sources before continuing your research, because local institutions might maintain accessible collections of the television programs being sought.

Check Availability of Programs for Loan from a Library or Archive   Network television newscasts and certain news specials are available via loan agreement from the Vanderbilt Television News Archive (A–23) and (for CBS news programs) from the National Archives and Records Service (A–14). At the moment, these are the only television materials that can be borrowed from an archive. Other libraries holding television materials should be contacted regarding their interlibrary loan policies.

Rent or Purchase Material from a Commercial Distributor   Film and video distributors, such as Time/Life and Films Inc., rent and sell some television documentaries and a few dramatic programs. Titles available from these major companies are found in the following sources: *The Video Source Book* and *The Video Programs Index* (R–19), *Educational Film Locator* (R–20), NICEM's *Index to Educational Videotapes and Index to 16mm Educational Films* (R–21), and *Film Programmer's Guide to 16mm Rentals* (R–22). Most libraries and media centers maintain these resources and additional catalogs from other distributors.

Several small companies not listed in the major finding aids sell old television programs either duplicated from a master, an original copy, or simply a copy. Quality of programs from these sources vary. For identification of the companies, see the annual "Video Software Marketers-Consumers" article in the June issues of *Videography*.[6] Only the names of the companies and genre of programs available are noted in this article, and consultation with *Videography* is advised for location of the distributors. In addition to these sources, past television product commercials of selected Clio Award winners are available for rent and sale.[7]

The ABC, CBS, and PBS networks have

their own in-house divisions, ABC Video Enterprises, CBS Resources Development and Production Department, and PBS Video, which distribute certain network programs. NBC contracts its distribution to an outside company, Films, Inc. Catalogs from these sources indicate titles available for rent or purchase (R–23).

Consult Major Television Archives on Holdings and Permission for Use If the television program is not available commercially, the researcher must travel to the archive that maintains a reference copy of the program. The chief exceptions to this in-house-use-only policy are, again, for network evening newscasts and most other news programs from the Vanderbilt Television News Archive (A–23), and for CBS newscasts and news specials from the National Archives and Records Service (A–14). Special loan agreements are involved to borrow materials from either of these archives.

An archive is a special library, and use of archive materials is usually restricted to scholarly research. Only the Museum of Broadcasting (A–12) also permits entertainment viewing on an individual basis. Archive staffs welcome serious researchers. To expedite service from these institutions, the following procedures are recommended:

1. Be prepared with substantial information about the selected programs to be viewed. The exact title for each national run is important, because it is the major entry, and in most instances the only entry, in archive catalogs. The original broadcast title is preferred, although copies of later versions or reruns may be all that are available, and may be cross-referenced to the original title.
2. Check existing finding aids to archive collections. Print catalogs of these collections are identified in the appendices to this article. For additional descriptions of archives, consult *Motion Pictures, Television and Radio: A Union Catalog of Manuscripts and Special Collections in the Western United States* (R–24), *Scholar's Guide to Washington, D.C. Film and Video Collections* (R–25), and *AFI Education Newsletter* (R–26).
3. Contact the archive directly regarding its collection if the program is not identified by the previously cited sources. There is a good possibility of being referred to another archive collection, and in these instances, the researcher should maintain accurate notes on the person providing information at each institution and exactly what information is conveyed.
4. Make all requests to use the facilities in writing. Some archives accept appointments by phone, but it is best to follow up with a letter including supporting documentation from your sponsoring institution. Because both archive staff and viewing facilities are limited, be as specific as possible regarding research needs and make appointments for viewing far in advance.

Under almost no circumstances will archive staff perform analysis of the collection for researchers. (See Archive Appendix for descriptions of archive collections.)

Determine Whether the Program Exists at All If the program is not in the collections of the archives identified in the Archive Appendix or in the alternative sources suggested by archive staffs, the researcher must determine whether the program exists at all. One procedure is to consult *Series, Serials and Packages* (R–7) for information on the current distributor of the program. When the title is not listed in the current edition, check back issues until the title is identified.[8] Contact the distributor or production company to negotiate use. If fees for viewing these resources are exorbitant, or if use is denied, or if the program is not listed in any issue of *Series, Serials and Packages*, the next step is to approach individuals who were involved in the original production, such as producers, talent, writers, sponsors, and advertising agencies. In many cases, these persons have obtained personal copies or own the rights to the television programs.

Requesting permission to view these materials is asking for a special consideration that may or may not be accommodated. It is helpful to remind individuals and distribution companies holding these rare programs that a donation of the show or episode from the series to a television archive would allow future use by all scholars and would relieve the current responsibility they now assume as sole source of a part of broadcasting history.

Contact the Television Archives Advisory Committee The Television Archives Advisory Committee, now part of the National Center for Film and Video Preservation, American Film Institute, is the primary organization interested in locating past television programming. When researchers have approached owners of unique television materials, the committee asks to be notified as a courtesy. The committee, representing the majority of archives and information sources identified in the Archive Appendix, meets annually to exchange information on archival television collections, management, and preservation controls. Reporting to the committee one's success or failure in finding a program not housed in an archive would be of mutual benefit to television archivists and researchers. Information should be sent to: National Center for Film and Video Preservation, American Film Institute, 2021 North Western Avenue, Los Angeles, CA 90027.

Current procedures for locating a past television program are complicated for many reasons. Program producers, creators, and owners have not offered financial assistance nor donated enough shows to television archives. Funds needed to store, preserve, and catalog, and to pay archive staff to perform these and reference services for a growing collection of audiovisual materials are enormous. Most of the accessible collections are located at universities, where external funding is necessary for them barely to survive, or at government institutions, which are inadequately funded to handle the massive amount of material held. In general, the budgets of most archives are modest, especially when compared to the responsibilities they have.

When additional monies become available,

catalogs of collections may then be created, distributed, and made accessible via a national data base of television program information. Yet, the identification of archival holdings is only one element that will simplify the location of television programs; the preservation of and access to all existing materials in cooperation with the industry are badly needed.

Future
of Television
Preservation

Recent developments indicate a brighter future in the preservation of television programs. New legislation guarantees the availability of current television programming; new archives are being established; past programs continue to be located; and national and international efforts to promote television and film preservation are gaining momentum.

Before 1978, most television programs were preserved if they (1) had future monetary value to the original production company or current distributor, or (2) were donated to an archive, or (3) were part of a private collection. The Copyright Act of 1976[10] changed this practice by establishing the American Television and Radio Archives at the Library of Congress,[11] by allowing libraries and archives to tape broadcast news programs off the air,[12] and by stipulating that television program copies be submitted as part of the registration process for copyright protection.[13]

Although some television productions have been deposited for copyright for many years, the new legislation will increase the flow of material. The American Television and Radio Archives, incorporated into the Motion Picture, Broadcasting and Recorded Sound Division of the Library of Congress (A–11), draws on the Register of Copyrights' materials for its collection. In certain cases, a notice of compliance to deposit a program can be sent to the copyright holder. Limited off-air taping also will be used to add to the archives' collection.

Two important provisions of the Copyright Act are permission for libraries and archives to tape "audiovisual news programs" off the air and to lend a limited number of these taped programs or excerpts. This section of the law is sometimes referred to as the "Vanderbilt Amendment." Practices of the Vanderbilt Television News Archive (A–23) are cited in *House Report* HR 941476 and *Senate Report* SR 94473 as appropriate interpretation and application of the statute. The adoption of this clause into law ended a three-year CBS lawsuit against Vanderbilt for copyright infringement by taping and lending network newscasts for use off the premises.[14] Certain libraries and archives now may house collections of television newscasts and news special events, as newspaper and news magazines back issues are stored. This is a major step in use of broadcast materials for teaching and in research.[15]

Other broadcast archives will continue to be created. Recently, the Jewish Archives of Film and Broadcasting was organized by the Jewish Museum to meet a specialized interest in the broadcasting field.[16] Private collections are slowly being made available to existing archives or are being established as separate archives. The Diamant Memorial Library of Classic Television Commercials at Brooklyn College is an example of such an arrangement (A–6).

Historic television shows and films continue to be discovered in Hollywood garages by heirs of television personalities or by people who bought the real estate, under tarps in warehouses,[17] and even found buried in ditches.[18] There is no reasonable way to know when materials like these will appear, but archivists are always prepared for the occasion. Newspapers and magazines mention these discoveries. The *American Film Institute (AFI) Education Newsletter* (R–26) also contains current information about archival resources in its "Announcements" and "Profile" sections.

A common problem among television archivists in the United States and around the world is the preservation of videotape. Although standards of archival storage of tape have finally been established,[19] the longevity of this medium is still unknown. The quality of videotape stock throughout the years has improved, as has videotape equipment. Each archive reports a different rate of deterioration for the many kinds of tapes on which programs are stored. Research into this area conducted by the Bureau of Standards resulted in a report issued in 1978.[20] The report concluded that videotape is not an archival medium for preservation, and thus that materials should be transferred to 16mm safety film, a costly and impractical suggestion. Videodisc was also mentioned as a possible alternative in future preservation because the nickel plate used to press the disc is regarded as an archival medium.[21] However, developments in the video field for moving images are progressing slowly. Even though the technology exists, the expense involved in making a master for a few copies is prohibitive. Videodiscs are inexpensive to the consumer because of the large quantity being distributed. This problem is similar to one in the past of preserving one copy of an out-of-print book, printed on poor stock, before the advent of photocopying and microfilming processes; the book would have needed to be typeset in order to make a few preservation copies, a cost most archives could not have undertaken.

The National Center For Film and Video Preservation was established in 1983 under an agreement with the National Endowment For The Arts and the American Film Institute with Robert Rosen as founding director. The purpose of the center is to provide a permanent mechanism for coordinating and implementing a national priority in media preservation. A major goal is to establish ongoing communication and interaction between the archival community and media production industry. In its initial stage, the NEA-funded aspects of the program focus on the film genre. The center assumed the role of secretariat for the Television Archives Advisory Committee and is working toward establishing a program for television preservation. The center is currently coordinating a design for the National Moving Image Data Base to include television as well as video and film. Television programs are acquired for deposit at the Library of Congress and other archives.[22]

The Board of Trustees at the Museum of Broadcasting, who represent the leadership of the broadcasting industry, are also concerned about preserving the media. In 1984, the museum hosted a special meeting chaired by Frank Stanton, former president of CBS. Participants were museum board members and other leaders in the field and videotape manufacturers who explored how the Museum of Broadcasting could assist in the preservation effort.

International efforts to address the problem of television preservation are currently under way. In October 1980, this issue was discussed at the Television Archives Advisory Committee meeting. Individual members of the committee also attended the International Federation of Television Archives (FIAT) conference held at the same time. The federation is an association of broadcasting companies' archival divisions from countries including France, England, Germany, Italy, the Netherlands, Chile, Brazil, Canada, and the United States; CBS is the only current institutional member from the United States with representation from the Library of Congress and National Archives and Records Service. FIAT meets twice a year to exchange information about preservation and archive operations and to develop continuing education programs for the staffs of member institutions.[23] Coordination between these two major television archive organizations led to planning for the widespread promotion of research and the development of an archival medium for television programs.

In October 1980, another important international measure was the adoption of the UNESCO resolution on the safeguarding and preservation of moving images.[24] The statement strongly presented the need, importance, and obligation for nations to preserve film and television materials. Recommended procedures for implementing protection for these media on national and international bases were also part of the resolution. Adoption of this policy helps archivists around the world gain support for acquiring and preserving television materials.

Television archivists have done a valuable job in locating, acquiring, protecting, cataloging, and, with hoped-for technological innovations, preserving television shows. In spite of these efforts, all past programs are still not available for research. Large gaps in the archival collections will never be filled for various reasons. Some live broadcasts were never recorded, videotape masters were erased, film and kinescope copies were destroyed, or distributors and private collectors are maintaining concealed collections. After fifty years of broadcasting, legislation finally ensures the preservation of current programming. But only through cooperation between the television industry, television archivists, private collectors, and you, the media researcher, can the years of missing programs be restored or ascertained to exist. In following the process of locating past television shows, the researcher may discover a new collection or establish a cooperative relationship with a program owner. Sharing this information with the television archivists is both a courtesy and an obligation to safeguard an important part of our nation's historic and cultural heritage.

Archive Appendix

This appendix summarizes the major television collections in archives throughout the United States. It is not intended to describe each archive's complete holdings. Some radio collections and script sources are identified.[25] Two television information organizations, Television Information Office (A–20) and Television News Study Center (A–21), are included because referral to television archives is part of their services. Two private collections, Political Television Commercial Archive (A–18) and Peter Vest Collection of the DuMont Network (A–17), are included because of the unique materials involved. Please note that a private collector has no obligation to open a collection for research or any other purpose.

Information for this section was gathered from on-site visits to most archives, from telephone inquiries, and from abstracts from the Television Archives Advisory Committee Profile of Assembled Archives questionnaire.

Because the materials are listed in this section does not necessarily mean that they may be viewed. In most archives, only a duplicate of the original program, called a reference copy, may be viewed for research.

Note: Read the body of this essay before contacting any of these archives.

Entry Format

Name

Address

Telephone number

Description of Medium:
> TELEVISION—all videotape formats, kinescope, and film.
> RADIO—all recording formats.
> PRINT—scripts, manuscripts, clipping files, etc.
> REFERENCE—assistance in locating resources besides archive's collection, print reference works, clipping files.

Description of Genre:
> NEWS—newscasts, specials, newsreels, documentaries.
> ENTERTAINMENT—variety, comedy, drama, sports, music.
> EDUCATION—programs designed specifically for instruction by television.
> COMMERCIALS—political and product.

Collection
> A brief description of the collections, including dates of broadcast.

Reference
> Nature of service by letter, phone, and/or walk-in inquiries and print reference material and periodicals.

Finding Aids
> Card catalogs, computer retrieval systems, lists, publications that identify the collection (accessible catalogs are identified also in the Reference Appendix).

Use
> Eligibility of users.
> In-house: Hours, appointment procedures, and playback facilities.
> Mail requests: Materials available for loan, purchase, rent, or lease.

Table of Entries

A-1

ATAS–UCLA Television Archives

The Academy of Television Arts and Sciences
  Foundation

Department of Theater Arts, University of
  California, Los Angeles

Melnitz Hall, Room 1438

Los Angeles, CA 90024

(213) 206-8013

TELEVISION/PRINT

ENTERTAINMENT/NEWS/COMMER-
  CIALS

Collection (1947–present)

Television: 20,000 titles concentrating on
drama series, such as *Hallmark Hall of
Fame, The Alcoa Hour*, and *Story Theater*,
and comedy-variety shows, such as *Texaco
Star Theater* (Milton Berle), *The Jack Benny
Show, The Smothers Brothers Comedy
Hour, Colgate Comedy Hour*, and Ernie
Kovacs programs. Variety of political com-
mercials and documentaries on John F. Ken-
nedy and Adlai E. Stevenson highlight the
news programs in this collection. Edward R.
Murrow's *See It Now*, David L. Wolper's
March of Time series, and other documenta-
ries, such as "Making of the President" and
"Race for Space," are also included.

Print: 4,000 teleplays of some of the programs in the collection are held in the Theater Arts Library along with thousands of
other documents on television history and
production. Contact Audree Malkin, Head
Librarian at the library, for use of these
materials.

(See A–22 for description of UCLA radio
archives.)

Finding Aids

Card catalog: 15,000 titles.

Print catalog: *A Catalog of the Study Collection of the Academy of Television Arts
and Sciences, UCLA Archives*, 1980 (R–27).

Use

In-house: Hours 9:00–5:00, Monday–Friday, by appointment only.

Playback facilities: (3) 16mm flatbed viewing tables, (4) 35mm flatbed viewing tables,

(2) ¾" videocassette players and monitors,
(2) ½" videotape players and monitors.

A-2

Alfred I. duPont–Columbia University
  Awards in Broadcast Journalism

701 Journalism

Columbia University

New York, NY 10027

(212) 280-5047

TELEVISION/PRINT

NEWS

Collection (1977–present, complete; 1968–
  76, partial).

Television: Archive of local and national
news, public affairs programs, and independent productions that are recipients of the
annual duPont Awards. Programs from the
beginning of the awards in 1942 are currently being acquired.

Print: Scripts, press releases, public response, etc., of the programs.

Finding Aids

Chronological list.

*Broadcast Journalism: The Alfred I.
duPont/Columbia University Survey*
(R–28).

Use

In-house: Hours by appointment only.

Playback facilities: (2) color monitors, (2)
¾" videocassette players.

A-3

ABC News Library Information Department

2040 Broadway, Main Floor

New York, NY 10023

(212) 887-4374

TELEVISION

NEWS

Collection

Newscasts: Videotapes of entire newscasts
(1976–present), kinescopes of entire newscasts (1971–1975), audiotapes of entire
newscasts (1963–present), film segments/
outtakes (1963–present), kinescope seg-

ments/outtakes (1971–1976), videotape segments/outtakes (1976–present).

News special events: Kinescopes (1966–1974), videotape (1976–present).

Other television news programs: Documentaries (film) (1965–present), *20/20* (1976–present).

Radio: [See National Archives (A–14), Museum of Broadcasting (A–12), and Library of Congress (A–11)].

Finding Aids

Newscasts and outtakes: Computer system (including daily stories) STAIRS (1963–present), card catalog (divided by subject, name, and location of individual film and video segments), transcripts (1963–present). Other television news programs: Documentaries (STAIRS), *20/20* (STAIRS).

Use

In-house: The archive's materials are stored at the Sherman Grinberg Libraries for a five-year period before being sent to ABC storage in Ft. Lee, New Jersey. Viewing is exclusively for ABC news staff. Outside researchers may use the Grinberg Library only to view materials for purchase/lease of outtake footage. Exceptions are rarely made to researchers for viewing since the operation is not designed as a reference library. A fee ranging from $500 to $1,000 per day is charged when approval is given for such research.

Playback facilities at Sherman Grinberg Film libraries: (3) color monitors, (3) ¾″ videocassette players, (2) 16mm flatbed viewing tables, (3) 35mm flatbed viewing tables.

Mail requests: Accepted only if items are specifically identified. Contact ABC Video Enterprises (R–23) for commercial distribution of programs.

Purchase/licensing of materials: All film and videotape newscast segments without the voice or image of an ABC News correspondent or reporter may be obtained via a licensing agreement.

Contact Sherman Grinberg Film Libraries, Inc., 630 Ninth Avenue, New York, NY 10036, (212) 765–5170, for prices on film and videotape segments, and royalty fees for commercial use of these materials.

A–4

American Film Institute
National Center for Film and Video Preservation
John F. Kennedy Center for the Performing Arts
Washington, DC 20566
(202) 828–4070
(The archives' administration is at the AFI Los Angeles address. Questions regarding the collection should be referred to the Washington, D.C., location.)

TELEVISION/REFERENCE/PRINT
ENTERTAINMENT/EDUCATION

Collection (1930s–present)

Television: Approximately 500 reels of entertainment television program series, such as the *Naked City*, *Abbott and Costello Show*, and *Fireside Theatre*. The AFI archival holdings are mostly deposited into the Library of Congress Collection (A–11), and informational inquiries on those titles should be referred to that archive.

Reference and Print: American Film Institute, Louis B. Mayer Library, 2021 North Western Avenue, Los Angeles, CA 90027, (213) 856–7658, has 800 scripts of comedy, dramatic, and some educational programs and of some made-for-television movies. Books, periodicals, and clipping files on subjects and personalities, and programs on television. Telephone and mail inquiries honored.

Use (Louis B. Mayer Library)

In-house: Hours 10:30–5:30, Monday–Friday.

A–5

Broadcast Pioneers Library
1771 N Street, N.W.
Washington, DC 20036
(202) 223–0088

TELEVISION/RADIO/PRINT/REFER-
ENCE
ENTERTAINMENT/NEWS/COMMER-
CIALS
Collection (1944–1956)
Television: 17 programs, including *The Clock*, *Eisenhower and Nixon*, and *Meet the Man*.
Radio: Approximately 250 broadcasts, 600 oral history interviews of broadcast pioneers, speeches, and radio-related programs
Print: 300 scripts of radio and television programs.
Photographs: 20,000 concerning television and radio.

Reference
Books, periodicals, and clipping files pertaining to radio and television broadcasting history. Papers and scrapbooks of broadcast pioneers. Mail and telephone inquiries honored. Referral service to other broadcast sources.

Finding Aids
Television: title list.
Radio: card catalog.

Use
In house: Hours 9:00–5:00, Monday–Friday, by appointment only.

A-6
Celia Nachatovitz Diamant Memorial Library of Classic Television Commercials
Brooklyn College
Bedford Avenue & Avenue H
TV and Radio Department
018 Whitehead
Brooklyn, NY 11210
(212) 780–5558
TELEVISION
COMMERCIALS
Collection
69 commercials (2 hours) donated by Lincoln Diamant.

Finding Aids
Television's Classic Commercials; The Golden Years, 1948–1958 (R-29). Contains detailed information about all of the commercials; scripts are included. Title list.

Use
Mail order: All commercials are available for purchase. Send 2 blank 60-minute, ¾″ videocassettes plus $50 duplication fee (must be submitted together) to Jill Burger, c/o library. Three weeks delivery.
In-house: Contact library for arrangements. Fees will be charged.

A-7
CBS News Archives
524 West 57th Street
New York, NY 10019
(212) 975–2834
TELEVISION/RADIO
NEWS
Collection
Newscasts: Videotapes of entire newscasts (January 1974–present), selected videotapes of entire newscasts (1960–1974), audiotapes of entire newscasts (1950–present), selected kinescopes of entire newscasts (1948–1960), film segments/selected outtakes used in newscasts (1950–present), videotape segments/selected outtakes used in newscasts (1959–present), videotape outtakes from newscasts (1959–present).
News special events: kinescope (1952–1959), videotape (1959–present).
Other news programs: Documentaries (*CBS Reports, CBS News Specials, CBS Special Reports*) (1950–present); *60 Minutes, Magazine, Face the Nation, In the News, 30 Minutes* (entire series).
Radio: Radio network newcasts (such as *World News* and *The World Tonight*) and news specials are available at the National Archives (A-14). The collection ranges from the mid-1930s to 1940s. The university has a detailed card catalog for the collection. The CBS News Archives holds the complete collection from the late 1950s to present, and materials are identified in a separate card catalog. Newscasts may be purchased by license agreement through CBS News Archives at a flat fee of $50 for reel-to-reel or audio-cassette tape. Collections of some CBS radio are located at the Museum of

Broadcasting (A–12), Library of Congress (A–11), and National Archives (A–14).

Finding Aids

Television newscasts, news programs, and outtakes: card catalogs (divided by subject, name, and location of individual film and videotape segments since 1953); transcripts (newscasts and news programs since 1963); computer (stores data from transcripts of all newscasts and public affairs programs since 1971 and every film and videotape assignment, whether aired or not, since 1975); *CBS News Television Broadcasts* (transcripts of all CBS news programs since 1963) and *CBS News Index* (index to transcripts since 1975) (See R–14).

Documentary films: internal shelf list.

Use

In-house: The archives' primary purposes are to provide data to the CBS News Division, to service purchase requests for available footage, and to assist outside television news researchers (priority in that order). Weekdays from 9:00–5:00, a special librarian is assigned to assist people not affiliated with CBS.

Researchers should call or write the archives to ascertain whether their research needs can be accommodated. Because the archives are not set up for large-scale public use, decisions are made on a case-by-case basis. When permission is granted, an appointment is arranged. Researchers are permitted to use the card catalog. Once selections are made, a fee is charged for the librarian's retrieval of materials, use of viewing facilities, and computer searches.

Playback facilities: (1) ¾″ videocassette player and monitor, (1) 16mm flatbed film viewing table, (1) 35mm flatbed film viewing table, (1) audiotape reel-to-reel player, (1) audiocassette player.

Mail requests: Accepted only if items are specifically identified. Contact CBS Broadcast International (R–23) for commercial distribution of programs. Consult the National Archives (A–14) for newscasts and news specials that are loaned from its collection.

Purchase/licensing of materials: Some film and videotape newscast segments without the voice or image of a CBS News correspondent or reporter may be obtained via a licensing agreement. Contact the CBS News Archives for prices on film and videotape segments and for royalty fees for commercial use of these materials.

A–8

George Eastman House
International Museum of Photography
Department of Film
900 East Avenue
Rochester, NY 14607
(716) 271–3361
TELEVISION
ENTERTAINMENT/NEWS

Collection

More than 50 titles of television shows from 1950s, including *Camel News Caravan, Person to Person, Tonight Show with Steve Allen, I Love Lucy, Hallmark Hall of Fame, Big Story, Dragnet, Mama,* and *Ding Dong School.*

Finding Aids

None.

Use

In-house: Only available to scholars who apply in writing for use of the collection. Hours: 9:00–5:00, Monday–Friday, by appointment only. Fees: $10 per hour for viewing.

A–9

George Foster Peabody Collection
Main Library
University of Georgia
Athens, GA 30602
(404) 542–7462
TELEVISION/RADIO
ENTERTAINMENT/NEWS/EDUCATION

Collection

Archive for radio and television entrants for and winners of the George Foster Peabody Radio and Television Awards for Distinguished Achievement and Meritorious Public Service (1940–present).

Television: 6,000 programs, including news, public affairs, children's programs, entertainment, and those that promote international understanding. 700–800 entries are received each year.

Radio: 12,000 titles with the same subjects as for television (1940–present).

Print: More than 200,000 scripts and other supporting documentation to programs (1940–present).

Finding Aids

Peabody Digest, listing all entries to most of the Peabody Awards competitions. Information on programs for years in which *Digest* was not printed is available at the archive.

Card catalog, OCLC (computer), title index, subject index, special subject biographies.

Use

In-house: Hours by appointment only. Playback facilities: Reference copies of programs from 1974–81 are available to be viewed at the Media Department of the main library. Viewing copies are ½″ videocassette; radio is audio-cassette.

Duplication: Programs may be duplicated only with the written permission of the copyright holder and through negotiation with the archive. Apply to Dr. William W. McDougald, School of Journalism and Mass Communications, University of Georgia, Athens, GA 30602.

A-10

House Broadcasting System
U.S. House of Representatives
Washington, DC 20515
(202) 225-8906
TELEVISION
NEWS

Collection   (March 19, 1979–present)

Videotape and audiotape copies of House floor proceedings.

Finding Aids

Congressional Record should be used to ascertain the exact date and time of material.

Use

In-house: No viewing or listening areas are available. Researchers are referred to Library of Congress, Motion Picture, Broadcasting and Recorded Sound Division (A-11) for use of audiocassette copies. No videocassette copies are available at this time.

Mail requests: All material is for sale; no rentals or loan service is offered. Requests should be in writing, including the date, time, and speaker(s) as printed in the *Congressional Record*, and sent to Clerk of the House, Office of Records and Registration, 1036 Longworth, H.O.B., Washington, DC 20515, (202) 225-1300.

Purchase fees: ¾″ videocassette: $104–30 minutes, $176–60 minutes; 1″ reel to reel (type C format): $184–30 minutes; $272–60 minutes, $24–30 minutes, $43–60 minutes, $32–30 minutes, $56–60 minutes. For further information, contact Joan Teague at (202) 225-8906.

A-11

Library of Congress–American Television and
   Radio Archives
Motion Picture, Broadcasting and Recorded
   Sound Division
James Madison Building, Room LM 336
2nd Street & Independence Avenue, S. E.
Washington, DC 20540
(202) 287–1000 Television/Video Film
(202) 287–7833 Recorded Sound
FILMS/TELEVISION/RADIO/PRINT/
   REFERENCE SERVICE
ENTERTAINMENT/NEWS/COMMER-
   CIALS/EDUCATION

Collection

Television: More than 25,000 titles on film, kinescope, videotape, and video disc, including entertainment, documentary, and news programs. More than 2,000 titles are added each year from programs registered in the Copyright Office and gifts from production companies (1949–present).

Radio: Approximately 50,000 recordings, including NBC news and entertainment programs since 1937; Armed Forces Radio

Service programs since 1942, which contain selections of radio news and entertainment shows of all networks; Office of War Information and Voice of America programming; National Public Radio Cultural Programming; and many off-air recordings (1924–present).

Print: Scripts, transcripts, and summaries of programs registered for copyright are available. Some scripts and transcripts are located in the Manuscript Division, (202) 287–5387.

Reference

Telephone, mail, and walk-in inquiries honored. Division has a reference collection of books and other publications about film, radio, television, and recording. Additional materials are available in the library's collection through the General Reading Room.

Finding Aids

Television: Title card catalog; *Catalog of Copyright Entries, Motion Pictures* (two volumes, 1950–1969) plus semi-annual supplements (includes television) (R–30); *Television Programs in the Library of Congress: Programs Available for Research as of December 1978* (R–30).

Radio: *Radio Broadcasts in the Library of Congress 1924–1941* (R–30), title card catalog, lists of specific collections.

Use

In-house: Only reference copies of materials are available for in-house use only by serious researchers. Write well ahead for appointment. Undergraduates must have a letter from faculty advisor. No charge for playback facilities.

Television: Hours: 8:30–4:30, Monday–Friday. Playback facilities: (3) 16mm flatbed viewing equipment, (3) 35mm flatbed viewing equipment, (1) ¾″ videocassette player and monitor, (1) ½″ VHS videocassette player and monitor, (1) ½″ Beta videocassette player and monitor, (1) video disc player and monitor.

Radio: Sound recordings are available for in-house use only by serious researchers. Hours: 8:30–5:00, Monday–Friday, walk-in service; 8:30–5:00, Saturday. Appointment

needs to be made during the week for Saturday use. Playback facilities: (2) audio cassette, (7) phono discs (2 have 78 rpm capability), (5) open reel, (1) 8-track.

A–12

Museum of Broadcasting
One East 53rd Street
New York, NY 10022
(212) 752–4690

TELEVISION/RADIO ENTERTAINMENT/NEWS/COMMERCIALS

Collection

Television: More than 9,000 titles from the major networks, and some from public television and foreign networks. Sampling of complete day of broadcasts from network affiliates and independent stations throughout the United States (1939–present).

Radio: 10,000 titles from ABC, CBS, NBC. Complete day broadcasts for September 21, 1939; D-Day 1944; VE Day 1945; VJ Day 1945; and assassination of Kennedy, November 22, 1963. NBC radio programs from 1927–1937; 1937–1969 are held at the Library of Congress (see A–11). Music and entertainment programs included (1920–present).

Print: 2,400 radio scripts; 1,600 are available for public use on microfiche (1927–present).

Finding Aids

Card catalog: In-depth cross reference of programs by title, subject, production credits, date, network, genre, and cast.

Print catalog: *Subject Guide to the Radio and Television Collection of the Museum of Broadcasting* (R–31).

Use

In-house: museum is open to the public for entertainment viewing. Some membership privileges. Allow members to reserve playback areas in advance. Serious researchers may make special arrangements with museum administration. All materials are for in-house use only. Hours: 12:00–5:00, Wednesday–Saturday, 12:00–8:00 Tuesday.

Playback facilities: (23) carrels with ½″ videocassette, monitor, and audiocassette playback; (3) large viewing rooms for special programs sponsored by museum; (63)-seat theater; (40)-seat video theater.

Fees: $3.00 donation requested from non-members; $2.00 students, $1.50 senior citizens, children under 13. Membership: $30 per year; $20 for students, senior citizens, and nonresidents; $40 family; $125 contributing.

A-13

Museum of Modern Art
Video Archives
11 West 53rd Street
New York, NY 10019
(212) 708-9689
TELEVISION
ENTERTAINMENT/EDUCATION/COM-
  MERCIALS

Collection
106 television programs about artists (1951–1974), 79 commercials (1953–1972), 95 videotapes by artists (1971–present).

Finding Aids
Lists by artists.

Use
Archives are not available for use at this time. Viewing facilities will be available when new museum building is completed. Contact archives for current information.

A-14

National Archives and Records Service
Special Archives Division
Motion Picture and Sound Recording Branch
Washington, DC 20408
(202) 786-0041
TELEVISION/RADIO
NEWS

Collection
Newscasts: CBS Evening Newscasts and *Morning News, Midday News, Newsbreak* (daily) (April 11, 1974–present). Department of Defense kinescopes—approxi-

mately 600 reels of television network news programs 1965–1976 that cover stories of interest to the Defense Department, including Vietnam, arms limitation, and foreign relations news.

News special events: *CBS News Special Reports* (April 1, 1974–present). ABC and NBC selected news special events (1976–1982). Collection includes State of the Union addresses, impeachment hearings, Humphrey memorial ceremony, Watergate hearings, 1976 Democratic and Republican conventions, 1976 election night, Carter's inauguration, Ford and Carter debates, and all televised presidential speeches.

Other television news programs: *Longines Chronoscope*, a weekly series of 15-minute interview television programs on the CBS network, originating in New York, from June 11, 1951, until April 2, 1955. (Eleanor Roosevelt, Henry Cabot Lodge, Jr., Joseph McCarthy, Robert Moses, Dean Rusk, and John Foster Dulles are among the 460 individuals interviewed.) These programs are on kinescope and in the public domain. American Enterprise Institute (AEI) *Public Debates of the 70's*, 30 videotapes of programs broadcast on local television stations from 1972 to 1975.

Other news resources: *Universal Newsreels*. (Entire library of newsreels from 1929–1967, except from 1941 to 1944. The archives is currently securing copies of these years to complete the collection.) Viewing copies are available from 1956 to 1967 and indexed in a card catalog. The earlier nitrate copies of the newsreels eventually will be copied onto videotape for public viewing.

Other newsreels: *March of Time* (Stock Film Library), 1935–1951; *Fox-Movietone*, 1957–1963; *Paramount News*, 1940–1957; *Hearst News of the Day*, 1963–1967. (Indexed in card catalog.) CBS-WTOP radio newscasts (Washington, D.C.) (1937–1955); NPR (National Public Radio) newscasts (1971–1973) (continuing donation, five years' delay); ABC radio network newscasts (1945–1967). Copies of WTOP newscasts and some other materials are available for purchase.

Finding Aids

Department of Defense Kinescopes: chronological shelf list.

CBS news and specials: *CBS News Index and CBS News Television Broadcasts* (R–14) since 1975, and *Television News Index and Abstracts* (R–13).

Longines Chronoscopes: chronological shelf list.

American Enterprise Institute: chronological shelf list.

Radio newscasts: chronological shelf list.

Use

In-house: National Archives is open to the public from 9:00 to 5:00, Monday–Friday, excluding holidays. Researchers should call the Motion Picture Section, (202) 786-0041, 0042, 0043, to identify materials to be viewed and to reserve playback facilities. The staff has experience helping researchers to use the collection effectively. Before entering the Motion Picture Section, all researchers must have a Researcher Identification Card. (This may be obtained from Room 230 on the second floor of the Archives Building, Pennsylvania Avenue entrance.) There is no charge for in-house viewing. At this time, compiled excerpts from newscasts are not available through the National Archives.

Playback facilities: Video: (1) ½″ reel-to-reel, (1) ¾″ videocassette, (1) color monitor; film: (2) 16mm flatbed film viewing table (Steenbeck), (4) 35mm flatbed film viewing table (Steenbeck); audio: (3) reel-to-reel (1) cassette; microform: (1) microfiche reader.

Mail requests: Only CBS News materials on ¾″ videocassette may leave the archives and are requested through standard interlibrary loan procedures. Orders are usually processed in fifteen business days. A fee of $5.00 is charged for postage on videocassette. Check archives for current fees.

Purchase of materials: *Longines Chronoscope, AEI Debates of the 70's*, and *Universal Newsreels* are available for purchase on videocassette. Check archives for current fees.

Regional archive branches: Evening network news programs and news specials may be viewed at presidential libraries and regional archive branches. Consult each center for specific procedures.[26]

The following presidential libraries have news programs other than those in the National Archives collection in Washington, D.C.: Lyndon B. Johnson Library, 2313 Red River Street, Austin, TX 78705, (512) 397-5137; John F. Kennedy Library, Morrisey Boulevard, Columbia Point, Boston, MA 02125, (617) 929-4500; Dwight D. Eisenhower Library, Abilene, KS 67410, (913) 752-4738; Gerald R. Ford Library, 1000 Beale Avenue, Ann Arbor, MI 48109, (313) 668-2218. For information on future presidential libraries, call (202) 523-3212 (Presidential Libraries Department of the National Archives).

A–15

NBC News Archival Services
30 Rockefeller Plaza
Room 902
New York, NY 10020
(212) 664-3271
TELEVISION
NEWS

Collection

Newscasts: Videotapes of entire newscasts (1975–present), selected videotapes and kinescopes of entire newscasts (1963–present), selected film and videotape segments (1950–1975), videocassettes from news bureaus (field cassettes) (1976–present), Stock Shot Library (1½ million feet of newsfilm) (1940–present), Space Library (110,000 feet of film donated by NASA, and NBC space materials) (1960–current).

News special events: Kinescope (1940–1950s), videotape (1950s–present) (both format dates not inclusive).

Other television news programs: Documentaries (more than 3,000) (1950s–

present); *Prime Time* (July 1979–present); *Today Show*, entire program (1976–present), selected features (1952–present); *Week-End* (Oct. 1974–June 1979); *First Tuesday* (Jan. 1969–Sept. 1971, Jan. 1973–Aug. 1973); *Chronolog* (Oct. 1971–July 1972).
Radio: (See Library of Congress A-11, and Museum of Broadcasting A-12.)

Finding Aids

Newscasts: Entire newscasts (May 1977–present: computer; April 1975–April 1977: log); features and stock footage (1970, Aug. 1974–current: computer; 1971–July 1974: computer, in process; 1963–1970s: log; 1951–1969: abstracts by date); videocassettes from bureaus (1976–May 1977: computer; Washington, D.C. bureau, 1976–1978: computer); Space Library (1961–present: computer).

News special events: Kinescope (1940–1950s: logs where available), videotape (1976–present: computer; 1950s–present: logs where available).

Other television news programs: Documentaries (1978–present: computer; 1950–1977: card catalog); *Prime Time* (July 1979–present: computer; *Today Show,* entire program (May 1977–present: computer), entire program (April 1975–April 1977: log), features (1963–1970s: card catalog); *Week-End* (Oct. 1974–June 1979: computer/card catalog); *First Tuesday* (Jan. 1969–Sept. 1971: computer/card catalog; Jan. 1973–Aug. 1973: computer/card catalog); *Chronolog* (Oct. 1971–July 1972: computer/card catalog).

Use

In-house: The purposes of the NBC Archival Services are to serve the NBC news division, assist outside researchers, and sell stock footage. Outside researchers should request use of the facility by mail, including references and purpose of study.
Fees: Rates subject to change. NBC staff assistance, $15.00 per hour; viewing, ¾″ videocassette, $77.00 per hour; viewing, 2″ quad videotape, $100.00 per hour; viewing, film, $25.00 per hour.

Mail requests: Contact Films, Inc., for available NBC documentaries (R–23)
Purchase/licensing of materials: All film and videotape newscast segments without the voice or image of an NBC news correspondent or reporter may be obtained via licensing agreement. Consult the archive for price information and royalty fees for commercial use of materials.

A–16

National Jewish Archive of Broadcasting
Jewish Museum
1109 Fifth Avenue
New York, NY 10128
(212) 860-1886
TELEVISION/RADIO/REFERENCE
NEWS/ENTERTAINMENT/EDUCATIONAL/COMMERCIALS

Collection (1949–current)

More than 500 television programs and 100 radio programs from American commercial broadcasting that have Jewish-related subjects. Foreign broadcasts also included, public broadcasting, and the complete video recording of the trial of Adolf Eichmann.

Finding Aids

Annotated list.
Computerized catalog (planned for 1985).

Use

By appointment only for serious research. Screenings of the collection are available to the public in the Jewish Museum's auditorium.

A–17

Peter Vest Collection from DuMont Television Network
P.O. Box 2306 CS
Pullman, WA 99163
(509) 332-4748
TELEVISION
ENTERTAINMENT/NEWS

Private Collection (1949–1956)

Approximately 200 television shows from DuMont Television Network. The kinescopes have been tramsferred to ¾″ video-cassette.

Finding Aids
Card catalog (in progress).
Transcripts (1,400 of all shows in the collection).

Use
Unavailable for use at this time. Contact Donald Zimmerman at above address for current information.

A-18

Political Television Commercial Archives
1821 Rosemary Road
Highland Park, IL 60035
(312) 831-2294
(312) 648-4400
TELEVISION/RADIO
COMMERCIALS

Private Collection (1952–present)
Contains 8,000 political commercials, mostly television, ranging from 10 seconds to 30 minutes in length. Campaigns range from candidates for President and other national offices to local election positions, such as for mayor, judge, and school board officials. Good samples of nationwide local elections. Some foreign commercials are also included.

Finding Aids
List.

Use
Limited in-house use. Contact Julian Kanter, Director of the Archives, for permission to use the collection.

A-19

Public Television Program Archive
Public Broadcasting Service (PBS)
475 L'Enfant Plaza. S.W.
Washington, DC 20034
(202) 488-5010
TELEVISION/PRINT
EDUCATION/NEWS/ENTERTAINMENT

Collection (1953–present)
50,000 nationally distributed programs:
NET (National Education Service) (1953–1970); syndicated programs from Educational Television Station Program Service (1965–1971); Public Broadcasting Service (1970–present); Public Television Library (1971–1980); PBS Video (formerly Public Television Library) (1980–present).

Finding Aids
Computer printout (1953–present).
Inventory list, by title (1953–present).

Use
In-house: Limited, since at this writing, the archive no longer is functioning. Consult Salome Swaim. Preferable to contact copyright owner of program for viewing permission.
Mail order: Consult *PBS Video Catalog* (R-23) for programs available for rent and sale.

A-20

Television Information Office
745 Fifth Avenue
New York, NY 10022
(212) 759-6800
TELEVISION REFERENCE
ENTERTAINMENT/NEWS/COMMERCIALS/EDUCATION

Reference
Large selection of books, periodicals, research studies, and clipping files covering a wide range of television-related subjects. Mail and telephone inquiries honored.

Use
In-house: Hours 9:30–5:00, Monday–Friday, by appointment only.

A-21

Television News Study Center
George Washington University
Gelman Library
2130 H Street, N.W.
Washington, DC 20052
(202) 676-7218
TELEVISION REFERENCE

Reference
Selection of all available finding aids to available television news programs. Refer

ral service to television news archive collections, in particular, the Vanderbilt Television News Archive. Finding aids include complete sets of *Television News Index and Abstracts* (R–13) and prepublication copies, *CBS News Index* and transcripts (R–14), and transcripts to *MacNeil/Lehrer Report* (R–17). Study guides available on location of news archive resources (R–32). Mail and telephone inquiries honored.

Use

In-house: Hours 8:30–10:00, Monday–Friday; 10:00–6:00, Saturday; 12:00–10:00, Sunday.

Playback facilities: The center provides video playback areas to television news researchers. Contact the Head, Reserves and Media Resources, to arrange for use of the study areas. One video carrel with ¾″ videocassette player and monitor. Fees may be charged for certain services.

A–22

UCLA Radio Archives
Department of Theater Arts
University of California, Los Angeles
Melnitz Hall, Room 1438
Los Angeles, CA 90024
(213) 825–7357
RADIO
ENTERTAINMENT/NEWS/COMMER-
CIALS

Collection (1932–present)

Radio: 10,000 programs, including a large collection of Jack Benny shows; *Fred Allen Show; Hallmark Playhouse; Hall of Fame; The Bing Crosby Show; Richard Diamond, Private Detective; George Burns and Gracie Allen Show; Beulah;* and *Arthur Godfrey Time* are among the series held in the archives.

Print: 1,700 radio scripts are held in the Theater Arts Library (see ATAS-UCLA Television Archive, A–1). Jack Benny's papers and most of his radio scripts are held in the Department of Special Collections.

Finding Aids

Card catalog in progress.

Use

In-house: Available for in-house use only by appointment. The archives is the process of developing public services and should be contacted for current information.

Playback facilities: (2) audiocassettes.

A–23

Vanderbilt Television News Archive
Vanderbilt University Library
Nashville, TN 37203
(615) 332–2927
TELEVISION
NEWS/COMMERCIALS

Collection

Newscasts: ABC, CBS, NBC: weekdays (Aug. 5, 1968–present), some weekends (1971–Dec. 2, 1978), most weekends (Dec. 9, 1978–present). From Aug. 5, 1968, to May 1, 1979, programs were recorded off-air onto 1″ reel-to-reel black-and-white video recorders, and on May 2, 1979, began to record in color onto ¾″ videocassette. On Dec. 9, 1978, George Washington University Library started to record weekend newscasts in color onto ¾″ videocassette for the Vanderbilt collection. Before that time, some of the weekend newscasts were taped. Beginning Jan. 1, 1977, all videotapes are electronically coded, displaying at the top of the screen the network, date, and time of broadcast.

News special events: ABC, CBS, NBC, PBS (Aug. 5, 1968). Includes Democratic and Republican presidential conventions, election night coverage, inauguration, and other programs about the electoral process; Congressional hearings, such as Watergate impeachment debate, Bert Lance hearings; Presidential Press Conference; and speeches.

Face the Nation, Issues and Answers, Meet the Press (1970–present).

Print: Transcripts from CBS lawsuit (1973–1976).

Finding Aids

Newscasts: *Television News Index and Abstracts* (R–12) (Aug. 1968–present).

Vanderbilt Television News Archive
APPLICATION FOR USE OF TAPE RECORDINGS
—please type or print clearly—

NAME_____TELEPHONE_____
      last   first   middle   area code/number

ADDRESS_____
       number   street   city   state   zip code

INSTITUTION REPRESENTED (if any)_____
                         name   address   department

PROFESSOR OR SPONSOR GUIDING STUDY (if any)_____
                                   name   title

TERM OF LOAN_____
        date needed   date pledged for return

MATERIAL REQUESTED_____
        (if lengthy order or compilation, use tabular form or otherwise list)

INTENDED USE OF MATERIAL_____

_____
(manner in which the material is to be used, including time and place of use and audience, is of interest to the Archive in evaluating its services)

TAPE FORMATS: Reel Formats: _____ 1 inch Ampex Type A   _____ ½ inch EIAJ-1
                  Cassette Formats: _____ ¾ inch   _____ ½ inch Beta   _____ ½ inch VHS
                  Audio Format: _____ cassette

NOTE: Depending on the extent and comprehensiveness of compilations, returned tapes may or may not be kept for later use. Unless the original user instructs otherwise, compilations will likely be erased.

Public law 94-553 includes provisions effective January 1, 1978, regarding copyright in audio-visual works and the archiving of television news broadcasts. Users of the Archive should be advised that some of the materials in the collection contain a notice of copyright and be guided by provisions of the statute in using materials from the Archive.

LOAN AGREEMENT

1. Tapes are on loan and are to be returned to the Vanderbilt Television News Archive by date specified above.
2. Use of this material is subject to the stated service charges, including costs of any tape damaged in use.

_____   _____
        signature   date

(Form for compilation tape orders)						
VANDERBILT TELEVISION NEWS ARCHIVE						
Please list items by network, chronologically, only one						
network per sheet. Copy form before use. NETWORK_____						

DATE	PAGE	START	STOP	TOTAL TIME	FOR VTNA	COMMENTS/ DESCRIPTION

News specials and other news programs: chronological shelf list.

Use

In-house: Hours 8:00–6:00, Monday-Friday; weekend appointments are available with special arrangements of archive staff. Write or call the archive to reserve viewing areas and to identify materials needed. A fee of $6.00 per viewing hour is charged for academic uses and $10.00 per viewing hour for other uses. Academic uses are considered to be uses by students, faculty, and other people connected with academic institutions for instructional and research purposes.

Playback facilities: (2): 1″ black-and-white, reel-to-reel video players and monitors; (2) ¾″ color videocassette players and monitors.

Mail requests: All newscasts and most news specials are loaned from the archive. Nothing is sold. Vanderbilt performs a special compilation service in which news segments selected by the researcher are edited onto a single tape. This unique service saves both time and money.

How to order: All requests for news items must be researched by the borrower. "Application for Use of Tape Recordings" (page 35), which is both an order form and loan agreement, must accompany all orders. Compilation orders require an additional form (included here) whereby the borrower lists each news item in chronological order by date, time, and descriptive heading for each network requested. *Television News Index and Abstracts* is the primary source for this information.

Formats available: 1″ reel-to-reel videotape; ½″ reel-to-reel videotape; ¾″ videocassette; ½″ videocassette; audiocassette.

Fees:	*Academic*	*Other*
Compilation tape (video and audio	$60 per hr.	$100 per hr.

| Duplicated video | $30 per hr. | $50 per hr. |
| Duplicated audio | $12 per hr. | $20 per hr. |

A–24

Wisconsin Center for Film and Theater Research
816 State Street
The University of Wisconsin
Madison, WI 53706
(608) 262–0585
TELEVISION
ENTERTAINMENT/NEWS/COMMER-CIALS
Collection (1948–present)
Television: Approximately 4,000 titles of entertainment series and specials, documentary series, news specials, and commercials
Print: More than 200 manuscript collections relating to film, television, and theater
Photographs: More than 1,000,000 items

relating to productions and individuals in film, television, and theater.
Finding Aids
Card catalog
Collections of the Mass Communciations History Center, and the Wisconsin Center for Film and Theater Research (R–33)
Sources for Mass Communications, Film and Theater Research: A Guide (R–33).
Use
In-house: All materials are available for use at Film and Manuscripts Archive, The State Historical Society of Wisconsin, 816 State Street, Madison, WI 53706, (608) 262–0585.
Hours: Film Archive, 10:00–4:30, Monday–Friday, by appointment only; Manuscript Reading Room, 8:00–5:00, Monday–Friday, some Saturdays.
Playback facilities: (5) 16mm flatbed film viewing tables, (1) 35mm flatbed viewing table, (1) ½″ reel-to-reel videotape player, (2) ¾″ videocassette players, (2) monitors.

Reference Appendix

The following list of reference materials pertains to books, periodicals, catalogs, and documents that will help researchers locate television shows. It is an annotated ordering list for academics and librarians to build a print collection of television research materials. Ordering procedures and information as of June 1984 are included where available.

General Television Program Reference Books
R–1   Vincent Terrace, *The Complete Encyclopedia of Television Programs*, 2nd ed., 2 vols. (Cranbury, N.J.: A. S. Barnes, 1978).
_____, *Television 1970–1980* (La Jolla, CA: A. S. Barnes, 1981).
R–2   Lester Brown, *The New York Times Encyclopedia of Television Programs* (New York: Times Books, 1977).
R–3   Tim Brooks and Earle Marsh, *The*

Complete Directory to Prime Time Network TV Shows 1946–Present, rev. ed. (New York: Ballantine, 1981).
R–4   Alex McNeil, *Total Television: A Comprehensive Guide to Programming from 1948–1980*, 2nd ed. (New York: Penguin Books, 1980).

Books and Periodicals That Identify Episode Titles
R–5   Nina David, *TV Season 1978–1979* (Phoenix: Oryx Press, 1980).
_____, *TV Season 1977–1978* (Phoenix: Oryx Press, 1979).
_____, *1976–1977* (Phoenix: Oryx Press, 1978).
_____, *TV Season 1975–1976* (Phoenix: Oryx Press, 1977).
_____, *TV Season 1974–1975* (Phoenix: Oryx Press, 1976). (Annual Publication)
R–6   Jeb H. Perry, *Universal Television,*

1950–1980 (Metuchen, N.J.: Scarecrow Press, 1983).

R-7   Titles available from the Broadcast Information Bureau (BIB)
Series, Serials and Packages: Domestic Edition; *Series, Serials and Packages: Foreign Language Edition* and supplement.
TV Feature Film Source Book and two supplements.
Ordering address: Broadcast Information Bureau, Inc., 100 Lafayette Drive, Syosset, NY 11791, (516) 496-3355.
Most local television stations subscribe to the BIB series and may be willing to donate the previous years' issues to your institution rather than throwing them away.

R-8   Larry James Gianakos, *Television Drama Series Programming: A Comprehensive Chronicle, 1959–1975* (Metuchen, N.J.: Scarecrow Press, 1978).
_____, *Television Drama Series Programming: A Comprehensive Chronicle, 1947–1959* (Metuchen, N.J.: Scarecrow Press, 1980).
_____, *Television Drama Series Programming: A Comprehensive Chronicle, 1975–1980* (Metuchen, N.J.: Scarecrow Press, 1981).
_____, *Television Drama Series Programming: A Comprehensive Chronicle, 1980–1982* (Metuchen, N.J.: Scarecrow Press, 1983).

R-9   *Television Index*, 150 Fifth Avenue, New York, NY 10011. Descriptive information on current network prime-time programs. Weekly publication since 1949. Subscription to service is necessary in order to use library services for past information.

R-10 *TV Guide*. Available from Triangle Publications, 100 Matsonford Road, Radnor, PA 19088. Past issues from April 1953 to 1979 are available on microfilm. *TV Guide 25 Year Index*, one volume that covers all material in *TV Guide* except for the program listings, has recently been released. Orders for past issues and the *Index* are to be sent to Cathy Johnson, Microfilm Library, c/o *TV Guide*.

R-11 Examples of books written about specific television series: Richard P. Adler, ed., *All in the Family: A Critical Appraisal* (New York: Praeger Publishers, 1979); also in paperback edition (Palo Alto, Cal.: Cambria Press, 1979). Gary Gerani and Paul H. Schulman, *Fantastic Television: A Pictorial History of Sci-Fi, the Unusual and the Fantastic from Captain Video to the Star Trek Phenomenon and Beyond . . .* (New York: Harmony Books, 1977). Bart Andrews, *Lucy and Ricky and Fred and Ethel: The Story of "I Love Lucy"* (New York: Dutton, 1967). Marc Scott Zicree, *The Twilight Zone Companion* (New York: Bantam Books, 1983).

R-12 Examples of reference work pertaining to particular genre are:
George W. Woolery, *Children's Television: The First Thirty-five Years, 1946–1981. Part I: Animated Cartoon Series* (Metuchen, N.J.: Scarecrow Press, 1983).
_____, *Children's Television: The First Thirty-five Years, 1946–1981. Part II: Live, Film, and Tape Series* (Metuchen, N.J.: Scarecrow Press, 1984).
Joel Eisner and David Krinsky, *Television Comedy Series: an Episode Guide to 153 TV Sitcoms in Syndication* (Jefferson, N.C.: McFarland, 1984).
Raymond William Stedman, *The Serials: Suspense and Drama by Installment,* 2nd ed. (Norman, Okla.: University of Oklahoma Press, 1977) (includes soap operas).

Identification Sources for Television News Programs

R-13   *Television News Index and Abstracts*
Abstracts of evening news programs for ABC, CBS, and NBC, with monthly and annual subject indexes. Distributed on three-month delay from current broadcast. Finding aid to Vanderbilt Television News Archive Collection (A-22). Annual subscription 12 issues plus index. Back issues on microfilm since 1972; August 1968–December 1971 on microfilm. Prepublication copies 15¢ per page.
Ordering address: Vanderbilt Television News Archive, Vanderbilt University Library, Nashville, TN 37203, (615) 322-2927.

R-14   *CBS News Index, CBS News Television Broadcasts*, and *Face the Nation.*
CBS News Index (finding aid to *CBS News Television Broadcast* transcripts) (1975–present).
CBS News Television Broadcasts (transcripts of all CBS News programs) (1963–present).
Face the Nation (separate transcripts and index of programs) (1954–present).
Ordering address: Microfilming Corporation of America, 1620 Hawkins Avenue, P.O. Box 10, Sanford, NC 27330, (800) 334-7501.

R-15   *Meet the Press.*
Microfiche transcripts of the NBC weekly news program beginning in 1957. Subscription includes transcripts and alphabetical listing of guests with program data.
Transcripts (1957–present), $1008 inclusive; individual year, $42.
Ordering address: Customer Service Department, Micro Photo Division, Bell and Howell, Wooster, OH 44691.

Current subscription for paper copy may be obtained from Kelly Press, Inc., P.O. Box 8648, Washington, DC 20011, (202) 529-1600. Back issues available since 1978.

R-16   ABC news programs.
Transcripts of the following news programs are available from *Journal Graphics*:
Nightline (Sept. 28, 1981–present), PO# 234, $2.00 each.
This Week with David Brinkley (Nov. 15, 1981–present), PO# 247, $3.00 each.
20/20 (April 30, 1981–present), PO# 2020, $3.00.
Close-Up (documentaries) (Dec. 21, 1981–present), PO# 770, $3.00 each.
Ordering address: *Journal Graphics* (note: use PO# corresponding to requested program), Ansonia Station, New York, NY 10023.

R-17   *Broadcast Review and Index.*
Index and transcripts of PBS's *MacNeil/Lehrer Report.*
Index (1976–present).
Transcripts (1976–present).
Ordering address: Microfilming Corporation of America, 1620 Hawkins Avenue, P.O. Box 10, Sanford, NC 27330, (800) 334-7501.

R-18   Television Documentaries.
William A. Bluem, *Documentary in American Television* (New York: Hastings House, 1965).
Charles Montgomery Hammond, Jr., *The Image Decade: Television Documentary, 1965-1975* (New York: Hastings House, 1981).

General Educational Film and Videotape Title Locators

R-19   *The Video Source Book* and *The Video Program Index.*
Annual publication.
Ordering address: The National Video Clearinghouse, Inc., P.O. Box

3, Department 40 AF, Syosset, NY 11791.

R-20   *Educational Film Locator*, 2nd ed., 1980.
Ordering address: R. R. Bowker Company, 1180 Avenue of the Americas, New York, NY 10036.

R-21   *Index to Sixteen-mm Educational Films*, 7th ed., 1980.
Index to Educational Video Tapes, 5th ed., 1980.
Ordering address: National Information Center for Educational Media (NICEM), University of Southern California, University Park, Los Angeles, CA 90007.

R-22   *Film Programmer's Guide to 16mm Rentals*, 3rd ed., 1980.
Ordering address: Reel Research, Box 6037, Albany, CA 94706.

R-23   Sources for catalogs of news programs for rent and/or sale produced by the television networks:
ABC: ABC Video Enterprises, 1330 Avenue of the Americas, New York, NY 10011, (212) 887-5706.
CBS: For information or in-house distribution, and for a copy of *The Best of Everything: CBS Broadcast International Program Catalog*, contact CBS Broadcast International, 51 West 52nd Street, New York, NY 10019, (212) 975-8585.
NBC: Films, Inc., 114 Wilmette Avenue, Wilmette, IL 60091, (800) 323-4222.
PBS: *PBS Video Catalog*, 475 L'Enfant Plaza, S.W., Washington, DC 20034, (202) 488-5220.

Sources That Describe Some Television Archives

R-24   Linda Mehr, ed., *Motion Pictures, Television and Radio: A Union Catalog of Manuscripts and Special Collections in the Western United States* (Boston: G. K. Hall, 1977). $27.

R-25   Bonnie G. Rowan, *Scholar's Guide to Washington, D.C., Film and Video Collections* (Washington, D.C.: Smithsonian Press, 1980).

Sources of Information about Discoveries of New Television Archive Collections

R-26   *The American Film Institute (AFI) Education Newsletter.* This publication was suspended with the May/June 1983 issue but may be published again by Fall 1984. Five issues per year. Complimentary subscription when placed on mailing list.
Ordering address: Education Liaison, American Film Institute, 2021 North Western Ave., Los Angeles, CA 90027, (213) 856-7725.

Catalogs to Television Archive Collections

R-27   Catalog to ATAS-UCLA Collection (A-1):
A Catalog of the Study Collection of the Academy of Television Arts and Sciences, UCLA Archives (San Mateo, CA: Redwood Press, 1980).

R-28   Marvin Barrett, ed., *Broadcast Journalism 1979-1981. The Eighth Alfred I. duPont/Columbia University Survey* (New York: Everest House Publishers, 1982). This is the most recent edition in a series of books published every two years. It reports on the duPont awards and trends in broadcasting.

R-29   Catalog of CND Commercial Library (A-6):
Lincoln Diamant, *Television's Classic Commercials: The Golden Years, 1948-1958* (New York: Hastings House, 1971).

R-30   Finding aid to some titles in the Library of Congress collection (A-11):
U.S. Copyright Office, Library of Congress, *Catalog of Copyright Entries, Motion Pictures, 1950-1969* (Washington, D.C.; U.S. Government Printing Office). Semi-annual supplements. *Television Programs in*

the Library of Congress: Programs Available for Research as of December 1978 (working title) (Washington, D.C.: Library of Congress, forthcoming, projected 1985).

James Smart, comp., *Radio Broadcasts in the Library of Congress* (Washington, D.C.: Library of Congress, 1982).

R–31 Catalogs to collection at the Museum of Broadcasting (A–12): *Subject Guide to the Radio and Television Collection of the Museum of Broadcasting*, 1979, 2nd ed. (available from museum).

R–32 Study guide exclusively locating television news archives: Fay Schreibman, *Television News Resources: A Guide to Collections* (Washington, D.C.: George Washington University, 1980).

Prepaid orders only. Order from: Television News Study Center, George Washington University, Gelman Library, 2130 H Street, N.W., Washington, DC 20052.

R–33 Catalog of collections at the Wisconsin Center for Film and Theatre Research (A–23):
Collections of the Mass Communications History Center and the Wisconsin Center for Film and Theatre Research. Order from the archive.
Sources for Mass Communications, Film and Theater Research: A Guide (Madison: State Historical Society of Wisconsin, 1981). Refers to print collections and if audiovisual materials are included.

Endnotes

1. The author thanks the following colleagues for their assistance in preparing this article: Lawrence Karr, former director, Preservation, at the American Film Institute; Erik Barnouw, Professor Emeritus, Columbia University; Barbara Humphreys at the Library of Congress; and the Television Archives Advisory Committee for their constant support and for filling out a painfully lengthy questionnaire about their archives; William Adams, Director, Television and Politics Study Program, and Michael Robinson, Director, Media Analysis Project, George Washington University, for taking time to review and criticize this work; Rosemary Hanes, a budding film archivist; and special thanks to Lawrence Lichty, Professor of Communications, University of Maryland, for sharing his knowledge in this field and for providing the environment in which to write this essay.

2. The American Film Institute holds an annual Film/TV Documentation Workshop designed for researchers, educators, and librarians. Some sessions describe how to locate film and television resources. Contact Anne G. Schlosser, Head Librarian at the Louis B. Mayer Library, American Film Institute, Los Angeles, for more information about the next workshop. (A–4). Also consult Fay C. Schreibman, *Broadcast Television: A Resource Guide*, Factfile #15 (Washington, D.C.: American Film Institute, 1983). This is a general guide to the various information resources about television.

3. Consult Peter Bukalski and Margaret Bults, eds., *The American Film Institute Guide to College Courses in Film and Television* (Princeton, N.J.: Peterson's Guides, 1980) for identification of the colleges that offer broadcast classes. The colleges are presented by geographic areas.

4. Examples of this are at Antioch College, the Antioch Television Communications Study Center, and at the Massachusetts Institute of Technology, the News Study Group, where selected news materials are maintained for specific research studies. The Annenberg School of Communications, University of Pennsylvania, holds a

particularly valuable collection of television programs. Since 1968, Annenberg has taped one week per year of prime-time entertainment programming, which is used as the basic material in research for Cultural Indicators. The best known of these indicators is on violence, which has been used in reports for the National Commission on Causes and Prevention of Violence, the Surgeon General's Scientific Advisory Committees on Television and Social Behavior, the White House Office of Telecommunications Policy, and others. The only access outside researchers may have to these materials is through contract agreement for Annenberg research staff to perform a particular analysis. The vast amounts of data already surveyed about these programs cover trends in television content and viewer conceptions of social reality. For more information, contact Nancy Signorielli, Annenberg School of Communications, University of Pennsylvania, 3620 Walnut Street C 5, Philadelphia, PA 19104.

5. This lists museums and historical societies that hold mostly donated local television news footage and have some entertainment programs.
California: Oakland Museum, 1000 Oak Street, Oakland, CA 94607, (415) 834-2413 (KPIX newsfilm, 1950--); Sacramento Museum, 1931 K Street, Sacramento, CA 95814, (916) 445-4209 (KCRA, 1950-1970+); San Francisco State University, Audio Visual Center, 1600 Holloway Avenue, San Francisco, CA 94132, (415) 469-2637 (KQED, 1960-1980); *Connecticut*: Wesleyan University Archives, Olin Library, Church Street, Middletown, CT 06457, (203) 347-9411 x2456; *District of Columbia*: Library of Congress (see description in Section III, C, 1, above); *Illinois*: Chicago Historical Society, Clark Street and North Avenue, Chicago, IL 60614, (312) 642-4600 (WGN, 1948-1977; *Kukla, Fran and Ollie,* 1948-1957); *Indiana*: Indiana Historical Society, 315 W. Ohio Street, Indianapolis, IN 46302, (317) 232-1882

(WRTV and WRBN, 1960-1970); Indiana State Library, 140 N. Senate, Indianapolis, IN 46204, (317) 232-3671 (WRTV and WRBN, 1972-1976); *Maryland*: Enoch Pratt Free Library and the University of Baltimore, Audio Visual Department, 400 Cathedral Street, Baltimore, MD 21201, (301) 396-5430 (WMAR, 1940s–current, in negotiation); *Massachusetts*: Boston University Libraries, Department of Special Collections, 771 Commonwealth Avenue, Boston, MA 02215, (617) 353-3696 (general programs); *Maine*: Bangor Historical Society, 159 Union Street, Bangor, ME 04401, (207) 942-5766 (local news collection); *Mississippi*: Mississippi Department of Archives and History, Box 571, Jackson, MS 39205, (601) 354-6218 (WLBT, 1954-1971 and 1974-1981); *New Jersey*: New Jersey Historical Society Library, 230 Broadway, Newark, NJ 07104, (201) 483-3939 (New Jersey Public TV, Trenton, 1970-present, in negotiation); *New York*: Buffalo and Erie County Historical Society, 180 Race Street, Buffalo, NY 14216, (716) 874-0670 (WKBW, WIVB, and WGR, 1962-present); St. Bernard's Seminary Library, 2260 Lake Avenue, Rochester, NY 14612, (716) 254-1455 (television programs and scripts of the *Bishop Fulton J. Sheen Show*); *North Dakota*: State Historical Society of North Dakota, North Dakota Heritage Center, Bismarck, ND 58505, (701) 224-2666 (WDAY, 1940s–1970s; Prairie Public Television: local interviews); *Ohio*: Ohio Historical Society, I-71 and 17th Avenue, Columbus, OH 43211, (614) 466-1500 (WCMH, 1967-1971; WTVN, 1965-1980; WGSF, 1966-1976; WBNS, 1952-1978); *Pennsylvania*: Temple University, Department of Radio, Television, and Film, Philadelphia, PA 19122, (215) 787-8423 (WPVI, 1958-1962. *Note*: The Library of Congress holds KYW, 1950-1970s); *Rhode Island*: Rhode Island Historical Society, 121 Hope Street, Providence, RI 02906, (401) 331-0448 (WJAR, 1952-1976; WPRI, 1962-1978; WTEV,

1973–1975); *Washington*: Seattle Folklore Society, 1810 NW 65th Street, Seattle, WA 98117, (206) 782-1919 (50 hours of kinescopes of blues musicians from 1960s, taped by local stations); University of Washington, Media Center, Seattle, WA 98195, (206) 543-2100 (KOMO, 1954–1970); *Wisconsin*: Nebel Public Museum, 129 S. Jefferson Street, Green Bay, WI 54301, (414) 497-3764 (WBAY, 1953–1976; WFRV, 1968–1970s); Wisconsin State Historical Society, 816 State Street, Madison, WI 53706, (608) 262-2283 (WMTV, 1971–1973; WISC, 1969–1975; WKOW, 1965–1979).

6. "Video Software Marketers-Consumer," *Videography* (June 1983): 30–36. Updated annually.

7. For more information, send requests to CLIO Awards, 336 E. 59th Street, New York, NY 10022.

8. Television Information Office (A–20) has one of the few complete sets of *Series, Serials and Packages* past issues.

9. The author is chairperson of the Profile of Assembled Archives Subcommittee, Television Archives Advisory Committee, and is interested in this information for the committee's files.

10. General Revision of Copyright Law, *Public Law* 94–553, October 19, 1976.

11. *American Television and Radio Archives Act*, sec. 113, 90 *Stat.* 2601–2602 (1976), 2 *U.S. Code*, sec. 170 (1976).

12. This should not be confused with the recent Supreme Court decision regarding off-air taping of television programs for home use known as the "Betamax Case." As a result of the lawsuit brought against SONY by MCA and Walt Disney Productions, the court ruled that anything broadcast may be taped in the home as long as the tapes are not used for commercial purposes. Institutions, including educational organizations, such as archives, libraries, and colleges, may tape and retain newscasts, news specials, and programs permitted to be taped by the copyright holder; entertainment programs, documentaries, and such news programs as *60 Minutes* may be recorded and retained for limited use; see *Guidelines for Off-Air Taping of Copyrighted Programs for Educational Use: Thirty Questions Librarians Ask* (Chicago: American Library Association, 1982). For more information on the issues involved in developing these guidelines with the television industry and educational community, consult U.S. Copyright Office, Library of Congress, *Conference on Video Recording for Educational Uses July 19–22, 1977* (Washington, D.C.: U.S. Government Printing Office, 1978); and U.S. Congress, House Committee on the Judiciary, *Off-Air Taping for Educational Use*, Hearings before the Subcommittee on Courts, Civil Liberties and the Administration of Justice, 96th Cong., 1st sess., 1979.

13. "Deposits of copies or phonorecords for Library of Congress," sec. 407(e), 90 *Stat.* 2579–2590 (1976), 17 *U.S. Code*, sec. 407 (1976).

14. For a bibliography on the CBS lawsuit against Vanderbilt, see William Adams and Fay Schreibman, eds., *Television Network News: Issues in Content Research* (Washington, D.C.: George Washington University, 1978), 109–110; and Cosette Kies, "The CBS–Vanderbilt Litigation: Taping the Evening News," in John Shelton Lawrence and Bernard Timberg, eds., *Fair Use and Free Inquiry* (Norwood, N.J.: Ablex, 1980).

15. Consult Robert Schmuhl, ed., *The Classroom and the Newsroom* (Bloomington: Indiana University, 1979), for samples of papers and curricula presented at these seminars.

The Television News Study Center at George Washington University (A–20) offers equal access to past newspapers and broadcast newscasts. Several departments have taken advantage of this unique resource. Contact William Adams, Public Administration Department, and Robert Lichter, Political Science Department, at George Washington University, and Lawrence Lichty, Radio-Television-Film Division, University of Maryland, College

Park, for detailed information about application of this resource in scholarly research and teaching.

16. "Jewish Archives of Film and Broadcasting Created," *New York Times* (March 16, 1980): 57. *Note*: Since the initial writing of this article in 1980, the author has become founding director of that archive; it opened on March 27, 1984.

17. The discovery of the Peter Vest collection (see A–16) is an interesting and yet typical story of how missing collections of television shows have been found. The discoverer, Donald Zimmerman, describes his discovery:

The kinescopes were originally produced as a means of storage and distribution of television material produced at the DuMont Telecenter in New York. Mr. Peter Vest was a make-up artist at that center for many years. The material in the collection was used and expendable in the eyes of the Network. The company felt the original negative material was surplus. Apparently, instead of the kines being hauled to the dump, Mr. Vest was permitted to take what he wanted home. During approximately 1950 to 1962 they were stored on Mr. Vest's patio covered by a tarp.

Members of the family took more than half of the collection to the dump after Peter's death in 1962. His wife, who died in 1972, had no interest in the collection. The remaining kines were trucked to a small town in Iowa. Mr. Alan Vest, Peter's brother, stored the collection in Schaller, Iowa, in a popcorn warehouse. They remained there for ten years.

I heard of the collection soon after my marriage to Linette C. Mogck of St. Cloud, Minnesota. Her aunt, Pearl Vest, is Alan Vest's wife. At first there was a degree of confusion about the collection. They were mentioned to me as, 'movies of Captain Video and other TV shows.' I recognized some of the titles, but I knew that they were live TV shows and not films. I believed that the stories were a matter of vivid imagination on the part of the less specialized Mr. Vest. Upon our visitation to Iowa in 1972 I found the reels and boxes to actually contain kinescopes of the DuMont Television Network. I knew the collection was very important to the history of television. After several months of correspondence and negotiations I was able to have the collection shipped to Pullman, Washington. I was named curator of the collection by Mr. Alan Vest which was dedicated to his brother, Peter.

Since 1973 I have tried to find funding to research the collection. For a long time I only knew that I had 3,000 pounds of materials. Not until September 1977 did I receive any grant money to begin the work. A very small grant from the National Endowment for the Arts has allowed the materials to be dubbed into videocassettes.

18. Sam Kula, "There's Film in Them Thar Hills," *American Film* 3 (July–August, 1979): 14–18. Rare nitrate films of serials and newsreels from 1903 to 1929, thought to be lost, were recently found buried in the Yukon. Nitrate film is extremely inflammable, and the films were placed in the ground as landfill.

19. James Wheeler, "The Long-Term Storage of Videotape" *SMPTE (Society of Motion Picture and Television Engineers) Journal* 92:6 (June 1983): 650–654.

20. U.S. Department of Commerce, National Bureau of Standards, *Transfer of Monochrome Video Information from Magnetic Tape to Motion Picture Film for Archival Storage*, NBS Special Publication 480–31 (Washington, D.C.: U.S. Government Printing Office, 1978).

21. "Firms Join Video Disc Upgrade Race," *Electronic News* (July 16, 1979): 19. For information regarding video disc technology, consult the following articles: S. Rolph, "Disc Revolution," *Datamation* (February 1980): 147–148; "Videodiscs: The Expensive Race to be First," *Business Week* (September 15, 1975): 58–61; "New Television (video discs)," *Forbes* (June 1, 1976): 24–29; Joe Roizen, "Future of Television," *Video Systems* (June 1979): 10–15.

22. Other activities of the National Center for

Film and Video Preservation are distributing grants from the American Film Institute Preservation Program/National Endowment for the Arts, acquiring films for deposit primarily at the Library of Congress and other archives, serving as Secretariat for the Film Archives Advisory Committee, and developing special programs to travel around the country that exemplify the need for moving image preservation. The Center is also continuing the *AFI Catalog* project of films from 1911-1920. For more information, contact National Center for Film and Video Preservation, American Film Institute, 2021 North Western Avenue, Los Angeles, CA 90027, (213) 856-7658.

23. For more information about the FIAT organization, contact Fernando Rubio, Secretaire General, Federation Internationale des Archives de Télévision, c/o RTVE, Centro Empresarial Somosaguas, Calle Saturno, 10-Madrid-23, Spain.

24. United Nations Educational, Scientific and Cultural Organization (UNESCO), Special Committee of Government Experts to Prepare a Draft Recommendation Concerning the Safeguarding and Preservation of Moving Images, *Draft Recommendation Concerning the Safeguarding and Preservation of Moving Images* (Paris: CC-80/Conf. 208/3, March 27, 1980).

25. For complete information on location of radio archives in the United States, see Marvin R. Bensman, "Obtaining Old Radio Programs: A List of Sources for Research and Teaching in Radio and Television History," *Journal of Popular Culture*, XII: 2 (Fall 1979): 360-367; John Eastman, "American History on the Record," *New York Times* (December 3, 1978): sec. D, 22; Lawrence Lichty, "Sources for Research and Teaching in Radio and Television History," *Performing Arts Resources*, 1 (New York: Drama Book Specialists, 1974): 218-231 (the entire volume concentrates on film, television, and radio archives); and *Radio and Television Program Sources* (Washington, D.C.: Broadcast Pioneers Library, forthcoming).

26. Regional branches of the National Archives and Records Services (not including the Presidential Libraries) are: (Atlanta area) 1557 St. Joseph Avenue, East Point, GA 30344, (404) 763-7477; (Boston area) 380 Trapelo Road, Waltham, MA 02154, (617) 223-2657; (Chicago area) 7358 South Pulaski Road, Chicago, IL 60629, (312) 353-0161; (Denver area) Denver Federal Center, Denver, CO 80225, (303) 234-5271; (Fort Worth area) 4900 Hemphill Street (office), P.O. Box 6216 (mailing), Fort Worth, TX 76115, (817) 334-5515; (Kansas City area) 2306 East Bannister Road, Kansas City, MO 64131, (816) 926-7271; (Los Angeles area) 24000 Avila Road, Laguna Niguel, CA 92677, (714) 831-4220; (New York area) Building 22-MOT Bayonne, Bayonne, NJ 07002, (201) 951-5591; (Philadelphia area) 5000 Wissahickon Avenue, Philadelphia, PA 19144, (215) 951-5591; (San Francisco area) 1000 Commodore Drive, San Bruno, CA 94066, (415) 876-9001; (Seattle area) 6125 Sand Point Way NE, Seattle, WA 98115, (206) 442-4502.

3

Analysis of Broadcast News Content*

Raymond L. Carroll

Radio and television are important sources of news and information for the American public.[1] Consequently, scholars and critics of the broadcast media are interested in the nature of broadcast news content and the effects it may have on its audiences. To that end, this essay discusses approaches to the objective study of the content of radio and television news. The intent is to acquaint readers with various approaches to broadcast news content research, indicating the scope and direction of past studies and the orientation of further research.

This essay categorizes broadcast news content studies by whether they described content, examined influences on the news, or considered effects it may have had on audiences. These categories provide a basis for assessing approaches to the study of broadcast news. The analysis of broadcast news should consider previous work, as research and theory building can be compared to paving a road with bricks. Each piece of worthwhile research is an increment in building or testing a theory. Thus, each useful study of news content provides another brick or contribution toward the goal of understanding the process and implications of broadcast journalism.

The Premise of Content Analysis

Content analysis is a research procedure that can lead to conclusions about attributes of broadcast news, but it is not criticism of the news. Harwood defined broadcast criticism as ". . . making statements in which an event is compared with a standard of the event."[2] Young asserts that the critic serves as an influence in ". . . forming, educating and often swaying public tastes or opinions."[3] But what distinguishes content analysis from criticism are the separate activities of *analyzing* and *appreciating* style. Paisley notes that "One *analyzes* patterns of use and nonuse, conjunction and disjunction, emphasis and understatement, and so on. One *appreciates* how effectively or satisfyingly the creator has dealt with his chosen form and content."[4] Smith clarifies this difference by categorizing the "ways of knowing" held by critics and scientists. Critics

*Assistance in preparing this essay was provided to the author through a grant from the Office of Research and Service of the School of Communication at the University of Alabama.

should be fair and accurate in using sources, but there is no arbitrary limit on the kinds of support that can be used to arrive at a critical judgment. Where critics are concerned with *evaluation*, scientists are concerned with *explanation.*[5]

Thus, both the researcher and the critic assess the content of broadcasting, but their criteria are different. The researcher's goal, explanation, can be achieved only through a systematic, objective, and quantitative approach to the content. Whether that description is pleasing or the subject of scorn is better left to the critic.

Characteristics of Broadcast News Content

The unique nature of broadcast news must be understood if one is to produce meaningful analyses of its content. First, it is important to observe that the broadcast media, although effective disseminators of news and information, are primarily entertainment or recreational in orientation. Many regular members of news program audiences are also heavy viewers of and listeners to entertainment. These nonselective or regular viewers and listeners tend to watch and listen not by the program, but by the clock. News programs, then, are a part of their ritual, constituting only a small portion of the total time they spend as members of the audience.[6]

Like print news, television news and radio news are varieties of journalism. All consist of accounts and analyses of current events and issues reported by on-the-scene observers employed by organizations established for that single purpose. All three media present their accounts in the context of dramatic structure, using similar themes, formulas, and symbols in recreating the actions that give meaning and identity to events.

But differences among the media are significant. For example, in comparison to newspapers, television news is more coherently organized and unified. This difference is a consequence of television's organization and presentation, in which time is the critical limi-

tation, as contrasted with newspapers, where space is the principal constraint.

The effect of handling time causes the broadcast to be limiting. The format of news programming is prescribed, appealing to a nonselective audience with stories that are short and fast-paced. Material chosen for a report must fit these demands.

Limitations of time for radio and television news mean that many more stories, in much greater detail, are presented in newspapers. Furthermore, newspaper news is not presented with the intention that the reader consume it all, where the broadcast news story (indeed, the entire program) is designed to be wholly consumed. Therefore, radio and TV program elements are unified—a tightly structured whole—whereas newspaper stories have little planned relation to one another.

News Content Questions

Just as there are notable differences between broadcast and print news, there are varied objectives and information provided in studies of broadcast news content. The researcher interested in this subject has some presumed objective for an investigation. Such a goal should be clearly articulated as the "research question": What does the investigator wish to find out? The research question is a guide to the most appropriate procedure for conducting the investigation. Consequently, content analysis may not prove the best method for achieving the stated goal for a study.

An investigation of broadcast news content should also have a clear conceptual or theoretical objective. An analysis limited to describing the content will have little value unless it fosters greater understanding of the nature of broadcast news. In other words, a content analysis should transcend the immediate study in order to add to our knowledge of the news process. If, for example, studies of television news coverage of the Vietnam conflict merely provide descriptions of what was broadcast, they would have little value beyond providing an historic record. But Bailey, for example, provides a general indication of network news anchor personnel performance and the amount of interpretation of the news they convey.[8] His findings can be compared with observations made in other studies, thus serving as a basis for a hypothesis about news content that can be tested in subsequent research. Recent studies of American television news coverage of the Iranian crisis provide a case in point. These theses should extend our understanding of the news process and also provide a useful record of news coverage of that story. That objective is more likely to be met if the literature of television coverage of the Vietnam conflict has been considered.

Therefore, any intended study should have a clearly stated purpose, indicating how an understanding of the broadcast news process, from conception of a story idea to reaction by an audience, might be furthered. The purpose should indicate the policy implications that might be given support or refutation as a result of the analysis.

How one determines what to study is, of course, influenced by personal interest. After a researcher has identified the aspect of news content to be analyzed and has stated the specific goal or research question, the pertinent literature should be reviewed before stating hypotheses that serve as tests of the question. (Much of the literature should be assessed before or during the process of determining the research goal in order to justify the study.) Such a foundation is necessary if the analysis is to contribute to knowledge on the subject. Consequently, research contributing to understanding the news process must consider the complex production requirements, political and economic influences on news organizations, and the nature of news recipients. Unless demands on news organizations and the effects of content are considered, content analysis will be superficial.[9]

Approaches to the Analysis of Broadcast News Content

The investigator should use some organized method of assessing the literature so that all pertinent reports of studies are considered in determining the scope of the new research. Any of several ways of categorizing these studies may prove workable.[10] The following discussion, based on Gerbner's system of "cultural indicators," represents root questions for the study of news content by classifying the literature according to a larger context. With this scheme, findings that transcend specific reports to apply to other research questions can be more easily identified.

Therefore, reports are classified according to whether they ask "What is?" "What is important?" "What is right?" or "What is related to what?" Research that addresses these content questions is categorized as (1) attention analysis, (2) emphasis analysis, (3) tendency analysis, or (4) structural analysis.

Studies of "What is?" report on the distribution and frequency of attention to content attributes. Studies of "What is important?" isolate the aspects important to the message system in analyzing content emphasis. Studies of "What is right?" are measures of tendency. They are concerned with how things are presented. Studies that ask "What is related to what?" analyze structure to determine relationships among components of the message system.[11]

Attention Analysis

News content studies that ask "What is?" report on the distribution and frequency of attention to content attributes. Many analyses provide accounts of content presented during specified periods of time; the question of attention to certain kinds of news content is the premise of other content research.

Many such analyses provide support for considering policy changes in broadcast news content (that is, what should be "done" about "what is"). Recommendations can be based on evidence that can be categorized by whether they examined emphasis placed on content, compared content attributes, analyzed trends in content, or provided a record of what was broadcast.

Emphasis Some studies consider *what* is given access but generally do not go so far as to assess reasons for stress or limitation in content. Most authors use their findings as evidence of needed policy changes. For example, Adams considered aspects of local television news content. In one report, he investigated local TV news emphasis on public affairs compared with other kinds of news. The second study examined TV station allocation of newscast time to coverage of the towns and cities in the viewing area. Similarly, Dominick considered the topic of representation of geographic areas of the country in network newscasts. Based on his findings, he suggested that newscasts should systematically allocate more time to regional reports.[12] Thus, implications for policy change can be drawn from analyses of emphasis in news content.

Content Comparisons Many analyses of broadcast news compare the content of one version of the news with others. For instance, most studies of network newscasts are comparisons of content, even though the purpose of the research may be broader. Still, some analyses make such comparisons their primary purpose. An example is Fowler and Showalter's examination of network evening news selection and treatment; their purpose was to determine whether network editors exercised a common news judgment in choice of stories and order of presentation.[13]

Trends An analysis may be concerned with "What is?" over time, identifying recurring patterns in broadcast news to observe a structure in the content.[14] Bailey reported trends in the networks' nightly news coverage of the Vietnam conflict. His analysis, limited to frequency, type, and subjects of stories, did not attempt to assess why content was manifested in the observed manner. Bailey made the important point that more work was needed to analyze television coverage of that war.[15]

Records At the least, an accurate record of the content of broadcast news coverage of some situation or event provides a basis for predicting the kind of content to be expected under similar circumstances during another period. Such records may help the historian accurately assess what information was disseminated during a particular period.

Most studies that provide such records are analyses of political broadcasts. Meadow and Jackson-Beeck, for example, compared the content of the nationally televised 1960 and 1976 presidential candidates' debates. Pepper provided another record of political events coverage with his analyses of network TV coverage of election returns.[16] The utility in describing attention given various subjects during specified periods of time may be in pointing to research questions not addressed in the immediate study.

Emphasis Analysis

Emphasis analysis examines aspects of television news content that may be determined by perceptual biases—"What is important?" These are studies of who decides what content to emphasize or to exclude from news programs. Content analysis cannot determine the nature of the decisions that might affect news content, but it can identify attributes that are the apparent results of such decisions. Thus, content analysis might be teamed with some other research procedure to ascertain the relationship between components in the news dissemination process.

Gatekeeper Studies An example of such a combination of methodologies is Bailey and Lichty's analysis of the NBC film report of the shooting of a suspected Viet Cong infiltrator on a Saigon street during the height of the Vietnam conflict. This gatekeeper study analyzed both the content of the report and decisions made by various news personnel that affected the version seen on the television sets tuned to the *NBC Nightly News.*[17]

Another perspective on the gatekeeper approach is in Robinson and McPherson's analysis of network television news coverage of the presidential election campaign before the 1976 New Hampshire primary election. The study could be considered a description of the process of decision making, even though it focused on network organizational attributes, assessing the behavior of network news departments through their coverage of the campaign.[18]

What Is Left Out A promising area in news content research lies in assessing the less obvious aspects of content: not what "is," but what "isn't." The values held by gatekeepers and their organizations can be clarified by assessing both the content that was broadcast and excluded. Lefever's missing news analysis considered the performance of network news reports and interpretation of national defense issues, asking whether the coverage was adequate and balanced and whether all major options and viewpoints were given fair presentation.[19] This interpretation could be considered an analysis of network ideological bias, but it illustrates that content studies can also address the implications of what is not given attention in the news.

Theme Analysis Robinson urged researchers to continue to look at news content systematically and also to consider different models of news instead of accepting only one approach to analysis.[20] One alternative goes beyond manifest content to consider symbols of interaction in news content. Bantz urged a descriptive-analytical approach instead of a statistical-predictive analysis, thereby identifying themes in broadcast news. Similarly, Smith examined news content on the basis of whether it was structured as a limited repertoire of consistent, predictable narratives, concluding that television news portrays political leaders as symbols of omnipotence. Bantz observed that particular themes (such as "loser") were present in news coverage of political campaigns, and Bormann asserted that the major themes change through the communication system of a campaign, providing a persona of the candidates to the American electorate.[21]

These and other studies of symbols and themes in news broadcasts offer an important alternative perspective for the study of news content. At the least, they point to attributes that can be tested through more traditional approaches to analysis of content.

Prediction Analysis A question frequently asked in relation to the use of content analysis techniques is whether one can predict the effects of the message. The answer may be yes—if an outside measure of the response of the audience to the content can be validly ascertained.[22] Outside measures considered here are found in research on agenda setting and causal analysis.

The process of agenda setting by a news medium can be described as presenting subjects in a broadcast that may tell the audience not *what* to think, but what to think *about*.[23] In an illustrative study, Williams and Semlak compared their content analysis of network television news with a survey of viewers to determine whether an agenda was set by watching. Similarly, McClure and Patterson compared heavy and light viewer salience of issues presented in newspapers and network television news programs. Another orientation to agenda setting is Burriss and Williams's study, which examined the effect of television on the treatment of newspaper stories. A related examination of intermedia agenda setting effect, by Malaney and Buss, compared news wire service and TV news coverage.[24]

Causal Analysis Even though effects-related studies are close to the approach of other studies cited earlier, some have used content analysis to examine the influence of content on audiences. And even though content analysis is not a test of causality, it can indicate possible effects. Thus, a study such as Levine's, which considered the possibility that "helplessness" could be learned from content, is mentioned here. Levine asked whether individuals who viewed helplessness models in news reports came to feel a lack of control over events.[25] Similarly, Haight and Brody investigated whether presidential broadcasting influenced public opinion about how the president was handling his job. They found that Nixon's use of television affected public opinion poll results.[26]

Tendency Analysis Tendency studies ask "What is right?"—Are certain people, themes, or subjects presented more positively than others? Perhaps the most common descriptor in such studies is whether content is biased toward or against a particular point of view. Bias, as described by Russo, is the quality of statements of opinion or of actual or supposed fact that would influence the viewer to support or oppose an official or his or her policy. Another interpretation of the concept of news bias is offered by Williams, who identifies qualities required to make findings of TV news bias remarkable. Williams asserts that establishing and clearly stating a norm of tolerable bias is both an investigator's right and a responsibility.[27]

One of the most controversial analyses of television news was by television critic Edith Efron, who concluded that network coverage of Richard Nixon during his 1968 campaign for the presidency was unfair. Stevenson et al. sharply criticized this conclusion for methodological flaws in the analysis.[28]

The news coverage of political campaigns has been the subject of many tendency or bias analyses, among the most extensive of which is Hofstetter's analysis of the 1972 presidential campaign. He found structural bias (discussed later) to be more prevalent than any instances of partisan favoritism.[29]

Structural Analysis Ideological bias in the news is important. The question of other kinds of biases leads to considering relationships among components of message systems. Thus, structural analysis examines the proximal or logical association of components in news content. These structures may favor certain kinds of broadcast news and information.

Probably the most frequently cited study of organizational influence on broadcast news content is Epstein's *News from Nowhere*. He describes the influence of a network news organization in great detail, but he does not actually deal with a detailed analysis of program content. Altheide, in *Creating Reality*, defines "news perspective" as the day-to-day operations of news work, which, by its organization, ingrains bias into the news report (for example, removing reports of events from their context would leave the report biased). Of the general organizational studies, only Gans, in *Deciding What's News*, has described an anal-

ysis of broadcast news content to support his thesis of what is required and why it is presented that way.[30]

Other researchers have observed that certain kinds of content will not generally be presented in television news due to a structural orientation (bias?) toward the visual content. For instance, stories may not be covered because they are too complex. A further bias is identified as television news preference for personifying and dramatizing.[31]

Another organizational influence was examined by Anderson. He attempted to determine the multimedia ownership influence on versions of news stories presented by broadcast stations and newspapers. Wirth and Wollert broached this question with regard to public interest programming.[32] McNulty also examined organizational requirements, considering the content of CBS News documentaries in relation to decision making within the organization that produced the programs.[33]

Visual Analysis Until recently, the visual content of news received little research attention. No doubt the reason for so few such analyses was the high cost for equipment and research time, but the price of this lack of research attention is a failure to consider a considerable body of information being conveyed to audiences of news programs.

The Vanderbilt Television News Archive and other such sources allow access to past television news broadcasts, and the home video recorders make convenient and relatively inexpensive study of current broadcasts feasible. But whether the researcher analyzes the visual and aural content from video recordings or by another method, several techniques can overcome many procedural difficulties. Fyock suggests a useful procedure that includes ways to handle very complex material, thus allowing analysts to surmount many problems inherent in visual analysis.[34]

A study can be limited by ignoring visual attributes; it can also be weakened by the way they are analyzed. Culbert suggests that researchers analyze the symbolic nature of visual content that may be present in (or edited out of) news reports. He stresses the need for placing visual material in a historic context. Another useful approach is Adams's proposal for analyzing three areas of inquiry in newscast visual content: *visual images*, as determined by factors outside the producer's control; *production factors*—those aspects of visual image usually under the technical control of news personnel; and *interaction* between visual and audio messages in newscasts.[35]

These perspectives are in some analyses of visual content of news broadcasts. The mechanics of television coverage of news were observed by Whale, who concluded that the equipment that permits visual presence is ultimately a hindrance to thorough coverage. Frank, who analyzed differences in nonverbal presentation of candidates in the 1972 presidential election campaign, found clear differences in the kinds of shots used to show candidates.

During the 1976 presidential campaign, several studies were made of the televised debates between Gerald Ford and Jimmy Carter. Tiemens analyzed differences in camera framing and composition, camera angle, screen placement, and reaction shots, which, he concluded, seemed to favor Carter. Another study, by Davis, concluded that Carter's greater eye contact with the camera served him well. Messaris, Eckman, and Gumpert also analyzed the debates, concluding that structural characteristics of television played a part in determining the nature of the confrontation between Ford and Carter.[36]

Other structural bias considerations have been observed by Jackson-Beeck and Meadow. In an exploratory study of communication content that is not manifest (issues and statements, for example), they considered such attributes as nervousness, speaking rate, and mistakes as conveyed during the 1976 presidential debates. They assessed the feasibility of examining types of broadcast content identified as "unintentional message transmission," "unconscious use of speech within the context of substantive messages," and nonverbal content such as body language. Their approach appears to have value in identifying content attributes that can, in turn, aid in understanding both message originators and the possible effects of news coverage on audiences.[37]

Such research goes beyond manifest content to assess attributes in news coverage that may be equal or more powerful influences on audience perceptions. They raise important questions for further study.

Analysis

Content analysis procedures are standard, as discussed in Alan Wurtzel's contribution to this volume. But news analysis may contain special problems of which the researcher should be aware. This discussion is, therefore, divided into five areas: (1) sampling, (2) units of analysis, (3) measurement, (4) validity, and (5) reliability. After considering these items, a procedure will be illustrated for analyzing news content that can increase the accuracy and reliability of the data.

Sampling

As Wurtzel pointed out in chapter 1, selecting the sample must consider variances in the normalcy of the content, such as seasonal differences and audience rating periods. In selecting a sample of news broadcasts, normalcy becomes a critical problem.[38] For instance, the three commercial networks only recently began broadcasting weekend news programs, and those are sometimes preempted by other broadcasts. Another consideration would be the ratings dark weeks, when no national network program ratings are ascertained. Many news specials and documentaries are usually scheduled during this period. In evaluating the content of network "instant news specials," one must consider the ABC regularly scheduled *Nightline* program, which usually covers news events that CBS or NBC might deal with in special broadcasts. On the local level, many television stations curtail their weekend news operations. Thus, if an important news story breaks on a day not included in the sample, representation of the news coverage by one network or station might be erroneous. For any of several possible reasons, those news programs might present the information on the next broadcast day. If such variations are not considered, then all sources may not be compared equitably.

Such sampling problems can be diminished, for network programs, at least, by checking the coverage of news stories in the *Vanderbilt Television News Archive Index*, which lists all network coverage or absence thereof. These patterns of coverage should be taken into account in selecting the sample.

Units of Analysis

Detail in content analysis is dictated by several considerations. Most important, the purpose for the study should indicate the specificity necessary. It should be sufficient to pursue the research question by testing hypotheses generated by it.

Resources available to the researcher are also important. If transcripts or recordings of the news content can be obtained, considerably greater detail for analysis is possible. However, the number of coders and the amount of time allocated for their efforts may limit the study.

Another consideration is the usefulness of detail that might be included. This consideration goes back to the purpose of the study (the research question). Visual detail might be analyzed, for instance, but is it pertinent to the researcher's goal? Some researchers have assumed that such detail would be included in their studies until they addressed the question of its pertinence.

The audience for the intended report should also be considered in deciding on the level of detail necessary. As reviewed earlier, there are a number of types of content analyses of broadcast news. Some studies consider bias in the several forms thus far identified; other studies are limited to describing what was broadcast. The audiences for these or other types of analyses might have different needs. For instance, once the *what* has been reported and assessed, audiences could be expected to demand studies with more specifically defined questions.

Thus, the unit to be analyzed may be as broad as the whole news program or the news story—or it may be as narrow as individual words in the news content. Selecting the appropriate unit depends on the research question and availability of primary data. Consequently, if the researcher wishes to determine what subjects were dealt with in news broadcasts over a period of time, the appropriate unit for analysis would most likely be the news story. But if the question is whether news treatment is favorable or unfavorable toward a particular point of view, perhaps the unit should be defined as statements, sentences, or even words. (A note of caution, though: The more specific the unit, the greater the likelihood that contextual meaning will be distorted.)

A second important consideration is the availability of data sources for analysis. Depending on the research question, secondary sources such as program listings in major newspapers or in *TV Guide* may suffice. Other sources of news content information are news program logs (rundowns) maintained by networks and radio and television stations. The scripts for these newscasts may also be available. In some cases, it may be possible to obtain access to the audio and, perhaps, to the video logging tapes many stations maintain. These tapes are a verbatim record of the news broadcasts. A valuable secondary source of information on network evening news content is the *Vanderbilt Television News Archives Index*. The index includes information on the length, principal participants, and a synopsis of news subject treatment in each network's news program. Depending on the purposes of the study, such summaries may be adequate sources of data. Of course, the unit of analysis could be no more specific than the story. Information sufficient for more detailed analysis could be obtained from audio or video recordings or from transcripts of the broadcasts.

Measurement

After establishing the unit of analysis and ascertaining the availability of data sources, the researcher should determine the appropriate units for coding. Content categories (often referred to as variables) are the operational measures for testing hypotheses formulated by the research question.

Categories in a content study should ". . . reflect the purposes of the research, be exhaustive, be mutually exclusive, independent and be derived from a single classification principle."[39] Coding can follow an archetypical statement plan, such as actor – act – object.[40] Another scheme, discussed more fully below, might be called a decision-level approach. Both coding schemes include a kind of flow chart for decision making. An advantage in using levels of abstraction is that the coder's decisions are made at the lowest level, giving the analyst more control over reliability and, perhaps, also validity of the measurements of the content.

Specificity of coding categories is an important concern. Categories could be so narrow they virtually replicate the raw data. On the other hand, the investigator may discover that initial categories are so broad that little distinction can be made between attributes. Thus, content coded according to specific categories would permit better explanation of trends occurring during short periods of time. Still, categories may be so narrow that they gather few cases in each division.

Resolution of these important concerns can be found in coding schemes where initial categories are aggregated into broader, more abstract levels for some phases of the analysis. For instance, it is possible to create indices by collapsing several content categories. As an example, one might be able to justify a favorable coverage index by coding such categories as "video or anchor report" with higher numerical ratings if the candidates were shown on the screen, and higher still if a candidate actually spoke during the report. If the report about a candidate was the lead story in the newscast, this fact might provide another increment in the index. By combining the rankings coded for various content categories, an index of prominence of candidate coverage could be obtained.

Another way to determine the appropriate range of content categories would be to allow for statistical manipulation. Factor analysis techniques, for instance, could identify a structure by which content categories tend to be associated, or "hang together."[41] The use of such an analysis must be determined before coding categories are established, however, to ensure that data appropriate to this kind of analysis are encoded.

The data coding procedure should accommodate the requirements and limitations of the computer analysis program package to be used (SPSS and SAS are two widely available statistical packages). Otherwise, the researcher may be frustrated in achieving desired manipulations of the data obtained in the content categories.

One advantage of a content coding form duplicated on a mimeograph machine is its low cost (forms can even be duplicated on the back of used paper). Each unit of analysis should be coded on a separate form and inserted into a loose-leaf notebook for easy reference. A portion of the page can be reserved for notes, making the coding forms into a reference book after the data have been punched onto computer cards.

Validity

Much has been made of the need for a thorough review of the literature and a careful statement of the question guiding the research. These are important aspects in establishing the validity of any study.

Validity, as the term is used in research, is the test of whether a study measures what it purports to measure. In content analysis, the question of validity is often a judgment call. But if credible (that is, widely accepted) and authoritative studies are cited as precedents, the validity of the proposed method of analysis will probably be satisfactory to most critics. The researcher is responsible for knowledge of all the literature pertaining to the procedures proposed for a study. Using Efron's *The News Twisters* as the standard in guiding the analysis would probably generate considerable negative criticism. Consequently, the researcher must be aware of the weaknesses in that study's methodology and of approaches accepted in the academic community.

Reliability

Reliability is the measure of consistency achieved in gathering the data for a study. The term indicates the likelihood that another researcher would obtain similar results using the same procedures. But consistency in intrastudy data coding is as important as interstudy reliability.

Reliability can be enhanced by using a panel of judges who agree on coding decisions. Coding can be done independently by judges who compare results, thus measuring intercoder reliability. Even if the analysis is conducted by a single coder, problems in consistency and thus in reliability can occur.[42]

For coding to be consistent, an index of the choices in each content category (a coding dictionary) should be compiled. Computers can be programmed to interpret word sequence according to the analyst's scheme,[43] but visual material or content context cannot be so easily identified. For instance, an angry reaction from the audience at a political rally could be interpreted as either positive or negative toward a candidate. The context of the reaction, perhaps made in response to a remark by some member of the audience, could clarify the direction. Similarly, the question of whether partisan or opposing audience members were shown in the news report should be addressed. Such content judgments can be made only by viewing a news story.

Still, when coding is done by persons rather than by machines, a communication problem is inherent. Judges must use a system that ensures consistency in coding according to predetermined criteria. When content category increments are devised in advance (as they must be if computer coding is done), there is less chance of communicating unreliable information among coders. Human inconsistencies — memory lapses, for instance — can affect the reliability of the coding process.

Another problem is inclusiveness. The subject of an analysis may change strategy or direction while the count is being made. Unanticipated content matter may be discovered, and it should be accounted for. When the object of the research is to make specific inferences about events and particular times and places, the analysis is made less precise if low frequency indicators are ignored.[44] Such tabulations may be valuable when the analyst has prior or independent knowledge of their meaning, role, and significance in the system under study. It would be important, for instance, to note the infrequency of discussion (that is, what is missing) of particular content in news programs if there is some outside measure of its importance.

On the other hand, since broad categories will permit better inferences when content is presented over a fairly long period of time, use of specific content coding criteria could result in many categories with few entries in each. Fewer categories, representing a larger number of the units of analysis, should foster more meaningful interpretation of trends in content.

The analysis of broadcast news coverage of a political campaign is a good example of the problem of unanticipated content increments. Even if a study is begun after the fact (after the election), it is unlikely that every campaign issue could be identified before the coding is started. There is no reason to ignore content, no matter how obscure, when it pertains to the research question. All such increments can be included in the analysis without lessening either coding efficiency or the clarity of the question that motivated the study.

Coding the Data

The function of computer cards is to feed data to a computer for analysis. Computer cards are useful for the incidental purpose of maintaining a coding dictionary of content categories. In content studies that use a computer for data analysis, a numeric code is assigned to each increment in a content category. To illustrate the use of computer cards in forming a coding dictionary for an analysis of news program "subjects," a three-digit code would allow up to 999 possible increments. (The content category, "subject," would be coded and punched in three sequential columns on computer data cards for analysis.)

Figure 3-1 shows how coding information for news program "subjects" could be displayed on computer cards to form a dictionary that accommodates *a priori* and unforeseen increments in a category. For accuracy, dictionary cards should be reserved for unforeseen increments and added to the "master deck." A code number is assigned to each new increment (program subject, in this case) when it is encountered during the coding process. If, for instance, "juvenile delinquency" was not anticipated as a subject before the coder encountered a program on that topic, it would be assigned the first unused dictionary card, say "006." Card number "006" would eventually be repunched to display that code number and the assigned increment, "juvenile delinquency."

The analyst can maintain a listing (printout) of the dictionary cards as a convenient record of all increments assigned in each content category. Cards with unassigned chronological numbers are included in the master deck and in the master listing. When new increments are encountered, the topic is written on the first unassigned numbered card and on the master listing beside the assigned code number. Thus, the analyst always has a double record for all coding assignments.

As new category increments are assigned code numbers, "master" cards would be punched. The original card would be placed in sequence in the master deck, replacing the numbered "blank" card. The master dictionary deck should be duplicated, sorted alphabetically, and distributed to each content coder. Dictionary decks can be stored in computer card boxes; cards can be divided alphabetically by inserting tabs in the decks. Since duplication and listing are so easily and inexpensively done at the computing center, each member of the research unit can receive current chronological and alphabetical listings of all coding dictionaries, along with duplicates of new entries for his or her card dictionary.

In studies examining many units of analysis

(which probably require a considerable time, a large team of coders, or both), there is a possibility of creating redundant category increments. For example, a program reporting on the Mafia may be encountered. Perhaps a previously assigned increment was "organized crime." Logically, programs about "the Mafia" would be coded as "organized crime." If a redundant category code is assigned, a simple computer instruction can combine all units coded as "Mafia" with those coded as "organized crime." In all probability, the redundancy would be discovered when the analyst scanned listings of the master dictionary deck. But, in any event, such an error could be rectified before performing any analysis of the data.

In Figure 3-1, some cards designate different titles for category increments (topics) having a common numerical code. The flexibility of the computer card dictionary allows analogous designations for a single increment. Thus, the coder who thinks of "liquor" when the original designation for that topic is "alcoholism" can still find and correctly code the increment. By updating the dictionary, these cards also serve as a cross-reference to similar but separate increments. The abbreviation "SA" on such cards indicates "See Also: 'another similar increment.' "

Accuracy of the Coded Data

When all units of analysis are coded and key-punched, the analyst should make data card listings for each content category. Computer programs can readily sort the data deck by numerical and alphabetical designations before listing the cards. Many computing centers can insert "blank" spaces on each side of columns of data representing each coded category, as shown in Figure 3-2. This procedure makes it easier to scan lists of data columns for errors. In Figure 3-2, the first three fields show the date for each broadcast (day, month, year).

If space is reserved on each card for a title or for other descriptive identification, coding errors can be more easily observed. For instance, a program entitled "Marriage and the Young" might be inadvertently coded with the subject

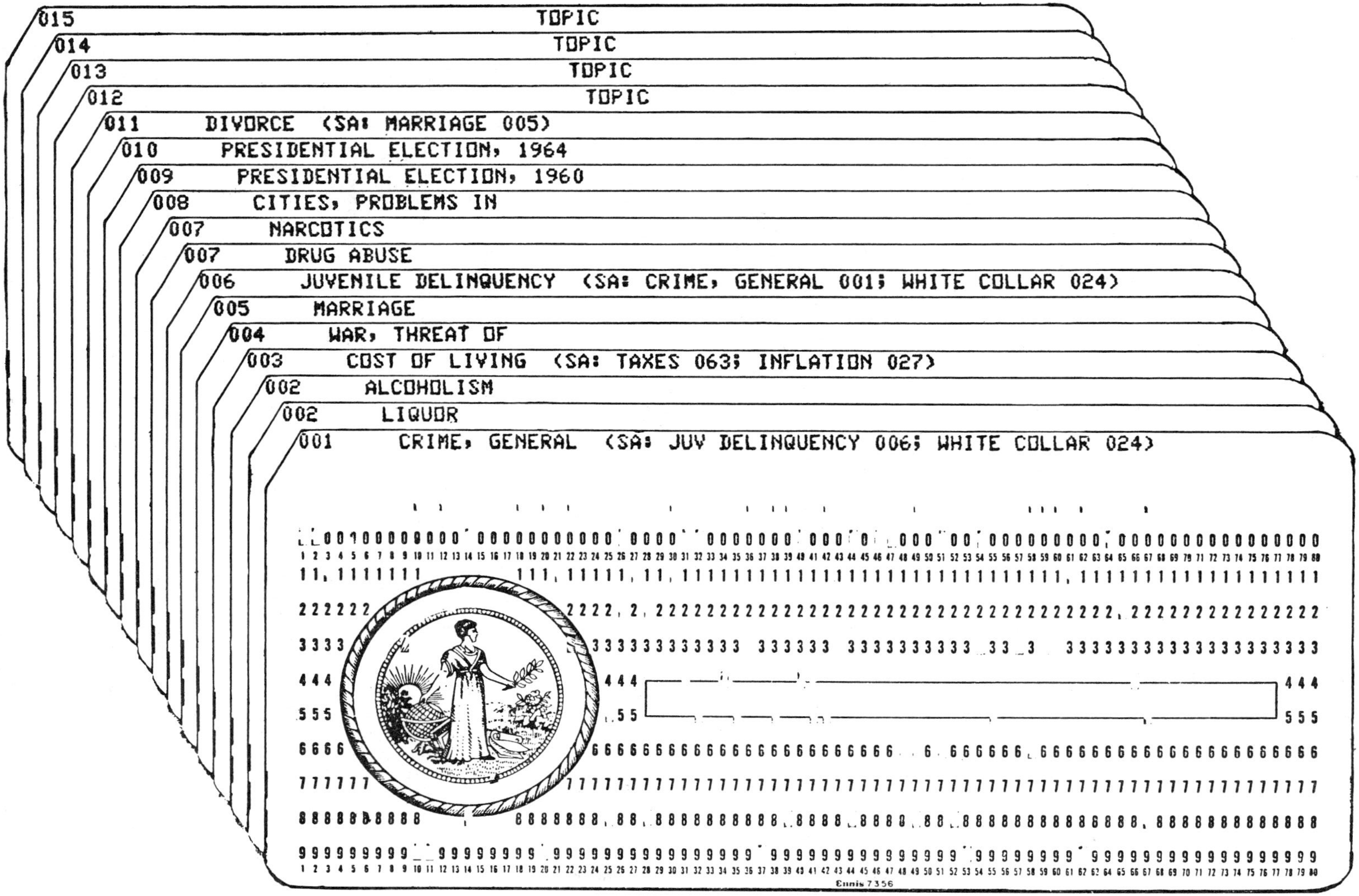

Figure 3-1 Coding Dictionary in Card Form

Figure 3-2 Listing of Content Data Cards

1773.	05	06	75	4	15	2000	3	2	1	16	42	50	1			5	2	1	FND OF THE HO CHI MINH TRAIL, THE (NPACT/BBC)	
1774.	24	06	75	4	05	2030	3	1	1	07	04		3				3	0	NOVA-WAR FROM THE AIR	R
1775.	10	08	75	2	10	1800	3	1	4	05	90		2		2		2	0	CONV W/ SEVAREID-FRANCIS FITZGERALD (FIRE-LAKE)	
1776.	19	09	75	4	05	1830	3	2	1	25	61		2				2	1	PEOPLE AT THE END OF THE TUNNEL, THE (REFUGEE)	
1777.	20	09	75	3	15	2330	3	3	1	25	61	63	2					1	WKND-NIGHTMARES IN THE DREAM FACTORY	
1778.	15	10	75	4	05	2200	3	1	1	27	54		2					1	SAY BROTHER (NAT'L ED)-VIETNAM	
1779.	18	10	75	2	05	1330	3	4	1	16	50		1				1	0	WAA-WHAT'S COMMUNISM ALL ABOUT (VN TAKE-OVER)	
1780.	28	12	75	2	10	1800	3	2	1	24	50		1				1	0	1975-A TELEVISION ALBUM (SVN REFUGEES, ARVN)	
1781.	05	01	76	3	30	2000	3	2	1	29	90							0	NEW WORLD-HARD CHOICES-AM. FOREIGN POLICY 1976	
1782.	31	01	76	4	10	2000	3	1	4	15	90		2	1				1	FIRING LINE: GEN WM. WESTMORELAND	
1783.	17	02	76	4	05	2000	3	1	4	15	90		2		1	5		1	BT LINES: DAVID HALBERSTAM	
1784.	30	03	76	3	15	2130	3	4	1	02	90		2					0	LIBERTY (HS KIDS PROTEST VN, KICKED OUT)	
1785.	02	05	76	2	10	1900	3	4	1	30	90							0	60M: HIRED GUN (MERCENARY, DECORATED IN VN)	
1786.	04	06	76	4	10	2000	3	1	4	15	90		2					0	FIRING LINE: THE INTIMATE LBJ (DORIS KEARNS)	
1787.	28	06	76	4	10		3	2	1	31	42		1					1	SIEGE OF DIEN BIEN PHU, THE	
1788.	03	12	76	3	10	2200	3	4	1	17	90		2				1	0	SOMETIMES SOLDIERS, THE	
1789.	09	01	77	2	10	1900	3	3	1	02	90		2					0	60M-AN AM TRAGEDY (KENT STATE, M/ANN DELVICCO)	
1790.	02	04	77	3	15	2330	3	3	1	35	95	91	0				3	0	WKND-A LONG WAY FROM HOME (DRAFT EVADE AMNESTY)	
1791.	85	06	77	2	10	2200	3	3	1	25	90		2				1	1	WHO'S WHO-THE MARSHAL'S PLAN (FX VP KY IN CAL)	
1792.	11	06	77	4	05	1830	3	1	4	15	90		2						BOOKBEAT-PATRICIA HANGEN (WIFE, WELLES)	
1793.	01	12	77	1	10	2200	3	2	1	28	54	92	2					1	ACU-CLASS THAT WENT TO WAR, THE	
1794.	25	12	77	2	10	1800	3	3	1	28	54	56	2					0	60M-PROFILE MAX FREEMAN (1ST VN VET TO HEAD VA)	R
1795.	17	01	78	2	10	2000	3	2	1	28	54		2			4		1	CNS-CHARLIE COMPANY AT HOME-THE VETERANS OF VN	
1796.	01	04	78	3	15	2330	3	3	1	25	61		2					0	WKND-SVNESE REFUGEES IN WDC (NITE CLUBS)	
1797.	11	04	78	4	10	2100	3	2	1	23	50		1			5		1	VIETNAM-PICKING UP THE PIECES (SAIGON NOW)	
1798.	20	04	78	4	10	2100	3	1	1	23	42	91	1				2	1	WORLD-VIETNAM-30 MONTHS AFTER THE 30-YEAR WAR	
1799.	26	04	78	3	10	2200	3	2	4	15	90		2	1		1		0	GERALD R. FORD-PRESIDENTIAL DECISIONS	
1800.	04	05	78	2	10	1000	3	3	1	10	91	83	2				1	0	MAG-HE'S ONLY MISSING (GIRL SEARCH-MIA FATHER)	
1801.	16	05	78	4	10	2200	3	2	4	15	90		2	2	3			0	SOME OF THE PRESIDENT'S MEN (VN & WGATE)	
1802.	07	06	78	2	10	2000	3	2	1	06	40		6			3	1	1	CNS: WHAT'S HAPPENING TO CAMBODIA? (E BRADLEY)	
1803.	11	06	78	1	10	2000	3	2	1	16	50	42	1				1	0	ANS: 1968—A CRACK IN TIME	
1804.	04	07	78	1	10	2200	3	3	1	10	93		2					1	20/20: PROFILE, ADM JAMES B STOCKWELL (POW)	
1805.	25	07	78	1	10	2200	3	3	1	28	90	54	2					0	20/20: AGENT ORANGE-I (EXPOSED GIS GET CANCER)	
1806.	16	01	79	2	10	2000	3	2	1	25	61		0					1	CR: BOAT PEOPLE, THE (VN REFUGEES IN MALAYSIA)	
1807.	18	02	79	4	10	2000	3	1	1	25	61	63	1					1	FYI: LEGACIES OF VN (BOAT PEOPLE, AGENT ORANGE)	
1808.	04	03	79	2	10	1800	3	3	1	25	61	63	4			4		0	60M: OUR SECRET ARMY (MONG TRIBE, POP BUELL)	
1809.	31	05	79	1	10	2200	3	3	1	23	63		5					1	20/20: ONLY THE SIDES HAVE CHANGED (G RIVERA)	
1810.	07	06	79	1	10	2200	3	3	1	23	01		6					0	20/20: BEHIND THE LINES (RIVERA: LAOS REBELS)	
1811.	23	06	79	2	10	1900	3	3	1	25	61		0					0	60M: THE ISLAND (EXCERPT, CR: THE BOAT PEOPLE)	
1812.	01	07	79	2	10	1900	3	3	1	25	61	63	4			5		0	60M: OUR SECRET ARMY (MONG TRIBESMEN IN LAOS)	R
1813.	09	08	79	1	10	2200	3	3	1	05	90		2	1	2			0	20/20: BAEZ & FONDA (STATUS 6 YR AFTER US OUT)	
1814.	19	08	79	3	10	1300	3	2	4	25	90		2					1	BOAT PEOPLE (SEA REFUGEES, W/R CLARK, US REP)	
1815.	04	09	79	3	20	2100	3	4	1	29	90		0					0	WP: NO MORE VIETNAMS, BUT . . . (OIL & FOR POL)	

END DATA.

QU,A, SUBTSDE TPES., IRES., 2000, 132, KEY/ / .A, KEY/ .A,KEY/ .A,KEY/ / .A
SORTSDE ESS 09/18-12:24
INPUT RECORD COUNT: 1815
OUTPUT RECORD COUNT: 1815

"organized crime." On spotting this apparent inconsistency in the listing, the analyst could refer to information from which the original coding decision was made to determine corrections to be made on the data card.

Title or other unit identification also facilitates anecdotal description as a supplement to numerical analysis. The listing is a guide to specific instances or patterns in the content and an index to finding direct quotations.

Analysis of Data

Very specific category increments can be coded, yet the study can accommodate the need for broader, more general concepts in the analysis. For example, Schutz constructed categories by breaking the decision process into dichotomous parts and rebuilding them in logical clusters of unitary traits.[45] Stone et al. also worked from a "dependent category" scheme, breaking down levels of abstraction so that coding was done at the most concrete level. Thus, at each level of abstraction, the analyst

had the option of more or less specific designation of content increments.[46] In ascension, each conceptual level served as an indicator of the lower levels of abstraction incorporated in the analysis. Carrying this concept forward, North et al. used such "entry words" as *United States* and *Soviet Union* in their study of international crisis. At their next level, the "tag concept" for those entry words was *nations*. At the third level, tag concepts were aggregated to become "generic language concepts." Thus, *nations* and other tag concepts were designated as *actors* in the international crisis.[47]

This concrete-to-abstract process, illustrated in Figure 3-3, represents the analysis of "inclusive" increments for the content category "news subject." Such entry words as "juvenile delinquency" and "white-collar crime" could be collapsed into the more general concept "crime." The resulting tag concepts could be aggregated to form a grander concept "law and order."

The level of abstraction could be ascended

Figure 3-3   Concrete to Abstract Coding Scheme

Entry Words Level 1	Tag Concepts Level 2	Generic Language Concepts Level 3
Juvenile Delinquency Organized Crime White-Collar Crime Political Kidnappings Street Crime (Muggings, etc) Rape Child Abuse	Crime	
F.B.I., The City Police Other Police Forces Other Federal Law Enforcement	Law Enforcement	
Lawyers Courts/Trial System Supreme Court of the U.S.	Judgment	LAW AND ORDER
Problems in Prisons Prisoner Rehabilitation Jails and Jail Problems Probation System Prison Parole Women in Prison	Penalty	

even higher than illustrated in Figure 3-3 by collapsing units that led to the *law and order* generic language concept with other third-level categories. This would create a fourth level of abstraction, such as *system order* or *social issues.*

Summary

The researcher who contemplates the analysis of broadcast news content should carefully appraise the findings of previous research in broadcast news in devising a research question and establishing precedents for the new study.

In proceeding with the content analysis, clear communication must be maintained among people working on an analysis (even if a single coder is involved). A computer card dictionary will enhance coding reliability and accommodate unforeseen content attributes. This documenting procedure also permits the delay of decisions about the level of content abstraction until coding is completed. The data thus obtained can be checked before they are analyzed by examining listings of the coded cards.

Findings from analyses that follow such a procedure of documentation are more likely to add a substantive increment to knowledge of broadcast news content.

Endnotes

1. Critiques of broadcast news in the Alfred I. duPont-Columbia University Survey of Broadcast Journalism series illustrate the importance that critics give broadcast news organizations and their responsibilities. At this writing, eight volumes under the editorship of Marvin Barrett have been published. See, for example, Marvin Barrett, ed., *Broadcast Journalism: 1979–1981* (New York: Everest House, 1982).

2. Kenneth Harwood, quoted in Lawrence W. Lichty, "What Does a Television Critic Write About?" *Journal of Broadcasting* 7 (1963): 353.

3. Elizabeth L. Young, "One Medium: Two Critics, Two Views," *Journal of Broadcasting* 11 (1966–1967): 41.

4. William J. Paisley, "Studying 'Style' as Deviation from Encoding Norms," in George Gerbner, Ole R. Holsti, Klaus Krippendorff, William J. Paisley, and Philip J. Stone, *The Analysis of Communication Content* (Huntington, N.Y.: Robert E. Kreiger Publishing Co., 1978), 135–136. Gerbner makes essentially the same point on p. 127.

5. Robert Rutherford Smith, *Beyond the Wasteland: The Criticism of Broadcasting* (Falls Church, Va.: Speech Communication Association, 1976), 3–4.

6. The reader is cautioned that analyzing news as a program viewed in isolation may result in the misleading implication that news content is the viewer's main source of information. See George Gerbner and Nancy Signorielli, "The World of Television News," in William Adams and Fay Schreibman, eds., *Television Network News: Issues in Content Research* (Washington, D.C.: George Washington University, 1978), 189–191.

7. These attributes are described in greater detail by: Robert M. Batscha, *Foreign Affairs News and the Broadcast Journalist* (New York: Praeger, 1975), 84–92; Gary L. Walmsley and Richard A. Pride, "Television Network News: Rethinking the Iceberg Problem," *Western Political Quarterly* 25 (1972): 434–450; and Paul H. Weaver, "Newspaper News and Television News," in *Television as a Social Force*, Douglass Cater and Richard Adler, eds. (New York: Praeger, 1975), 81–94. Attributes of broadcast program structure and appeals are described by Lawrence W. Lichty, *Broadcast Program and Audience Analysis* (Madison, Wis.: American Printing and Publishing, 1975).

8. George Bailey, "Interpretive Reporting of the Vietnam War by Anchormen," *Journalism Quarterly* 35 (1976): 319–324.

9. See George Gerbner, "On Content Analysis and Critical Research in Mass

Communication," *Audio-Visual Communication Review* 6 (1958): 91, for an overview of the concept of analyzing content in the context of its system.

10. William Adams provides a useful description in "Network News Research in Perspective: A Bibliographic Essay," in *Television Network News*, 11–46.

11. George Gerbner, "Toward 'Cultural Indicators': The Analysis of Mass Mediated Public Message Systems," in Gerbner et al., *The Analysis of Communication Content*, 123–132.

12. William C. Adams, "Local Public Affairs Content of TV News," *Journalism Quarterly* 55 (1978): 690–695; and "Local Television News Coverage and the Central City," *Journalism of Broadcasting* 24 (1980): 253–265; Joseph R. Dominick, "Geographical Bias in National TV News," *Journal of Communication* 27 (Autumn 1977): 94–99.

13. Joseph S. Fowler and Stuart W. Showalter, "Evening News Selection: A Confirmation of News Judgment," *Journalism Quarterly* 51 (1974): 712–715.

14. Herbert J. Gans, *Deciding What's News* (New York: Pantheon, 1979), 5.

15. George Bailey, "Television War: Trends in Network Coverage of Vietnam, 1965–1970," *Journal of Broadcasting* 20 (1976): 147–158.

16. Robert G. Meadow and Marilyn Jackson-Beeck, "Issue Evolution: A New Perspective on Presidential Debates," *Journal of Communication* 28 (Autumn 1978): 84–92; Robert Pepper, "An Analysis of Presidential Primary Election Night Coverage," *Educational Broadcasting Review* 7 (1973): 159–166; and "Election Night 1972: TV Network Coverage," *Journal of Broadcasting* 18 (1976): 27–38.

17. George A. Bailey and Lawrence W. Lichty, "Rough Justice on a Saigon Street: A Gatekeeper Study of NBC's Tet Execution Film," *Journalism Quarterly* 49 (1972): 221–229, 238.

18. Michael J. Robinson and Karen A. McPherson, "Television News Coverage before the 1976 New Hampshire Primary: The Focus of Network Journalism," *Journal of Broadcasting* 21 (1977): 177–186.

19. Ernest W. Lefever, "CBS and National Defense, 1972–73," *Journal of Communication* 25 (Autumn 1975): 181–185; and *TV and National Defense; An Analysis of CBS News, 1972–1973* (Boston, Va.: Institute for American Strategy Press, 1974).

20. Michael J. Robinson, "Future Television News Research: Beyond Edward Jay Epstein," in *Television Network News*, 197–212.

21. Charles R. Bantz, "Television News: Reality and Research," *Western Speech Communication* 39 (1975): 123–130; "The Critic and the Computer: A Multiple Technique Analysis of the ABC Evening News," *Communication Monographs* 46 (1979): 27–39; and "The Rhetorical Vision of the *ABC Evening News*; June 12 to July 10, 1972," *Moments in Contemporary Rhetoric and Communication* 2 (1972): 34–37; Robert Rutherford Smith, "Mythic Elements in Television News," *Journal of Communication* 29 (Winter 1979): 75–82; Ernest G. Bormann, "The Eagleton Affair: A Fantasy Theme Analysis," *Quarterly Journal of Speech* 59 (1973): 143–159.

22. See a discussion on "Drawing Inferences About Receivers," by Wayne A. Danielson, "Content Analysis in Communication Research," in *Introduction to Mass Communications Research*, Ralph O. Nafziger and David M. White, eds. (Baton Rouge: Louisiana State University Press, 1963), 197–199.

23. The concept of agenda setting and television news content analysis is discussed in William C. Adams, "Network News Research in Perspective: A Bibliographic Essay," in *Television Network News*, 19–20. The seminal work on this subject is Maxwell E. McCombs and Donald L. Shaw, "The Agenda-Setting Function of Mass Media," *Public Opinion Quarterly* 36 (1972): 176–187.

24. Wenmouth Williams, Jr., and William

Semlak, "Campaign '76: Agenda Setting during the New Hampshire Primary," *Journal of Broadcasting* 22 (1978): 532–540; Robert D. McClure and Thomas E. Patterson, "Television News and Political Advertising: The Impact of Exposure on Voter Beliefs," *Communication Research* 1 (1974): 3–31; Larry L. Burriss and Jeanne P. Williams, "Use of Network News Material by Cross-Owned Newspapers," *Journalism Quarterly* 56 (1979): 567–571; Gary D. Malaney and Terry F. Buss, "AP Wire Reports vs. CBS-TV News Coverage of a Presidential Campaign," *Journalism Quarterly*, 56 (1979): 602–610.

25. Grace Ferrari Levine, " 'Learned Helplessness' and the Evening News," *Journal of Communication* 27 (Autumn 1977): 100–105.

26. Timothy R. Haight and Richard A. Brody, "The Mass Media and Presidential Popularity: Presidential Broadcasting and News in the Nixon Administration," *Communication Research* 4 (1977): 41–60.

27. Frank D. Russo, "A Study of Bias in TV Coverage of the Vietnam War: 1969 and 1970," *Public Opinion Quarterly* 25 (1971–72): 539; Alden Williams, "Unbiased Study of Television News Bias," *Journal of Communication* 25 (Autumn 1975): 190–199. John C. Merrill provides useful categories for analyzing bias in news content in "How Time Stereotyped Three U.S. Presidents," *Journalism Quarterly* 42 (1965): 563–570.

28. Edith Efron, *The News Twisters* (Los Angeles: Nash Publishing Co., 1971); Robert L. Stevenson, Richard Eisinger, Barry M. Feinberg, and Alan B. Kotok, "Untwisting *The News Twisters:* A Replication of Efron's Study," *Journalism Quarterly* 50 (1973): 211–219.

29. C. Richard Hofstetter, *Bias in the News: Network Television Coverage of the 1972 Election Campaign* (Columbus: Ohio State University Press, 1976); "News Bias in the 1972 Campaign: A Cross-Media Comparison," *Journalism Monographs* 58 (November 1978).

30. Edward Jay Epstein, *News From Nowhere: Television and the News* (New York: Random House, 1973); David L. Altheide, *Creating Reality: How TV News Distorts Events* (Beverly Hills, Calif.: Sage Publications, 1976); Herbert J. Gans, *Deciding What's News* (New York: Panthcon, 1979).

31. Useful observations are made by John Weisman, "Stories You Won't See on the Nightly News," *TV Guide* (March 1, 1980): 4–8; Michael Novak, "The Inevitable Bias of Television," in *Survey of Broadcast Journalism: 1970–1971*, Marvin Barrett, ed. (New York: Grossett & Dunlap, 1971), 121–132; and Paul H. Weaver, "Is Television News Biased?" *The Public Interest* 26 (Winter 1972): 57–74.

32. James A. Anderson, "The Alliance of Broadcast Stations and Newspapers: The Problems of Information Control," *Journal of Broadcasting* 16 (1971–72): 51–64; Michael O. Wirth and James A. Wollert, "Public Interest Program Performances of Multi-Media Owned Stations," *Journalism Quarterly* 53 (1976): 223–230.

33. Thomas M. McNulty, "Vietnam Specials: Policy and Content," *Journal of Communication* 25 (Autumn 1975): 173–180.

34. James A. Fyock, "Content Analysis of Films: New Slant on an Old Technique," *Journalism Quarterly* 45 (1968): 687–691.

35. David Culbert, "Historians and the Visual Analysis of Television News," in *Television Network News*, 139–153; and "The Vanderbilt Television News Archive: Classroom and Research Possibilities," *The History Teacher* 8 (November 1974): 7–16; William C. Adams, "Visual Analysis of Television News," in *Television Network News*, 139–153.

36. John Whale, "The Distant Scene: Foreign News on Television," *Television Quarterly* 8 (Summer 1969): 56–62; Robert S. Frank, "The 'Grammar of Film' in Television News," *Journalism Quarterly* 51 (1974): 245–250; Robert K. Tiemens, "Television's Portrayal of the 1976 Presidential Debates: An Analysis of Visual Content," *Communication Monographs* 45 (1978):

362–370; Leslie K. Davis, "Camera Eye-Contact by the Candidates in the Presidential Debates of 1976," *Journalism Quarterly* 55 (1978): 431–437, 455; Paul Messaris, Bruce Eckman, and Gary Gumpert, "Editing Structure in the Televised Versions of the 1976 Presidential Debates," *Journal of Broadcasting* 23 (1979): 359–369.

37. Marilyn Jackson-Beeck and Robert G. Meadow, "Content Analysis of Televised Communication Events: The Presidential Debates," *Communication Research* 6 (1979): 321–344.

38. Wayne A. Danielson addresses the problems of sampling, establishing units of analysis, coder reliability, and validity of the results of content analysis of news in "Content Analysis in Communication Research" in *Introduction to Mass Communications Research*, Ralph O. Nafziger and David M. White, eds. (Baton Rouge: Louisiana State University Press, 1963). A good discussion of sampling considerations, units of analysis, content categories, and analysis of television news content is provided by Lawrence W. Lichty and George A. Bailey, "Reading the Wind: Reflections on Content Analysis of Broadcast News" in *Television Network News*, 111–137.

39. Ole R. Holsti, *Content Analysis for the Social Sciences and Humanities* (Reading, Mass.: Addison-Wesley, 1969), 95.

40. For an example, see Gans, *Deciding What's News*, 8–15.

41. See Robert Edward Mitchell, "The Use of Content Analysis for Explanatory Studies," *Public Opinion Quarterly* 31 (1967): 235–236, for a discussion of the use of factor analysis in the coding scheme. For a more general discussion of factor analysis and other statistical techniques in content analysis, see Richard W. Budd, Robert K. Thorp, and Lewis Donohew, *Content Analysis of Communications* (New York: Macmillan, 1967), 72–90.

42. William C. Schutz offers suggestions for increasing reliability in judging content in "On Categorizing Qualitative Data in Content Analysis," *Public Opinion Quarterly* 22 (1958–59): 503–515. Also see William A. Scott, "Reliability of Content Analysis: The Case of Nominal Scale Coding," *Public Opinion Quarterly* 19 (1955): 321–325.

43. Philip J. Stone, Dexter C. Dunphy, Marshall S. Smith, and Daniel M. Oglivie, *The General Inquirer: A Computer Approach to Content Analysis* (Cambridge, Mass.: MIT Press, 1966), 85–95, 134–206. See their definition and discussion of the construction and uses of dictionaries in content analysis. See also L. Carroll DeWeese III, "Computer Content Analysis of Printed Media: A Limited Feasibility Study," *Public Opinion Quarterly* 40 (1976): 92–100.

44. Alexander L. George, "Quantitative and Qualitative Approaches to Content Analysis," in *Trends in Content Analysis*, Ithiel De Sola Pool, ed. (Urbana, Ill.: University of Illinois Press, 1959), 20–24.

45. Schutz, "On Categorizing Qualitative Data," 504–509.

46. Stone et al., *The General Inquirer*, 145–146.

47. Robert C. North, Ole R. Holsti, M. George Zaninovich, and Dina A. Zinnes, *Content Analysis* (Evanston, Ill: Northwestern University Press, 1963), 6, 131–135.

4
*Attitude Measurement**

John E. Hocking

Even though no one has ever seen an *attitude*, the concept is extremely useful for social scientists in a wide variety of disciplines, including broadcasting research. This essay introduces issues relevant to using attitudes as variables in empirical broadcasting research, including what attitudes are, why they are important, and, particularly, how they are measured.

As many writers have pointed out, attitudes are probably measured more successfully than they are defined. Allport reviews sixteen definitions of the term *attitude* before offering a seventeenth of his own.[1] Other writers have listed as many as thirty such definitions.[2] An excellent discussion of definitional issues is presented in McGuire's chapter on attitudes in *The Handbook of Social Psychology*.[3] The present discussion will rely on Simon's definition: An attitude is a relatively enduring predisposition to respond favorably or unfavorably toward an attitude object.[4]

An attitude object is the thing toward which the attitude holder is predisposed to respond. This could be a physical object, another person, a social practice, a political institution, an ethnic or national group, an abstract concept—in short, almost anything.

For attitudes to be useful to social scientists, they must be relatively enduring. This is not to suggest that attitudes do not change over time. Of course they do, but the changes are usually not of a capricious nature.

As predispositions, attitudes exist inside people's minds and thus cannot be observed directly. Their existence must always be inferred from observations of behaviors. We cannot observe people's attitudes toward the Rolling Stones. However, we can observe people standing in line for six hours to buy Stones' concert tickets; buying and playing Stones' albums; verbalizing the opinion that the Stones are the world's greatest rock and roll band (opinions are usually defined as verbal manifestations of attitudes); indicating on a music preference questionnaire that the Stones are their favorite group; and so on. The researcher infers from these behaviors that the people observed probably have a relatively enduring predisposition to behave favorably toward the

*The author would like to think Steve McDermott, Linda McAlister, and Dan Everett for comments on an earlier version of this essay.

Rolling Stones — that is, they have favorable attitudes toward the group.

Finally, attitudes vary both in direction (favorable or unfavorable) and intensity (slightly unfavorable, strongly favorable, etc.).

Why Measure Attitudes?

Attitudes are important variables in broadcasting research in at least three ways. First, audience attitudes can be thought of as influencing other variables of interest to broadcasting researchers. A researcher might be interested in the ways attitudes toward blacks influence choices to watch or not watch television programs that feature black characters. Attitudes were used in this way by Hur in his study of the impact of the television series *Roots* on black and white teenagers.[5] He found that whites with favorable attitudes toward blacks were more likely to watch the series than were whites who had less favorable or unfavorable attitudes. This use of attitudes treats them as independent variables — attitudes are conceived of as the cause of or as antecedent to or "predictor of" the dependent variable — media exposure, in this case.

Second, audience attitudes can be thought of as influencing or mediating the effects that media have on audience members. Differing audience attitudes toward blacks may explain the different effects of exposure to the program featuring black characters. *Roots* may have different effects on a racist viewer than on a viewer who has a favorable attitude toward blacks. Hur, for example, found that whites who viewed *Roots* and who had favorable attitudes toward blacks indicated that the series was more enjoyable, more entertaining, and more informational than did white viewers with less favorable attitudes.[6] Using attitudes in this way treats them as mediating variables — variables that help explain the fact that independent variables such as media exposure and attention affect different people differently.

Finally, and perhaps most important, attitudes themselves can be thought of as being influenced by the media. Broadcast researchers are interested in the effects of the broadcast media on listeners and viewers. Do political commercials affect voting? Do soap operas affect the career choices of young women? Do children who watch Saturday morning television programs influence their parents' cereal- and candy-buying habits? These are important broadcast research questions. The independent variable implied in each question is the level of exposure and/or attention paid to some part of the broadcast media. The dependent variable — the thing the researcher believes to be affected by the independent variable — is, in each case, audience behavior. Unfortunately, from the researcher's point of view, the affected behaviors may be difficult to observe in a systematic manner. Voting behavior occurs in private. Career choices may be made years after exposure to soap operas. The researcher may not be present in the supermarket when the child asks the parent for a particular brand of cereal. This difficulty of assessing the impact of the media on audience behaviors is, to some extent, alleviated by substituting audience attitudes as the dependent variable. Attitudes were used in this way in Atkin's study of the effects of broadcast news programming on children.[7]

It should be pointed out, however, that although attitudes are frequently used as dependent variables within the context of a particular study, from the broader standpoint of the questions concerning media effects on audience behaviors, attitudes are intervening variables. Researchers construct intervening variables to account for internal and unobservable psychological processes that in turn account for overt (and observable) behavior. Thus, attitudes can be thought of as intervening between the stimulus — exposure to the media — and the response — voting, career choosing, parent influencing, and so on. In other words, the researcher postulates that the media do not have a direct effect on behavior but rather affect audience members' attitudes, which, in turn, affect behavior. Thus, it is assumed that someone who has a highly favorable attitude toward a particular political candidate is more likely to vote for him or her than is a voter who has a less favorable attitude. Is this assumption justified? The answer, as we shall see, is a qualified "yes."

The Relationship between Attitudes and Behaviors: A Caveat

Inasmuch as attitudes are predispositions to behave, it seems reasonable to assume that, when given the opportunity, people will behave toward attitude objects in ways that are consistent with their attitudes. Someone who has a favorable attitude toward the Rolling Stones ought to say so, buy and play their records, attend their concerts, and so on.

Surprisingly, most empirical studies of the relationship between attitudes and behaviors have found that attitudes and action are, at best, only weakly related.[8] The most famous study examining the attitude-behavior relationship was conducted in the 1930s by Richard LaPiere.[9] He was interested in the relationship between prejudice (negative attitudes toward a particular group) and discrimination (negative behaviors directed toward the group). Hotel managers were asked in a mail questionnaire if they would allow a Chinese couple to stay in their establishment. Many said no. However, when the same managers were confronted later with an actual Chinese couple requesting lodging, they contradicted their earlier expressed attitude and allowed the couple to stay.

Why are attitudes and behaviors so often poorly correlated? First, situational factors can exert powerful influences on overt behaviors. A particular situation might constrain an individual from engaging in a desired behavior or it might require a behavior that is contrary to the person's attitude. Someone who does not have the means (money or time) to attend a Rolling Stones concert probably will not attend even though he or she has a favorable attitude toward the group.

Second, specific behaviors are seldom the result of a single attitude. Whether we attend the Stones concert might be influenced by our attitude toward the Stones, toward rock and roll concerts in general, toward waiting six hours in line for tickets, and toward all the alternatives we might do with the time and money required to attend the concert. Obviously, some people who like the group very much are not going to be at the concert. And a few people who have unfavorable attitudes toward the group are going to be in attendance, perhaps because of their favorable attitude toward a member of the opposite sex who wanted to see the Stones.

Does the apparently weak relationship between specific attitudes and behaviors limit the usefulness of the attitude concept to the broadcast researcher? Somewhat. Does the weak relationship invalidate its usefulness? Definitely not. Most researchers believe that, other things being equal, people who have favorable attitudes toward something will behave more favorably toward that something than will people who have less favorable or unfavorable attitudes toward it. The problem, of course, is that other things are seldom equal. The intent here is to alert the reader to the complexity of the attitude-behavior relationship. Even though there is seldom a simple one-to-one relationship between attitudes and behaviors, attitudes will continue to be useful variables for scholars of the broadcast media.

Measurement Reliability and Validity

To have confidence in the result of empirical broadcast research, the researcher, as well as consumers of the research, must believe that the measures used were reliable and valid. This section discusses these important aspects of measurement.

Reliability

Reliability refers to the extent to which a measure yields data—numbers—that are consistent, dependable, stable, and predictable. The word *reliability* is used by measurement experts in much the same way as it is used in other contexts. A reliable employee, for example, is one whose behavior is dependable and predictable; he or she will perform on the job next week just as today. The unreliable employee is not so predictable. He or she may perform reliably today but next week may not show up for work.

To understand measurement reliability, think of a person's response to any attitude scale or question as having two separate components. One component of the response is systematic: repeated applications of the test yield identical responses. This component can be considered as representing the true attitude of the respondent. The second component is random and does not reflect the respondent's attitude. Perhaps a question was worded ambiguously or a respondent sneezed as she indicated her response, causing her pencil to miss the intended mark. Whatever the reason, responses to all attitude measures are to some extent affected by this random component. This nonsystematic random fluctuation is measurement unreliability. The more a response is a result of systematic factors, the more reliable is the measure. Conversely, the more the response is a result of random factors, the less reliable the measure.

A completely unreliable measure would not measure anything; it would provide random data. If an attitude measure were repeatedly given to respondents and each respondent's responses bore no relation to his or her earlier responses, the measure would be completely useless—it would not be measuring anything. Data from such a measure would be uninterpretable. To the extent that the responses were identical each time the measures were given—or to the extent that any changes in respondents' answers were systematic—the measure would be reliable. It would be measuring something, even if it were not what the researcher intended.

All attitude-measuring instruments are imperfectly reliable. Several factors detract from reliability. First, unclear or ambiguous test instructions or specific questions can contribute to measurement unreliability. Ambiguous questions can be interpreted in more than one way; and since such alternative interpretations are frequently random, they increase unreli-

ability. Thus researchers attempt to write instructions and specific questions clearly and unambiguously. Most researchers pretest attitude questionnaires on small groups of respondents who are similar to the respondents to be used in the actual study. Poorly worded items can thus be identified and rewritten or eliminated.

A second way to increase reliability is to increase the number of specific measures of the same attitude. As the number of questions increases, any random component in a respondent's answers to specific questions becomes less influential in determining the respondent's overall score. The random fluctuations on individual questions tend to cancel each other as the number of questions increases. Also note that as additional measures of the same attitude are added, reliability increases in generally systematic and predictable degrees.

Another factor that can increase measurement reliability concerns the circumstances in which the measures are administered. Most researchers have experienced the frustration of examining a questionnaire that appears to have been filled out completely at random. Properly motivated respondents are not likely to do this. Thus, researchers make every effort to motivate respondents to fill out questionnaires or to answer interviewer questions in a conscientious manner. For this, as well as for ethical reasons, respondents should feel free to decline to participate in the research.[10] Finally, measures should be administered under well-controlled and standardized circumstances. Measurement reliability usually decreases as the number of different circumstances under which the measures are administered increases. For example, if the instructions to respondents about how to answer questions differed, even slightly, from administration to administration, then measurement reliability could be reduced.

An effort is made in most media research to assess the reliability of the measures used. This assessment is frequently included in the research report to give the reader additional information for interpreting and evaluating the research. This assessment frequently takes the form of a reliability coefficient, denoted r_{xx}, which has a range of 1.0 (completely reliable) to 0 (completely unreliable).[12]

Validity

Validity concerns the general issue of whether a measuring instrument (such as a questionnaire) measures what its user thinks it measures. Although this is a common way to think about validity, it should be emphasized that there are several kinds of measurement validity, and any measure is valid, if at all, only in the context of a particular use to which it is put.

The three major types of measurement validity are content validity, criterion-related validity, and construct validity. There also are corresponding procedures for estimating how valid a measure is.

The content validity of an attitude measure addresses the issue of whether the specific measures used are relevant to, and representative of, the content of the object toward which attitudes are being measured. A researcher might be interested in measuring attitudes toward the tax-exempt status of religions. It would be possible to construct hundreds of relevant statements (called *items*) about this issue, and respondents could be asked to indicate the extent to which they agree or disagree with each statement. (These are Likert-type scales, described below.) However, the researcher cannot ask respondents to answer hundreds of items. He or she must select a sample from the list of possible statements for inclusion in the actual measure. To the extent that the items included are representative of all possible relevant items, the measure will have content validity.

Whether a measure has content validity is, to some extent, a subjective judgment. The relevance and representativeness of specific items should be independently judged by several experts in the content of the attitude object — perhaps members of the clergy for the religion example. An item that states: "The Genesis version of the Bible should be taught in the public schools," probably would not be rele-

vant to the content of the church taxation issue. The statement, "Church income and property should be taxed like that of any private business," probably would be.

The basic idea of criterion-related validity is that a measure is valid to the extent that it enables the researcher to predict the respondent's score on other measures believed to measure the same thing, or to predict a particular behavior of interest. The concern is not really with what is being measured as long as the measure predicts relevant respondent behavior or responses on the second measure. For instance, if the goal of a research project is the practical concern of estimating voter turnout, a measure yielding responses that allow the researcher to do this accurately is valid, regardless of what it is measuring. The interest is more in the criterion itself (voter turnout) than in the relationship between what is being measured and the criterion. Thus, a measure labeled the *attitude toward voting scale* might include items about past voting behavior, campaign interest, attention to campaign advertising, political party affiliation, and education level. Although this scale measures a variety of things, it would have criterion-related validity if responses could be combined or weighted in such a way that voting could be accurately predicted. Criterion-related validity is often more useful in applied research than in theoretical or pure research.

Construct validity is a complex and controversial subject. As Kerlinger writes, "It bores into the essence of science . . . it is concerned with the nature of reality and the nature of properties being measured. . . ."[13] In short, construct validity is concerned with what is being measured.

The most easily understood method for estimating construct validity is the known-groups technique. If the definition of the attitude being measured leads the researcher to expect that two groups of potential respondents will differ in their attitudes toward the object, a valid measure of the attitude should yield predictably different scores for the two groups. Thus, a measure of attitudes toward the progressive income tax might be validated by giving the test to two groups who are likely to differ on this issue—liberal Democrats and conservative Republicans—and showing that the liberal Democrats, as expected, score higher (indicate more favorable attitudes) than do conservative Republicans.

A second approach to estimating construct validity involves showing that scores on an attitude measure behave in theoretically expected ways in relation to other variables. For example, a broadcast researcher may hypothesize that the degree of attention that audience members pay to television commercials is influenced by attitudes toward the product or service being advertised (favorable attitudes lead to attention). If the measure of attitudes toward the product is correlated with measures of attention, this would be evidence for both the validity of the attitude measure and the usefulness of the theory on which the hypothesis is based. The researcher might also have theoretical reasons for expecting the attitude measure not to correlate with certain other variables. Demonstrating that the two variables were unrelated would be further evidence of the construct validity of the attitude measure. In other words, if relationships between a measure and other variables that are predicted by the theory are found, but other relationships that are not predicted are not found, then the pattern of results is evidence for the construct validity of the measure.

How are reliability and validity related? Reliability is a necessary but not sufficient condition for validity. That is, for a measure to be valid, it must be reliable; but a reliable measure is not necessarily valid. For example, if a researcher were interested in assessing a group of respondents' attitudes toward President Ronald Reagan, and if he or she asked them how many children the President had, the resulting answers would probably be reliable but invalid data. Answers would be likely to be consistent and dependable. Respondents who today indicate that Reagan has four children would be likely to respond in the same way next week, too. But this response, "four," would probably not reflect their attitude toward Reagan.

Levels of Measurement

In measuring height, the notion that an object three feet tall is half as tall as something six feet tall is taken for granted. Similarly, it is clear that the difference between three feet and four feet is the same as the difference between six feet and seven feet. It is thus tempting to conclude that someone who has an attitude of "6" toward something is twice as favorable as someone who has an attitude of "3," and that the difference between an attitude of "3" and one of "4" is the same as the difference between an attitude of "6" and one of "7." Depending on the level at which we measure an attitude, these conclusions may or may not be warranted.

The four levels of measurement are nominal, ordinal, interval, and ratio. Nominal measurement involves assigning numbers to categories that have qualitative rather than quantitative differences. In effect, the number is used to name the category. If one basketball player wears a number 32 on his or her back, and another wears number 16, there is no implication that 32 has more of something than 16, let alone that he or she has twice as much of it. The numbers only differentiate and name the two players.

Variables of interest to the broadcast researcher that would typically be measured at the nominal level include sex, race, geographic region, political party affiliation, and medium of exposure (radio, TV, magazines, etc.). The advantage of calling something "1" and "2" instead of male and female is that variables so labeled can then be analyzed, related, compared, and so on, with the use of special statistics for nominal scores.

Attitudes are usually measured at least at the next level of measurement complexity, the ordinal level. This level involves indicating the order of magnitude of measurements. The basic relationship expressed by ordinal data is that of "greater than" or "less than." For instance, a respondent asked to rank order the sources of news information toward which he or she was most favorable, might say, "television first, newspapers second, radio third, other people fourth, and magazines fifth." The researcher might assign a "1" to television, a "2" to newspapers, and so on. This procedure is ordinal measurement, because nothing is implied about the size of the difference in the favorableness of the respondents toward sources that are adjacent along the scale. The difference between the respondent's attitudes toward television and newspapers might be large or small, and it might or might not be the same as the difference between the respondent's attitudes toward other people and magazines. Further, nothing is implied about the absolute magnitude of the respondent's attitudes toward the five news sources. He or she could be highly favorable or not at all favorable toward all five.

Interval measurement meets the same criteria as ordinal measurement. In addition, the distance between adjacent scores are of equal intervals. The difference between two respondents whose attitudes are "8" and "10" toward some attitude-object is the same as the difference between two other respondents whose attitudes toward the same object are "3" and "5." Although the issue is somewhat controversial, the numbers derived from most attitude scales are treated as interval data.[14] This measurement allows the researcher to use more powerful statistics, which increase the chance of finding relationships between attitudes and other variables of interest.[15]

The fourth level of measurement complexity, ratio measurement, meets all criteria of interval measurement and also has a meaningful absolute zero point. Broadcast researchers use such ratio measures as number of hours of television viewing. This is ratio measurement because it is conceivable for someone to watch zero hours of television during some specified time period. There is some question, however, whether attitudes should be measured with ratio measures.[16]

Attitude Measurement Scales

The most common way attitudes are measured in broadcast research is with scales. Scales can be used on questionnaires that respondents fill out themselves, in face-to-face interviews, or, with slightly more difficulty, in telephone interviews.[17]

Many of the scales described here must be constructed according to elaborate procedures and pretested before being put to the substantive use for which they are being created. When constructing attitude scales, the respondent group and the circumstances under which the scales are pretested should be as similar as possible to the eventual respondents and circumstances that will be part of the actual research. If, for example, the respondents who participate in the actual study are to have their anonymity protected, then respondents who participate in the measure-construction phase of the research should also be assured that their responses will be kept anonymous.

All scales described, if constructed and used properly, can be reliable and valid measures of attitudes.

Semantic Differential

The semantic differential (SD) scale is a general technique for measuring the meaning that an object has for an individual. Using the technique involves placing the name of the object at the top of a series of seven-point scales that are anchored by bipolar adjectives. The respondent is asked to rate the object by placing a check somewhere along each scale. For example, the following scales might be used to measure attitudes toward Ronald Reagan.

Ronald Reagan

good :__:__:__:__:__:__:__: bad
unfair :__:__:__:__:__:__:__: fair

The semantic differential, developed by Osgood and his associates, has been widely used as an attitude measure.[18] Using a statistical procedure called factor analysis, the Osgood group found that three general factors or dimensions of meaning—activity, potency, evaluation—seem to be measured by the semantic differential. The evaluative factor is generally assumed to measure attitudes. The bipolar adjectives that typically anchor the evaluative scales include: pleasant-unpleasant; valuable-worthless; honest-dishonest; nice-awful; clean-dirty; fair-unfair; and good-bad. Most measurement experts suggest, however, that a unique and appropriate set of anchoring adjectives be developed for each new attitude object and respondent group.[19]

The scales are scored by assigning a "1" if a respondent's mark is placed in the space next to the negative side of the scale, a "2" if the mark is in the next space over, and so on, up to "7," if the mark were next to the positive side of the scale. Typically, scores from several scales are added together to determine a composite score for each respondent.

Thurstone Scales

This approach is named for its main inventor, Louis Leon Thurstone.[20] Scales created through this technique are also called *equal appearing interval* scales. Constructing these scales involves five steps. (1) Writing at least 100 statements about the attitude object. The statements should be a representative sample of all possible meaningful statements about the object—some should be very favorable, some very unfavorable, some moderately favorable, and so on. (2) These statements (items) are sorted by a number of judges (usually at least thirty) into eleven categories that appear to the judges to be equal distances apart. (3) The categories are assigned numbers from "1"—very unfavorable—to "11"—very favorable. For each statement, a value is calculated that is either the mean or median of the category positions in which the item was placed. (4) A measure of the degree of agreement between judges about the correct category to which to assign each statement is calculated for each item. (5) A small number of items (usually between twenty and thirty) are selected for use on the final scale. Items are selected that represent

all points on the eleven-point continuum and for which there was high judge agreement.

The respondent in the actual research is instructed to select each item with which he or she agrees. His or her score is either the mean or median of the scale values for the items with which he or she agrees. If the scale has been properly constructed, then each respondent should agree with only a few items that should have values that are similar and reflect his or her "true" position on the attitude continuum. The following are examples of Thurstone items designed to measure attitudes toward any school subject.[21] The scale values for each item would not appear on an actual questionnaire.

Scale Values

10.2	I would rather study this subject than eat.
8.5	This subject is a good subject.
5.5	I haven't any definite like or dislike for this subject.
2.6	This subject reminds me of Shakespeare's play—"Much Ado About Nothing."
1.6	This subject is a waste of time.

Likert-type Scales

Likert-type scales are also named for the principal developer of the technique through which they are created, Rensis Likert.[22] They are also called *summated rating* scales. Likert items are widely used to measure attitudes, in part because they are considerably easier to create than are Thurstone items.

Creating Likert-type scales involves these steps: (1) A large number of statements about the attitude object are generated that represent all points (favorable to unfavorable) along the attitude continuum. (2) Respondents are asked to indicate along a five- (or sometimes seven-) point scale the degree to which they agree or disagree with each statement. For favorable statements about the attitude object, a "strongly disagree" response is scored "1," "disagree" is scored "2," "neither agree nor disagree" is scored "3," "agree" is "4," and "strongly agree" is "5." The scoring process is reversed for negative statements. Each respondent's answers to the specific items are summed to produce his or her total score. (3) A variety of techniques can be used to select the smaller number of items (usually around twenty) that are used on the completed measure. All techniques involve selecting items to which an individual's responses tend to agree with his or her total score for all the items. In other words, if a respondent is favorable toward the attitude object as indicated by his or her overall score, a good item is one that also has yielded a favorable response from this subject. If a subject is negative toward the object, the response to the specific item should be equally negative.

Examples of Likert-type items designed to measure attitudes toward feminism appear in Figure 4–1.[23]

Guttman Scaling

Guttman scaling, named for its principal developer, Louis Guttman,[24] is sometimes called scalogram analysis or cumulative scaling. The basis of Guttman scaling is the notion that items can be arranged on a continuum such that a respondent who agrees with a particular item will also agree with all items expressing favorable (or unfavorable), but less extreme, positions toward the attitude object. Thus, statements have to be written so that acceptance of a very favorable item does not preclude acceptance of less favorable items. To meet this criterion, all items on a Guttman scale must either be positive or negative toward the attitude object, differing only in magnitude of favorableness or unfavorableness. The technique through which items are analyzed and selected for a Guttman scale is sometimes called the Cornell procedure.[25]

Respondents are scored according to the number of statements with which they indicate agreement. Someone who agrees with most or all the statements, including those of high magnitude, receives a high score. Someone who agrees with only a few (or no) statements, necessarily those that are of low magnitude, receives a low score.[26]

The following is an example of a Guttman scale designed to measure attitudes toward fluoridation:[27]

Least favorable:

A. It is all right for people to drink fluoridated water if they wish to.
B. If people want fluorine in their water but can't afford it, it is all right for the city to pay for it.
C. The city should publicize the

Figure 4-1 Examples of Likert-style Items

Women should be given equal opportunities with men for vocational and professional training.

____	____	____	____	____
strongly disagree	disagree	neither agree nor disagree	agree	strongly agree

Note: The same scales would follow each item.
There is no particular reason that a woman standing in a crowded bus should expect a man to offer a seat.
It is naturally proper for parents to keep a daughter, on the average, under closer control than a son.
Women should accept the intellectual limitations of their sex.
The general belief that women are by nature too high-strung to hold certain jobs is no more true than many of our superstitions.

availability of free fluorine for
those who want it.

D.   The city should add fluorine to the
water so that all people get it automatically.

Most favorable:

E.   The city government should
require that all citizens drink some
fluoridated water every day.

Multidimensional Scaling

Multidimensional scaling (MDS) is a class of
techniques that use information about how
similar or how different objects are, or are perceived to be, in order to place them into special
relationships with one another.[28] MDS is based
on the work of Torgerson and Gulliksen.[29]

When MDS is used to measure attitudes, respondents are given a list of attitude objects
and asked to make judgments about the perceived dissimilarity between each object. They
are provided with an arbitrary psychological
yardstick to apply in making their judgments
of the distances between the objects. The yardstick is in the form: If object *X* and object *Y*
are *U* units apart, then how far apart are object
A and object *B?* In order to compare each attitude-object with every other object, the respondent is required to make $n(n-1)/2$
separate judgments, where *n* is the number of
attitude objects. Thus, if there were five attitude objects on the list, ten judgments would
be required $[5(5-1)/2 = 10]$—ten objects
would require forty-five judgments.

To use MDS meaningfully in measuring attitudes, the researcher must know respondents
to be favorable toward at least one attitude object on the list.

Media researchers Barnett, Serota, and Taylor used MDS to examine attitude change during a 1974 congressional election.[30] Random
samples of voters were given an MDS questionnaire that included the following psychological yardstick: *If John F. Kennedy and
Dwight D. Eisenhower are 10 political inches
apart, how far apart are:*

Crime Prevention and the Republican
Party _____

Crime Prevention and Inflation _____
Inflation and the Republican Party _____

The complete list of attitude objects used by
the researchers included: (1) crime prevention;
(2) integrity and honesty in government; (3) the
Republican Party; (4) inflation; (5) the Democratic Party; (6) Democratic candidate; (7)
campaign reform; (8) busing; (9) ME; (10) Republican candidate.

ME was assumed to be the object toward
which the respondents would be highly favorable, although the authors point out that other
concepts such as "my vote" or "the ideal candidate" may have been superior. The larger the
number of "political inches" the respondents
perceived between themselves (ME) and a particular object, the more negative they were assumed to be toward the object.

The MDS questionnaire was administered
to random samples of voters at three times during the campaign. Based on the spatial configurations of the relationships between the
objects found at the first administration, the
researchers were able to advise one candidate
about what advertising messages would be
most likely to move him in the voters' collective
abstract spatial configuration toward issues
the voters favored and toward "ME," the voters themselves.

Figure 4-2 displays a three-dimensional arrangement or "plot" of the relationships between the ten attitude objects at the time of the
first administration of the questionnaire. The
numbers of the figure correspond to the numbers of the attitude objects listed above. This
arrangement is designed so that the distance
between any two objects approximates the average distance between the objects indicated by
the group of respondents on the MDS questionnaire.

The MDS procedure was also shown to be a
better predictor of the election results than was
a companion question, "If the election were
held today, whom would you vote for?" traditionally used in political opinion polling.

MDS is a relatively new procedure and has
not been widely used as an attitude measure in
broadcast research. Nonetheless, it has been

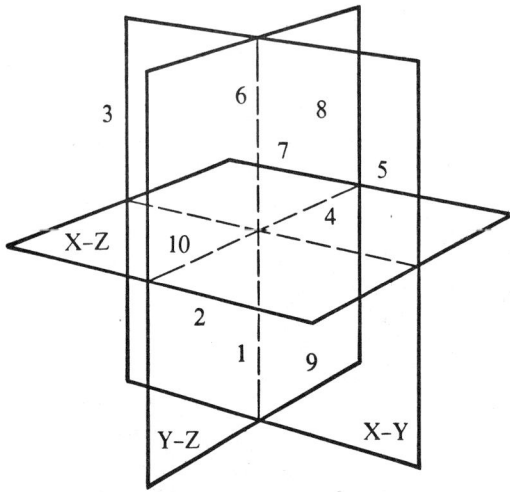

Figure 4-2 A geometric approximation of the distances between each attitude object at the first administration of an MDS questionnaire before a 1974 Michigan congressional election. (Barnett, Serota and Taylor, "Campaign Communication and Attitude Change, *Human Communication Research* Volume 2 [1976]: p. 233. Reprinted by permission of International Communication Association.)

demonstrated to be a viable measurement technique that in some research applications can be superior to more traditional scaling.[31] Its use will likely increase in the future.

Hybrid Scales

The scales presented thus far have generally been described in their pure form. Researchers, however, frequently use modifications of

the various scale construction techniques or combine features of several measures. This section presents a small and nonrandom sampling of these hybrid scales.

A study by Atkin and Block that examined the impact of alcohol advertising on audience attitudes toward alcohol used three different types of scales.[33] First, attitudes toward the persons appearing in the ads were measured as in Figure 4-3.

Next, respondents were asked about their attitudes toward particular brands of beer, as in Figure 4-4.

Finally, respondents were asked about their attitudes toward a brand of bourbon, as in Figure 4-5.

The Roper Polling Organization used the following modification of a Thurstone-type measure to assess the public's view on one aspect of the energy crisis:[33]

Here is a list of statements about the gasoline shortage (respondent given card). Which *one* of those statements comes closest to expressing your opinion?

A. There is a very real shortage, and the problem will get worse during the next 5 to 10 years.
B. There is a real oil shortage, but it will be solved in the next year or two.
C. There was a short-term problem, but it has been largely solved and there is no real problem any longer.
D. There never was any real oil shortage—it was contrived for economic and political reasons.

Polling organizations frequently measure attitudes with questions that have dichoto-

Figure 4-3   Attitudes toward ad spokespersons as measured by Atkin and Block.

Rate the people (or person) in each ad by circling the number that most accurately reflects your view.

Not Trustworthy	0	1	2	3	4	5	6	7	8	9	10	Most Trustworthy
Not Competent	0	1	2	3	4	5	6	7	8	9	10	Very Competent

For each of the following beers, draw a circle that shows whether your attitude is positive or negative.

	Very Negative	*Negative*	*Neutral*	*Positive*	*Very Positive*
Budweiser	– –	–	o	+	+ +
Miller	– –	–	o	+	+ +
etc.					

Figure 4-4   Attitude toward brands of beer from Atkin and Block.

mous response options. NBC News asked the following question of a national sample of adults:[34]

> The new treaty between the United States and Panama calls for the United States to turn over ownership of the canal to Panama at the end of this century. However, this treaty has to be approved by the Senate. Do you favor or oppose approval of this treaty by the Senate?

The technique of asking the respondent a direct question about his or her attitude and providing scaled response categories is common. Hocking used this procedure to measure attitudes toward a particular rock and roll band (not the Rolling Stones) and toward rock music in general[35] (see Figure 4-6).

Other Attitude Measures

Open-ended Questions

Open-ended questions differ from closed questions in that the respondent is not given a set of categories from which to select a response. Examples are, "How do you like the way the Supreme Court of the United States is doing its job these days?" and "How do you feel about the Soviet invasion of Afghanistan?"

Depending on the nature of the research project, open-ended questions can be useful as attitude measures. They may enable the researcher to discover respondent attitudes that may not have been anticipated when the measurement instrument was designed. They offer the potential for the researcher to gain a richer insight into the nuances of feeling that sample members may hold toward the object in question. The use of open-ended questions can also be an effective means of increasing rapport with the respondent by allowing him or her to express his or her views in more detail. For this reason, it is generally a good idea to include a few open-ended questions on attitude measuring instruments. Many respondents find long lists of closed-ended scale items boring or frustrating to fill out.

Open-ended questions also have certain disadvantages and thus should be used judiciously. They are time consuming—both to gather initially and to interpret later. Some respondents ramble and give answers that are long and/or irrelevant. It is often difficult reliably to code (assign numbers) to responses. Also, data derived from open-ended questions frequently do not meet all the interval mea-

Figure 4-5   Attitude toward one brand of bourbon as measured by Atkin and Block.

Do you think Wild Turkey is a good brand or a bad brand of bourbon? Give it a rating score between 0 and 10—10 is the highest possible score.

| Bad Brand | 0 | 1 | 2 | 3 | 4 | 5 | 6 | 7 | 8 | 9 | 10 | Good Brand |

How would you evaluate the overall quality of this band?

Extremely		Extremely
Bad	:__:__:__:__:__:__:__:__:__:	Good

In general, how much do you like rock and roll music?

Dislike		Like
a Lot	:__:__:__:__:__:__:__:__:__:	a Lot

Figure 4-6 Attitude toward a rock and roll band as measured by Hocking.

surement assumptions and thus should be treated with less powerful statistics (see endnote 15).

Unobtrusive Measures

All paper-and-pencil measures of attitudes, whether self-administered or administered face-to-face or in phone interviews, to some extent obtrude on the respondent. The respondent is aware that his or her attitudes are being measured. This awareness has the potential to affect responses, especially when the attitude object is one for which some responses are perceived to be more socially desirable than others. For example, broadcast researchers have found that television audiences indicate verbally that they have very favorable attitudes toward educational television. These reports, however, are apparently influenced by respondents' beliefs about the social desirability of their answers, since other measures of the same attitudes (such as ratings) are not consistent with these verbal reports.

In their book on unobtrusive measures, Webb and his associates argue that this, as well as other potential shortcomings of using "reactive" measures (questionnaires and interviews), can be minimized by using measurement techniques that do not require respondent awareness of the fact they are being measured.[36] A further theme of their book is that a shortcoming of much social research is the reliance on single measures. They point out that all measures are imperfect. "If a proposition can survive the onslaught of a series of imperfect measures, with all their irrelevant error, confidence should be placed in it."[37] They argue that unobtrusive measures can be important supplements to interviews and ques-

tionnaires. They describe three broad categories of such measures: physical traces, archives, and observations.

Physical traces include erosion, in which the degree of selective wear on some material yields the measure; and accretion, in which the measure is some deposit of materials. Examples: A measure of the popularity of exhibits in Chicago's Museum of Science and Industry was derived by finding that the floor tiles around the hatching-chick exhibit were replaced every six months. Tiles at other exhibits lasted years before replacement was required. One researcher measured the readership level of advertisements by counting the number of different fingerprints on the pages.

Archives include the ongoing, continuing records of a society, and episodic and private records. Examples: Library records were used to examine one effect of introducing television into a community. Withdrawals of fiction titles dropped, but nonfiction titles did not. One researcher attempted to measure air passenger anxiety by examining records on the sale of alcoholic drinks in airports after major air crashes.

Observations involve simply watching behavior and inferring that the person observed has an attitude consistent with the behavior. For instance, racial attitudes in two colleges were compared by observing the grouping of blacks and whites in classrooms. The degree of fear created by ghost stories was measured by observing the shrinking diameter of a circle of children.

Perhaps the most widely known unobtrusive measure in broadcasting research is Bandura's use of the Bobo doll in investigating the impact of violence in the broadcast media.[38]

The independent variable in a series of studies was exposure to broadcast materials that either did or did not depict violent acts. The dependent variable was the number of times that the child viewers struck a Bobo doll placed nearby. Bandura demonstrated, at least within the limited context of his procedures, that media violence can contribute to viewer violence.

Obviously, the researcher is limited in using observations as attitude measures by the pragmatic necessity of using behaviors that can be elicited from research participants. This is the reason for the reliance on paper-and-pencil measures and on interviews in the overwhelming number of broadcasting studies using the attitude concept.

Summary

This essay introduced attitude measurement. Attitudes were defined, and their use in broadcasting research as independent, mediating, and dependent variables was explained. The concepts of measurement reliability and validity were discussed, as were the four levels of measurement complexity: nominal, ordinal, interval, and ratio. Commonly used measurement techniques were described, including semantic differential scales, Thurstone scales, Likert scales, Guttman scales, multidimensional scaling, hybrid scales, open-ended questions, and unobtrusive measures.

Endnotes

1. Gordon W. Allport, "Attitudes," in Carl A. Murchison, ed., *Handbook of Social Psychology* (Worcester, Mass.: Clark University Press, 1935), 789–884.
2. Erland Nelson, "Attitudes, I: Their Nature and Development," *Journal of General Psychology* 21 (1939): 367–436.
3. William J. McGuire, "The Nature of Attitudes and Attitude Change," in Garner Lindzey and Elliot Aronson, eds., *The Handbook of Social Psychology*, 2nd ed., Vol. 3 (Reading, Mass.: Addison-Wesley, 1969), 136–314.
4. Herbert W. Simons, *Persuasion: Understanding, Practice and Analysis* (Reading, Mass: Addison-Wesley, 1976), 80.
5. K. Kyoon Hur, "Impact of 'Roots' on Black and White Teenagers," *Journal of Broadcasting* 22 (1978): 289–307.
6. Ibid.
7. Charles K. Atkin, "Broadcast News Programming and the Child Audience," *Journal of Broadcasting* 22 (1978): 47–61. Measuring the attitudes of children creates special problems for the broadcasting researcher. These problems are discussed in the essay by Meyer and Hexamer in this volume.
8. A. W. Wicker, "Attitudes vs. Actions: The Relationship of Verbal and Overt Behavioral Responses to Attitude Objects," *Journal of Social Issues* 25 (1969): 47–66. See Kerry Thomas, ed., *Attitudes and Behavior* (Baltimore: Penguin, 1971), for a book of readings about the attitude-behavior relationship.
9. Richard T. LaPiere, "Attitudes vs. Actions," *Social Forces* 13 (1934): 230–237.
10. For a discussion of ethical issues, see Committee on Ethical Standards in Psychological Research, *Ethical Principles in the Conduct of Research with Human Participants* (Washington, D.C.: American Psychological Association, 1973).
11. For an introductory and clear discussion of the correlation coefficient, see Edward W. Minium, *Statistical Reasoning in Psychology and Education* (New York: John Wiley & Sons, 1970), 130–152.
12. Fred N. Kerlinger, *Foundations of Behavioral Research*, 2nd ed. (New York: Holt, Rinehart & Winston, 1973), 456–476. Kerlinger's book includes thorough and very readable discussions of reliability and validity, as well as of other measurement issues.
13. Ibid., 473.
14. See Kerlinger, 438–441, for a discussion.
15. Nominal and ordinal data require the use of "nonparametric" statistics, which are less powerful than parametric statistics, which require interval data. See Kerlinger, 286–288, for a discussion.

16. Depending on how attitude is defined, it may or may not make sense to conceive of an individual as having a "zero" attitude toward an attitude object. However, whether or not an absolute zero point on an individual's internal attitude continuum makes conceptual sense, it is possible to measure attitudes at the ratio level. For example, a broadcasting researcher could use the number of hours per week a viewer watched crime shows as a measure of attitude toward this type of programming. This would be ratio measurement, because a respondent could indeed watch zero hours—and one who watched four hours has watched twice as much as someone who watched two hours.

17. An excellent discussion of the advantages and disadvantages of phone versus face-to-face interviewing versus mail questionnaires, and so on, is found in C. A. Moser and G. Kalton, *Survey Methods in Social Investigation*, 2nd ed. (New York: Basic Books, 1972).

18. Charles Osgood, "The Nature and Measurement of Meaning," *Psychological Bulletin* 49 (1952): 197–237. Charles Osgood, George J. Suci, and Percy Tannenbaum, *The Measurement of Meaning* (Urbana: University of Illinois Press, 1957).

19. Donald K. Darnell, "Semantic Differentiation," in Philip Emmert and William D. Brooks, eds., *Methods of Research in Communication* (New York: Houghton Mifflin, 1970), 181–196.

20. L. L. Thurstone and E. J. Chave, *The Measurement of Attitude* (Chicago: University of Chicago Press, 1929). It would be difficult to overemphasize the influence of the writings of Thurstone on the development of attitude measurement and psychometric theory in general. A diverse range of ideas and techniques are attributed to him and the "method of equal appearing intervals" originally described in his 1929 paper with Chave is only one of many Thurstone techniques.

21. E. B. Silance and H. H. Remmers, "An Experimental Generalized Master Scale: A Scale to Measure Attitude Toward Any School Subject," in Marvin E. Shaw and Jack W. Wright, eds., *Scales for the Measurement of Attitudes* (New York: McGraw-Hill, 1967), 295. The Shaw and Wright book contains 175 separate attitude scales and is an excellent resource.

22. Rensis Likert, "A Technique for the Measurement of Attitudes," *Archives of Psychology* 140 (1932): 1–55.

23. Clifford Kirkpatrick, "The Construction of a Belief Pattern Scale for Measuring Attitudes Toward Feminism," in Shaw and Wright, 279–287.

24. Louis Guttman, "A Basis for Scaling Qualitative Data," *American Sociological Review* 9 (1944): 139–150.

25. See Louis Guttman, "The Cornell Technique for Scale and Intensity Analysis," *Educational and Psychological Measurement* 7 (1947): 247–280.

26. William A. Scott, "Attitude Measurement," in Gardner Lindzey and Elliot Aronson, eds., *The Handbook of Social Psychology*, 2nd ed., Vol. 2, 224. Scott's chapter is a comprehensive treatment of attitude measurement.

27. Ibid., 222.

28. Joseph B. Kruskal and Myron Wish, *Multidimensional Scaling* (Beverly Hills: Sage, 1978), 7.

29. Warren S. Torgerson, *Theory and Methods of Scaling* (New York: John Wiley & Sons, 1958). Harold Gulliksen, "Paired Comparisons and the Logic of Measurement," *Psychological Review* 53 (1946): 199–213.

30. George A. Barnett, Kim B. Serota, and James A. Taylor, "Campaign Communication and Attitude Change: A Multidimensional Analysis," *Human Communication Research* 2 (1976): 227–244.

31. For another application of MDS by broadcasting researchers, see Byron Reeves and M. Mark Miller, "A Multidimensional Measure of Children's Identification with Television Characters," *Journal of Broadcasting* 22 (1978): 71–86.

32. Charles K. Atkin and Martin Block,

"Content and Effects of Alcohol Advertising," Technical Report #1 to the Bureau of Alcohol, Firearms and Tobacco, November 1979.

33. Al Richman, "The Polls: Public Attitudes Toward the Energy Crisis," *Public Opinion Quarterly* 43 (1979): 577–578.

34. Bernard Roshco, "The Polls: Polling on Panama: Si; Don't Know; Hell, No!," *Public Opinion Quarterly* 42 (1978): 557.

35. John E. Hocking, Duane G. Margreiter, and Cal Hylton, "Intra-audience Effects: A Field Test," *Human Communication Research* 3 (1977): 243–249.

36. Eugene J. Webb, Donald T. Campbell, Richard D. Schwartz, and Lee Sechrest, *Unobtrusive Measures: Nonreactive Research in the Social Sciences* (Chicago: Rand McNally, 1966).

37. Ibid., 3.

38. Albert Bandura, Dorothea Ross, and Sheila Ross, "Imitation of Film-mediated Aggression Models," *Journal of Abnormal and Social Psychology* 66 (1963): 3–11.

Additional References

Dawes, Robyn M. *Fundamentals of Attitude Measurement*, New York: John Wiley & Sons, 1972.

Edwards, Allen L. *Techniques of Attitude Scale Construction*, New York: Appleton-Century-Crofts, 1957.

Guilford, J. P. *Psychometric Methods* (2nd ed.), New York: McGraw-Hill, 1954.

Nunnally, Jum C. *Psychometric Theory*, New York: McGraw-Hill, 1967.

5
Ethnographic Studies of Broadcast Media Audiences

James Lull

Despite the fact that most media consumption occurs at home, little social research on broadcasting has been conducted there. The family home is an intimate location. Particularly in this country, where emphasis is placed on privacy, the idea of invading the home to do social research does not appeal to most researchers. To date, naturalistic studies of families have been rare. Naturalistic studies of broadcast audiences conducted in homes are even less common.

There are some exceptions. An observational study of seventeen "normal" and disturbed families was undertaken by two Boston psychiatrists and their associates.[1] Henry wrote about five psychiatrically disturbed families after living with each for one week.[2] Lewis lived with Mexican and Puerto Rican families, observed their activities in relation to their histories, interviewed them, and reconstructed their realities in his written accounts.[3]

The famous videotaped ethnography of the William Loud family was aired on public television. More recently, Wilkes documented the lives of *Six American Families* for public television. He also wrote a short book about these families and the method he used.[4] Lull developed a typology of the social uses of television by living with families and documenting their communication habits.[5] Reid provided a symbolic interactionist interpretation of children's time spent watching television commercials using observations collected in homes.[6] Other researchers have also begun to collect ethnographic data on media audiences.[7] Naturalistic studies of audience behavior probably will be undertaken more frequently in the future.

This essay provides specific methodological suggestions for researchers who intend to conduct observational studies of broadcast audiences. Data also are presented regarding the effect of the observer on the family unit, with special attention to potential disturbances of family television viewing.

Methodological Issues

The ethnographer of family audience behavior must be concerned with: (1) sampling, (2) observational techniques, (3) stages of data collection, and (4) organizing and presenting data. This discussion focuses on lessons learned from research conducted during the past several years in Wisconsin and California, where observations and interviews of more than 300 families have been made for periods of three to seven days each.

Sampling

Depending on the number of families required, the sampling can be very time consuming and frustrating. Nonetheless, as many as 90 observers have been placed simultaneously in families previously unknown to them.[8] Through trial and error, an effective means has been found for locating families who will permit extended observations in their homes.

Random phone calls or neighborhood surveys conducted to contact families initially have not worked well. Even the most conservatively dressed representative with the most apparently benign intent has been unable to convince subjects to open their doors for observation. Contact through some agency of importance to the family is usually necessary to gain access. These agencies include religious and educational institutions, places of work, community service groups, and clubs. If the agency is of great importance to the family (as in the case of religious or vocational institutions), then families in the sample are likely to be homogeneous.

Civic groups and clubs represent a wider range of family types. Even though there may be less emotional commitment to these organizations when compared with religious or vocational groups, most families still honor a basic commitment to community groups and respect the desires of their leaders, thereby increasing the likelihood that they will agree to participate. Groups such as girls clubs, boys clubs, Parent Teacher Associations, and community nursery schools have been especially cooperative. Some family research requires that children of a particular age be present in the home, and these agencies can be helpful.

A successful approach to gaining groups' cooperation has been first to call their adminis-

trators, explaining the essential nature of the research program and requesting to address the next board meeting. At the board meeting, the general nature of the research project is explained, and the cooperation of the group is requested. The researcher's affiliation with a local university and the noncommercial nature of the investigation are persuasive factors. The researcher describes an interest in studying "communication in families" or "family life" (never mentioning mass communication or television viewing).

The executive group is asked to endorse the research project and to provide access to telephone lists of their members or to allow a personal appeal for volunteer subjects at the next meeting of the general membership. Telephone calls, in which the research project is identified as being conducted cooperatively with the group, have been more productive of willing families than have been speeches to the general membership of these community groups. Both approaches have been effective, however. Depending on the project and the group, 25 to 35 percent of the families contacted initially have been willing to participate.

From families that agree to serve as subjects, an additional 10 to 20 percent will not provide usable data for various reasons. Oversampling is necessary for studies that involve many observers and families. No effort has yet been made to determine whether the kinds of families who self-select into samples for ethnographic studies are different from those who do not cooperate. Sampling procedures have generated an assortment of family types. Whether this assortment is representative of American families overall is a methodological consideration that has not been investigated.

Families have not been paid when students do the observing and when the length of time involved is short. When inconvenience to the family is great, as in week-long stays, families have been paid a small amount of money and asked to provide food. Arrangements have sometimes been made, particularly with farm families, for the observers to perform certain work tasks in order to compensate for the inconvenience they may cause.[9] Observers have not always slept at subjects' homes. Little data seem to be lost if the researcher leaves at bedtime and returns the next morning.

Observational Techniques

The particular theoretical and conceptual concerns that motivate a research project determine what qualifies as observational evidence and what the manner for documentation of family data should be. Naturalistic studies in communication, such as those that analyze conversational form, may require precise documentation of verbal interaction. Audio- and videotape recorders have sometimes been used to document conversations, but this technique has rarely been used in home settings.

The use of electronic recording equipment to study family television viewing has been tried at least once but with limited success. In a study by Bechtel and his associates, television cameras were placed on top of the television sets of a small sample of families in order to document their behaviors while viewing.[10] Microphones were placed around the room in order to record conversations and personal reactions to the shows. The scope of this research project was limited only to the characteristics of eye contact, physical movement, and talk patterns while viewing. These are interesting considerations, but the ethnographer usually wants to learn more about the environment in which these behaviors are taking place.

It is technically possible to pin small cordless microphones on each family member while a slow speed, multitrack audiotape recorder documents everything said during the observational period (one track on the recording unit assigned to each person). The difficulties with this approach are that the equipment is expensive and the researcher has no record of where the taped comments were made. This latter problem can be overcome by continual note-taking by the observer. In spite of the problems, such a technical device may prove to be suited to studying family life.

Currently, the most effective method for documenting the activities of family life is still written notes made by the observer. Note-taking in the presence of families is an awkward task that must be done in a way that attracts minimum attention. Student observers may have an advantage since they can take notes in the guise of homework chores. This technique has often worked well in the study of media audience behavior, since many families spend their evenings in front of the television set. The student observer, also seated in the viewing area but surrounded by homework, can easily take notes on interpersonal interaction that accompanies viewing. It is helpful to document conversations as they unfold, a goal facilitated by taking notes in this fashion.

The natural breaks occurring during observational studies give the researcher time to take detailed notes about what transpired during the preceding minutes or hours. Reconstruction of the scene is more accurately accomplished when opportunities are created to take notes during the actual observational period. Additional notes can be made at bedtime. At first, many families are sensitive to observer note-taking, and it is sometimes difficult to be unobtrusive during early stages of the research. Note-taking becomes less troublesome during later stages of data collection.

Stages of Data Collection

An ethnographer studying family life at home must first decide the length of the observational period for each family. The time unit must be sufficiently long to understand the family and to insure that the behaviors observed are not staged for the researcher's benefit, thereby obscuring valid identification of concepts and relationships. On the other hand, observation should cease when the important characteristics of social structure and process have been identified and documented. Seven days is often an excellent, time for reasons that will be discussed later. At least three days per family seems to be the minimum.

It is necessary to establish rapport with family members sufficient to insure the gathering of valid self-reports and accounts by subjects of the perceived attitudes and behaviors of others. The privacy of the home and the small number of subjects involved in family research may make the observer's presence more conspicuous than in other settings. Nonetheless, the observer who is accepted into the family system can provide "camera-like views of the movements, conversations and interactions" in a way no other social research method can rival.[11]

When researchers live in the homes of families, "stages of familiarity" or "stages of trust" develop. These stages vary from observer to observer and from family to family, but some basic techniques can help standardize the sequence of events and the time they require.

The process typically develops in three stages. In the first stage, spanning roughly the first two days of observation, family histories, biographical sketches, and descriptions of the physical environment are the primary elements recorded. Time can be spent effectively noting everyday objects, such as home furnishings, clothing, ornaments, tools, domestic appliances (particularly the location of television and radio receivers), and other machinery.[12] This is a natural and convenient development since the researcher immediately encounters the physical aspects of the environment when the observational period begins. It is perhaps best to document these items right away anyway, since their appearance may be more striking at first than later, when the researcher has become accustomed to the surroundings.

Families often begin to reveal much of their past and present during the first day or two of observation. This revelation of personal information is often produced with little or no stimulation and makes the situation more relaxed. The researcher may feel more comfortable by saying something personal at this time, although specific references to the objectives of the research program should not be made.

Interaction sequences, family routines, communication habits, particular media uses, and more detailed personal information become accessible to the researcher during the second stage of the research. Using a seven-day model for the period of observation, the second stage typically begins late in the second day or during the third day. The researcher begins to feel that the interpersonal dramas unfolding are normal.

During this second stage, the observer must create and sustain rapport with family members while maintaining the disinterested eye and ear of the objective observer-reporter. He or she must also understand each family member's acts from the actor's perspective while retaining an objective attitude toward the "actor and the action scene."[13] The close quarters of family studies can make the adjustment of the observer to the subjects, and their adjustment to him or her, difficult. The observer must engage in enough conversation and physical activity to appear and feel normally situated in the place of study, yet he or she must not lead conversation or direct behavior. Families can be asked directly not to alter their routines to accommodate the observer. Families must be confident that they are not being judged or evaluated by comparison to an external behavioral norm.

In research conducted in Wisconsin and California, observers participated in family routines for the duration of the observation periods. They ate with families, performed household chores, played with the children, and engaged in group entertainment, particularly television watching. A successful method for achieving rapport with family members during the second stage was for the observer to participate in activities that were important to each individual. For instance, ethnographers of dairy farm families should be prepared to help milk the cows, do the barnyard chores, assist in housework, and play with the young children. These behaviors help the observer become accepted by each member of the group. Such gestures should not be sustained to the point where they begin to interfere with the natural manner in which the activities are conducted. These moments of sharing labor have also proven useful for gathering additional information by means of informal questioning.

Validity and reliability checks on specific observations, concepts, behavioral rules, or theory are usually the last data-gathering responsibilities in family research. This third stage occurs after the last day of observation has been completed. Independent interviews are conducted with each family member. These question-and-answer sessions should be recorded on audiotape. They are unlike others that take place in social research since by this time an unusual degree of rapport has been established between the observer and family members. This atmosphere contributes to relaxed, productive, and revealing interview sessions. During these sessions, family members are typically willing to comment at length about their feelings regarding the issues raised by the observer and to report their beliefs and opinions about other family members.

Organization and Presentation of Data

Three or four forms of raw data typically exist at the conclusion of the research period. Written materials include the notes taken by the observer during the time spent with individual families. The observer also has written a summary at the end of each observation day. Another form of written material sometimes used is a standardized interview schedule, administered to each family member during the final stage of data collection. Audiotape recordings are made by interviewing each family member at the conclusion of the observational period. Written transcripts are then made from the tape recordings. With these materials at hand, the ethnographer organizes and writes a report.

Written reports conform to one of three basic plans. First, if the ethnographer has studied family life with specific *a priori* research hypotheses in mind, the most effective way to report the findings is to organize the evidence around these hypotheses. In exploratory, interpretive, or phenomenological works, the report can focus on individual family members or on communications phenomena distilled from the raw data. Third, a combination of these approaches may be appropriate.

Some reports are book-length manuscripts. For instance, in one lengthy ethnography of family communication and mass media habits, each family was discussed in terms of its (1) family structure and communication patterns, (2) family media habits, (3) media habits of individual family members, and (4) particular communications phenomena (such as use of mass media to establish and demonstrate interpersonal dominance, parasocial interaction with television and the maintenance of marriage, television and exploration of interpersonal possibilities, natural viewing rights, regulation of program viewing, and successful role enactment).[14]

A simple but useful technique is to type all observational and interview notes that will be used in compiling the final ethnographic report. After carefully reviewing the data for themes to be explored in the analysis, observations and interview comments are sorted by first cutting the typewritten pages into units of one observation each. Then the researcher rearranges the bits of data into topics with the proper internal consistency in each.[15] Samples of conversation and descriptions of interaction patterns can be used to illustrate conceptual focal points. These data help the ethnographer of communication demonstrate the internal validity of areas to be developed theoretically. Finally, accurate and concise use of language facilitates ethnographic reporting, making the work credible and potentially useful to a wide range of readers.

Observer Obtrusiveness: Some Recent Findings

A common criticism of ethnography is that the presence of an observer in a naturalistic environment must affect those who are observed, altering their behavior and thereby distorting the nature of the phenomena under study. The existence or magnitude of this problem has yet to be documented empirically; nonetheless, many researchers assume it to be true. Of course, every method of data collection in social research interferes in some way with the natural behavior of the individuals studied. In experimental or survey research, the investigator creates an unnatural event (the experiment with its artificial setting or the survey that solicits verbal re-creations of reality). In ethnography, the investigator documents naturally occurring behavior but risks interference by being present.

Table 5-1 Was Your Behavior Affected by Observer's Presence?

	Yes	%
Fathers (n = 68)	14	20.6
Mothers (n = 82)	17	20.7
Children (n = 179)	48	26.8
N = 329	79	

In a study of audience members' uses of television, 85 trained observers were sent for three days into the homes of families unknown to them.[16] Observations of family communication, including media use, were made the first two days. On the third day, the observer asked a standard set of questions of each family member seven years of age or older. The interview schedule included questions about possible effects of the observer's presence in the home.

Fathers and mothers were equally likely to say that the observer's presence affected their behavior (Table 5-1), with one of five indicating that they behaved differently. Children said they were only slightly more likely to be affected by the observer.

Family members reported three major categories of altered behaviors (Table 5-2). Most family members who said their behavior was different indicated that they were nicer, more polite, or more formal than usual. This finding may, in part at least, be due to the short period of observation in this study.

Family members more frequently believed that someone other than themselves was affected by the presence of the observer (Table 5-3). Generally, the person named as affected was one of the children. The child was usually said to be more animated or talkative, ploys apparently used to gain the observer's attention (Table 5-4). Respondents said the altered behaviors of other family members fell into three main categories: (1) animated–attention–seeking–talkative, (2) nice–polite–formal, and (3) shy–nervous–quiet–inhibited. The reactions reported about other family members were similar to the behaviors that emerged from the self-reports.

Respondents strongly indicated that their television viewing was not altered because of the observer (Table 5-5). Parents and children both reported that, with few exceptions, their television habits did not differ with the observer in the home. This is an encouraging finding for ethnographers of audience behavior, since it indicates that even though some audience members modify their behavior with the observer present, these changes apparently do not involve the disruption of routine pat-

Table 5-2 How Was Your Behavior Affected by the Observer's Presence?

	f	%
No difference	250	75.9
Nice–polite–formal	38	11.5
Animated–attention–seeking–talked more	12	3.6
Shy–nervous–quiet–inhibited	16	4.8
Stricter	2	0.6
Talked to observer	4	1.2
Didn't specify difference	7	2.1
	329	100.0

Table 5-3   Who Acted Differently?

	f	%	*% (of individuals in subgroup)*
Father (n = 68)	18	5.5	26.5
Mother (n = 82)	24	7.3	29.3
Child (n = 179)	87	26.4	48.6
Nobody	200	60.8	
	329	100.0	

Table 5-4   How Did That Person Act Differently?

	f	%
No difference	250	75.9
Nice–polite–formal	38	11.5
Animated–attention–seeking–talked more	12	3.6
Shy–nervous–quiet–inhibited	16	4.8
Stricter	2	0.6
Talked to observer	4	1.2
Didn't specify difference	7	2.1
	329	100.0

terns of television use. In the few cases when television watching was reported to be altered, the distribution of changes revealed no systematic trend (Table 5-6). Among the viewers who indicated that their amount of viewing changed, about the same number said they watched *more* television as *less* when the observer was in the home. Only two of the 329 who were questioned said that the television was turned off, on, or to a particular channel in order to accommodate the observer.

Summary

Ethnographic research is an interpretive enterprise whereby the investigator uses observation and in-depth interviewing to grasp the meaning of communication by analyzing the perceptions, shared assumptions, and activities of the social actors under scrutiny. This essay provides some specific practical suggestions for observing families in their homes. The recommendations are intended to illus-

Table 5-5   Was Your Television Viewing Different because of Observer?

	Yes	%
Father (n = 68)	11	17.2
Mother (n = 82)	12	14.7
Children (n = 179)	22	12.3
	45	

Table 5-6 What Were the Differences in Family Television Viewing?

	f	%
No difference	286	86.9
Watched more	18	5.5
Watched less	13	4.0
Watched different shows	1	0.3
Different viewer arrangement	4	1.2
Different viewer time	2	0.6
Advantage for child	2	0.6
More talk/activity	1	0.3
TV for observer	2	0.6
	329	100.0

trate particular approaches to studying the behavior of broadcast media audiences. These recommendations do not exhaust the possible ways of conducting family ethnographies, nor has every methodological issue been discussed.

Since ethnographic studies of audience behavior involve spending time in the natural environment where media messages are consumed, a discussion of the effects of the observer on family members has been presented. Data from a recent mass observation study demonstrate that the presence of the observer does not severely disrupt the normal behavior of families. Television viewing habits are infrequently disturbed under these conditions, and the changes that do occur are not systematic.

Endnotes

1. David Kantor and William Lehr, *Inside the Family* (San Francisco: Jossey-Bass Publishers, 1975).
2. Jules Henry, *Pathways to Madness* (New York: Vintage Books, 1965).
3. Oscar Lewis, *Five Families* (New York: Basic Books, 1959); Oscar Lewis, *La Vida* (New York: Random House, 1965).
4. Paul Wilkes, *Six American Families* (New York: Seabury/Parthenon Press, 1977).
5. James Lull, "The Social Uses of Televi-

sion," *Human Communication Research* 6 (1980): 197–209.
6. Leonard N. Reid, "Viewing Rules as Mediating Factors of Children's Responses to Commercials," *Journal of Broadcasting* 23 (1979): 15–26.
7. Timothy P. Meyer, Paul J. Traudt, and James A. Anderson, "Nontraditional Mass Communication Research Methods: An Overview of Observational Case Studies of Media Use in Natural Settings," *Communication Yearbook* 4 (1980): 261–275.
8. James Lull, "Family Communication Patterns and the Social Uses of Television," *Communication Research* 7 (1980): 319–334.
9. The idea of inconvenience may be stressed too strongly. In most cases, families say they enjoy the presence of the observer. Many report that they miss him or her when the observation period is over. In some cases, lasting friendships have been made between the observer and the observed as a result of the research.
10. Robert Bechtel, C. Achelpohl, and R. Akers, "Correlates Between Observed Behavior and Questionnaire Responses on Television Viewing," *Television and Social Behavior*, *4*, E. A. Rubinstein, G. A. Comstock, and J. P. Murray (eds.) (Wash-

ington, D.C.: U.S. Government Printing Office, 1972): 274–344.

11. Lewis, *Five Families*, xxii.

12. John Madge, *The Tools of Social Science* (London: Longman, Green and Co., 1953), 140–141.

13. Aaron Cicourel, *Method and Measurement* (New York: The Free Press, 1974), 50.

14. James Lull, "Mass Media and Family Communication: An Ethnography of Audience Behavior," unpublished doctoral dissertation (Madison: University of Wisconsin, 1976).

15. It may be useful at this time to ask the family to comment on the validity of the conceptual or theoretical structure that has developed during this process.

16. Lull, "Family Communication Patterns and the Social Uses of Television," 1980.

Studies of the mass communication process using physiological responses as measures are relatively rare, but an abiding suspicion that important and otherwise unavailable information lies hidden in the human subconscious gives these studies great appeal. On the whole, such studies depend on measuring involuntary changes in the sympathetic nervous system as indicators of information processing ongoing in the central nervous system. The theoretical constructs to which physiological measures have been said to relate include emotional arousal, habituation, orienting, and attention.

Interest in physiological measures endures because of these features:

1. Physiological devices are completely stable. . . . This means that significant variability in the obtained data reflect changes within the subject and not in the measuring. . . .
2. Physiological measures can be monitored continuously over time. . . .
3. Physiological measures are derived solely from the individual, in contrast to many measures of social behavior which are defined relative to the responses of a group. This means that greater differentiation of an individual's behavior in a social situation can be made by examining both socially directed behavior and bodily activity.[1]

6
Physiological Responses to the Media

James E. Fletcher

The Three Nervous Systems

Exciting fields of the life sciences today are the neurosciences—anatomy, biochemistry, and physiology—in which significant discoveries about the human nervous system are occurring with such frequency that keeping up becomes a major investment in time and study materials. For study purposes, the human nervous system can be divided into the central nervous system, the limbic system, and the autonomic system.

The Central Nervous System

The central nervous system of human beings differs from that of other animals. The spinal cord provides a two-way path for nervous impulses to the body's striped muscles (muscles that move the skeleton) and for sensory signals from the receptors of pain, temperature, touch, movement, and so forth. Sitting atop the spinal cord and amounting to an intricate elaboration of the cord are the structures of the brain—the neocortex (cerebrum), midbrain, cerebellum, and hindbrain (pons and medulla oblongata). These structures must work in the communicating adult; the neocortex of the cerebrum draws the lion's share of attention as the seat of learning, memory, feeling, language, and expression.

The Limbic System

The existence of the limbic system had been postulated in 1878 by the French anatomist Broca, but it was named only about thirty years ago by MacLean.[2] The limbic system's functions are still not completely understood. This system consists of fifty-three regions and thirty-five associated tracts lying in a circular arrangement immediately below the cerebral cortex. Its connections to the central nervous system and to the autonomic system are extensive, and its influence on them and on the endocrine system is important. The limbic system has a role in the harmonious integration of these systems in the body's response to its environment. To date, systematic study of the limbic system and its role in human communication has hardly begun.

The Autonomic System

The autonomic nervous system is identified structurally by its connections to the smooth, involuntary muscles of the body; it includes pathways running parallel to and outside of the spinal cord. Outside of the brain, it consists of two sometimes opposed subsystems—the parasympathetic and sympathetic nervous systems.

The parasympathetic system consists of nervous pathways extending from both ends of the spinal cord. From the head, these pathways are extensions of the cranial nerves; the largest is the tenth cranial nerve—the vagus. The parasympathetic system is also marked by the postganglionic synaptic transmitter chemical—acetylcholine. That is, when a neural signal crosses the synapses that flow from the ganglia of the parasympathetic system, the chemical acetylcholine forms to transmit the signal across the synapse. Hence, parasympathetic pathways are also called cholinergic.

The sympathetic nervous system is identified by a system of ganglia lying parallel to and outside of the spinal cord. Most postganglionic synapses of the sympathetic nervous system are characterized by the chemical noradrenaline as the synaptic transmitter. The exceptions are the nerves connecting the sympathetic system to the liver, adrenal glands, and sweat glands; these sympathetic nerves are cholinergic like those of the parasympathetic system. Because the postganglionic synaptic transmitter substance for most of the sympathetic system is noradrenaline, the sympathetic nervous system is sometimes labeled adrenergic.

As a general rule, the parasympathetic system is classified as anabolic, "concerned with conservation, accumulation and storing of bodily energies."[3] The sympathetic system is catabolic, "serving to facilitate all internal processes that aid muscular efficiency."[4]

The sympathetic nervous system is more frequently involved in studies of communication; this system alters the body to take in more information from the environment and prepares the body to respond.

How Physiological Responses Are Measured

The typical physiological recording device is represented in Figure 6-1.

The transducer, which converts some form of physiological energy into electrical energy, is the starting point of the measurement. In many cases, the physiological measurement of interest is an electrical signal in the body, which is picked up by electrodes.

This signal from the electrodes or transducer passes through a signal conditioner preamplifier, which modifies the physiological signal, making it easy to record or interpret. For example, the signal conditioner may be an integrator, which is a kind of electronic measuring cup. The integrator is used with signals

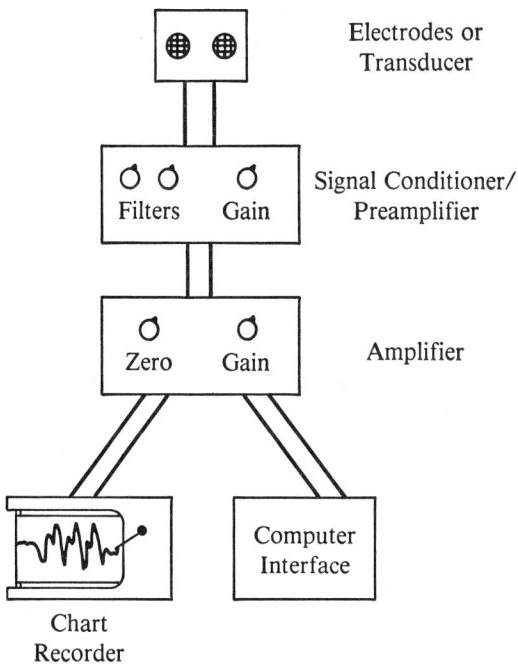

Figure 6-1 Schematic diagram of physiological recorder.

that have no characteristic shape but are indicators of gross nervous activity in some part of the body. When the integrator is in the circuit, a smooth line representing volume of electrical activity will appear on the chart recorder. Another important kind of signal conditioner is a filter, which allows only some electrical activity to pass. The filter might filter out all but a particular frequency or signal, or it might allow only fast rather than slow signals to pass. Most signal conditioners/preamplifiers include a line current filter, which can remove from the recording any effect of 50 or 60 hertz variation from the electrical power line.

The amplifier is the key component of the system because amplification must be noise-free, distortion-free, and high gain. The special amplifiers used in physiological recording are called d.c. amplifiers, designed to amplify very small, low-frequency signals.

The chart recorders used in physiological recording are single channel (one pen) or multichannel (more than one pen); each channel

may be curvilinear or rectilinear. In a curvilinear channel, the path of the pen point is the chord of a circle. This recording method is less costly but does bend the shape of the response recorded. A rectilinear pen writes perpendicularly to the direction of the chart paper's movement through the recorder. A rectilinear pen provides a true picture of the shape of a physiological response but costs more.

Many students of communication physiology prefer to interface the physiological recorder directly to a computer, which reduces the time required to analyze the resulting record.[5]

Central Nervous System Measures

Three common physiological measures from the central nervous system are: eye movement, alpha wave, and electromyogram.

Eye movement Eye movement indicates the viewer's relative interest in the parts of a visual image. The eyes' scanning movement is recorded photographically or electrically. The photographic method places a small lamp in front of the eye, which is reflected by the cornea's relatively flat central portion. As the eye moves, the reflected light also moves, providing a continuous trace of movement that can be recorded by a motion picture camera or television camera/recorder. In some eye movement apparatus, the subject's head must be held stationary in a brace or with a mouthpiece bitten during viewing.

The electrical measurement of eye movement requires two channels of electrophysiological recording. The eye, electrically speaking, bears a polarity roughly like that of a battery, negative pole at the back of the eyeball, positive pole at the front. If an electrode is placed immediately to the right of the right eye and another to the left of the left eye, then as the eyes turn to the right the right electrode becomes positive and the chart recorder produces the wave form seen in Figure 6-2.

As the eyes turn to the left, the right electrode becomes negative with respect to the left electrode, with the resulting wave form shown in Figure 6-3.

The up and down movement of the eyes is

Eye Straight . . . Ahead   Eye Turned Right

Figure 6-2 Electrical recording of eye movement (curvilinear).

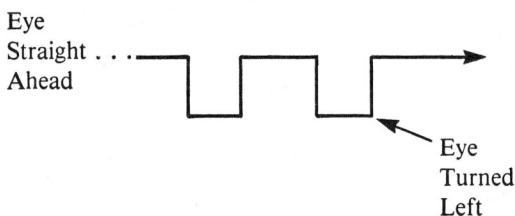

Figure 6-4 Electrical recording of muscle contraction (rectilinear).

recorded in a separate channel from a second pair of electrodes, one above and one underneath one eye.[6]

Electromyography Electromyography is the electrical recording of muscle potentials. As striped (skeletal) muscles contract, the surface of the muscles changes polarity. The common method of measuring this phenomenon is to place one electrode over the belly of the muscle, the other at a reference site (such as the earlobe). The contraction of the muscle appears in the resulting chart recording as an irregular series of bursts, something like Figure 6-4.

With an integrator in the coupler, the recording looks like Figure 6-5.

Each spike on the chart recording corresponds to emptying an electronic measuring cup that accumulates irregular activity. A commonly measured muscle is the frontalis, which reaches from the eyebrow back over the top of the head. The activity of the frontalis muscle is taken as an index of postural tension or anxiety.[7]

Electroencephalography — the alpha wave Electroencephalography, as the name implies,

involves recording the potentials arising from the surface of the brain itself. So far as communication studies are concerned, the so-called alpha-wave of the electroencephalogram has been most frequently studied. This electrical activity has a recurrent frequency of eight to thirteen hertz (cycles per second) and is a relatively large signal recorded from the occipital region (back point of the head to right or left of midline). One electrode is positioned on the scalp in the occipital area (special miniature electrodes are used for recording EEG), the other at a reference site, such as the earlobe. The self-report of a subject who is generating the alpha wave is that of restful alertness, not focused on immediate surroundings. The trace on the charge recorder (rectilinear) for the alpha wave may appear like that in Figure 6-6.

A number of options are possible as signal conditioners. A filter can separate the band of alpha frequencies producing a chart trace (rectilinear) like Figure 6-7. Or, a more involved electronic circuit may yield percent time alpha, the proportion of all EEG activity in a unit of time that is alpha wave activity.[9]

Autonomic Measures

The most frequently used autonomic measures are pupil response, heart rate, respiration rate,

Figure 6-3 Electrical recording of eye movement (rectilinear).

Eye Straight . . . Ahead

Eye Turned Left

Figure 6-5 Muscle contraction recorded with an integrator (rectilinear).

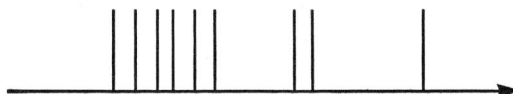

Figure 6-6 Electroencephalographic recording.

Horizontal scanning of conventional video camera

blood pulse volume, skin conductance, and skin potential.

Pupil response, changes in the size of the eyes' pupils, are triggered by signals in the sympathetic nervous system and are taken as indices of attention. They have been and are used in advertising research and program testing.[10]

Pupil response is an increased opening of the pupil followed by a gradual recovery. It is recorded by a motion picture camera or a special television camera focusing on the eye. If a film camera is used, then the vertical opening of the pupil is measured on a projection screen and relative changes in pupil size are the data entering analysis. The video camera used to record pupil response is a vertical scanning camera, as contrasted with horizontal scanning in the conventional video camera. See Figure 6-8.

The part of the camera scan traversing the image of the pupil is darker; this dark area is electronically measured and recorded on a paper chart. Video devices for this sort of pupil response measurement are reliable and precise but relatively expensive.[11]

Heart rate can be taken as a measure of attention (the heart rate response) or as an indicator of overall anxiety.[12] The physiological

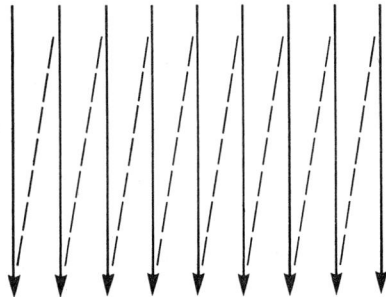

Vertical scanning of eye monitor video camera

Figure 6-8 Scanning of eye camera contrasted to that of regular video camera.

measure taken may be the familiar electrocardiogram or a conditioned, direct reading of heart rate. The electrocardiogram (EKG) indicates the heart's contractions as the electrical polarity of the heart's surface changes during contraction. This electrical activity of the heart can be picked up from electrodes placed anywhere on the body; a common electrode pattern is placing one electrode at the right ankle, the other at the left wrist. A chart trace of the EKG (curvilinear) from this combination of electrodes might look roughly like Figure 6-9, called Lead II by clinical cardiologists).

The various components of the heart contraction are designated by the letters *P, Q, R,*

Figure 6-7 Alpha frequencies in the electroencephalogram.

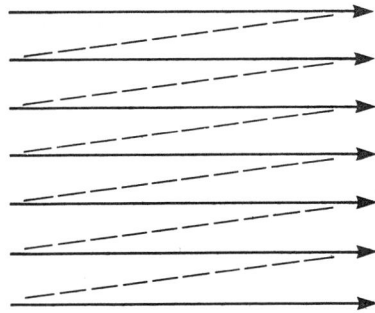

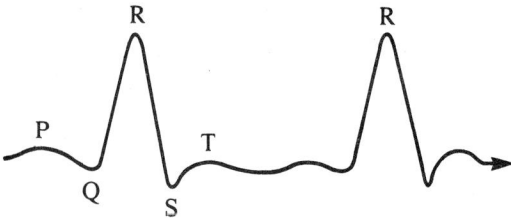

Figure 6-9   Electrocardiogram.

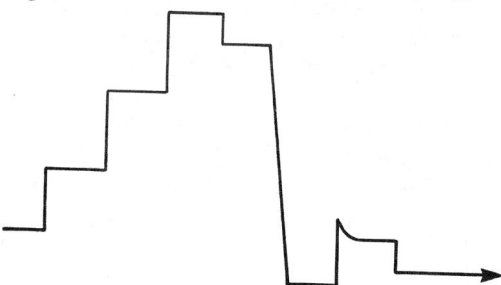

Figure 6-11   Electrical recording of respiration (curvilinear).

S, and *T*, as indicated. The datum of interest is the *R–R* interval, or interbeat interval (IBI), the time between heart contractions. If the signal conditioner/preamplifier includes a cardiotachometer, the EKG is converted to a chart trace like that in Figure 6-10. The height of each plateau indicates the rate of heart contraction for that beat. It is uncommon for a series of heart beats to be all at exactly the same rate. In a cardiotachometer trace, the heart's response to communication is readily visible.[13]

Respiration is the rate at which air is taken into the body. As part of attention, respiration rate suddenly slows or pauses then accelerates and returns to level. Respiration is one of the easiest measures to take. One method involves attaching a rubber tube around the chest. As the subject inhales, the pressure of the air inside the tube increases; this increase is recorded on the chart paper. A simpler technique is to attach a thermistor (a transducer that translates temperature into electrical signals) to the interior of the nostril. Exhaled air passing over the thermistor is warmer; inhaled air is cooler.

A recording of respiration (curvilinear) might look like Figure 6-11. Respiration can also be electronically translated by signal conditioner/preamplifier to respiration rate, with the resulting trace something like that of heart rate.

Blood pulse volume and pulse rate can be recorded by a method known as photoplethysmography, an inexpensive and robust autonomic measure. It is the result of monitoring the blood supply in the capillaries just below the skin. When those capillaries are full of blood, they absorb more light; when they are not full, they absorb less light. The photoplethysmograph transducer contains a small lamp that illuminates the capillary bed beneath it. In the same transducer, a photoreceptor picks up the light reflected back from the capillaries and produces a chart trace (curvilinear), as in Figure 6-12.

Pulse rate is the time distance between peaks in the record; blood pulse volume is the

Figure 6-12   Curvilinear recording from photoplethysmographic transducer.

Figure 6-10   Cardiotachometer recording.

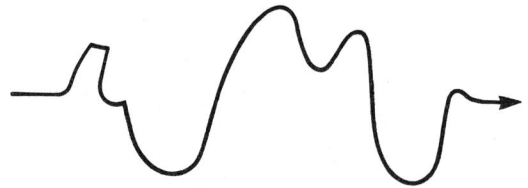

relative pulse-by-pulse height of the recorded trace. Blood pulse volume is taken as an index of attention, and average pulse rate can provide an index of physiological arousal or readiness to respond.[14]

Electrodermal measures include skin resistance, skin conductance, and skin potential. The oldest recorded physiological measure is the electrodermal, sometimes called GSR (galvanic skin response).[15] The phenomenon being measured is a change in the permeability of the skin to the potassium ion.[16] Two effector systems are apparently involved, both from the sympathetic nervous system. One system generally raises the permeability of the skin by activating sweat glands, and the other increases the absorbing qualities of the sweat ducts.[17] These changes in the skin are interpreted to index attention, physiological arousal, and resistance to learning.[18] Electrodermal activity can be measured by passing a small electric current through the skin, recording the resistance or conductance changes that occur with changes in skin permeability. An alternative is to measure the potential difference between the surface of the skin and the interstitial fluids.

Skin conductance is the preferred method of measuring the electrodermal response when taken to index attention. Two small silver/silver chloride electrodes are attached to the palm-side, second joints of the index and middle fingers of the same hand. Each electrode is filled with a surgical jelly, which is .05m sodium or potassium chloride. The electrode is held in place by an adhesive collar. A constant voltage of .2 volts is placed across the electrodes. Skin conductance change is manifest as a change of current passing in the circuit.[19] The typical short duration response would appear as a chart trace (rectilinear), like Figure 6-13. The height or amplitude of the trace is the datum recorded. Amplitude is first converted to its logarithm.[20] The average log amplitude of skin conductance change is the measure taken as representing the subject's response to a message.

Skin resistance is measured as is skin conductance and produces a similar chart trace,

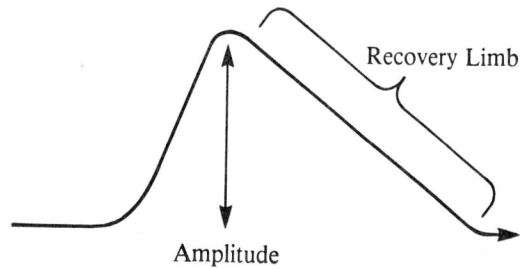

Figure 6-13 Short duration skin conductance response.

except that a constant current rather than constant voltage is applied to the electrodes. For accuracy and safety, care must be taken that current at each electrode is in the range 4–10 μamps/cm^2.[21] The response amplitudes of each response are first converted to conductance (reciprocal of resistance), then treated as conductance measurements.[22] The resulting measure is referred to in the methodological literature as average log conductance change (log Δc).

Skin potential measurements reflect the same autonomic responses as do skin conductance and skin resistance measures. But in skin potential, the skin responses are measured without the addition of a small current to the body. Skin potential is measured from two electrodes, one on the palm or finger (the active site) and one on the inside forearm (the reference site). The reference site requires some special preparation: the skin is abraded slightly with an emery board and electrode paste rubbed in before the electrode is attached. The effect of this preparation of the reference site is to short the reference electrode to the fluids beneath the skin. The two electrodes together measure the potential difference in millivolts between the interstitial fluids and the surface of the palm or finger. The two principal characteristic traces for this measure are seen in Figure 6-14. The uniphasic response and the negative-going component of the diphasic response in a skin potential record are the same responses that appear as the amplitude of skin conductance and skin resistance records.

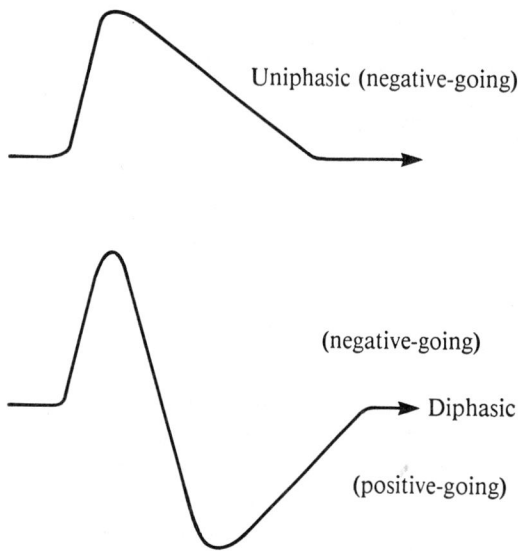

Figure 16-14   Two characteristic traces of the skin potential response.

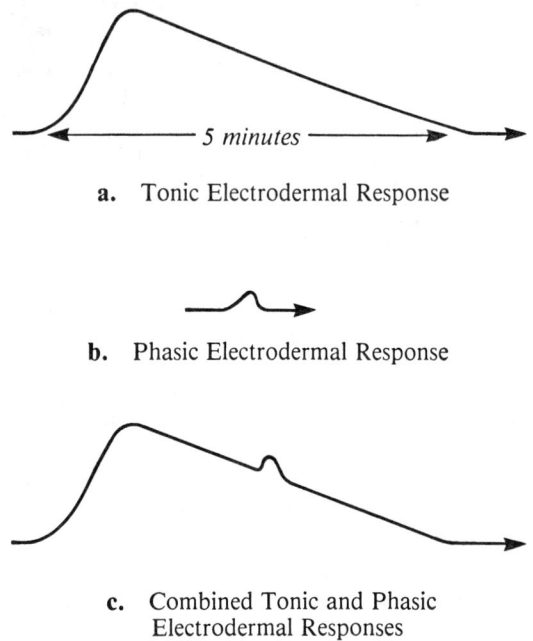

Figure 6-15   Tonic and phasic electrodermal responses.

The positive-going component of skin potential response is related to the steepness of the recovery limb of the skin conductance and skin resistance responses. Both seem to reflect autonomic activity at least partly independent of negative-going skin potential and of the amplitude of the skin conductance and resistance records.

Long- and Short-Duration Responses

Long- and short-term autonomic responses are of great potential interest to the communication scholar. Lynn reviews the evidence for long or tonic (generalized) reactions and short or phasic (localized) reactions to stimuli.[23] The tonic responses are of long duration and may last for as long as an hour in the case of someone awakened to alertness from sound sleep. The phasic responses are of shorter duration, perhaps two seconds. This relationship can be clarified by looking at Figure 6-15. In most physiological recording of natural behavior in human beings, tonic responses are seen only as shifts in base level, since the duration of physiological recording may be relatively brief — matters of minutes.

Law of Initial Values (LIV)

A law of initial values is assumed to operate in physiological records.[24] This law states that the size of a response to a stimulus will be a function of the prestimulus level of the responding system. All else being equal, the higher the prestimulus level, the smaller and more frequent the responses.

In light of the distinction between tonic and phasic responses, the law of initial values might be restated as the larger the tonic response, the smaller and more frequent the phasic responses that are superimposed on the tonic response.

Autonomic Channel Limit

The law of initial values suggests that there is a limit to the possible size of autonomic responses to a stimulus. The reason that phasic responses must be smaller following a tonic response is that a ceiling effect begins to operate.

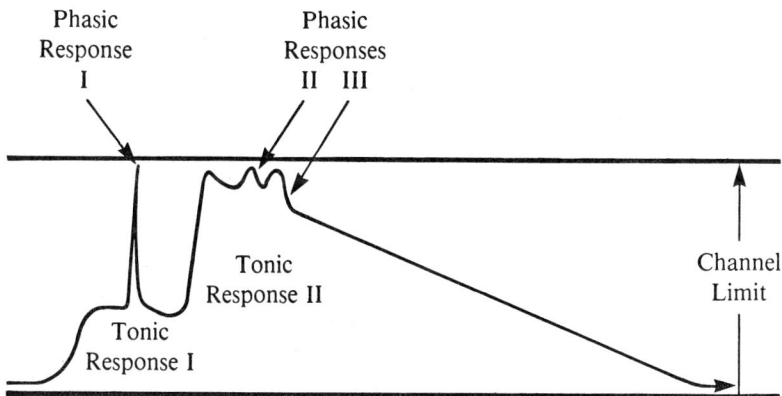

Figure 6-16 Autonomic channel limit is inferred by the law of initial values.

Interpreting Physiological Responses

The two principal interpretations of the commonly recorded physiological measures of an individual's attending to media messages are arousal and attention. Some writers represent these two concepts as rival explanations of the same phenomena. Here, however, arousal will be considered an adequate explanation of tonic autonomic responses, and both tonic and phasic responses can be interpreted as attention.

Arousal

According to Van Toller, the term *arousal* was introduced in the 1930s by Duffy.[25] Arousal refers to a general activation of the sympathetic nervous system by a mechanism, or system of mechanisms, in subcortical areas of the brain. Arousal is a general, as opposed to specific, reaction to stimuli, a kind of energizing of the body for response. Lindsley connected the notion of arousal to an activation theory of emotion.[26] This position and others related to it hold that arousal is a generalized condition of alertness underlying the intensity or strength of all human behavior.[27]

Since the late 1950s, however, there has been growing opposition to arousal as an interpretation of sympathetic nervous response.[28] The bulk of this criticism has been on the basis that attention, particularly as defined by the orient-

ing response (OR), provides a better explanation of sympathetic nervous response.[29]

Attention — The Orienting Response

Soviet neuropsychologist E. N. Sokolov has described three reflexive responses that the individual's autonomic nervous system makes to sensory information — orienting, adaptive, and defense responses.[30]

The adaptive response is described as a local protective mechanism that triggers a specific local response to a specific change in the stimulus environment. An example is the reflex that closes the pupil of the eye as scene illumination increases. Since adaptive reflexes involve relatively fixed relationships between local stimuli and subcortical responses, they hold little interest for the student of communication process and will not be considered further here.

The notion of the orienting response has stimulated as much research and writing in psychophysiology as has any other idea in the past several decades. Sokolov defined the orienting response (OR) as a nonspecific reaction that better prepares ("tunes") a sensory end-organ to receive information from a new stimulus.[31]

Physiologically, the process is something like this. When the sensory end-organ generates neural information about a new stimulus in the immediate environment, neural messages arrive at the cerebral cortex, where they are compared with stored recollections, or neuronal models, of earlier neural information.[32] If there is a match between the incoming sensory information and the cerebral neuronal models, then an inhibition signal is sent from the cerebrum to the reticular activation system (RAS) of the subcortex. The RAS, in turn, restores the relative insensitivity of the sensory apparatus to prestimulus levels.

If, on the other hand, there is in the cortex a mismatch between incoming sensory information and the stored neuronal models, an activation signal goes to the RAS, which, in turn, "tunes," or sensitizes the sensory end-organs through the sympathetic system. As a consequence, a greater volume of sensory information about the new stimulus will enter the cerebrum. This activation signal from the RAS to the sympathetic system is the orienting response (OR).

As a result of greater volume of sensory information entering the cerebrum after the OR, a new neuronal model will be formed in the cerebrum. Then, a match between incoming neural information and the new neuronal model will occur. The match sends an inhibition signal to the RAS, causing the OR to disappear. The inhibition of the OR to a new stimulus after a neuronal model has been formed is called *habituation*.

The neuronal models formed in this mismatch–OR–habituation process must be stored in number enough to reflect all the variety of experience with which an individual must deal, including physical characteristics of stimuli, words, syntax, meaning, and attitudes. This process is summarized in the graphic model in Figure 6-17.[33]

Maltzman and Raskin list the specific physiological measurements related to the OR as "depression of cortical alpha rhythm, the galvanic skin response, pupillary dilation and a complex vasomotor response consisting of cephalic vasodilation and peripheral vasoconstriction."[34] The reasoning of a number of workers connects the OR to the consciousness-

Figure 6-17   A graphic model of the process of the orienting response. (Copyright © 1971, The Society for Psychophysiological Research. Reprinted with permission of the publisher from "The Orienting Response as an Index of Mass Communication Effect," by J. E. Fletcher, PSYCHOPHYSIOLOGY, 1971, *8*, 699–703.)

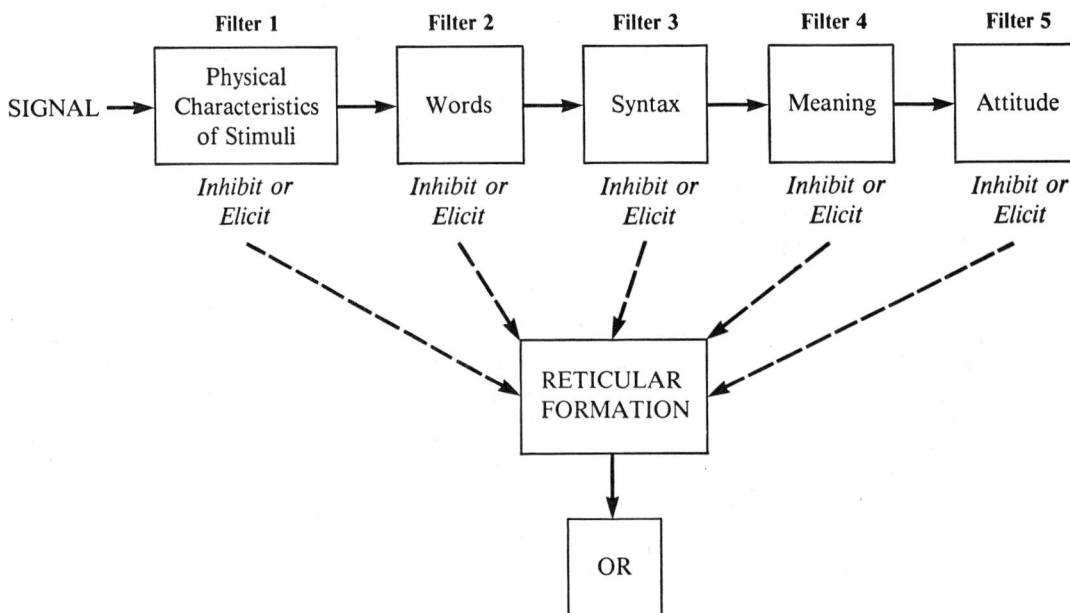

centered concept of attention.[35] Attention has been thought to facilitate response and memory and to be a prelude to effective communication.[36]

In terms of information processing, the OR can be viewed as the process by which external stimulation becomes internalized, and neuronal models can be equated with cognitions. The OR indicates that relatively more information is being taken in from the environment — an excellent definition of attention.

The OR and Entropy One inference possible from the neuronal model explanation of the OR is that the set of neuronal models in the cerebral cortex has some finite probability of matching incoming neural information from a given communication environment. The values of these neuronal models, together with the associated probabilities that the models will inhibit the OR, can be taken to represent the negentropy[37] or combined certainties of the individual in a given stimulus environment, since, if the models match all incoming information, no new models need to be formed, and the pattern of stored cerebral experience satisfactorily accounts for, or organizes, the individual's communication surroundings. To establish a numerical value for each of the thousands of neuronal models and their associated probabilities of relevance to even a narrowly defined set of communications would be extremely difficult, if not impossible.

But, since attention (the OR) is elicited whenever the cerebrum does not have models adequately conforming to incoming sensory information, the OR can be viewed as an index to entropy or combined uncertainties of the stimulus environment, the relative probability that the OR will be elicited and the mathematical complement of cerebral negentropy. Attention (the OR) is thus an index of the entropy in a communication environment.

When studying the likely effects of alternative media messages, the probability that some elements of a message will elicit the OR is equivalent to the probability that the cerebrum will take in for processing the neural information that the OR will generate. If the messages are persuasive in objective, then those parts of the message requiring the listener's attention (elicit ORs) should be those important to the sender's persuasive intent. If other than the persuasive parts of the message elicit attention, the eliciting parts of the message may be said to be distracting. If, on the other hand, only the message parts important to the persuasive objective of the sender elicit attention, then the message can be said to be without distractions.

Attention Triggered by More than Novelty

Berlyne early recognized that novelty alone is not a sufficient explanation of the stimulus characteristics triggering the OR.[38] Some message features he identified as demanding attention are intensity, color, indicating stimuli, novelty, surprisal, complexity, uncertainty, incongruity, and conflict.[39] These features can be simplified to three: (1) message features that to the individual are unpredictable (because they are novel, incongruous, inherently uncertain, or greater or smaller than expected in some respect); (2) message features that imply an obligation to act, either mentally or physically (because the receiver's name is called; a reference group norm is invoked; other previous experience involving threat or action is evoked); and (3) message features that are directly at odds with the policies or states then governing the receiver's behavior.[40]

Phasic and Tonic ORs Recall the long-term (tonic) and short-term (phasic) division of autonomic responses. Do these two varieties of response distinguish varieties of attention (ORs) as well? Yes. Most of the discussion above, which reviews the attention-demanding features of messages, deals with phasic ORs — short-term attention. Tonic ORs can be viewed as setting the cerebral capacity to attend to sensory information demands. As tonic OR increases, the frequency of information demand from the cerebrum (phasic OR) will also increase, but the amplitude of information demands (ORs) will decrease (law of initial values). As individual capacity to attend to information increases, demands for information increase in frequency, but the amount of information (size of the phasic OR) demanded will be reduced. If two messages are presented, as an illustration, and if tonic attention is equal to both, the message producing the largest average phasic attention will produce the greatest retention. If, on the other hand, phasic attention to two messages is equal, then the message producing high tonic attention will be better retained. Some support for this corollary appears in a review by Levonian in which long-term memory was reported to be facilitated by situations suggesting tonic and phasic ORs were simultaneously occurring.[41] Other evidence that the communication setting in which a message occurs is important in defining the information demand values of a message is provided in a study by Kennedy (1971), in which the effectiveness of television commercials was shown to be influenced by the television program setting in which they were shown.[42]

It should also be apparent that tonic attention must be a function of the sum of the phasic attention demanded by competing messages in the environment. This principle is important in studying relaxation messages, where the purpose of relaxation routines is to produce messages that reduce the information demands associated with a communication setting.

In the case of popular music, for example, what is it about such music that accounts for the common assertion by devotees that familiar music is relaxing? Familiar music has low information demand values, since neuronal models of its characteristics had to be well established before it could become familiar, and relatively small or no phasic ORs are elicited by music that is familiar. In a communication setting where such music is present, the sum of the information demand values of all of the messages in the setting will decline. Hence, tonic ORs should decline in a setting characterized by familiar music. This result does indeed occur, as reported in a study of popular radio music.[43]

Curvilinearity of Attention and Retention

More than three decades ago, Trenaman reported his research of several years on the interest levels of listeners to information programs of the BBC and their ability to recall the content of the programs.[44] He found the relationship between self-reported and listener interest in a program and retention of the content of a program to be curvilinear, as illustrated in Figure 6-18.

When interest in a radio program was very low, retention of program content was also low—the common expectation. Often not anticipated was that retention was also low when interest was high.

The extreme of high interest might be the sleeping explorer who awakens to find a tarantula crawling up an arm. He or she is, no doubt, interested in the tarantula, but surprise or alarm will impede ability later to produce a good sketch of the tarantula.

It is possible that the relationship of attention to retention is also curvilinear, so that both high and low levels of attention produce low retention. This result might occur if whatever cerebral neural traffic is required to establish neuronal models must traverse the same channels as incoming sensory information, imposing a ceiling on the combination of cerebral and sensory information that can be simultaneously transmitted in the cerebrum. When attention is increased to its upper limit, intra-brain communication can be suppressed, inhibiting retention.

Figure 6-18 Curvilinear relationship of retention and interest.

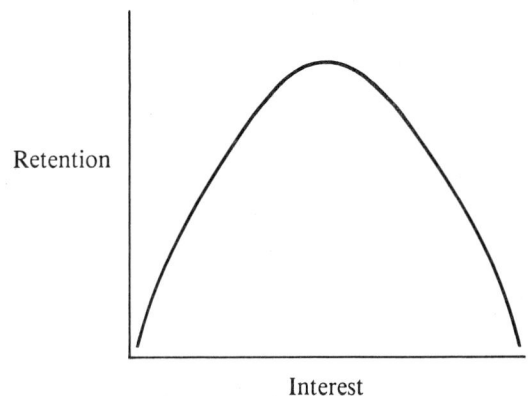

The optimum situation for learning—or retention—would appear to be when attention is moderate, leaving unused channel space for intrabrain information processing.

Of concern to message researchers is the problem of determining whether the message used as stimulus in a study is on the ascending or descending portion of the relationship curve between attention and retention. For the most part, the messages of radio and television (to the extent they have been studied) appear to fall on the ascending portion of the curve of this relationship. As attention increases, so does retention.[45]

Another hint as to whether the level of attention is in the range of increased attention/increased retention can be provided by the defense response (DR).

The Defense Response

The defense response (DR), named by Sokolov, has been identified with the "startle" reaction described in American and European literature.[46] The DR is manifest in a momentary but marked increase in heart rate and blood pressure and positive-going skin potential.[47] It appears when the body is mobilized to resist. For example, subjects in an avoidance conditioning group experienced greater defense responses.[48]

Evidence also exists that retention of a message is lower when the DR is elicited.[49] The defense response is usually accompanied by an increase in the number of phasic ORs, so that an increase in sensory input to the cerebrum can occur at the same time as reduced cerebral efficiency. Since reduced efficiency, in turn, can occur in greater or lesser degree before total attention occurs, it is different from the enervating, high levels of attention described above. Nevertheless, its dysfunctional effect on retention is real and can provide insights into information processing overload. Because the autonomic indicators of the DR are relatively sensitive, they can index levels of central nervous processing overload that occur within such small message elements as words and camera shots.

Some Study Design Considerations

Researchers prefer to use physiological variables in repeated measures study designs. In such designs, all subjects are exposed to each of a series of messages under study with order of message presentation rotated and balanced across subjects.[50] Physiological measures will vary much more among subjects than will the paper-and-pencil instruments used in communication research. A subject's measurement that is analyzed as to sources of variability in the measure consists of:

a. Response produced by the test stimulus
b. + Response increment or decrement characteristic of the individual respondent's response style
c. + Influence of the communication environment
d. + *Error of Measurement*
e. = Measurement score recorded.

It is (b) above that is at issue in repeated measures design. The factorial design by way of contrast requires a different group of subjects to be exposed to each test message. In the factorial design, (b) and (d) are not separable. As a result, high variance between individuals increases the error component in factorial designs. Since such high variance characterizes physiological measures, use of a factorial design materially reduces the probability that a difference in the responses produced by two or more test messages will be detected in a significance test.

Laboratory Setting

It will also be apparent that physiological measures are appropriate primarily to laboratory research. The reason is not that the measures are difficult to use outside the laboratory, but that the influence of communication environment is considerable when a dependent measure is highly sensitive. The proper way to reduce the confounding influence of communication environment is by holding it constant—to the extent possible—in a laboratory study.

Production Variables Research

Message and Program Testing

The objective of message and program testing is to select from a set of messages or message elements those that will be included in a mass communication. In television advertising, for example, a set of possible television commercials is prepared in execution form—perhaps as a comic strip or as a slide/tape show. These commercials are then shown to test audiences whose responses help the advertiser select which alternative should become a finished commercial.

Later, when the commercial is in rough cut, more testing can indicate the strong and weak points of the composition, editing, or sound.

Academic research in this area is properly addressed to (1) development of improved testing procedures and (2) the discovery of principles of effective mass communication.[51] The research is organized in similar ways in both cases. In the first sort of research, message stimuli are held constant while dependent measures and analytic routines are systematically varied. In the latter, dependent measures and analytic routines are held constant while message stimuli are systematically varied.

In both instances, the repeated measures design is employed, with message stimuli presented in each possible order to an equal number of subjects. Each subject is presented the stimuli and measured individually.

Cultural Acceptance

For academic and industrial purposes, it is important to judge the acceptability of a message or program in light of a specified group's cultural standards. The identifying feature of this research problem is the recognition that cultural standards are defined across the group in question—as opposed to being defined in a designated or recognized individual. As a consequence, individual responses to the message or program in question are noise, while the responses characteristic of the group are signal.

Mass registration of physiological responses as demonstrated by Hagfors is appropriate for studies of cultural standards.[52] In these studies, groups of forty subjects were measured simultaneously as they viewed feature films. Subgroups of twenty were recorded into a single channel of physiological measurement. Some of these subjects' responses were additive because they occurred at the same time and in the same direction. Others were not additive and appeared to cancel one another.

It can be argued that Hagfors's additive responses were those that were socialized. Suppose that identical twins have always been exposed to Object I in exactly the same way. One might describe the response as socialized. As traces on a physiological chart, these might appear as in Figure 6-19.

On the other hand, suppose that the twins are exposed to Object II after age twenty-two, when each has married and moved to a different city. It is no longer anticipated that the object will produce responses at the same time and in the same direction for both twins. The

Figure 6-19   Additive nature of responses of theoretical twins identically socialized.

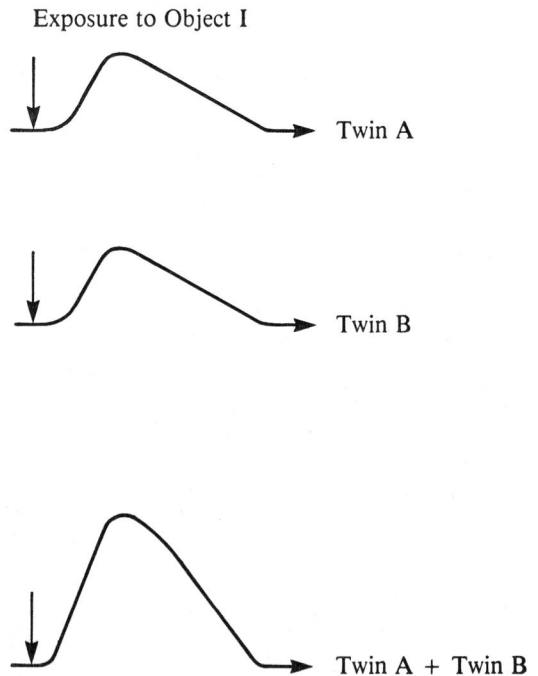

Exposure to Object I

Twin A

Twin B

Twin A + Twin B

situation might appear in a physiological chart as in Figure 6-20. In this case, the prominent additive response does not appear.

Hagfors's recordings were records of the relatively socialized responses of a group — cultural standards. Certain identifiable patterns of socialized response appeared to characterize his audiences of Finnish feature films. Figure 6-21 shows the pattern that characterized best-liked film passages and that Hagfors labeled *beta*.[53] An indicator of the promise of this technique is that quantity of the *beta* pattern when considered with scores from a mood checklist produced multiple correlations in excess of +0.90 with actual box office records of the films involved. Figure 6-22 shows the actual pattern of a part of a Finnish comic film.[54]

Summary

The physiological responses of interest to communication researchers are primarily those of the autonomic system. Short-duration responses are referred to as phasic; longer-duration responses are called tonic. The most popular interpretations of these responses pro-

Figure 6-21 Hagfors's *beta* pattern.

ceed from conceptions of the orienting response (OR) and the defense response (DR). Phasic ORs are best interpreted as attention — information being taken into cerebral processing. Tonic ORs are best interpreted as capacity to attend.

Cognitive efficiency and the OR seem to be related in a curvilinear fashion. Very high attention and capacity to attend are associated with poor retention.

The DR appears to reduce information processing efficiency, and it is sensitive to low orders of such inefficiency.

Studies involving physiological measures need to be cast as repeated measures designs with stimuli presented in balanced order.

Physiological measures may be particularly appropriate to studies of media production variables.

Figure 6-20 Additive nature of response of theoretical twins dissimilarly socialized.

Exposure to Object II

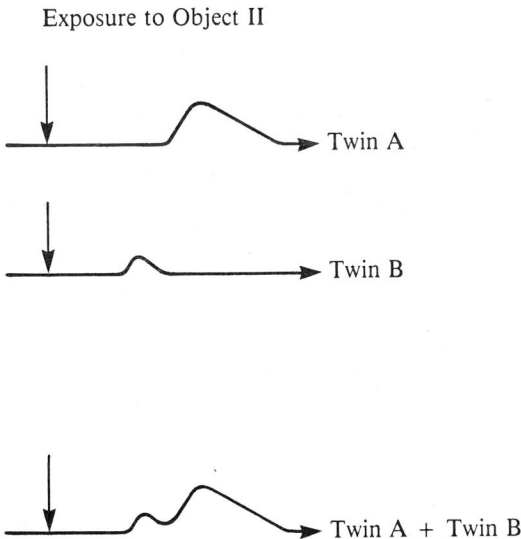

Endnotes

1. David Shapiro and Andrew Crider, "Psychophysiological Approaches in Social Psychology," in Gardner Lindzey and Elliot Aronson, eds., *The Handbook of Social Psychology*, 2d ed., vol. 3 (Reading, Mass.: Addison-Wesley, 1969), 6–7.
2. P. D. MacLean, "Psychosomatic Disease

Figure 6-22 Trace of Finnish comic film.

and the 'Visceral Brain': Recent Developments Bearing upon the Papez Theory of Emotion," *Psychosomatic Medicine* 11 (1949): 338–353.

3. C. Van Toller, *The Nervous Body: An Introduction to the Autonomic Nervous System and Behavior* (Chichester, England: John Wilcy & Sons, 1979), 29. An excellent reference on the ANS.

4. Ibid., 28.

5. Some of the better-known suppliers of physiological measurement apparatus are: Gulf & Western Applied Science Laboratories, 335 Bear Hill Road, Waltham, Massachusetts 02154; Med Associates, Inc., Box 47, East Fairfield, Vermont 05448; LBV Corporation, Box 2221, Lehigh Valley, Pennsylvania 18001; Coulbourn Instruments, Box 2551, Bldg. P12, Lehigh Valley, Pennsylvania 18001; Lafayette Instrument Company, P.O. Box 1279, Lafayette, Indiana 47902; Grass Medical Instruments, Quincy, Massachusetts 02169; Beckman Instruments, Inc., Electronic Instruments Division, 3900 River Road, Schiller Park, Illinois 60176; Stoelting Company, 1350 South Kostner Avenue, Chicago, Illinois 60623.

6. For more detail, consult Brian Shackel, "Eye Movement Recording by Electrooculography," in P. H. Venables and Irene Martin, eds., *A Manual of Psychophysiological Methods* (Amsterdam: North Holland, 1967), 299–334.

7. See O. C. J. Lippold, "Electromyography" in Venables and Martin, 245–297.

8. For a brief discussion, refer to James Hassett, *A Primer of Psychophysiology* (San Francisco: W. H. Freeman, 1978), 91–98.

9. Consult Hassett, 100–126; J. H. Marginson, P. St. John Loe, and C. D. Binnie, "Electroencephalography," in Venables and Martin, 351–402; Curtis Marshall, "Research Electroencephalography," in Clinton C. Brown, *Methods in Psychophysiology* (Baltimore: Williams and Wilkins, 1967), 221–233.

10. See H. E. Krugman, "Some Applications of Public Measurement," *Journal of Marketing Research* 1 (1964): 15–19; Richard

S. Halpern, "Application of Pupil Responses to Before and After Experiments," *Journal of Marketing Research* 4 (1967): 320–321; H. E. Krugman, "A Comparison of Physical and Verbal Responses to Television Commercials," *Public Opinion Quarterly* 29 (1965): 323–325.

11. See G. Hakerem, "Pupillography," in Venables and Martin, 335–349.

12. For an example of the latter see Martha L. Knight and Richard J. Borden, "Autonomic and Affective Reactions of High and Low Socially-Anxious Individuals Awaiting Public Performance," *Psychophysiology* 16 (1979), 209–213.

13. See Hassett, 56–59; Jasper Brener, "Heart Rate," in Venables and Martin, 13–131.

14. See Clinton C. Brown, "The Techniques of Plethysmography," in Brown, 54–74; Joseph Weinmen, "Photoplethysmography," in Venables and Martin, 185–217.

15. E. Neumann and R. Blanton, "The Early History of Electrodermal Research," *Psychophysiology* 6 (1970): 453–475.

16. Robert Edelberg, "Electrical Properties of the Skin," in Brown, 1–53.

17. R. Edelberg, "The Information Content of the Recovery Limb of the Electrodermal Response," *Psychophysiology* 6 (1970): 527–539.

18. James E. Fletcher, "A Physiological Approach to the Study of Human Information Processing," paper presented to the International Congress of Communication Sciences (Berlin, June 1977); "Old Time GSR and a New Approach to the Analysis of Public Communication," *Quarterly Journal of Speech* 59 (1973): 52–60.

19. David T. Lykken, and Peter H. Venables, "Direct Measurement of Skin Conductance: A Proposal for Standardization," *Psychophysiology* 8 (1971): 656–672; D. C. Fowles, M. G. Christie, R. Edelberg, W. W. Grings, D. T. Lykken, and P. H. Venables, "Publication Recommendations for Electrodermal Measurements," *Psychophysiology* 18 (1981): 232–239.

20. Ernest A. Haggard, "On the Application of Analysis of Variance to GSR Data: I. The Selection of an Appropriate Measure," *Journal of Experimental Psychology* 39 (1949): 378–392.
21. Edelberg, "Electrical Properties," 13–17.
22. Fletcher, "The Orienting Response as an Index of Broadcast Communication Effect," *Psychophysiology* 8 (1971): 699–703.
23. R. Lynn, *Attention, Arousal and the Orientation Reaction* (Oxford: Pergamon, 1966), 4–5.
24. J. Wilder, "The Law of Initial Values in Neurology and Psychiatry," *Journal of Nervous and Mental Disorders* 125 (1957): 73–86.
25. Van Toller, 84–87.
26. Consult discussion in Hassett, 16–19.
27. Some illustrations include: R. S. Lazarus and E. Alfert, "Short-Circuiting of Threat by Experimentally Altering Cognitive Appraisal," *Journal of Abnormal and Social Psychology* 69 (1964): 195–205; R. S. Lazarus, J. C. Spiesman, A. M. Mordkoff, and L. A. Davison, "A Laboratory Study of Psychological Stress Produced by a Motion Picture Film," *Psychological Monographs* 76 (1962): 553; E. McGinness and H. Aiba, "Persuasion and Emotional Response: A Cross Cultural Study," *Psychological Reports* 16 (1965): 503–510; J. B. Cooper and D. N. Singer, "The Role of Emotion in Prejudice," *Journal of Social Psychology* 44 (1966): 241–247.
28. Hassett, 18; Van Toller, 87; J. Flanagan, "Galvanic Skin Response: Emotion or Attention," *Proceedings of the 75th Annual Convention of the American Psychological Association* 2 (1967): 7–8.
29. A useful bibliography in assessing these arguments is Nicholas J. Carriero et al., *An Annotated Bibliography on the Literature Dealing with the Physiological Correlates of Cognitive Performance* (Aberdeen Proving Ground: U.S. Army Human Engineering Laboratory, June 1978).
30. E. N. Sokolov (S. W. Waydenfeld, trans.), *Perception and the Conditioned Reflex* (Oxford: Pergamon, 1963).
31. Sokolov, 11.
32. Sokolov, 282–294.
33. "The Orienting Response," 699–703.
34. Irving Maltzman and David C. Raskin, "Effects of Individual Differences in the Orienting Reflex on Conditioning and Complex Processes," *Journal of Experimental Research in Personality* 1 (1965): 1.
35. D. E. Berlyne, *Conflict, Arousal and Curiosity* (New York: McGraw-Hill, 1960); Maltzman and Raskin; Lynn; Fletcher, "Old Time GSR," 52–60.
36. William James, *The Principles of Psychology* I (New York: Dover, 1950) (originally published 1890), 424–425; C. I. Hovland, A. A. Lumsdaine, and F. D. Sheffield, *Experiments on Mass Communication* (New York: Wiley, 1949), 81.
37. J. Y. Kim, "Feedback in the Social Sciences: Toward a Reconceptualization of Morphogeneses," in B. D. Ruben and J. Y. Kim, eds., *General Systems Theory and Human Communication* (Rochelle Park, N.J.: Hayden, 1974), 213.
38. D. E. Berlyne, M. A. Crow, P. H. Salapatek, and J. L. Lewis, "Novelty, Complexity, Incongruity, Extrinsic Motivation and the GSR," *Journal of Experimental Psychology* 66 (1963): 560–567.
39. *Conflict, Arousal and Curiosity*, 96–103.
40. See in addition J. G. O'Gorman, "The Orienting Reflex: Novelty or Significance Detector?" *Psychophysiology* 16 (1979): 253–262; Alvin S. Bernstein, "The Orienting Reflex as Novelty and Significance Detector: Reply to O'Gorman," *Psychophysiology* 16 (1979): 263–273; Irving Maltzman, "Orienting Reflexes and Significance," *Psychophysiology* 16 (1979): 274–282.
41. E. Levonian, "Retention over Time in Relation to Arousal during Learning: An Explanation of Discrepant Results," *Acta Psychologica* 36 (1973): 290–321.
42. J. R. Kennedy, "How Program Environment Affects TV Commercials," *Journal of Advertising Research* 11 (1971): 33–38.
43. James E. Fletcher, "Attention, Retention, Meaning and Popular Music," paper pre-

sented to annual meeting of the Speech Communication Association, San Francisco, December 1976.

44. Joseph Trenaman, "Understanding Radio Talks," *Quarterly Journal of Speech* 37 (1951): 173–178.

45. See, for example, J. M. Caffyn, "Psychological Laboratory Techniques in Copy Research," *Journal of Advertising Research* 4 (1964): 349–350; X. Kohan, "A Physiological Measure of Commercial Effectiveness," *Journal of Advertising Research* 8 (1968): 46–48; H. E. Krugman, "Some Applications of Pupil Measurement," *Journal of Marketing Research* 1 (1964): 15–19; Richard S. Halpern "Application of Pupil Responses to Before and After Experiments," *Journal of Marketing Research* 4 (1967): 320–321; Krugman, "A Comparison of Physical and Verbal Responses to Television Commercials," *Public Opinion Quarterly* 29 (1965): 323–325; Krugman, "Brain Wave Measures of Media Involvement," *Journal of Advertising Research* 11 (1971): 3–9; Fletcher, "The Orienting Response as an Index of Broadcast Communication Effect."

46. See Lynn, 8–10.

47. David C. Raskin, H. Kotses, and J. Bever, "Autonomic Indicators of Orienting and Defensive Reflexes," *Journal of Experimental Psychology* 80 (1969): 424–433.

48. S. R. Shnidman, "Avoidance Conditioning of Skin Potential Responses," *Psychophysiology* 6 (1969): 38–44.

49. P. E. Thetford, M. E. Klemme, and H. E. Spohn, "Skin Potential, Heart Rate and Span of Immediate Memory," *Psychophysiology* 5 (1968): 166–177; J. Wilcott, "Correlation of Skin Resistance and Potential," *Journal of Comparative and Physiological Psychology* 51 (1958): 691–696; C. I. Notarius, T. J. Burns, L. J. Ingraham, C. Wemple, and S. Kollar, "Facial Expressivity, Self-Reported Emotional State, Heart Rate and Skin Potential Response in a Provocative Interpersonal Situation," *Psychophysiology* 17 (1981): 312 (abstract).

50. James E. Fletcher, "Empirical Studies of Visual Communications; Some Methodological Considerations," paper presented to the annual meeting of the Speech Communication Association, Minneapolis, November 1978. ERIC Document ED166737.

51. James E. Fletcher, "Academic Research in Retrospect: A Final View," *Feedback* 21 (Summer 1979): 14–17.

52. Carl Hagfors, *The Galvanic Skin Response and Its Application to the Group Registration of Psychophysiological Processes* (Jyvaskyla, Finland: Jyvaskyla Yliopostio, 1969).

53. Ibid., 98.

54. Ibid., 103.

During the 1970s, economic analysis became increasingly important in the decision-making process at the FCC. This conclusion is easily illustrated by examining the Prime-Time Access and Cross-Ownership Rules, deregulation of distant signal importation and exclusivity for cable, and the deregulation of radio. The role of economic analysis has been to develop theoretical and empirical models to assess the impact of new telecommunication services, to measure the consequences of concentration of ownership and control, and most recently to analyze the behavior of the television networks. This essay explores two important methods of economic research. The first method examines regression analysis that permits the researcher to identify the determinants of important economic phenomena in broadcasting. The second method explains some available operational techniques for measuring market concentration.

7
Economic Methods of Broadcast Research

Barry R. Litman

Regression Analysis

Regression analysis is one of the most important tools for statistical analysis of economic issues in the media. It permits the estimation of functional relationships between a dependent variable and one or more independent (explanatory) variables. The following exposition is a basic summary review of simple and multiple regression analysis. The interested reader can consult a standard statistics text for greater detail on these models.[1]

Begin with a functional relationship derived from economic or communication theory between a random dependent variable Y and a fixed independent variable X.[2] Consider TV station profits (before taxes) to be the dependent variable and the corresponding market size of the station to be the independent variable. Since market size is limited to positive values ranging from 10,500 ADI television households in the smallest market to 6.43 million TV households in New York City, it is said to be a fixed independent variable. (ADI, Area of Dominant Influence, is an area designated by Arbitron Ratings to include all areas where the preponderance of television viewed is to the stations of the area so designated.) The hypothesized functional relationship is that TV station profits are positively related to the size of the market in which the station is located.

It is now necessary empirically to estimate the shape and magnitude of this functional relationship from a sample of observations. Suppose the sampling procedure is to choose one station randomly from each of the 214 ADI markets. A scatter diagram for this two-variable model is shown in Figure 7-1. For each value of X (market size), there is a dispersion of values for Y (station profits).[3] This dispersion of values results from a number of random causes (such as quality of management or sales effort), each producing a small deviation of the Y value from what it would be if the relation were perfectly deterministic.

To simplify the analysis, assume that the dispersion of the y values is normally distributed for each fixed value of X, that the variance for each normal distribution is identical for each fixed value of X, and that the observed values of Y are independent of each other.[4] In Figure 7-1, note that for a market size of 200,000 households, the corresponding observed y values will be clustered around the mean y value of $1 million, with relatively fewer points near the extremes of $1.6 million and $.4 million. The expected value of station profits $E(y)$ for a market with 200,000 TV households is best represented by the mean of y, $1 million. Follow the same procedure for each fixed value of X (i.e., $x = 300,000$, $x = 400,000$, etc.), and the means of y are then connected, as in Figure 7-1, to form a straight line. This straight line, the regression line, represents the estimated functional relationship between the dependent (Y) and independent (X) variables. In mathematical terms, the regression line is written as $E(Y) = \hat{Y} = a + bX$, where a is the Y-intercept, b is the slope of the equation, and $E(Y) = \hat{Y}$ is the expected value of the dependent variable.

For an equation estimated to have more than one independent variable, the technique is known as multiple regression analysis. In the context of the previous example, it may be important to add another possible explanatory variable to help account for the variation in station profits in the sample. Add a second independent variable, X_2, which represents whether the station is a network affiliate or an

Figure 7-1   Distribution of sample Y values.

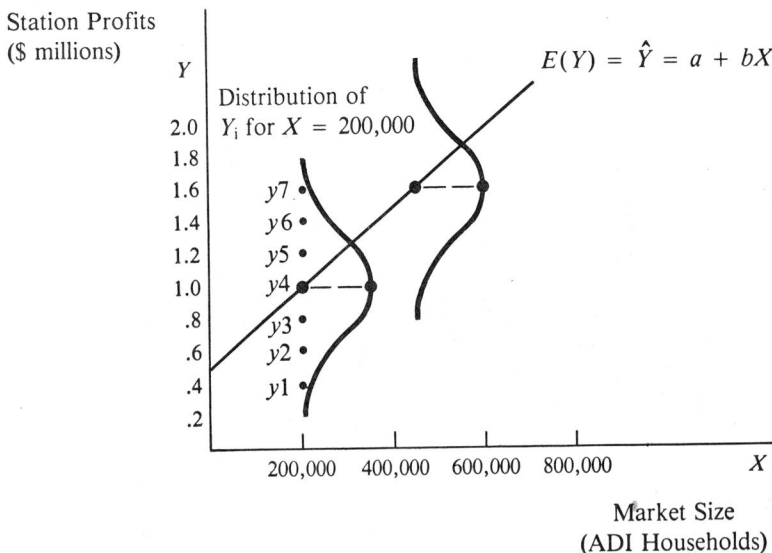

Station Profits
($ millions)

Market Size
(ADI Households)

independent station. Since network affiliates receive high quality programming from their respective networks, their ratings (and hence revenues) can be expected to be higher than those of independent stations, which are responsible for their own programming. Thus, one expects a positive correlation between network affiliation and station profits.

In estimating this multiple regression equation, add one further assumption to the simple linear regression model: All explanatory variables are independent of each other. Serious violations of any of these assumptions will reduce the reliability of the regression estimates.[5] The multiple regression equation is expressed as:

$$E(Y) = \hat{Y} = a + b_1 X_1 + b_2 X_2$$

Rather than a regression line, as illustrated in Figure 7-1, one now has a regression plane in three-dimensional space.

To facilitate estimating regression equations for either the simple or multiple regression case, statisticians have developed a technique known as least squares estimation. The principle of the least squares technique involves minimizing the sum of squared deviations of the observed values of Y from the mean of Y. Simply, one must find the value of the mean that makes the required sum of deviations as small as possible. It has been demonstrated repeatedly that this estimation technique yields the best linear unbiased estimator (BLUE) of the underlying population regression line (plane).[6]

For the case of simple regression, the technique of least squares estimation generates two equations frequently called the "normal equations."[7] In mathematical terms, they are represented as:

$$na + b \Sigma x = \Sigma y$$
$$a \Sigma x + b \Sigma x^2 = \Sigma xy$$

where n = number of individual observations, and x and y are the actual values of those individual observations. These equations can be solved for the constant term (a) and the coefficient of the X variable (b), yielding:

$$b = \frac{n \Sigma xy - \Sigma x \Sigma y}{n \Sigma x^2 - (\Sigma x)^2}$$

$$a = \frac{\Sigma y}{n} - \frac{b \Sigma x}{n}$$

Since a and b are the principal components of a linear regression equation, the formal estimation is now complete with $E(Y) = \hat{Y} = a + bX$. Suppose $a = \$50,000$ and $b = 1.5$; one can now substitute values for X (say, 2 million households) and obtain the best estimate of the expected station profits (\$3.05 million).

The procedure is identical for multiple regression analysis, but the solution of the normal equations is more difficult. With two independent variables, the normal equations would be:

$$na + b_1 \Sigma x_1 + b_2 \Sigma x_2 = \Sigma y$$
$$a \Sigma x_1 + b_1 \Sigma x^2_1 + b_2 \Sigma x_1 x_2 = \Sigma x_1 y$$
$$a \Sigma x_2 + b_1 \Sigma x_1 x_2 + b_2 \Sigma x^2_2 = \Sigma x_2 y$$

To solve these equations for the constant term and b coefficient requires the use of sophisticated matrix algebra.[8] Fortunately, many computer software packages and several programmable calculators can perform the necessary calculations and yield the multiple regression estimating equation.

Once the regression equation has been estimated, one can determine how closely it fits the observed data—how reliable it is as a predictive tool. This process can also be thought of as measuring the amount of improvement (or reduction in the total error) due to the regression line (plane). Variations in the observed values of y are partly due to changes in the explanatory variable(s) and partly due to the impact of random disturbances. To decompose the total variation of Y into its explained and unexplained components, one uses the means of Y ($\bar{Y}$) for the entire sample as the base for comparison, since this grand mean would be the estimator for Y if no regression line were used. Figure 7-2 shows that the total variation (error) for any observed y (say y_1) is the distance between the observed point and the regression line (known as unexplained error) and the distance between the regression line and $\overline{Y}$ (known as the explained error). In mathematical terms, we have:

$$(y_1 - \overline{Y}) = (y_1 - \widehat{Y}) + (\widehat{Y} - \overline{Y})$$

| total error | unexplained error | explained error |

This equation applies only to a single observation y_1. To compute a summary measure for all sample observations, which is not dependent on positive or negative values, square both sides of the equation and sum over all the observations in the sample. This process is represented mathematically as:[9]

$$\Sigma(Y - \overline{Y})^2 = \Sigma(Y - \widehat{Y})^2 + \Sigma(\widehat{Y} - \overline{Y})^2$$

| total sum of squares | unexplained sum of squares | explained sum of squares |

The closeness of fit of the estimating equation is then easily found by calculating the coefficient of determination. The coefficient of determination (R^2) equals the explained sum of squares divided by the total sum of squares. It can range from 0 to 1; zero implies that no improvement is attributed to the regression, and

1 implies that all variation in the dependent variable is explained by the estimating equation (completely determinate). Most equations in the social sciences have an R^2 somewhere in the .25 to .75 range, with .50 being considered a reasonably good fit for cross-sectional data. For multiple regression, the same procedure is followed with only a difference in interpretation. R^2, now called the coefficient of multiple determination, measures the closeness of fit (or reduction in error) of the regression plane to the observed y values and relative to the plane going through ($\overline{Y}, \overline{X}_2, \overline{X}_2 \dots \overline{X}_k$).

The last important test is to determine whether the coefficients of the independent variables are important individual contributors in explaining the variance in Y. The coefficients have different meanings, depending on whether one is using simple or multiple regression. In simple regression, the coefficient b is the slope of the equation and measures the change in $\widehat{Y}$ resulting from a unit change in X. In multiple regression analysis, the b coefficients are interpreted as measuring the change in $\widehat{Y}$ resulting from a unit change in the corresponding X variable, all other independent variables held constant.

This procedure allows one to isolate each independent variable and test its separate impact on Y, having held all other influences constant. This is the social scientist's equivalent to the pure scientist's method of laboratory con-

Figure 7-2 Explained and unexplained errors.

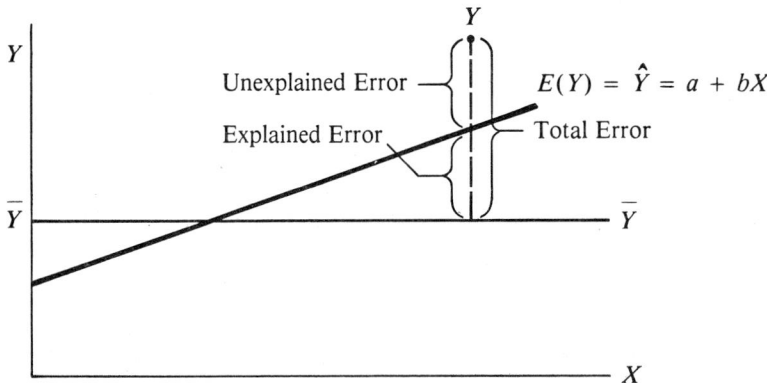

trol. Thus, multiple regression analysis permits one to measure the impact on Y of a large number of explanatory forces acting simultaneously; it also allows each variable to be examined in isolation. Thus, it is a powerful statistical tool.

To test for significance of each b coefficient, the null hypothesis states that the coefficient equals zero—that is, it contributes nothing or is totally unimportant in explaining the variation in the dependent variable. The alternative hypothesis can be that $b \neq 0$ or is positive or negative, depending on *a priori* theory. The calculated test statistic has a t distribution and equals the b coefficient divided by its standard error, $t = b/S_b$.[10] The statistical test procedure is the same for any t test. For example, if one has set up the alternative hypothesis as $t \neq 0$, then the two-tail test is appropriate and the 5 percent level of significance is used (2½ percent in each tail). The acceptance region for the null hypothesis is:

$$-t_{n-k-1,\ 2\frac{1}{2}\%} \leq \frac{b}{S_b} \leq t_{n-k-1,\ 2\frac{1}{2}\%}$$

(where k is the number of independent variables in the equation and n is the sample size).

If the calculated t statistic falls outside this region, the null hypothesis is rejected, and one believes with a 95 percent rate of certainty that the X variable significantly contributes towards explaining the variation in the dependent Y variable. Often, the researcher is interested only in the coefficient (and impact) of a single explanatory variable. Nevertheless, it is imperative that the full model be estimated so that the simultaneity of forces be permitted to exert its collective influence on the dependent variable. It is also important that the researcher have *a priori* theories and hypotheses concerning the expected sign of each coefficient for the independent variables.

Applications

Telecommunication researchers have used multiple regression analysis in many different economic contexts. Most applications have involved policy issues or explanations of business practices or phenomena. An in-depth analysis of several studies here illustrates the usefulness and importance of this statistical technique.

In a recent study, Litman[11] attempted to estimate a ratings function for theatrical films first broadcast on network television during the 1976–77 season. He hypothesized that the TV ratings of theatrical movies (the dependent variable) were functionally related to a number of independent variables measuring the quality of the film in its theatrical run, the critics' evaluation of the film, the elapsed time between the film's theatrical release and network showing (age), and binary variables[12] representing the day of the week and season in which the film was scheduled. The results, in Table 7-1, conform fairly well to the *a priori* hypotheses concerning the expected signs of the coefficients. Only the age variable and binary variable for Friday telecasts were insignificant at the 5 percent level. The R^2 of .657 means that nearly two-thirds of the variance in ratings is explained by the independent variables in the regression model.

It may be instructive to interpret a few of the coefficients in Table 7-1. The variable X_2 (adjusted theatrical rentals) has a coefficient of .095. This means that for every $1 million increase in theatrical rentals (adjusted for inflation) of a film during its theatrical run, one expects the network rating to rise by .095 rating points (all other independent variables remaining the same). Hence, if a network were considering telecasting one film with theatrical rentals of $10 million and another with rentals of $20 million, the $10 million differential could be expected to increase network ratings by 10 × .095, or .95 of one rating point.

Similarly, if the film were scheduled for the peak viewership periods of fall or winter, its expected rating would be 4.677 rating ponts higher than films telecast during the spring and summer months. The average picture in the sample has an age of 3.741 years, an adjusted rental of $6.66 million, and a star rating of 2.59 stars. If this film were shown during the

Table 7-1   Regressions on Ratings of Theatrical Movies [Dependent Variable: Ratings of theatrical movies shown during the 1976–77 season (rating points)]

Explanatory Variables	Coefficients
X_1-Age (Years)	−.027
	(−.161)
X_2-Adjusted Theatrical Rentals ($ Millions)	.095
	(4.148)**
X_3-Star Ratings (# stars)	−1.193
	(−3.162)**
X_4-Season $\left(\begin{array}{l}\text{1 if fall or winter}\\\text{0 if spring or summer}\end{array}\right)$	4.677
	(5.669)**
X_5-Sunday $\left(\begin{array}{l}\text{1 if Sunday}\\\text{0 if otherwise}\end{array}\right)$	6.562
	(5.819)**
X_6-Monday $\left(\begin{array}{l}\text{1 if Monday}\\\text{0 if otherwise}\end{array}\right)$	6.066
	(5.122)**
X_7-Wednesday $\left(\begin{array}{l}\text{1 if Wednesday}\\\text{0 if otherwise}\end{array}\right)$	1.992
	(1.795)*
X_8-Friday $\left(\begin{array}{l}\text{1 if Friday}\\\text{0 if otherwise}\end{array}\right)$	−.722
	(−.711)
Constant	15.096
	(10.285)**
R^2	.657
Sample Size (N)	118

t = statistics in parentheses
*Significant at the 5% level for a one-tail test
**Significant at the 1% level for a one-tail test

Source: Barry R. Litman, "Predicting TV Ratings for Theatrical Movies," *Journalism Quarterly* 56 (1979), p. 592. Reprinted by permission from Autumn 1979 *Journalism Quarterly.*

fall season on a Sunday night, it would earn expected ratings equal to:

$$\widehat{Y} = 15.096 - (.027 \cdot 3.741) +$$
$$(.095 \cdot 6.66) - (1.193 \cdot 2.59)$$
$$+ (4.677 \cdot 1) + (6.562 \cdot 1)$$
$$= 23.77 \text{ rating points}$$

Regression analysis is sometimes used as an input to public policy decisions. An example of such use is the cross-ownership question. During the early 1970s, this hot issue questioned whether daily newspapers should be permitted to own broadcast outlets in the same local area where the newspaper operated. The commission had historically permitted such ownership as part of its policy of local ownership of broadcast stations. The Justice Department charged that cross-ownershp concentrated control of the marketplace of ideas into relatively few hands and thus raised prices to advertisers. The broadcast lobby countered by saying that the joint businesses operated separately and with independent editorial boards, and also that the many voices in the marketplace of ideas competed with other media for advertising dollars.

Owen[13] tested the hypothesis that cross-ownership was related to the prices charged to advertisers in both the newspaper and television markets. To isolate the impact of cross-ownership, Owen first had to specify the complete model — all factors that jointly determine newspaper and television advertising prices. The television price model will be considered in greater detail.

Owen theorized that the price per unit of time (the dependent variable) was functionally related to the quality of the station's programs, its potential reach, the demographic value of the market to advertisers, and various ownership configurations. In more specific terms, the highest hourly prime time rate depended on the market size and whether the station was a VHF or UHF (reach); whether the station was an affiliate or an independent (quality of programming); median income of consumers in the market (demographic value); and finally, whether the station was cross-owned or competed in the market with cross-owned stations (ownership configurations).[14]

The results in Table 7-2 closely conform to Owen's hypotheses. He used a log linear transformation[15] for his nonbinary variables in order to make them conform to the linearity

assumed in regression procedure. His R^2 equals .71, a good fit for cross-sectional analysis. The crucial variable in the analysis is the cross-ownership binary. Owen found that cross-owned TV stations (everything else held constant) had higher advertising prices by about 15 percent than did stations not owned by local newspapers. In conjunction with his other result that cross-owned newspapers charge advertising prices about 10 percent higher, Owen notes, "No economist will be surprised to find that monopolists charge monopoly prices. It is, nevertheless, interesting to confirm empirically this basic theoretical proposition."[16]

Owen's results were challenged by Lago[17] and others on the grounds that his regressions omitted two key variables measuring the newspaper's circulation and the TV station's audience rating. These variables were thought to be crucial determinants of the advertising prices of newspapers and television stations, respectively. When Lago included these variables, the cross-ownership binary turned out to be insignificant for both the newspaper and TV price

Table 7-2 Regression Results: Effect on Television Prices of Joint Ownership [Dependent Variable: Logarithm of Highest Prime Time Hourly Rate]

Explanatory Variables	*Coefficient*	*t-statistic*[a]
Square of log population	0.0539	23.7
Household income	0.000057	2.5
Joint newspaper ownership[b]	0.151	2.5
VHF–UHF status[b]	0.540	9.1
Network affiliation status[b]	0.420	4.8
Competes with combination owned stations[b]	0.0741	1.6
Intercept	7.790	43.2

R^2 = .71
Sample Size = 496
[a]*t*-statistics greater than 2.516 are considered significant at a .01 confidence level; *t*-statistics greater than 1.960 are considered significant at a .05 confidence level; and *t*-statistics greater than 1.645 are considered significant at a .10 confidence level.
[b]Binary variables

Source: Bruce M. Owen, "Newspaper and Television Station Joint Ownership," *The Antitrust Bulletin* 18 (1973), p. 806. c Federal Legal Publications, Inc., 157 Chambers St., New York, NY 10007. Antitrust Bulletin: XVIII, p. 806.

regressions. In other words, the cross-owned newspapers and TV stations charge no higher prices than similarly situated outlets owned by other interests.

The important feature of this debate is that including or excluding a certain variable greatly influenced the policy recommendations. This example illustrates how this statistical technique can be misused, unless the complete model is specified and each variable justified by *a priori* theory.

An important use of multiple regression analysis is the measurement of supply and demand functions. The estimation of demand functions is particularly important to broadcasters and advertisers, because the supply of advertising minutes is generally fixed and thus demand determines the market price. The typical demand function is expressed in the following terms, with the expected signs of the coefficients listed above each independent variable.[18]

Quantity demanded for product A $(Q_A) =$

f [Price of A $(\overline{P}_A)$, Price of substitutes for A

$(P_{B_1} + {}_{B_2} + ..._{B_k} +)$, Price of complements for

$A(P_{\overline{C}_1, \overline{C}_2...\overline{C}_k})$, Income $(\overset{+}{I})$,

Population $(P\overset{+}{o}p)$, Tastes $(\overset{+}{T})$, time $(\overset{+}{t})$].

Quantity demanded is:
(a) Inversely related to price, since decreases in price (*ceteris paribus*) cause consumers to feel wealthier and at the same time divert income away from higher priced substitute goods toward the purchase of good A;
(b) Directly related to the price of substitute goods, because, as their prices increase, the consumer switches out of them and into other goods, including good A;
(c) inversely related to the price of complementary goods (goods used in conjunction with another good, such as coffee and cream), since increases in the complements' prices reduce their consumption as well as the product they are tied to;

(d) Directly related to income, since higher income means the consumer can afford more of all goods, including good A;
(e) Directly related to population, since the greater the potential number of consumers, the greater is the total need for the product in question;
(f) Directly related to fashion trends for the good in question;
(g) Influenced positively or negatively by institutional policies;
(h) Directly related to peak buying seasons and inversely related to off-peak seasons.

In addition, economists are concerned with the price elasticity of demand, which is the relative responsiveness of quantity demanded to price (*ceteris paribus*).[19] In mathematical terms, it is:

price elasticity of demand

$$(\eta_d) = \frac{\% \, \Delta Q_A}{\% \, \Delta P_A} = \frac{\dfrac{\Delta Q_A}{Q \text{ base}}}{\dfrac{\Delta P_A}{P \text{ base}}}$$

$$= \frac{\Delta Q_A}{\Delta P_A} \cdot \frac{P \text{ base}}{Q \text{ base}}$$

Since

$$\frac{\Delta Q_A}{\Delta P_A}$$

is the coefficient of the P_A independent variable in the multiple regression equation, we can evaluate this coefficient at an appropriate price and output base (usually the means of the variables) to determine the elasticity. If

$$|\eta_d| > 1$$

the output of the good is responsive to changes in price, or elastic. If

$$|\eta_d| < 1$$

the good is unresponsive to changes in price, or inelastic. If

$$| \eta_d | = 1$$

there is a proportionate response, or unit elasticity. Inelastic goods tend to be necessities, to account for only a small percentage of one's income, or to have few available substitutes. In other words, inelastic goods provide the consumers with little choice and will not significantly curtail purchases (Q_A) with increases in price. This fact favors the supplier, who has a greater ability to raise prices without fear of losing customers to a substitute good. The opposite holds for elastic goods.

Bowman[20] estimated the advertisers' demand for network television time using a multiple regression model. His formulation of the demand function uses price per home per minute as the dependent variable. Price depends on: (a) the number of minutes of network advertising watched per month by all households; (b) the level of disposable income per month; (c) the season of the year; and (d) the unemployment rate, which is a proxy measure for slack in the economy. Bowman's sample is a time series of monthly observations for all the variables for the period of 1964–69.

The results of his estimation closely conform to *a priori* theory. Only the unemployment variable was insignificant. Using the log linear transformation, the statistical fit (R^2) of his equation was .943. Bowman discovered that the elasticity of demand for network television was .73, indicating that it is an inelastic product with few close substitutes.[21] He also found that the aggregate demand for advertising shifts up before Christmas (peaking in October) and reaches its lowest levels in the summer. Bowman correctly notes that knowledge of elasticity measurement is crucial to FCC policymakers who are considering policies affecting the supply of advertising minutes. Changes in the supply of advertising minutes cause movements along the demand curve, and the impact on revenues can be estimated by knowing the elasticity of demand in the relevant region. Examples of such policy changes are the Prime-Time Access Rules (1970), the proposals seeking to decrease the amount of advertising time on children's programming, and the recent abandonment of the NAB commercial time limits due to the threat of antitrust litigation.

Multiple regression analysis has also been applied to broadcasting in other interesting contexts listed here. The interested reader is encouraged to sample these articles.

1. Litman[22] has developed a model to examine the issue of whether network-owned television stations (O&Os) carry as much public service programming as non-network-owned stations and also a model that examines the determinants of who watches and contributes to television evangelists.
2. The FCC Network Inquiry Group has developed a model to examine the determinants of the station clearance rate for network programming.
3. Levin[24] and Blau, Johnson, and Ksobiech[25] have models predicting the selling price of television stations.
4. Wirth and Thompson[26] have developed a model that examines the determinants of the cost of license renewal.
5. Park, Johnson, and Fishman[27] have developed a model to explain the variation in television station profits.

Measures of Concentration in Telecommunication

Many important and controversial issues with which the FCC has historically dealt involve questions of concentration of ownership in the telecommunication industries. Consider the history of FCC rulemaking in such areas as chain ownership, multiple ownership, cross-ownership, and prime-time access. Each lengthy proceeding involved questions of concentration of power at the national or local level. The commission has historically favored a decentralized system of ownership in the United States on the theory that "the right conclusions are more likely to be gathered out of a multitude of tongues than through any kind of authoritative selection."[28] These questions of concentration of control within and between telecommunication industries will become increasingly important with the emergence and viability of such new services as pay cable, direct broadcast satellites, subscription television, videocassettes, and video discs. This section examines some economic techniques used to measure the degree of concentration in various telecommunication markets.

First, let us briefly review the economic concept of market structure. The essential difference between a competitive and noncompetitive market is in the distribution of power between the market and the firm. In a competitive market, all power resides in the market mechanism; it is the ultimate regulator of conduct. The firm is a slave to the forces of supply and demand; it has few choices to make and no power to enforce its decisions. The market compels good performance, and consequently one expects the lowest level of prices, the greatest degree of allocative efficiency and cost effectiveness, and the most rapid introduction of new products and technology under the perfectly competitive ideal market structure. On the other hand, the firm in a noncompetitive market has considerable control over its economic destiny. It has significant power, as well as flexibility and discretion over price, output, advertising, and research and development expenditures. The market mechanism has been shortcircuited and stripped of some of its regulatory powers. The results are usually higher prices, misallocation of society's resources, excessive costs, and retardation of technological change.

Economists have defined such concepts as *perfect competition*, *oligopoly*, and *market* with theoretical precision; but it has not been easy to apply these abstractions to the context of real world industries. To prove concentration of power, the first step is to define the relevant market in which the industry or several industries operate. Without such a definition, it would be impossible to detect whether there has been or threatens to be a "substantial lessening of competition or a tendency to create a monopoly."[29] The case of cross-ownership will highlight these problems.

Does the relevant product market include all forms of local advertising (daily newspapers, television, radio, weekly newspapers, etc.), or is each of these media separate and distinct? If one argues the former, then cross-ownership can substantially lessen competition in the local advertising market. If one argues the latter, then cross-ownership is irrelevant, since the two media do not directly compete with each other. The question of defining the relevant market turns on whether newspapers and, say, television stations are close substitutes in the minds of local advertisers. The cross-elasticity of demand is a generally accepted economic test for measuring the degree of substitutability between any two products.

The cross-elasticity of demand is the relative responsiveness of changes in the quantity of one good (newspaper advertising) in regard to changes in the price of another good (television advertising).[30] If the two goods are substitutes, then an increase in the price of TV advertising should cause advertisers to switch some expenditures from television into newspapers. In mathematical terms, the cross-elasticity of demand can be expressed as follows:

Cross elasticity of demand for good A with respect to good B

$$(\eta_{A,B}) = \frac{\% \, \Delta Q_A}{\% \, \Delta P_B} = \frac{\dfrac{\Delta Q_A}{Q \text{ base}}}{\dfrac{\Delta P_B}{P \text{ base}}}$$

$$= \frac{\Delta Q_A}{\Delta P_B} \cdot \frac{P \text{ base}}{Q \text{ base}}$$

Unfortunately, economists only describe cross-elasticity measurements in the rather general terms of *strong* or *weak*. It is generally considered that goods with cross-elasticities near one are strong substitutes, and those approaching zero are weak. The cross-elasticity of demand can be easily calculated from the estimated demand function described in the first part of this chapter. Since

$$\frac{\Delta Q_A}{\Delta P_B}$$

is the coefficient corresponding to one of the independent variables in the multiple regression equation, it is simple to evaluate this coefficient at an appropriate output and price base to derive the measure of cross-elasticity. This procedure can be followed for all independent variables considered to be substitute goods for the product in question. Regrettably, no such calculations were ever made in the long cross-ownership proceeding.

Once the relevant product market has been identified, the next step is to develop a measure for the concept of market concentration. It is known from economic theory that a concentrated market structure will have a relatively small number of large and powerful firms. To determine the size distribution of sales or assets, several alternative measures are available.[31]

First, one could simply count the number of competitors operating in the product market. In the case of cross-ownership, if broadcast outlets, daily and weekly newspapers and magazines are included as part of the product market, then counting each competitor separately might give the impression of a large number of media voices (competition). Rosse and Dertouzas,[32] following this procedure in counting the number of media voices for New York City, discovered 459 separate voices. The problem with this measure is that each media voice is given an equal weight, which masks the heavy influence of the television and daily newspaper outlets. Another example is to count the number of radio stations in Chicago and label this a competitive market without considering differences in wattages among AM stations and differences between AM and FM stations.

A second technique frequently used to illustrate concentration of power within a market is the Lorenz Curve,[33] which graphically highlights inequality of market shares among firms (or program categories). Suppose one wishes to illustrate the fact that network programming is superior to syndicated fare, and that, as a result, network affiliates earn a disproportionately higher share of audience (and revenues) during prime time.

Examination of the Arbitron audience share for the New York market for the November 1981 sweeps reveals ten active stations during prime time. The three VHF affiliates accounted for a 72 percent share of the audience; the three VHF independents accounted for 22 percent; and the other four stations (two public and two UHF independents) accounted for 6 percent. If audience shares were equally distributed, then the three VHF affiliates, which accounted for 3/10 or 30 percent of all stations in the market, should have earned a 30 percent audience share. The fact that they earned more than twice that share while the lowest four stations (representing 40 percent of all the stations) earned only a 6 percent share indicates a maldistribution of audience shares in New York City during prime time.

The Lorenz Curve for these data appears in Figure 7-3. The 45° line represents perfect equality; that is, 10 percent of the firms earn 10 percent of audience share, 20 percent of the firms earn 20 percent, and so on. The bowed-out curve represents the true distribution of shares. The more the Lorenz Curve departs from the 45° line, the greater the inequality of audience shares among the firms. One problem is associated with the use of Lorenz Curves. When there are relatively few firms in an industry—say, four—and market shares are almost evenly split among the four firms, the Lorenz Curve will nearly coincide with the 45° line. It would be wrong, however, to label this a competitive industry since the number of firms is so small. Under these circumstances, this technique should not be used to assess concentration among the three networks or within a three- or four-station market.

The most frequently used measure of concentration is the four- or eight-firm concentration ratio—a measure of the cumulative market share of the top four or eight firms in an industry or a market. Comparisons over time are often made to see if this concentration ratio has increased, thereby implying a greater degree of monopoly power within the industry. Handy rules to use with concentration ratios are: If the four-firm ratio is equal to or greater than 50 percent, or if the eight-firm ratio is equal to or greater than 75 percent, then the in-

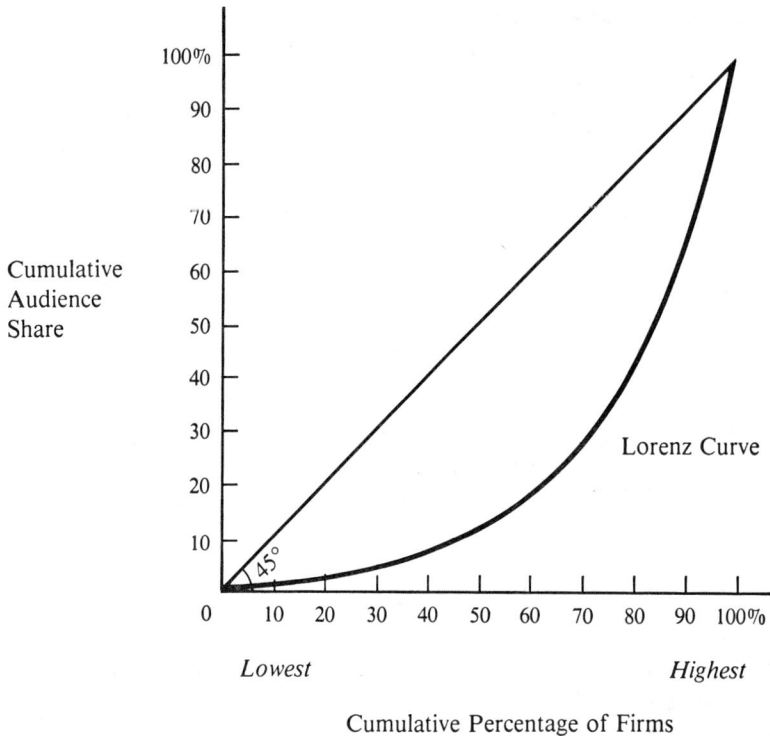

Figure 7-3   Lorenz Curve of audience share distribution.

dustry or market is highly concentrated; If the four-firm ratio is between 33 and 50 percent, or if the eight-firm ratio is between 50 and 75 percent, then the industry or market is moderately concentrated. All other cases indicate the presence of some degree of competition within the industry or market. This sort of measure has been frequently used to assess national concentration of ownership among multiple cable system owners.

One problem with the concentration ratio is that it can hide inequality of power within its own group. Two radio markets can have identical four-firm concentration ratios of, say, 40 percent; yet, in one market, the distribution might be 25, 5, 5, 5, while in the other it may be 10, 10, 10, 10. These two different distributions might have different meanings in terms of the nature of competition, even though the concentration ratios are the same.[34] Also, it is possible that the four- or eight-firm ratio might be relatively constant over time, but wide swings in individual firm market shares may have simultaneously occurred. These wide swings over time will have a different meaning than if the firms maintained constant shares over the time interval.

Another useful measure of concentration is the Herfindahl-Hirschman (H-H) Index, which is calculated by summing the squared market shares of all firms in an industry or market. This index is desirable because it increases as the number of firms declines and also as inequality among those firms rises.

Thus, to the extent that monopoly power is correlated positively with both fewness of sellers and inequality in their sizes, the Herfindahl-Hirschman Index comes close to being an ideal composite measure.[35]

The H-H Index equals one, if there is a pure monopoly, and approaches zero if there is an approximation to perfect competition. Suppose there were four firms, each splitting the market in equal shares; then the H-H Index would be .25. As a rule of thumb an H-H Index greater than .20 indicates a significant degree of concentration within the industry; an H-H Index between .10 and .20 indicates a moderate degree of concentration within the industry. The H-H Index for the New York television market described above turns out to be .194, a fairly high degree of concentration during prime time.

In a recent article,[36] Litman calculated H-H indices for the distribution of network time among nine program types for the 1974–78 television seasons. The results are displayed in Table 7-3; the index ranges from .140 to .190, indicating a fairly high concentration of time among a few program types. This model was used as evidence to support the proposition that the networks imitated each other rather than presenting a balanced schedule of programming. The decrease in the H-H Index after the 1975 season also demonstrates that the ascendency of ABC shook the industry and caused the networks to do more counterprogramming and take more chances with infrequently used program types.[37]

A final method of measuring concentration is the market share stability technique. The basic theory behind this technique is that in an oligopoly market structure, firms will attempt to forge a spirit of cooperation, express or tacit, and come to an oligopoly consensus concerning the mutually beneficial prices, the distribution of market shares, and standardization of industry-specific practices.[38] To the extent that this consensus is complete in all areas of contact, the industry will be in a state of equilibrium, and market shares will be stable over time. On the other hand, if the industry has difficulty in establishing consensus, or if the agreement is inequitable to some firms, one should expect a disequilibrium state of widely fluctuating market shares over time. Hence, stability of market shares will be a proxy value for a shared monopoly power over time, and instability will indicate a competitive environment.

The value of this measure derives from the

Table 7-3 Aggregate Network Diversity (1974–1978 Seasons)

Program Types	1974–75*	1975–76*	1976–77*	1977–78*	1978–79*
General Drama	7.9%	9.1%	7.6%	10.6%	9.1%
Variety–Comedy	4.6	6.8	10.6	7.6	7.6
Western–Early American	7.9	4.6	4.6	7.6	4.6
Action–Adventure	10.3	12.1	6.1	6.1	6.1
Situation Comedy	13.5	15.9	18.9	21.2	18.9
Mystery–Suspense	29.4	33.3	22.7	16.7	15.2
Feature Films	23.0	15.2	20.5	18.2	27.3
Science Fiction	0.0	0.0	4.6	7.6	6.1
Other	3.2	3.0	4.6	4.6	5.3
Herfindahl-Hirschman Index $H = \sum_{i=1} \text{program share } (S_i^2)$	.184	.190	.156	.140	.159

*Fall season schedule.

Source: Barry R. Litman, "The Television Networks, Competition and Program Diversity," *Journal of Broadcasting* 23 (1979), p. 403. Reproduced with the permission of the *Journal of Broadcasting*.

fact that it gives a more accurate picture of the dynamic process of change within an industry or market than does an examination of four- or eight-firm concentration ratios. The measure is calculated as the sum of the absolute value of change in market shares for all firms between two or more specific points in time. In mathematical terms, this is:

$$\sum_{i=1}^{n} \left| S_i^t 0 - S_i^t 1 \right|$$

where S_i is the share of the ith firm, and t_{0-1} represents the time interval under investigation. Prisuta[39] and Litman[40] have recently used this market-share stability technique to assess the degree of competition during the local television newscast. One problem associated with the technique is that, under certain circumstances, a finding of market share stability can give an erroneous impression of significant market power and the corollary of poor economic performance. Hence, this measure is best used in conjunction with one or more of the other techniques. Regrettably, no absolute standard has yet emerged to delineate market stability from instability.

Summary

This essay has examined several techniques that economists use to analyze telecommunication issues. Regression analysis is a flexible tool used to examine the functional relationship between a dependent variable and one or more independent variables. By specifying a complete regression model, one can measure the individual and collective influences of a number of explanatory variables on a dependent variable of economic interest. This form of analysis is useful for estimating demand functions, for predicting some economic phenomena, as well as for isolating certain variables that have important policy ramifications.

The second methology related to several different techniques economists use to measure concentration of control (or of any other phenomenon) in the media. The first task was to delineate a relevant product market that contained close substitute goods. The measure used was the cross-elasticity of demand. Then, a number of similar methods were explained for indexing the degree of monopoly power within markets. These measures include Lorenz Curves, concentration ratios, the Herfindahl-Hirschman Index, and a market-share stability index.

The use of economic analysis in examining media issues is in its infancy. There must be a refinement of the techniques and a greater concentration of effort before its true value will be established in the marketplace of ideas.

Endnotes

1. The following books are recommended: Taro Yamane, *Statistics: An Introductory Analysis*, 2nd ed. (New York: Harper and Row, 1967); Jan Kmenta, *Elements of Econometrics* (New York: Macmillan, 1971); and Hubert M. Blalock, Jr., *Social Statistics*, 3rd ed. (New York: McGraw-Hill, 1979).
2. The basic sources for this statistical section are Yamane, op. cit., and Kmenta, op. cit.
3. The capital letters X and Y generally refer to the X and Y variables. The lower case letters x and y refer to specific observations of those variables.
4. These characteristics are known as the basic assumptions of regression analysis; see Kmenta, op. cit., 202.
5. For greater detail on these problems and methods of alleviating them, see Kmenta, op. cit., chap. 8.
6. The maximum likelihood technique yields equivalent results and is used when the distribution of y values is known to be normal; see Kmenta, op. cit., chap. 7.
7. Yamane, op. cit., chap. 14.
8. Ibid., chap. 22. Yamane also has a nice discussion of the more complex case when k independent variables are used.
9. Kmenta, op. cit., 230–231.

10. Yamane, op cit., chaps. 14, 22; also see Kmenta, chap. 7. Note that most statistical packages for regression analysis routinely print out the *b* coefficients, the constant term, R^2, and *t* values for each independent variable.

11. Barry R. Litman, "Predicting TV Ratings for Theatrical Movies," *Journalism Quarterly* 56 (1979): 590–595.

12. A binary variable takes on the value of 1 or 0. Usually the value of one is an affirmative answer to the implied question in the variable. An example of this would be the season binary used in this study. Each movie that was telecast in the fall or winter months would receive a 1, and all other seasons a 0.

13. Bruce M. Owen, "Newspaper and Television Station Joint Ownership," *The Antitrust Bulletin* 18 (1973): 787–813.

14. Ibid., 805–806.

15. A log linear transformation is frequently used in estimating demand or quasi-demand functions. To perform this transformation, simply take the logarithm (base 10) of the dependent and of each continuous independent variable.

16. Owen, op. cit., 813.

17. Armando M. Lago, "The Price Effects of Joint Mass Communication Media Ownership," *The Antitrust Bulletin* 16 (1971) 789–813. Also see Walter S. Baer et al., *Concentration of Mass Media Ownership: Assessing the State of Current Knowledge* (Santa Monica: Rand, 1976), Appendix.

18. For more detail on the economic theory, see Paul A. Samuelson, *Economics*, 10th ed. (New York: McGraw-Hill, 1976), chap. 4.

19. Ibid., chap. 20.

20. Gary W. Bowman, "Demand and Supply of Network Television Advertising," *The Bell Journal of Economics* 7 (1976): 258–267.

21. Ibid., 262.

22. Barry R. Litman, "Measuring Divestiture of Network Owned Television Stations: An Econometric Approach," *The Antitrust Bulletin* 25 (1980): 363–376; also Litman, "Proselytizing the Masses: The Economics of Televangelism," paper presented at meetings of the Broadcast Education Association (April 1983).

23. FCC Network Inquiry Special Staff, "An Analysis of the Network-Affiliate Relationship in Television," (October 1979): chapter 5.

24. Harvey J. Levin, *The Invisible Resource: Use and Regulation of the Radio Spectrum* (Baltimore: Johns Hopkins Press, 1971), Appendix C.

25. Robert T. Blau, Rolland C. Johnson, and Kenneth J. Ksobiech, "Determinants of TV Station Economic Value," *Journal of Broadcasting* 20 (1976): 197–208.

26. Michael O. Wirth and Lawrence Thompson, "The Cost of TV and Radio License Renewals," paper presented to the Broadcast Education Association, April 1980.

27. R. Park, L. Johnson, and B. Fishman, "Projecting the Growth of Television Broadcasting: Implications for Spectrum Use" (Santa Monica, Calif.: Rand, 1976).

28. *U.S. v. Associated Press* (52 F. Supp. 362, 372 [1943]).

29. This language is used in the Clayton Antitrust Act of 1914 as amended (15 *U.S.C.A.* S 14).

30. Edwin Mansfield, *Microeconomics: Theory and Applications*, 2nd ed. (New York: W. W. Norton, 1975), chap. 4.

31. The best discussion on these subjects is F. M. Scherer, *Industrial Market Structure and Economic Performance* (Chicago: Rand McNally, 1971), chap. 3.

32. James N. Rosse and James Dertouzas, "Economic Issues in Mass Communication Industries," in FTC, *Proceedings of the Symposium on Media Concentration* Vol. 1 (December 1978): 182.

33. The Lorenz Curve was originally used to illustrate the unequal distribution of income in the United States.

34. Scherer.

35. Ibid., 52.

36. Barry R. Litman, "The Television Net-

works, Competition and Program Diversity," *Journal of Broadcasting* 23 (1979): 393–410.

37. Ibid., 403–404.

38. Barry R. Litman, "Market Share Instability in Local Television News," *Journal of* *Broadcasting* 24 (1980): 499–514.

39. Robert H. Prisuta, "Local Television News as an Oligopolistic Industry: A Pilot Study," *Journal of Broadcasting* 23 (1979): 61–68.

40. Litman, "Market Share Instability."

This essay acquaints the reader with methods of audience segmentation, beginning with what segmentation is and what value it has. The nature of the data that the segmenter works with will be discussed, along with several measures that can be calculated from these data. Next, some major methods of analysis used in segmentation are briefly described. Finally, examples of segmentation research that illustrate the application of these methods are presented. This essay does not show how to perform the statistical analysis required for each method; rather, it shows how these techniques are applied, the types of questions the techniques are best suited to answer, and how to apply the output of these analyses to the original purposes of the research.

8
Techniques for Audience Segmentation

Jonathan Gutman

Approaches to Audience Segmentation

Segmentation in audience research refers to the process of dividing a large mass of potential viewers into smaller, homogeneous subsets. The expectation is that these smaller subgroups will prefer and view different types of programs. Audience segmentation also permits the researcher to probe more deeply into the desires and satisfactions of specific groups of audience members. Potential program material can be evaluated more effectively by testing it among audience segments that will ultimately choose to view the program when it is aired.

Bases for segmentation can be discussed as general versus situation specific and as objective versus inferred. Figure 8-1[1] depicts this dual classification system.

The two criteria for successful segmentation are that: (1) groups will be homogeneous with respect to some designated quality; and (2) a group identified in one market by a given segmentation measure will be similarly identified in any other market. The first criterion implies that any basis used for segmentation (see Figure 8-1) will result in people similar on that basis being grouped together as a segment. The second criterion implies that the basis for segmentation will apply to persons in regions other than the one used to develop the segmentation scheme. Other essays in this book dis-

Viewer Characteristics

	General	*Situation Specific*
Objective	Demographic Factors (Age, Stage in Life Cycle, Sex, Place of Living, etc.) Socioeconomic Factors	Viewing Patterns (Heavy, medium, light) Channel and Program Loyalty Patterns
Inferred	Personality Traits Life Style	Attitudes Perceptions and Preferences

Figure 8-1 Alternative bases of audience segmentation.

cuss the variables in each of these cells, variables available to the audience segmenter. This essay outlines the methods and data demands associated with implementing the various segmentation approaches.

Comments on Viewing Behavior

A discussion of viewing patterns precedes the discussion of techniques and data needs since the segmenters' ultimate interest is in behavior. Any method of segmentation must ultimately rely on behavioral differences for its justification. Of course, the researcher can segment viewers on the basis of the amount of their viewing behavior and then describe the characteristics of viewers in each behavioral segment. Nielsen and Arbitron periodically publish demographic profiles of heavy, medium, and light viewers. Other studies have sought to understand light versus heavy viewers in terms of personality traits.[2]

Another approach to analyzing behavior focuses on viewing choices. The program types in television[3] can be determined by content analysis or by using similarity ratings or preference data, as previously cited. However, in dispute is the existence of viewer-types, viewers devoted to specific types of programs. If preference data are analyzed, identifiable program types do emerge; but if actual viewing data are analyzed, program types are rarely obtainable. Suggestions as to why there may not be viewer types for specific types of programs are that:

1. People do not always watch what they prefer; set control, family dynamics, availabil-

ity (near a TV set when preferred program is on).
2. People do not always like what they watch; much viewing occurs because others are viewing. Viewing occurs because a given program represents the least objectionable choice.

This absence of viewing segments devoted to program types is explained in Goodhardt and Ehrenberg's[4] Law of Duplicated Viewing, which states: "The percentage of the audience of any TV program who watch a given TV program on another day of the same week is approximately equal to the rating of the latter program times a constant."[5] Header, Klompmaker, and Rust[6] disagree with this view in their analysis of some Simmons data on viewing in the United States (data from Goodhardt et al. are based on viewing in the United Kingdom). This essay will not resolve these conflicting views, but duplicated viewing might be solely a function of rating (percentage of homes with televisions tuned to a given station) and not of program content. The burden of proof is on the segmenter to show that the segments created using the techniques described below do display significantly different viewing behaviors.

Measures Used in Segmentation Research

Measures of Association

In general terms, segmentation research rests on analysis of measures of association and proximity. The measure of association used most frequently is the product-moment correlation coefficient. The product-moment or Pearson coefficient is an index of the pattern of variation between any two vectors. For example, two people may have the following scores (using a 7-point scale) on several variables (personality traits, attitudes, etc.):

	Variables					
Person	*1*	*2*	*3*	*4*	*5*	*6*
A	5	7	6	5	6	5
B	1	3	2	1	2	1

The correlation between these two people would be 1 — a perfect correlation; yet person B is obviously lower on all variables than is person A. The high correlation would result in grouping together people with similar patterns of change in magnitude across variables (see Rummel[7] for a discussion). The use of such a coefficient would not matter if one were forming correlations among the columns of such persons by variables matrices: one is interested in which variables co-vary. This example, although it might represent an extreme case, shows the dangers in using coefficients reflecting pattern only. Most people who correlate highly across variables will tend to have similar scores on an absolute basis. The segmenter, however, should check the relations among people in the same segments on the variables used in the segmentation attempt to determine whether they really belong together before proceeding with analysis.

Other types of coefficients consider magnitude as well as pattern (see Rummel[8] for a discussion). In the final analysis, the researcher often must determine options in terms of objectives.

Proximity Measures —
Distance and Matching

Having discussed correlation measures, we now turn to distance measures. One basic decision the segmenter faces is whether to use correlation or distance to capture resemblance among respondents (see Cronbach and Gleser[9] for a discussion of this issue). Two types of distance measures predominate — Euclidean or Manhattan (city block). The formula for computing these distance measures is:

$$d_{gi} = \left[\sum_{i=1}^{x} \left| S_{il} - S_{gl} \right|^{a} \right]^{1/a}$$

d_{gi} = distance between case i and g on variable L

x = number of variables on which distance between cases is to be calculated

S_{il} = score for case i on variable 1

S_{gl} = score for case g on variable 1

a = an exponent

If a is 2, the formula computes the Euclidean distance; if a is 1, the city block distance is calculated. Given the following data for two persons' preferences for four programs:

	Preference for Program			
Person	*1*	*2*	*3*	*4*
A	5	3	1	2
B	3	4	3	5

the Euclidean distance between persons A and B would be:

$$[(5\text{-}3)^2 + (3\text{-}4)^2 + (1\text{-}3)^2 + (2\text{-}5)^2]^{1/2}$$

$$= [18]^{1/2} = 4.24$$

Distance measures are usually clustered or scaled, as opposed to being factor analyzed; but it is possible to transform the d_{gi} measures so they will be analogous to correlation coefficients (varying between 0 and 1) by dividing all distances by the maximum distance,

$$d^{s}_{gi} = 1 - \frac{d_{gi}}{dmax}$$

where d^{s}_{gi} is the scaled distance and *dmax* is the largest distance in the matrix (see Rummel[10] for an illustration of this approach).

Before discussing specific matching indices typically used in analyzing viewing data, the nature of such a matrix should be discussed. Typically, the matrix to be analyzed would have viewers as rows and programs represented as columns. Analysis can be made of relations among the rows of such a matrix, or column relations can be analyzed just as in giving people factor scores and then clustering the factor scores, or in clustering principle components obtained through factor analysis.

The values in such a person-by-program matrix would be zeros and ones, where 1 represents viewing, and zero represents not viewing. Many measures of similarity and distance are possible,[11] but a few are more frequently used than others. Consider first the types of relations between any two given rows: 1,1; 1,0; 0,1; 0,0. A 1,1 means both persons watch show 1; a 1,0 indicates person 1 watches program 1 and person 2 does not; 0,1 is the reverse of the 1,0 situation; and 0,0 means neither person watched show 1. Two matching types of similarity indices are most common—counting the number of 1,1 and 0,0 pairs, or all matches that can be divided by the total number of relations. The other index involves counting the 1,1's (two people watching the same show, referred to as duplicated pairs) and dividing by the sum of 1,1; 0,1; 1,0 relations.

Consider the following matrix of three persons by five programs, where 1 indicates viewing and zero is nonviewing:

Persons	*Programs*				
	a	*b*	*c*	*d*	*e*
A	1	1	1	1	0
B	1	1	0	0	0
C	1	0	0	0	1

The above matching indices are calculated below:

All Matches

	A	B	C
A			
B	.6		
C	.2	.6	

$$\text{A-B} = \frac{1,1 + 1,1 + 0,0}{5}$$
$$= 3/5 = .6$$

$$\text{A-C} = \frac{1,1}{5}$$
$$= 1/5 = .2$$

$$\text{B-C} = \frac{1,1 + 0,0 + 0,0}{5}$$
$$= 3/5 = .6$$

1,1 Matches Only

	A	B	C
A			
B	.5		
C	.2	.33	

$$\text{A-B} = \frac{1,1 + 1,1}{1,1 + 1,1 + 1,0 + 1,0}$$
$$= 2/4 = .5$$

$$\text{A-C} = \frac{1,1}{1,1 + 1,0 + 1,0 + 1,0 + 0,1}$$
$$= 1/5 = .2$$

$$\text{B-C} = \frac{1,1}{1,1 + 1,0 + 0,1}$$
$$= 1/3 = .33$$

Note that A-C and B-C have the same number of 1,1 matches—one each. However, A-C shows more differences (1,0; 0,1) than does B-C.

The choice between the two indices should be made based on the researcher's feeling about the meaningfulness of weak matches (0,0). Does the fact that two people do not watch the same programs contribute meaningfully to their similarity? Do we wish to emphasize similarity among respondents in clustering at the expense of differences that might exist among them?

Methods of Audience Segmentation

Many sources for learning about techniques can be used to segment viewing audiences. This section describes the major analytical approaches (factor analysis, clustering, Q-methodology, multiple discriminant analysis, and multidimensional scaling) and how to implement them. The research methodology of studies using these techniques is discussed by demonstrating the flow of analysis.

The choice among analytic techniques for segmenting audiences largely depends on the nature of the data to be analyzed. However, as a general distinction, cluster analysis and multidimensional scaling are more oriented toward defining who is a member of each segment; the other techniques provide more information on the criteria used to form the segments.

Factor Analysis

Any matrix can be factored; that is, any table of numbers can be analyzed for its set(s) of patterned variation. We will assume that a matrix consists of people as rows and programs viewed or preferred, personality traits, attitudes possessed, or life style, as columns. Our interest in such a matrix might be in the correlation between two variables as one moves down the columns from person to person (e.g., the correlation between person A and B, B and C, etc.)—see Figure 8-2. Or, our interest might be in the correlation between two rows as we consider the correlation between person A and B, B and C, etc., across variables. The former perspective is called R-factor analysis; the latter, Q-factor analysis.

The correlation matrix is basic to most applications of factor analysis. In R-factor analysis, the variables or columns of the matrix represent the values factored. In Q-factor analysis, the correlations among people (rows) are factored. Factoring a matrix means searching for linear combinations among the variables (or people) as expressed in the correlation matrix. The factor loading matrix is one key output of factor analysis. It contains the correlations between the variables (in R-type) or people (in Q-type) and the linear combinations (factors) that best reproduce the correlation coefficients in the original matrix.

The factor matrix is rotated to obtain a more desirable solution. One popular criterion for rotation, simple structure, attempts to maximize the number of high loadings in each factor while minimizing the number of factors with high loadings for each variable. If using the R-type approach, people (rows) can be given scores on the factors (dimensions). These factor scores can then be clustered to form segments. If using Q-type factor analysis, the researcher must determine from the original variables what makes the people loading on each factor similar (more will be said about this when discussing Q-methodology). Rummel[12] and Gorsuch[13] contain useful discussions of this analytical technique.

The two major approaches for using factor analysis in audience segmentation as specified above are: (1) factor the variables, give people scores on the factors, then cluster people using the factor scores (or use factor scores to describe respondent groups formed on other bases, such as viewing); and (2) factor the people across the original set of variables, then calculate profiles for people loading on the same factors (this approach will be discussed in the context of Q-methodology). One reason for using the first approach is that the patterns of relationship among the variables might not be clear, as often occurs when trying to segment audiences on attitudes, life style, or personality. Respondents might be asked to respond to many items, because the researcher does not know precisely which items are critical. Factor analysis can tell the researcher which items occur together or are answered in similar patterns by respondents. Once these common patterns of response are identified, the researcher can eliminate unneeded items and can tell which items pertain to particular areas of interest. The researcher may wish to use many items but to combine the ratings on subsets of items for greater stability. Using factor scores also helps equalize the impact of the various subsets of items in terms of their contribution to differences among people. If one area had ten items and another only five, the

Figure 8-2 Data matrix for factor analysis.

Person	1	2	3	4
		Variable		
A	3	4	5	3
B	4	5	3	3
C	3	3	5	4
D	5	4	3	3

former would have twice the impact of the latter.

For example, Frank and Greenberg[14] administered to respondents 139 leisure interest and activity items and 59 needs satisfied by leisure interests, all to be rated on a four-point rating scale. Through principle components analysis (a type of factor analysis), the 139 items were reduced to 18 interest factors and the 59 need items were reduced to nine factors. The 18 interest factor scores were subsequently used to group the respondents into segments. The nine need factors helped identify the nature of the segments.

In another study, Villani[15] collected responses on 214 personality and life-style items to be used in assessing television program audiences. Although these items were based on previous research as well as on theory, factor analysis was used "to determine independent psychographic measures and appropriate weights for aggregating individual statement scores to form trait scores."[16] Thirteen personality trait factors and 51 life-style factors were obtained. The associated factor scores were used to measure respondents' level of possession of these traits and life-style variables in subsequent analyses.

Factor analysis can also be used to create predetermined groups that serve as a basis for profiling audience subsets.[17] Villani[18] used factor analysis to reduce raw viewing frequencies for 78 prime-time television programs into 19 program types. In her analysis, regression was used to analyze the relationship between the viewing factor score for a particular program type and 68 variables (4 demographic variables, 13 personality factor scores, and 51 life-style factor scores). Other researchers have suggested adjusting raw viewing behavior or program preferences for personal and scheduling variables before factor analysis is applied.[19]

The reader is encouraged to consider Ehrenburg and Goodhardt's[20] alternative to factor analysis. They suggest analyzing the actual relationships in the observed data by asking what relationship, if any, holds across different subgroups of data. This is done by rearranging the order of the variables by the average size of the correlations in each row or column and by superimposing on this numerical ordering any ordering that initial inspection or previous knowledge may suggest. Reducing the correlations to a single digit allows any pattern existing in the data to be seen. Various *a priori* orderings can be tried out. At the least, such an approach would give the researcher a feel for the data that he or she would not get using traditional factor analysis.

Cluster Analysis

Cluster analysis offers a direct approach to separating people into groups so that people within groups are more similar to each other than to people outside their group. One primary decision of the cluster analysis user is what measure of resemblance between people to use. The section covering proximity measures discusses the alternatives.

Having selected a measure of resemblance, the researcher must select a computation routine for clustering the profiles. Of the many computer programs available to perform cluster analyses, two main types stand out—hierarchical and nonhierarchical. The hierarchical approach begins with each point as a separate cluster. The two closest points are then placed in a cluster. Then, either another point is joined to this cluster or two separate points form a new cluster (depending on which set of points is closest together). Analysis proceeds until all points are joined in a single large cluster. The BMDP[21] clustering programs, the most readily available, offer three options for building up clusters: single linkage (defining distance between clusters as the shortest distance from a point in one cluster to a point in another cluster); complete linkage (uses the longest distance between objects in two clusters as the measure of cluster distance); and average linkage (uses the average distance between objects in clusters as a measure of cluster distance). The nonhierarchical methods select cluster centers and assign objects within prespecified limits to these nodes.

One could cluster either raw values (personality, attitudes, life style, viewing behavior) or factor scores derived from these values. The Frank and Greenberg[22] study used a hierarchical clustering algorithm to cluster respondents into 14 segments based on 18 interest factors obtained from 139 items. The 14 segments were then used as the basis for a cross-tabulation foundation analysis to examine how they differed.

Plummer[23] reported on a cluster analysis of 1,200 male heads of household using 300 AIO (activity, interest, and opinion) measures. His approach for interpretation of clusters represents one method of interpreting clusters:

> Among men, the six-cluster solution appeared to be the most meaningful, as further clustering produced either very small or difficult-to-interpret clusters. The cluster analysis generated a "cluster" mean score on each of the 300 AIO items with a resulting F ratio to indicate the level of differentiation between clusters. For each AIO item with a significant F ratio, the two clusters with the highest mean scores and the two clusters with the lowest mean scores were selected. Examination of each cluster's array of high and low mean AIO items provided an empirical lifestyle profile for each cluster.[24]

At the beginning of this quotation, note that the number of clusters was at issue. The question of how many clusters there ought to be can never be answered. The choice must be made in light of interpretability and the desired degree of group similarity (often referred to as amalgamation distance). The remainder of the quotation refers to the development of cluster profiles so as to "name" or identify the nature of the clusters. These clusters then became the bases for viewing behavior analysis.

Discriminant Analysis

Before discussing Q-technique, which differs from the other segmentation procedures, a brief comment will be made about two other methods for segmenting audiences—discriminant analysis and multidimensional scaling.

The multiple discriminant analysis technique addresses whether profiles for two or more audiences are truly different. Massy[25] demonstrated this use of discriminant analysis using FM station audiences. Forty-seven measures on 239 families were reduced to 12 variables using factor analysis. The 12 variables were then used to predict which station each family listened to (was tuned to at time of interview).

The actual station listened to became the group to which each family was assigned. The resulting discriminant function equation was then used to predict to which station each family listened. A comparison of the predicted station with the actual station distinguished the station profiles (for the 12 variables). That is, if we can correctly predict to which station people listen (correctly predict group membership) on the basis of demographic and life-style variables, then that station audience must differ from other stations' audiences. Johnson[26] demonstrates how audience members might be plotted into the same space as objects.

In another radio format study, Lull et al.[27] used multiple discriminant analysis to identify "which demographic indices provide the most information in differentiating types of listeners for the formats." Two significant discriminant functions emerged from the analysis (primarily revolving around age and education).

Multidimensional Scaling

Multidimensional scaling (MDS) can be used for segmenting audiences in several ways. The task in nonmetric MDS is to work backward from a set of rank-ordered interobject distances (e.g., rated dissimilarities for pairs of objects from most to least similar) to find the number of dimensions and the configuration of points such that the ranks of their computed interpoint distances most closely match the ranks of the input data. The way different persons perceive television programs can be the basis not only for arranging the programs in an *n*–dimensional space but also for arranging the viewers in the same space.

Preference data can also be the basis for arranging people in *n*–dimensional space. A preference matrix of persons by programs can be used to generate a person-by-person matrix of Euclidean distances between people. This matrix can be input to a scaling program (e.g., TORSCA, POLYCON,[28] etc.), which will array the people points. It is also possible to use a rank-order preference matrix of persons by programs to array both programs and people in the same (joint) space. Needless to say, implementing these procedures is complex. The cited sources can serve as a guide to this approach.[29] There are definite limits as to the number of stimuli (objects plus respondents) that can be used in these techniques, and this is a major drawback in applying these techniques to segmentation analysis.

Q-technique

Q-technique is more than Q-factor analysis (correlating people), as Stephenson's[30] books indicate. Mechanically, the factor analytic aspects of the analysis are the same as obverse factor analysis, but the generation of the data sets it apart from traditional forms of analysis. Factor analysis, as we have seen, can be applied to many types of data — preference ratings of programs, attribute ratings for program, viewing choices, self-assessments as in life-style analysis and so on. Q-technique implies that people are responding to statements or other materials that allow respondents to project something about themselves into their responses.

At the heart of Q-methodology is the forced-choice method. The respondents rank order rather than rate many statements. To facilitate making the statements, respondents are asked to sort statements into a given number of classes on a quasi-normal frequency basis. The rows of the persons-by-statements matrix containing the rank values are correlated, then factored. The loadings in the rotated factor matrix indicate which respondents cluster together. Interpreting clusters is similar to cluster analyses, wherein cluster profiles are generated. In this case, prototypical sorts are generated by obtaining an average sort for a person most representative of each cluster.

Understanding Q-technique means understanding how statements are structured for Q studies. Fisher's methods for experimental designs provide a basis for composing a sample that represents the (hypothesized) chief variables assumed to be relevant to a given behavioral domain.[31] In the same fashion that people are selected to represent levels in a factorial design (e.g., two levels of sex — males, females; two levels of age — under and over 40), statements can be selected to represent the levels of factors. This implies that the researcher should have some theoretical basis for the study, rather than merely throwing together a bunch of statements to use (this would be an unstructured Q-sample).

As an example of the Q approach to audience segmentation, a study that the author conducted[32] using Q methodology will be discussed. Its basis was the functional purpose television plays in a person's life. A basic dimension on which statements were selected was whether they pertained primarily to program content or to noncontent-related reasons for viewing. Three types of noncontent areas were included: (a) escaping, (b) facilitating interaction, and (c) escaping boredom. Among content-related reasons were: (d) culture, (e) technical information, (f) keeping current, and (g) entertainment. Six statements were generated for each of the seven levels of the "Use Factor" (see Table 8-1). These statements were written by the author, although they need not have been; they could have been collected from articles or from short essays on "Why I Watch Television" written by a sample of viewers.

The statements were given to respondents who read them and separated them in three piles — descriptive of this other viewing, nondescriptive, and a neither category. Ultimately, the respondents had to sort the 42 statements into nine categories using the following distribution:

Most de-scriptive								Least de-scriptive
2	3	4	7	10	7	4	3	2

Factor analysis is the analytic technique most frequently used to determine the patterns

Table 8-1   Statements Reflecting Uses of Television

Statement Number	Category Number	
6	e	Watching television to learn about what stores to shop at
10	b	Watching television to give me something to talk about with my friends
14	b	Watching television with my family because it's a good way for the family to be together
16	c	Watching television because I am alone in the house
23	g	Watching television because TV is more interesting than other things I could do
24	b	Watching television to help fill in the lulls in conversation when company is visiting
26	g	Watching television because the programs I watch are very good
28	d	Watching television to listen to people with some of the finest minds in the country
29	g	Watching television because I enjoy it
30	a	Watching television to be alone when I can't be
31	c	Watching television because it requires so little effort
33	a	Watching television as a substitute for having company or going out to visit
35	a	Watching television because I'm too tired to visit with the family
37	g	Watching television for its entertainment value
38	a	Watching television to avoid having to think up things to say to others whom I may be with
42	d	Watching television to learn things that improve my mind
46	b	Watching television because other members of the family do
47	f	Watching television to stay in tune with new clothing fashions
49	c	Watching television when I have things to do that I don't want to do
51	e	Watching television to learn how to play sports better
54	c	Watching television because it occupies my time

Table 8-1   (cont.)

Statement Number	Category Number	
56	c	Watching television to pass an hour between other activities
57	c	Watching television because there is nothing else to do
59	f	Watching television to keep abreast of national and international events
60	f	Watching television to keep informed about new ideas
61	d	Watching television to see programs about science or history
63	d	Watching television to see symphony orchestras and ballet groups I wouldn't otherwise be able to see
66	d	Watching television to see programs about famous painters or sculptors
69	e	Watching television to learn about what products to buy
71	f	Watching television for in-depth coverage of specific topics
72	e	Watching television to learn what's on sale
77	e	Watching television to learn how to become handier around the house
78	d	Watching television to see fine plays
79	g	Watching television to see my favorite TV series
81	f	Watching television to keep up to date on local news
83	a	Watching television to avoid having to play with the children
88	b	Watching television because I can learn how to get along better in social situations
89	f	Watching television to find out about tomorrow's weather
91	b	Watching television when I have friends over because it's easier to spend time with others when I have the TV on
93	a	Watching television to avoid having to put up with anyone
95	g	Watching television because I like to watch my favorite TV personalities
97	e	Watching television to improve my ability at doing the things I like to do

of similarity among people in the data. Schlinger[33] suggests guidelines for determining from the loading which persons shall be used to represent which factors (a minimum loading of 3 × 1/√N [three times the standard error of a zero order correlation] and significant loadings squared being twice the squares of the two next largest loadings).

A matrix of the ranking of 42 statements by 29 persons was factored using a principle components analysis with varimax rotation (see Table 8-2). The underlined loadings are those that met the previously mentioned criteria.

The sorts of the persons selected to represent the factors are weighted in proportion to their loadings on the factors (see Schlinger and Stephenson[34]). These factor arrays represent prototypical sorts of a person with a high loading on each factor (see Table 8-3). Interpretation is made after ordering the statements from low to high for each factor type and reviewing the differences. It is helpful if the statements used in the sorts represent replications of factors in an experimental design. Then, both the statement and the level it represents in the experimental design aid in interpretation.

Table 8-2 Rotated Factor Loadings[a]

Respondents	I	II	III	IV	V	VI
1	15	29	17	− 09	<u>60</u>	06
2	16	06	01	11	<u>83</u>	06
3	− 02	23	04	50	64	23
4	31	07	− 10	07	09	15
5	22	57	− 01	38	45	− 14
6	40	30	19	<u>59</u>	− 02	05
7	40	27	− 07	16	46	56
8	46	47	40	18	05	28
9	<u>77</u>	12	− 00	25	10	− 16
10	<u>50</u>	03	− 01	66	02	00
11	− 25	<u>48</u>	18	13	35	18
12	65	− 15	01	34	26	08
13	<u>70</u>	02	31	25	23	− 02
14	16	− 02	21	09	13	<u>81</u>
15	21	16	32	<u>65</u>	26	04
16	24	01	<u>76</u>	13	22	15
17	− 05	06	19	− 04	03	<u>83</u>
18	75	06	05	− 01	12	47
19	13	<u>80</u>	14	18	17	− 22
20	<u>66</u>	21	41	17	− 21	24
21	<u>57</u>	50	31	16	16	11
22	37	<u>60</u>	12	11	40	31
23	<u>66</u>	12	39	15	16	06
24	<u>20</u>	14	<u>70</u>	20	05	10
25	17	25	<u>73</u>	13	− 04	31
26	13	33	19	<u>75</u>	09	06
27	52	38	44	05	32	− 09
28	10	<u>68</u>	07	25	06	41
29	<u>76</u>	<u>26</u>	30	10	06	15

[a]Decimal points omitted.

Table 8-3 Factor Score Arrays for Prototypical Factor Types for Six Factors

Statement Number	I	II	III	IV	V	VI
6	5.0	5.2	7.1	6.8	6.7	7.0
10	4.4	7.4	6.8	5.3	6.5	3.5
14	6.2	5.0	5.4	5.7	3.7	4.0
16	5.7	6.4	5.0	5.3	5.5	4.5
23	6.4	4.6	6.1	3.8	4.0	6.0
24	8.0	7.8	6.6	5.2	5.0	5.0
26	3.2	2.9	5.9	2.6	2.7	6.5
28	3.3	4.8	5.6	2.4	5.0	7.5
29	5.4	2.9	2.8	3.5	3.2	2.5
30	6.8	6.3	5.3	6.0	5.0	4.9
31	6.0	3.9	5.2	7.8	3.7	4.5
33	7.8	5.9	6.9	5.5	4.3	5.5
35	7.6	5.0	7.6	5.3	5.3	5.0
37	3.0	1.7	2.9	2.7	2.5	2.5
38	6.1	7.9	8.4	6.6	5.7	7.1
42	3.0	6.4	1.7	3.8	4.0	1.5
46	6.9	3.7	3.2	5.0	6.4	4.0
47	4.4	6.9	5.8	4.5	8.2	5.5
49	6.6	4.3	6.3	5.4	5.3	4.3
51	4.3	6.1	6.4	6.9	2.3	5.9
54	6.0	5.1	3.1	5.5	5.5	3.4
56	4.3	3.2	3.5	5.2	7.5	2.9
57	7.0	3.1	8.0	5.8	7.2	3.5
59	1.4	2.1	3.3	1.8	1.3	4.1
60	4.3	5.7	1.3	4.4	5.5	1.0
61	3.0	3.4	2.9	3.5	6.2	6.9
63	4.2	5.5	4.3	4.3	8.5	7.6
66	5.2	5.4	4.0	5.6	4.7	8.5
69	5.0	5.8	6.0	6.5	7.2	3.9
71	3.2	3.0	3.3	4.0	5.5	5.0
72	5.4	7.3	6.3	6.9	6.0	4.5
77	5.0	6.1	5.7	8.2	5.7	5.1
78	3.7	4.6	4.3	2.2	7.5	5.1
79	3.2	2.7	3.6	1.8	2.5	4.5
81	2.3	5.0	2.8	3.6	2.3	3.1
83	5.9	6.7	5.3	7.3	4.7	7.9
88	4.8	6.0	5.9	6.7	5.0	4.5
89	2.9	3.5	5.2	5.9	2.3	4.1
91	6.8	6.4	5.6	6.2	6.5	7.1
93	7.6	5.4	5.0	7.2	5.7	8.5
95	4.7	3.1	4.4	1.8	2.7	6.0
97	4.0	5.6	5.4	5.2	5.0	5.5

Neff and Cohen restate Stephenson's claim for the factorial approach to generating statements for Q studies:

First, it is possible to apply the powerful techniques of the analysis of variance to a single sorting array. Second, items have specified meanings (they represent the cells of the variance design). Third, the amount of error involved in sorting the items is also specified in the within-cell or replication variance.[35]

If several statements represent a level of a factor in an experimental design structure, any differences in categories to which these statements were sorted can be treated as error or randomness in sorting. This error can become the basis for determining whether respondents were internally consistent.

Neff and Cohen suggest analyzing the Q-sort data by treating the statements as replicates of the factors (statement categories). The uses of television referred to in the statements in Table 8-1 are treated as seven levels of the "Use Factor," each replicated six times. Following Neff and Cohen, the factorial design was primarily assumed to be a means to obtain systematic coverage of the various potential uses of television. To ascertain the degree to which the statements fit the factorial structure, a variance analysis of each person's Q-sort could be carried out.

Using the data reported in Gutman's[36] study, the first question to ask in this analysis concerned the internal consistency the respondents demonstrated in their Q-sorts. Neff and Cohen suggest using an F ratio of $(N/N\text{-}1)\sigma/MS_w$. The variance is fixed by the Q-sort constraints; therefore, the numerator of the F ratio equals 4.0 (σ comes from the distribution used in the Q study). If the denominator equals the within-cell variation, the more homogeneous the scores given statements within the same "use category," the larger the F ratio. With ∞, 35 (7 levels times 6 replications minus $1 - 7 \times [6 - 1] = 35$) degrees of freedom, the F ratio has to exceed $1/56$ for significance at the .05 level. Of the 29 subjects, 12 sorts were internally consistent; at the .10 level, 15 sorts had

significant internal consistency levels.

Two aspects of these Q-sorts are apparent — the statements probably reflect the groups to which they belong; and improvement or refinement in the statements is desirable. Neff and Cohen also suggest a revised method for carrying out Stephenson's suggested variance analysis of the Q-sorts. Using their procedures, in which the variance (4) becomes the denominator after adjustment by a sampling fraction — $(N - K)/(N - 1)$ — all the sorts were found to be significant. That is, at a gross level, all the sorts contained significant differences among the statement means by "use" category. Therefore, even though all subjects were not internally consistent, their sorts were not completely random.

Unfortunately, much of this significance seems due to the differences in social desirability among the various uses of television viewing. The forced nature of Q-sorting compensates for this to some extent.

One frequent criticism of Q-technique is the ipsative or forced-choice nature of the data. The sorting method results in rank order data wherein responses are not independent. Technically, these data violate correlational and analysis of variance assumptions. Many researchers feel strongly about this. Stephenson feels that large samples of statements reduce the impact of this problem (also see Kerlinger[37] on this point). Fletcher[38] has raised the issue of stability in criticizing Q-analysis as an audience segmentation technique. He makes the point that the correlations among respondents depend for their stability on the number of statements respondents are asked to sort. In the case of a sixty-four card sort, the 95 percent confidence interval ranges from .25 to .75 (the standard error of a correlation coefficient is $1/\sqrt{N\text{-}1}$; the confidence interval is $r \pm Z(SE)$ or $.5 \pm 2[1/\sqrt{64\text{-}1}]$).

As these are valid arguments presented both for and against the use of Q-technique, the reader will have to adopt a position he or she feels comfortable with. The author has found the forced-choice nature of the method useful in that people must choose how they want to represent themselves. It helps control for social desirability bias and other forms of response bias. Of course, ranking does eliminate elevation (mean level of response on a scale from consideration as well as scatter standard deviation). The researcher interested in comparative levels of response on life-style items for different viewer groups is advised not to use ipsative measures such as these. Kerlinger and others feel that the large number of statements used in Q-sorts reduces the impact of the interdependence created by the ranking procedure on the degrees of freedom.

Summary

This essay discussed many ideas about audience segmentation and techniques for carrying out audience segmentation research. Readers interested in audience segmentation must become proficient in at least two areas. The first area is substantive, involving knowledge of human behavior, how people function, and what role viewing or listening plays in their lives. The second area is technical, including the techniques discussed here.

This essay introduces the application of these techniques and indicates what the researcher is attempting to do when segmenting audiences and how the various statistical techniques relate to those objectives.

Although the purpose behind the segmentation attempt will dictate its approach, there are two basic approaches. The researcher can segment audience members on their behavior and use demographic and psychographic variables as profile data. In the reverse approach, audience segments created by using demographic and psychographic variables are examined for their differential viewing or listening behavior.

The author wishes to leave the reader with one overriding thought—people try to make the best choices they can. If we cannot understand these choices, the fault lies with our methods, not with the people. Finding meaningful, actionable audience segments is not easy. The researcher must bring to it all he or she knows about human behavior. All perspectives, from communication theory to psychology, sociology, anthropology, and consumer behavior, have to be brought to bear on the problem if success is to be achieved.

Endnotes

1. Ronald E. Frank, William F. Massy, and Yoram Wind, *Market Segmentation* (Englewood Cliffs, N.J.: Prentice-Hall, 1972), 27.
2. Jonathan Gutman, "Self-Concepts and Television Viewing among Women," *Public Opinion Quarterly* 37 (1973): 388–397.
3. G. J. Goodhardt, A. S. C. Ehrenberg, and M. A. Collins, *The Television Audience: Patterns of Viewing* (Great Britain: Saxon House, 1974); Ronald E. Frank and Marshall G. Greenberg, *An Interest-Based Segmentation Study of Television Audiences* (Marketing Department Working Paper Series No. 79–003: The Wharton School, Philadelphia, Pa., 1978); Ronald E. Frank, James C. Beckwell, and James D. Clokey, "Television Program Types," *Journal of Marketing Research* 8 (1967): 204–211; Dennis H. Gensch and B. Ranganathan, "Evaluation of Television Program Context for the Purpose of Proportional Segmentation," *Journal of Marketing Research* 11 (1974): 390–398; Ronald E. Frank and Marshall G. Greenberg, "Zooming in on TV Audiences," *Psychology Today* 13 (October 1979): 92–103.
4. G. J. Goodhardt and A. S. C. Ehrenberg, "Duplication of Television Viewing Between and Within Channels," *Journal of Marketing Research* 6 (1969): 169–178.
5. Ibid., 177.
6. Robert S. Header, Jay E. Klompmaker, and Roland T. Rust, "The Duplication of Viewing Law and Television Media Scheduling," *Journal of Marketing Research* 16 (1979): 333–340.
7. R. J. Rummel, *Applied Factor Analysis* (Evanston, Ill.: Northwestern University Press, 1970), 301.
8. Rummel, op. cit.

9. L. Cronbach and G. Gleser, "Assessing Similarity Between Profiles," *Psychological Bulletin* 54 (1953): 456–473.

10. Rummel, op. cit., chap. 22.

11. Timothy Joyce and C. Charron, "Classifying Market Survey Respondents," *Applied Statistics* 50 (1976): 191–215.

12. Rummel, op. cit.

13. Richard L. Gorsuch, *Factor Analysis* (Philadelphia: W. B. Saunders Company, 1974); see also James R. Smith and Roger K. Blashfield, "Reporting Factor Analysis in Mass Media Research: A Review of Methods," *Journal of Broadcasting* 21:2 (1977): 187–197.

14. Frank and Greenberg, 1978, op. cit.

15. Kathryn E. A. Villani, "Personality/Life Style and Television Viewing Behavior," *Journal of Marketing Research* 12 (1975): 432–439.

16. Villani, op. cit., 433.

17. Joseph T. Plummer, "Life Style Patterns," *Journal of Broadcasting* 16 (1971–72): 79–89.

18. Villani, op. cit.

19. Frank, Beckwell, and Clokey, op. cit.; Gensch and Ranganathan, op. cit.

20. A. S. C. Ehrenberg and G. V. Goodhardt, *Factor Analysis: Limitations and Alternatives* (Cambridge, Mass.: Marketing Science Institute, 1976), 35.

21. W. J. Dixon and M. B. Brown, eds., *BMDP-77, Biomedical Computer Programs—P Series* (Berkeley: University of California Press, 1977).

22. Frank and Greenberg, 1978, op. cit.

23. Plummer, op. cit.

24. Plummer, op. cit., 86.

25. William F. Massy, "Discriminant Analysis of Audience Characteristics," *Journal of Advertising Research* 5 (1965): 39–48.

26. Richard M. Johnson, "Multiple Discriminant Analysis: Marketing Research Applications," in Jagdish N. Sheth, ed., *Multivariate Methods for Market and Survey Research* (Chicago: American Marketing Association, 1977), 65–79.

27. James T. Lull, Lawrence M. Johnson, and Carol E. Sweeny, "Audiences for Contemporary Radio Formats," *Journal of Broadcasting* 22 (1978): 439–454.

28. F. W. Young, *Polycon Users Manual—A Fortran-IV Program for Polynomial Conjoint Analysis* (Chapel Hill, N.C.: L. L. Thurstone Psychometric Laboratory Report No. 104, 1972).

29. P. E. Green and F. J. Carmone, *Multidimensional Scaling and Related Techniques in Marketing Analysis* (Boston: Allyn and Bacon, Inc., 1970); P. E. Green and V. R. Rao, *Applied Multidimensional Scaling: A Comparison of Approaches and Algorithms* (New York: Holt, Rinehart & Winston, 1972).

30. William Stephenson, *The Study of Behavior* (Chicago: The University of Chicago Press, 1953); William Stephenson, *The Play Theory of Mass Communication* (Chicago: The University of Chicago Press, 1967); see also Fred N. Kerlinger, *Foundations of Behavioral Research* (New York: Holt, Rinehart & Winston, 1973), chap. 34.

31. Stephenson, op. cit., 1953, chap. 4.

32. Jonathan Gutman, "Television Viewer Types: A Q Analysis," *Journal of Broadcasting* 22 (1978): 505–516.

33. Mary Jane Schlinger, "Cues on Q-Technique," *Journal of Advertising Research* 9 (1961): 53–60.

34. Schlinger, op. cit., 57; Stephenson, op. cit., 1953, 174–179.

35. W. S. Neff and J. Cohen, "A Method for the Analysis of the Structure and Internal Consistency of Q-Sort Arrays," *Psychological Bulletin* 68 (1967): 361–368.

36. Gutman, op. cit., 1978.

37. Kerlinger, op. cit., 595.

38. James E. Fletcher, "Evaluation of Foley's Q-Sort As a Technique for Audience Segmentation," *Western Speech* 39 (1975): 13–19.

9
Sustaining Causal Inference

Joseph R. Dominick

Broadcasting research, like all social science research, is concerned with explanation. A major part of the explanatory process makes cause–effect statements about specific variables in the environment. One method of arriving at cause–effect relationships is the experiment. By manipulating certain independent variables, an investigator can usually isolate the individual effects of separate antecedent variables on a single dependent variable. By using randomization, the experimenter can rule out with reasonable certainty possible unknown disrupting influences. Thus, after carrying out a well-designed experiment, the investigator can draw causal inferences on the basis of the results with some confidence.[1]

Unfortunately, this situation becomes more complex when studying observational or correlational data, especially in the survey situation where many unknown and outside influences usually operate. It is difficult to rule out the importance of these variables through randomization, and the investigator usually does not have adequate information about the temporal sequence involved. Unlike the laboratory situation, the survey researcher usually does not positively know whether variable *A* preceded variable *B*, or vice versa. Because much broadcasting research falls into the survey category, this essay presents a brief overview of the problem of drawing causal inferences from correlational data. Even though correlation does not prove causation, the survey researcher's situation is not hopeless. Thus, this essay first discusses several important concepts underlying the notion of causality and then briefly discusses commonly used statistical procedures that might sustain a causal inference based on nonexperimental data.

The Meaning of Cause and Effect

For an extended discussion of the philosophical implications of the concepts *cause* and *effect*, readers should consult the many writings on these topics.[2]

In general, saying that one event "causes" another posits a crucial link between these two events. A change in the cause variable directly produces a change in the effect variable. This change in the cause variable can be used to explain and understand the change in the effect variable. Thus, if we set a lighted match in a pile of gunpowder, and the powder explodes, we can say that the heat generated by the match and not some other factor is responsible for the explosion.

Many writers have examined the cause-effect relationship by introducing the idea that certain conditions are *necessary* for others to follow and that some conditions are *sufficient* for others to follow. A necessary condition is one that must be present for some subsequent event to occur, although such a condition does not guarantee that the subsequent event will happen. For instance, being at least eighteen years old is necessary for a person to vote (the subsequent event), but being at least eighteen does not guarantee that the individual will indeed vote. On the other hand, a *sufficient* condition is one that will always result in a subsequent event's occurrence. For example, arriving late at school may be a sufficient condition for being sent to the principal's office. Of course, other factors, such as being unruly in class, might also culminate in a trip to the same office. Thus, arriving late is a sufficient but not a necessary cause.

Two additional considerations complicate matters. In the first place, most variables used in mass communication research are not as neat and dichotomous as those in the above examples. Instead, they tend to be continuously distributed. Several writers have persuasively argued that where we dichotomize these variables can lead to substantially different conclusions about the nature of a causal relationship.[3] Moreover, it is common to use statements of probability in discussing cause and effect. For instance, if you are exposed to someone with the flu, your chances of coming down with this illness are increased. We might say that such exposure "causes" you to become ill, although not all people so exposed will contract the flu. Similarly, running a stop sign increases the chances that a driver will be involved in a traffic accident. In this sense, running stop signs "causes" accidents, even though not all drivers who run stop signs are involved in mishaps. Consequently, this activity is neither a sufficient nor a necessary cause. We can now see that determining whether one event causes another is not easy. Nonetheless, scientists have developed a useful formal system for demonstrating cause and effect, even though it does not satisfy all the issues raised here.

Conditions for Demonstrating Cause and Effect

Time Order

We can speak of causation only when the cause precedes the effect. For example, we might want to know why people perspire. From our observations, we notice that when the temperature increases, people start to perspire. Temperature increase preceded perspiration. This is one reason we know that increased temperature causes perspiration rather than the other way around.

In survey research, many variables are not easily classified into temporal order. When we collect data during a survey, our measurement of variables is usually simultaneous. Sometimes we can use logic to argue that A precedes B. For example, when correlating years of education with income level, we can usually assume that education came before income level. On the other hand, some cases are not this clear-cut. When studying the relationship between IQ and athletic ability, it would be difficult to argue which came first. Additionally, in some situations, two variables seem to cause one another. We might, for example, expect that social isolation might cause increased television viewing; but it is also possible that excessive viewing might prompt social isolation. Such situations are examples of *reciprocal causation*. There seems to be a clear back and forth interplay: a change in A produces a change in B, which, in turn, affects A. Without several surveys at different times, it would be difficult to assess the relative strength of each causal direction.

Association

Causation can be said to occur only if some tendency for a change in *A* results in a change in *B*. If temperature increase did not produce an increase in perspiration, there would be considerable doubt as to the cause-and-effect relationship between these two variables. Thus, when we say that two variables are associated, we mean that a change in one is accompanied by an anticipated and predictable change in the second. Various correlational statistics are useful in determining the degree of association between two variables. Remember, however, that not all variables that are related in a statistical sense are related in a cause–effect fashion; but a necessary condition of determining cause and effect is mutual association.

Alternative Causes

Before we can attribute effects to causes, we must fulfill another necessary condition. In order to infer causation, we must eliminate all other possible causal interpretations. For example, consider the situation in which three different groups of individuals are given large quantities of scotch and soda, brandy and soda, and whiskey and soda, respectively. On the basis of the first two criteria mentioned in this section, we might plausibly conclude that soda causes inebriation. The drinking of soda preceded the inebriation, and the amount of soda consumed was related to increased inebriation. The actual cause of the inebriation, however, was due to the presence of a hidden third variable — alcohol — in the process.

This example illustrates that a causal relationship can be questioned if it is possible to find another causal variable that makes more sense in explaining the phenomenon. An important function of theory is to help us discover and test important alternative variables as other causes of the concept under investigation. It is true, however, that we cannot investigate the many alternative causes and thus can never conclusively prove that a causal relationship exists. Nonetheless, if we can rule out plausible alternatives, then we can have more faith in the causal validity of the relationship under consideration.

Causal Processes

Before discussing the particular statistical techniques for sustaining causal inference, let us consider the problem's possible complexity. It is unlikely that a single independent variable will be the sole cause of a dependent variable. Human behavior and attitudes are usually too complex to allow for such a simple explanation.

Indirect and Multiple Causation

In broadcasting research, as in most social sciences, the variables we want to explain often involve multiple causes. As we shall see, we can follow certain statistical procedures to test for the importance of the role of several independent variables. Even though we consider the possibility of multiple causation, we should never expect to explain fully all the variance in our dependent variable. The inevitable errors in sampling, data collection, and measurement will reduce our capacity to explain.

Additionally, causation may be indirect. An independent variable, *A*, might affect dependent variable *C* directly *and* indirectly, through another independent variable, *B*. In studying cause and effect, we usually try to distinguish between variables having a direct effect on the dependent variable and those having both direct and indirect effects.

Arrow Diagrams

A common way to diagram causal processes is to use a system of arrows. An arrow indicates that one variable is thought to affect another; the direction of the arrow shows the presumed direction of influence. (We will later enlarge on these arrow diagrams until they become path diagrams.) Figure 9-1 shows a simplified version of a model that might be used to explain a child's prosocial behaviors. Setting aside the substantive validity of the model, let us examine the usefulness of arrow diagrams in explaining a complicated causal relationship.

Child's
Academic
Achievement

Parent's
Education
Level

Child's
Prosocial
Behaviors

Child's Viewing
of Prosocial
TV Programs

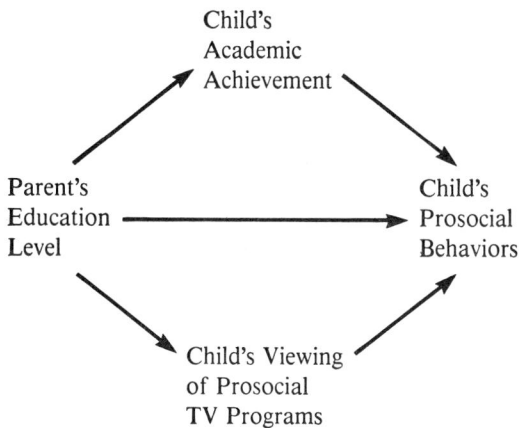

Figure 9-1   Sample arrow diagram.

Parents' education is seen to be a direct cause of the performance of the child's prosocial behaviors and also exerts indirect effects through its influence on the child's viewing of prosocial TV programs. Academic achievement and viewing prosocial TV are posited to be in a causal relationship. When planning causal analysis, such useful arrow diagrams encourage the researcher to think in causal terms and to list all the relevant variables that can be included in an explanation and to begin to trace the possible causal processes.

We should now emphasize that the techniques of sustaining causal inference discussed below are not magical manipulations that will produce order and clarity from a mass of data. These techniques depend on sound theory for guidance. Identifying the key variables in an arrow diagram and describing the causal patterns are difficult and require the help of a well-developed theory. Thus, inferring cause and effect using the techniques presented below is not recommended for exploratory research.

Having looked at some problems and promises of causal analysis, let us now examine some commonly used techniques. The first pair of techniques are useful in cross-sectional analysis, where the investigator has data from only one time period. The second set of techniques has been used when longitudinal data were available. The following sections presume a knowledge of basic correlational and regression techniques.

Partial Correlation

The easiest technique to use in sustaining a causal inference is partial correlation. Recall that one condition for cause and effect was mutual association. If it can be shown that the first-order correlation between the two variables was spurious (both the independent variable and the dependent variable were related to a third variable that induced a common relationship), then we can reject the notion of one causing the other. (The formulae for computing partial correlation coefficients can be found in most basic statistics texts.) Remember, however, that the causal model posited by the researcher will bear on the interpretation of the partial r. For example, should the disappearance of the correlation be interpreted as supporting an intervening model of cause (where A causes B, which, in turn, causes C) or a spurious model (where B causes both A and C)?[4]

Path Analysis

Path analysis was developed by geneticist Sewall Wright as a technique for studying the direct and indirect influences of variables presumed to be causes of other variables assumed to be effects. In survey research, where the investigator cannot manipulate or randomize, interpretations must be made with caution. Correlations can suggest cause–effect linkages, but explanation is arrived at on the basis of theory and logical analysis. Once the analysis has been conducted, the investigator must decide whether the data are consistent with an explanatory scheme. If they are inconsistent, then doubt is cast on the theory. If they are consistent, the explanatory model is supported. This, however, is not the same as proving a theory. For example, it is plausible that the same data can be consistent with two contradictory models. To use a concrete illustration, here are two competing models:

(1) $A \rightarrow B \rightarrow C$ (2) $B \rightarrow A \rightarrow C$

Model 1 suggests that A causes B, which, in turn, causes C. Model 2 suggests that B causes A. Correlations among the variables in these models could be consistent with both theories. Suppose, however, that A precedes B in time. Support might then be inferred for Model 1. In any case, the reason for deciding in favor of this particular explanation resides outside the data. Thus, path analysis and the other techniques discussed below cannot "discover" causes. They are more useful in testing theory than in generating it.

Path Models and Diagrams

Consider the causal diagram in Figure 9-2. The variables with no straight arrows drawn to them (X_1 and X_2) are called *exogenous* variables. Variables with arrows pointing to them (X_3, X_4, and X_5) are *endogenous* variables. (Endogenous variables may also have arrows originating from them.) The curved double-headed arrow between X_1 and X_2 indicates that these variables may be correlated with one another but not causally linked. In Figure 9-2, W, Y, and Z represent *latent* (or disturbance) variables. Path analysis assumes that the variation in the endogenous variables is never completely explained by the causal antecedents. Thus, while X_3 and X_4 explain some variation in X_5, other variables, not accounted for in the system, are also causing X_5. W, Y, and Z represent the causal variables missing from this analysis. These latent variables are important because under specified conditions,[5] the arrow from the latent variables to the endogenous variable is identical to the familiar coefficient of alienation, $1-R^2$, where R is the multiple correlation coefficient for a particular endogenous variable. In addition, the presence or absence of intercorrelations among the latent terms has important implications for the type of causal system posited.

Recursive systems   Figure 9-2 represents a particular type of causal system. Note that the

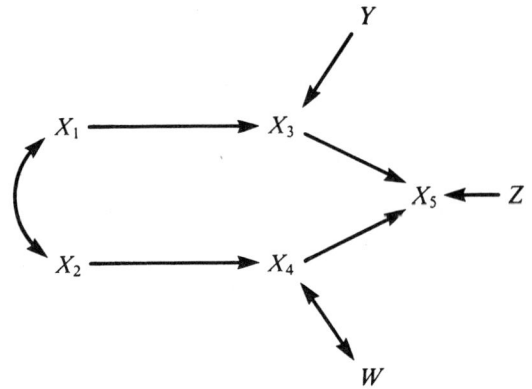

Figure 9-2   Path diagram illustrating a recursive model.

linkages are one-way; there is no mutual association among variables. The model posits that X_1 influences X_3 but that X_3 does not influence X_1. When the system is made up entirely of one-way linkages, and there are no correlations among the latent variables, we have a *recursive* system. Recursive systems have the simplest structure and require the easiest mathematics. Unfortunately, these advantages are offset by the presence of the strong assumptions that no mutual influence is present and that the latent variables are not correlated.

Rules for Reading a Path Diagram Wright's simple system for reading a path diagram consists of two definitions and three instructions. The definitions are: (1) any correlation between two variables can be decomposed into a sum of simple and compound paths; and (2) a compound path is equal to the products of the simple paths comprising it. The three instructions are:

1. No path may pass through the same variable more than once.
2. No path may go backward on (against the direction of) an arrow after the path has gone forward on a different arrow.
3. No path may pass through a double-headed arrow more than once in a single path.

A path coefficient can be thought of as a measurement representing the independent effect of each causal variable on each endoge-

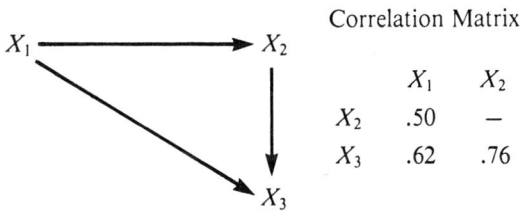

Figure 9-3 Path diagram for three variables.

Correlation Matrix

	X_1	X_2
X_2	.50	—
X_3	.62	.76

nous variable, provided everything else is held constant. Put another way, the path coefficient between variable *A* (assumed cause) and variable *B* (assumed effect) tells how much of a change in *B* will result from a one unit change in *A*, assuming everything else is held constant. The usual symbol for a path coefficient is *p* with two subscripts. The first subscript indicates the effect (dependent) variable; the second, the cause (independent) variable. Thus, in Figure 9-2, p_{31} indicates the direct effect of variable X_1 on variable X_3.

Finding Path Coefficients Path coefficients can be found in a straightforward manner using the familiar concepts of multiple regression. In fact, path coefficients are usually expressed as standardized regression coefficients. Consider the simple three variable path diagram in Figure 9-3.

Each endogenous variable (X_2 and X_3) can be represented by an equation consisting of the variables on which it is assumed to depend and a term representing the latent variables. The letter *U* represents these latent factors. Thus, in Figure 9-3, we can write three regression equations:

$$X_1 = U_1$$

$$X_2 = a + b_1 X_1 + U_2$$

$$X_3 = a + b_1 X_1 + b_2 X_2 + U_3$$

where *a* is the intercept point and the *b*'s are the appropriate betas as used in ordinary multiple regression. Now we will standardize our variables, setting $a = 0$ and rewriting the form of the equations as follows:

$$Z_1 = U_1$$

$$Z_2 = p_{21} Z_1 + U_2$$

$$Z_3 = p_{31} Z_1 + p_{32} Z_2 + U_3$$

where the *p*'s are the standardized regression coefficients. We assume that the latent factors are not intercorrelated, and that they do not correlate with the variables in the equations in which they appear. With the information from Figure 9-3 and these equations, we can calculate the *p*'s for this model. First, let us take p_{21}, the coefficient indicating the effect of X_1 on X_2. Recall that:

$$r_{12} = \frac{1}{N} \Sigma Z_1 Z_2$$

Substituting the above equation for Z_2 in the *r* formula:

$$r_{12} = \frac{1}{N} \Sigma Z_1 (p_{21} Z_1 + U_2)$$

or

$$r_{12} = p_{21} \frac{\Sigma Z_1 Z_1}{N} + \frac{\Sigma Z_1 U_2}{N}$$

But

$$\frac{\Sigma Z_1 Z_1}{N}$$

is simply the variance of a set of standard scores that equals one, and the correlation between variable 1 and U_2 is assumed to be zero. Thus,

$$r_{12} = p_{21}$$

That is, the path coefficient from X_1 to X_2 equals r_{12}, which can be found from inspecting the correlation matrix. Note that two paths lead to variable X_3 (p_{31} and p_{32}).

$$r_{1-3} = \frac{1}{N} \Sigma Z_1 Z_3$$

Substituting for Z_3 and simplifying by omitting the latent variable yields:

$$r_{13} = \frac{1}{N} \Sigma Z_1 (p_{31} Z_1 + p_{32} Z_2)$$

or

$$r_{13} = p_{31} \Sigma \frac{Z_1 Z_1}{N} + p_{32} \frac{\Sigma Z_1 Z_2}{N}$$

$$r_{13} = p_{31} + p_{32} r_{32}$$

We can read r_{13} and r_{12} from the correlation matrix, but this equation still has two unknowns and cannot be solved. But it is possible to construct a second equation involving the same unknowns and treat the two as simultaneous equations and solve them using techniques of basic algebra. The second equation:

$$r_{23} = \frac{1}{N} \Sigma Z_2 Z_3$$

Again substituting:

$$r_{23} = \frac{1}{N} \Sigma Z_2 (p_{31} Z_{21} + p_{32} Z_2)$$

$$= p_{31} \frac{\Sigma Z_2 Z_1}{N} + p_{32} \frac{\Sigma Z_2 Z_2}{N}$$

$$r_{23} = p_{31} r_{12} + p_{32}$$

As a consequence:

$$r_{12} = p_{21}$$
$$r_{23} = p_{31} r_{12} + p_{32}$$
$$r_{13} = p_{31} + p_{32} r_{12}$$

From the data in the correlation matrix, it is now possible to solve for the *p*'s.

$$p_{21} = r_{12} = .5$$

and

$$.62 = p_{31} + (.5) p_{32}$$
$$.76 = (.5) p_{31} + p_{32}$$

Solving these two simultaneous equations gives us:

$$p_{31} = .32$$
$$p_{32} = .60$$

and these values have been substituted in Figure 9-4.

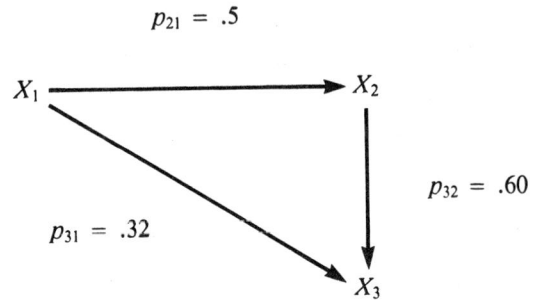

$$p_{21} = .5$$
$$p_{31} = .32$$
$$p_{32} = .60$$

Figure 9-4   Path diagram with path coefficients computed from data in Figure 9-3.

Analyzing a Correlation

One advantage of path analysis is that it allows us to decompose a given correlation into its direct and indirect components. A procedure for analyzing correlations is illustrated by applying it to Figure 9-4. Recall the original equations:

$$r_{12} = p_{21}$$
$$r_{13} = p_{31} + p_{32} r_{12}$$
$$r_{23} = p_{31} r_{12} + p_{32}$$

A glance at Figure 9-4 reveals that variable 2 is affected solely by variable 1. The r_{12} relationship is due completely to the direct effect of variable 1 on 2, as indicated by p_{21}. Now examine the correlation between variables 1 and 3. Since $p_{21} = r_{12}$, we can substitute and obtain:

$$r_{13} = p_{31} + p_{32} p_{21}$$

Clearly, r_{13} is composed of two elements: a direct effect (p_{31}) and an indirect effect through variable 2 $(p_{32} p_{21})$. Using the same procedure for r_{23} yields

$$r_{23} = p_{31} p_{21} + p_{32}$$

As a general rule, the total indirect effect in a correlation is found by subtracting its direct effect from the correlation between it and the dependent variable. Table 9-1 summarizes the findings for our current example.

Table 9-1 Decomposition of Correlations in Figure 9-3

Bivariate relationship	X_1X_2	X_1X_3	X_2X_3
Original r	.50	.62	.76
Direct causal effect	.50	.32	.60
Indirect causal	—	.30	—
Total causal effect	.50	.62	.60
Noncausal (spurious)	—	—	.16

Note that the decomposition of r_{23} led us to calculate the quantity $p_{32}p_{21} = .16$. This is a legitimate mathematical operation, but it is not a substantive effect, since it violates the causal ordering among variables. According to Figure 9-4, X_1 influences X_2, and not the reverse. Thus, .16 is listed as a noncausal (spurious) component of the total X_2X_3 relationship. Any interpretation of indirect effects must be made with the original model in mind. Not all indirect effects may be meaningful under the posited model.

Model Testing

Another application of path analysis is to determine whether a pattern of correlations is consistent with a specific model. As we have seen, using path coefficients, we can generate the entire correlation matrix for all the variables in the system. Caution: When a given theoretical model has all variables connected by paths, the original correlation matrix will be reproduced regardless of the causal model employed by the investigator. As a result, reproducing the correlation matrix when all the p's are used will not help a researcher choose a specific model. But what if the researcher were able to delete certain paths (in effect, setting $p = 0$)? With this technique, the correlation between two variables whose connecting path is deleted is seen as composed entirely of indirect effects. If, after deletion, the p's closely reconstruct the original r matrix, one might conclude that the original pattern of correlations is more consistent with the revised and more parsimonious model. This does not mean, however, that the model is true. In many instances, competing models might be equally parsimonious and equally successful in reconstructing the r matrix.

If after the deletion of some paths, we find large discrepancies between the original r matrix and our reconstruction, we conclude the new model is not appropriate. We should also keep in mind that there are no rules as to what constitutes a "good" approximation of the original matrix. Some writers suggest a discrepancy of $< .05$ as a rule of thumb, but even this could be exceeded in some situations in which the theoretical justification was strong enough.[6]

Perhaps the best way to illustrate this technique of model fitting is with a hypothetical example. (The data in this example are borrowed from political science.) Consider the three competing models of a four-variable relationship diagramed in Figure 9-5. Table 9-2 contains the original r matrix.

For simplicity, we will report the path coefficients directly. First let us examine Model A. The relevant p's are $p_{21} = .50$ and $p_{31} = .74$. From the model, $r_{23} = p_{31}p_{21} = (.74)(.50) = .37$. Since the original r as seen in Table 9-2 was .64, it seems apparent that this model will not do an adequate job. Turning next to Model B, we will try to reproduce r_{31}. In this model, $p_{32} = .64$ and $p_{21} = .50$. From the diagram, $r_{13} = p_{32}p_{21} = (.64)(.50) = .32$. Since the orig-

Figure 9-5 Three competing models for the interpretation of a causal system.

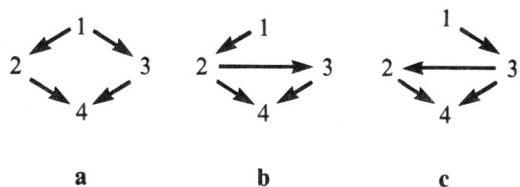

a   b   c

Table 9-2   Correlations among Variables in Figure 9-5

	X1	X2	X3
X2	.50		
X3	.74	.64	
X4	.65	.72	.82

inal *r* was .74, this model is ripe for rejection.

Next, let us examine Model C. The relevant *p*'s are $p_{31} = .74$, $p_{23} = .64$, $p_{42} = .33$, and $p_{43} = .61$. Reproducing r_{12}:

$$r_{12} = p_{31}p_{23} = (.74)(.64) = .47$$

$$\text{(original } r = .50)$$

So far, so good.

Reproducing r_{14} (note the total number of possible paths):

$$r_{14} = p_{42}p_{23}p_{31} + p_{43}p_{31}$$

$$= (.33)(.64)(.74) + (.61)(.74)$$

$$= .61 \text{ (original } r = .65)$$

Given the small discrepancies, Model C seems most appropriate.

Nonrecursive Systems

This discussion has assumed a causal system with a simple structure. Figure 9-6 shows that this path diagram incorporates a new feature.

Figure 9-6   Causal model of a nonrecursive system.

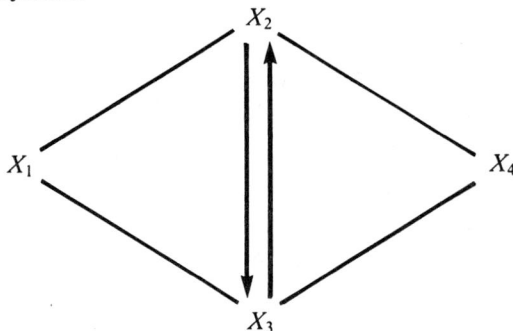

Variables X_2 and X_3 are linked by reciprocal or mutual causation. They both affect each other.

Unfortunately, the presence of nonrecursive systems such as that in Figure 9-6 makes it impossible to use the standard least squares regression procedures, and new techniques must be used to estimate the path coefficients. It is possible to use matrix algebra to calculate these estimations, but a discussion of this technique is beyond the scope of this essay. Readers interested in pursuing this topic should consult the reading list presented by Capella.[7]

Cautions in Path Analysis

A potential user of path analysis should remember several cautions when deciding to use and in interpreting the results of this technique. One problem is multicolinearity (highly correlated independent variables). The presence of highly related predictor variables may lead to sizable standard errors for the regression coefficients. In addition, path analysis is susceptible to wrong interpretation if there is low measurement reliability. Using unreliable measurements would affect calculation of slopes, thus giving wrong estimations of the path coefficients. This difficulty is compounded, because one variable measured with low reliability can affect the estimate of several path coefficients. Lastly, there are situations where the unstandardized regression coefficients may be more appropriate to use than the standardized coefficients.[8]

Examples from Broadcasting Research

Path analysis has not been extensively used in broadcasting research probably due more to the rudimentary state of theory than to a lack of methodological skill. Nonetheless, it may be useful to examine one or two of the existing examples to see the technique's actual applications. LeRoy and Ungurait[9] present a path model to account for the reasons behind an individual's voluntary contact with a broadcast station; they found that education was a key variable in the process. Christiansen[10] used path analysis to specify the conditions under which television role models were likely to be important sources of information for adolescent job aspirations. While the final model was not very successful in explaining a great deal of variation in the dependent variable, the path analysis findings did support much of the earlier research results. Johnson[11] constructed a path analysis of the influence of several antecedent variables on the acquisition of political information. Even though television availability had some direct effect on the dependent variable, the most potent predictor variable was the level of family politicization (see Figure 9-7).

Panel Data

In some broadcasting research situations, an investigator has measured two (or more) variables on a number of individuals at two (or more) times. This approach is the longitudinal or panel technique. At least two different approaches are appropriate for sustaining a causal inference in this situation.

Multiple Regression

The first technique uses ordinary multiple regression analysis. Multiple regression equations can be constructed to calculate the strength of a relationship between a presumed dependent variable at Time 2 and presumed predictor variables at Time 1. The situation is then reversed, and the corresponding *beta* weights can be examined to see if they are consistent with a specific causal ordering.

Cross-Lagged Correlation

Another research technique appropriate for sustaining a chain of causal inference from panel data is cross-lagged correlation (also referred to as time-lagged correlation). Examine Figure 9-8 and assume that we have two different variables (A and B) measured at two different times; six possible correlations are present. The correlations between variables at the same time (rA_1B_1 and rA_2B_2) are *synchronous* correlations. Correlations between the same variable at different times are *auto correlations*. Of most interest are the correlations along the diagonal, the cross-lagged correlations (rA_1B_2 and rB_1A_2). Comparing these two correlations allows us to answer this question: Is A a stronger cause of B than B is of A? If, indeed, A is a stronger cause of B, then we would expect that $rA_1B_2 > rB_1A_2$. Conversely, if B causes A, then $rB_1A_2 > rA_1B_2$. This is because an effect should be more correlated with a

Figure 9-7 Johnson's model of politicization. (Norris Johnson, "Television and Politicization: A Test of Competing Models," *Journalism Quarterly* Vol. 50 (1973): p. 455. Reprinted by permission from Summer 1982 *Journalism Quarterly.*

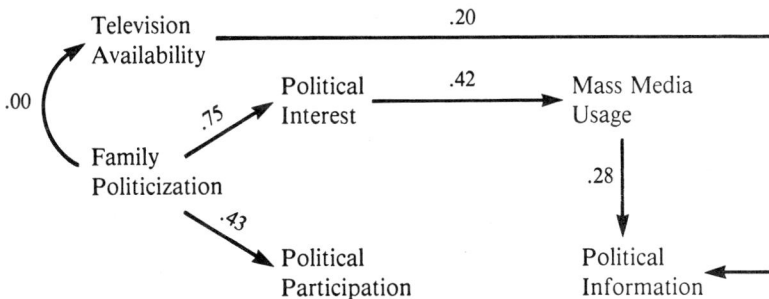

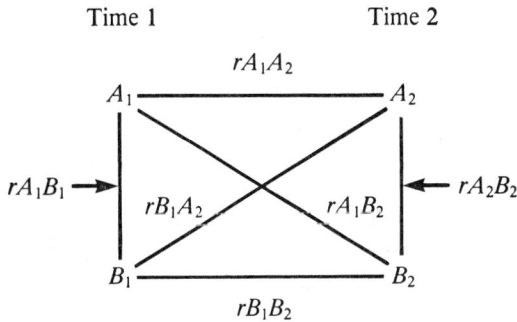

Figure 9-8 Model for cross-lagged correlation.

prior cause than with a subsequent cause. Note that this technique does not establish A as the sole cause of B. It simply allows for a comparison between relative causal hypotheses.

· Even though this logic has certain intuitive appeal, cross-lagged correlation should be used with caution. To illustrate, let us redraw Figure 9-8, but we will adopt the path analysis notation discussed in the previous section (see Figure 9-9).

According to the rules of path analysis, the correlations rA_1B_2 and rB_1A_2 can be analyzed as follows:

$$rA_1B_2 = pB_2A_1 + rA_1B_1 \, pB_2B_1$$

$$rB_1A_2 = pA_2B_1 + rA_1B_1 \, pA_2A_1$$

Obviously, the cross-lagged coefficients are not simple functions of their underlying causal parameters, pB_2A_1 and pA_2B_1. For example,

Figure 9-9 Path analysis model for cross-lagged correlation.

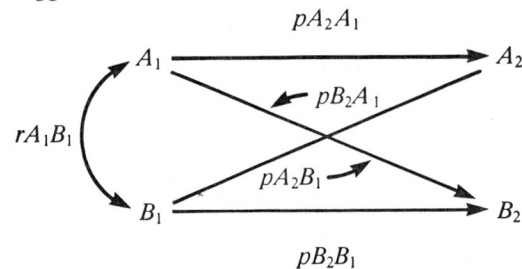

let us fill in path coefficients, as displayed in Figure 9-10.

Calculating the correlation coefficients from the p's gives $rA_1B_2 = .72$ and $rB_1A_2 = .48$, leading to a conclusion opposite from that of the path diagram. Because of this problem, some writers have recommended that the cross-lagged correlations should be compared only after partialling out the initial state of the variables. This procedure would seem indicated, especially when much of an individual's score on A_2 or B_2 is due to A_1 or B_1. The conclusion as to the relative effects of the variables would then be based on comparing partial r's ($rA_1B_2 \cdot B_1$, and $rB_1A_2 \cdot A_1$). This technique bears some similarities to the approach of path analysis.[12]

Other problems must also be considered. Changes in the reliability of measurement of the variables may influence the interpretation of the cross-lagged r's. If one variable increases in reliability from Time 1 to Time 2, all other things being equal, there is a chance it will mistakenly be assumed to be an effect rather than a cause. For example, in Figure 9-8, if A_2 is measured more reliably than A_1, all correlations involving A_2 will be higher than those including A_1, including $rB_1A_2 > rA_1B_2$. Because of this, several researchers have urged that a "correction for communality" should be incorporated into the calculations.[13]

To make matters murkier, it is not necessarily true that only two causal hypotheses are in competition ($A \rightarrow B$; $B \rightarrow A$). A causal relationship can be either positive or negative. An increase in A can result in an increase in B or a decrease in B. Thus, in actuality four hypotheses must be logically considered: $A \xrightarrow{+} B$; $A \rightarrow$

Figure 9-10 Path coefficients for model shown in Figure 9-9.

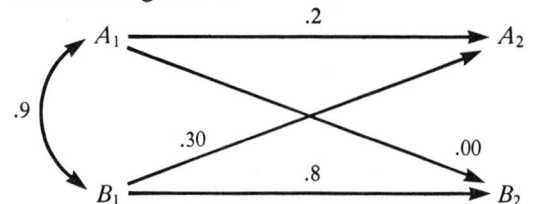

B; $B \overset{+}{\rightarrow} A$; $B \rightarrow A$. To untangle this situation, certain authors have suggested computing a "no cause comparison base" against which each cross-lagged value could be compared. Thus, one would use the lagged auto correlations and the synchronous cross correlations to estimate what each cross-lagged correlation would be in the absence of $A \rightarrow B$ or $B \rightarrow A$ causation. The obtained cross-lagged correlations would each be compared to this value rather than to each other. Thus, an investigator could confirm two separate rival hypotheses at one time, and each hypothesis might be either positive or negative. (Of course, at some time, some of the four competing hypotheses can be ruled out on theoretical grounds as implausible.) One method of obtaining this no-cause baseline is shown below. Using Figure 9-8, the baseline statistic could be found by:

$$\text{Baseline} = \frac{rA_1B_1 + rA_2B_2}{2} \left(\sqrt{\frac{rA_1A_2}{r_a} \times \frac{rB_1B_2}{r_b}} \right)$$

where r_a and r_b are the internal consistency components of the reliability coefficients for each variable. If we found, for example, that the baseline statistic was .45 and both rA_1B_2 and rB_1A_2 were .60, then we would conclude that $A \overset{+}{\rightarrow} B$ and $B \overset{+}{\rightarrow} A$, assuming the .15 difference is significant. Had each been .30, our conclusion would have been $A \rightarrow B$ and $B \rightarrow A$. Had rA_1B_2 been .60 and rB_1A_2 been .45, then $A \overset{+}{\rightarrow} B$. Unfortunately, the adequacy of this estimation procedure has been questioned.[14]

Given these concerns, it appears that cross-lagged correlations should be used to sustain causal inferences with some caution. When stationarity exists, that is, $rA_1A_2 = rB_1B_2$ and $rA_1B_1 = rA_2B_2$, the causal model would seem to have maximum interpretability. But there is doubt even in situations that demonstrate stationarity, since Campbell and Cook have shown that the presence of an unknown third variable that in fact causes the relationship between A and B will lead to mistaken assumptions about causality derived from the cross-lagged r's.[15] As a general rule, perhaps, the technique of cross-lagged correlation should not be used alone in arguing for a certain causal position but should be presented along with other techniques, such as path analysis or multiple regression, as a contributing argument for inferring cause.

Examples from Broadcasting Research

Probably the best known example of the use of cross-lagged correlation is the study by Eron et al. reported in the Surgeon General's Report on Television and Social Behavior. Eron and his colleagues had earlier determined the amount of TV violence viewing and aggression of 875 third graders. Ten years later, when the respondents were nineteen years old, comparable data were obtained from 460 of the original 875 subjects. The cross-lagged correlation among boys for TV violence viewing in the third grade and aggressive tendencies at age nineteen was .31, and the relationship between aggressive behavior in the third grade and television violence viewing at age nineteen was .01, indicating support for the proposition that viewing causes aggression.[16] (Eron's conclusions were also supported by a path analysis of the same data done by an independent investigator.) In another example, Atkin[17] used cross-lagged correlation to demonstrate that the viewing of news programs at Time 1 led to greater political knowledge at Time 2, rather than the reverse. (Atkin also used the multiple regression technique mentioned above to support this conclusion.) Other examples can be found in the work of Chaffee et al.[18] and in an earlier study by Atkin.[19]

Summary

No statistical strategy can allow for completely confident causal inferences. The best a researcher can hope for is a pattern of data that supports the causal model. Any model of cause and effect represents a particular and subjective point of view about the relationship between variables. Whether it makes sense depends on our knowledge of the subject matter. To paraphrase Wright, all methods of sustaining causal inference discussed in this essay will not accomplish the impossible task of deducing causal relationships from correlation coefficients. These techniques will allow an investigator to determine whether a proposed interpretation is consistent with the data.

Endnotes

1. Note, however, that many philosophers of science have correctly pointed out that causality cannot strictly be proven beyond all doubt, no matter what the empirical evidence.
2. See, for example, Bertrand Russell, "On the Notion of Cause," *Proceedings of the Aristotelian Society* (New Series) 13 (1913): 1–26; P. A. Suppes, *A Probability Theory of Causality* (Amsterdam: North Holland, 1970); D. Gasking, "Causation and Recipes," *Mind* 64 (1955) 479–487; E. G. Boring, "The Nature and History of Experimental Control," *American Journal of Psychology* 67 (1954) 573–589; K. R. Popper, *The Logic of Scientific Discovery* (New York: Basic Books, 1959); and Thomas Cook and Donald Campbell, *Quasi-Experimentation* (Chicago: Rand McNally, 1979).
3. Hubert Blalock, *Causal Inferences in Nonexperimental Research* (Chapel Hill: University of North Carolina Press, 1964), 33.
4. See Michael Walizer and Paul Wiener, *Research Methods and Analysis* (New York: Harper and Row, 1978), 295–328, for a discussion of this problem.
5. Specifically: no mutual causation, standard scores, and no correlation between latent factors.
6. See Herbert Asher, *Causal Modeling* (Beverly Hills, Calif.: Sage Publications, 1976), 40.
7. Joseph N. Capella, "An Introduction to the Literature of Causal Modeling," *Human Communication Research* 1 (1975): 362–377.
8. Asher, op. cit.
9. David LeRoy and Donald Ungurait, "Ascertainment Surveys: Problem Perception and Voluntary Station Contact," *Journal of Broadcasting* 19 (1975): 23–30.
10. John E. Christiansen, "Television Role Models and Adolescent Occupational Goals," *Human Communication Research* 5 (1979): 335–338.
11. Norris Johnson, "Television and Politicization: A Test of Competing Models," *Journalism Quarterly* 50 (1973): 447–455.
12. David R. Heise, "Causal Inference from Panel Data," in Edgar Borgatta and George Bohrnstedt, eds., *Sociological Methodology*, (San Francisco: Jossey-Bass, 1970), 3–25.
13. D. A. Kenny, "Cross-Lagged and Synchronous Common Factors in Panel Data," in A. S. Goldenberger and O. D. Duncan, eds., *Structural Equation Models in the Social Sciences* (New York: Seminar Press, 1973).
14. S. Rickard, "The Assumptions of Causal Analysis for Incomplete Sets of Two Multilevel Variables," *Multivariate Behavioral Research* 7 (1972): 317–359.
15. Cook and Campbell, *Quasi-Experimentation*, especially chap. 7.
16. Leonard Eron et al., "Television Violence and Child Aggression: A Followup Study," in George Comstock and Eli Rubinstein, eds., *Television and Social Behavior*, Vol. III, *Television and Adolescent Aggressiveness* (Washington, D.C.: U.S. Government Printing Office, 1970), 35–136.
17. Charles Atkin and Walter Gantz, "Television News and Political Socialization," *Public Opinion Quarterly* 42 (1978): 183–198.
18. Steven Chaffee et al., "Mass Communication and Political Socialization," *Journalism Quarterly* 47 (1971): 647–659.
19. Charles Atkin et al., "News Media Exposure, Political Knowledge and Campaign Interest," *Journalism Quarterly* 54 (1976): 230–238.

Annotated Bibliography

Herbert Asher. *Causal Modeling.* Beverly Hills: Sage Publications, 1976. *This short monograph, one paper in the Sage quantita-*

tive applications series, is a good introduction to path analysis. It covers recursive and nonrecursive systems and is written in a straightforward manner.

William D. Berry. *Nonrecursive Causal Models*. Beverly Hills, Calif.: Sage Publications, 1984. *Another monograph in the Sage series, this paper examines models from all of the social sciences.*

Edgar F. Borgatta, ed. *Sociological Methodology, 1969*. San Francisco: Jossey-Bass, 1969. *The first four chapters deal with path analysis and the study of change. This is a good introduction to the area with emphasis on problems in interpretation.*

Joseph N. Capella. "An Introduction to the Literature of Causal Modeling," *Human Communication Research* 1 (1975): 362–377. *In addition to a short summary of the basic principles of causal modeling, Capella presents a reading list that can be used to self-teach more advanced methods of causal modeling.*

Thomas Cook and Donald Campbell. *Quasi-Experimentation*. Chicago: Rand McNally, 1979. *Chapter 1 presents a lucid discussion of the problems involved in making cause-effect statements and summarizes various philosophical viewpoints on causal matters. Chapter 7 discusses path analysis and some problems with cross-lagged correlation.*

Fred Kerlinger and Elazar Pedhazur. *Multiple Regression in Behavioral Research*. New York: Holt, Rinehart and Winston, 1973. *This basic text in multiple regression contains a section on recursive path analysis, complete with examples.*

Ronald Kessler and David Greenberg. *Linear Panel Analysis: Models of Quantitative Change*. New York: Academic Press, 1981. *This is the best book available for learning the techniques of panel research. It contains an excellent discussion of the perils of cross-lagged correlation.*

C. C. Li. *Path Analysis: A Primer*. Pacific Grove, Calif.: Boxwood Press, 1975. *This is the best single source for learning path analysis. Chapters one through six introduce multiple regression, standardized variables, structural equations, and recursive path analysis. The book is clearly written and well-organized, with abundant examples. The author is a biologist so three chapters of examples come from population genetics, one chapter treats examples from the social sciences.*

B. Claire McCullough. "Effects of Variables Using Panel Data: A Review of Techniques," *Public Opinion Quarterly* 42 (1978): 199–220. *This book discusses path analysis use for cross-lagged data as well as other less-used panel techniques.*

Norman Nie et al. *Statistical Package for the Social Sciences*. New York: McGraw-Hill, 1975. *Chapter 21 is a basic overview of the principles of recursive path analysis.*

10
Developing Mass Communication Research Models

Roger D. Wimmer

The word *model* refers to many things, such as a child's plastic airplane or a person who demonstrates a fashion designer's new clothing styles, or an architect's detailed scale version of a bridge or building. A model is a representation of something else. The child's plastic airplane and the architect's scaled replicas represent the real, larger objects; the fashion model represents how other people might look wearing the designer's fashions.

In these examples, the model is important either in demonstrating an idea or object, in saving time or money in construction of an object, or in providing a miniature of a larger item so that details can be inspected or possible errors or difficulty anticipated. The simplest model is static, that is, not concerned with changes over time. A more complex, dynamic model is used when time and uncertainty are included. In each case, simplification of a new object or concept has taken place. Models are valuable in mass communication research because they can simplify complex processes.

The preceding essays have demonstrated that research in mass communication can cover a wide variety of topics. However, regardless of the specific area under investigation, one characteristic is always present: complexity. In every communication analysis, researchers deal not only with complex communication situations, but also with human subjects who add further complications. Subjects under investigation often defy predictions developed through research (as with predictions of presidential contests from a study of how voters used the media for political information); communication messages and situations refuse to remain static (as indicated by the changing use of words and phrases and their accepted meanings); and researchers deal with constantly changing media (as shown, for example, by the technological developments in television, including satellites and videotape recording systems).

The complexity of mass communication research is not a barrier to investigation. Instead, it is an opportunity for explanation. Researchers in the communications field, as in all scientific research, hold prediction as a primary goal of research. On the way to prediction, researchers must gain understanding and the ability to explain. Developing a model is often the first step in many studies.

Mass communication research models, as with models of the communication process, can be developed in many ways. A simple mathematical model might take the form $A = B + C$, or a sophisticated and complex verbal model might involve several paragraphs. This essay introduces mass communication research models[1] in six steps: the definition of *model*, the value of models in mass communication research, classification of models, a morphology of models, the goals and objectives of model development, and the criteria necessary for developing a model.

Definition

Most dictionary definitions of the word *model* incorporate three commonplace usages: as a noun to imply representation, as an adjective to imply a degree of perfection or idealization, or as a verb to indicate what something is like. Fundamentally, a model represents a simplified version of reality.[2]

Capella[3] suggests that a model ". . . consists of a set of formally stated relationships among concepts." Sereno and Mortensen[4] suggest that a model is ". . . an analogy, a representation of relationships that supposedly determine the nature of a given event." Sereno and Mortensen stress that a communication model consists of an idealized description of an event, and that a model only replicates, or duplicates in abstract terms, the important features of a communication event.[5] In relation to this idea, Barnlund[6] indicates that a physical or symbolic model eases researchers' handling of the many variables in a given communication situation.

A simplified model might provide insight into a problem of mass communication. This is the same simplification process as in the child's plastic airplane or the architect's scaled replica: a complex situation is represented by only a few parts.

Each preceding definition provides some basis for understanding; a combination of the ideas may provide a statement more applicable to the material described here. In this essay, a model is considered to be a physical or symbolic representation of the relationships among concepts or phenomena or their parts, usually with the intent of explanation and/or prediction.

The astute reader may recognize that the definition of *model* is closely related to another important term: *theory*. The similarity of these two terms has been controversial for a number of years.

Theory has been defined by Kerlinger as a:

> . . . set of interrelated constructs (concepts), definitions and predispositions that present a systematic view of phenomena by specifying relations among variables, with the purpose of explaining and predicting the phenomena.[7]

The two definitions are close, but the differences are important. Marketing researcher Ralph Day suggests that the difference between theory and model is one of semantics, since the word *theoretical* has come to mean the opposite of *practical* and *useful*.[8] Day suggests that in place of the word *theory*, most researchers have substituted the word *model*. Simon[9] suggests that a model is actually a mini-theory, and that the terms *model* and *theory* are often used interchangeably. Nevertheless, other considerations more rigorously separate the two terms.

Capella notes that a model is usually the first step in the development of theory, focuses on more limited problems than a theory and may comprehend a single, particular system rather than an entire class of systems.[10]

Another way to differentiate theory and model is to note that a model is often considered a subcategory of a theory. That is, the word *theory* is often used in the same sense as the biological term *genus*, whereas a model might be compared to a species. A theory tends to state a broad relationship between variables or events, and this relationship can be understood by application of several different models.

Finally, consider the element of testing. A theory, according to scientific principles, must be testable. This is not a necessity for a model. A model in most research is a set of assumptions or postulates that are not directly tested but are used to generate testable hypotheses.

To summarize, different types of models exist. In mass communication research, models are generally used as a beginning step in the development of understanding the media. Without models, mass communication research would be more complicated. A model helps focus an investigation and leads to the development of theories of mass communication.

The Value of Models

In mass communication research, models can be constructed to represent relationships and interactions between the media and consumers of the media, or the effects of the media in different communication environments, among others. For example, a researcher might develop a model of the interaction between young television viewers and scholastic achievement in various school subjects. The model, a verbal model in this case, might be: Increased viewing of television causes a decrease in scholastic performance.

At first glance, this model may appear to be a hypothesis, but in fact, the model is too broad. A hypothesis would need to include information concerning what constitutes an increase in viewing and what constitutes a decrease in performance. In addition, not enough information is now available to allow testing this problem. The statement is too simple to be considered anything more than a model.

Simplicity, or parsimony, is a primary value of a model. Models generally do not include all variables involved in the real situation; rather, they provide a simple picture of what might exist.

However, although models may simplify a research situation, they can at the same time create difficulty. Some models might overlook or distort important variables. For instance, returning to the example of increased televi-

sion viewing and decreased scholastic performance, such a model might be detrimental because of what it neglects. It does not consider other possibilities that might influence poor performance in school; television might be blamed (because of the simplified model) for something on which it may have little, if any, influence. This oversimplification amounts to distortion, and an analysis based on this model may produce distorted results.

A further potential problem in model development is that a model might hide the real purpose of a research study. Again to the example: The model might hide a real interest in teacher effectiveness in the classroom rather than in an outside influence of television. That is, models are developed with definite goals in mind (see essay 9 in this book).

One additional complication with model development is the tendency of models to become more complex as additional relationships and variables are added to the initial model. As researchers look beyond the basic model and its applications, they consider further applications of the model, naturally adding more variables. However, for any model to be of value, it should be as simple as possible. The purpose of model development is simplification of reality; and the simpler the model is, the better it will be understood.

Although distortion through simplification might occur, the primary value of a model is its ability to handle many variables in a simplified manner to form a logical starting point for research. A model alone will not answer a research question. Instead, a model helps focus a researcher's ideas about an object or phenomenon.

Classification of Models

This essay discusses three main model categories: (1) micro-macro models, (2) static-dynamic models, and (3) deterministic-probabilistic models.[11]

Micro-Macro Models

A micro model focuses on small details of a particular situation or phenomenon. A macro model is used for a broader perspective and encompasses a variety of events or phenomena. In other words, the macro model examines the relationships between a phenomenon and the system of which it is a part, whereas the micro model examines relationships and constructs interior to the phenomenon of interest.

Reid[12] used a micro-model approach to analyze the factors involved in a child's response to television commercials. The phenomena of interest were effects of television on the audience. Using a micro approach, Reid isolated a specific demographic group and a particular aspect of the media for analysis. He sought to discover whether differences in children's responses to television advertising and parents' handling of those responses are mediated by the parents' concern for their child's consumer development and by parents' enforced viewing rules. Extrapolating Reid's verbal description yields the pictorial micro model in Figure 10-1. The model indicates that Reid's approach isolated a specific aspect of a phenomenon: media effects. The model allowed for flexibility of empirical analysis where a variety of details could be investigated.

The macro model involves a broader topic; a researcher can make broader generalizations about a given situation. Minute details are often sacrificed for simplicity.

Larson's[13] macro-model study investigated the broadcast brokerage industry. Considering that brokerage firms had not been analyzed be-fore Larson's study, the area could not justifiably be dissected for scrutiny of individual variables. Larson considered the entire industry—a broad-based analysis—including the history and development of broadcast brokerage firms and the methods companies use to acquire properties for clients.

Static-Dynamic Models

A model is either static or dynamic depending on the time restriction placed on it. A static model represents a system or phenomenon at a single time; a dynamic model attempts to represent a system or phenomenon at successive times. An analysis of a ten-year history of broadcast advertising revenues for a particular station is considered a static model, since the revenue figures are fixed; the figures cannot change and are considered at a single time.[14]

On the other hand, if a model represents the effects of the past ten years of advertising on the income of the current year, the model is dynamic: the variables contained in the time frame are not fully determined and can change. This model represents a dynamic situation, not one measured at a specific time.[15]

The differences between static and dynamic models are shown in Figures 10-2, 10-3, and 10-4. A static communication model might be pictured as in Figure 10-2. This simple model represents communication sent by a communicator then received by another individual or

Figure 10-1 Reid model of media effects.

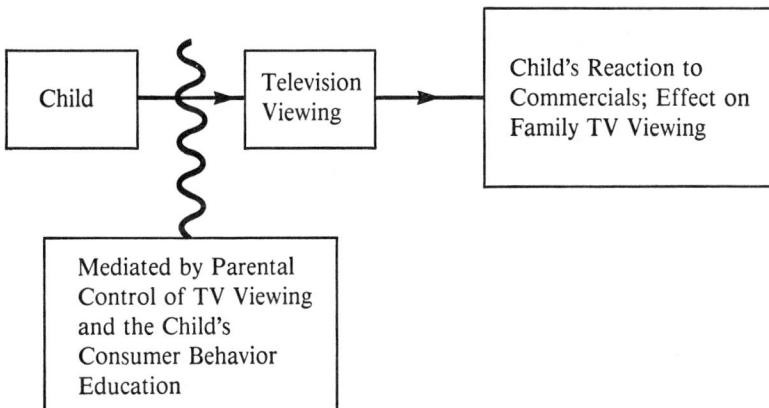

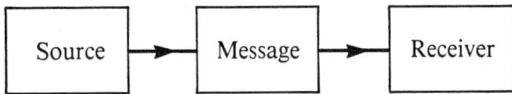

Figure 10-2 Simplified static model of communication.

group in the same form. We know that communication in real life does not operate on this level. Countless forms of interference exist between the source and receiver, not to mention that the receiver under most conditions can provide some feedback to the source.

A more complete model of the communication process, developed by Shannon and Weaver,[16] more accurately represents communication (see Figure 10-3). Although this model by Shannon and Weaver more accurately depicts the process nature of communication by adding other variables and more closely indicates the dynamic nature of the process, the model might still be too simple. Communication represents an ongoing and interactive process. A further addition to Figure 10-3 demonstrates a more dynamic approach to model development in communication. See

This dynamic model indicates the inevitable interference between a source and receiver and adds the possibility of feedback. The static models in Figures 10-2 and 10-3, in varying degrees, allowed for little or no interaction be-

tween source and receiver and did not portray communication as a process. The process approach is more clearly seen in the dynamic model in Figure 10-4.

Deterministic-Probabilistic Models

Models in this third category consider the relative uncertainty of an event or situation. A model that considers the possibility of further influential variables is considered probabilistic. Also called a stochastic model, the probabilistic model takes into account the possibility of additional influences; the deterministic model does not.

Assume an interest in the broadcast engineering problem of adding another television channel in a particular market (commonly called a drop-in). A deterministic model, or the if-then approach, might be: Another channel in the market will interfere with other channels currently in operation. A probabilistic model including intervening variables might consider other such variables as market size, revenue losses or gains for other stations, and potential audience size—not all of which can be unequivocally specified. The probabilistic model includes uncertainties; it is not an if-then approach.

A Morphology of Models

Models can take different forms and shapes, four of which are: verbal or prose models, pictorial models, mathematical models, and sim-

Figure 10-3 Shannon-Weaver model of communication. (Claude E. Shannon and Warren Weaver, *The Mathematical Theory of Communication* (Urbana: The University of Illinois Press, 1964) p. 34, Figure 1. Reprinted by permission of the University of Illinois Press.)

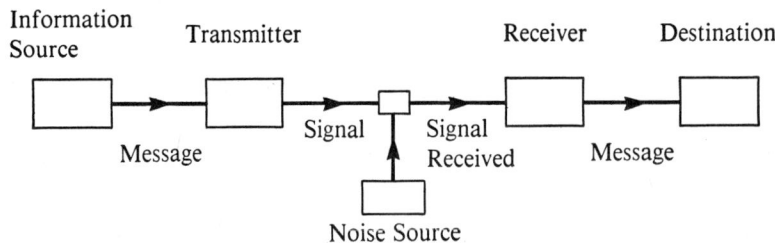

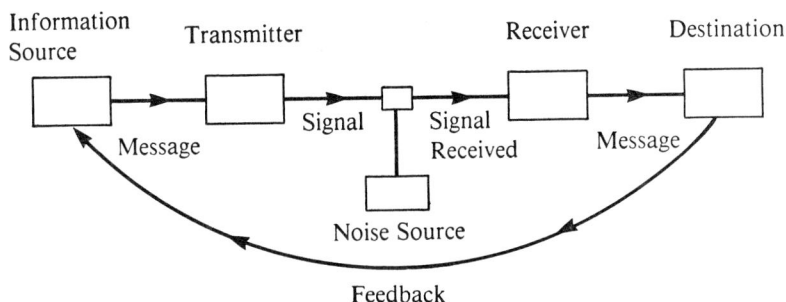

Figure 10-4 Dynamic model of communication.

ulation models. However, keep in mind that other model forms do exist.

Verbal or Prose Models

The verbal model is often the least confusing approach to initial model development, but this form can become as complex as any other form. Often, a broad verbal model is developed with the intention of refining during later stages of research.

The verbal model in Figure 10-5 demon-

Figure 10-5 Example of verbal model.

> Given that station advertising rates have not been increased in three years, what effect will a 10 percent increase in all rates have on the station's revenues from time sales, and on its advertisers?

Possible Paths

1. If rates remain the same, losses will increase due to inflation and increased operating expenses.
2. If rates are raised, competing stations may follow suit. This will lessen the effect of our raise on advertisers.
3. An increase in rates will no doubt make some advertisers angry. Some will cancel contracts, others may refuse to buy time, others may reduce current schedules.
4. Rates may be raised five percent this month, and five percent in six months to alleviate hardships on advertisers.

strates that this approach is not always simple. The question the model asks is: Should our radio station raise advertising rates by 10 percent? It is clear that a variety of responses are possible. A term more appropriate than *simple* when describing verbal models is *preliminary*, although further model development or refinement might not always be required. A verbal model may, in fact, be the only model required in a particular research problem.

Lasswell's[17] classic model of communication demonstrates another approach using a verbal model. Although the Lasswell model might appear too simple, an analysis of a communication situation using the model can involve a complex array of statements.

Mathematical Models

A mathematical model frequently offers a great deal of parsimony and precision to the model development process because symbols and numbers can represent ideas or objects. In Figure 10-7, the model considers the anticipated revenue for the station and the revenues with a 10 percent rate increase. Obviously, this

Figure 10-6 Lasswell's verbal model of communication

> Who?
> Says What?
> In Which Channel?
> To Whom?
> With What Effect?

model could include other variables that would increase its complexity, but Figure 10-7 serves as an example of the mathematical approach.

Figure 10-7 shows a basic characteristic of mathematical models: they generally do not allow for extraneous variables (such as canceled advertising contracts in the example). The model attempts to present a closed rather than open representation of a system or phenomenon. Mathematical models are usually precise and do not allow for ambiguity. Einstein's famous $E = MC^2$ allows for little flexibility, although other considerations, such as entropy, must be included at some point.

Mathematical models can be used in many ways in media research. Chaffee and Wilson[18] developed a mathematical model to investigate entropy and agenda diversity in community newspapers in Wisconsin. Portrayal of violence on television is measured and based on a mathematical model.[19] Sprafkin and Rubinstein[20] used a simpler mathematical model to investigate children's television viewing habits and prosocial behavior.

Networks and other media-related organizations use mathematical models for several areas of decision making. For example, a decision to produce a pilot might be determined by using the mathematical model[21] in Figure 10-8.

Although mathematical models can be tested and analyzed through various statistical methods, the approach does have drawbacks. In many cases, a detailed verbal description, or a secondary model, must further explain the mathematical approach.

Efficiency and simplicity are also problems

Figure 10-7   Simple mathematical model.

$A = B + C$

where:

A = Station revenue

B = Expected station revenue at current rates

C = Revenue anticipated with rate increase

$$(1 - t) A \left[BV + (1 - s) CDL - K \right] > P$$

where

P = Cost of the pilot production

V = Present value of expected broadcast revenue of an accepted pilot during the network run

L = Present value of expected broadcast revenue of an accepted pilot in off-network syndication

K = Present value of the opportunity cost of producing the expected number of episodes of an accepted pilot

B = Program owner's share in broadcast revenue from network run

D = Program owner's share in revenue from off-network syndication broadcast after payment of distributor's fee

t = Profits tax base

A = Probability a pilot will be accepted by the networks

C = Probability that an accepted pilot will be released into off-network syndication

s = Network's share in profits from off-network syndication

Figure 10-8   Example of model used in mass communication.

with the mathematical model. By eliminating the possibility (in many cases) that other variables can be involved, some mathematical models have limited use in the mass communication field. The mathematical model often cannot represent the dynamic nature of communication. The hard sciences of physics, chemistry, and others use the mathematical approach more because these research areas deal with more static concepts and objects.

Pictorial Models

The pictorial model is an appropriate technique when a variety of possible solutions need to be explained in a simple manner. Pictorial models are also excellent representations of concepts and objects for nontechnical individuals to use as quick reference to a complex problem (see Figures 10-1, 10-2, and 10-3).

One form of the pictorial model approach is the algorithm, or flow chart, shown in Figure 10-9. Flow charts have become popular since the advent of high-speed electronic computers; many researchers in all fields use them in model development. Computer programmers use detailed flow charts to show the path of decision making a computer must follow in order to solve a problem.[22] The flow chart presents to the computer a series of if-then statements in order to make a decision: if one thing happens, then go to the next step; if it does not occur, use an alternative route.

As Figure 10-9 indicates, the algorithm chart method can be used in our example of increasing advertising revenues through a rate hike. The sales manager could develop, or map out, the possible decisions (and their consequences) that could arise with an increase in advertising rates. A simplified pictorial model allows for a quick glance at a complex problem.

Simulation Models

The simulation approach to model development is an expanding method for problem solving in many research fields. This approach might not be the best method in our advertising example, but it should not be excluded while considering the problem.

In each form, the simulation attempts to re-enact a real situation and allows participants or researchers to play at decision making without facing the consequences of the real situation. A simulation is basically an opportunity to practice or run through the decision-making process. The model represents a system from which the behavior of the system over time can be inferred.[23] For example, space scientists, notably at NASA, simulate with computers the atmosphere and characteristics of space and space flight. These simulations help technicians prepare space vehicles and astronauts for conditions they might encounter in space.

By using real flight conditions simulated in ground-based training facilities, airline pilots can learn how to operate aircraft under stress conditions without endangering passengers. The Federal Aviation Administration also uses simulations to re-enact conditions under which an aircraft crashed in order to determine what went wrong.

Simulation is not restricted to space flight and air travel. Many commercial products and organizations prepare simulation exercises for management personnel, office workers, and many professions dealing with decision making and people. Some parlor games invite players to simulate being lost in the wilderness or receiving a large inheritance.

All simulations are instructive because participants can enter a situation, react to problems and situations, and make decisions without facing any harm: the simulations are imaginary. The advertising example used in this essay could also benefit from a simulation model. For example, the sales manager could present the problem of increasing advertising rates to station personnel, who could then discuss potential problems and benefits. This procedure could also be used with advertisers who would be affected by the rate increase. Feedback gained from such a simulation would enable the sales manager to plan ahead in the decision-making process.

Another simulation approach is the Delphi Technique, used to arrive at consensus about future developments.[24] In the 1950s, the Rand Corporation established the Delphi Technique to "obtain the most reliable consensus of opinion of a group of experts . . . by a series of intensive questionnaires interspersed with controlled opinion feedback."[25]

The Delphi Technique takes its name from the ancient Greek Oracle of Delphi, where a blind seeress would transmit forecasts from Apollo to those who consulted her. As Bachner and Khosla state:[26]

In this case, "blind" is the key word because those who participate do not know who else is participating; thus, bias, which sometimes results when one may say something just to be opposed to someone else . . . is reduced. The

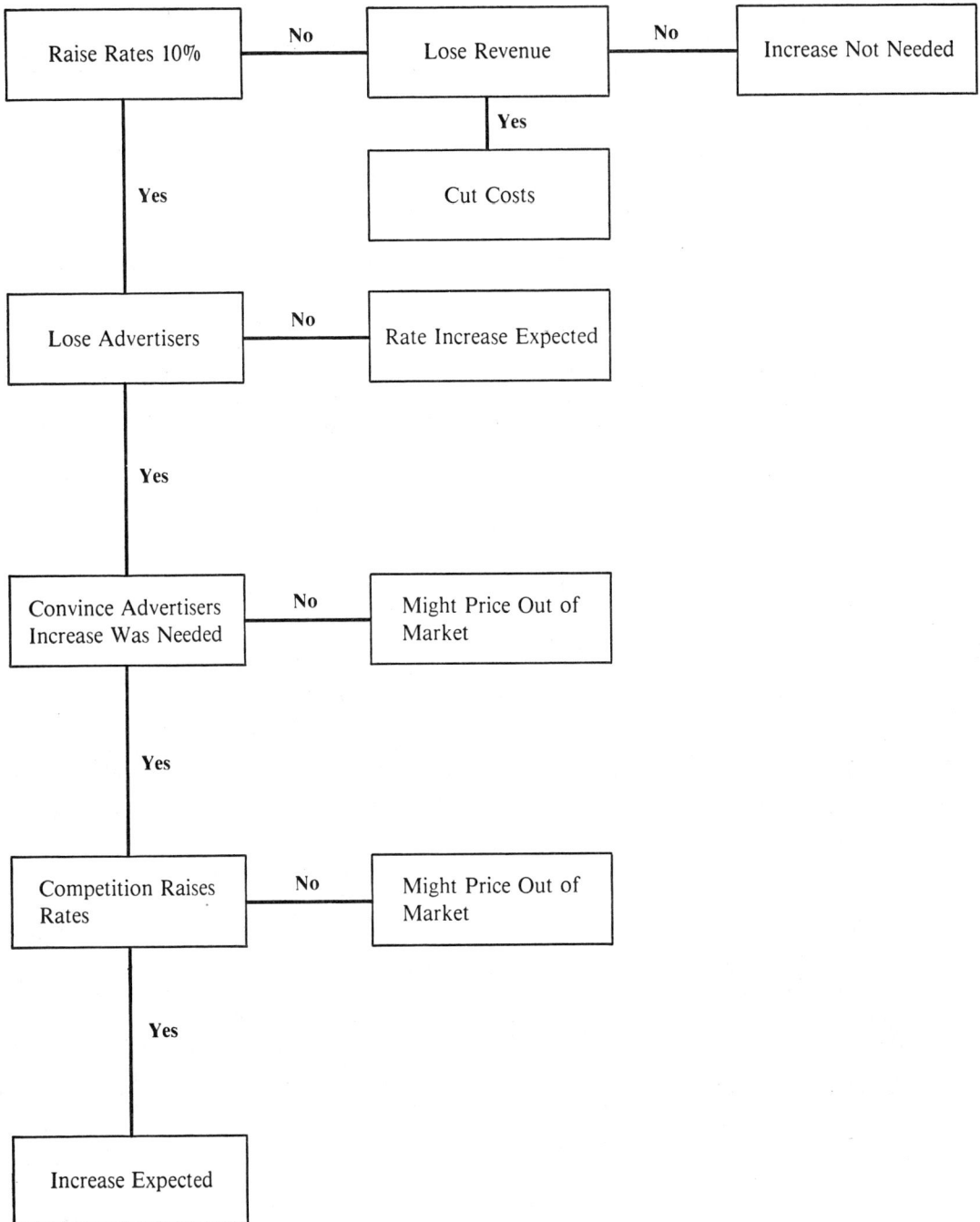

Figure 10-9   Example of pictorial (flowchart) model.

person running the Delphi program, therefore, would select recognized experts in a given subject or subjects but would not tell any of them who else is participating.

The Delphi Technique involves sending out questionnaires to subjects who respond to the qualitative items. These responses are summarized and returned to the participants. Further comments are received and again summarized. This procedure continues until the experts reach a consensus. Because of the time and expense involved, the Delphi Technique is limited to large companies or organizations that can afford the expenditures. It is easy to see how the Delphi Technique can be used in mass communication research, such as in programming decisions, future directions for broadcasting, or ramifications of particular FCC decisions.

Objectives of Model Development

A communication model, as noted, can be constructed for a variety of reasons. Some models are designed to add general knowledge to a given area, others are intended to help solve a specific problem, and others are constructed to show what a final product might look like. Whichever purpose is intended for a model, the objectives for using such a procedure are similar.

The first step in model development is to determine the specific purpose for the model: (1) classification; (2) descriptive or explanatory; and (3) predictive. The choice depends on the nature of the research and on what goal has been established for the research.

A classification model attempts to develop procedures to identify classes, groups, or types of data. A researcher might wish to classify the various types of radio stations into specific categories of advertising revenue. A classification model, if clearly defined, would allow for such identification.

A good classification model allows a researcher to: (1) examine individual groups of things or events or data and simplify the information to improve research techniques, and

(2) compare similarities and differences among groups to create new categories of importance. For example, a researcher might be interested in reclassifying what is meant by *major market* in broadcasting. A model could include information other than the usual population of a town or city; other variables might be included in the way market classification is established.

The descriptive or explanatory model approach is used most often in mass communication research since it is intended to explain phenomena. For example, a descriptive model could try to explain how viewers process information gained from the media and how they use that information in daily life.

A descriptive model can help solve a problem or even make a general contribution to knowledge. It can suggest hypotheses for further research or help determine what data should be collected.[27]

Predictive models are designed to predict future events. Since prediction is a primary goal in all areas of research, this model is used often. In mass communication, a researcher might want to predict audience size, advertising revenues, or media use. However, the predictive model is not better than other approaches. A classification or descriptive model might need to be developed in order to collect enough information to use the predictive approach.

Goals of Models

In general, research models are constructed with two criteria in mind. First, the model should be convenient in the sense that it aids in the research process. Developing a model that complicates and slows down research does little for the advancement of knowledge. Second, a model should follow logically with current knowledge in the area. Designing a model for research purposes that conflicts with current information is not an intelligent use of knowledge. To use a simple example, a researcher who designs a model to test whether "the earth is the center of the solar system" would not be reasoning with current data. Although this is an exaggerated example, it is not uncommon to see model development (and research) based on an ivory tower approach, where a researcher disregards the current state of information. Research following the ivory tower approach often rediscovers data or renames concepts or objects—an illogical approach to scientific research.

Criteria for Model Building

Regardless of the type of model developed, or for what purpose, recognized criteria should guide any model development procedure. The criteria are flexible to allow them to fit any type of model under consideration.[28]

1. A mass communication model should have the ability to generate solutions to mass communication problems. This sounds simple, but the model developed should be precise enough to investigate the problem without including irrelevant or unnecessarily redundant information.

2. Mass communication models should be designed so that they help us understand the nature of the mass media. That is, all models should help in some way with understanding the processes, uses, or effects of mass communication—as well as understanding the research procedures of hypothesis development, data collection, and data analysis.

3. Mass communication models need to limit the number of variables to be considered. Parsimony, or simplicity, is the key. Working with small problems involving a limited number of variables is usually more productive than developing a model nearly as complex as the phenomenon. Research usually proceeds more quickly when a major problem is broken down into its component parts.

4. All mass communication models should be developed to avoid ambiguous variables. In other words, any word or phrase or mathematical statement must be defined both theoretically and operationally. An operational definition of a variable or concept assigns meaning to the term. For example, an operational definition of the term *cake* is the recipe from which it is made.

Summary

Model development in mass communication research is an important step in understanding the role and function of the mass media in our society. As a partial summary of the material discussed in this chapter, consider some of the more important research uses of models.

First, mass communication models provide a frame of reference for solving communication problems. Models help focus any research study, and, through systematic model development, mass communication researchers are better able to collect valuable information for investigation. Models provide an excellent starting point for research.

A second important use of models is to help explain complex relationships existing between the many variables usually present in mass communication investigations. Through model development, researchers are better able to view relationships between variables such as the media and consumers. Models are an important exploratory tool.

Third, models may help researchers make predictions. For example, researchers interested in the effects of the mass media during political campaigns may make substantial gains in understanding through model development based on previous elections. Forecasting any presidential election, for example, depends entirely on models developed in previous years.

A fourth important use of models is in theory construction. Any theory, regardless of what field is mentioned, must be based on a substantial amount of information. Model development is an effective method of organizing data collection.

A final important use of models is to help eliminate irrelevant information involved in a research study. Considering that model development is usually the first step in research (whether the model is simple or complex), researchers must look at the problem under investigation; researchers can learn a lot about a problem through model development before the investigation actually begins.

Endnotes

1. This chapter is a preliminary discussion of models. For further information, see: H. Sachman, *The Delphi Culture* (Lexington, Mass.: Lexington Books, 1975); J. Fowles, ed., *Handbook of Futures Research* (Westport, Conn.: Greenwood Press, 1978); H. M. Blalock, *Social Statistics* (New York: McGraw-Hill, 1972); D. E. Hewes, "Finite Stochastic Modeling of Communication Processes," *Human Communication Research* 1 (1975): 271–283; E. Nagel, *The Structure of Science* (London: Routledge, 1961); A. Kaplan, *The Conduct of Inquiry* (San Francisco: Chandler, 1964); K. W. Deutsch, "On Communication Models in the Social Sciences," *Public Opinion Quarterly* 16 (1952): 365–380.

2. J. M. McLean, "Simulation Modeling," in J. Fowles, ed., *Handbook of Futures Research* (Westport, Conn.: Greenwood Press, 1978), 329.

3. Joseph N. Capella, "Research Methodology in Communication: A Review and Commentary," in Brent D. Rubin, ed., *Communication Yearbook I* (New Brunswick, N.J.: Transaction Books, 1977), 38–53.

4. Kenneth K. Sereno and C. David Mortensen, *Foundations of Communication Theory* (New York: Harper & Row, 1970), 56.

5. Ibid.

6. Dean C. Barnlund, "A Transactional Model of Communication," in Kenneth K. Sereno and C. David Mortensen, eds., *Foundations of Communication Theory*, (New York: Harper & Row, 1970), p. 86.

7. Fred N. Kerlinger, *Foundations of Behavioral Research* (New York: Holt, Rinehart and Winston, 1973), 9.

8. Ralph L. Day, ed., *Marketing Models* (Scranton, Pa.: International Textbook Company, 1964), 4.

9. J. L. Simon, *Basic Research Methods in Social Sciences*, 2nd ed. (New York: Random House, 1978), 64.

10. Capella, op. cit., 39.

11. William F. Massy, "Model Building in Marketing: An Overview," in Robert Ferber, ed., *Handbook of Marketing Research* (New York: McGraw Hill, 1974), 504–506.

12. L. N. Reid, "Viewing Rules as Mediating Factors of Children's Responses to Commercials," *Journal of Broadcasting* 23 (1979): 15–26.

13. T. L. Larson, "Aspects of Market Structure in the Broadcast Brokerage Industry," University of Utah, 1979.

14. Massy, op. cit., 509.

15. See, for example, B. R. Litman, "Alternative Measures of Competition in Broadcasting: The Market Share Instability Technique," presented at the 1980 Broadcast Education Association Convention, Las Vegas, Nevada.

16. C. Shannon and W. Weaver, *The Mathematical Theory of Communication* (Urbana: University of Illinois Press, 1949).

17. H. D. Lasswell, "The Structure and Function of Communication in Society," in L. Bryson, ed., *The Communication of Ideas* (New York: Harper and Brothers, 1948).

18. S. Chaffee and D. Wilson, "Media Rich, Media Poor: Two Studies of Diversity in Agenda Holding," *Journalism Quarterly* 54 (1977): 466–476.

19. See the *Journal of Broadcasting*, Volume 21 (1977) for several discussions of the Gerbner Violence Index.

20. J. Sprafkin and E. Rubinstein, "Children's Television Viewing Habits and Prosocial Behavior: A Field Correlational Study," *Journal of Broadcasting* 23 (1979): 265–276.

21. R. Noll, M. Peck, and J. McGowan, *Economic Aspects of Television Regulations* (Washington, D.C.: The Brookings Institution, 1977).

22. See N. Stern, *Flowcharting: A Tool for Understanding Computer Logic* (New York: John Wiley & Sons, 1975).

23. J. M. McLean, "Simulation Modeling," 329–352.

24. J. P. Bachner and N. K. Khosla, *Marketing and Promotion for Design Professionals* (New York: Van Nostrand Reinhold Co., 1977), 49.

25. N. Dalkey and O. Helmer, "An Experimental Application of the Delphi Method to the Use of Experts," *Management Science* 9 (1963): 458.

26. Bachner and Khosla, op. cit., 49.

27. Massy, op. cit., 509.

28. W. Lazer, "An Investigation of Marketing Models," in M. L. Bell, ed., *Marketing: A Maturing Discipline* (New York: Macmillan, 1960), 47–53.

This essay defines policy and policy research and separates policy research from its theory-building counterpart. It discusses the potential importance of policy research and its value for both the public and the researcher. It also discusses the logic and methodology of policy research and the most appropriate research and statistical designs to use when conducting it. The role of policy research in the policy process is examined, with special attention given to the FCC. The writing style necessary for maximum exposure of research in the policy arena is discussed and suggestions offered for making research more visible to decision makers.

11
Policy Research

Robert H. Prisuta

Policy and Policy Analysis

Public policy has been defined as "whatever governments choose to do or not to do."[1] This general definition can be appropriately applied to the formulation of communications policy in the United States and other countries. Congress, the courts, the federal regulatory commissions, and the executive branch are involved in the complex process of communications policy development.[2]

The motivation for policy development is also complex. It can stem from political pressures, self-interest, traditional preconceptions, anecdotal evidence, and so on. It can also arise from systematic policy analysis, in which various alternatives are evaluated with empirical data in an effort to arrive at the most efficient policy, as defined by previously agreed on objective criteria.

Policy analysis is the focal point of policy research, which provides an opportunity to become directly involved in the communications policy process. Policy analysis goes beyond the traditional academic tendency to observe, study, and comment on phenomena without directly affecting them. It carries with it a *modus operandi* different from that of theoretical, scholarly research. Its rewards and its risks are different as a result.

A Definition of Policy Research

Goals

Policy research has three basic concerns: (1) measuring the impact of current and past public policies, (2) predicting the impact of future policies, and (3) making this knowledge available to decision makers.

Structure and Logic

Policy research differs substantially from theoretical research, which is preponderantly deductive. A general theory is formulated, from which specific hypotheses are derived and tested. Support for the hypothesis (albeit in an indirect way, stemming from failure to reject the null hypothesis) leads to support for the theory by inference. In policy research, the logic is often inductive. A specific problem or question is raised, leading to a broader, more general approach to the issue. Since government reacts to specific problems or pressures, the research question must be solution-oriented.

Theoretical research is complex; policy research strives for simplicity. Theory building calls for application of empirical results to a refinement and addition to a basic theory, in an attempt to account for all factors and explain as much variance as possible in the variable under study with a given set of predictors. The concern of policy research is the opposite. It attempts to establish what the impact of a particular policy is, was, or will be. It seeks the bottom line without concern for the intervening variables.

Theoretical research tends to be conservative. The researcher must be certain that the null hypothesis can be rejected before accepting results as valid. In the policy environment, the necessity to choose between significantly different alternatives in a limited span of time prevents such a tentative approach.

The major difference between the two is intent. Scholarly research seeks to build theory; policy research seeks to answer specific questions. Both use the same methodology. Sampling, surveys, experimental techniques, and statistical analysis are all part of policy research. The difference is in how these methods are applied. Theoretical research seeks knowledge as a way of understanding complex phenomena; policy research attempts to answer such specific questions as, "Should this action be taken?" "What form of action is appropriate here?" or "To what extent should this course of action be followed?"

The Importance of Policy Research

It is a recent development in the practice of governments to ask questions about the impact of policy.[3] As a result, the researcher faces some hurdles in getting the message across. A basic challenge is the skeptic with the real-world orientation who views academic research as esoterica and abstraction, asking "What does it mean?" or "What relevance does this have for the problem before us?"

Often, such a skeptic is an attorney, trained in verbalization and rhetorical logic rather than in quantitative, statistical logic; or an economist, critical of the allegedly soft data and controversial operational definitions of the communications researcher.

It is hoped in empirical research that objective and systematic procedures will yield more useful information than other methods. Good policy research therefore has several obvious benefits—it can lead to public policies that increase public benefit and reduce public costs.

For the researcher interested in making findings policy-relevant, the main issue is packaging—not just the final product, but the entire research operation—so it can receive maximum attention from a small but important audience—the decision makers.

For too long, communications scholars have been aloof from the policy area. They are usually unaware of the details of government procedure and may not be sure of the specific issues being dealt with at a particular time. Most government agencies, however, like the Federal Communications Commission, tend to rely on information submitted to them. These commissions do publish requests for information, but the requests are not widely distributed or noted. As a result, the commission may be unaware of relevant research findings available in the academic community.

Most communications scholars limit their published findings to peer review through scholarly journals and academic meetings. This material is designed for colleagues who already have the conceptual and methodological background necessary to understand it. Information in popular form is usually presented in the classroom or to consultant clients.

Advantages of Academic Policy Research

Despite the use of internal policy research at the congressional and regulatory agency level, the outside contributions of the academic community are essential to more enlightened policy analysis. The resources of academia are one reason. Strong academic departments have the staff, data processing hardware and software, motivation, time, support, and environment necessary for undertaking complex research projects.

The atmosphere of the academic community is a second factor. Political pressures are fewer, and credibility of the researchers is higher than in a government research environment. This input from a separate, independent source, well equipped to deal with the research questions involved in an issue, is important to good policy analysis.

Access to Decision Makers

Policy research may be an important, growing area, and academic research centers may be suited to perform it, but getting access to the decision makers is a crucial hurdle in the process. Key decision-makers do not look for information but expect it to be delivered to them. The aspiring policy researcher must therefore become familiar with how a regulatory agency gathers information.

Thanks to the new Administrative Proce-

dures Act (5 U.S.C.), this process is now more formal and open to greater public scrutiny. These improvements in formality and access permit initial input by the researcher and have the potential for review of other submissions, which the researcher can then react to individually.

Two basic means of access are available to the researcher. The researcher can take a direct and active role by attempting to initiate a policy or policy change or can become involved in an ongoing issue by submitting material as comments or reply comments.

Petitioning

Taking an active role is the petitioning process. Under current administrative law and FCC policy, any concerned individual or group can file a petition urging commission action in a specific area. A petition for rulemaking recommends a specific rule change or addition. A petition for an inquiry requests a formal investigation of an issue. The inquiry is usually used when an issue is too complex and/or it is felt that too little is presently known about it for a rulemaking to be advantageous.

Specific information on format and style can be obtained from the commission's Office of Consumer Affairs. The following checklist of basic guidelines will enhance the petition's chances of acceptance.

A brief introduction presenting the overall intent of the petition along with a summary of its rationale is the appropriate way to begin. Next comes historical and legal background. A review of *Pike and Fisher*, law reviews, journals, and other legal reference materials will be appropriate here. Then, a brief review of previous empirical literature will be helpful. The information based on your research will be the major portion of the document.

Finally, you must draw conclusions from your research in terms of specific policy changes and state those changes with specific reference to appropriate sections of either the Communications Act or FCC rules and regulations. This final portion might be the most difficult. Academics are accustomed to interpreting the results of their work in abstract, theoretical terms, rather than in the specifics of policy. In this regard, a joint filing may be of value. At the least, consulting a colleague familiar with law, regulation, and policy will be valuable. A legally oriented colleague will be able to structure the proposal in the practical, specific terms and concepts with which policy makers are accustomed to dealing.

The work of Abel and Saxton exemplifies this approach. Their research centered on equal opportunity/affirmative action in the broadcast industry. Testing the allegation that broadcasters inflated job rankings by giving women official-sounding and managerial titles without related responsibilities, they compared the listing on the stations' reporting forms with those in *Broadcast Yearbook*. They predicted that the number of women listed in the yearbook, which is used as an industry guide to key station personnel, would be smaller than the number listed on the FCC forms. They found a significant difference between the two, supporting the idea that some broadcasters might be giving female employees better sounding titles in order to make their affirmative action results look good.

The traditional approach to research stopped here. Rather than submitting the findings to a journal or presenting them at a convention, Abel and Saxton filed a petition for rulemaking with the FCC, calling for a revised reporting form with more specific job categories and job information. They outlined the FCC's EEO enforcement history, other research findings, and the rationale for their rulemaking. They then provided a specific model of the type of form they wished to see the FCC adopt, followed by the research material itself.

The result was significant. Instead of gathering dust on a library shelf, or being heard by a handful of peers at a convention, the petition was the impetus to a major, wide-ranging investigation of commission EEO policy and future options in this area. Other petitioners joined, and significant time and effort were allocated considering new EEO policy.

Under the Administrative Procedures Act, a regulatory agency such as the FCC must con-sider any petition brought before it. Even a petition dismissed at an early stage in the policy process will be read and evaluated by a staff member and reasons for its rejection provided.

Comments and Reply Comments

A less direct and active approach is also available. In addition to initiating procedures, it is possible to comment on any ongoing issue before the commission. The commission files both formal and informal comments when considering an issue. The most effective procedure is to file comments that are formatted and substantive enough to be categorized as formal, thus receiving more than the cursory attention given to the informal comments, usually consisting of the handwritten letters submitted by private citizens.

When a petition is accepted, a formal docket is created, into which all formal comments are entered and then opened to the public. When preparing action on the docket, the staff must read, summarize, and evaluate each formal comment filed and indicate how it was considered in the final decision recommended to the commission. The commission also publishes a list of the comments received. Any interested observer can file a comment, examine what others have said, and file reply comments on any docket.

The best way to use this procedure is to keep informed via the trade press on the issues up for consideration. Then, by contacting the Consumer Assistance Office, the researcher can obtain the docket number, filing deadlines, and list of public comments to date. The researcher can also be placed on a mailing list to receive information about upcoming issues that the commission might consider. Copies of particular filings can also be requested for further examination.

By comments, the commission means not just expository material, but all evidentiary data used in making a policy decision. There are obviously several flaws in this approach. One problem is the lack of knowledge about it. Many academics, observers, and other interested parties feel incorrectly that comments and/or material published in other places, such as scholarly journals, will be read by decision makers. The staff applies little outside of docket material to its deliberations, relying on intuitive judgment. The commissioners approach an issue in the same way, relying on the staff summary and on information from their own offices. Therefore, it is essential to get one's material into the docket.

The second problem is the lack of systematic and objective submission of data to the docket, or what the survey researcher might call response error (the experimenter might call it a selection problem). Only people aware of the inquiry/rulemaking and motivated to submit information are represented. By using the docket comments as a gauge of opinion, the commission omits those who do not know about the docket or those who do not file comments.

Often, the broadcasters are well represented in the docket file. For instance, a recent inquiry into public service announcements (PSAs) drew many comments with evidence to back up their claims from various broadcast stations that thought they were doing a good job and did not need any government prodding in this area. Naturally, stations not doing a good job would not file this information. Therefore, the docket provided an inaccurate indication of what was happening. Even though several communications researchers have worked with PSAs in their analysis, these data are not usually submitted to the docket, where they might make a valuable contribution.

Also, the process is adversarial. As a result, docket filings reflect certain human response tendencies. Filings against a proposed rulemaking or inquiry usually outnumber those supporting it, since it is easier to motivate a negative reaction than a positive one.

The Research Agenda

Given these weaknesses in the information-gathering process, the researcher must keep advised of developments on the policy agenda. Often, the agenda for theoretical research and policy research are entirely different, which makes the process difficult. For instance, the commission recently focused on the dereg-

ulation of radio. The commission therefore needed information on radio audiences, their use of the medium, its effect on them, listening patterns, and so forth. Most researchers have neglected radio, however, studying the more contemporary and fashionable medium of television. The commission has also examined employment patterns in the equal employment opportunity/affirmative action areas, with an eye to revising these regulations. But broadcast research tends to be content oriented rather than structurally oriented, despite the obvious social aspects of the latter.

Keeping in Touch with the Policy Process

Several steps are necessary to keep informed. Some of these are obvious. Reading the fine print in the trade publications is a must. Your reading should also include the Federal Register, which lists upcoming agendas and requests for proposals, and the Action Alert, which describes all upcoming FCC business. For additional output, the commission's Consumer Assistance Office can be of value.

Informal contacts are important. Contact other people who have filed material or people who might do so or could contribute if they did. Fight the tendency of academics to work in isolation. Contact commission staff directly.

Even though each government organization works differently, an example of FCC procedure will make the point. A petition accepted for consideration is assigned a contact person who gathers material on the petition and formulates a general position for the commission to take. This person is usually an attorney; additional empirical research support is usually supplied. A call to the Policy and Rules Division will determine which attorney, engineer, and/or policy researcher is working on a particular document. Once you have this information, in addition to filing the material, send a copy to these people, following it up with a telephone call and/or letter so that you can discuss your contributions with them personally. You can clarify elements of your research they do not understand or deem relevant. You will also assure maximum visibility for your material and be able to get some help on the timing, style, and emphasis of possible future filings.

Also, circulate your material to other key interested parties in the docket and to the commissioners themselves. It may be best to limit your submission to a commissioner who is more involved in that particular issue than others (information you derive from reading the trade press), so that it will be read at the staff assistant level, with a verbal summary passed on to the commissioners. Should someone comment on your submission, remember that you have the opportunity to respond.

The timing of a submission is important. Ascertaining which topics are ripe to be acted on is a subtle process that can be observed with the right combination of close commission watching and personal contact with staff. A document submitted to an active docket is obviously more valuable than one submitted to a dead-end issue.

Writing the Policy Document

Docket submissions require a writing style different from that in scholarly journals since they are for a different audience. The biggest difference in writing style is a greater focus on the consequences of research findings rather than a mere statement of these findings, with perhaps some discussion of their theoretical implications.

Organization

A scholarly article usually states a problem and its rationale, summarizes previous research and literature on the problem, presents hypotheses to be tested, and describes the methodology used to test the hypotheses. The data and results of the hypothesis testing are then presented, with some tentative and limited conclusions drawn.

A docket submission should be different. Results and implications should be clarified early in the paper and complexities included later or in footnotes or appendices. Statements and style should be clear, direct, simple, and jargon-free, even at the risk of oversimplifying or overgeneralizing.

When addressing comments to an inquiry or rulemaking already under way, the best procedure is to follow the direction of the notice itself. The notice usually contains a series of questions to which information and answers are sought. Other questions are implicitly contained in the body of the document.

A filing presented in this manner is easier for the staff to compare with other material in the docket and keeps their attention.

Repetition is also important. The broadcast news story is a better model than the scholarly broadcast article. The article's introduction should contain the major conclusions and recommendations, which can be amplified and discussed in detail later and again summarized at the close of the article.

Style

Remember that you are writing for a lay audience. The fact that your audience lacks full familiarity with communication terms, symbols, and jargon does not mean, however, that they lack opinions on the issues. Their opinions often result from personal experiences, anecdotal data, and/or philosophical or intuitive judgments. The academic article that goes against the grain and is counterintuitive might be rejected on its form alone.

A good approach is to delete jargon and the qualifications and tentative statements common to research attempting to build on theory. Be direct, general, and attempt to get a few key points across.

Be direct in discussing the policy ramifications of your research. Do not count on policy makers to draw inferences from it, since they are not used to dealing with this type of material. At the risk of restating the obvious, indicate what you think are the most self-evident points.

Supporting material should be kept out of the way. Literature reviews, tables, methodological discussions, citations, and the like should appear in footnotes or appendices. Footnoting is preferable to notation in the

Modern Language Association or American Psychological Association style; it is more familiar and seems more precise. Remember that the policy maker is interested in conclusions, and this interest should be facilitated. Supporting material can always be examined later, and a few appendices or long footnotes go a long way toward uncluttering the copy for readability. Another idea is to precede a long document with an executive summary, a few pages summarizing the text following.

Methodological Considerations

Statistical analysis also should be considered carefully. Most policy makers do not have a firm grasp of statistical techniques or concepts. Such terms as *significance* may be misunderstood, and probabilistic thinking may have to be clarified. Keep in-depth statistical analysis at the basic level, reporting only the most important results in the body and relegating other information to footnotes or appendices. Repeating data displayed in tables within the text may seem redundant but is necessary. Do not count on tables to carry the message; highlight them and describe the most important information in the body of the text. Tables present a maze of numerical information to the untrained observer and might be ignored or misunderstood if left unexplained.

In designing policy research projects, recall a general bias among policy makers—that surveys are more generalizable and reliable than are laboratory experiments. Field experiments are also preferable to the lab, but less preferred than surveys. The field survey is considered, at the intuitive level, to be more consistent with real life; other types of research are of limited value because of their artificial or laboratory conditions. Even though such negative experimental effects as the Hawthorne Effect are now thought by academics to be less a problem for validity than once imagined,[4] experiments are seen as artificial by policy makers. The more your research can be demonstrated to have occurred in a natural environment with limited artificial constraints, the more it will be recognized as valid, despite the precision and control of a laboratory experiment.

The same holds true for statistical analysis. Some tests might be precise and accurate; however, more powerful and robust tests will make the product more acceptable. Tests indicating significance more easily than others are generally considered to be more powerful tests. They run the risk of ascribing significance to a relationship where there is none, but they are less likely to miss a significant relationship where one actually exists; missing such a relationship is considered the worse of the two evils in policy research. This attitude contrasts with theoretical research, where falsely disproving the null hypothesis is considered a greater problem. Robust tests maintain their value even if some of their assumptions are violated. This flexibility is important in policy research, since policy makers are seeking information of value under many conditions and circumstances. Some elegant, complex, and precise statistical analysis is more often subject to a highly conditional environment, since more assumptions must be met. Thus, the robust test, capable of generating accurate data under a wider variety of conditions and circumstances, is preferred in the policy environment.

As a consequence, correlation and regression analysis seem to be favored over analysis of variance and similar nonlinear analytical techniques. Linear concepts are easier to deal with because of their capacity for graphic representation, their tendency to assume causal and/or directional flow, and the degree to which they can be used in trend analysis. The preference for survey and field research, the prominence of econometrics, and the complexity of ANOVA techniques are probably all factors in this unstated preference.

Econometrics have also given the social researcher concepts for describing and choosing among policy alternatives. Policy can and should be discussed in terms of its human cost effectiveness and cost-benefit balance, as opposed to theoretical abstraction. Cost effectiveness analyzes the effectiveness of different policies given identical costs. Cost-benefit analysis considers the marginal, or increased, value and cost of a particular program as it is extended. It is reasoned that the scope of a program should be enlarged until it costs more to expand the program than the benefits it provides.[5]

Other Considerations

Research Directions

Current approaches to policy provide an additional challenge to the communications scholar. Sensitivity to First Amendment considerations and political pressures has led to a deemphasis of content regulation, which has been countered by an emphasis on regulation of industry structure, business practices, personnel matters, institutional tendencies and procedures, and so on. For most of its history, communication research has taken the direct route of examining and discussing communication from a content-oriented perspective. Even in recent years, despite the recognition of the complex social, psychological, and other factors impacting on human communication, emphasis has centered on content rather than on the overall communication process.

To have maximum policy input, the researcher must focus on the research's noncontent aspects, even if dysfunctional effects of certain communication outcomes are determined by many intervening variables. Now, the researcher must emphasize these variables and seek change in areas other than direct regulation of content.

Personal Factors

The difficult decision to enter the policy environment includes making professional value choices. Academic research, with its emphasis on theory building and knowledge generation for its own sake, will have little direct policy impact. Therefore, the researcher must bend the internalized rules under which he or she has been trained.

There are benefits and risks both to the communications discipline in general and to the individual scholar for participating in policy research. The benefits include increased visibility and credibility for the discipline and the researcher plus the potential for greater research funding and placement opportunities for students. More effective competition with economics and the more traditional social sciences for these scarce resources is likely. The personal satisfaction of seeing one's work applied directly to real problems and having a positive impact on society is another benefit. Social benefits from an organized, systematic, and objective approach to increasing the information available for policy decisions are also possible. The more accurate information a policy maker has to work with, the greater the chances of making the right decision. It is a small but important step toward the experimenting society that other researchers have advocated.

There are risks as well. Other academic researchers may scoff at the weaker methodology and lack of theory-oriented analysis. People conducting research involving sensitive topics may be accused of taking sides and selling out to business, government, or whoever is sponsoring the study or looks favorable in the result. On volatile issues, the researcher can be caught between two hostile sides. In general, the researcher seeking policy relevance for his or her work must be resigned to frequent, hostile, and uninformed criticism of both methodology and findings.

The natural resources for good policy research exist in the communications field. The periodicals and journals of the discipline are filled with articles that apply to policy decisions yet that are unused because their approach is perceived as tangential, ambiguous, and tentative or because of the impenetrability of jargon. Providing clear and direct versions of this material to the right parties would ensure a greater role for communications research in the policy environment.

Summary

Policy research is concerned with measuring and predicting the impact of current and future public policy and making this information available to decision makers. The methodology and research techniques are similar to those of theoretical research, yet important differences in the two exist.

Policy research is less conservative in its approach and less methodologically complex and rigorous. Its approach is inductive rather than deductive. It strives for simplicity and flexibility of design in order that a few basic questions may be answered. In doing so, it sacrifices the completeness of results that complex theory-building may require.

The policy researcher must be active if he or she is serious about making significant contributions to policy decisions. The policy arena is unfamiliar with empirical analysis and makes no special effort to seek it out. Research presented to the policy maker must be clear, to the point, jargon-free, and stylistically streamlined. Tentative and overly complex conclusions must be avoided. Specific questions the policy maker might have must be answered directly.

Even though this approach sacrifices to some extent the goals and intent of theoretical research, it holds the potential for increased impact for the research performed by the communications scholar.

Endnotes

1. Thomas R. Dye, *Understanding Public Policy* (Englewood Cliffs, N.J.: Prentice-Hall, 1972), 1.
2. Erwin G. Krasnow and Lawrence D. Longley, *The Politics of Broadcast Regulation* (New York: St. Martin's, 1978), 27.
3. James S. Coleman, *Policy Research in the Social Sciences* (Morristown, N.J.: General Learning Press, 1972), 1.
4. Donald T. Campbell and Julian C. Stanley, *Experimental and Quasi-Experimental Designs for Research* (Chicago: Rand McNally, 1963), 18.
5. Otto Eckstein, *Public Finance* (Englewood Cliffs, N.J.: Prentice-Hall, 1973), 20.

Additional References

Riecken, Henry W., and Robert F. Boruch, eds. *Social Experimentation*, New York: Academic Press, 1974.

Rossi, Peter H., and Walter Williams, eds. *Evaluating Social Programs*, New York: Seminar Press, 1972.

12

Assessing Consumer Information Needs

John E. Bowes

The past decade has been a time of consumer unrest, if not outright dissatisfaction. Government, corporation, and public utility have been chastened in the face of organized protest. Consumer protection agencies have been established or strengthened at all government levels. Corporations have initiated hot lines to handle complaints and information requests and have increased institutional advertising to convince the public of their worth. Utilities scramble to explain rate hikes and conservation needs.[1] The media, print and broadcast alike, have tried to research consumer information needs to serve their audiences better, to increase circulation, and to meet public service pressures from community and government.[2]

Such efforts have largely been intuitive occasionally hurried responses to alleged consumer information needs. Little of the established advice on measuring information needs, as we will discuss later, has held up well across most situations that professional communicators face. The few conceptual designs that help information professionals cope with consumer information problems often have been suspect in terms of their applicability to real-life settings. The pressures of the past decade have made the development of better models and measures of consumer information needs a matter of increased urgency.[3] Most communication researchers realize that American industry and big government have a communication gap with the citizen. There is less agreement on how best to identify the consumer's information needs and to bridge existing information gaps. Unfortunately, broadcasters cannot shun the problem. Public service responsibilities and the popularity of news magazine programs featuring consumer issues command their attention.

This essay critically reviews assumptions and methods traditionally used to determine information needs, particularly as they confront broadcasters. The first part outlines several difficult problems in many consumer information need assessments. A second section examines several useful models—efforts to cope with the problems previously described—in the context of actual field research. Our interest is not in providing strict cookbook instructions for curing the ills of consumer need assessment; rather, it is to offer some basic conceptual directions and practical examples of how broadcasters and others in similar roles can make these assessments more faithful representations of consumer information needs.

Problems in Determining Consumer Information Needs

Not everyone has questions for your answers or problems for your solutions. Only some people see information as a solution to their needs—consumer or otherwise. Asking questions is recognizing that solutions are information-based; it is almost a reflexive act of the educated and self-reliant. Studies of economically and educationally disadvantaged groups, for example, suggest that fatalism, luck, or the intervention of an outside force share attention with information seeking as a way to resolve problems.[4] In one study of "problem perception" in audience ascertainment research, 10 percent of respondents could not name a single national or local problem. These individuals tended to be urban minorities with minimal education and economic security—people who often need consumer information the most.[5] In short, the population's need for and use of consumer information vary considerably. In many instances, especially in giving information to low-income clients, people needing information the most are least likely to attend to and use it effectively. This situation frustrates information providers.

Not everyone has the same questions. Many information providers cannot understand variability. After all, normative assumptions about the typical media consumer provide comforting targets for programming and advertising campaigns. The broad appeal campaign is satisfying in that one information set handles most people and costs are minimized. But the cost in ultimate effectiveness among people most needing the information can be considerable.

Communication scholars have recognized this point and have moved from hypodermic media concepts based on direct, powerful informational and attitudinal influence to a view encompassing the variability of motivation and need among the audience. The question of media influence on needs and their satisfaction focuses more on what the consumer wants than on what media provide.[6]

Unfortunately, this viewpoint learned by academic researchers has had only limited impact on people outside this group. Information needs are still largely adduced through normative research more intent on finding similarities than in segmenting the audience into differing target groups with different needs and receptivity to information. Broadcast public affairs and consumer information consequently remain "mass" in a wholly undifferentiated way. However, advertisements and increasingly entertainment content are often sculpted for specialized audiences. The increase in advertising effectiveness from targeting well-defined audiences has been amply demonstrated. An equally attentive effort should be made for consumer information needs.

Situations affect information needs. The normative trap extends beyond averaging audience and perceived needs to the situation in which the need arises. Detailed information might be useful in one instance because the solution is complex and time available permits study. Another situation might present an emergency, requiring fast advice, free of much detail via electronic media. Timing, public access, and the ability to tailor to individual need must be considered.

One example of this accommodation is the practice of providing taped information via telephone by insurers, consumer agencies, and government. Callers can select information on a variety of topics from a live operator who then connects them to the playback machine.[7] Of course, the caller determines when and where contact is made. The ability to choose tapes allows some matching of message to specific need and time for an extended reply from the recorded expert. The speed of access suits the crisis nature of many medical problems. The system also offers a level of anonymity to the caller in asking about personal matters. Periodically tabulating the frequency of requests by tape as well as requests made but not matched by appropriate tapes provides a crude but useful running evaluation of the system.

The careful reader will doubtless find problems with this system. People seek medical advice as much for the personal contact and concern of the provider as for the information itself and see little comfort in a taped message. The tape for a medical question cannot restate answers in simpler terms or add detail. However, the system accommodates a variety of needs in some situations.

A Seattle television station uses this approach in cooperation with a voluntary group to resolve consumer-merchant disputes and warn about shoddy business practices.[8] Trained volunteers maintain a call-in service to answer individual problems. The broadcaster has a successful vehicle to advertise the service and can gather case studies from call records for feature stories. The records, when aggregated weekly, indicate trends and changes in consumer problems. The service has stopped fraud schemes and faulty civic services.

Both projects provide systems that can define information needs for particular users; the situation produces the need and strategies that yielded effective solutions. Neither project used traditional information campaign formats or unusual technologies or practices. Both avoided untested assumptions about what the public needs to know.

Information providers can have less in common with their clients than they think. Social scientists are sensitive to observer-actor confusion: mixing up one's own perception of information needs with those of the observed subjects of study. The ideal of an information need study is to reflect needs as the client perceives them. Inarticulate, frightened clients are common where information may be most needed. Clients often seek resources, services and emotional support rather than information. Pressure to attend and follow information may not be understood as helpful and may be viewed as a barrier.[9]

Observer-actor confusion is common in checklist efforts to survey information needs. Respondents who are not allowed to reply in their own words must reply in terms imposed by survey makers. This occurrence can circumscribe the true variety of needs among the population: questions focus answers.[10] Tests comparing checklists and fixed-response questionnaires against situations where consumers are free to respond in their own terms show the bias of the former.[11] Much depends on the researcher's skill in anticipating to a reasonable degree the likely categories of need present in the sample. Yet it is the situation of not being able to discern needs that first prompts the research!

This dilemma has been best treated by combining open or free-response questions with more structured items that aid recall and confront respondents with competing categories when ranking needs. The critical impact of question-asking approaches is best shown by Greenberg et al.'s study of ascertainment methodologies.[12] The importance of community problems determined by frequency of mention among a sample responding to open-ended items showed no relationship to importance determined by selecting problems from possibilities provided in a close-ended question. The broadcaster must use open-ended items to catch new, unanticipated problems as well as close-ended lists to prompt recall and provide comparison.

Communication may not occur at the beginning of the job but at the end. Many broadcasters may see their job beginning with construction of a media message and ending with its successful receipt. Viewing consumers as passive recipients (attentive or not) of media information ignores their active, situational use of the information. But to understand this activist stance, one should consider events that lead to as well as result from communication. What circumstances induce people to seek information? What leads them to prefer certain kinds of sources over others? For the information professional, this view acknowledges that information for consumer needs must respond to situations. For the researcher, this view implies that communication is the consequence of events, not necessarily a beginning that ends in consumer problem-solving. In the same way that new program decisions are rooted in audience analysis and in the demography of particular audience tastes, consumer information needs must be treated by continuously testing current assumptions about the audience for new trends and need situations.

There is an additional perspective—the easily forgotten cliché that communicating needs is a reciprocal process—that consumer information professional and client must maintain a dialogue. This process permits information programs to be adjusted to changing needs and situations. It also suggests that information professionals may have to help people articulate needs, just as responses help articulate information programs.

This point suggests an important conceptual confusion about consumer information needs. In one sense, *need* implies a consumer actively seeking sources and assistance. In a different sense, the information professional may sense an unrealized need. Is an unrealized need really a consumer information need? Perhaps it is, as attested to by the profusion of outreach information programs spawned by social service agencies. But, as suggested earlier, if consumers do not see needs in information terms, the professional's task differs from when they do. What becomes important in this distinction is prior concern, perhaps interest of the consumers in their need. Information professionals often hope to provoke need when none is apparent. In short, the distinction between information seeker and provider becomes blurred when the provider attempts to recruit seekers.

In summary, our brief critique of consumer information need research developed the following points:

- *Information is not universally viewed as the solution to problems.* Even though information can lead to solutions, its value in this role might not be recognized. The assumption that receipt of information leads to consumer action is faulty.
- *Professional communicators frequently are caught in a normative trap*, assuming a homogeneity to their clients/audience that does not exist. More important, responsiveness of consumer information programs to such differences might be the key to their effectiveness.
- *Observer-actor confusion can allow inadvertent substitution of the researcher's view* for that of the consumer. The subtlety of question-asking is an important aspect of this problem.
- *Communication may be more effectively viewed as the outcome* or result of preceding events, rather than as the beginning of the professional communicator's job. Understanding the evolution of information needs is a key to the communication strategy used in responding to them.
- *Communication on information needs is a reciprocal process.* Communication professionals might have to create community discussion of needs and elicit feedback information once programs are operative to see if modification and adjustment are needed as conditions change.
- *Consumers recognizing their needs should be distinguished from those who do not.* One must consider consumers' previous concerns about problems. Building a sense of need where it exists wastes resources.

Useful Models and Research Examples[13]

Developing conceptual models useful to information professionals has been a slow process and their application in the broadcast environment has been glacial. Several prominent corporate researchers have lamented the apparent missing link between their research on information policy and the research of the academic community. As one writer stated, "Academic and business research are sometimes so divergent, it is difficult to believe that they are addressing the same kind of task."[14] Carter finds both camps doing similar things and vulnerable to the same criticism—they are not generating enough good questions with both conceptual and applied payoffs.[15] By offering several conceptual alternatives to traditional normative research, one risks the suggestion that the examples are blanket prescriptions for doing good research. Instead, they should serve as examples only of meeting certain criticisms voiced above, constrained by time, situation, and budget. The intent is to encourage readers to experiment with potentially better methods of conceiving social reality in their research.

One familiar approach to consumer information needs is what one public relations research specialist, Glenn Broom, labels the "corporate-public definitional-agreement approach."[16] In this context, public relations operationally includes measurement, analysis, and influence of public concern. Its purposes are to determine gaps between the institutional and public point of view and then to close the difference via a persuasive campaign. The object is to create a shared opinion or agreement based on persuasive communication from information provider to consumer.

The risk is that agreement measures only similarity of evaluation. There is no certainty that the principals share the same object or definition of what is being evaluated. Two parties can agree, without realizing that each has different referents in mind. The danger is that disillusionment and misunderstanding replace short-term apparent satisfaction of information needs when the information provider and consumer discover that they constructed agreement on different anchors.

An example might clarify matters. The Interior Department commissioned the author and a colleague to study the extent to which the public, community leaders, and state officials in North Dakota agreed on regional development.[17] Initially, agreement appeared quite high. All parties saw regional development as a positive venture. The difficulty, when examined, was that each party based a favorable evaluation on different ideas. Citizens saw enhancement of the local economy and jobs for youth. State officials saw increased revenues from industry and energy. Community leaders, the pivot of information flow between citizens and government, saw enhancements to tourism, local industry, and schools. On the sur-

face, agreement seemed strong. But intensive discussions revealed that citizens were worried about crowding in schools, farmers were concerned about hiring labor in competition with high wages from new industry, and state government was worried about competition for water between farmers and industry. It was clear that advantages for one group could be disadvantages for another. Also, many negative issues were submerged in information about advantages, aimed at securing agreement.[18] Most citizens of the region had not heard enough about negative impacts to begin asking questions about them, and they had not carefully considered their neighbors' competing needs. The region's media also had not realized the conflicts embedded in apparent support. They reported government press releases, reinforcing the climate of consensus.

Critical to this study were orientations toward regional development shared by major subgroups in the population. Agreement was meaningless without the sharing. To measure its level, we needed to assess the orientations of the three major subgroups involved in regional planning. What characteristics did each group assign to regional development? This approach was developed from Chaffee and McLeod's interpersonal coorientation model,[19] wherein the information specialist examines the characteristics assigned by each group and each group's estimate of the characteristics assigned by others.

By contrasting the view each group estimated for the other two against the view reported by those groups, the error in sharing perceptions could be calculated. Information programs could then be structured to address these gaps, trying, in effect, to raise awareness of major differences people had underlying their apparent agreement. In practice, the study's results forced better disclosure of negative impacts to citizens and leaders. Community leaders were least accurate in perceiving the viewpoint of major parties involved in the development, so the state government relied on them less as a guide to citizen information needs and opinions.

Even if information professionals know

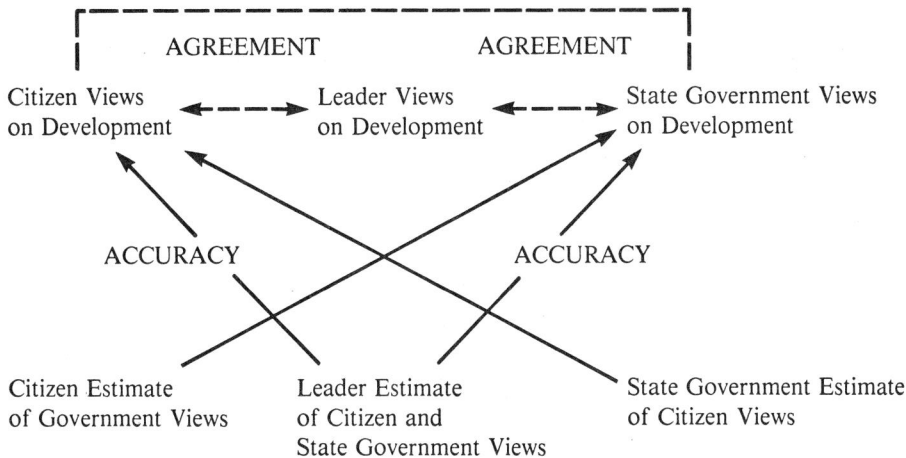

Figure 12-1 Coorientation measurement model showing relationships among three groups involved in regional development assessment.[20]

their clients' perspectives and needs, a problem remains in choosing and evaluating media to reach them. Media are selected for many reasons that have been extensively measured, including cost, readability, design, and interest. The volumes of readership research testifies to the importance of selecting the right channel. But the situations motivating us to access information vary. It is hard to make blanket statements about people's source preferences in the face of such flux. What can be learned from the situations that lead consumers to want information in the first place?

Grunig's study, conducted among employees of the National Bureau of Standards (NBS) in Maryland examined information seeking in sixteen situations.[21] Four major concepts were operationalized:

- Problem Recognition: The extent one recognizes something is "missing or indeterminate" in a situation and stops to consider it.
- Constraint Recognition: The limits one perceives on personal freedom to act or construct one's own behavior.
- Referent Criterion: The extent to which one knows what to do in a problem situation.
- Involvement Level: The range of communication behavior from active information-

seeking to passive processing in behalf of a problem situation.

These variables were grouped into sixteen combinations characterizing how situations can be perceived. Hypotheses were developed about the nature of communication in each combination. For example, in the highly decentralized NBS organization, it was hypothesized that professional employees would actively seek information relevant to their own research but only passively process information on administrative and other organization-wide problems. Other hypotheses were formulated for administrative and nonprofessional employees. From the data obtained, it was possible to construct profiles of employee types based on their situational use of information (e.g. for research, administrative matters, etc.). One could then identify which information sources (supervisors, various in-house publications) each employee type found most useful.

This study concluded that employee media contained much information about situations that employees did not perceive as involving them. Second, the study isolated employee profiles that differed in information needs and strategies necessary to serve those needs. These profiles and the situational variables on which they were built provided a useful conceptual basis for suggesting revisions in NBS's strategies for in-house media based on a better knowledge of how employee information needs arise.

Extending this approach to the broadcast treatment of consumer information needs suggests careful selection of target audiences based on situations in which this type of transmission best accommodates certain needs. To a degree, this has already been determined through trial and error with ratings. Traffic information is useful to commuters listening to car radios. Weather information is useful in the morning and late evening for planning. In short, Grunig suggests moving from a largely intuitive trial-and-error approach to an approach that systematically researches specific target audiences in terms of situation, timing, media used, and need.

The consumer's motivation to seek information is often a critical variable in information need studies. Surely information need implies existing consumer motivation. In practice, information professionals attempt not only to determine needs but also to promote need to serve some goal. For the social program advocate, it is not practical to discover and fulfill consumer information needs if no consumer action or change results. The connection between behavior and consumer interest or concern is difficult to examine. Advertisers, for example, are familiar with testing the effects of various advertisements in promoting a new product. Monitoring sales from stores before and after the ad or between comparable districts receiving different advertisements provides some evidence on the strength of this link. But for many information needs assessments, such a process is too costly and involves behaviors less visible and easily counted as new product purchases. Moreover, even in such clear-cut situations, the influence of interest, concern, or motivation remains elusive.[22]

A study of attitudes toward garbage disposal alternatives by Stamm, Dervin, and Laing[23] illustrates an attempt to examine linkages among concern, knowledge, media use, and a willingness to act. Did knowledge promote concern about the environment, or did concern lead to gaining more knowledge? To what extent does media exposure influence or become influenced by concern and knowledge about environmental matters? What is the joint influence of these forces on willingness to adopt environmentally sound solid waste handling practices (such as use of returnable containers, avoiding throw-away paper products, sorting garbage for recyclables)? The literature contained little *a priori* rationale for claiming one causal sequence over the other. To cast some empirical light on the question, the strength of seven correlational models were tested, each examining a different sequence. Indices of knowledge and concern about solid waste management were developed and tested in all possible sequential and simultaneous patterns to see which best fit the data.

The sequence of events has strong implications for what steps policy makers take in dealing with the public's information needs. Common approaches are to increase knowledge or to provide information to close the gap between concern and willingness to act (see Figure 12-2a).

The results did not clearly favor this pattern over other possible orderings, but knowledge and concern both strongly and positively impacted willingness (Figure 12-2b). Media, when added to the model, showed strong links to knowledge and forged an indirect link to willingness. Concern, by comparison, was not strongly enhanced by the media and seemingly made its own contribution to willingness (Figure 12-3).

Figure 12-2 Causal patterns for three variable system.

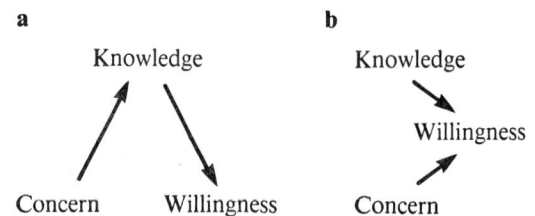

Media ──────────→ Knowledge

Knowledge ↘

Willingness

Concern ↗

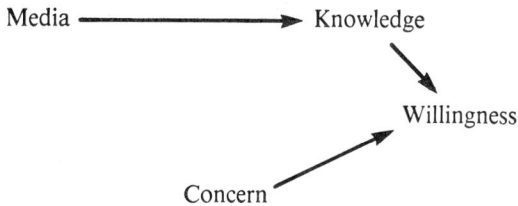

Figure 12-3 Possible causal pattern for four-variable model.

It is difficult to equate the concern of this study with information need, but the suggestion of motivation exists in both concepts. These findings suggest that both concern and knowledge contribute to desired outcomes (environmentally sound practices), but that media seem to influence knowledge without arousing concern. In this sense, campaigns designed to satisfy existing needs and concerns might have influence, whereas campaigns that attempt to generate both need and the knowledge to satisfy the need might be less successful. The question deserves further study and it should spur information professionals to clarify their use of need: whether they intend both to create and satisfy it or to respond to an established prior need. The public information announcements that broadcasters help produce and transmit often seem to assume need and an attentive public. This presumption should not go untested.

Edelstein's[24] decision-making context is another useful conceptualization of information need. Based on a model of cognitive processes by Carter,[25] Edelstein asked respondents to specify problems and possible solutions in their own words, indicating which solutions they could accept, would reject, or were undecided on. For solutions that could not be decided, respondents were asked if they had questions and needed additional information. Respondents were asked to explain whether available information was helpful and to describe the usefulness of existing information sources in helping them resolve indecision.

From this information, it was possible to characterize the complexity of the respon-

dents' decision making. Did they have only single reasons for supporting or rejecting alternative solutions or were multiple reasons given? Were reasons mixed (both positive and negative) or were they either positive or negative?

The study demonstrated complexity to be a powerful predictor of communication behaviors. People with complex as opposed to unidimensional (simple) structures, for example, were more likely to perceive interpersonal communication as an opportunity to exchange information and points of view. They were more likely to find some sources (especially television) and content not useful and to have lower overall use of the mass media. This example of people who differ cognitively in solving the same problem shows the variability of source preference and content sophistication that must be satisfied in effectively meeting information needs. It may suggest to broadcasters that they alone cannot efficiently meet some information needs.

The common thread throughout these studies is a better recognition of how individuals differing situationally, cognitively, and in terms of motivation vary in using information sources. We have also examined how information providers can be better evaluated in terms of their recognition of consumer perspectives. Several studies by Dervin have attempted a comprehensive integration of these characteristics in examining "sense-making."[26]

According to Dervin, successful information providers come to "understand how people make sense in their lives and on their jobs regardless of whether or not they use our (information) institutions at all or use them in ways we expect them to."[27] Many efforts to make sense fall short of informational professionals — thinking of oneself, consulting friends, and complaining are informal mechanisms. Complaining might not solve problems but the complainer might feel better. What are evident in this view are the informality and the responsiveness of the information seeker to the demands of the moment and resources at hand. What is in jeopardy in this view is the formal, institutional structure — experts, libraries, classroom instruction. These places are not as responsive to the moment and situation when information is needed.

If one accepts this perspective, what are the implications for people trying to discover and serve consumer information needs? Dervin[28] recommends the following steps:

- Allow the respondent to identify troublesome real-life situations where it was necessary to understand what was happening. This assures the relevance of the information need topics to the respondent's life, contrasting to the checklist approach where need structure is provided by the information provider.
- Try to find out what happened to the respondent in an actual information need situation. What gaps in information were encountered; when in the course of events was information sought? Knowing this, the provider may have insight into how information should be provided.
- Ask how the individual obtained and used information, and from what sources in particular situations. This is in contrast to traditional methods of asking people how often they use institutional information sources without regard to the situation they were in.
- Determine the unique questions the individual wants information for. A traditional classification of "neighborhood problem" may actually be for the individual a "bad neighbor's barking dog." There is a social overlay here that is not comparable to another identically cast "neighborhood problem" such as too much traffic on local streets. The steps an information professional might recommend in each instance could vary greatly.
- Emphasize the personal sense-making of the individual—how one resolved confusion, attained understanding. Traditional research has focused on information needs when the individual did not necessarily view his or her problem in just that way. Delivery of information cannot be assumed a sufficient solution to a problem situation. One has to be able to apply information to problem solutions in a way that can be personally managed and understood.

Essentially, this perspective asks those studying information needs to move closer to the client—to understand that information resources are not always used as we expect, that people cope with information sources as they are, not as we might wish them to be. For the broadcaster, these recommendations suggest a direct form of monitoring consumer needs: that personal contact with people expressing problems in their own terms and setting is desirable for people directly responsible for consumer information programs. Operation of telephone action lines, attendance at community meetings, and monitoring of civic agencies that receive consumer questions (libraries, extension agents, schools) are means of achieving this less idealized, more realistic view of consumer information needs.

Summary

The central theme of this discussion has been the making of normative assumptions in consumer information research. A failure to appreciate the heterogeneity of consumers has resulted in research that, although successful in describing the market for well-targeted products, has not been as successful in describing the market for information. One should not confuse methods at the root of creating need as market demand for commodities with trying to determine existing needs from frequently inarticulate, hard-to-understand people. This confusion of purpose and mindset is possibly a prejudice of well-educated professionals: to see others as they see themselves—people who question and seek solutions with information.

The research described has, on the whole, broken with much of the conventional wisdom of marketing and public opinion research. Each study attempts to apply basic communication concepts such as reciprocation, shared understanding, decision-making, and process. In doing so, it is possible to picture consumer information needs more realistically. Grunig's findings suggested which publications were most useful to employees in certain situations. Bowes and Stamm's studies showed distortions in a communication network between the citizen and government presumed to be accurate. The work of Stamm and his colleagues attempted to discern causal links among elements in a process of information use and knowledge-building leading to a willingness to be environmentally sound in handling solid waste. Edelstein attempted to describe cognitive states that lead to information seeking in behalf of decision making. Dervin discussed the informal and situational nature of consumer information seeking as a contrast to prevalent institutional and normative methods of handling consumer information needs.

Collectively, these approaches signal change from traditional descriptive methods. But even though they are tied to conceptual models of communication, these studies are applied in purpose and outcome. As an approach, each study can find many practical applications for the broadcaster. Their methodologies are rarely complex and can be carried out with reasonable ease in the field. The cost they represent is largely an investment in understanding their conceptual perspectives—a minor expense for real gains in explanatory power and the improved chance that consumer information needs assessed are real and not artificial.

Endnotes

1. Harry O'Neill, "Survey Research as a Public Relations Tool," *Public Relations Review* 3 (1977): 17–35.
2. Mary Ann Heller, "Problems in Ascertainment Procedures," *Journal of Broadcasting* 21 (1977): 427–433.
3. Walter K. Lindenmann, "The Missing Link in Public Relations Research," paper presented to the Public Relations Division, Association for Education in Journalism, Seattle, Washington, August 1978.
4. Julian R. Rotter, "Generalized Expectancies for Internal Versus External Control of Reinforcement," *Psychological Monographs* 80 (Whole 609, 1966); see also: R. K. Ackoff, "Toward a Behavioral Theory of Communication," *Management Science* 4 (1958) 218–234; Brenda Dervin, "The Communication Behaviors of the American Urban Poor: A Summary of Research and Suggestions for Future Research," Project CUP, Report #13, Department of Communications, Michigan State University, East Lansing, Michigan (1970).
5. David J. LeRoy and Donald F. Ungurait, "Ascertainment Surveys: Problem Perception and Voluntary Station Contact," Communication Research Center, Florida State University (mimeo, undated).
6. Sidney Kraus and Dennis Davis, *The Effect of Mass Communications on Political Behavior* (University Park: Penn State Press, 1978).
7. The system described is operated by Blue Cross of King County (Seattle), Washington, and is typical of similar systems elsewhere. The affective and technical cost/benefits of telephone conferencing and information systems are outlined in: Robert Johansen, Jaques Vallee, and Kathleen Spangler, *Electronic Meetings: Technical Alternatives and Social Choices* (Menlo Park, Calif.: Addison-Wesley, 1979).
8. This system, known as Action Northwest, is sponsored by KING Broadcasting, Seattle, Washington.
9. Brenda Dervin et al., "The Development of Strategies for Dealing with the Information Needs of Urban Residents: Phase I—Citizen Study," Final Report, Project #L0035JA, U.S. Department of Health, Education and Welfare, Office of Education, Office of Libraries and Learning Resources, April 1976.
10. For a popularized but nonetheless competent account of question (and other) bias in questionnaires, see Michael Wheeler, *Lies, Damn Lies and Statistics* (New York: Liveright, 1976).

11. Alex Edelstein, "Have We Reached the Pollenium?", School of Communications, University of Washington, Seattle, 1978 (mimeo). Prepared as a chapter for Lee Thayer, compiler, *Ethics, Morality and the Media: Reflections of American Culture*, New Edition (New York: Hastings House, 1980).

12. Bradley Greenberg, Thomas F. Baldwin, Byron Reeves, Lee Thornton, and Jack Wakshlag, "Methods of Ascertaining Community and Community Leader Needs," (Technical report submitted to the Office of Communication Research, Corporation for Public Broadcasting), Department of Communication and Television-Radio, Michigan State University, East Lansing, Michigan, November 1974.

13. It is not possible to organize examples illustrating the individual problems summarized in the previous paragraphs. Rather, the conceptual design of each study described might account for several criticisms made.

14. Neil Bruce Holbert, "Research: The Ways of Academe and Business," *Business Horizons* (February 1976): 36; see also: James E. Grunig and Robert H. Hickson, "An Evaluation of Academic Research in Public Relations Research," *Public Relations Review* 2 (Spring 1976): 31–43.

15. Richard F. Carter, "Response from a Communications Researcher," *Public Relations Review* 5 (Spring 1979): 45–47. This paper was one of several responses to Lindenmann (see endnote 3).

16. Glenn M. Broom, "Coorientational Measurement of Public Issues," *Public Relations Review* 3 (Winter 1977): 110–119. The reader is encouraged to review the balance of this volume, which contains a series of articles devoted to measuring the effectiveness of public relations.

17. John E. Bowes and Keith R. Stamm, "Evaluating Communication with Public Agencies," *Public Relations Review* 1 (Summer 1975): 23–37. For a detailed report of this study, see: John E. Bowes and

Keith R. Stamm, "Development Priorities in the West River Region, North Dakota: A Social Attitude and Communication Analysis," Communication Research Center, University of Washington, Seattle, Washington (October 1974).

18. Keith R. Stamm, "Strategies for Evaluating Public Relations," *Public Relations Review* 3 (Winter 1977): 120–128.

19. Steven H. Chaffee and Jack M. McLeod, eds., "Interpersonal Perceptions and Communication," special edition of the *American Behavioral Scientist* 16 (March–April 1973): 484.

20. Note that not all possible accuracy comparisons were made in this study. Omitted were citizens' and agencies' estimates of community leaders; thus, accuracy measures could not be made for these two groups with respect to community leaders. This limitation was primarily necessitated by the length of interview that would otherwise have resulted.

21. James E. Grunig, "Evaluating Employee Communications in a Research Operation," *Public Relations Review* 3 (Winter 1977): 61–82.

22. See: Raymond Bauer, "The Limits of Persuasion," *Harvard Business Review* (September–October 1958): 105–110; Herbert Krugman, "An Application of Learning Theory to TV Copy Testing," *Public Opinion Quarterly* 26 (1962): 626–634; and Herbert Krugman and E. L. Hartley, "Passive Learning from Television," *Public Opinion Quarterly* 34 (1970): 184–190.

23. Keith R. Stamm, Brenda Dervin, and Robert Laing, "Applying Communication Research to Environmental Policy Decisions: Seattle's Solid Waste Planning," School of Communications, University of Washington, Seattle, Washington, 1975 (mimeo).

24. Alex Edelstein, "Attribute Structure, Education and Communication with Respect to Vietnam," a paper presented to the International Communications Division, Association for Education in Journalism, Washington, D.C., August 1970.

25. Richard F. Carter, "Communication and Affective Relations," *Journalism Quarterly* 42 (1965): 203–212.
26. In Vernon Palmour, Patricia Rathbun, William H. Brown, Brenda Dervin, and Patricia M. Dowd, *Information Needs of Californians*, prepared for the California State Library, March 1979. For an earlier conceptual organization and literature review of this area, see: Brenda Dervin, "The Everyday Information Needs of the Average Citizen: A Taxonomy for Analysis," chapter 2, in Manfred Kochen and Joseph Donohue, *Information for the Community* (Chicago: American Library Association, 1976), 19–38.
27. Ibid., 30.
28. Ibid., 34–35.

Additional References

Atkin, Charles K. "Anticipated Communication and Mass Media Information Seeking," *Public Opinion Quarterly*, 36 (Summer 1972): 188–196.

Baldwin, Thomas F., Bradley S. Greenberg, Martin P. Block, John B. Eulenberg, and Thomas A. Muth. "Michigan State University-Rockford Two-way Cable Project: System Design, Application Experiments and Public Policy Issues," Volume I, Summary of the Final Report, NSF Grant #APR75–14286, Department of Telecommunications, Michigan State University, East Lansing, Michigan, June 1978.

Bogart, Leo. "Changing News Interests and the News Media," *Public Opinion Quarterly* 32 (1968): 560.

Bowes, John E., Keith R. Stamm, Kenneth M. Jackson, and Jeff Moore. *Communication of Technical Information to Lay Audiences*, Prepared for Union Carbide Corp. under contract #W–7405–ENG–26 to the U.S. Department of Energy, Office of Waste Isolation as Report #Y/OWI/SUB–78–22337 by the Communication Research Center, School of Communications, University of Washington, May 1978.

Chaffee, S. H., and J. M. McLeod. "Individual vs. Social Predictors of Information Seeking," *Journalism Quarterly* 50 (1973): 237–245.

Dervin, Brenda. "Information: An Answer for Every Question? A Solution for Every Problem?" *Journal of Broadcasting* 20 (1976): 323–344. This special section contains two relevant articles: Brenda Dervin, "Strategies for Dealing with Human Information Needs: Information or Communication?" and John E. Bowes, "Media Technology: Detour or Panacea for Resolving Urban Information Needs."

Dervin, Brenda. "Communication Behaviors as Related to Information Control Behaviors of Low Income Adults," unpublished doctoral dissertation, Department of Communications, Michigan State University, East Lansing, Michigan, 1971.

Edelstein, Alex. *The Uses of Communication in Decision-Making: A Comparative Study of Yugoslavia and the United States*, New York: Praeger, 1974.

Gee, Gerald M. *Urban Information Needs—A Replication: A Report of the Syracuse/Elmira Study*. Final Report from the Center for Study of Information and Education, Syracuse University, to the U.S. Office of Education, Division of Library Programs, Contract #OEG–72–5405, 1974.

Greenberg, Bradley, and Brenda Dervin. *The Use of Mass Media by the Urban Poor*, New York: Praeger, 1970.

Hunt, J. McV. "Motivation Inherent in Information Processing and Action." In J. Harvey, ed., *Motivation and Social Interaction*, New York: Ronald Press, 1963, 35–94.

Katona, G., and E. Mueller. "A Study of Purchase Decisions," in Lincoln Clark, ed., *Consumer Behavior: The Dynamics of Consumer Reaction*, New York: New York University Press, 1955.

Nelson, P. "Information and Consumer Behavior," *Journal of Political Economics* 78 (1970): 311–329.

Parker, E. B., and William J. Paisley. "Patterns of Adult Information Seeking," Stanford University Institute of Communications Research, 1966.

Rees, Matilda, and William J. Paisley. "Social and Psychological Predictors of Information Seeking and Media Use," Report of the Institute for Communication Research, Stanford University, September 1967, 107 pp.

Surlin, Stuart H. "Ascertainment through Community Leaders," *Journal of Broadcasting* 18 (1974): 97–107.

Tipton, L. P. "Effects of Writing Tasks on Utility of Information and Order of Seeking," *Journalism Quarterly* 47 (1970): 309–317.

Wade, Serena, and Wilbur Schramm. "Mass Media as a Source of Public Affairs, Science and Health Knowledge," *Public Opinion Quarterly* 33 (1969): 197–209.

Warner, Edward S., Ann D. Murray, and Vernon E. Palmour. *Information Needs of Urban Residents.* Final report of the Regional Planning Council of Baltimore, Maryland, and Westat, Inc., of Rockville, Maryland, to the U.S. Office of Education, Division of Library Programs, Contract EOC-0-71-455, December 1973.

II
Research Problems: Theoretical and Applied

Agenda setting is the mass media's ability to tell people what to think about, but not what to think.[1] More precisely, the media, while performing their news function, determine which issues will receive order and time/space emphasis based on a set of objective criteria. These media agenda are then communicated to their respective audiences. If the media can affect or set agendas, the audience will prioritize or ascribe levels of importance to issues corresponding to the media emphases. For example, if a television network continually emphasizes issues related to the Third World by leading with and devoting the most time to these stories, its viewers should also believe the Third World to be most important. If the second issue in emphasis is the SALT negotiations, then viewers should perceive the treaty as the second most important issue. If the media set agendas, then the media and audience agendas should be highly correlated or similar.

The general findings of most studies on the agenda setting function support this notion—the media do set personal agendas. However, many conditions are contingent to this effect. For example, commitment to a candidate affects how the media set personal agendas during political campaigns. Other contingent conditions include, but are not limited to, audience: (1) need for information, (2) salience (personal importance of issues), (3) age, (4) education, and (5) political involvement. Many conditions contingent to the agenda-setting function involve political campaign variables because most of this research has been conducted in campaign environments. Political campaigns provide an ideal setting for agenda-setting research for two reasons. First, messages are designed to have specific effects. Candidates are continually attempting to set political agendas through access to the news media, personal appearances, and paid political announcements, to name a few. Second, campaigns have a definable beginning and an end with a measurable, terminal behavior—the vote.

Because most agenda-setting studies are conducted in political campaigns, they begin before election day. The typical study begins

13
Agenda-Setting Research

Wenmouth Williams, Jr.

with the collection of the media agenda(s). The three television network newscasts and the local daily newspapers are the most common media considered in these studies, primarily because they have the most impact on the greatest number of voters. This data collection process is usually started about two to four weeks before the audience survey.

Two strategies for surveying the audience are common to the typical agenda-setting study. First, registered voters have been randomly sampled. For obvious reasons, political researchers are only interested in studying effects the media have on people eligible to vote. Second, some studies involve a random sampling of all adults (over eighteen years of age) in a community because they are considered potential future voters or because the researchers are interested in studying both voters and nonvoters.

Audience agendas are determined in a variety of ways. During the audience survey, each respondent is asked to list the most important issues relevant to the political campaign in terms of interpersonal and intrapersonal perceptions. Interpersonal agendas are constructed from responses to an open-ended question such as:

When talking to others, what is the most important presidential campaign issue?

A question measuring the intrapersonal agenda might be:

What do you feel is the most important political campaign issue, to you personally?[2]

The reason for differentiating interpersonal and intrapersonal agendas will be discussed later.

The media and personal agendas are then constructed from content analyses. The result is two rank orderings of issues. The media agenda is comprised of categorized issues rank ordered by the amount of space or time devoted to all issues within the category. The personal agenda is constructed by totaling the number of respondents naming each issue as most important within the category of issues.

Categories are then rank ordered according to the number of mentions each issue receives. For example, one issue category common to most agenda-setting studies is the economy. This category might be comprised of stories on the inflation rate, the prime interest rates, and the gross national product. If ABC covers these three issues and devotes one minute to each during the media survey period, a total of three minutes would be assigned to the economy category. Two other categories of issues common to most agenda setting studies would be foreign affairs and the government. If two minutes and one minute were devoted to these categories respectively, the ABC agenda would look like this:

ABC AGENDA

Issue	Time	Rank
1. Economy	3 minutes	1
2. Foreign affairs	2 minutes	2
3. Government	1 minute	3

The audience agenda is constructed by summing the number of mentions an issue within each category receives in the audience survey. A hypothetical agenda of 225 respondents might look like this:

AUDIENCE AGENDA

Issue	Mentions	Rank
1. Economy	100	1
2. Foreign affairs	75	2
3. Government	50	3

The agenda-setting effect is usually determined by computing a Spearman Rho rank order correlation between the audience and media agendas. In the preceding example, the correlation would be 1.00, a perfect relationship. The conclusion would be that ABC set the audience agenda in the hypothetical study. The logic is that the ABC agenda preceded the audience agenda. Therefore, it is likely that ABC affected its audience's perception of issue importance.

Perfect correlations between media and personal agendas are rarely, if ever, found because of the contingent conditions mentioned earlier, measurement error, coding reliability, and validity, or even the methods of collecting data. The data collection procedures for determining media and personal agendas are discussed below.

Collecting and Analyzing Personal Agendas

Two issues are relevant to the discussion of agenda setting research when collecting and analyzing personal agendas. The first issue, briefly discussed in the introduction, concerns the conceptualization of the personal agendas as either interpersonal or intrapersonal. The second issue involves the operationalization of the personal agendas.

Personal Agenda Conceptualization

The personal or audience agenda has been conceptualized as either intrapersonal or interpersonal. This distinction is made because researchers have believed that the electorate uses two types of issues when making political decisions. The first type, intrapersonal, is comprised of issues personally important to the respondent but not usually discussed with other people. Conversely, the interpersonal agenda is comprised of issues used in conversations. The latter group of issues may or may not be personally important in the political decision-making process. For example, one voter may believe that relations with Communist China are important but may only discuss the economy with friends. Unfortunately, no studies have determined which agenda is most important in voting decisions.

Research has been conducted to determine, in part, which conceptualization is most relevant to the agenda-setting process. An early study by McCombs found some, but not perfect, overlap between interpersonal and intrapersonal agendas of college students.[3] A more recent study by Semlak and Williams found a +.91 correlation between the intrapersonal and interpersonal agendas of central Illinois residents.[4] The difference between these two

results can be explained by differences in survey populations and environments. The McCombs study surveyed college students not involved in a political campaign.

In terms of the agenda-setting function, research has found that the media generally have the most impact on the interpersonal agenda.[5] In fact, many studies have found that the media provide the stimulus for discussion, in general. However, these effects might be affected by the type of media considered: newspapers might have the most impact on intrapersonal agendas, and the broadcast media could most affect the interpersonal agenda.[6] The research question should guide the decision of how to measure the personal agenda.

Personal Agenda Operationalizations

At least five different operationalizations or methods of measuring personal agendas have been used in previous agenda setting studies:

1. Asking the respondent to name the most important issue (open ended).
2. Asking the respondent to rank order a predetermined list of issues (closed ended).
3. Asking respondents to rate a list of issues.
4. Using paired comparisons in a predetermined list.[7]
5. Asking respondents to link issues to one another.

The open-ended operationalization of the personal agenda, described in the introduction, is the most common.[8] The obvious problem with this measurement strategy is that it favors the more educated audience or the person best able to verbalize important issues. The advantage is that the respondent is not forced to respond with an issue selected by the researcher, as in the closed-ended technique.

Closed-ended operationalizations require the respondent to evaluate a list of issues preselected by the researcher.[9] Usually listed are issues emphasized by the media and determined by a content analysis immediately before the audience survey. The disadvantage of the closed-ended item is that it could preset the respondent; that is, the person could respond with an important issue when none of the issues mentioned in the question are actually perceived as important. An advantage could be for the less educated respondent who cannot verbalize important problems but can select important issues from a structured list.

The third operationalization of the personal agenda is rating issues.[10] These ratings might be of a preselected list or of an issue elicited from the respondent by an open-ended question. For example, the respondent might be asked to rate on a Likert-type scale (with answers ranging from very important to very unimportant) his or her perceived importance of a selected list of issues (closed ended). The second alternative requires the respondent to rate an issue on a Likert scale after it is elicited by an open-ended question. These strategies offer an additional benefit from the single open- or closed-ended question because parametric statistics can be applied to the rating responses. Also, rating questions can indicate issue saliency, an important precondition to the agenda-setting function.[11]

A fourth method for measuring the personal agenda is using paired comparisons. Each issue of a preselected list is paired with every other issue, and the respondent is asked which issue in each pair is more important.[12] Using the hypothetical list of three issues discussed earlier, a paired comparison list would look like this:

Pair	First Ranked Issue
1. Economy–Foreign affairs	1. Economy
2. Economy–Government	2. Economy
3. Foreign affairs–Government	3. Foreign affairs

Every time a respondent names an issue, when compared to its match, as most important, it receives a value of one (1). A two (2) is assigned for the second ranked issue in each pair. These values are then summed. In the preceding example, the summed totals would be:

Issue	Total
1. Economy	2
2. Foreign affairs	3
3. Government	4

The advantage of this procedure is that issues are compared to one another in terms of their relative importance to the respondent, a benefit not possible in the other operationalizations. Also, interval level data, making parametric statistical analyses possible, allow for more sophisticated tests of agenda setting. However, the paired comparisons technique suffers from the same disadvantages of all closed-ended strategies. Further, measuring the personal agenda takes longer in the interview, an important commodity in survey research.

If time is not crucial and the researcher wants to know more than just the one or two important issues perceived by the respondent, Edelstein's content-free interview schedule can be used. Briefly, this technique allows the researcher to determine how the respondent really feels about selected issues. Probes in the questionnaire require the respondent to give alternatives to the identified problem, evaluations of these proposals, the reasoning responsible for these evaluations, and the desired solutions.[13] Using this technique in an agenda-setting study, Benton and Frazier argued that the media can affect not only perceptions of most important issues (level I), but also subissues (level II) and possible solutions (level III). By comparing agendas in these three levels to what a daily newspaper and the three television networks were communicating, Benton and Frazier could tell how the media affected the various levels of what they labeled "information holding." Considering only levels II and III, they found newspapers influential; television did not impact on the personal agendas.[14] The conclusions from this study are that perceptions of issue importance are complex and that the media can have more than a simple agenda-setting effect. Analyses of the personal agenda, such as conducted by Benton and Frazier, are necessary for the researcher interested in these complex processes.

Based on this discussion, the decision concerning which operationalization to use depends on the research question posed by the investigator. Exploratory studies of an electorate should probably use an open-ended strategy. Other operationalizations would restrict the variance of answers possible in the study. Closed-ended questions are most appropriate for less educated populations and when the researcher is interested only in perceptions of issues presented by the media. The other operationalizations are necessary when sophisticated research questions are posed that necessitate sophisticated analytic techniques.

In terms of validity, Semlak and Williams found statistically significant correlations between agendas elicited by the open-ended and closed-ended questions. When the perceived salient issues, determined by including only issues that respondents rated as very important, were considered, the correlations were still statistically significant. This finding suggests that both operationalizations had predictive validity in this study.[15] Unfortunately, no research, to date, has assessed the actual validity of the other three methods of measuring the personal agenda. The same criticism applies to determining the media agenda.

Collecting and Analyzing the Media Agenda

The collection and analysis of the media agenda have been separated for purposes of discussion. The collection decision involves issues relative to what media content to collect and when to begin the collection process. Decisions in the analysis stage must consider from where to collect this information and what methods of data synthesis to use. Naturally, these decisions must be guided by the researcher's initial research question.

Collecting the Media Agenda

Two perplexing issues of collecting the media agenda are what to collect and when to start. The answer to the first question, like all research decisions, depends on the research

question. If the researcher is primarily interested in investigating the general agenda-setting effect, all the media available in the study market must be considered. For example, if the study is to be conducted in a major market, local and national television newscasts and daily newspapers must be included in the research design. However, radio newscasts probably would not be important. If the market has no local television station, other media sources for local problems should be considered. For example, a study by Williams and Larsen found radio and cable access newscasts had a measurable impact on personal agendas.[16]

The second issue—when to begin collecting the media content—has received considerable attention. Logically, this part of the study must precede the collection of the audience survey. The question is, how far in advance must the researcher begin the media survey? McCombs, Becker, and Weaver suggest four months as the optimum time lag.[17] Unfortunately, such a long period is suitable only for specific types of research and pragmatic only in a limited number of studies. When time is limited, the collection of media data must also be limited. Given this problem, Semlak and Williams investigated the relative impact of collecting media data for three, six, and nine weeks before the audience survey. They found the media agenda to be very stable within the three week time period. Most correlations between media agendas for the three time periods were statistically significant. Because of the stability across time periods, Semlak and Williams argue that a three-week lag between starting the media and audience surveys should be sufficient.[18] However, this conclusion presupposes that nothing important occurs during this time. An event like a political assassination could produce an unstable agenda, making a longer time lag necessary.

In terms of a direct test of the impact these time lags have on personal agendas, a secondary analysis of the Semlak and Williams data was conducted. The results showed little variation when the media and personal agendas were correlated, further supporting the preceding discussion. Naturally, this analysis does not consider the overall impact a more lengthy media survey would have on the personal agenda. For example, would the media survey conducted by McCombs et al. show more of an agenda-setting effect than the agendas considered by Semlak and Williams? Further research in this area should answer this question and assist with the analysis of the media agenda.

Analyzing the Media Agenda

A variety of content analytic schemes have been used to measure the manifest and latent media agendas.[19] The most common strategy groups issues into categories, thus only measuring manifest or intended content. These categories are then ranked using the procedure discussed in the introduction. Using another simple content analytic scheme, Funkhouser determined the emphasis of national issues in three weekly news magazines by counting the number of stories dealing with each issue in the *Readers' Guide to Periodical Literature.*[20] Both the category and Funkhouser strategies are advantageous in their relative simplicity. Even though the content analysis process is time consuming, these strategies take little time compared to the more sophisticated techniques designed to measure both manifest and latent content. These more sophisticated techniques, described below, include: (1) the Greenfield Experiment, (2) verbal and nonverbal strategies, (3) the matrix approach, (4) visual analyses, and (5) other strategies.

Greenfield Experiment   Using the work of Funkhouser and an index developed by Greenfield for a basis, Beniger counted the number of stories dealing with various national issues from the year 1900 as a measure of social indicators. He argues that this content analytic technique is a fairly objective measure, citing as evidence the corresponding increases in drug-related stories and teenage drug deaths in the late 1960s. The value of this strategy, according to Beniger, is its suitability for dividing broad issues into their components.[21] For example, the economy, as a national issue, comprises concerns about inflation, jobs, and the price of gold. A second value of the Greenfield

Experiment is the ability to identify cycles of media issue emphasis.

Beniger concludes that future uses of this content analysis strategy might be applied to the *New York Times Index* and *TV Guide*. Unfortunately, such shortcuts to collecting media data base, as originally noted by Funkhouser, make the researcher dependent on the index compilers. The researcher should collect original data when possible. However, analyses such as Beniger's preclude such a systematic procedure. Therefore, the real value of the Greenfield Experiment is its ability to synthesize vast amounts of data. When the research question does not mandate such synthesis, more systematic content analytic tools, such as verbal and nonverbal strategies, are available.

Verbal and Nonverbal Strategies   The content analysis of verbal and nonverbal communication events on television was the focus of research conducted by Jackson-Beeck and Meadow. Their four-category matrix included the following communication content: (1) physiological and body language variables, (2) nonfluent vocal cues, (3) metaphors and imagery, and (4) manifest content. They used four data sources to analyze the 1960 and 1976 Presidential debates to compare and contrast the issues and candidates. For example, Carter stressed natural resources (analysis of manifest content) and talked much faster than Ford with more vocal errors (nonfluent vocal cues content). The latter finding, according to Jackson-Beeck and Meadow, supports the overall evaluation of Carter's performance as being more "nervous" than Ford's.[22]

The value of this content analytic technique to agenda setting research probably is in the analysis of metaphors and imagery. The use of salient metaphors could subconsciously affect a person's perception of the candidate. Another measure of latent meanings of news involves building an issue matrix.

Matrix Approach   The typical agenda-setting study considers the manifest content without regard to special emphases of selected stories. For the broadcaster, special emphases might include story placement or the use of visuals. The print journalist also uses story placement along with headlines and pictures to emphasize important issues. The print journalist, unlike the broadcaster, can also use related or secondary issues for explanatory purposes. For example, inflation can be explained in terms of relations with Israel. The print journalist has more flexibility because he or she has more column inches than the broadcaster has time. Unfortunately, few agenda-setting studies have considered what Greendale and Fredin call the relational approach to analyzing the news.[23]

The relational approach decomposes newspaper stories into most important and associated issues. Considering the first example in the preceding paragraph, inflation would be the most important issue and unemployment would be the associate. Using this distinction, Greendale and Fredin categorize each issue in terms of direction of influence. An issue with no associate is labeled an isolate. The most important issue has a prominence relation to the associate. Inflation is prominent to unemployment. Finally, unemployment has a contextual relation to inflation. Using this content analytic strategy, both the manifest content (analyses of most important issues) and latent connections (prominence and contextual relations) can be analyzed.

The value of this strategy is its ability to uncover regularly mentioned issues that rarely are most important in a given story. For support of this conclusion, Greendale and Fredin turn to an analysis of some 1976 election data collected by the Institute for Social Research. In terms of the prominence relation in the newspapers, coverage of the campaign, Watergate was an associate issue to the prominent issue—a Democratic landslide. For respondents surveyed around election day, Greendale and Fredin found Watergate to be an associate for confidence in government, government performance and competence, and government power issues. Other differences in issue relations were found between the newspaper and the respondents.

The relational approach could also be used in the analysis of broadcast content. Some stories could contain both a most important and

associate issue. In this instance, the strategy is directly applicable. Issue relations might also be analyzed in terms of story placement. A television newscast often juxtaposes related stories. For example, one news block might consist of reports from Iran, Afghanistan, and Communist China. Treating relations as sequences of stories might reveal patterns similar to the ones identified by Greendale and Fredin. Other strategies might include an analysis of visual techniques used by the broadcaster to emphasize selected stories.

Visual Analysis   A final content analytic approach designed to measure latent meaning considers the visual element in a broadcast news program. Two applications of this approach, conducted by Frank[24] and Hofstetter,[25] studied the 1972 Presidential campaign, considering story placement, videotape, and other visual techniques used to emphasize either McGovern or Nixon. The studies did not uncover any consistent biases in candidates' treatment.

Williams and Semlak's study of the 1976 Presidential campaign linked these visual emphases to agenda setting. Separate media agendas constructed for first and second stories, chroma key, sound-on-film, rear-screen projections, and videotape stories were correlated to the personal agendas. Story placement had the most impact on the personal agendas; static visuals like chroma key were second in influence.[26] The conclusion is that latent meanings in the news, in this case measured by visual analyses, can affect perceptions of issue importance. Similar findings might also result from using other latent content analytic techniques.

Contextual Analysis   One element missing from most studies on agenda setting is the context or frame of reference that a specific story receives in the media. For example, stories concerning relationships between Egypt and Israel are given a Middle East referent; issues dealing with crime statistics can be given a domestic frame. During political campaigns, news editors face the problem of competing frames of reference. Stories that could easily be given a Middle East frame also are relevant to the ongoing campaign process. So, stories included in the media agenda are given either their regular frame or one that gives the story meaning in terms of the campaign. News stories with a campaign frame are directly related to a specific campaign. For example, Ronald Reagan's opinion of relationships between Egypt and Israel, if specifically mentioned in a news item, would have had a campaign frame in 1980. If no specific reference to a candidate's position is made, the story is communicated in its regular frame.

Application of framing to the agenda-setting process was the subject of a series of studies conducted by Williams, Shapiro, and Cutbirth. Essentially, they found that stories with a political frame were more likely to affect personal agendas of campaign issues than were stories with no reference to the Presidential race.[27] Furthermore, media agendas with campaign frames enhanced the effect of relevant antecedent and intervening variables discussed later in this essay. The conclusion is that the context of issues in the media agenda directly affects how people perceive them.

Two other variables relevant to a contextual analysis of media content are obtrusiveness and duration. Obtrusive issues can be directly experienced by respondents in a survey; unobtrusive issues cannot. For example, problems with local school systems can be directly experienced; they are obtrusive. Conversely, relationships between Egypt and Israel cannot be directly experienced; they are unobtrusive. Duration refers to the time an issue has been included in media agenda.

Zucker's examination of both obtrusiveness and duration found the media to have their greatest agenda-setting effect for unobtrusive issues.[28] The reasoning is that respondents would not know about an issue, or its importance, without the mass media. Everyone can directly experience poor roads or economic conditions; they do not need the media to explain their importance. Other studies[29] confirm these findings.

Duration also is an important content variable. Zucker found that the longer an issue remained in the media agenda, the less impact it had on personal agendas. However, an issue highlighted by an event will be perceived as a new issue and have an impact on personal agendas. For example, the Equal Rights Amendment was a part of most media agendas for some time. The impact of this coverage increased when significant events occurred, such as ratification votes in key states, such as Illinois.

Other Content Analytic Tools Any discussion of media content analysis must include some of the organized efforts to collect and code it. For a more detailed discussion, see essays 1 and 3. For example, media archives such as at Vanderbilt University record and publish summaries of the three network newscasts. These summaries are housed in many libraries across the country. Care must be exercised when using just the summaries to construct the media agenda because they are often too short for extensive analyses of latent content and sometimes can be misleading even for the coding of manifest content.

Organized efforts to code newspaper content also are under way. Janowitz discusses the *Trend Report*, a mass content analysis of 200 representative daily newspapers. This analysis differs from the television archives in that stories are actually coded into relatively sophisticated categories. The results of these analyses have been used as indicators of social change.[30] Since any study of agenda setting must also, by definition, be a study of social change, content analyses such as the *Trend Report* could affect this area of research.

After the researcher has decided the conceptual and operational definitions of the personal agenda and the type of media survey appropriate to answer the research question, the next step is to select the best statistical analysis. Again, this decision should be considered in terms of the research question.

Statistical Analyses

Two basic statistical analyses have been popular in research studying the agenda setting function: (1) correlational and (2) causal. Since most past studies have been correlational, most of this discussion involves these tests. A more detailed examination of causal statistics is found in essay 9.

Correlational Analysis

The most common statistical test of agenda setting is the Spearman Rho rank order statistic discussed earlier. Other nonparametric statistics are Kendall's Tau and Gamma. Some studies have attempted to make the agendas interval-appearing by computing the percent of respondents naming issues within each category and then correlating these agendas to the media with a Pearson product-moment statistic.[31]

Partial correlations have also been used in these studies to identify the preconditions to the agenda-setting function. Two procedures have been used. First, true partial correlations (using percentages for interval appearing scales) have been computed. This technique controls by partialing out the effects of selected variables. For example, the effect of education on the relationship between the newspaper and personal agendas can be statistically eliminated using this technique.

The second method of controlling the effects of preconditions in agenda setting is to compute agendas for individual categories of variables. For example, the researcher might want to determine the effect of education. Two agendas could be computed: one for the very educated and one for the very uneducated. A hypothetical example would look like this:

Very Educated	*Very Uneducated*
1. Foreign affairs	1. Economy
2. Government	2. Government
3. Economy	3. Foreign affairs

These two agendas would then be correlated with the newspaper using the Spearman Rho. If the correlations were .95 for the very educated agenda and .42 for the very uneducated, newspapers would be said to have an agenda-setting effect on the former, but not the latter. A further control would be to consider only

newspaper readers when constructing these personal agendas. Nonreaders might suppress the true agenda-setting process.

Causal Analyses

The intention of causal analyses is to identify possible causal links between the media and personal agendas. Such analyses can be conducted with cross-sectional or panel studies. In cross-sectional design (one-shot survey), one causal statistic is path analysis. An example is Weaver and Wilhoit's study designed to measure political activities on senatorial news coverage. They found causal links between staff and state size and the senator's ability to obtain media visibility.[32]

One method of determining causal relationships in panel studies is cross-lagged correlations. This technique uses partial correlations to determine the direct impact of the media at one time on the personal agenda at the same time and at a later time. For example, McCombs's study attempted to determine whether television or newspapers had the greater agenda setting impact. Registered voters, the three television networks, and the daily newspapers were surveyed in June, October, and November 1972. A diagram of one analysis in the McCombs study might look this:

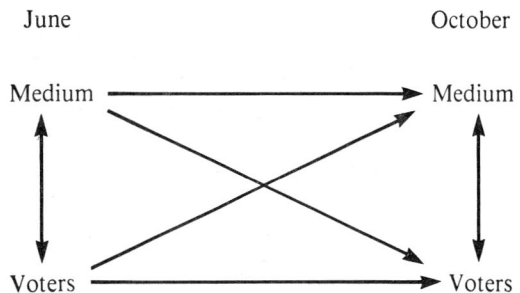

To determine the causal link between a medium in October and voters in November, partial correlations were computed for each arrow. The correlation from the medium in October to the voters in November should be greater than a baseline statistic and the synchronous correlations (computed between the medium and the voters at the same time). In terms of newspaper influence, the cross-lag between June and October was greater than both the synchronous correlations and the cross-lag from voters in October and the medium in June. This finding shows the causal link between newspaper and personal agendas during an election year. Similar findings did not result from the analysis of television's impact on voters.[33]

Research using statistical tests in these two broad categories reveals an agenda-setting effect. Correlational studies document the relationships between the media and personal agendas; causal analyses uncover causal links between what the media emphasize and what voters perceive as important. Let us now use this information to begin building an agenda-setting theory.

Agenda-Setting Theory

Many studies on the agenda-setting function conclude that the media can and do affect perceptions of issue importance. This effect has been found in the political environment and in off-election years. Fairly recent research has begun to synthesize the results of past studies, with the desired product being a theory of agenda setting.

McCombs, in a review of agenda-setting research, suggested two methods of theory construction. The first method is the hypothetico-deductive approach. The researcher, using common sense or speculation, posits and tests bivariate (two variable) relationships. Without sufficient information to predict precisely how these variables will interact, the researcher posits crude relationships. The second, slower approach is matrix building, in which the researcher uses past studies and systematically tests bivariate relationships through precise hypotheses.[34]

The actual theory-building process involves both approaches. The researcher systematically builds matrices of bivariate and multivariate relationships and also uses intuition to test other variables. The result is a matrix or matrices of variables that describe the preconditions to the agenda-setting process. Using this approach or approaches, Williams and Semlak suggest building two matrices: one for antecedent variables and one for intervening variables.

Antecedent Variables

Antecedent variables come before a proposed bivariate relationship. For example, a person's sex is an antecedent variable, no other variables can cause it. In agenda setting, antecedent variables come before the media-perception bivariate relationship. Using the hypothetico-deductive approach, researchers might suggest a number of antecedent preconditions using political campaigns. Most of these suggested variables have been used in past political communication studies to identify the active, interested voters and include a person's political involvement, civic activity, vote intention, professional activity, presidential campaign interest, and opinion leadership. The first four variables have been successfully linked to agenda setting.[35]

These results can now be used to add other antecedent variables to the matrix. Because variables that can distinguish politically active voters or the early deciders in a campaign from the inactives or nonvoters are preconditions to agenda setting, other variables can be suggested (matrix approach). For example, the number of elections in which a respondent voted is a measure of political activity that might also be related to agenda setting.[36]

Political activity variables might also suggest antecedent conditions to agenda setting in off-election years. For example, research shows the politically active voter engaging in more discussions involving politics. Using this reasoning, the researcher could systematically identify people who are more likely to discuss current events and could determine whether the media affect these discussions (interpersonal agenda) and what the person perceives as personally most important (intrapersonal agenda).

The hypothetico-deductive approach has also been important in identifying the most important antecedent precondition to agenda setting—salience, or the need for information. Many studies show that people who most need information regularly use the media for news and are most affected by the media when structuring their personal agendas. For example, using high and low relevance and uncertainty as antecedents, Weaver found that need for information was linked to media use; voters with high relevance and uncertainty (high need) used the media more than voters with high relevance and low uncertainty (moderate need) or low relevance (low need). Linking to agenda setting, voters with a high need for information had agendas more similar to the daily newspaper and network television newscasts than did voters with a moderate or low need for information.[37]

The list of variables in the antecedent matrix is extensive. The intention of this discussion is not to present each one, but to show how the hypothetico-deductive and matrix building approaches to theory construction have been used to identify variables antecedent to the agenda-setting process. These approaches have also been used to construct an intervening matrix.

Intervening Variables

The intervening variable comes between the media-perception relationship. The most logical intervening variable in the agenda-setting process is media use. The more attentive people are to the news media, the more likely they are to have their personal agendas affected. Many studies using the hypothetico-deductive approach have found such a relationship.[38] The amount of news coverage given to a special issue also affects perceptions of the importance ascribed to the issue.[39] In both instances, the need for information was a crucial antecedent variable.

Other variables can be added to the intervening variable matrix using a general conceptualization of media use for a basis. For example, the mass medium most often used as a source of information for perceived impor-

tant issues could enter into the agenda-setting process. Such was the finding in the Williams and Semlak study discussed earlier. Respondents' agendas were most affected by their preferred television network newscast.[40]

Media use has also been used as a basis for considering political knowledge in the intervening matrix. Hypothetically, the same people who use the media for information because they have a high need should also know the most about their government. Williams and Larsen tested this, with positive results.[41] However, more sophisticated measures of political knowledge must be developed.

As with the antecedent variable matrix, construction of the intervening variable matrix has benefitted from both the hypothetico-deductive and matrix-building approaches. Basically, the hypothetico-deductive approach is best for adding variables to both matrices that, at first consideration, seem unrelated to existing variables in the matrix. The matrix-building approach is beneficial in systematically guiding agenda-setting research by forcing the researcher to use past studies to formulate more specific hypotheses.

Summary

The agenda-setting process, like all communication processes, is complex because of the necessary preconditions. These preconditions have been identified through various methods of media and personal agenda collection and analysis. The media data collection methods range from simple inspections of media summaries such as *Readers' Guide* to the more rigorous strategies of issue coding in the verbal and nonverbal strategies. Measuring the personal agenda can be as simple as asking people to name their most important issue to investigating how they perceive connections between issues. Statistical analyses also have a wide range of sophistication, from simple rank-order correlations to complex path analysis.

The result of these studies has been the not-so systematic identification of preconditions to the agenda-setting process. Let us hope that future research will continue to identify these preconditions so that a theory of agenda setting can be developed.

Endnotes

1. Bernard C. Cohen, *The Press, The Public and Foreign Policy* (Princeton, N.J.: Princeton University Press, 1963), 13.
2. These questions are taken from Wenmouth Williams, Jr., and William D. Semlak, "Campaign '76: Agenda Setting During the New Hampshire Primary," *Journal of Broadcasting* 22 (1978): 531–540.
3. Maxwell E. McCombs, "A Comparison of Intra-Personal and Inter-Personal Agendas," paper presented to the annual meeting of the International Communication Association, New Orleans, 1974.
4. William D. Semlak and Wenmouth Williams, Jr., "Methodological Problems of Agenda Setting Research," paper presented to the annual meeting of the Speech Communication Association, Washington, D.C., 1977.
5. Lee B. Becker, Maxwell E. McCombs, and Jack M. McLeod, "The Development of Political Cognitions," in Steven H. Chaffee, ed., *Political Communication: Issues and Strategies for Research* (Beverly Hills, Calif.: Sage Publications, 1975), 21–64.
6. Maxwell E. McCombs, "Elaborating the Agenda Setting Influence of Mass Communication," paper prepared for the *Bulletin of the Institute for Communication Research*, Keio University, Tokyo, Japan, 1976.
7. Semlak and Williams, op. cit.
8. For example, see Maxwell E. McCombs and Donald L. Shaw, "The Agenda Setting Function of the Media," *Public Opinion Quarterly* 36 (1972), 176–187.
9. Jack M. McLeod, Lee B. Becker, and James E. Byrnes, "Another Look at the Agenda Setting Function of the Press," *Communication Research* 1 (1974): 131–183.
10. For example, see Robert D. McClure and Thomas E. Patterson, "Television News and Political Advertising: The Impact of Exposure in Voter Beliefs," *Communication Research* 1 (1974): 3–31.
11. David H. Weaver, "Political Issues and Voter Need for Orientation," in Donald L. Shaw and Maxwell E. McCombs, eds., *The Emergence of American Political Issues: The Agenda-Setting Function of the Press* (St. Paul: West Publishing Co., 1977), 107–120.
12. Maxwell E. McCombs, "Working Papers in Agenda Setting," University of North Carolina, 1973.
13. Alex S. Edelstein, "Decision-Making and Mass Communication: A Conceptual and Methodological Approach to Public Opinion," in Peter Clarke, ed., *New Models for Mass Communication Research* (Beverly Hills, Calif.: Sage Publications, 1973), 81–118.
14. Mark Benton and P. Jean Frazier, "The Agenda Setting Function of the Mass Media at Three Levels of 'Information Holding,' " *Communication Research* 3 (1976): 261–274.
15. Semlak and Williams, op. cit.
16. Wenmouth Williams, Jr., and David C. Larsen, "Impact of the News Media: Agenda Setting in an Off Election Year," *Journalism Quarterly* 54 (1977): 744–749.
17. Maxwell E. McCombs, Lee B. Becker, and David H. Weaver, "Measuring the Cumulative Agenda-Setting Influence of the Mass Media," paper presented to the annual meeting of the Speech Communication Association, Houston, 1975.
18. For example, see Leonard Tipton, Roger D. Haney, and John R. Baseheart, "Media Agenda-Setting in City and State Election Campaigns," *Journalism Quarterly* 52 (1975): 15–22.
19. The debate between the objective measurement of manifest or intended content and the latent meaning has been a major concern of content analysts. For an in-depth discussion of this and other related issues, see Ole R. Holsti, *Content Analysis*

for the Social Sciences and Humanities (Reading, Mass.: Addison-Wesley Publishing Co., 1969).

20. G. Ray Funkhouser, "The Issues of the Sixties: An Exploratory Study in the Dynamics of Public Opinion," *Public Opinion Quarterly* 37 (1973): 62–75.

21. James R. Beniger, "Media Content as Social Indicators: The Greenfield Index of Agenda Setting," *Communication Research* 5 (1978): 437–453.

22. Marilyn Jackson-Beeck and Robert G. Meadow, "Content Analysis of Televised Communication Events: The Presidential Debates," *Communication Research* 6 (1979): 321–344.

23. Susan C. Greendale and Eric S. Fredin, "Exploring the Structure of National Issues: Newspaper Content and Reader Perceptions," in Paul M. Hirsch, Peter V. Miller, and F. Gerald Kline, eds., *Strategies for Communication Research* (Beverly Hills, Calif.: Sage Publications, 1977), 167–186.

24. Robert Frank, *Message Dimensions of Television News* (Lexington, Mass.: Lexington Books, 1973).

25. C. Richard Hofstetter, *Bias in the News: Network Coverage of the 1972 Election Campaign* (Columbus: Ohio State University Press, 1976).

26. Wenmouth Williams, Jr., and William D. Semlak, "Structural Effects of TV Coverage on Political Agendas," *Journal of Communication* 28 (1978): 114–119.

27. Wenmouth Williams, Jr., Mitchell Shapiro, and Craig Cutbirth, "Framing in 1980 Presidential Campaign," *Journalism Quarterly* 60 (1983): 226–231.

28. H. G. Zucker, "The Variable Nature of News Media Influence," In B. D. Ruben ed., *Communication Yearbook 2* (New Brunswick, N.J.: Transaction Books, 1978).

29. L. Erbring, E. N. Goldenberg, and A. H. Miller, "Front-Page News and Real World Cues: A New Look at Agenda-Setting by the Media," *American Journal of Political Science* 24 (1980): 16–49; David H. Weaver, Doris A. Graber, Maxwell E. McCombs, and C. H. Eyal, *Media Agenda-Setting in a Presidential Election: Issues, Images, and Interest* (New York: Praeger Publishers, 1981).

30. Morris Janowitz, "Content Analysis and the Study of Sociopolitical Change," *Journal of Communication* 26 (1976): 11–21.

31. For example, see Tipton, Haney, and Baseheart, op. cit.

32. David H. Weaver and G. Cleveland Wilhoit, "Agenda Setting for the Media: Determinants of Senatorial News Coverage," paper presented to the annual meeting of the International Communication Association, Chicago, 1975.

33. Maxwell E. McCombs, "Newspapers Versus Television: Mass Communication Effects Across Time," in Shaw and McCombs, op. cit., 89–106.

34. Maxwell E. McCombs, "Agenda-Setting Research: A Bibliographic Essay," *Political Communication Review* 1 (1976): 1–7.

35. Williams and Semlak, *Campaign '76*.

36. Ibid.

37. Weaver, op. cit.

38. Ibid.

39. David H. Weaver, Maxwell E. McCombs, and Charles Spellman, "Watergate and the Media: A Case Study of Agenda Setting," *American Politics Quarterly* 3 (1975): 438–472.

40. Williams and Semlak, *Campaign '76*.

41. Williams and Larsen, op. cit.

14
Uses and Gratifications: Quasi-Functional Analysis

Alan M. Rubin

One goal of mass communication research is to identify and explain the uses and functions of the mass media. Uses and gratifications is one perspective that examines the role of mass communication for individuals, groups, and society. It focuses on what people do with the mass media, rather than what the mass media do to people.[1] Uses and gratifications is grounded in a functional paradigm of social influence and seeks to explain mass communication impact by emphasizing motives for and consequences of media use.

Functionalism and Mass Communication

A functional approach to mass communication study envisions the relationships among individuals, the media, and society as a series of systems and subsystems whose various components are integrated and interrelated. In other words, a change in any part would affect the other system components and the system as a whole. For example, the growth of cable television outlets or the introduction of new video technology in the home could alter present patterns of consumer viewing behavior, family relationships, advertisement placement, television station programming, and broadcast industry operations. They could also affect other communication media, avenues of entertainment and information, government regulation, and society as a whole.

The Concept of Function

Function is a concept describing the relationship and interdependence of a part of a system to the whole system. The terms *function* and *functionalism* have their roots in the biological, behavioral, and social sciences. In biology, for example, an organ (such as a blood cell) functions as part of a system or organism (such as a human being). Each organ performs certain behaviors vital to the organism's survival and is interdependent with the system's other organs. In cultural anthropology, cultural artifacts are interdependent as they contribute to the functioning of the entire culture. For example, two government functions for a society are to ensure order and preserve stability.[2]

Following from the work of cultural anthropologists, an analogy between the biological organism and the social organism clarifies the meaning of functionalism. Table 14-1[3] summarizes this analogy. As depicted in the table, functionalism is concerned with individual units of a system, the structure of or relationships among these units, the activities or behaviors of these units, and the functions or consequences of a unit performing these activities. A social system is an organization in which integrated and interdependent parts perform certain tasks to maintain or alter the whole system. The mass media of a society is one such social system or subsystem.

For a social system, the concept of function depicts the effects of certain units (such as consumers or media organizations) performing various activities (such as consuming or transmitting news and entertainment messages) on individuals, groups, or the entire society. Performing these activities is generally regarded to be intentional and can have functional or desirable effects (such as an informed citizenry's being the product of news presentation and consumption) or dysfunctional or undesirable effects (such as the creation of anxiety in individuals or undue disruption in society resulting from news presentation and consumption) toward the achievement of an overall purpose. A certain structure or series of relationships ex-

ists among individuals, groups, and organizations (such as among television viewers, social groups, media organizations, advertisers, and regulators). In addition, different social systems have different structures (such as authoritarian or libertarian societal systems) that aim at accomplishing different goals (such as furthering political ideology or providing a government watchdog).

The Evolution of Mass Communication Research

Functional paradigms of mass communication processes have evolved as alternative explanations of the media behavior of individuals within social systems. In contrast, traditional or classical media effects research largely assumes the influence of media messages on passive audience members. Before turning to the various functional approaches to mass communication research, it would be beneficial to consider briefly the evolution of media effects research.

Media effects research seeks to determine how messages affect an audience's thoughts, attitudes, or behaviors. Psychological and sociological models provide the basis for such investigations. Psychological models of media effects, derived from stimulus-response or behavioristic theories of persuasion and social influence, typically assume isolated audience members who are the targets of media messages. These messages are often intended by

Table 14-1 An Analogy between Biological and Social Organisms

	Biological Organisms	*Social Organisms*
Units	The biological cell	The individual person
Structure	Relationships between biological cells	Relationships between individuals and groups
Activities	Observed behavior of biological cells	Observed behavior of individuals and groups
Functions	The role of the behavior of cells in maintaining or altering biological structure. The association between the effects of the behavior of cells and the needs of the biological structure.	The role of the behavior of individuals and groups in maintaining or altering social structure. The association between the effects of the behavior of individuals and groups and the needs of the social structure.

their sender to influence audiences. Not surprisingly, this approach has been labeled the hypodermic needle model or bullet conception of media influence.[4] The orientation was expanded to include individual differences (such as individual attitudes and knowledge serving as selective filters) as potential intervening factors.

Studies from the 1920s through the 1940s on the potential influence of radio[5] and the effects of propaganda[6] initially fostered this line of research. Some contemporary television and violence research also follows from this model. Media effects studies seek to isolate a set of factors (such as source characteristics or message structures) that would enable researchers to explain and predict whether a certain message would have a positive or negative effect on a receiver. A principal deficiency of media effects research is its focus on short-term, immediate, and measurable changes in the thoughts, attitudes, or behaviors of individuals.

A voting behavior study of the 1940 Presidential campaign created an awareness that not all individuals have direct links to all media messages.[7] Social influence was found to be important in the mass communication process. The initial concept, the two-step flow of communication, postulated the role of opinion leaders acting as intermediaries between the media message and other audience members. This finding prompted questioning the fundamental individualistic assumption of psychological media effects models.

Sociological models of media effects underscore the role of the social structure and personal relations in the mass communication process. They shift the focus of media effects research from direct to indirect influence. Among the variables thought to intervene and mediate media effects are social categories, or demographic and cultural groupings of individual audience members (such as age, gender, race, and social class groups), and social relations (such as the norms and values of reference groups).[8] The principal assumption of these models is that social factors are significant in determining how people select and respond to media messages.

The work of Klapper, who synthesized prior media effects research findings, provides additional support for models of indirect media influence.[9] Klapper's phenomenistic perspective proposes that personal and social influence intervenes between the media message and an individual's response so that, in most instances, mass communications intended to persuade actually reinforce existing attitudes. These mediating factors include individual predispositions and selective perception processes, group norms, interpersonal dissemination of messages, opinion leadership, and the workings of the mass media in a commercial system of free enterprise.

The Functions of Mass Communication

Functionalism has been applied to mass communication study in many ways since the 1940s. Some adaptations have proved more useful than others in considering the dynamic potential for the interaction of units (such as the viewer and the television medium or program) within the larger social system. Three basic perspectives on the functions of mass communication have evolved: an inventory of media activities, functional analysis, and uses and gratifications.

An inventory of media activities, developed by Lasswell in the late 1940s,[10] emphasizes the functions of mass media content, rather than audience uses of that content. The media are treated as a single entity rather than as separate units within the social system. Lasswell maintained that the media perform certain activities for the society and, in so doing, produce effects that may be common to members of that society. This perspective inventories three major media activities: surveillance, correlation, and transmission. For their audience, the media survey the environment (a news function), correlate or interpret events in the environment (an editorial function), and transmit social norms and culture (a socialization function). Entertainment was added as another media activity several years later.[11]

A second approach, an outgrowth of the media activities inventory, considers the link of functional analysis to mass communication. Functional analysis is the study of structure and process, focusing on how a system performs and on the consequences of a given activity for the system as a whole. The system can be investigated on a macro level, in which the society is the social system of study with the mass medium, its content, and the individual being subsystems of the society. The system also can be examined on a micro level, in which a mass medium, its content, or the individual is the social system of analysis. In both cases, functional analysis is concerned with interactions within a system and with the effects of changes among the parts of the system.[12] With a focus on the individual as a system, these component parts could be needs, values, attitudes, interests, tastes, motives, behaviors, and the like.

As a form of scientific explanation, functional analysis seeks to understand the role of behavior pattern or sociocultural institutions in maintaining a system's balance and dynamics.[13] An activity or behavior that is part of the system is analyzed in terms of its consequences for the development, maintenance, or adjustment of the system as a whole. The unit's behavior that contributes to the system's balance or maintenance is functional. Behavior that is harmful or disturbs the system's equilibrium is dysfunctional. Merton expanded this positive-negative dichotomy to include functions or dysfunctions that are intended or manifest consequences and those that are unintended or latent consequences.[14]

Wright synthesized Merton's notion of consequences with the inventory of media activities and outlined a functional paradigm for considering the role of the mass media in society. Employing this framework, the investigator would ask: "What are the (1) manifest and (2) latent (3) functions and (4) dysfunctions of mass communicated (5) surveillance [news] (6) correlation [editorial activity] (7) cultural transmission (8) entertainment for the (9) society (10) individual (11) subgroup (12) cultural systems?"[15]

The Uses and Gratifications Perspective

In his 1963 Presidential address to the American Association for Public Opinion Research, Klapper argued that mass communication research has focused too often and too long on trying to determine whether the media have some specific effect.[16] Media effects research promotes a tendency to envision narrowly the connection between the message and receiver as being a static, one-to-one, cause-and-effect relationship. Klapper endorsed functional analysis tied to the uses and gratifications perspective as the appropriate research procedure for examining the actual role of mass communication in the lives of media audiences. The essence of functionalism is that an object is best defined by its use. As Katz has suggested, even the most potent media content ordinarily cannot influence an individual who has no use for the message in relation to his or her social and psychological environment.[17]

At present, uses and gratifications is more an individual, consumer-oriented approach to the study of mass communication than a society-oriented approach. In examining the mass communication process, the uses and gratifications perspective first looks at the receiver of media messages and attempts to explain the interactive communication behavior between the message consumer and the media. As consumers, audience members are regarded as participants in the mass communication process; they are not acted on by the media but rather actively use a medium and its content. Audience motives (or motivations) stem from underlying needs, and individual media behavior evolves from these motives for needs-satisfaction. Media behavior, in turn, produces certain gratifications or consequences for individuals. Effects that result from the use of media messages, then, are indirect. Media consumption also is linked to functional alternatives in the social context (such as other media or interpersonal channels) in the attempted gratification of needs.

Assumptions of the Perspective

The logic of the uses and gratifications perspective rests on five assumptions and three objectives outlined by Katz, Blumler, and Gurevitch[18] and summarized in Table 14-2.

The initial assumption is that audience members are active participants in the mass communication process. Media use is goal-directed, purposive behavior. This view is in contrast to the alternative theme of the media effects models that typically do not regard media behavior as the expression of an underlying motive or need. According to uses and gratifications, audience members choose to use certain media or types of media content on the basis of their expectations. For example, an individual may choose to watch a particular network or local television news program or to read a certain newspaper column in order to acquire information needed for instrumental decision-making, such as voting or investing money.

Second, mass media use is interpreted as a response to the perceived needs of audience members. Uses and gratifications recognizes

the role of intervening variables. Audience predispositions and social interaction factors produce viewer expectations for gratifying needs through the use of certain media. How adequately needs are met through media consumption varies with the individual. Perhaps only a portion of human needs can be satisfied by media use. The media compete with and are supplemented by functional alternatives (such as interaction with friends or family) in gratifying needs. For example, a need for companionship can be satisfied by using television, by being with friends, or by a combination of several sources. The need to reduce uncertainty about what product to buy or to determine what movie to see also could be satisfied by interaction with various people, as well as by media use.

Third, audience initiative for selecting media content for needs-gratification is emphasized. Individuals use the media rather than the media using them.[19] Or, rather than the media overpowering people, individuals select the media or media content to satisfy their needs.[20] The audience member determines which of the many messages relayed by the mass media he or she will select or consume. This initiative mediates audience patterns of media use, demands placed on the media and other external organizations (such as advertisers and policy

---

Table 14-2 Assumptions and Objectives of the Uses and Gratifications Perspective

Summary of Assumptions

1. Mass media use is largely goal-directed behavior.
2. Mass media use can be interpreted as a response to the felt needs of audience members.
3. Initiative lies with the individual audience member for mass media selection and use.
4. Individual audience members can account for their own communication motives and gratifications.
5. Value judgments concerning cultural significance should be suspended while audience motives and gratifications are explored on their own merits.

Summary of Objectives

1. To determine how individuals use the mass media for the gratification of needs.
2. To explain the motives and gratifications of individuals for specific media behavior.
3. To explore the functions or consequences of media use in order better to understand the mass communication process.

makers) for certain content, and the effects of the mass media.

Fourth, individual audience members know and can verbalize their own interests and motives. In terms of the methodology typically used to examine audience uses and gratifications, audience self-report accounts are thought to supply sufficiently accurate information about reasons for and gratifications derived from media use. This viewpoint, of course, may raise some questions concerning the possibility of identifying latent tendencies as well as manifest behaviors in a functional framework. Both open-ended questions (in which individuals are asked to indicate their reasons for using a mass medium) and closed-ended response categories (in which individuals are asked to indicate how similar a given motivation statement is to their own reasons for using the medium) have been used to determine motives.[21]

Fifth, a contrast is drawn to the study of popular culture by specifying that value judgments about the cultural significance of media or content should be withheld while audience motives and gratifications are explored on their own merits. Audience use of the media must first be explored and understood before considering these use patterns in relation to questions of cultural meaning and significance.

Objectives of the Perspective

In addition to the approach's five assumptions, uses and gratifications has three principal objectives. First, it seeks to discover how individuals use the mass media to gratify their needs. In effect, it transfers the inquiry of mass communication research from what the media do to people to what people do with the media. The functional underpinnings of the perspective assume that the individual audience member is an active seeker, selector, and user of messages to gratify personal needs, interests, and expectations.

Second, uses and gratifications seeks to explain the motives or reasons for specific media behavior. Why, for example, does the individual watch television news reports instead of (or

in addition to) reading the newspaper? What motives for information, entertainment, or interaction are fulfilled by television viewing (or radio listening)? What alternative vehicles are provided by friends, family members, other social groups, or additional mass media? These questions represent a brief segment of how individual motives can be explored.

Third, uses and gratifications emphasizes the functions or consequences of media use as a means to understand the mass communication process. In a natural communication environment, exposure to messages is largely a matter of voluntary choice. The pattern of media consumption warrants considering the motives underlying selection and use of messages, as well as the needs-gratification derived from attending to a medium and its content.

This third objective ties uses and gratifications to functional analysis by stressing the consequences of a certain behavior pattern for the individual. Therefore, the unit of analysis is generally the individual audience member. The structure is the active, integrative relationships among the individual, the societal system, the mass medium, its content, and alternative communication channels. The activities include the individual's observed behavior in using the medium or other sources to gratify felt needs. The functions include the consequences of this behavior pattern for the individual and eventually for other societal subsystems (such as the media themselves for programming decisions, or regulators and interest groups for policy initiatives).

A Uses and Gratifications Paradigm

Uses and gratifications has been described as an "umbrella" perspective under which several models are found.[22] Rosengren, though, outlines a basic paradigm for uses and gratifications research by which the uses and gratifications investigator must consider many elements and relationships[23]: (1) Certain basic biological and psychological human needs interact with different combinations of (2) personality and social individual characteristics and (3) the societal structure that surrounds the individual. This interaction of needs, individual characteristics, and societal structure results in different combinations of (4) felt individual problems that vary in intensity and (5) perceived solutions to these problems. These problems and solutions constitute (6) different motives for problem-solving or gratification-seeking behavior and result in different patterns of (7) media consumption and (8) other behavior. Together, media and other behavior produce (9) different patterns of gratifications and nongratifications and possibly affect (10) the individual's characteristics and ultimately (11) the structure of society, including media, social, political, cultural, and economic structures.

Research Phases
of the Perspective

Curiosity about mass media appeals and gratifications began in the relatively early days of empirical mass communication research. Media uses research has coexisted with media effects research. Three periods or research phases in uses and gratifications research can be identified.[24]

Investigations of why people use the mass media date from the 1940s. Lazarsfeld, pointing to gratifications research as a way to study the appeals of radio programs,[25] felt that it would consider these elements: audience members' description of the media experience (such as which parts of a program they preferred); the researcher's conceptualization (with attention to audience members' replies) about why the consumer uses the medium; theoretical expectations to identify the gratifications or satisfactions that audience members derive from certain programs; potential generalization as to whether the same gratifications are prevalent among other audience members; and frequency distributions of gratifications among different audience groups.

Three collections of radio and communication studies edited by Lazarsfeld and Stanton form the bulk of the early gratifications investigations.[26] Many of these studies were concerned with identifying the gratifications that individuals seek from selected media content. Gratifications were examined from the per-

spective of the consumer of the content. In contrast to media effects investigators, who largely ignored individual motives for behavior while focusing on the impact of persuasive communications, uses and gratifications researchers primarily seek to explore audience needs and motives as variables that intervene before media impact.

Typical of early mass communication gratifications research is a series of empirical investigations with different focal points: radio listening motives;[27] listener use of radio serials;[28] children's use of comics;[29] reader use of the newspaper;[30] and adolescent use of news sources.[31] The findings of a few of these studies will be summarized briefly.

Herzog examined the appeals of a successful radio quiz program, "Professor Quiz."[32] The qualitative analysis involved detailed listener interviews that isolated four program appeals: competition (to compete with the contestant or co-listener); education (to acquire knowledge, perhaps to enhance a person's social status when conversing with others); self-rating (to ascertain a person's own abilities); and sport (to enjoy the context).

The objective of another Herzog study was to learn about the effects of daytime radio serials on regular female listeners.[33] Five probable listener characteristics were conjectured: individuals who are isolated from their communities are more frequent listeners; the intellectual range of the listeners is not as broad as that of nonlisteners; individuals experiencing similar personal problems are especially attracted to the serials; people beset with anxieties and frustrations receive solace and compensation from listening; and listening to the serials is a special case of using radio as a habitual source of entertainment. Herzog identified three types of gratifications obtained by listening to these daytime serials: emotional release (a chance to cry or to enjoy the happy or sad surprises); wishful thinking (compensation for gaps or failures in the personal lives of listeners); and obtaining advice (learning appropriate behavior patterns).

Children's reading of comics was the subject of a Wolfe and Fiske study.[34] They found that comics become a substitute for what maladjusted, insecure children lack in life (for example, Superman becomes a father figure). Also, reading comics satisfies actual developmental needs in normal children by providing a means of ego-strengthening. Wolfe and Fiske observed three stages in comic reading for normal children: finding objects for fantasy in the funny animal stage; identifying with comic heroes in the adventure stage; and seeking real adventure, information, and the means for coping with the actual world in the true comics stage.

A 1945 newspaper delivery strike in New York City provided the context for studying gratifications derived from reading the newspaper.[35] Berelson attempted to go beyond the common-sense notion that newspapers function to keep people informed. He discovered five major uses of the newspaper: for public affairs information and interpretation (providing serious news and editorial opinion); as a tool for daily living (acquiring instrumental information, such as movie listings, radio logs, and stock reports); for respite (providing a means of escape from personal problems, psychological relaxation, and boredom relief); for social prestige (enabling individuals to appear informed by supplying information for conversations); and for social contact (providing personal advice, guides to morality, insight into the lives of others, and indirect contact with celebrities). Berelson also noted a few supplementary newspaper uses: they provide a sense of assurance to counter feelings of insecurity; they are inexpensive and readily available; and their reading becomes ritualistic, time-filling, and habitual behavior.

These early uses and gratifications studies have several commonalities.[36] They use similar methods asking people to provide open-ended motivation statements about why they use a particular medium or content. They are more qualitative than quantitative in that they group verbalized motives into categories without regard to their frequency distribution among media consumers. Although occasionally identifying demographic or personality characteristics, the studies generally do not explore the

relationships among psychological and sociological needs and motives for and gratifications derived from media use. These early investigations, therefore, provide less than a developed or integrated functional framework by which to conceptualize the mass communication process.

The second period in uses and gratifications research began toward the end of the 1940s and continued into the 1960s. Research began to explore media use patterns in relation to social and psychological motivations, gratifications, and functions.

Lasswell and Lazarsfeld and Merton made significant attempts at specifying the functions of mass communication. As discussed earlier, Lasswell proposed three principal functional activities of the mass media: surveillance of the environment; correlation of the parts of that environment; and transmission of social heritage.[37] Lazarsfeld and Merton suggested that the mass media perform two specific functions and one dysfunction.[38] The status conferral function is grounded in the belief that media presentations automatically enhance and legitimize the social status and prestige of individuals and groups. The ethicizing function sees the role of the media as an enforcer of society's social norms and values. The narcotizing dysfunction views the media as substitutes for social action by creating an illusion of political participation via the transmission of abundant information.

Other investigations present an array of actual and potential functions and dysfunctions of the mass media for the individual. For example, television viewing provides a sense of parasocial interaction with celebrities.[39] Television offers audience members opportunities to withdraw or escape from unpleasant life experiences.[40] Escapist television viewing may help children relieve feelings of discontent and better understand themselves; the same mass media use, however, could have different consequences for different audience members.[41] Mass media entertainment reduces anxiety created by mass media news and provides a perspective that makes the news less threatening to audience members.[42] The portrayal of occupational roles on television emphasizes certain stereotypes that children use to formulate perceptions of people who fill these social roles.[43] Television serves as an agency of socialization by reinforcing existing attitudes and values and by providing a set of norms for solving personal problems.[44] Television's importance lies in its pleasurable aspects or play function, rather than in its transmission of information.[45] The mass media shape audience members' perceptions of political reality by highlighting certain issues and events, setting the agenda for political campaigns, and influencing the salience of political attitudes, events, and issues.[46]

Two important studies of this period examined the role of television in the lives of children. Himmelweit, Oppenheim, and Vince, in a comprehensive inquiry into the effects of television on British children,[47] observed a variety of appeals of television for children: television is a readily available medium; it serves as a time filler; it offers satisfaction for children by providing a sense of being informed; it offers security and reassurance by presenting familiar themes and formats; it furnishes a means of excitement, escape, and identification; and it presents friendly personalities. Schramm, Lyle, and Parker's extensive examination of television for American and Canadian children[48] concluded that it is not possible to specify whether television viewing, in general, is good or bad, or if it has a particular effect on children. They noted that, for children television viewing radically reorganizes leisure behavior; provides immediate as opposed to delayed gratifications by meeting needs for fantasy experiences more than needs for reality experiences; performs a social function by providing a vehicle of entertainment, escape, and information; and it latently functions to produce incidental increments in learning from fantasy programs (such as learning the names of popular singers).

This second phase incorporates many interests exploring the links among media consumption and the social and psychological attributes of audience members. These studies primarily were not intended or designed to be uses and gratifications investigations and did not systematically explore the relationships among needs, motives, and consequences of media use. However, they do develop conceptual thought concerning functional mass communication research by at least inferring, if not explicitly stating, the associations between uses and functions of the media. The studies of this period surround Klapper's previously cited endorsement of functional analysis tied to uses and gratifications models for exploring and understanding mass communication.[49] These investigations also provide a conceptual link between early gratifications research and the third phase of uses and gratifications inquiry.

There has been a renewed international interest in uses and gratifications research since the early 1970s. In particular, several typologies of mass media motives and functions have been formulated to conceptualize the seeking of gratifications as variables that intervene before media effects. A few examples of these category structures will be summarized.

Rosengren and Windahl devised a functional scheme proposing several media functions for the individual.[50] Their model incorporates motives for using functional alternatives, including change, compensation, escape, and vicarious experience; relations between the audience and actors of mass communication, including detachment, parasocial interaction, solitary identification, and capture; and identification of media content in terms of proximity to reality, ranging from noninformative fictional content (such as drama) to nonfictional content that supplies explicit and concrete information (such as news).

McQuail, Blumler, and Brown proposed a framework that offers a similar set of television functions[51] including using television for: diversion, including escape from problems and the routine, as well as emotional release; personal relationships, comprising companionship and social utility; personal identity, including personal reference, reality exploration, and value reinforcement; and surveillance, consisting of news and information.

A series of recent studies have used and

adapted a similar set of viewing motive scales that provide a more systematic examination of television's [52] uses. Greenberg's prototype of these scales investigates the viewing motives of British children and adolescents.[53] In a preliminary project, reasons for viewing television were elicited from children and adolescents via written essays. A series of 31 empirical scales were then constructed to represent the principal viewing motives located in the essays. Along with sets of other questions regarding demographic information, television viewing behaviors, and aggressive attitudes, these scales were presented to 726 children and adolescents, ages nine, twelve, and fifteen, in a London school district. The respondents indicated the degree of similarity between the viewing statements and their own reasons for watching television. These responses were factor analyzed, producing several categories of motives for television use: for learning, as a habit, for arousal, for companionship, for relaxation, to forget, and to pass time. Viewing motives were then correlated with the other demographic and viewing behavior and with aggressive attitude variables.

A Research Illustration

An overview of one uses and gratifications investigation should clarify how such a research inquiry can be accomplished. A study by the author explored the relationships between television use and other television viewing and demographic variables and considered the compatibility of several of Greenberg's findings for a group of American children and adolescents.[54] This partial replication of the Greenberg study used many of the same television use scales. In order to select which scale to use, a questionnaire with all 31 viewing motive items was pretested. The pilot investigation revealed that completing all 31 viewing motive scales was a tedious task for younger children. Therefore, the three highest-loading items from each of Greenberg's eight initial viewing motive categories were selected and used in the actual investigation. In other words, along with other questionnaire items, the study used 24 viewing motive scales.

The survey was administered during regular class sessions at various elementary, junior high, and high schools in an Illinois community. In selecting the schools and classes for the sample, attempts were made to include students of various ability levels who represented the racial and socioeconomic composition of the community. Questionnaires were completed by 401 children and adolescents, ages nine, thirteen, and seventeen.

In addition to the 24 viewing motive scales, the questionnaire included an open-ended television viewing reason question and other items about television viewing behaviors (level of viewing and program preferences), television attitudes or perceptions (perceived realism of television content and affinity with the medium), and sociodemographic traits (age, gender, race, and social class). Eventually, partial correlation analysis was used to compare responses to the television use scales with the other variables in the investigation. A few summary findings will be mentioned briefly; these results are reported elsewhere and are not pertinent to the present descriptive narrative of how viewing motives can be determined in a uses and gratifications inquiry.

The children and adolescents in the sample were asked to indicate how similar each of the 24 television motive statements was to their own reasons for viewing television across four response options: "a lot," "a little," "not much," and "not at all" like their own reasons for watching television. Answers were coded so that a "4" indicated a high level and "1" reflected a low level of identification with each motive statement. Table 14-3 presents the actual viewing motivation instrument used in this investigation.

Responses to each of the 24 viewing motive items were intercorrelated and factor analyzed. To be retained, a factor had to contain at least two principal loadings. Two motivation items were discarded since they failed to load strongly on any factors. Six television viewing motive factors emerged from the principal components analysis. Table 14-4 summarizes the factor-analyzed data. Each item's largest factor loading and corresponding number

Table 14-3   Television Viewing Motives Instrument

Here are some reasons that other people gave us for watching TV. Please tell us how each reason is like your own reason for watching television. (Put one check in the correct column for each reason.)

I WATCH TELEVISION . . .	*A Lot*	*A Little*	*Not Much*	*Not At All*
1. Because it relaxes me	_____	_____	_____	_____
2. So I won't be alone	_____	_____	_____	_____
3. So I can learn about things happening in the world	_____	_____	_____	_____
4. Because it's a habit	_____	_____	_____	_____
5. When I have nothing better to do	_____	_____	_____	_____
6. Because it helps me learn things about myself	_____	_____	_____	_____
7. Because it's thrilling	_____	_____	_____	_____
8. So I can forget about school and homework	_____	_____	_____	_____
9. Because it calms me down when I'm angry	_____	_____	_____	_____
10. When there's no one to talk to or play with	_____	_____	_____	_____
11. So I can learn how to do things I haven't done before	_____	_____	_____	_____
12. Because I just like to watch	_____	_____	_____	_____
13. Because it passes the time away	_____	_____	_____	_____
14. So I could learn about what could happen to me	_____	_____	_____	_____
15. Because it excites me	_____	_____	_____	_____
16. So I can get away from the rest of the family	_____	_____	_____	_____
17. Because it's a pleasant rest	_____	_____	_____	_____
18. Because it makes me feel less lonely	_____	_____	_____	_____
19. Because it teaches me things I don't learn in school	_____	_____	_____	_____
20. Because I just enjoy watching	_____	_____	_____	_____
21. Because it gives me something to do	_____	_____	_____	_____
22. Because it shows how other people deal with the same problems I have	_____	_____	_____	_____
23. Because it stirs me up	_____	_____	_____	_____
24. So I can get away from what I'm doing	_____	_____	_____	_____

from the instrument presented in Table 14-3 are indicated. The figures following the factor identification in Table 14-4 represent the percentage of the common variance explained by each factor and the internal reliability of the factor. The six factors accounted for 47 percent of the total variance.

The investigation also attempted to assess the reliability and validity of the television viewing motive scales. Uses and gratifications investigations have been criticized for assuming scale reliability and validity. By contrast, many early gratifications studies merely posed an open-ended question asking respondents to state their reasons for using a particular mass medium or its content. In this study, test-retest reliability procedures indicated that responses to the several tested motivation items were consistent for a subsample of the children and adolescents. As mentioned, for the purpose of assessing convergent validity of the viewing motive scales, the children and adolescents in this sample were also asked the following open-ended question:

We are interested in the reasons why you watch television. For example, what are the reasons why you like to watch TV?

I watch television because _____
_____
_____

This open-ended viewing motives question was asked before presenting the television use scales so as not to bias the responses. As discussed earlier, a person's ability to verbalize reasons for using a mass medium is a major assumption of the uses and gratifications perspective. Therefore, the open-ended question enabled consideration of two points: whether children and adolescents could state their viewing motives and whether these verbalized motives would be consistent with responses to the viewing motive scales. In other words, are the responses provided by the television use scales valid measures of a person's television viewing motives?

To assess validity, two independent coders placed the responses to the open-ended questions into appropriate categories of viewing motives. The frequency of mention of open-ended reasons within each category of motives was then statistically compared to the mean responses for the viewing motive factors. In other words, both sets of data were rank ordered according to the number of mentions on

Table 14-4   Principal Factor Loadings of Viewing Statements

Viewing Motive Factor	*Factor Loading*	*Viewing Motive Factor*	*Factor Loading*
Factor 1 [25%, .81]		*Factor 2* [22%, .80]	
Learning—Things (11)	.67	Habit (12)	.66
Learning—Myself (14)	.67	Pass time (21)	.65
Learning—Myself (22)	.63	Habit (20)	.62
Learning—Things (19)	.62	Pass time (5)	.60
Learning—Myself (6)	.62	Pass time (13)	.49
Learning—Things (3)	.44	Habit (4)	.45
Factor 3 [16%, .75]		*Factor 4* [16%, .73]	
Companionship (18)	.70	Forget/Escape (24)	.69
Companionship (2)	.66	Forget/Escape (8)	.65
Companionship (10)	.56	Forget/Escape (16)	.58
Factor 5 [12%, .76]		*Factor 6* [9%, .62]	
Arousal (15)	.73	Relaxation (17)	.54
Arousal (7)	.56	Relaxation (1)	.49

Note: The numbers in parentheses refer to the viewing motive statement items in Table 14-3.

the open-ended question and the mean scores on the viewing motive scales. Computation of a Kendall Coefficient of Concordance indicated that the rankings of the two methods were consistent, lending support for the convergent validity of the motive scales. Because validity questions are important for all social science research, including uses and gratifications mass communication investigations, the author also used a similar procedure in a subsequent investigation of adult television viewing motives.[55] That study also supported the validity of the television use scales.

In the current study, then, the factor analysis identified six apparently valid reasons for children's and adolescents' use of television: for learning, as a habit or to pass time, for companionship, to forget or escape, for arousal or excitement, and for relaxation. Based on mean responses, viewing to pass time was the most salient reason for using television among this sample, along with watching television for relaxation and arousal.

Finally, Pearson product-moment correlations and partial correlations were computed to relate the viewing motives to the investigation's other variables. Age was found to be a significant correlate of the salience of viewing motives. Younger children generally identified more strongly with each viewing motive than did adolescents. Several significant associations among the viewing motives and levels of television watching, program preferences, television affinity, and perceived realism were also observed. For example, viewing to learn was a strong positive correlate of perceived television realism, and habitual viewing or watching to pass time was a significant negative correlate of public affairs and news program preference and a strong positive correlate of television affinity. From this type of uses and gratifications research, then, it is possible to gain a more comprehensive understanding of the motives and behaviors of audience members within the mass communication process.

Assessment of the Perspective

The basic uses and gratifications paradigm is concerned with the systematic and functional study of mass communication. According to Katz, Blumler, and Gurevitch, uses and gratifications seeks to analyze: "(1) the social and psychological origins of (2) needs, which generate (3) expectations of (4) the mass media or other sources, which lead to (5) differential patterns of media exposure (or engagement in other activities), resulting in (6) need gratifications and (7) other consequences, perhaps mostly unintended ones."[56] These gratifications and consequences can produce additional motives for and expectations of media use and social interaction, as the cycle repeats and continues. To date, however, no investigation has been able to achieve a true functional analysis of this process. In fact, uses and gratifications research largely remains at a developmental stage. Because of a series of obstacles, the perspective has not yet achieved the status of functional analysis advocated by Klapper several years ago. Several of these hurdles and criticisms of the perspective will be summarized.[57]

First, the methodology of functionalism itself has been criticized as being directed at stable rather than dynamic systems of rapid change. This view sees the functional analyst exploring only simple, stable systems and offering broad, sometimes even trivial descriptions of the system's operation (for example, a description such as "television is entertaining").

Second, the functional orientation of uses and gratifications has raised questions about investigators' ability to explain or predict beyond the individual unit. In short, uses and gratifications research treats the functions of mass communication from the perspective of the individual message consumer. The argument is sometimes made that because of varying cultural factors, research may be limited to explaining the behavior of a single person rather than a mass media audience. The same media content or experience can be used differently by separate individuals and can have different functions and dysfunctions for these people.

Third, investigations have produced their own typologies of audience motives and functions. Critics of the perspective contend that research has been compartmentalized as investigators focus on a variety of media functions or uses for individuals within a particular culture or demographic group. This has hindered integration and synthesis of results and has hampered conceptual development.

Fourth, critics have argued that uses and gratifications research has lacked both a relevant theory of social and psychological needs and an adequate conceptualization of how cultural and environmental factors contribute to selecting communication sources or gratifying needs. What is required is the systematic exploration of the origin and gratification of needs, which would consider the creation of individual needs; the expectation, selection, and use of communication sources to gratify these needs; and the consequences of this pattern of communication behavior.

Fifth, investigators universally have not agreed on the meaning of the perspective's major concepts (such as motive, gratification, and function). There are several results of this confusion: terms such as *motives* and *gratifications* are not used consistently; distinctions between gratifications sought and those received have not been totally obvious; there has been confusion as to what constitutes antecedent, intervening, and consequent variables in the process; and consequences and functional alternatives have not been systematically explored.

Finally, although the approach rests on an assumption of active audience involvement in the mass communication process, audience members seldom have been studied as active message consumers or processors. Uses and gratifications research generally has used questionnaires and individuals' self-reports of their motives and media behaviors. As discussed earlier, the validity of data gathering and the reliability of self-report data also have been questioned.

Many of these criticisms of the perspective are valid and need to be addressed in future research. Uses and gratifications is still a relatively young approach and needs continued, substantial, and systematic research efforts. In

recent years, criticism has begun to be addressed and considered in research designs. Uses and gratifications researchers have begun to consider more directly the perspective's conceptual underpinnings and problems. Systematic lines of inquiry have begun to examine consistent research questions, following a progressive path of development.

For example, one research direction has considered the associations between gratifications sought and gratifications obtained when using the media or their content.[58] These investigations have proposed discrepancy and expectancy models of uses and gratifications. A related research direction has compared media uses or gratifications across several media or between media and media content.[59] Another research direction has examined the social and psychological circumstances of media use.[60] These investigations have looked at a variety of factors affecting how consumers used the media, including personality variables, the family viewing context, social activity, interpersonal interaction, and life-position.

Another direction has examined the interrelationships among media use motives, media behaviors, and media attitudes or perceptions.[61] A significant finding from this line of research is that motives are not isolated and independent entities but comprise sets of interrelated media uses. In particular, two types of media use structures have been identified across several studies for the television medium, a popular television program, and for different groups of respondents. Ritualized television use indicates heightened affinity with the medium and habitual viewing of substantial quantities of television (rather than any specific programs) for time consumption, companionship, entertainment, and similar interrelated reasons. Instrumental television use indicates more selective viewing of news, talk, and magazine-type programs for informational reasons but does not mean substantial television affinity or viewing levels. Obviously, the consequences of ritualized and instrumental uses of the media should differ.[62]

The complexity of the uses and gratifications perspective provides no shortcuts or simple answers to questions of media impact. Over the long term, the goal of uses and gratifications is similar to that of media effects research: to explain the consequences or impact of mass communication. Uses and gratifications models, however, provide a more encompassing and demanding view of the workings of the process, the multitude of factors involved, the complexity of their interaction, and the active role of message consumers as the core of the system.

Uses and gratifications has the potential for more fully explaining and understanding the mass media's role in social influence processes. Theoretically, uses and gratifications provides a broader, more inclusive approach for exploring media behavior of individuals by directly linking activity to structure and function. It addresses the process by which human needs are gratified through communication use and the consequences of media use in the process. The approach emphasizes the dynamism and complexity of mass communication processes. It recognizes the role of functional alternatives (such as interpersonal interaction) complementing, supplementing, or displacing media use for needs-gratification. It has shunned single variable, cause-and-effect models of some media effects orientations for potentially more meaningful explanations of human behavior. The functional underpinnings of the approach call for a more comprehensive understanding of the impact of mass media messages by providing a possible range of effects (the use of channels and messages can have manifest and latent, functional and dysfunctional consequences for individuals, groups, and society) and the dynamics of change in the system (structures and activities can support or cause stress on the system or subsystems).

The assumptions and assertions of the uses and gratifications perspective have important implications for programmers and policy makers.[63] Active audience involvement with the media and the role of functional alternatives indicate that individuals will differentially use the media and their content to gratify felt needs and interests. These separate needs of individuals and social groups of individuals (such as demographic and psychographic groups), as well as the potential discrepancy among needs, expectations, and actual media content, should be recognized in programming and policy decisions. Because of the differential needs, interests, tastes, expectations, and motives of individuals and groups, it would be imprudent for media policies to be formulated solely on the basis of a uniform set of assumed audience sentiments.

In addition, differential motives, media expectations, and media exposure patterns should result in varied consequences or effects. Uses and gratifications researchers can point to the functions or beneficial consequences of media use that can be considered in policy formulation, as compared to media effects researchers who have tended to produce a catalogue of negative media effects that sometimes results in prior restraint and the replacement of content judged harmful with content deemed beneficial. The answers are not that simple.

Summary

Uses and gratifications focuses on the motives for and consequences of media use. It is grounded in functionalism with its concern for the interaction of units, structure of relationships, activities, and consequences for the social system. Functional paradigms for mass communication study have evolved as a means of improved understanding of the process, as compared to the media effects approach that is based on both psychological and sociological models of influence. Three basic functional perspectives have included inventories of media activities, functional analysis, and uses and gratifications. Uses and gratifications assumes goal-directed, active audience members who live in a social world and who have certain felt needs and expectations; they turn to the media or other communication sources to gratify these needs and motives. The perspective intends to explain how individuals use the media to gratify their needs and the motivations for and consequences of this behavior.

Three phases in uses and gratifications study include early gratifications investigations of the 1940s, exploration of media functions of the late 1940s through 1960s, and contemporary uses and gratifications typologies and systematic lines of inquiry since the early 1970s. The perspective recognizes the dynamics and complexities of the mass communication process and, by so doing, has realized problems in its application and development. Uses and gratifications offers a broad and heuristic approach to mass communication study and has important implications for researchers, programmers, and policy makers.

Endnotes

1. J. T. Klapper, "Mass Communication Research: An Old Road Resurveyed," *Public Opinion Quarterly* 27 (1963): 515–527.

2. N. S. Timasheff, *Sociological Theory: Its Nature and Growth*, 3rd ed. (New York: Random House, 1967).

3. J. Rex, *Key Problems of Sociological Theory* (London: Routledge and Kegan Paul, 1965).

4. This discussion could be expanded to consider systems models also, but this would be beyond the scope of the present essay.

5. H. Cantril and G. W. Allport, *The Psychology of Radio* (New York: Harper, 1935); H. Cantril, H. Gaudet, and H. Herzog, *The Invasion from Mars* (Princeton, N.J.: Princeton University Press, 1947).

6. H. D. Lasswell, *Propaganda Technique in the World Wars* (New York: Knopf, 1927).

7. P. F. Lazarsfeld, B. Berelson, and H. Gaudet, *The People's Choice* (New York: Columbia University Press, 1944).

8. M. L. DeFleur and S. Ball-Rokeach, *Theories of Mass Communication*, 4th ed. (New York: Longman, 1982), 183–198.

9. J. T. Klapper, *The Effects of Mass Communication* (Glencoe, Ill.: Free Press, 1960).

10. H. D. Lasswell, "The Structure and Function of Communication in Society," in L. Bryson, ed., *The Communication of Ideas* (New York: Harper, 1948), 37–51.

11. C. R. Wright, "Functional Analysis and Mass Communication," *Public Opinion Quarterly* 24 (1960): 605–620.

12. A. M. Rubin, "A Developmental Examination of the Uses of Television by Children and Adolescents," (Ph.D. dissertation, University of Illinois, 1976).

13. C. Hempel, "The Logic of Functional Analysis," in L. Gross, ed., *Symposium on Sociological Theory* (Evanston, Ill.: Row, Peterson, 1959), 271–307.

14. R. K. Merton, *Social Theory and Social Structure*, 3rd ed. (New York: Free Press, 1968).

15. Wright, op. cit., 610.

16. Klapper, "Mass Communication Research."

17. E. Katz, "Mass Communication Research and the Study of Popular Culture," *Studies in Public Communication* 2 (1959): 1–6.

18. E. Katz, J. G. Blumler, and M. Gurevitch, "Uses of Mass Communication by the Individual," in W. P. Davison and F. T. C. Yu, eds., *Mass Communication Research: Major Issues and Future Directions* (New York: Praeger, 1974), 11–35.

19. W. Schramm, J. Lyle, and E. Parker, *Television in the Lives of Our Children* (Stanford, Calif.: Stanford University Press, 1961).

20. E. Katz, M. Gurevitch, and H. Haas, "On the Use of the Mass Media for Important Things," *American Sociological Review* 38 (1973): 164–181.

21. Ethnography also has been proposed as an approach for observing audience uses and gratifications. See, for example, J. Lull, "The Social Uses of Television," *Human Communication Research* 6 (1980): 197–209.

22. J. G. Blumler, "The Role of Theory in Uses and Gratifications Studies," *Communication Research* 6 (1979): 9–36; S. Windahl, "Mass Communication at the Crossroads," in G. C. Wilhoit and H. de-Bock, eds., *Mass Communication Review*

Yearbook, Volume 2 (Beverly Hills, Calif.: Sage, 1981), 174–185.

23. K. E. Rosengren, "Uses and Gratifications: A Paradigm Outlined," in J. G. Blumler and E. Katz, eds., *The Uses of Mass Communications: Current Perspectives on Gratifications Research* (Beverly Hills, Calif.: Sage, 1974), 269–286.

24. Rubin, op. cit.

25. P. F. Lazarsfeld, *Radio and the Printed Page* (New York: Duell, Sloan and Pearce, 1940).

26. P. F. Lazarsfeld and F. N. Stanton, eds., *Radio Research 1941* (New York: Duell, Sloan and Pearce, 1942); P. F. Lazarsfeld and F. N. Stanton, eds., *Radio Research 1942–1943* (New York: Duell, Sloan and Pearce, 1944); P. F. Lazarsfeld and F. N. Stanton, eds., *Communications Research 1948–1949* (New York: Harper, 1949).

27. H. Herzog, "Professor Quiz: A Gratification Study," in Lazarsfeld, *Radio and the Printed Page*, 64–93; B. R. McCandless, "A Study of Non-Listeners," in Lazarsfeld and Stanton, eds., *Radio Research 1942–1943*, 407–418.

28. R. Arnheim, "The World of the Daytime Serial," in Lazarsfeld and Stanton, eds., *Radio Research 1942–1943*, 507–548; H. Herzog, "What Do We Really Know about Daytime Serial Listeners?" in Lazarsfeld and Stanton, eds., *Radio Research 1942–1943*, 3–33; W. L. Warner and W. E. Henry, "The Radio Daytime Serial: A Symbolic Analysis," *Genetic Psychology Monographs* 37 (1948): 7–69.

29. K. M. Wolfe and M. Fiske, "The Children Talk about Comics," in Lazarsfeld and Stanton, eds., *Communications Research 1948–1949*, 3–50.

30. B. Berelson, "What 'Missing the Newspaper' Means," in Lazarsfeld and Stanton, eds., *Communications Research 1948–1949*, 111–129.

31. F. J. Meine, "Radio and the Press among Young People," in Lazarsfeld and Stanton, eds., *Radio Research 1942–1943*, 189–223.

32. Herzog, "Professor Quiz."

33. Herzog, "What Do We Really Know about Daytime Serial Listeners?"

34. Wolfe and Fiske, op. cit.

35. Berelson, op. cit.

36. Katz, Blumler, and Gurevitch, op. cit.

37. Lasswell, "The Structure and Function of Communication in Society."

38. P. F. Lazarsfeld and R. K. Merton, "Mass Communication, Popular Taste and Organized Social Action," in Bryson, ed., 95–118.

39. D. Horton and R. R. Wohl, "Mass Communication and Para-Social Interaction," *Psychiatry* 19 (1956): 215–229.

40. L. I. Pearlin, "Social and Personality Stress and Escape Television Viewing," *Public Opinion Quarterly* 23 (1959): 255–259.

41. E. Katz and D. Foulkes, "On the Use of the Mass Media as 'Escape': Clarification of a Concept," *Public Opinion Quarterly* 26 (1962): 377–388.

42. H. Mendelsohn, "Socio-Psychological Perspectives on the Mass Media and Public Anxiety," *Journalism Quarterly* 40 (1963): 511–516.

43. M. L. DeFleur, "Occupational Roles as Portrayed on Television," *Public Opinion Quarterly* 28 (1964): 57–74.

44. W. Gerson, "Mass Media Socialization Behavior: Negro-White Differences," *Social Forces* 45 (1966): 40–50.

45. W. Stephenson, *The Play Theory of Mass Communication* (Chicago: University of Chicago Press, 1967).

46. M. E. McCombs and D. L. Shaw, "The Agenda-Setting Function of the Mass Media," *Public Opinion Quarterly* 36 (1972): 176–187.

47. H. Himmelweit, A. N. Oppenheim, and P. Vince, *Television and the Child* (London: Oxford University Press, 1958).

48. Schramm, Lyle, and Parker, op. cit.

49. Klapper, "Mass Communication Research."

50. K. E. Rosengren and S. Windahl, "Mass Media as a Functional Alternative," in D. McQuail, ed., *Sociology of Mass Communications* (Middlesex, England: Pen-

guin, 1972), 166–194.

51. D. McQuail, J. G. Blumler, and J. R. Brown, "The Television Audience: A Revised Perspective," in McQuail, ed., 135–165.

52. C. R. Bantz, "Exploring Uses and Gratifications: A Comparison of Reported Uses of Television and Reported Uses of Favorite Program Type," *Communication Research* 9 (1982): 352–379; S. T. Eastman, "Uses of Television Viewing and Consumer Life Styles: A Multivariate Analysis," *Journal of Broadcasting* 23 (1979): 491–500; B. S. Greenberg, "Gratifications of Television Viewing and Their Correlates for British Children," in Blumler and Katz, eds., 71–92; P. Palmgreen and J. D. Rayburn, "Uses and Gratifications and Exposure to Public Television," *Communication Research* 6 (1979): 155–179; A. M. Rubin, "Television Usage, Attitudes and Viewing Behaviors of Children and Adolescents," *Journal of Broadcasting* 21 (1977): 355–369; A. M. Rubin, "Television Use by Children and Adolescents," *Human Communication Research* 5 (1979): 109–120; A. M. Rubin, "An Examination of Television Viewing Motivations," *Communication Research* 8 (1981): 141–165.

53. Greenberg, op. cit.

54. Rubin, "Television Use by Children and Adolescents."

55. Rubin, "An Examination of Television Viewing Motivations."

56. Katz, Blumler, and Gurevitch, op. cit., 14.

57. J. A. Anderson and T. P. Meyer, "Functionalism and the Mass Media," *Journal of Broadcasting* 19 (1975): 11–22; L. B. Becker, "Measurement of Gratifications," *Communication Research* 6 (1979): 54–73; Blumler; J. W. Carey and A. L. Kreiling, "Popular Culture and Uses and Gratifications: Notes Toward an Accommodation," in Blumler and Katz, eds., 225–248; P. Elliott, "Uses and Gratifications Research: A Critique and a Sociological Alternative," in Blumler and Katz, eds., 249–268; Greenberg; Katz, Blumler, and Gurevitch, op. cit.; C. Pryluck, "Functions of Func-

tional Analysis: Comments on Anderson-Meyer," *Journal of Broadcasting* 19 (1975): 413–420; Rubin, "An Examination of Television Viewing Motivations"; D. L. Swanson, "The Uses and Misuses of Uses and Gratifications," *Human Communication Research* 3 (1977): 214–221; D. L. Swanson, "The Continuing Evolution of the Uses and Gratifications Approach," *Communication Research* 6 (1979): 3–7; Windahl.

58. J. J. Galloway and F. L. Meek, "Audience Uses and Gratifications: An Expectancy Model," *Communication Research* 8 (1981): 435–449; P. Palmgreen and J. D. Rayburn, "Gratifications Sought and Media Exposure: An Expectancy Model," *Communication Research* 9 (1982): 561–580; P. Palmgreen, L. A. Wenner, and J. D. Rayburn, "Relations Between Gratifications Sought and Obtained: A Study of Television News," *Communication Research* 7 (1980): 161–192; P. Palmgreen, L. A. Wenner, and J. D. Rayburn, "Gratification Discrepancies and News Program Choice," *Communication Research* 8 (1981): 435–478; L. A. Wenner, "Gratifications Sought and Obtained in Program Dependency: A Study of Network Evening News Programs and 60 Minutes," *Communication Research* 9 (1982): 539–560.

59. C. R. Bantz, W. R. Elliott, and C. P. Quattlebaum, "Similarities in Patterns of Media Use: A Cluster Analysis of Media Gratifications," *Western Journal of Speech Communication* 43 (1979): 61–72; Katz, Gurevitch, and Haas; A. Lichtenstein and L. B. Rosenfeld, "Uses and Misuses of Gratifications Research: An Explication of Media Functions," *Communication Research* 10 (1983): 97–109; D. E. Payne and A. H. Caron, "Anglophone Canadian and American Mass Media: Uses and Effects on Quebecois Adults," *Communication Research* 9 (1982): 113–144.

60. H. Adoni, "The Functions of Mass Media in the Political Socialization of Ado-

lescents," *Communication Research* 6 (1979): 84–106; J. W. Dimmick, T. A. McCain, and W. T. Bolton, "Media Use and the Life Span," *American Behavioral Scientist* 23 (1979): 7–31; F. Korzenny and K. Neuendorf, "Television Viewing and Self-Concept," *Journal of Communication* 30 (1980): 71–80; J. T. Lull, T. Miyazaki, "Housewives and Daytime Serials in Japan: A Uses and Gratifications Perspective," *Communication Research* 8 (1981): 323–341; A. M. Rubin and R. B. Rubin, "Contextual Age and Television Use," *Human Communication Research* 8 (1982): 228–244; R. B. Rubin and A. M. Rubin, "Contextual Age and Television Use: Reexamining a Life-Position Indicator," in M. Burgoon, ed., *Communication Yearbook 6* (Beverly Hills, Calif.: Sage, 1982), 583–604.

61. S. T. Eastman, G. M. Lometti, B. Reeves, and C. R. Bybee, "Investigating the Assumptions of Uses and Gratifications Research," *Communication Research* 3 (1977): 321–338; A. M. Rubin, "A Multivariate Analysis of '60 Minutes' Viewing Motivations," *Journalism Quarterly* 58 (1981): 529–534; A. M. Rubin, "Television Uses and Gratifications: The Interactions of Viewing Patterns and Motivations," *Journal of Broadcasting* 27 (1983): 37–51; A. M. Rubin and R. B. Rubin, "Older Persons' TV Viewing Patterns and Motivations," *Communication Research* 9 (1982): 287–313.

62. Windahl, op. cit.

63. E. Katz, *Social Research on Broadcasting: Proposals for Further Development* (London: British Broadcasting Corporation, 1977); Katz, Blumler, and Gurevitch, op. cit.; H. A. Mendelsohn, "Behaviorism, Functionalism and Mass Communication Policy," *Public Opinion Quarterly* 38 (1974): 379–389.

What Does Television "Cause"?

In the thirty years we have lived with television, there has been a steady proliferation of media research. Questions of spuriousness aside, it seems safe to say that from the beginning one thing television has caused is research. Most money for investigations has been allocated to marketing and advertising endeavors. Findings from these studies are rarely disseminated directly, although presumably the results are reflected in the shape and structure of the mass-produced symbolic environment in which we live.

The outcomes sought by commercial research are generally straightforward, and there is seldom need for complex conceptualizations of independent or dependent variables. Does advertisement X increase sales in product Z more than does advertisement Y? Do people say they like or will buy the product after seeing the ad? For what segments of the population will the ad be most effective?

We do not wish to criticize the goals and intents of such studies. We do wish to argue that market researchers' techniques and methods have often been inappropriately applied in the scholarly investigation of the social effects of television. Ironically, much of that kind of methodology was developed by social scientists in the 1940s and 1950s, when research on persuasive communication — propaganda, attitude change and the like — was the rage.[1]

Although there are innumerable variations on the typical experimental scenario, the usual design calls for assessing the differences between the state of receivers before and after exposure to some message, and for comparing these differences with a control group who have not received the message.

Much television research, particularly on questions of viewer aggression and violence, can easily fit into some form of this design.

Some early classic studies examined homes or entire areas before and after television became available to them.[2] Even today, researchers hope to locate some isolated group without television; in such a fortuitous natural experiment, pretelevision beliefs and behaviors

15
*Television and Enculturation**

Larry Gross
Michael Morgan

*This paper is derived from the theoretical and methodological work of the Cultural Indicators Project, directed by George Gerbner and Larry Gross, at the Annenberg School of Communications, University of Pennsylvania. The data reported here were gathered and analyzed under a grant from the National Institute of Mental Health, MH–21196 and written in 1980. The authors particularly wish to thank Dr. Robert Hornik and Hannah Kliger for their work on the family viewing context indices.

would be compared with what happens after television, perhaps with another unexposed group serving as a control. However, at the present level of world communication saturation, this type of research may do little but clarify various theoretical questions about the introduction of television to the few remaining corners of the earth. It is difficult to see how the results of such studies can elucidate the consequences of television in societies where it has been ubiquitous for the entire lifetime of half the population. Indeed, before and after community studies provide useful data about responses to technological novelty; but television is no novelty to our children.

As the possibility of finding these unexposed islands all but disappeared, investigators turned to the laboratory. But by and large, experimental or quasi-experimental approaches, whether they compare pre- versus postexposure or experimental versus control groups or something else, by definition overlook the pervasiveness of television and its invisible role in daily life. Two critical aspects—the content of television and the context of viewing—can hardly be validly reconstructed.

This essay discusses both content and context in some detail. At this point, however, we will voice our reservations about the kinds of dependent variables that have preoccupied researchers. Here is another example of the unfortunate similarities between much commercial and academic media research; investigators have spent much time and energy essentially seeking short-term behavioral or attitude change. Nearly thirty years ago, Lazarsfeld noted that "the real problem is the cumulative effect of television, what it does to children six years, not six minutes, later."[3]

Implicit in much popular and scientific debate is the notion that television is disruptive, even dangerous. Yet, it is unlikely that television does—or could—threaten, transform, or weaken conventional beliefs, norms, behavior, or morality. Rather, we assert that television is the dominant cultural arm of the established socioeconomic-industrial order. It provides continual celebration of the status quo.

The steady, ongoing cultivation of images, assumptions, and beliefs about life and society may be a more important and widespread consequence of exposure than are discrete instances of short-term change. Consider the issue of violence. If the most likely and menacing effect of television violence were the instigation and imitation of actual violence, elaborate research studies would not be needed; the average sibling, parent, and teacher would be reeling from the blows of television-stimulated aggression. There are rare (but widely publicized) apparent cases of serious imitative violence, but the eighty or so million people who watch each evening obviously do not respond to what they see by knifing or shooting each other.

Television violence can be more fruitfully conceptualized as a demonstration of power—a simple and inexpensive way to show vividly the winners, the losers, and the rules of the game. A more subtle result of cumulative exposure to systematic and formulaic symbolic violence may be the generation of fear and ultimately acquiescence to the power that can be achieved because of it.

The substance of the consciousness cultivated by television is not so much comprised of specific attitudes and outlooks as it is by broad, underlying assumptions about the facts of life. This consciousness is only one way our society has developed to explain the world to ourselves and our children; yet the socially constructed version of reality presented on television bombards all classes, groups, and ages with the same perspectives at the same time. The world view embedded in television drama may not differ appreciably from images presented in other media, and its rules of the social hierarchy may not be easily distinguishable from those imparted by other powerful agents of socialization. What makes television unique is its ability to standardize, streamline, amplify, and share with virtually all members of society common cultural norms that had been local, parochial, and selective cultural patterns.

Television as Enculturation

Socialization has been defined as "the process by which the individual acquires the culture of his or her group, and internalizes (in some measure) its social norms, thus leading the person to take into account the expectations of others."[4] On a more global level, socialization is not just the transmission of cultural norms and values but also "the process of becoming human."[5] Other researchers have framed it as "the whole process" of the development and acquisition of "specific patterns of socially relevant behavior and experience."[6]

In their unanimous use of the word *process*, these writers underscore that socialization is ongoing throughout life. When an individual experiences some life or status change (becoming a college student, losing employment, having a child) new roles, norms, and expectations become operative. Some have been previously learned, to be sure; others become salient only at the specified time; and our institutions and support systems are better prepared to deal with some transitions than with others.

Within this complex, elusive, continual process, we wish to isolate two conceptually distinct (but clearly overlapping) phenomena: socialization and enculturation. Neither supersedes or subsumes the other, and it is probably impossible to separate the two operationally. Yet, on some level, a worthwhile distinction can be made.

In short, the aspects of the process that are more like socialization relate to the specific patterns of thought and action. The facets that are more like enculturation impinge on becoming human. For the sake of this discussion, then, socialization refers to more specific, salient, issue-oriented patterns; enculturation is cast as more basic, general, and underlying.

Television may exert an independent contribution to both socialization and enculturation. For example, with regard to dating behavior, Gerson[7] found television's influence both in the acquisition of norms (in our terms, socialization) and also in the reinforcement of values (in our terms, enculturation).

Further, the DeFleurs[8] found that television not only provides a potent source of occupational status knowledge (socialization) but also engenders stereotyped beliefs about the world of work (enculturation). Finally, in our recent studies on television and aging,[9] we found that television cultivates (especially among the young) conceptions about the quality of older people's lives (socialization) and also the notions that the number of older people is declining and old age begins relatively early in life (enculturation).

In matters of socialization, television has a lot of competition. All of society's institutions, including schools, family, religions, and peer groups, are forceful agents of organization and control. In general, television should be most influential when the viewer has either no other contact (direct or mediated) with a given topic or when the television version is most congruent with the immediate environment. The specific lessons may or may not be learned, depending on a wide variety of powerful conditioning, antecedent, or mediating variables.

On the other hand, television's contribution to enculturation may be more universal, unobstructed, and enduring. Through its status and functions as chief creator of synthetic cultural images, the stories it tells to most people, most of the time, may have implications for the deeper, invisible, rarely questioned assumptions we all have that color and help inform the meaning of what we think, say, and do.

We live in an environment of symbols that sustains the most distinctively human aspects of our existence. Gerbner[10] has defined communication as "interaction through messages." These messages are produced and comprehended through shared complex symbol systems, which, in turn, give rise to the symbolic environment of a culture. Human thought and behavior derive a large part of their definitions and significance, potentials and limitations, and associations and relationships from this environment.

When these messages are mass produced (the analogy between the assembly line and network television programming is not forced), we have a collective symbolic environment that transforms the sources of consciousness and the context of social behavior. According to Gerbner and Gross, "The first and longest lasting organization of the symbolic world was what we now call religion." Through common rituals and mythologics, the symbol systems make people "perceive as real and normal and right that which fits the established social order." The most prized and sought-after goal is access to the cultural organs that embody and embrace all aspects of existence and experience and that are taken for granted in a culture.

> The nearly universal, non-selective and habitual use of television fits the ritualistic pattern of its programming. You watch television as you might attend a church service, except that most people watch television more religiously.[11]

This conceptualization of television also fits Berger's analysis of how enculturation "seeks to ensure a continuing consensus concerning the most important features of the social world." He notes that both children and adults "forget" the rules, the structures, and the ideals of what is socially legitimated; they need to be "reminded," and "the legitimating formulas must be repeated." To Berger, religion has provided a monumentally powerful means of accomplishing this task, so essential for the maintenance of culture.

> Indeed, it may be argued that one of the oldest and most important prerequisites for the establishment of culture is the institution of such 'reminders.' . . . Religious ritual has been a crucial instrument of this process of 'reminding.' Again and again it 'makes present' to those who participate in it the fundamental reality-definitions and their appropriate legitimations.[12]

Therefore, the heart of the analogy, and the similarity of the social functions, of television and religion may lie in the ritualistic repetition of messages that define the world and legitimate the social order. Again according to Gerbner, the "dominant agencies of communication produce the messages that cultivate the dominant image patterns. They structure the public agenda of existence, priorities, values and relations."

In this way, what is collectively defined, structured, valued, and related may be seen as a kind of superego, in that to some extent we must either conform to it or deviate from it; but we cannot avoid having to deal with it.

Most reasons for this are obvious. Television is more pervasive than other media. Children today were watching television before they could read or probably even speak. The number of hours devoted to it is unprecedented. Also, unlike print media, television does not require literacy from its audience. Unlike the movies, television runs continuously. Unlike radio, television can show as well as tell. Each characteristic is significant in itself, and their combined force is overwhelming.

But that is not all. For both children and adults, television offers a nonstop stream of facts and impressions about the way of the world, the constancies and vagaries of human nature. Most impressions appear as entertainment, but entertainment is the most broadly effective educational fare in any culture.

To be sure, the normal adult viewer is not likely to be unaware of the fictive nature of television drama. Yet it is not hard to find many large and important components of our knowledge of the real world (contemporary and historical) that can be traced in whole or in part to fictional symbolic representations. Regardless of personal experience, we all have ideas about what occurs in operating rooms, courtrooms, corporate board rooms, and the like, as well as strong images of the people in them.

The point is that no matter how aware we are that we are seeing a made-up story, and no matter how much we ascribe credibility or refuse to suspend our disbelief, the narrative action occurs against a highly naturalistic real-world background. Nothing impeaches the basic reality of television fiction.

According to Worth and Gross,[13] to recognize an event as symbolic is to see it as intentionally articulated along the lines of known and established conventions of communicative behavior. However, if we perceive the event as natural, we make a different assumption and invoke a different interpretive strategy; natural events are governed by the facts of life, not by the conventions of art. The inherent realism of television drama, although not natural in the sense of objective truth, makes us susceptible to such assessment errors. All of us are fooled some of the time, and some of us may be fooled all of the time.

Children have a particularly strong belief in the unmediated, inherent reality and truth of photographic and filmic images. Messaris and Gross[14] report studies showing that children will respond to a story shown to them in the form of photographic slides by stating that it was real, an actual depiction of actual events. When probed for the basis of their judgments, the children point to the premise of the assumption of realism. They know the story is real because photographs show reality; the camera does not lie.

The myths and rituals children absorb from television represent assumptions about the structure of reality and the meaning of being human that may endure throughout life. Specific attitudes and opinions and roles will vary over time, often with little continuity. In terms of such particular issues, television may be more or less effective at various points in the life cycle, or for certain groups, and so on. But the underlying sense of the shape, contours, and shadings of the world outside the family that television brings so relentlessly and effortlessly may be far from fleeting. In another sense, television serves to "spread and stabilize social patterns, to cultivate not change but resistance to change. . . . Its function is, in a word, enculturation."[15]

The Cultural Indicators Approach

The arguments that lead us to question the orthodox effects research designs do not suggest easy alternative solutions. At the same time, any hope of achieving even a partial solution must rest on reformulating the way much research has considered television. The title of our project, *Cultural Indicators*, embodies the belief that television drama can be taken and studied as a reflection and manifestation of the culture that it may also help shape and maintain.

Cultural indicators research begins with message system analysis, a flexible but precise tool for making orderly, objective, and cumulative observations of programming content. The technique allows us to identify almost any aspect of the television world so that we can then test its contribution to viewers' conceptions of the real world. The instrument of analysis does not attempt subjective interpretations of single incidents, evaluations of artistic merits, or ratings of individual programs. Instead, message system analysis reveals centrally controlled production policies by monitoring the prevalence, rate, structure, and distribution of clear and common terms. We have collected such content data annually since 1968.

The rationale for this type of analysis stems from sharp disagreement with the kinds of independent variables often manipulated in television research. Television is all of a piece and interwoven into a wider net of social institutions and values. We are arguing that the important stimulus or treatment is the entire world of television drama.

Our concern is with the total system of messages to which total communities are exposed. Unlike individual programs or incidents, the aggregate system provides bases for interaction and common assumptions and definitions (though not necessarily agreement) among large and otherwise heterogeneous publics. Studies using individual episodes, no matter how clean the design and clear the results, are of limited value because they ignore the fundamental feature of television drama: it consists of a vast, complex, and integrated system of characters, events, and relationships; its effects cannot be measured with regard to any single program (or set of programs) seen in isolation. What we study does not reflect what any individual sees but what large communities absorb over long periods of time. Having begun to describe and enumerate reliably many elements, relationships, and emphases of this system, we embark on the main focus of this paper, cultivation analysis.[16]

Cultivation analysis tries to assess television's contribution to viewers' beliefs, behaviors, and values based on the delineation of the central and critical facts of life in the world of television. If everything people knew were learned from television drama, their perceptions of the world would differ sharply from the real world. Beliefs about population parameters, the chances for success and happiness, the likelihood of encountering violence— all are portrayed differently by TV and census statistics.

The basic hypothesis of cultivation analysis is that the more time one spends living in the world of television, the more likely one is to report conceptions of social reality that can be traced to television portrayals. One frequently used strategy is to select issues and instances from our message system data bank exemplifying television's distortions. We then question various samples of children, adolescents, and adults about their beliefs and perceptions on such issues. Responses to these questions allow us to assess the degree to which the more frequent viewers are more likely than less frequent viewers to give answers reflecting television's image of the world. These patterns can then be examined in light of various controls (age, sex, education, occupation, IQ, use of other media, peer group integration) to determine the extent to which television's influence may be seen as independent, complementary, or contrary to these other major social variables.

A basic premise of cultivation analysis is that what happens to most people, most of the time, is more important than individual or discrete effects for policy decisions. Small effects might be satisfactory where a 1 percent increase in market share might represent millions of dollars in sales. But the study of how to change behavior and attitudes has neglected the steady cultivation of assumptions and perspectives that gives meaning to all issues, ideas, and actions. That is why we emphasize the common, underlying, and aggregate.

Our comparisons of light and heavy viewers have been fruitful. Even with other variables held constant, heavy viewers of all ages consistently are more likely to give television answers (responses more congruent with the television image than with the facts). Heavy viewers tend to see the world as more violent, to overestimate their chances of being involved in violence, and to express interpersonal mistrust. They also are significantly more likely to hold stereotyped notions about sex roles and age roles.

As repeatedly stressed, we are seeking to elucidate aggregate patterns and relationships between amount of viewing and audience conceptions of reality. As part of this analysis, we always implement controls for major demographic variables that might threaten our inferences by causing both heavy viewing and the clusters of outlooks revealed in television answers. These controls have primarily been used to guard against spuriousness; for the most part, the relationships we observe stand up well under such controls.

Recently, however, we have begun to go a step further. Even though the variables we hold constant do not explain the associations, the patterns are not identical across subgroups. These conditioning and mediating variables offer considerable theoretical promise for cultivation analysis; by examining between-group differences in terms of factors that might enhance or diminish associations, we can begin to understand which groups, on which issues, are more and less susceptible to the cultivation process.

For example, we have found that younger people are more vulnerable to television's negative portrayals of the elderly;[17] that the negative relationships among television viewing, IQ, and school achievement are stronger for boys;[18] that adult women are more likely than adult men to show evidence of the cultivation of sex-role stereotypes;[19] and that children in less cohesive peer groups (or none at all) show stronger associations between viewing and images of violence.[20] We have also found that the cultivation of fear seems most pronounced in high-crime urban areas, where the environment is presumably most congruent with television.[21] Finally, television viewing seems to cultivate distinctly conservative political outlooks, particularly among people who see themselves as liberal.[23]

Our latest findings about subgroup differences come from a three-year longitudinal study of adolescents attending a public school in suburban/rural New Jersey. This study involves six waves of questionnaires, in-depth personal interviews, and questionnaires completed by panel members' parents.

We are presently exploring the role of the family context of viewing in the cultivation of a variety of beliefs, notions, and images. Using many variables, we have constructed four reliable and internally homogeneous indices to reflect different aspects of that context. We focus on this context because laboratory studies inherently neglect it; although the general influence of the family decreases during adolescence, comparing different viewing patterns both brings us closer to understanding television viewing and effects in their natural setting and helps isolate groups with varying vulnerability. The dimensions tapped by the indices are:

1. Protectiveness: five variables (from the parents' questionnaires) reflecting parents' tendency to restrict their children's viewing; higher scores indicate that the parents have rules about what their children watch and when they watch, as well as specific shows that are prohibited (alpha = .83).
2. Utility: four variables reflecting the parents' tendency to see television as providing good information to their children and as teaching them about reality; also, having specific shows that they actively encourage (alpha = .59).
3. Conflict: five variables measuring students' and parents' reports of the extent of arguing about what, when, and how much they watch (alpha = .53).

4. Independence: four variables measuring students' access to television in terms of who selects what they see; also includes a ratio of the number of sets to the respondent's number of siblings (alpha = .63).

Our dependent variables for these analyses are related to fear, crime, and interpersonal mistrust. In the most recent violence profile, we accented the finding that these relationships withstand powerful controls; here, we will see whether meaningful subgroup patterns emerge. The two indices are:

1. Violence index: comprised of seven variables measuring perceptions of chances involvement in violence, the percentage of police in the labor force, the percentage of violent crimes, the tendency for police to respond to violence with violence, etc. (alpha = .51).
2. Mean world index: five variables reflecting notions of fear and interpersonal mistrust, such as the beliefs that you can't be too careful in dealing with people, they will take advantage of you if they get the chance, and that walking alone in a city at night is dangerous (alpha = .55).

Table 15-1 shows correlations (simple and controlling for socioeconomic status) between amount of viewing and scores on these two indices in the second and third years of the study, within context groups. Clearly, context makes a difference, even when adding the SES control. Relationships with both variables, both years, are much stronger among students whose parents are not restrictive and protective of their viewing. The difference between the two subgroups in the second year for the mean world index is particularly striking.

The relationship between amount of viewing and the violence index is not much different for students whose parents do and do not seem to encourage viewing. Yet, when the parents treat the medium in a positive manner, apparently using television to help socialize their children, the relationship between viewing and the mean world syndrome of mistrust and fear absolutely disappears.

Table 15-1 Simple and Partial Correlations of Television Viewing[1] with Violence and Mean World Indices, within Different Viewing Contexts[2]

| | Second Year | | | | Third Year | | | |
| | VIOLENCE INDEX | | MEAN WORLD INDEX | | VIOLENCE INDEX | | MEAN WORLD INDEX | |
	Simple r	Controlling for SES[3]	Simple r	Controlling for SES	Simple r	Controlling for SES	Simple r	Controlling for SES
Overall	.21**	.16**	.16**	.14*	.23**	.19**	.15*	.14*
Protectiveness								
Low	.29**	.24*	.41**	.36**	.23*	.19*	.30**	.25*
High	.19*	.14	−.09	−.08	.19*	.11	−.03	−.03
Utility								
Low	.20*	.16*	.24*	.21*	.24*	.15	.24**	.22*
High	.24*	.20*	.01	.00	.22*	.21*	.00	.00
Conflict								
Low	.17*	.14	.10	.08	.27***	.25**	.02	.01
High	.25**	.19*	.22*	.20*	.17	.12	.30**	.29**
Independence								
Low	.17*	.15*	.10	.12	.10	.08	.10	.11
High	.23*	.14	.18*	.13	.40***	.34***	.19*	.15

* = p < .05   ** = p < .01   *** = p < .001

[1]Reported television exposure "on an average day," in hours, each year; reliability estimates range from .70 to .80.

[2]Overall N = 216; indices are dichotomized by a median split. Cell N's vary around 100, due to missing data.

[3]Socioeconomic status (SES) measured by the father's occupational prestige (Duncan scale) and education (Hollingshead scale); reliability = .86

The presence of conflict in the home concerning viewing also impinges on the mean world relationship but not the association with the violence index. When there is arguing over television, heavy viewing strongly goes with higher levels of mistrust; when arguments are absent, the relationship is only moderate in the second year and gone in the third.

Finally, whether respondents or their siblings or parents select viewing fare does not make as dramatic a difference. Nonetheless, there is a fairly consistent tendency for students who select their own shows to manifest considerably stronger patterns of association between television viewing, fear, and mistrust.

To a certain extent, the data imply that the less parents are involved in their children's viewing, the stronger the effects. The involvement can either be positive or negative; particularly with the mean world index, students whose parents neither restrict nor explicitly encourage viewing show the most striking relationships. At the same time, when there is arguing and conflict, as opposed to simply regulation, the effects are exacerbated.

In contrast to these relatively sharp differences, content preferences of the students are highly ambiguous. The between-group differences based on students who prefer certain kinds of programming over others are inconsistent. However, this supports our contention that television is all of a piece and that the entire system of messages has more impact than do selective and isolated genres and variations.

These analyses also support Brown and Linne's[23] contention that "the family acts as a filter to the child's experience of television. Furthermore, this filtering process actually affects the type of influence television has on a child." Finally, the results point to the flexibility of cultivation analysis for uncovering theoretically relevant conditioning and mediating influences on the implications of heavy viewing.

Longitudinal Cultivation Analysis

The attractions of longitudinal research go beyond our distrust and disinterest in demonstrating effects that are observed six months after a child is shown a particular television program. When we began our longitudinal study of adolescents, we felt that by gathering information on a variety of dimensions and tracing patterns over time, we could achieve insight into the intricacies of association, correlation, and perhaps even causes and effects.

The prospects looked good. While Lazarsfeld,[24] Schramm et al.,[25] and others have frequently called for long-term longitudinal studies, Chaffee[26] persuasively finds pragmatic, conceptual, and statistical problems with long-term research that would "cut across radically different phases in child development." Reducing the scope of time involved, he argues that a "longitudinal study extending over two or three years within a homogeneous life-cycle period . . . would seem highly desirable." The implication is that such a study would provide less ambiguous tests of causality. Our three-year adolescent study meets those criteria and even employs multiple methods of data collection.

But now that we are into these longitudinal analyses (although not nearing completion), the implications of cultivation theory have led us to rethink some of the aims and expectations for longitudinal treatments of television's contribution to conceptions of social reality.

On one level, there is a statistical limitation. Most popular and useful techniques for longitudinal analysis (e.g., complex causal modeling; covariance structure analysis; regression with an interaction term; and even cross-lagged partial correlations, which we reject outright for various reasons) are implicitly based on the assumption of linear relationships. The more we examine functional forms in cultivation patterns, the more deviations from linearity we find; and path coefficients of zero may mask a powerful nonlinear relationship. Even when models are corrected for attenuation, television's influence may appear distorted or underestimated.

A more serious problem is a conceptual paradox, impossible to resolve through statistical manipulations. Another fundamental premise of longitudinal analysis is that the goal is to ascertain whether change in X leads to change in

Y. In other words, does an increase in viewing lead to an increase in a given television answer?

There are two ways of looking at this question; one traces patterns of concurrent change, the other examines patterns of lagged change. For either approach, the first step is to partition the sample into four groups of viewers, corresponding to the changes and stabilities in their viewing from one time to another. Based on a light-heavy median split at Time 1, the four types of viewers are: relatively light viewers both times; light the first time but heavy the second; heavy the first time but light the second; heavy viewers both times. In other words, there are two groups of stable viewers (consistently light and consistently heavy) and two groups of changing viewers (those who increase from light to heavy viewing and those who decrease from heavy to light).

The scores on the dependent variable can then be plotted across time for each group. With two waves of data, the concurrent patterns can be examined; the goal is to see what trends accompany changes and stabilities in viewing. Do people who increase viewing (light to heavy) simultaneously become more likely to give a television answer? Do those who reduce viewing (heavy to light) become less likely to respond that way? What accompanies consistently light or heavy viewing? These questions can be addressed by looking at how the scores on some dependent variables differ over time for the four groups of viewers.

With three waves of data (or more), it is possible to look at lagged change, often held to be a more powerful method of assessing causality. The effect of a change in viewing may not be immediately accompanied by change in the dependent variable; that change may be delayed. Therefore, when we look at lagged change, we are attempting to see if a change in viewing from Time 1 to Time 2 has any impact on dependent variable scores from Time 2 to Time 3. The four viewing groups are categorized as before, only here the dependent variable scores are plotted from Time 2 to Time 3.

Both techniques provide a means of seeing whether a change in viewing leads to a change in some perspective of the world, usually in terms of whether an increase in viewing foreshadows greater likelihood of perceiving the world in accordance with television's imagery. The only difference is that concurrent patterns look for change that accompanies simultaneous changes in viewing, whereas lagged patterns reveal whether the effect occurs at some later time.

Yet, we have argued extensively (as have others) that if one is looking for media effects, then looking for change is off the mark. We contend that the primary consequence of television is the stabilization and reinforcement of conventional values and morality.

To illustrate the complexities of this paradox and to offer a tentative solution, we present some preliminary data from our ongoing longitudinal analysis of the cultivation of sex-role stereotypes. The dependent variables are indices comprised of variables asked each year concerning respondents' opinions on who should hold full-time jobs in a family, whether society discriminates against women, whether women are happiest taking care of a family and raising children, and so on; reliability estimates range from .55 to .65.

The cross-sectional results are presented in Gross and Jeffries-Fox.[27] Although that article reports that the same-time associations are stronger for boys (heavy viewing goes with expressing more sexist attitudes), our longitudinal treatments show that the boys' association washes out whereas the girls' is surprisingly robust. We shall therefore present only data for girls here.

The case of adolescents and sexism is doubly problematic. Relative levels of both viewing and sexism (i.e., in general low-high terms) are virtually constant across the three years. Almost all change that does occur is a decrease, on both variables. (The well-documented decline in viewing during adolescence is probably maturational; the decline in sexism may follow from both maturational and historical phenomena.)

Therefore, rather than expecting change in sex-role stereotypes, we anticipated that steady heavy viewers (and the few who become heavy viewers) would show no change; that is, heavy viewing may help sustain the higher levels of sexism of earlier adolescence. Those who live less in the television world, where men outnumber women three to one and women rarely work, may be the ones who change. Thus, lack of change in the face of powerful social and maturational influences could be evidence of a more striking effect.

Figure 15-1 shows changes and stabilities in sexism in terms of changes and stabilities in viewing, for both lagged and concurrent change. For lagged change, the patterns are straightforward and provocative. Consistently heavy and consistently light viewers end up highest and lowest, respectively, on the index of sex-role stereotypes. The changing groups manifest a pattern completely against the change leading to change hypothesis but strongly support the notion of reinforcement and maintenance. First-year heavy viewers increase slightly in sexism regardless of whether they remain heavy viewers or become light. Further, the increases for the first-year heavy viewers (2.7 points for those who become light,

Figure 15-1 Lagged and concurrent changes in sexism scores for changing and stable viewers (girls only).

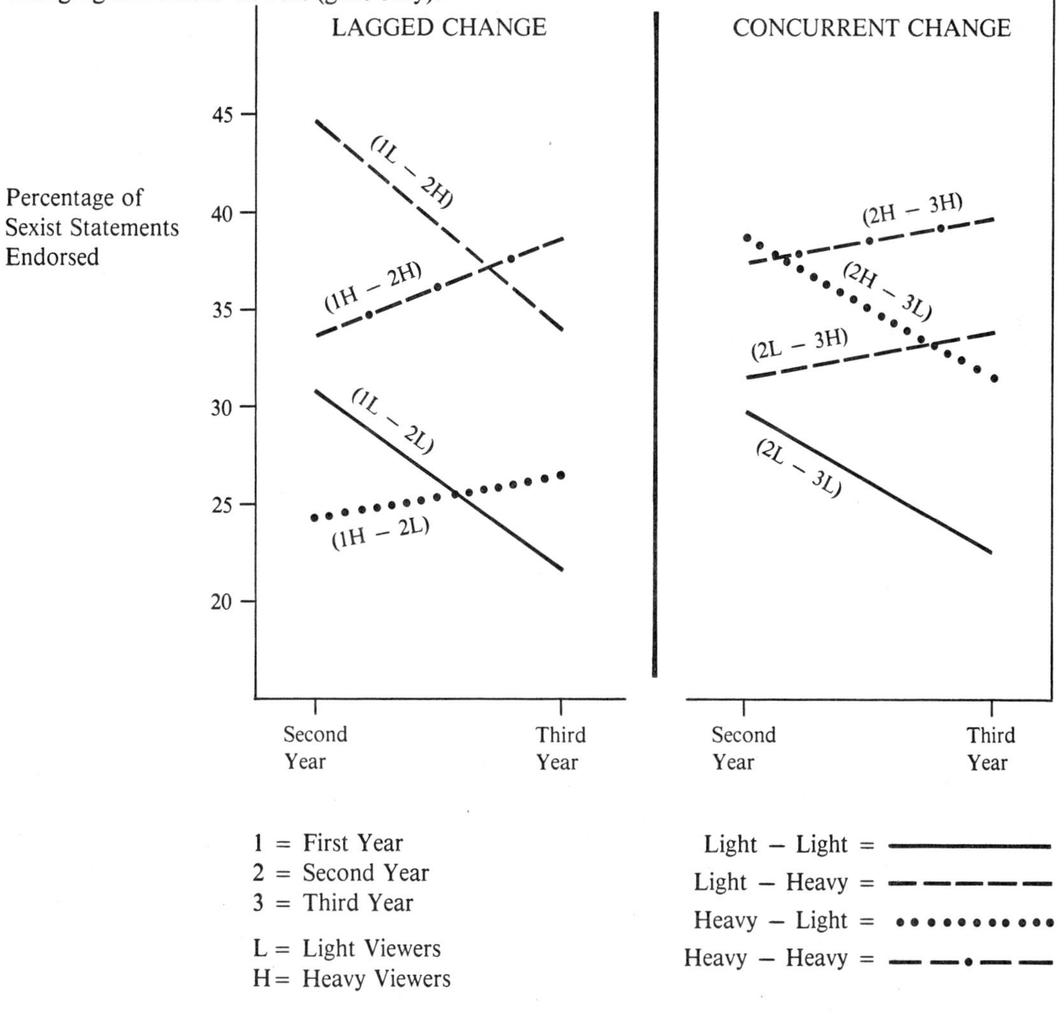

4.7 for those who remain heavy) are less than the decreases for first-year light viewers (9.0 points for those who remain light, 10.3 points for those who become heavy). In short, change in viewing makes less difference than initial level.

For concurrent change, on the other hand, there is support for the change leading to change notion. Light viewers at Time 2 have close sexism scores, and both are lower than the scores of Time 2 heavy viewers, which are also close. Yet, the light viewers who become heavy in the third year do increase on sexism by 2.5 points, whereas those who remain light drop almost 7 points. Similarly, a change from heavy to light viewing is accompanied by a decrease of more than 8 points, whereas those who stay heavy viewers increase 1.6. Thus, for girls, a change in viewing level does accompany a change in sexism. Those who become heavy viewers endorse a greater number of sex-role stereotypes; those who become light endorse fewer. Yet, consistently heavy viewers barely change, and consistently light viewers show a marked decrease.

Because younger students and those with lower IQs both increase viewing and appear to be more sexist, these patterns could be partly or entirely due to age and IQ. However, when age and IQ are removed from sexism scores, the changing and stable viewing groups manifest virtually the same pattern with the residual scores as they do with the raw scores.

From the lagged-effect perspective, early viewing is all that counts; heavy viewers increase and light viewers decrease regardless of change or stability in viewing. Looking at concurrent change, girls who increase viewing also increase on sexism. By removing the effects of IQ and grade, we see that television appears to make a notable independent contribution to the development of sex-role stereotypes among adolescent girls. While there is at least some evidence supporting the change leading to change notion (but only concurrently), the dominant features of viewing and sexism patterns over time is preservation, continuance, and reinforcement — in short, cultivation.

Do these patterns allow the inference of

causality? We are not sure. In any case, the causal question may be fundamentally insoluble. The point is not so much whether television viewing is a distinct, decisive, and isolated agent of causality, as it is the direction of the contribution it makes. Our longitudinal analyses are now expanding further into the areas of life course and family expectations, occupational and educational aspirations, and a variety of social reality conceptions. As these analyses proceed, we expect to continue to find that television cultivates assumptions that fit its socially functional myths.

Summary

This article began with a discussion of the role of television as the dominant cultural arm of the established socioeconomic-industrial order. Television has come to play a central role in the processes of socialization (acquisition of norms) and enculturation (acquisition and reinforcement of values) of members of our culture. As such, the appropriate way to conceptualize and detect the effects of exposure to television might be in terms of stability rather than of changes in attitudes and behavior.

This approach and methods were illustrated with examples from a three-year longitudinal study of adolescents. Looking first at a series of measures of parental involvement in their children's viewing, we find that the lower the level of such involvement, the stronger the evidence for cultivation. By *cultivation* we mean viewers' expression of conceptions of social reality that match the patterns and values found in television drama.

The article then discussed longitudinal analyses of data from the three-year study and discussed some conceptual and methodological challenges involved in attempting to trace effects over time. Looking at the adolescent girls' responses on items combined into a sexism index, we showed how the dominant patterns emerging over the three-year period are those of television's role in preserving and maintaining sexist views.

Endnotes

1. See, for example, William J. McGuire, "The Nature of Attitudes and Attitude Change," in G. Lindzey and E. Aronson, *The Handbook of Social Psychology* (Reading, Mass.: Addison-Wesley, 1969), 136–314; "Persuasion, Resistance and Attitude Change," in I. deS. Pool and W. Schramm, eds., *The Handbook of Communication* (Chicago: Rand McNally, 1973). Also, Arthur R. Cohen, *Attitude Change and Social Influence* (New York: Basic Books, 1964).

2. H. T. Himmelweit, A. Oppenheim, and P. Vince, *Television and the Child* (London: Oxford, 1958); W. J. Schramm, J. Lyle, and E. Parker, *Television in the Lives of Our Children* (Stanford, Calif.: Stanford University Press, 1961).

3. Paul F. Lazarsfeld, "Why Is So Little Known about the Effects of TV and What Can Be Done?" *Public Opinion Quarterly* 19 (1955): 243–251.

4. Charles R. Wright, *Mass Communication: A Sociological Perspective*, 2nd ed. (New York: Random House, 1975).

5. D. H. Wrong, "The Oversocialized Conception of Man in Modern Sociology," *American Sociological Review* 26 (1961): 183–193.

6. Edward Zigler and Victoria Seitz, "Changing Trends in Socialization Theory and Research," *American Behavioral Scientist* 21 (1978): 731–756.

7. W. Gerson, "Mass Media Socialization Behavior: Negro-White Differences," *Social Forces* 45 (1966): 40–50.

8. Melvin L. DeFleur and Lois B. DeFleur, "The Relative Contribution of Television as a Learning Source for Children's Occupational Knowledge," *American Sociological Review* 32 (1967): 777–789.

9. George Gerbner, Larry Gross, Nancy Signorielli, and Michael Morgan, "Aging with Television: Images on Television Drama and Conceptions of Social Reality," *Journal of Communication* 30 (1980): 37–47.

10. George Gerbner, "Communication and Social Environment," *Scientific American* 227 (1972): 153–160.

11. George Gerbner and Larry Gross, "Living with Television: The Violence Profile," *Journal of Communication* 26 (1976): 172–199.

12. Peter L. Berger, *The Sacred Canopy* (Garden City, N.Y.: Doubleday, 1966), 29, 31, 40.

13. Sol Worth and Larry Gross, "Symbolic Strategies," *Journal of Communication* 24 (1974): 27–39.

14. Paul Messaris and Larry Gross, "Interpretations of a Photographic Narrative by Viewers in Four Age Groups," *Studies in the Anthropology of Visual Communication* 4 (1977): 99–111.

15. Gerbner and Gross, op. cit.

16. For a more extended discussion of message system analysis, see George Gerbner, "Cultural Indicators: The Third Voice," in G. Gerbner, L. Gross, and W. Melody, eds., *Communications Technology and Social Policy* (New York: Wiley, 1973), 555–573. For a series of interchanges on the violence profiles, see articles by D. M. Blank and by G. Gerbner et al. in the *Journal of Broadcasting* 21 (1977): 273–303. For other discussions of the methodology, see George Gerbner et al., "Cultural Indicators: Violence Profile No. 9," *Journal of Communication* 28 (1978): 176–207; also see essay in this volume.

17. Gerbner, Gross, Signorielli, and Morgan, op. cit.

18. Michael Morgan and Larry Gross, "Reading, Writing and Watching: Television Viewing, IQ and Academic Achievement," *Journal of Broadcasting* 24 (1980): 117–133.

19. Nancy Signorielli, "Television's Contribution to Sex-Role Socialization," paper presented at the Seventh Annual Telecommunications Policy Research Conference, Skytop, Pennsylvania, April 1979.

20. Nancy F. Rothschild, "Group as a Mediating Factor in the Cultivation Process among Young Children." Unpublished

M.A. thesis, The Annenberg School of Communications, University of Pennsylvania, (1979).

21. George Gerbner, Larry Gross, Michael Morgan, and Nancy Signorielli, "The 'Mainstreaming' of America: Violence Profile No. 11," *Journal of Communication* 30 (1980): 10–29.

22. George Gerbner, Larry Gross, Michael Morgan, and Nancy Signorielli, "Charting the Mainstream: Television's Contributions to Political Orientations," *Journal of Communication* 32 (1982): 100–127.

23. J. R. Brown and O. Linne, "The Family as a Mediator of Television's Effects," in Ray Brown, ed., *Children and Television* (Beverly Hills, Calif.: Sage, 1976), 184–198.

24. Lazarsfeld, op. cit.

25. Schramm, op. cit.

26. Steven H. Chaffee, "Television and Adolescent Aggressiveness (overview)," in G. A. Comstock and E. A. Rubinstein, eds., *Television and Social Behavior*, Vol. III (Washington, D.C.: U.S. Government Printing Office, 1972), 1–34.

27. Larry Gross and Suzanne Jeffries-Fox, "What Do You Want to Be When You Grow up, Little Girl?" in G. Tuchman, A. K. Daniels, and J. Benet, eds., *Hearth and Home: Images of Women in the Mass Media* (New York: Oxford, 1978), 240–265.

Questions about the amount of violence in the mass media, particularly television programming, have been voiced since the advent of the media. Senate hearings about television violence were held as early as 1954. These concerns stem from fears that television violence leads to aggressive behavior, particularly among young people. An equally controversial subject has been how to define, measure, isolate, and analyze that violence. This essay examines ways television violence has been measured, including violence indices. The discussion is limited to television, even though there has been research about violence in other mass media. It also is limited to studies of American television.

Two rich information sources about television — its content and effects — are the 1972 six-volume report of the Surgeon General's Scientific Advisory Committee, *Television and Social Behavior*, and its 1982 two-volume update, *Television and Behavior: Ten Years of Scientific Progress and Implications in the Eighties*. These reports cover research projects conducted between 1967 and 1980 on a wide variety of television-related topics. This discussion draws up findings of these studies.

Violence in television programming has been studied in many ways. In a considerable body of research, the assessment of violence is the main issue; that is, the goal is to ascertain the amount of violence in television programming. Another large body of research, concerned with violence in programming as a side issue, assesses effects of programming, usually violent programming. Measures of violence are used to define experimental conditions; that is, the amount of violence is an independent variable. This research will be discussed briefly in reference to how violence is defined and/or measured.

This essay also examines definitions of violence and the ways violence is unitized. During the past twenty years, violence has probably been defined almost as many times as it has been examined. Since violence is complex, it can be and is defined in many ways. Researchers have also developed many ways to isolate discrete acts of violence in programming. The

16
*The Measurement of Violence in Television Programming: Violence Indices**

Nancy Signorielli

*Some of the discussion in this essay is based on the theoretical and methodological framework of the Cultural Indicators Project at the Annenberg School of Communications, University of Pennsylvania. The results of recent Cultural Indicators research also appeared in George Gerbner, Larry Gross, Michael Morgan, and Nancy Signorielli, "The 'Mainstreaming' of America: Violence Profile No. 11," Journal of Communication 30 (1980): 3. I particularly would like to thank Heather Harr-Mazar, Wendy Wolfenson, Larry Gross, and Michael Morgan for their help in preparing this essay.

discussion of definitions and unitization rules also elaborates on some controversy surrounding this research. The major thrust of this essay is methodological. Findings are presented briefly.

The Assessment of Violence in Television Programs

Researchers have assessed violence in television programs in four basic ways: (1) content analyses using trained coders and specific rules and definitions; (2) ratings or consensual measures in which people (experts as well as everyday) rate the amount of violence in programs; (3) studies in which the researcher predetermines which programs are violent; and (4) studies using combinations of (2) and (3). This last set of studies usually focuses on issues (motivation, prosocial, etc.) other than violence. Tables 16-1 and 16-2 list studies using the first two methods. The third and fourth areas are not included because they are not concerned with measurement issues *per se*. Moreover, the methods actually used in these studies are usually similar to those in (1) and (2).

Content Analysis

Although most people would agree that there is violence on television, there is no consensus about the degree or amount. To rely on people's perceptions or opinions raises important questions, including problems of selective exposure and differences in what to consider violence. Adequate and accurate assessment of the amount of violence in television programming can be achieved only through systematic research that includes quantification of this phenomenon. Methodologically, content analysis provides a procedural framework that can be used to conduct this type of research.

Content analysis has been defined as "any technique for making inferences by systematically and objectively identifying specified characteristics of messages."[1] The first step in content analysis is to design an appropriate recording instrument; for television programming, the set of observations that must be made for all programs in the sample. This recording instrument also includes the definitions and rules used to code these programs. Content analysis data are generated by coders trained to use this instrument; that is, they are taught to observe a phenomenon in a particular way. Thus, coders' personal opinions should not be apparent; in a rigorous content analysis any trained coder will generate the same data. Moreover, this objectivity can and should be measured via reliability analysis. Thus, the researcher is assured that the data reflect actual properties of the material under investigation and not ambiguities contributed by the uncertainties in the instrument or coder idiosyncracies.

The study of television violence through content analysis usually includes examining several aspects of this phenomenon. Most of these analyses try to measure violence precisely. Thus, the content analysis recording instruments include a definition of violence and rules to isolate and count the number of times violence occurs. These rules, the unitization procedures, specify what constitutes a discrete act of violence—when it begins and when it ends.

Since 1954, many content analyses have assessed television content (see Table 16-1).[2] The earliest important studies, conducted by Dallas Smythe[3] and Sidney Head,[4] coded programs "off the air." They found that in the early 1950s there was a considerable amount of violence in New York City television programming.

Clark and Blankenburg[5] assessed violence in television drama over a longer time, 1953 through October 1969. The authors, using *TV Guide* synopses as source material, stated that their measure or assessment of violence is probably underestimated, particularly in regard to television comedies. Since the source material is limited, the research only assessed general levels of violence; a specific count of violent actions could not be done. Clark and Blankenburg found a high level of violence that appeared to be cyclical. There were peaks in 1955, 1959, 1963, and 1967, with especially high levels in the late 1950s.

Table 16-1 Measuring Violence Via Content Analysis

Authors	Phenomenon	Who Codes	Definition	How Used
Cultural Indicators Gerbner Gross Signorielli Morgan Jackson-Beeck	annual weekly samples of prime-time, weekend-daytime network dramatic programs	trained coders (12–16)	yes	To ascertain content on number of basic issues, such as violence, aging, sex-roles, and minority presentation
Harvey Sprafkin Rubinstein	week long sample of prime-time programs (video-taped)	trained coders	yes	To determine the impact of family viewing time policy on content; to isolate prosocial and aggressive behavior
Schuetz Sprafkin	week-long sample of Saturday A.M. commercials (video-taped)	two trained raters	yes	To isolate prosocial behavior in children's TV commercials
Deiner DeFour	12 adventure programs	30 trained undergraduates	yes	To answer question: Does television content enhance program popularity?
Franzblau Sprafkin Rubinstein	week-long sample of prime-time programs (video-taped)	four trained raters	yes	To ascertain amount of sexually aggressive (e.g., rape, aggressive touching) behavior in TV programs
CBS, Office of Social Research	samples of prime-time programming	trained coders	yes	To ascertain the amount of violence in programming

Table 16-1 (Cont.)

Authors	Phenomenon	Who Codes	Definition	How Used
Slaby Quarforth McConnachie	week-long sample of programs (off-air)	undergraduates (trained & practiced)	yes (Gerbner-based)	To assess violence on TV and attribute to major sponsors
Dominick	week-long sample of prime-time programs (off-air)	7 trained coders	yes	To ascertain portrayal of criminal victims and law enforcement on TV
Clark Blankenberg	TV Guide Synopsis (1953–1969)	coders	yes	To ascertain trends in amount of violence in prime-time programs
Head	13-week sample of programs (4 episodes/ programs) (off-air)	4 coders	yes	To analyze TV content
Smythe	samples of programs (off-air)	trained coders	yes	To ascertain content of tele-vision programs on basic issues

Table 16-2 Measuring Violence Via Ratings

Authors	Type of Phenomenon Directly Observed	Who Observes	Provided Definition	How Results Used
Murray Cole Fedler	list of programs	teenagers	their own; half before, half after rating	Determine whether teenagers who watch television, especially violent programs, possess characteristics different from teenagers who prefer less violent programming
Greenberg Gordon	list of programs	TV critics, public (adults)	half	To determine how much violence TV critics perceive in programming in comparison to that perceived by viewers
Abel Beninson	list of programs	children and their mothers	half	To determine if there is agreement between children and their mother's perception of violence
Israel Robinson Smith	list of programs programs list	TV critics, graduate students graduate students	half yes	To ascertain demagogical characteristics of viewers of violent programs To determine if "bad" drivers have a greater preference for viewing violent TV programs than "good" drivers
Loye	lists	psychiatrists, psychologists, parents, etc.	unknown	To measure psychological effect of watching different types of dramatic content

239

Researchers have used content analysis to isolate different aspects of violent content.[6] Dominick[7], examining crime and law enforcement in prime-time programming, found that two-thirds of the programs portrayed at least one crime. He also found that violent crimes were the most prevalent; murder, assault, and armed robbery made up 60 percent of television crimes. Moreover, television tended to overrepresent crimes directed against people rather than property[8] and to underrepresent violent crimes between family members.

The results of content analyses have been put to several interesting uses. Slaby, Quarforth, and McConnachie[9] related television violence to the people who sponsor it. They assessed the amount of violence on television and determined the rate of violence attributable to major commercial sponsors. They found 2,796 violent episodes in 376 hours of programming, or 7.43 episodes per hour. The range of violent actions was quite large—from none to 22.5 per hour.

One grassroots movement concerned with ascertaining the amount of violence in programming grew out of the research of Slaby, Quarforth, and McConnachie. In 1976, the National Citizens Committee for Broadcasting (NCCB) set up a monitoring system to determine which companies were sponsoring the most and least violent programming. NCCB consulted with experts to set up a system and used a commercial monitoring firm to gather the data. They reported the results of this project in *Media Watch*, their bi-monthly newsletter.

Another grassroots movement of about the same time was the National PTA's TV Action Center. Given two years without national coverage, this project may no longer exist. This project used thousands of PTA members throughout the country (two units from each state) as monitors who noted instances of gratuitous violence (violence used to maintain interest, violence not necessary for plot development, and glorified violence). They also looked for instances of sexploitation as well as for sexual, age, and racial or ethnic stereotypes. In a yearly TV program review guide,

the PTA listed the least and most violent programs and sponsors, as well as descriptions of individual programs based on monitors' opinions.

The PTA project raised the level of public consciousness about TV violence. Its drawback was that the monitoring was not objective; the PTA wanted their monitors to elicit personal opinions about programming. The PTA did supply some definitions and a short training program, but it did not measure the reliability of the codings. Thus, the results of the monitoring project should be viewed cautiously.

A third monitoring project has examined television violence for the past three years. In 1980, building on previous work of the NCCB and PTA, the National Coalition on Television Violence (NCTV) was founded. Like NCCB, this organization consulted with experts to set up monitoring procedures. The NCTV reports its findings in a quarterly newsletter, *NCTV News*. NCTV, however, uses its own staff of monitors to gather data. NCTV also links advertisers with violent programs and reports advertisers who sponsor the least violent as well as the most violent programs. Finally, NCTV encourages members to write to companies praising them or complaining about their advertising practices.

The networks, especially CBS, have also been active in this area. Since 1972, the Office of Social Research at CBS has conducted an annual content analysis of prime-time network dramatic programming that counts incidents of violence within programs and as a result has been concerned with definitional and unitization issues. The results of these analyses are presented in Comstock et al.[10] Typically, they find considerably less violence than nonindustry-conducted analyses—differences that often result from methodological, definitional, and unitization issues to be discussed later.

The Cultural Indicators Project

The most long-term and extensive content analysis of television programming that includes the study of violence is the Cultural Indicators Project at the Annenberg School of Communications, University of Pennsylvania (often referred to as the Gerbner research). This research began in 1967–1968 with a study for the National Commission on the Causes and Prevention of Violence. It continued under the sponsorship of the Surgeon General's Scientific Advisory Committee on Television and Social Behavior, the National Institute of Mental Health, the White House Office of Telecommunications Policy, the American Medical Association, the National Science Foundation, and other agencies.

The research consists of two interrelated parts: (1) message system analysis—the annual content analysis of prime-time and weekend-daytime network television dramatic programming, and (2) cultivation analysis—determining conceptions of social reality television viewing tends to cultivate in different groups of viewers.[11] The analyses provide information about the geography, demography, character profiles, and action structure of television drama and focus these images and lessons on specific issues, policies, and topics.

The content data on which Cultural Indicators bases its reports are gathered on issues other than violence. Rigorously trained two-person coding teams generate the content data. During training, each pair independently codes a series of ten programs that have been coded by the entire message system analysis staff, returning one joint coding for each program. Each pair then meets with a staff member to discuss difficulties encountered. When the month-long training has been completed, coder-pairs begin to code the annual sample of prime-time and weekend-daytime (children's) network dramatic programming. During both the training and data-collection phases, coder-pairs monitor their assigned videotaped programs as often as necessary, rescreening portions as needed. All programs in the sample are coded independently by two separate coder-pairs to provide double-coded data for reliability testing.

Reliability measures are designed to ascertain the degree to which the recorded data reflect the properties of the material being studied and not observer bias or instrument ambiguity. The Cultural Indicators reliability assessment consists of calculating an agreement coefficient for each content item in the recording instrument. Only items meeting acceptable levels of agreement are included in subsequent analyses.[12]

The data do not reflect what one person sees but what large communities absorb over long periods of time. Thus, the research does not attempt to interpret individual programs, networks, or productions, nor to draw conclusions about artistic merit. The analysis isolates the patterns and symbolic structures in the samples. The purpose of this content analysis is to provide systematic, cumulative, and objective observations of the relevant aspects of the world of television drama.

Cultural Indicators has published annual reports[13] on violence in television programming and has developed an index used to compare the levels of violence in different programming genres. This discussion focuses only on some methodological issues and controversies surrounding this research.

Measuring Violence via Ratings

The second type of study that generates measures of the amount of violence in programs uses people (experts such as television critics as well as average people) to rate the degree of violence within programs. The raters are given lists of television programs and asked to rate programs with which they are familiar on a three- or five-point violence scale. These studies often manipulate whether raters are given a definition of violence; most studies have found that it does matter. For example, Greenberg and Gordon[14] and Abel and Beninson[15] found that adult raters who were given a definition rated programs as more violent than the raters not given one. For children, though, the opposite was true—those without a definition rated programs as more violent. Other experimental conditions include having raters generate their own definition of violence either before or after completing the rating task.[16]

The best known rating study is by Greenberg and Gordon[17] as part of the Surgeon

General's three-year study of television. This research compared the ratings made by television critics with those of the public (adults). Greenberg and Gordon also manipulated, for the public, whether a definition of violence was supplied (the critics were given a definition and also asked to supply their own if it differed). They found unanimity between the critics and the public about the twenty most violent shows in the 1969 television season. Moreover, the critics judged programs as more violent than did the public. Finally, violence ratings increased when raters were given a definition of violence.

It thus appears that requiring raters to adhere to an explicit definition may inflate perceived violence levels. It should be stressed that absolute levels are misleading and not the central issue. A primary value of systematic research is that it provides a way to compare trends reliably over time. Agreements or disagreements about individual programs are less important than the phenomena contained in the total, coherent system or messages.

Key Issues: Definitions, Unitization, and Sampling

Measuring violence rests on three key issues that are also the basis for disagreements about the findings of violence-related content analyses: (1) the way violence is defined and what to include as violence; (2) the way violence is isolated or unitized; and (3) the nature of the sample.

Definitions of Violence

The rating studies revealed that when raters were given a definition of violence, programs were usually rated as more violent. Thus, the way violence is defined is an important methodological issue. Although almost every study supplies its own definition of violence, most definitions have a common core that includes physical hurting and/or killing. Some specific definitions used in this research are given below.

The most widely used[18] definition was developed for the Cultural Indicators Project. Violence is "the overt expression of physical force (with or without a weapon, against self or other) compelling action against one's will or pain of being hurt or killed, or actually hurting or killing."[19] The definition of violence used in the CBS monitoring project is "the use of physical force against persons or animals, or the articulated, explicit threat of physical force to compel particular behavior on the part of a person."[20] The PTA isolates gratuitous violence, defined as "violence to maintain interest, violence not necessary for plot development, glorified violence."[21] PTA monitors are instructed to focus primarily on violence to persons, to property, and to laws. Clark and Blankenburg[22] define violence as "physical acts or the threat of physical acts by humans designed to inflict physical injury to persons or damage to property." Harvey, Sprafkin and Rubinstein[23] and Scheutz and Sprafkin[24] focus on aggression, rather than violence, which they define as "acts involving the use of force, threat of force, or intent of force against others."

As noted, some ratings studies manipulated whether raters were given a definition of violence before the rating task. These definitions also focus on physical violence, such as hurting. Smith defined a violent program as "a program where usually at some point the action results in injury or destruction to some object, animal, or human. The injury may be psychological or physical . . . a result of verbal or motor action."[25] Greenberg and Gordon[26] and Abel and Beninson[27] used the same definition, "how much fighting, shooting, yelling or killing there usually is in the show." Finally, some rating researchers had the raters define violence—either before or after rating the programs. Again, physical violence predominates. For example, Murray, Cole, and Fedler[28] found that teenagers' definitions of violence generally involved three types of acts:

1. Physical: Violence to persons, damage to property
2. Mental: Psychological and emotional (e.g., fear and hatred)
3. Verbal: Verbal abuse

These definitions are remarkably similar, stressing primarily physical force, including hurting and killing. One basic difference is whether the definition includes violence to property and emotional or psychological violence. Cultural Indicators, CBS, and Greenberg and Gordon do not, but most others do. These differences seem to have been accepted, and no major arguments have arisen because of them. The arguments that do exist are between industry-related research and the Cultural Indicators study. The differences focus not on the definition of violence *per se* but on whether to include certain forms of violence, such as comic violence, accidents, or acts of nature.

The network researchers (CBS[29] and NBC[30]) argue against including these disputed forms. Cultural Indicators research, on the other hand, records all incidents of violence if they meet the criteria in the definition and coding instructions.[31] In regard to comic violence, Cultural Indicators records all violence occurring in a realistic or serious context along with violence in a fantasy or humorous context. CBS, however, would not count as violence events "in a context which would ordinarily produce laughter" and violence that is "not of a serious character." The network critics attack the inclusion of comic violence with the supposedly disarming example of a pie in the face. Cultural Indicators, however, classifies as violence only the credible indication or actual infliction of overt physical pain, hurt, or killing. Thus, if a pie in the face does that, which depends on the specific incident, it is violence and would be recorded as such.

Substantial empirical evidence indicates that a comic context is an effective form in which to convey serious lessons.[32] Moreover, CBS has been quick to point out that children can learn (perceive) pro-social messages in comic context.[33] Although CBS may assume that children will only pick up "good" messages in a "humorous context," Cultural Indicators does not.

The second definition-related contention is whether to include accidents and/or acts of nature. Again, the networks argue against their inclusion (except those occurring in a violent context, such as someone killed in an accident while escaping from a crime[34]) without offering a reason other than that accidents are not reasonable types of violence. Cultural Indicators research has always included both violence occurring due to accidents and/or acts of nature because, in fact, there are no accidents in fiction. The author invents (or producer inserts) dramatic disasters, accidents, and acts of nature for a purpose—often to eliminate or incapacitate a character. Moreover, the pattern of violent victimization revealed through these occurrences may be a significant part of television violence. It is hardly accidental that certain types of characters are accident- or disaster-prone in the world of television. These patterns may also have significant effects on some viewers' conceptions of life and on their own risks in life. Therefore, a person concerned with the full range of potential significant consequences from violence in television programming must identify and report all types of violence that fit the strict definition.

Unitization of Violence

The second area of disagreement about how to measure violence is how to isolate specific incidents of violence. Where does a violent action start and where does it end? Although any decision is somewhat arbitrary and open to debate, these researchers must operationalize the concept in the most appropriate, meaningful, simple, and comprehensible way.

In the tradition of content research since the first studies of the 1950s, Cultural Indicators' coding instructions specify that a violent action is a scene of some violence confined to the same participants. If a scene is interrupted by flashback or shifts to another scene but continues in real time, it is still the same episode. Any change in the cast of characters, such as a new agent of violence entering the scene, starts another episode.

The CBS study, which is essentially the only other major study (aside from the NCCB and NCTV monitoring[35]) that measures violence levels and counts the number of actions within programs, defines a violent action somewhat similarly: "one sustained, dramatically continuous event involving violence, with essentially the same group of participants and with no major interruption in continuity."[36] The major difference between the two rules is the ambiguous inclusion of the word *essentially* in the CBS instructions. Moreover, since the criteria for demanding the essential set of agents are not specified, the CBS study seems to present an arbitrary and subjective manipulation of the unit of analysis. In fact, CBS's instructions to coders are vague on this issue:

> A violent incident is not absolutely synonymous with an "act." One incident might include brief breaks in the action, as in a protracted chase scene, interrupted by pauses for regrouping and reloading or acts of violence by more than one person, as, for example, in a fight scene involving several people.

Because of these differences, the findings of these two major studies differ, but in a predictable way. CBS, as expected, finds less violence than does Cultural Indicators.[38]

Sampling

Another area of considerable debate and criticism of Cultural Indicators research is the nature of the sample used for the annual message system analysis—a single week of programming broadcast in the fall of each season. In particular, CBS has argued that there is no such thing as a typical television week. Cultural Indicators, knowing the dangers of using too small a sample, has conducted sampling studies to assess the representativeness of a one-week sample. These studies include an initial analysis in 1969,[39] repeated spring-season test samplings in 1975 and 1976, and an analysis of seven weeks of fall 1976 prime-time programming.

In the 1976 study, violence-related content data were collected for seven consecutive weeks, including the week originally selected for the fall 1976 sample of prime-time programming. Many statistical routines, including several analyses of variance, led to the same conclusion—each sample week yielded

basically similar findings. That is, there were no significant differences by week for dependent measures such as the number of violent actions, the duration of violence, and the significance of violence. There were, however, significant main-effects for program-related variables, including network, type of program, time of broadcast, and new or continued program; but there were no significant interactions. Thus, for example, the networks differed significantly overall from each other on these measures (see Table 16-3) but not on a week-by-week basis. Moreover, for the number of violent actions, the network rankings are remarkably stable during this time period. We found the same rank-order of the three networks no matter which week was chosen, except for one instance when ABC and CBS were tied.

These studies thus indicate that even though a larger sample may increase precision, given our operational definitions and multidimensional measures that are sensitive to many significant aspects of television violence, the one-week sample yields remarkably stable results with high cost-efficiency.

Indices of Violence

Indices abound in American culture. Most Americans are aware of economic indices, such as the Consumer Price Index, and, recently, the Pollution Index has been gaining recognition.

In research, indices are usually developed and used as data reduction devices. Basically, an index's usefulness is its ability to reduce a lot of data to a simple number that is easy to interpret and understand. An index has been defined as "a type of composite measure that summarizes several specific observations and represents some more general dimension."[40]

Most studies that measure violence in television programming are not concerned with indices. As noted, the rating and predetermined studies label programs from very violent to not violent. When researchers want more sophisticated data, they use the number of violent actions as a measure of the degree of violence in different programming genres. Ratings and the number of acts are useful because they give a very general measure of the amount of violence in programming.

But violence is a complex phenomenon; and a sophisticated analysis involves attending not only to specific actions but also to whom is hurt, who does the hurting, and so on. Thus, although simple measures such as the number of violent incidents reveal fluctuations in the basic levels of violence, by itself this type of measure does not yield rich analytic information.

Since 1969, Cultural Indicators research has developed and reported, on a yearly basis, an Index of Violence combining several violence-related measures and calculated for many genres of programs. It is not, however, calculated for the individual programs within the yearly samples.

The Cultural Indicators Violence Index contains three sets of direct observational data. These measures reveal the extent to which violence occurs at all in the program sample (prevalence), the frequency and rate of violent episodes (rate), and the number of roles calling for characterization as violents, victims, or both (role).

Prevalence ($\%P$) is the percent of programs containing any violence in a particular sample of programs. Rate expresses the frequency of

Table 16-3 Analysis of Seven Weeks of Fall 1976 Programming

	Test Sample Week						Fall 1976	Total
	1	*2*	*3*	*4*	*5*	*6*		
Total								
No. of programs	58	58	57	58	61	56	61	409
No. of violent acts	345	342	365	365	341	294	342	2,394
Rate (acts per program)	5.9	5.9	6.4	6.3	5.6	5.2	5.6	5.9
ABC								
No. of programs	20	20	19	19	20	19	19	136
No. of violent acts	114	107	112	132	116	106	110	797
Rate (acts per program)	5.7	5.4	5.9	6.9	5.8	5.6	5.8	5.9
CBS								
No. of programs	22	21	22	21	21	23	24	154
No. of violent acts	90	91	130	97	66	102	84	660
Rate (acts per program)	4.1	4.3	5.9	4.6	3.1	4.4	3.5	4.3
NBC								
No. of programs	16	17	16	18	20	14	18	119
No. of violent acts	141	144	123	136	159	86	148	937
Rate (acts per program)	8.8	8.5	7.7	7.6	8.0	6.1	8.2	7.9

Analysis of Variance Results

	F	*df*	*p*
Week	.248	6	ns
Network	11.989	2	p<.001
Week by network	.342	12	ns
Residual		380	

violent actions or episodes in units of programming and in units of time. The number of such episodes divided by the total number of programs (violent or not) yields the rate per program (R/P). The rate per hour (R/H) is the number of episodes divided by the number of program hours in the sample. The latter measures the concentration or saturation of violence in time and compensates for the difference in rates between a long program unit, such as a movie, and a short one, such as a ten-minute cartoon.

Role is the portrayal of characters as violents (committing violence) or victims (subjected to violence) or both, and yields several measures. They are percent of violents out of all characters in a sample; percent of victims out of all characters in a sample; all those involved as violents or victims or both ($\%V$); percent of killers (those who commit fatal violence); percent of killed (victims of lethal violence); and all those involved in killing, either as killers, killed, or both ($\%K$).

The findings from these data are combined to form the index. This index is the sum of the five measures: the percent of programs containing any violence ($\%P$), twice the rate of violent incidents per program ($2R/P$), twice the rate of violent incidents per hour ($2R/H$), the percent of characters involved in any violence ($\%V$), and the percent of characters involved in killing ($\%K$). That is,

$$VI = (\%P) + (2R/P) + (2R/H) + (\%V) + (\%K).\text{[41]}$$

Prevalence, rate, and role are thus reflected in the index, giving it a multidimensional quality sensitive to a variety of measures of violence portrayals and lending to it a stability not easily altered or manipulated by superficial script changes. The Index itself is not a statistical finding but illustrates trends and facilitates gross comparisons.[42]

The Cultural Indicators Violence Index has been intensely criticized. CBS has criticized the Index because it includes a set of measures rather than only a single indicator, such as the number of violent actions, and because the different measures may move in different directions. But this criticism basically says that the Violence Index is faulty because it meets the criteria of an index. The same criticism should be leveled at any set of comprehensive indicators, such as the GNP, the Dow Jones, many labor statistics, or even the weather forecast. Critics fail to realize that the primary usefulness and strength of an index are that it combines measures of different aspects of a complex phenomenon. Cultural Indicators reports have consistently presented all components of the Violence Index separately as well as in combination. Thus, people who wish to assess or use this index have access to each component and can observe individual as well as combined movement. Moreover, researchers can use these data to develop their own indices.

Testing the Index

The components of the Violence Index have consistently achieved high intercoder reliability; during the last eleven years, the agreement coefficients for individual items range from .65 to .86. Most importantly, the Violence Index meets the critical statistical and empirical requirement of an index: unidimensionality and internal homogeneity. A major criticism of the Violence Index has been that it may be combining apples and oranges, that it mixes together disparate and unrelated dimensions.[43] If, indeed, the Index's components are not measuring the same thing, then it is wrong to combine them; but if they are manifestations of the same underlying dimension, then the Index yields a measure of television violence more reliable and valid than any individual term.

In short, the Index provides a highly reliable measure of television violence, particularly in prime-time programs. Factor analysis reveals only one factor underlying the five components of the Index for both early evening (8–9 P.M. EST) or late evening (9–11 P.M. EST) programs. In terms of internal homogeneity, Cronbach's alpha for all prime-time samples from 1967 to 1978 is a very high .89. Thus, the

Table 16-4   Reliability Coefficients for the Violence Index

	UNWEIGHTED INDEX			WEIGHTED INDEX		
	raw alpha	standard-ized alpha	theta	raw alpha	standard-ized alpha	theta
All Program Data						
(N = 162)	.70	.76	.82	.75	.78	.82
8-9 P.M. EST (N = 60)	.69	.85	.86	.74	.85	.86
9-11 P.M. EST (N = 60)	.74	.88	.88	.79	.88	.86
Weekend Day (N = 42)	.69	.66	.71	.65	.66	.71
Prime-Time total						
(N = 120)	.75	.89	.89	.80	.89	.89

The unit of observation is the time period (8-9 P.M., 9-11 P.M., and weekend daytime) for each network. The reliability estimates are based on all fall samples (1967–1978), the two spring samples (1975 and 1976), and the six-week special sample (1976; for prime-time only).

The unweighted index estimates represent reliability obtained by adding up the five components (percent of programs containing violence, rate of violent acts per hour, rate of violent acts per program, percent of characters involved in violence, and percent of characters involved in killing).

The weighted index doubles the absolute value of two items: acts per hour and rate of violent acts per program.

The raw alpha indicates the reliability the index would have when its components are added up (in raw form).

The standardized alpha indicates the reliability the index would have if the items were standardized before being added up. That is, the index would have this reliability if the raw scores were subtracted from the mean and divided by the standard deviation.

The theta indicates the reliabililty the index would have if the items were both standardized and weighted by their factor score coefficients before they were added up. This is generally the maximum reliability possible to achieve in a given index.

items are measuring a single dimension, and they are measuring it quite well (see Table 16-4).

Critics have also argued that the weights used in creating the Index are arbitrary and unjustified. Yet the Violence Index produces lower reliability estimates when the rate of violent acts per program and per hour are not weighted by two. In each time period (and overall), as shown in Table 16-4, weighting these two components adds about .05 to the alpha.

Finally, in weekend-daytime programs, the internal homogeneity is somewhat lower, but still acceptable (alpha = .66). This is primarily due to one item: the percent of characters involved in killing. In general, weekend-daytime programs have the highest rates of violent acts and the greatest number of programs containing violence, but they also have the smallest proportion of characters involved in killing. In fact, within weekend programs, killing is negatively related to the rate of violent acts per hour. Evidently, children's shows contain a lot of nonlethal violence; and when killing does appear, it seems to be accented as a central action while other aspects of violence are downplayed.

Despite this qualification, these items clearly provide a reliable, unidimensional, internally homogeneous, and efficient measure of television violence.

Summary

Over the past quarter century, there has been considerable concern about and research on television violence. Violence has been assessed in two ways—through content analysis and rating procedures. Content analysis provides objective and quantitative measures of violence; ratings give judgments that reflect raters' personal opinions.

Two controversial issues were discussed—how violence is defined and unitized. Specifically, debate has centered on whether to include violence that occurs in a comic context, or violence that is the result of an accident and/or act of nature, and how to isolate (unitize) discrete acts of violence within a program. These issues are important because differences in their conceptualization have led to predictable differences in the research results.

Although most researchers have focused on only one aspect of violence (the frequency of violent actions) this is not the whole picture. Violence is a complex phenomenon involving specific actions and relating to lessons of victimization, risk, fate, and power. Consequently, its assessment should combine several violence-related measures. The annual Cultural Indicators Violence Index does this: it incorporates measures of the prevalence, rate, and role of violence in television programming. The Index is a simple measure reported both as a summary figure and in terms of its individual components. It is not a statistical finding but serves to illustrate trends and to facilitate gross comparisons.

The Cultural Indicators Violence Index and its components have revealed that, during the past decade, despite year-to-year changes for specific networks, various time-periods, and individual genres, the amount of violence in the entire system of television's messages has remained remarkably consistent. Thus, it is reasonable to expect that television programs will continue to feature violence at the fairly high levels that have been observed since 1967.

But there is more to the problem than the quantity of violence that television presents, and Cultural Indicators research does not call for the total elimination of television violence. Symbolic violence is a story-telling device that can serve many purposes. Our task is more to monitor and interpret than to judge, but we report our findings in terms of general standards of equity, fairness, and justice. Our concern is with the kinds of violence shown, the systematic and resilient patterns of who commits violence and who is victimized. These lessons of power, powerlessness, risks, and fates may be critical mechanisms of social control. The roles of both the violent and the victim can be learned by the viewers. In cultivating among the many a fear of the power of the few, television violence may achieve its greatest effect.

Endnotes

1. Ole R. Holsti, "Content Analysis," in Gardner Lindsay and Elliot Aronson, eds., *The Handbook of Social Psychology*, Vol. 2 (Reading, Mass.: Addison-Wesley, 1968), 601.

2. There are several good reviews of this literature. See, for example, William R. Catton, "The Content and Context of Violence in the Mass Media," in Robert Baker and Sandra Ball, eds., *Mass Media and Violence, A Staff Report to the National Commission on the Causes and Prevention of Violence* (Washington, D.C.: U.S. Government Printing Office, 1969), 423–452.

3. Dallas Smythe, *Three Years of New York Television 1951–1953* (Urbana, Ill.: National Association of Educational Broadcasters, 1953); "Reality as Presented on Television," *Public Opinion Quarterly* 18 (1954): 143–156.

4. Sidney Head, "Content Analysis of Television Drama Programs," *Quarterly of Film, Radio and TV* 9 (1954): 175–194.

5. David G. Clark and William B. Blankenberg, "Trends in Violent Content in Selected Mass Media," in George Comstock and Eli Rubinstein, eds., *Television and Social Behavior*, Vol. 1, *Media Content and Control* (Washington, D.C.: U.S.

Government Printing Office, 1972), 188–243.

6. See, for example, Susan Franzblau, Joyce N. Sprafkin, and Eli Rubinstein, "Sex on TV: A Content Analysis," *Journal of Communication* 27 (1977): 164–179; and Stephen Schuetz and Joyce N. Sprafkin, "Portrayal of Prosocial and Aggressive Behaviors in Children's TV Commercials," *Journal of Broadcasting* 23 (1979): 33–40.

7. Joseph R. Dominick, "Crime and Law Enforcement in Prime-Time Television," *Public Opinion Quarterly* 37 (1973): 243–250.

8. According to U.S. statistics, most crimes are directed at property rather than people. See, for example, *Criminal Victimization in the United States, 1974, A National Crime Survey Report* (Washington, D.C.: U.S. Government Printing Office, 1974).

9. Ronald G. Slaby, Gary R. Quarforth, and Gene A. McConnachie, "Television Violence and Its Sponsors," *Journal of Communication* 26 (1976): 88–96.

10. George Comstock, Steven Chaffee, Nathan Katzman, Maxwell McCombs, and Donald Roberts, *Television and Social Behavior* (New York: Columbia University Press, 1978).

11. This research design has been documented in a number of publications. The best description of the methodology appears in George Gerbner, Larry Gross, Marilyn Jackson-Beeck, Suzanne Jeffries-Fox, and Nancy Signorielli, "Cultural Indicators: Violence Profile No. 9," *Journal of Communication* 28 (1978), 176–207. The conceptual framework is presented in George Gerbner, "Cultural Indicators: The Third Voice," in George Gerbner, Larry Gross, and William Melody, eds., *Communications Technology and Social Policy* (New York: John Wiley, 1973). The essay by Larry Gross and Michael Morgan in this book ("Television and Enculturation: What Does Television Cause?") describes cultivation analysis. Further re-

finements are presented in George Gerbner, Larry Gross, Michael Morgan, and Nancy Signorielli, "The 'Mainstreaming' of America: Violence Profile No. 11," *Journal of Communication* 30 (1980): 3; and "Charting the Mainstream: Television's Contributions to Political Orientations," *Journal of Communication* 32 (1980): 100–127.

12. Five computational formulae are used; their variations depend on the scale type of the particular variable being analyzed. Except for their respective scale-appropriate sensitivity to deviations from perfect agreement, the coefficients make the same basic assumptions as the prototype for nominal scales devised by Scott (1955). Thus, in the case of a binary variable, all formulae yield identical results. For the derivation of the formulae and a discussion of their properties, see Klaus Krippendorff, "Bivariate Agreement Coefficients for the Reliability of Data," in E. F. Borgatta, ed., *Sociological Methodology: 1970* (San Francisco: Jossey-Bass, 1970). Also see George Gerbner, Larry Gross, Michael Morgan, and Nancy Signorielli, "Violence Profile No. 11: Trends in Network Television Drama and Viewer Conceptions of Social Reality" (Annenberg School of Communications, University of Pennsylvania, 1980).

13. George Gerbner and Larry Gross, "Living With Television: The Violence Profile," *Journal of Communication* 26 (1976) 173–199; George Gerbner, Larry Gross, Michael Eleeny, Marilyn Jackson-Beeck, Suzanne Jeffries-Fox, and Nancy Signorielli, "TV Violence Profile No. 8: The Highlights," *Journal of Communication* 27 (1977): 171–180; George Gerbner et al., "Cultural Indicators: Violence Profile No. 9," op. cit.; and George Gerbner, Larry Gross, Nancy Signorielli, Michael Morgan, and Marilyn Jackson-Beeck, "The Demonstration of Power: Violence Profile No. 10," *Journal of Communication* 29 (1979): 177–196; George Gerbner, Larry Gross, Michael Morgan, and Nancy

Signorielli, "The 'Mainstreaming' of America: Violence Profile No. 11," *Journal of Communication* 30 (1980): 10–29.

14. Bradley S. Greenberg and Thomas F. Gordon, "Critics and Public Perceptions of Violence in Television Programs," *Journal of Broadcasting* 15 (1970–1971): 24–43.

15. John D. Abel and Maureen E. Beninson, "Perceptions of TV Program Violence by Children and Mothers," *Journal of Broadcasting* 20 (1976): 355–363.

16. Randall L. Murray, Richard R. Cole, and Fred Fedler, "Teenagers and TV Violence: How They Rate and View It," *Journalism Quarterly* 47 (1970): 247–255.

17. Greenberg and Gordon, op. cit.

18. The Cultural Indicators' definition of violence was also used by Slaby, Quarforth, and McConnachie, op. cit., and in the NCCB and NCTV monitoring projects.

19. Gerbner et al., "Violence Profile No. 11," op. cit.

20. Office of Social Research, CBS, Inc., "Network Prime-Time Violence Tabulations for 1976–1977 Season" and "Instructions to Coders," 15.

21. Individual Monitoring Form. National PTA TV Action Center, 700 N. Rush St., Chicago, Ill. 60611.

22. Clark and Blankenberg, op. cit.

23. S. E. Harvey, J. N. Sprafkin, and E. A. Rubinstein, "Prime-Time Television: A Profile of Aggressive and Prosocial Behaviors," *Journal of Broadcasting* 23 (1979): 179–189.

24. Schuetz and Sprafkin, op. cit.

25. James R. Smith, "Television Violence and Driving Behavior," *Educational Broadcasting Review* 3 (1969): 23–28.

26. Greenberg and Gordon, op. cit.

27. Abel and Beninson, op. cit.

28. Murray, Cole, and Fedler, op. cit.

29. David M. Blank, "The Gerbner Violence Profile" and "Final Comments on the Violence Profile," *Journal of Broadcasting* 21 (1977): 273–279, 287–296.

30. Thomas E. Coffin and Sam Tuchman, "Rating Television Programs for Violence: A Comparison of Five Surveys" and "A Question of Validity: Some Comments on 'Apples, Oranges and the Kitchen Sink,' " *Journal of Broadcasting* 17 (1972–1973): 3–20, 31–33.

31. The Cultural Indicators replies to these critiques are in the following articles: George Gerbner, Larry Gross, Michael Eleeny, Marilyn Jackson-Beeck, Suzanne Jeffries-Fox, and Nancy Signorielli, "The Gerbner Violence Profile — An Analysis of the CBS Report" and "One More Time: An Analysis of the CBS 'Final Comments on the Violence Profile,' " *Journal of Broadcasting* 21 (1977): 280–286, and 297–303; and Michael F. Eleeny, George Gerbner, and Nancy (Tedesco) Signorielli, "Apples, Oranges and the Kitchen Sink: An Analysis and Guide to the Comparison of 'Violence Ratings' " and "Validity, Indeed!" *Journal of Broadcasting* 17 (1972–1973), 21–30, 34–35.

32. See, for example, Albert Bandura, Dorothea Ross, and Sheila Ross, "Transmission of Aggression through Imitation of Aggressive Models," *Journal of Abnormal and Social Psychology* 63 (1967): 575–582; Albert Bandura, Dorothea Ross, and Sheila Ross, "Imitation of Film Mediated Aggression Models," *Journal of Abnormal and Social Psychology* 66 (1963): 3–11; Glenn Thomas Ellis and Francis Sekura III, "The Effects of Aggressive Cartoons on the Behavior of First Grade Children," *Journal of Psychology* 81 (1972): 7–43; O. I. Lovas, "Effect of Exposure to Symbolic Aggression on Aggressive Behavior," *Child Development* 32 (1961): 37–44; Richard Haynes, "Children's Perceptions of 'Comic' and 'Authentic' Cartoon Violence," *Journal of Broadcasting* 22 (1978): 63–70.

33. "They Learn while They Laugh," a CBS-published public relations booklet extolling the educational virtues of its children's programming, including cartoons, undated.

34. Office of Social Research, CBS, Inc., op. cit.

35. For the most part, the NCCB project used Cultural Indicators methodology and unitization rules.

36. Office of Social Research, CBS, Inc., op. cit.

37. Ibid.

38. The differences in the results of the two studies are discussed in Comstock, et al., op. cit.

39. Michael F. Eleeny, "Variations in Generalizability Resulting from Sampling Characteristics of Content Analysis Data: A Case Study" (The Annenberg School of Communications, University of Pennsylvania, 1969).

40. Earl R. Babbie, *Practice of Social Research* (Belmont, Calif.: Wadsworth, 1973), 495.

41. The rates were weighted by a factor of two in the Cultural Indicators index so as to increase their importance. That is, the rates are usually small numbers (on the order of 4 to 9), and weighting increases their contribution to the index.

42. The National Citizens Committee on Broadcasting (NCCB) has reported two indices that are based essentially on the Cultural Indicators methodology. Note, however, that in some of their reports, NCCB distinguishes between the Gerbner definition (including comic violence, accidents, and acts of nature) and a definition not including these types of actions. The NCCB program index is the sum of (1) the ratio of incidents of violence in a program to the total number of incidents and (2) the ratio of the time of violence (in minutes and tenths) in the program to the total time of violence in prime time. This index is used to rank programs from least to most violent. Advertisers are ranked by an index made by summing (1) the ratio of the length of violent programming by an advertiser to the total length of programming with violence in prime time, (2) the ratio of the number of incidents of violence in programming sponsored by the advertiser to the total number of violent incidents in prime time, and (3) the ratio of the length of violent incidents sponsored by the advertiser to the total length of violent incidents (in minutes and tenths) in prime time. ("Prime Time Violence Profiles," National Citizens Committee for Broadcasting and BI Associates, 1976).

43. Coffin and Tuckman, 1972, op. cit.

Additional References

Diener, Ed, and Darlene DeFour. "Does Television Violence Enhance Program Popularity?" *Journal of Personality and Social Psychology* 36 (1978): 333–341.

Israel, H., and J. P. Robinson. "Demographic Characteristics of Viewers of Television Violence and News Programs," in Eli A. Rubinstein, George A. Comstock, and John P. Murray. *Television and Social Behavior*, Vol. IV. *Television in Day-to-Day Life: Patterns of Use* (Washington, D.C.: U.S. Government Printing Office, 1972) 87–128.

Loye, David, Roderic Gorney, and Gary Steele. "An Experimental Field Study," *Journal of Communication* 27 (1977): 206–216.

Scott, William A., "Reliability of Content Analysis: The Case of Nominal Scale Coding," *Public Opinion Quarterly* 17 (1955): 321–325.

17
Assessing Impacts on Children

Timothy P. Meyer
Anne Hexamer

Background

For almost as long as radio and television have been part of American society, concern has been expressed about their effects on children and adolescents. This concern has been reflected from local and regional levels through inquiries and policy proposals at the national level.

Fear of broadcasting's negative effects has characterized the three most recent decades. Television came under scrutiny in the 1950s. Early fears centered on the medium's effects on reading, schoolwork, vision, juvenile delinquency, and so on. The early to mid-1960s found TV on trial as a source of antisocial behavior among children. In 1968 and 1969, following the assassinations of John Kennedy, Martin Luther King, Jr., and Robert Kennedy, a National Committee on the Causes and Prevention of Violence was formed. This committee examined the role of television in contributing to the frequency of violent acts and the degree to which it contributed to an atmosphere that encouraged, facilitated, and/or condoned violence. The decade of the 1970s provides ample evidence of the fears and anxieties still manifest toward the assumed negative impact and consequences of certain kinds of television content.

In late 1971 and early 1972, the U.S. Surgeon General's Scientific Advisory Committee on Television and Social Behavior issued its summary report on the impact of television on youth. This report and its supporting five volumes of studies funded by a million and a half dollars created considerable controversy and public debate. The nature of the findings was the root of the controversy, which we discuss later; the important point here is that national attention was again drawn to how television was affecting the behavior of the nation's children.

Spurred on by citizens' media reform groups, such as Action for Children's Television, the issue of television's effects on children began to intensify. As the 1970s drew to a close, the Federal Trade Commission (FTC) announced a major policy-making inquiry proposing the elimination or reduction of televised commercials directed at children. Again, assuming that commercials produced harmful effects on some children, the general issue of television impact was spotlighted. Not to be outdone by their federal agency counterparts, the Federal Communications Commission (FCC) launched another inquiry into the topic of children's television. As the 1980s began, both investigations were in progress. By 1981, however, both inquiries had been suspended or delayed.

The 1980s: TV Continues on the Hot Seat

During the 1980s, television's accountability will continue to be questioned. Policies will continue to be prepared, amended, and rewritten relative to the outcomes of the various inquiries. Concerns will move to television's alleged culpability in areas other than antisocial behavior and commercials. Decline in college SAT scores has been attributed at least partly to the TV generation's watching more and reading less. Children's learning of stereotypes—occupational, sex-role, age, and racial—continues to be questioned, with television usually being condemned for negligence. The effects of electronically sophisticated shows on children's classroom learning is being debated. Teachers complain about being unable to compete with shows like *Sesame Street, The Electric Company, Zoom,* and *3, 2, 1, Contact.* A corollary issue is that the tightly edited, frenetically paced nature of many children's shows contributes to such children's learning problems as lack of task persistence, hyperactivity, and disruptive behaviors.

Last in this abbreviated list is the topic of sexually oriented TV content and its effects on children and adolescents. With the proliferation of home video recorders, disk machines, and pay cable programming, the appearance of explicit sexual acts on the home screen is becoming a reality in many American households. The apparatus for receiving such content is present in 40 percent of all U.S. households as of 1983. How children and adolescents are affected by exposure to these materials will be a growing interest.

The list of issues involving television and its effects on both children and adolescents is extensive and impressive. The consequences of determining impacts on children are significant and far-reaching. The reasons for a preoccupation with TV's impact on children serve as the focus of the next section.

Children: A Special Audience

Children have long been recognized as a special audience. For many years, the now defunct voluntary code of the National Association of Broadcasters had a separate section on children, acknowledging their relative innocence and the ease with which unscrupulous producers might exploit them. Children pose an added social responsibility for broadcasters.

The courts have also called attention to children as exceptions to various laws and interpretations bearing directly on proper uses of broadcast channels in programming to an audience. Noted First Amendment scholar Thomas Emerson aptly summarized the legal status of children regarding broadcast content:

> The system cannot and does not treat children the same as adults. The world of children is not the same as the world of adults, so far as a guarantee of untrammeled freedom of the mind is concerned. The reason for this is, as Justice Stewart said in Ginsburg, that a child is not possessed of that full capacity for individual choice which is the pre-supposition of First Amendment guarantees. He is not permitted that measure of independence, or able to exercise the maturity of judgment, which a system of free expression rests upon. This does not mean that the First Amendment extends no protection to children; it does mean that children are governed by different rules.[1]

Children Versus Adults: Some Basic Differences

The differences between adults and children in legal proceedings are based on the well-known, commonsense notion that children, as they develop into adults, must learn to deal with an increasingly greater variety of events in their environment. And, if past experience becomes a learning device that modifies children's ongoing interactions with the environment while acquiring and evaluating basic day-to-day experiences, children are as prepared as most adults to make sense out of the world. Understanding is going through nearly constant and often rapid change, as the children learn to grasp some workings of people, objects, and places in their environment. Klapper observes, "the classic literature of child development . . . indicates that children perceive environmental stimuli in markedly and predictably different ways than do adults."[2] Her own research, and that of others, has shown that "children's perceptions of television content are indeed different from those of adults. . . ."[3] Collins has effectively demonstrated differences among children of different ages in ability to recall program content in proper sequence (as it is presented in a program) and to comprehend the meaning of many actions in various programs.[4]

How Children Differ from Adults: Different Perspectives

The awareness that the child's behavior has a cognitive structure or organizational pattern to be described independently of the degree to which it corresponds to the adult culture is at least as old as Rousseau. There are two major theoretical notions about the source of distinctions between a child and an adult. One theoretical approach to investigating and describing the child's frame of reference seeks qualitative developmental differences in the thought processes of children of various ages and/or at certain stages. Work by Flavell, Kohlberg, Bruner et al., and Piaget represent this approach.[5] The other major theoretical explanation for child/adult differences emphasizes the quantity and nature of experiential differences of the two groups. In essence, adults and children engage in the same basic processes, but adults have the benefit of learning from more and different experiences than children. Research in this area is represented

by Bronfenbrenner, Mayer, Wittrock, Bandura, and Gewirtz.[6]

Developmental differences among children are thus examined from two distinct theoretical and research perspectives. Learning theories of development favor continuity rather than stage categories of a child's development. This difference depends on the kind of analysis being made rather than on descriptions of a child's sequence of learning behaviors. Learning theory assumes that the mechanisms of learning are preformed and function in a consistent manner throughout life. By contrast, cognitive developmental theory (Piaget) proposes a predetermined and fixed sequence of stages of cognitive structure that develop in the child's information processing through interaction with the environment.

Cognitive developmental approaches differ from learning primarily by accepting four basic assumptions:

1. Development involves transformations of cognitive structures for the child. A distinction is made between behavior changes or learning in general and basic changes in the child's mental structures. Cognitive structure refers to the rules used for processing information and connecting events experienced by the child in the environment. These structures thus undergo changes not explained by other factors such as repetition of events in the environment or associational or conditional learning.

2. Development of cognitive structure is the result of a qualitative interaction between the child and the environment rather than a direct result of either maturity or continued learning. Cognitive developmental theory rejects the notion of mental structures that are innate patterns with which the child is born.

Piaget's biological orientation provides an adaptive model for the interaction between the child and the environment. Each encounter with the world around the child has two aspects—assimilation and accommodation. A child thus adapts what is learned from a given event by integrating the information into a particular way of looking at the world (assimilation); the child also adapts himself or herself to the specific environment presented (accommodation).

3. Specific stages are proposed to represent the transformations of mental structures through the processes of assimilation and accommodation. The core of the cognitive developmental approach is the children's progression from stage to stage. Stages have the following characteristics: (a) they imply distinct differences in the way children think or go about solving problems; these differences are manifest when the same children try to solve the same problem at a later stage; (b) the sequence of stages is invariant in development: cultural factors may increase, slow, or stop development, but they do not change its sequence; (c) each stage is a structured whole representing an underlying organization of thought that differs from other stages. A child in the concrete operations stage approaches the solution to a problem in a different way from a child who is in the formal operations stage. In this case, a concrete operations child might solve a problem in a specific situation but would be unable to generalize the properties of the experience to another situation at another time. The child in formal operations would be able to make such a generalization.

The stage concept is meaningfully and usefully applied to developmental patterns. This value of the stages concept is maintained even though future research and theorizing may alter some notions, such as the qualitative nature of change or level of analysis associated with one or more stages.

4. The fourth assumption of cognitive developmental theory is that the direction of development is toward an underlying stability for the child when interacting with the environment. The child passes through qualitatively different stages of thought that differ from the adults' approach in that most adults approach problems with a predictably consistent analysis, whereas children of various ages display different approaches to finding solutions. Moreover, experience in dealing with problems sometimes makes little difference in finding problem solutions by children in a particular

stage; therefore, the environment alone appears to be minimally effective in prompting a child to change his or her approach. Each new problem will be approached in the same way as in the past, despite repeated failures in arriving at an acceptable solution. Experience is, of course, important to the child's learning about the environment, but the impact of that experience apparently does not immediately or directly alter children's patterns of thought.

Children pass through four basic stages in ordered sequence. These stages and their corresponding age levels are described here.

Age Range (in years)	Stage Description
0–2	*Sensorimotor Development:* The child's senses develop along with coordination of body functions; the child learns object permanence (a ball that rolls behind a chair is still there even though it cannot be seen), but operations are limited mostly to the immediate environment/child interactions.
2–7	*Preoperational Thought:* Language development begins; the child learns to manipulate symbols in his or her mind, a kind of mental experimentation that eliminates the need for many trial-and-error experiences; experiences are still tied to the present environment, however.
7–11	*Concrete Operations:* The process of logical deduction begins and develops; the child can now manipulate concrete concepts mentally but still has problems generalizing principles derived from experiences to different situations; operations are also thought to be limited to only one or a few central facets of a process as opposed to being able to

deal with the entire process considered as a whole.

11-15   *Formal Operations:* The child now fully develops the ability to reason in the abstract, to assess implications from a combination of events, to test logical propositions, and to test mental hypotheses fully; the key here is the child's ability to manipulate symbols in a logical manner but still in the abstract.

Note that Piaget has criticized many American psychologists for overemphasizing the stage concept as if each stage represented independent units. He stressed the continuous flow from one stage to another, showing some evidence of the previous stage and some evidence of the next stage, and that, even though children differ in their rates of development (a seven-year-old may be capable of formal operations, for example), the essence of stage theory is that children must go through the first stage before the second, the second before the third, and so on. The specific sequence is more important than the length of time one child or a group of children appears to spend at any one stage.

Corresponding to stages in cognitive development, Kohlberg has suggested stages of moral development through which children progress.[7] These moral stages derive from the specific motives children use in moral reasoning regarding situations that confront them. Kohlberg posits three basic levels of moral development: (1) moral values rest in the presence or absence of punishment or reward for behaving in a certain way; something is good if it is rewarded or bad if it is punished; what motivates children at the earliest level, then, is the avoidance of punishment or the attainment of desired rewards for their actions as determined by the authority figures in their environment (parents); (2) moral value rests in performing good or right roles (being a good student at school), maintaining the conventional order by not disrupting or by cooperating to keep order, and maintaining the expectancies of peers

and authorities. In essence, what is right is determined by what is expected of children when they find themselves in various roles; (3) moral value resides in the child's conformity to shared or sharable standards, rights, or duties; the conscience dictates what appears to be right in a given situation; situational ethics also operate, with what is right or wrong being a function of the specific conditions present, as opposed to a "something is either right or wrong" approach that characterizes earlier moral reasoning. Each level, of course, corresponds to stages in cognitive development. Level one operates usually up through age six; level two from seven to eleven years of age; and level three from twelve years of age on. As in cognitive developmental stages, children can arrive at a given level at different ages, but the child progresses in the specified order of levels of development.

Conclusion

Children differ substantially from adults in the way they look at and deal with the world around them. Television and, to a lesser extent, radio are integral parts of nearly every child's environment. They provide children with a continuing flow of activity, with obvious effects on what they think and believe and how they behave. But since they perceive their world differently from adults, children must be dealt with as an audience separate from older groups. The special sense that children make of their world offers the broadcast researcher unique but challenging opportunities. The following sections describe how researchers study children.

Research Methods in Assessing Broadcast Impact on Children

The researcher studying the impact of broadcast content on children can choose many basic research methods. These methods include experiments, both in and outside the laboratory (field experiments); surveys, conducted face-to-face in school or household settings, by telephone, or via the mail (parents usually fill out the questionnaire or answer the telephone interviewers' questions pertaining to their children's media-related behaviors); and descriptive studies of children observed in a natural environment, such as school and/or their households. Studies can be short or long-term, assessing immediate impact or allowing time to elapse between measurement periods in an attempt to determine the durability of impact and/or changes in behavior. Each approach is discussed in subsequent sections; some examples of each are indicated here.

A classic laboratory study measuring short-term effects of television on children is that of Stanford psychologist Albert Bandura, in collaboration with Dorothea and Sheila Ross; Hicks reported a long-term laboratory experiment, building on Bandura's research.[8] Two excellent examples of a field experiment are the study by Huston-Stein and Friedrich, conducted in a preschool setting, and the study by Feshbach and Singer in private schools and boys' homes.[9] The longitudinal approach is exemplified by the work of Lefkowitz, Eron, Walder, and Huseman; the short-term survey approach is represented by Ward and his associates.[10] Descriptive studies of children and media in natural settings include the study by Murray and those by Lull and Traudt and discussed by Meyer, Traudt, and Anderson.[11]

All approaches to researching the impact of broadcasting on various groups in the audience have strengths and limitations. Any approach attempting to measure and explain the complex processes through which media effects occur is subject to certain limitations urging caution on those who would use the findings. Research investigating child/media interrelationships has a brief history. To date, no concrete body of undisputed fact or knowledge exists, only hypotheses or guesses, some with limited or no empirical support.

Experimental Methods

The experiment is one basic method used in broadcast research. Drawing heavily from advances in the social and behavioral sciences, mainly psychology, communication investigators have relied on experimental designs and their accompanying statistical tools to analyze their data. Experimental hypotheses or predictions of certain specified relationships are tested with the primary goal of presenting cause-and-effect statements pertaining to the conditions and concepts (variables) being studied.

For example, many researchers have tried to measure some effects of watching televised violence on the aggressive behavior of children. The main hypothesis or prediction is that a group of children observing television violence would behave more aggressively as a result than would another separate group who viewed a nonviolent program or segment. Both groups, therefore, would be exposed to some TV content, either violent or nonviolent, and their aggressive behavior would be measured following viewing. The amount of aggressive behavior displayed by the two groups would then be compared statistically to discern a reliable difference (one probably not due to chance) between the two groups and to see which group behaved more aggressively on the average.

Experiments are done to verify and identify relationships among specific, definable events or occurrences in the environment. These events are labeled and treated by researchers as variables. A common variable is the one in the preceding example — violent versus nonviolent TV content. The amount of content can vary (more or less), as can the type of violence (physical versus verbal, a fist-fight versus a gunfight, etc.).

Experiments work with two different kinds of variables — independent and dependent. The experimenter chooses to manipulate one or more independent variables and to observe the outcome of that manipulation on a dependent variable. Thus, in the previous experiment, one independent variable, violent versus nonviolent TV content, was manipulated by the researcher; the effect was then observed on the measure of viewers' aggressive behavior, the dependent variable. The relationship between the variables is hoped to be a causal one: seeing TV violence can cause viewers to become more aggressive in their behavior.

If the causal assumption is to be verified, the experimenter must successfully rule out, to the extent possible, other events or factors (variables) that might have caused the differences observed on the dependent variable. The experiment must, therefore, introduce at least some elements of control. Some variables are actively controlled by the researcher (such as the age range of participants and the setting for each participant); other variables are assumed to be equally distributed across experimental groups. For example, some children might behave more aggressively than others before participating as subjects in the study. If most of these high aggressors were in the violent TV group, this previous difference rather than the TV content could have caused the higher average aggression. Experiments control for such differences by assigning subjects to experimental groups at random. Random assignment means that each subject has an equal chance of being placed in the violent or the nonviolent TV group. With this procedure, it is unlikely that all or even most of the high aggressors would be in the same group.

Experiment results demand that the conditions under which effects are observed be as accurately and completely specified as possible. This requirement means that differences in conditions may produce different effects. Science also demands that findings be capable of reproduction. When findings are retested under the same conditions, the process is called replication. Replication is a safeguard in the scientific process that prevents a chance or coincidental result from being attributed to the causal relationship the experiment was supposed to be testing. Successful replication depends on careful and exacting specifications of conditions and variables and adds credibility to the cause/effect relationship reported by the scientist. When replication does not take place, or when results are not successfully reproduced, the relationship remains tentative, questionable, or both.

The key to useful laboratory experiments is the complete, accurate, and reproducible specifications of variables and experimental conditions. Variables must be defined via operationalizing. Operational definitions enable an observer to recognize and measure the behavior. An operational definition of aggression, for example, is the frequency of hitting an inflatable bobo doll with a mallet or the number of electrical shocks given by a TV viewer to another participant after seeing either a violent or nonviolent TV segment. The key definition is aggression—either as it characterizes the behavior of TV actors or of viewers in the experiment.

Validity is the most important attribute in evaluating experimental operational definitions. The behavior as represented and measured in the laboratory must be isomorphic to the behavior as it occurs outside the laboratory—the two behaviors must be equivalent. Hitting a bobo doll with a mallet must be equivalent to a set of behaviors that occur in the real world that would be termed aggressive or violent (striking another person). If there is no equivalency, or if the equivalency is highly questionable, the results are known as experimental artifacts—products unique to the laboratory setting but inapplicable to the actual behavior that the experiment was to represent. Much criticism of laboratory studies of media effects is that the experiment's variables and conditions do not effectively simulate or approximate those occurring naturally outside the laboratory. Thus, the argument goes, experimental findings are interesting but irrelevant.

The Bandura, Ross, and Ross study mentioned is a classic experimental study of television's effects on children. These investigators were interested in measuring the degree to which preschool children would imitate the behavior of models either on TV or in real life. One group of children saw an adult model pummeling a bobo doll with a mallet; another saw the same model on film (projected through a TV receiver); a third saw a cartoon figure engaging in the same behaviors; a fourth group observed no models at all and served as a control group. The control group enables a researcher to compare subjects exposed to the different kinds of content to a group experiencing manipulation of the independent variable.

Following exposure to the model, children were observed for a twenty-minute period as they played with toys in the room where the model had performed. Other toys were also provided besides the ones used by the model. Two unseen observers monitored each child's behavior at five-second intervals through a one-way mirror.

The dependent variables included imitative aggression, specific behaviors performed by the children that were performed by the model; nonimitative aggression, including behaviors toward the bobo doll not performed by the model; aggressive gun play, including aiming a toy gun and firing imaginary shots or throwing darts. The independent variables were, in addition to the model (real life, real life on film, cartoon figure), sex of child and sex of model. Differences were predicted regarding the amount and types of modeling effects; males were expected to be more aggressive than females; real-life models were expected to be more imitated than the film model, with the cartoon figure producing the least imitative behavior. All three models were predicted to produce greater amounts of imitative behavior in comparison to the control group.

Bandura et al. used Stanford University preschool children ranging in age from three to six years. Differences among these ages were not examined, despite enormous developmental differences between three- and six-year-olds. Commenting on Bandura's use of these children, Mendelsohn observed that as children of university professors, the participants do not represent the larger population of children and are "almost certain to manifest changes as a direct result of exposure."[12]

This type of experiment has many limitations; the central argument is what is being measured: is it imitation of aggressive models, or is it the imitation of models at play with some toys? The authors interpret their results to mean that children can learn novel aggressive behaviors from exposure to a real life or mediated model. There is little question that the children displayed evidence of what they saw. The question is: was it aggression?

In reporting the results of their study, the authors point out that the experimenter and a nursery school teacher who knew the participating children rated each child before the study on a series of rating scales. That called for judgment of each child's display of physical aggression, verbal aggression, aggression toward inanimate objects, and of aggressive actions in the face of provocation. These observations of children's aggressive behavior were based on the children's interactions and behavior in their nursery school environment. The experimenter and teacher knew the children well and had worked with them daily. When these aggression ratings were correlated with the aggression displayed by each child in the experiment (pounding on the bobo doll, etc.), the authors reported no relationship between the ratings of aggressive behavior and the behavior observed in the experimental play period. That is, children rated as being very aggressive in their nursery school environment were just as likely to display a lot of, very little, or no imitative aggression during the experimental play period.

The lack of correlation suggests that the behaviors being measured were not aggressive and may have been the children's propensity to imitate socially approved play with various toys as sanctioned by adults. If aggression involves a purposive act to harm or injure another person, and if the researchers measured children imitating models in a play environment with inanimate objects, then there is no relationship between aggression and the children's play activities. This may be a classic case of definitions of aggression that are not isomorphic. Aggression, principal behavior of focus in the experiment, was not effectively simulated in the experiment. The construct of aggression in the experiment (how it was operationalized) was not isomorphic to aggressive behavior as manifest by children outside experimental boundaries and conditions.

Experiments in broadcast research are valuable because they provide an opportunity to explore important relationships among key variables. They enable the construction and testing of cause-and-effect hypotheses and thus can contribute a great deal to our understanding of how broadcast content affects children. To be effective, however, experiments must simulate conditions that are excellent approximations of real world conditions and behaviors. The example of measuring aggression is one variable that has posed persistent problems of simulation and measurement for media researchers.

The other major problem frequently overlooked is the pattern by which children are exposed to or watch television. In most experiments, children are directed to watch television as part of the study. In their natural viewing environment, such involuntary exposure is seldom if ever present. Children also have many competing outlets for their time and attention in their own environments (such as toys and friends). This competition is controlled out of the experiment to make findings less ambiguous. Again, the isomorphic relationship appears to be violated, but if it is considered, results from many media experiments might turn out differently than reported.

Survey Methods

The goals of description and explanation are addressed by survey methods; causality and prediction were more directly sought with experimental methods. The greatest strength of questionnaires and interviews for research may be the freedom from confining hypotheses and variable manipulation. The value of survey research is the richness of its interpretation and explanation. The contribution of data to be interpreted and explained is confined by the definitions, designations, and collection methods of the social scientist. The weakness of survey methodology is the obscurity of these self-imposed constraints. Children's survey responses present researchers with interpretation problems that are magnified and unique when contrasted with surveys of adults.

The child's reasoning, attitudes, and concepts as described earlier are strikingly dif-

ferent at different ages/stages. Although researchers as adults have gone through these developmental changes, they did not pass through those stages with the awareness or ability to characterize the changes. Neither can they introspectively access their unreorganized memories of thoughts and impressions for current analysis. Childhood becomes foreign to adults when they try to examine its character through research methodologies.

The problems of interpreting children's responses are especially evident in examining the child's lack of facility with language, his or her comprehension of vocabulary and interviewer/questionnaire meaning as presented, his or her ability to express an understanding of various concepts, and ability to express oneself in a way understood by the adult in the survey context. This language problem inevitably invades research involving children and television and can affect almost every step in the research process.

The difficulties of language facility fall broadly into two areas: competence and performance. Competence, the ability to verbalize one's thoughts, includes such skills as sentence construction, labeling abstract concepts, and possessing an adequate vocabulary. Since language is one of the most complex human faculties, it develops later, and younger children (in preoperational and concrete operational stages) have the most difficulty responding to researchers' questions.

For example, when asked "What is a television commercial?" a child who is three to six years old may not respond or may reply that he or she does not know but may be able to point them out while viewing.[13] The selling intent is the most crucial distinction between a television program and a commercial—the one sought by researchers evaluating a child's understanding. However, researchers have been hampered in their assessments by the discrepancy between understanding and ability to articulate, between a functional salience or relevance for making the distinction (between programs and commercials) and a definition of the distinction. Because a child does not respond to a specific question about television does not necessarily mean that the child has no understanding of the concept. It may mean that the child has not acquired sufficient vocabulary or language facility to respond verbally. Selecting among alternative pictures to answer the interviewer's question may be necessary to gain a meaningful response from some children.

The child's performance in response to the researcher may also be related to the child's tendency to be shy with strangers. Many young children (three to six years old) often will not respond to adults they do not know, especially when asked questions they have never been asked. Many stare blankly at the researcher or give the easiest response to strange questions by saying, "I don't know." Racial and ethnic differences also may contribute to the researcher's problems of interpreting survey data. These differences should be recognized in studies involving ethnic or racial differences between interviewers and children. Children's facility with language (influenced by ethnicity, experience, and developmental level) may seriously affect the interpretation of meaning as they attempt to articulate ideas and attitudes in response to the researcher's questions.

A lot of evidence supports the suggestion that what a young child is willing or able to verbalize is not a true indicator of what the child understands.[14] The understanding vocabulary of young children is generally larger than the active speaking vocabulary. Questions demanding that a child be able to explain with expressive language the meaning of terms may be inappropriate for use with young children in assessing what the child cognitively processes or comprehends. When appropriately and thoroughly questioned, children show broad nuances of meaning in their judgments, responses, and reasoning about the meaning of their media experiences. Simple questions invariably produce simple answers; and even though simple answers are easier to understand and act on than complex answers, complexity is the inescapable characteristic of the process through which children relate to the media.

Generalized questions pose analysis and interpretation problems that make the implications of results very ambiguous. General *yes/no* questions encourage an answer that is easy for the child to deal with, but they do not prove the child's own definition of what the researcher means by his or her terms. For example, children have ideas of what they mean by "to tell the truth" when they respond to a researcher's question about television commercials. However, the child's definition may differ from the adult meaning or the researcher's interpretation of what constitutes truth in television commercials. Adults probably judge truth in advertising based on what is said or implied about the product's performance (does it do what the commercial claims it does?); most children have a different standard of truth.[15] To them, being truthful means the introduction of fantasy or make-believe elements. For children, being truthful or lying is associated with something they like a great deal or dislike a lot. Since true is a good quality and lying a bad quality, the like = true and dislike = false or lie connections emerge as significant dimensions partially explaining the overall result that commercials do not always tell the truth.

An important issue in survey research with children is whether age-related increases in performance of various responses are a function of greater verbal abilities in older children. Ward, Reale, and Levinson[16] made a significant effort to classify children's expressions of judgment about television into levels of fundamental awareness. Reference to the coding of responses, however, illustrates that greater language facility was required of the child for him or her to be credited with higher awareness of the purpose of television commercials, for instance.

Close scrutiny of Ward's examples of children's responses reveals problems in his coding scheme and overall categorization that prohibit considering the data as evidence for separating verbal skills and higher-level information-processing skills for purposes of that study. The awareness of selling motive is spread across different categories, while perspective-taking differentiates the responses.

Perspective-taking noted in language behavior may not reflect awareness of television commericals' selling motive.

Responses to the interviewer's questions are coded into two significantly different categories as defined by the researchers.

- Question: When you watch TV you must see a lot of commercials. What is a TV commercial?
- Coded Responses for Medium Awareness: They sell stuff; They sell toys; They tell you their product is best; Shows you things so you know what to buy.
- Coded Responses for High Awareness: They want you to buy their products; They make people look nice and liking their product so you'll want to buy it.
- Question: Why are commercials shown on television? Is there any other reason they're on TV?
- Coded Responses for Medium Awareness: To sell things; To get you to buy stuff and make you believe theirs is the best.
- Coded Responses for High Awareness: To talk you into buying things; They want people to know a product and its qualities so they'll buy it.

Do these responses indicate different levels of awareness or differences in the degree of articulation? The consequences of interpreting these ambiguous nuances have had great impact on policy deliberations. The Federal Trade Commission and Federal Communications Commission have relied on social science findings to guide their inquiries and regulation decisions. However, the assumptions and limitations of this research should not be forgotten or ignored.

To the extent that surveys and interviews traditionally rely on language, media researchers must be cautious in surveying children. Experiments or qualitative study or hybrid methods using games to operationalize variables, or other alternative methods should be carefully weighed.

Alternative Methods

Differing explanations and interpretations of the child-media relationship present researchers with a dilemma of direction. Some researchers may attempt to force a choice among competing theories. Others may attempt to accommodate differing explanations from a more holistic perspective with altering situations or contexts. The use of one methodological approach and not another changes the means by which one perceives the reality under study.[17] Also, the reality to which a researcher has applied a method may itself be determined by the perspective suggested by the method used.

Contemporary philosophers of science have moved from determinism to concerns about the social construction of knowledge and reality.[18] Theorists have shifted from reifications to definitions of process and change. These fundamental shifts are also evident in the mass communication literature.[19] Miller addressed this notion of process in communication: "Process implies a continuous interaction of an indefinitely large number of variables with a concomitant, continuous change in the values taken by these variables."[20]

However, the mainstream methodological options are not conducive to this twentieth-century notion of communication as a process.[21] The alternative methods currently under discussion in the field are basic qualitative approaches—long-term observational analysis and in-depth interviewing of individuals and their family members or confederates.

Some qualitative analysis has usually preceded all research, providing the hypotheses or other questions for investigation. This analysis, which may have emerged from casual observation or intuitive insights, often is not reported. The legitimization of this analysis is expected to provide a formal grounding for more adequate exploration and explanation of the communication process.

This formal grounding is especially needed in child-broadcast relationships. The adult and child have qualitatively different frames of reference; this difference may be more significant than the normal difference between two people of the same age. Therefore, casual observation, introspection, and intuition alone may be deficient guides for the researchers in applying theory and understanding the child and his or her relationship to the media. Thus researchers of the child and media must ground their qualitative explorations and analyses, perhaps beginning with careful descriptions of observer perspectives. Explicit derivative explanations of observations from defined theoretical preferences and personal biases would advance qualitative studies for reference by researchers who may be predisposed toward other methods of investigation.

Conclusion

The choice to use one research method is, at the same time, also a choice against employing competing methods. Each method reveals differing strengths and weaknesses for a given research effort. Each method yields a perspective of value. Methodological orientations, strengths, and weaknesses are critical considerations in studying children and the media. The child-adult differences make this area of study especially challenging and demanding.

Broadcast Research and Children: Protecting Rights and Ethical Issues

This essay has clarified the difficulties researchers encounter when assessing television's impact on children. The problems, however, are conceptual and methodological. Legal and ethical difficulties also should be mentioned.

Legally, researchers using children in their studies must comply with restrictions and provisions from the federal level (Department of Health and Human Services guidelines) to university and school/community policies that require additional obligations. First and foremost is the issue of parental/guardian consent and total awareness. Researchers must obtain written permission from parents/ guardians; these forms must also clearly indicate the nature of the study, what is expected of

the child, what information will be sought and why, and what will be done with the information. Any unusual procedures must be spelled out or legal action may be brought against the school and/or researchers.

Ethical concerns are also important. Children can be easily exploited. Some types of research with children can be politically and personally sensitive. Studies, for example, may look for racial or sex differences in how much and what is comprehended by children who view a given TV program. Race as a research variable is often important as a predictor of different types of media effects, but the ethical dimension is relevant at the level of how race differences are presented and interpreted. If children of one race or sex have lower retention scores, such differences should not be interpreted to imply that one group is smarter or brighter than another. Such differences are usually due to children of different races or sexes having a different orientation or set of past experiences with the content. Intelligence is not the issue but can appear to be an appropriate inference, unless the researcher takes care to prevent it.

Summary

The work of researchers in assessing the impact of broadcasting on children requires innovation, tenacity, careful thought, and the capacity to assimilate the impressive bodies of literature, thought, and inquiry from what often seem like divergent areas. Research, to be comprehensive and potentially meaningful, must consider work in child development, media process and effects, and research methodology. Because children differ from adults in many crucial respects, the researcher must also be willing to pursue a variety of methodological approaches to discover more about how children interface with television and radio. Approaches should not be thought of as competitive in the sense that one is best or right and others inappropriate or wrong: rather, each approach presents a unique way of examining some of the same phenomena. Distinct methodological pitfalls should be avoided, and the researcher investigating child-media relationships must be open-minded and willing to learn from various approaches.

With a relatively new field and the pressure to provide answers to perhaps unanswerable questions posed by anxious policy makers at the FCC or FTC, it is easy to rush into data collection and generalization. The true scientist is never satisfied, however, that his or her findings or even a whole body of findings represent the best or a completely accurate picture of events being studied. This spirit needs to be reemphasized so that it is not lost by both researchers of the child-media relationship and those who use the findings. Dealing with children makes for an ambiguous situation. Children are a special audience and demand special considerations in assessing the impact of broadcasting on their development and socialization.

Endnotes

1. Thomas I. Emerson, *The System of Freedom of Expression* (New York: Columbia, 1970), 496–597.
2. H. L. Klapper, "Twenty-Ninth AAPOR Conference Proceedings," *Public Opinion Quarterly* 38 (1974): 436.
3. Ibid.
4. W. Andrew Collins, "Children's Comprehension of Television Content," in Ellen Wartella, ed., *Children Communicating: Media and Development of Thought, Speech, Understanding* (Beverly Hills, Calif.: Sage, 1979), 21–52.
5. J. H. Flavell, *Cognitive Development*, (Englewood Cliffs, N.J.: Prentice-Hall, 1977); Lawrence Kohlberg, "Stage and Sequence: The Cognitive Development Approach to Socialization," in D. A. Goslin, ed., *Handbook of Socialization Theory and Research* (Chicago: Rand McNally College Publishing, 1969); Jerome S. Bruner, R. R. Oliver, P. M. Greenfield, J. R. Hornsby, H. J. Kenney, M. Maccoby,

N. Modiano, F. A. Mosher, D. R. Olson, M. C. Potter, L. C. Reich, and A. M. Sonstroem, *Studies in Cognitive Growth: A Collaboration at the Center for Cognitive Studies* (New York: John Wiley, 1966); and Jean Piaget, *The Language and Thought of the Child* (Cleveland: Meridan, 1955).
6. Urie Bronfenbrenner, *The Ecology of Human Development: Experiments by Nature and Design* (Cambridge: Harvard University Press, 1979); R. E. Mayer, "Information Processing Variables in Learning to Solve Problems," *Review of Educational Research* 43 (1975): 525–541; M. C. Wittrock, "Learning as a Generative Process," *Educational Psychology* 11 (1974): 87–95; Albert Bandura, "Social-Learning Theory of Identificatory Processes," and Jacob L. Gewirtz, "Mechanisms of Social Learning: Some Roles of Stimulation and Behavior in Early Human Development," in David A. Goslin, ed., *Handbook of Socialization Theory and Research* (Chicago: Rand McNally College Publishing, 1969), 213–262, 57–212.
7. Kohlberg, op. cit.
8. Albert Bandura, Dorothea Ross, and Sheila Ross, "Imitation of Film-Mediated Aggressive Models," *Journal of Abnormal and Social Psychology* 66 (1963): 3–11; David Hicks, "Imitation and Retention of Film-Mediated Aggressive Peer and Adult Models," *Journal of Personality and Social Psychology* 2 (1965): 97–100.
9. Aletha Huston-Stein and Lynette Friedrich, "Television Content and Young Children's Behavior," in J. P. Murray, E. A. Rubinstein, and G. A. Comstock, eds., *Television and Social Behavior, Vol. 2: Television and Social Learning* (Washington, D.C.: U.S. Government Printing Office, 1972), 202–317; Seymour Feshbach and Robert D. Singer, *Television and Aggression: An Experimental Field Study* (San Francisco: Jossey-Bass, 1971).
10. Monroe Lefkowitz, L. D. Eron, L. O. Walder, and L. R. Huseman, "Television

Violence and Child Aggression: A Follow-up Study," in G. A. Comstock and E. A. Rubinstein, eds., *Television and Social Behavior, Vol. 3: Television and Adolescent Aggressiveness* (Washington, D.C.: U.S. Government Printing Office, 1972), 35–135; Scott Ward, G. Reale, and D. Levinson, "Children's Perceptions, Explanations and Judgments of Television Advertising: A Further Exploration," in E. A. Rubinstein, G. A. Comstock, and J. P. Murray, eds., *Television and Social Behavior, Vol. 4: Television in Day-to-Day Life: Patterns of Use* (Washington, D.C.: U.S. Government Printing Office, 1972), 468–490.

11. John P. Murray, "Television in Inner-City Homes: Viewing Behavior of Young Boys," in E. A. Rubinstein, G. A. Comstock, and J. P. Murray, eds., *Television and Social Behavior, Vol. 4: Television in Day-to-Day Life: Patterns of Use* (Washington, D.C.: U.S. Government Printing Office, 1972), 345–394; James Lull, "The Social Uses of Television," *Human Communication Research* 6 (1980): 162–170; Paul J. Traudt, "Television and Family Viewing: An Ethnography," unpublished Master's Thesis, University of Utah, 1979; Timothy P. Meyer, P. J. Traudt, and J. A. Anderson, "Non-Traditional Mass Communication Effects Research Methods: Observational Case Studies of Media Use in Natural Environments," in D. Nimmo, ed., *Communication Yearbook IV* (New Brunswick, N.J.: Transaction, 1980); J. Lull, "A Rules Approach to the Study of TV and Society," *Human Communication Research* 9 (1982): 3–16; see also *Journal of Broadcasting* 4 (1982) for additional examples of qualitative approaches.

12. Harold Mendelsohn, "Behaviorism, Functionalism and Mass Communications Policy," *Public Opinion Quarterly* 38 (1974): 379–389.

13. Thomas R. Donohue. L. L. Henke, T. P. Meyer, and M. J. Lohghlin, "Problems in Researching Young Children: A Case of Lost or Misunderstood Meaning," Research Report, New England Television Research Center, University of Hartford, August 1978.

14. Bruce F. Gardner, *Development in Early Childhood: The Preschool Years* (New York: Academic Press, 1964).

15. Donohue et al., op. cit.

16. Ward et al., op. cit.

17. Ray C. Rist, *The Invisible Children: School Integration in American Society* (Cambridge: Harvard University Press, 1978).

18. B. Aubrey Fisher, *Perspectives on Human Communication* (New York: MacMillan, 1978).

19. Meyer et al., op. cit.; D. Cushman, "The Rules Perspective as a Theoretical Basis for the Study of Human Communication," *Communication Quarterly* 25 (1977): 30–45; David H. Smith, "Communication Research and the Idea of Process," *Speech Monographs* 39 (1972): 174–182.

20. Gerald Miller, *Speech Communication: A Behavioral Approach* (Indianapolis: Bobbs-Merrill, 1966), 33.

21. Lull, 1980, 1982; Smith, op. cit.

Additional References

Sources marked with an asterisk (*) include major bibliographies or literature reviews.

Achenbach, Thomas. *Research in Developmental Psychology: Concepts, Strategies, Methods,* New York: Free Press, 1978.

Brown, J., J. Cramond, and R. Wilde. "Displacement Effects of Television and the Child's Functional Orientation to Media," in J. Blumler and E. Katz, eds., *The Uses of Mass Communication*, Beverly Hills, Calif.: Sage, 1974, 93–112.

Bryant, Peter. *Perception and Understanding in Young Children: An Experimental Approach,* New York: Basic Books, 1974.

*Comstock, George. *Television and Human Behavior: The Key Studies,* Santa Monica, Calif.: Rand, 1975.

*Comstock, George and Marilyn Fisher. *Television and Human Behavior: A Guide to the Pertinent Scientific Literature,* Santa Monica, Calif.: Rand, 1975.

*Comstock, George, Steven Chaffee, Nathan Katzman, Maxwell McCombs, and Donald Roberts. *Television and Human Behavior*, New York: Columbia, 1978.

Greenberg, Bradley. "Gratifications of Television Viewing and Their Correlates for British Children," in J. Blumler and E. Katz, eds., *The Uses of Mass Communications,* Beverly Hills, Calif.: Sage, 1974, 71–92.

Journal of Broadcasting 25 (1981), 327–407. An update on the Surgeon General's Report on the Impact of TV Violence is discussed by researchers and critics: Collins, Dorr, Rice, Singer, Rubinstein, Anderson, and Siruta.

*Liebert, Robert, J. M. Neale, and E. S. Davidson. *The Early Window: Effects of Television on Children and Youth,* 2nd ed., Elmsford, N.Y.: Pergamon Press, 1982.

*Nobel, G. *Children in Front of the Small Screen,* Beverly Hills, Calif.: Sage, 1975.

*Roberts, Donald. "Communication and Children: A Developmental Approach," in I. de Sola Pool, W. Schramm, F. W. Frey, N. Maccoby, and E. B. Parker, eds., *Handbook of Communication,* Chicago: Rand McNally College Publishing Co., 1973, 174–215.

Tucker, David, and J. Saffelle. "The Federal Communications Commission and the Regulation of Children's Television," *Journal of Broadcasting* 26 (1982): 657–670.

Ward, Scott, D. B. Wackman, and E. Wartella. *How Children Learn to Buy: The Development of Consumer Information Processing Skills,* Beverly Hills, Calif.: Sage, 1977.

Reasons for Concern: Media Saturation

American mass media transmit messages to millions of individuals, transcending geographic locations and socioeconomic statuses. Never in human history have so many individuals had exposure to such a wide variety of communication, and never before have so few individuals had such power to create universal images, lend national significance to isolated events, and shape national and individual values. America's mass media form the world's first communication colossus.

The United States dominates the world with popular forms of mass media, since our facilities for developing and using popular media outstrip those of most countries. Our general media wealth can be more fully appreciated when contrasted with that of other countries. In Bangladesh, for example, a ball-point pen is a symbol of wealth; in this country, *Books in Print* lists more than two hundred thousand books available. Algeria has ten television sets for every thousand inhabitants; the United States has nearly five hundred sets for every thousand persons. The USSR publishes about six hundred newspapers; the United States publishes more than 1,700 dailies.[1] This omnipresence of American mass media makes it a social concern.

An examination of individual media tells the story of media penetration. In 1981, American book publishers' estimated net sales were nearly eight billion dollars. In 1982, they published more than 50,000 books.[2]

In the United States, 1,435 evening newspapers and 346 morning dailies have a combined circulation of more than sixty-two million readers. Sunday newspapers number some 650 with a total circulation of more than fifty million. In addition, approximately 10,000 weekly newspapers in the United States serve interest groups, ethnic groups, and small communities.

American magazines are also powerful in terms of individual exposure. Readership figures for some magazines are large. *TV Guide*, for example, has a circulation of more than twenty million, and *Reader's Digest* boasts a circulation of nearly eighteen million. These figures do not represent all readers, since a magazine circulates among family members

18
The Mass Media and Sex-Role Socialization

Linda J. Busby

and friends, and one copy may be read by a hundred or more library patrons. Ideas in mass circulation magazines are assimilated by millions of people from the Atlantic to the Pacific and beyond.

Reader's Digest is published in six editions: the United States; Western Europe, and Scandinavia; Latin American; Asian and African; Australian and New Zealand; and Canadian. *Vogue* magazine of fashion and beauty hints is published in Australia, Britain, France, Italy, and in the United States. *Cosmopolitan* magazine is distributed throughout the Spanish speaking world as *Cosmopolitan En Español*. *Time* magazine has six editions, including the Atlantic edition, which covers Europe; the Asian edition; the South Pacific edition; and the United States edition. Magazines are powerful vehicles for transmitting social values and attitudes.

Film is also a powerful medium because it is used primarily by the nation's youth. Studies indicate that persons under thirty years of age comprise approximately 75 percent of the audience for commercial films.[3]

United States films are also likely to introduce American lifestyles to foreign audiences. Estimates indicate that United States films dominate 60 percent of the world's motion picture playing time. In some countries, United States films dominate most offerings.[4]

Books, newspapers, magazines, and films constitute healthy evidence of our mass media prosperity, but radio and television are the most frequently used media. In the United States, there are 1,695 radios for every one thousand individuals and 472 television sets for every one thousand population. Over 98 percent of all American homes have at least one television set, which is estimated to be on for more than six hours a day on the average.

The number of people who experience the same television phenomenon at any time is staggering. An estimated one hundred million people watched the 1982 Super Bowl telecast;[5] in April 1977, an estimated ninety million viewers watched the special *Jesus of Nazareth*.[6] On Saturday evening, January 15, 1972, more than twenty-five million Americans watched Edith and Archie Bunker on *All in the Family*.[7]

George Gerbner, television critic and researcher, has written: "Television is the new religion. . . . It is religion in the sense of preindustrial, pre-Reformation religion, in the sense of one's having no choice—a cosmic force or a symbolic environment that one was born into and whose assumptions one accepted without much question."[8]

Indeed, American mass media are big businesses, and the penetration of books, newspapers, magazines, films, radio, and television into the daily lives of Americans has caused concern. Do mass media have effects on us as individuals? What effects do the media have on our sex-role socialization?

Media Effects: Sex-Role Socialization

The notion that the mass media are important socialization forces has strong supporting evidence. Baxter and Kaplan wrote: "A growing body of research evidence suggests that television plays an important role in socialization, especially for the young viewer."[9] Researchers have reported that the content in other forms of media (storybooks and textbooks, for example) is an important socialization source. Studies have long verified that children model behavior they see in the mass media.[10] But do the media have a particular sex-role socialization effect? Some evidence suggests an affirmative answer to this question. Schramm, Lyle, and Parker,[11] in their landmark study of children and television, found marked sex differences in how children use mass media: ". . . girls early turn toward programs which relate to the responsibilities they will assume in adolescence and adult life. Boys, on the other hand, maintain boys' taste for adventure, excitement, and physical combat well into adolescence."

Hale, Miller, and Stevenson found that adolescent girls showed more incidental learning from a film depicting a domestic situation than did adolescent boys.[12] The researchers concluded that the girls were looking for roles that they would be assuming later in life.

Lyle and Hoffman in 1972 found that male preschool children could identify more male TV characters than could female preschoolers and the female children could identify more female TV characters than could the male children.[13] They noted: "Boys generally seemed to show an earlier preference than girls for action programs—which, incidentally, usually feature the strong male characters. The girls in the first grade were already fond of the family situation comedies in which women predominate or are coequal with the male lead. . . ." These researchers found also that black children could identify more black characters than could white children. A definite race and sex variable functioned in the youngsters' abilities to identify television characters.

Maccoby, Wilson, and Burton in 1958[14] found that male viewers spent more time watching the hero and that female viewers spent more time watching the heroine in romance movie scenes involving just the male and female leading characters. Sprafkin and Liebert found similar results with first- and second-grade children.[15]

In a study of seventh graders exposed to a class B entertainment movie, Maccoby and Wilson found that boys remembered aggressive content better, and girls remembered romantic content better.[16] Boys remembered the aggressive actions of the hero but not those of the heroine. Maccoby and Wilson noted: "We see then that similarity between viewer and actor, both in role (for example, sex) and in preferred action system, influences which elements of movie content will be absorbed." Again, Sprafkin and Liebert reported similar findings in their 1978 research.[17] Girls attended 78 percent of the time to female characters exhibiting sex-typed behavior but only 52 percent of the time to females performing non-sex-typed behavior.[18]

Goff, Goff, and Lehrer added a new dimension to this research,[19] using the Bem Sex-Role Inventory to assess and classify the sex role of TV viewers and TV characters. They found that viewer sex-role, not viewer sex, was strongly related to the viewer's perception of the TV character. These researchers suggest that the viewer's perception of his or her sex-role may be an important factor in the viewer's perception of sex-role characteristics of TV characters.

Beuf, in a 1974 study of sixty-three children between the ages of three and six, attempted to answer three questions: How do children perceive familial and occupational roles?[20] Do children begin to limit their life options because of mental association between role and sex? What influence do television programs have on these ideas? Using an interview technique with the children, Beuf discovered:

- More than 70 percent of the boys and 73 percent of the girls chose stereotypical careers for themselves.
- 65 percent of the heavy television viewers compared with 50 percent of the moderate viewers selected stereotyped careers for themselves. "Children who were more moderate viewers appeared to exert a wider range of choice in career selection than the heavy viewers."
- The children saw the world divided into male and female tasks and gave the male tasks higher ratings of importance. "The envy of male pursuits shown by the girls, and the reluctance of the boys to entertain for a moment the idea of what they would do if they were girls, pointed to the hierarchical arrangement that children perceive in the roles."

At least one other study found that girls who are heavy television viewers have more sex-role stereotype beliefs than do girls who view less heavily.[21]

Another study of television and sex-role effects by Miller and Reeves used a questionnaire survey of 200 grade-school children.[22] Three hypotheses were examined:

1. Boys would nominate more television characters as models for their own behavior than would girls.
2. Boys would nominate more same-sex char-

acters as models for their own behavior than would girls.

3. Children who exposed themselves to television content portraying women in counter-stereotypical occupations would perceive these occupations as more appropriate for women in real life.

Miller and Reeves found that boys did name more television characters as models for their behavior than did girls. The hypothesis that boys would nominate more same-sex models than girls was also supported. The authors noted: "The best evidence for the hypothesis probably lies in the fact that no boy nominated opposite-sex models, while 27 percent of the girls who nominated models chose one or more male characters."

The researchers also confirmed their third hypothesis, that exposure to female counter-stereotypical roles correspondingly altered real-life perceptions. These authors concluded: "The findings support the assertion that television can shape children's sex-role perceptions. Children do nominate television characters as people they want to be like when they grow up. There is ample evidence that children can learn through imitation and it is reasonable to assume that they will imitate particular people whom they say they want to be like. Since children chose primarily characters of their own sex and those characters are highly stereotyped, television must either directly or indirectly reinforce the stereotypes."

Researchers have found also that male and female youngsters use different standards for identifying with media characters. Reeves and Greenberg found that physical strength and activity level of TV characters predicted identification for boys and physical attractiveness was the single predictor for girls.[23] Miller found that boys perceive television characters they want to be like as physically strong and dynamic and girls perceive their chosen models as physically attractive.[24] Greenberg et al. also reported that physical attractiveness predicted identification for girls, but not for boys.[25]

Frueh and McGhee hypothesized that the amount of time a child spent watching television would be significantly related to the strength of that child's acceptance of traditional sex roles.[26] Using eighty children from kindergarten through sixth grade as subjects, the researchers found support for the hypothesis, concluding: "High amounts of television watching are clearly associated with stronger traditional sex-role development. The lack of interaction effect suggests that this relationship holds equally for boys and girls, and that it does not change with increasing age."

As mentioned in the Reeves and Miller study, some evidence suggests that children exposed to nonstereotypical sex roles remember the nonstereotypical information and are more likely to endorse nonstereotypical sex roles than are children not exposed to the information. In 1975, Atkin and Miller prepared television commercials with women in typically male occupations.[27] The commercials, embedded in half-hour television cartoon programs, were shown to grade-school children. The researchers found that the children who saw the nonstereotypical commercials were more likely to endorse the occupations as appropriate for women than were the children who saw other commercials. O'Bryant and Corder-Bolz reported similar results using specially designed commercials and elementary school children as subjects.[28]

Davidson, Yasuna, and Tower also found that media content with few sex-role stereotypes had a positive effect on reducing children's sex-role stereotypes.[29] These researchers showed five- and six-year-old girls a television program with few sex-role stereotypes and reported: "Results indicate that girls who viewed the low-stereotyped program received significantly lower sex-role stereotype scores than did girls in the high and neutral conditions. . . ."

In a study of black children's learning of work roles from television commercials, O'Bryant and Corder-Bolz found that six- and seven-year-old black girls showed greater preference for traditionally male jobs following TV exposure to women in such roles.[30] Students in one group saw specially prepared commercials featuring a woman as a pharmacist, a welder, a butcher, and a laborer. The other group saw regular TV commercials with a woman as a telephone operator, a model, a file clerk, and a manicurist. The children viewing women in nonstereotypical roles indicated a greater preference for traditional male-oriented jobs than did the group viewing regular commercials with women in typical female-oriented jobs.

This research reported that specially designed TV content could reduce sex-role stereotyping in viewers. Similar results have been reported using the print media. Flerx, Fidler, and Rogers found that preschoolers exposed to a brief illustrated story involving egalitarian sex-role models reduced their stereotypic thinking.[31] The egalitarian story was more effective on the attitudes of female children than on the attitudes of the male children. Egalitarian sex-role models in films, however, produced more enduring attitude changes about children's play activities than did the storybook models.

Schau reported findings similar to Flerx, Fidler, and Rogers.[32] More than one thousand grade-school children were exposed to stories with reversed sex-role occupations. The researchers found that the stories were effective in reducing the occupational sex-role stereotypes of the children, reporting: "The stories worked equally well for boys and girls at all three grade levels. . . . In addition, the instrument . . . also changed attitudes toward increasing flexibility. . . . The project shows that at least some aspect of children's attitudes can be changed using reading materials within a school system, even when the teachers themselves may be sexist."

McArthur and Eisen reported slightly different findings using storybooks as a medium for investigation.[33] Preschoolers heard either a stereotypic story depicting male but not female achievement behavior or a reversal story depicting female but not male achievement behavior. After hearing a story depicting male achievement, boys were found to persist longer on a task, and girls demonstrated a nonsignifi-

cant trend to persist longer on a task after hearing a story depicting female achievement behavior. Boys were less likely to recall the female character's behavior, and both boys and girls indicated a greater identification with same-sex characters. Kropp and Halverson's sample of pre-school-age girls preferred stories with female characters and traditional female activities and boys preferred male characters and traditional male activities.[34] Children of both sexes objected to stories with characters of their sex engaging in sex-inappropriate behavior.

Whether children remember nonstereotypical information better than stereotypical information is questionable when research from a variety of studies is examined. Koblinsky, Cruse, and Sugarawa, in examining "Sex Role Stereotypes and Children's Memory for Story Content,"[35] found that, in remembering textbook materials, children exhibited selective memory for stereotypic sex-role content. Children of both sexes remembered more masculine sex-typed traits and male characters' behaviors and more feminine sex-typed traits and female characters' behaviors. (Bryan and Luria also reported that their grade-school subjects remembered more same-sex tasks than opposite-sex tasks regardless of the sex of the model.[36])

Koblinsky, Cruse, and Sugarawa speculate that children find stereotypical traits and behaviors easier to remember because by an early age sex stereotypes are established and children use them as an organizational frame for remembering other types of information. They concluded: "This discovery does not diminish the importance of utilizing nonsexist materials but does suggest the need to develop additional strategies for reducing the bias in children's memory for sex-role information."

Barkley et al. found results similar to those of Koblinsky et al. and of Bryan and Luria.[37] Using children four to eleven years old as subjects, these researchers showed videotapes of adult males and females engaged in same-sex and opposite-sex stereotypic behavior. The researchers found that girls imitated feminine behavior more than did boys, regardless of the sex of the model displaying the feminine behavior. Also, boys imitated modeled masculine behavior significantly more than did girls, again, regardless of the model's sex.

Tan found that adolescent girls exposed to a series of television commercials for beauty products indicated that the commercials had an immediate impact on their attitudes toward themselves.[38] When asked to rate characteristics important "for you personally," these adolescent girls rated beauty characteristics as more important than did subjects who had seen the neutral commercials.

Moving in a different research direction, Jennings, Geis, and Brown investigated the impact of television commercials on adult women,[39] using instruments to evaluate the women's self-confidence and independent judgment. Two matched series of commercials served as stimuli. One set of advertisements consisted of four ads from the commercial networks; the other series consisted of four commercials, identical in every respect except that each role was portrayed by a person of the opposite sex. Fifty-two college women viewed either the traditional or reversed-role commercials. The women who saw the nontraditional versions of the commercials showed more independent judgment in follow-up testing. Also, when asked to deliver a speech, the women who viewed the role-reversed commercials were judged to show greater confidence in speech delivery.

The researchers suggested that repeated exposure to nonstereotypic commercials might help produce positive and lasting behavior changes in women, also noting: "At minimum, it can be concluded that a social environment presenting images of important women produced more competence and confidence in women subjects than an environment of subservient women role models."

What all the research suggests is that many factors lead to sex-role stereotyping, which is multifaceted. To understand it and to develop strategies for eliminating sex-role stereotyping that may limit life options and social mobility

for both children and adults will require more research and analyses.

Williams, LaRose, and Frost found that sex-role stereotyping stems from a variety of factors.[40] Media content is not the only, nor necessarily the primary, factor. These researchers did find, however, that counterstereotypical roles in TV programming could help reduce the child's sex-role stereotyping if (1) the child understands the character's behavior or intention; (2) the character is an attractive model to the child; (3) "significant others" are shown interacting and evaluating the main character's behavior or attitudes. These researchers argue that:

> If this hypothesis is supported, then the quantities of males and females shown on television are considerably less important than the qualities portrayed. Behavior will be most apt to be emulated from dramatic and realistic contents (not variety shows, not cartoons) where a character has the attributes for high modeling potential but, more important, where sufficient content is presented to convey evidence of personal and social reinforcement for the behavior.

To summarize the research findings regarding the media's impact in the sex-role socialization process, several observations can be supported.

- Media users personalize media content and thereby become directly involved in it.
- Sex of the media user is an important factor in the user's use and recall of media content.
- Under some circumstances, youngsters model behavior they see in the media.
- Boys use physical strength and dynamic action as criteria for selecting media models; girls use physical attractiveness as the criterion in selecting media models.
- Youngsters who are heavy television users have more stereotypical notions of sex roles than do youngsters who are light or medium television users.
- Some research indicates that nonstereotypical sex-role models in media used by chil-

dren lessen the children's stereotypic sex-role attitudes.

- Some research indicates that children learn stereotypic sex roles so thoroughly that they depend on the stereotypes as an organizational frame for remembering media content.
- Some research indicates that counterstereotypical media content can be used to increase women's self-confidence and independent judgment.
- Research indicates that sex-role stereotyping is multifaceted and that we may not understand all the facets.
- Finally, researchers are beginning to believe that, as the various facets of sex-role stereotyping are understood, media content can be used to alleviate some of its negative aspects.

Media Content Examined

If mass media content does play a part in sex-role socialization, what content in the mass media contributes to the socialization process? Mass media content studies have been conducted on nearly every media form, including television programs, comic books, children's textbooks, films, magazines, and newspapers. The studies' conclusions are two: (1) women are underrepresented in media content; (2) women who do appear in media content have limited roles.

Content study was the first research methodology used to document the status of women in the various media. Advertising was one of the first forms of media content to be examined, perhaps because it contains much material to examine and because the content is discrete—a one-minute commercial or one magazine page.

One landmark content study of sex roles in advertising, by Courtney and Lockeretz,[41] examined seven general-interest magazines (*The New Yorker, Time, Look*, etc.) and used cross-tabulation to record such data as number of male and female workers in the ads, number of ads showing only men or only women, and types of products in which males and females were identified. They reported:

- Women were rarely shown in out-of-home working roles.
- Not one woman was shown as a professional or high-level business person.
- Women rarely ventured far from home by themselves or with other women.
- Women were shown as dependent on men's protection.
- Men were shown regarding women as sex objects or as domestic adjuncts.
- Females were most often shown in ads for cleaning products, food products, beauty products, drugs, clothing, and home appliances.
- Males were most often shown in ads for cars, travel, alcoholic beverages, cigarettes, banks, industrial products, entertainment media, and industrial companies.

Courtney and Lockeretz concluded: "The data suggest that feminists are at least partially justified in saying that advertisements do not present a full view of the variety of roles women actually play in American society." Sexton and Haberman's findings in a study of advertising in *Good Housekeeping, Look, Newsweek, Sports Illustrated*, and *TV Guide* from 1951 to 1971[42] were similar to those of Courtney and Lockeretz.

Roberts's study of advertising and fiction in *Ladies Home Journal* from 1960 to 1962 and from 1974 to 1976 found that women in fiction appeared to remain consistently traditional in the two periods but some advertisements in the second period showed women in nondomestic, active, nontraditional roles.[43] Women were still most likely to be in ads for beauty products and household products, but some women appeared in roles more fully indicating the roles of women in society.

Goffman[44] examined many ads in the print media and observed that in print advertising: (1) a woman is taller than a man only when the man is her social inferior; (2) a woman's hands are seen just barely touching or caressing—

never grasping or manipulating; (3) when a photograph illustrates instructions, the man is always instructing the woman; (4) when an advertisement requires someone to lie on a bed or on the floor, the person is almost always a woman or a child; (5) women are repeatedly shown drifting from the scene while in close physical contact with a man. In another study, the researchers reported: "The overwhelming conclusion of the magazine and television monitoring studies is that advertising still portrays women in traditional roles."[45]

In a 1981 study of male roles in advertising, Skelly and Lundstrom[46] found that: "In general, men have increasingly been portrayed in less stereotyped roles, but in women's magazines the 'manly' activities were replaced by more decorative roles." These researchers concluded that advertising featuring men appears to be gradually moving toward a decrease in sex-role stereotypes, but the process appears to be slow.

Another landmark study, published in the *New York Times Magazine* in 1972,[47] was a report of a content study of television advertising conducted by the National Organization of Women (NOW). This study is significant for several reasons: (1) It placed the issue of sex-role content in the media in a respectable public forum, thus creating general public interest; (2) it introduced the use of content study by a pressure group intent on reforming the media; (3) the findings were interesting and presented in a provocative format.

Hennessee and Nicholson, authors of the *New York Times* article, reported that NOW monitored 1,241 television commercials during a one-and-one-half year time period. NOW found:

- 37.5 percent of the ads showed women as men's domestic adjuncts.
- 22.7 percent demeaned housework.
- 33.9 percent showed women as dependent on men.
- 24.3 percent showed women as submissive.
- 16.7 percent showed women as sex objects.
- 17.1 percent showed women as unintelligent.

- 42.6 percent showed women as household functionaries.

A 1972 Dominick and Rauch study using more traditional research methods[48] examined more than 1,000 television ads and used cross-tabulations and chi square tests to analyze the findings. They reported:

- Women were seven times more likely to appear in ads for personal hygiene products than not to appear.
- 75 percent of all ads using females were for products found in the kitchen or in the bathroom.
- 38 percent of the females in these television ads were shown inside the home, compared to 14 percent of the males.
- Men were significantly more likely to be shown outdoors or in business settings than were women.
- Twice as many women were shown with children as were men.
- 71 percent of the women in the ads were judged to be between twenty and thirty-five years old; only 43 percent of the men were in this age group.
- Men over fifty years old outnumbered women over fifty by a factor of two.
- 56 percent of women in the ads were judged to be housewives.
- 43 different occupations were coded for men, 18 for women.
- Of 946 ads with voice-overs, only 6 percent used a female voice; a male voice was heard on 94 percent.

In general, the content analysis of advertising, whether print or electronic, has found that women in the advertisements are associated with domesticity and submissiveness, while males are associated with more worldly roles and with dominance. Research completed in the early 1980s indicates that there may be less sex-role stereotyping in advertising, but the process of change is slow.

In examining more lengthy media content, researchers found that women were underrepresented in number and, when represented, were seen in limited roles. Tedesco, examining the roles of women in prime-time television,[49] found that males greatly outnumbered females and that males were frequently cast as heroes while females were frequently cast as victims of violence. Other findings from the Tedesco study included:

- Females were more often cast in light or comic roles, while males were portrayed in more serious roles.
- More than half of the female characters were married, compared to less than one-third of the male characters.
- Almost two-thirds of the female major characters were unemployed, while approximately one-third of the males were unemployed.
- Males had more violent roles than did females, but females were frequently the victims of violence.
- Male characters were more powerful, smart, rational, tall, and stable, while females were more attractive, fair, sociable, warm, happy, peaceful, and youthful.

More recent studies report similar results; see Greenberg et al., for example.[50] Another study conducted by Seggar, Hafen, and Hannonen-Gladden found that white women had increased in numbers on prime-time TV, but black females have become almost invisible in TV content.[51]

Many content studies of television programming have found that age is a major determinant of the number of women in programs. Gerbner et al. document this fact and observe:

The age distribution of females, compared to males, favors young girls and women under 35. While women are most concentrated, with almost a third of their total number, in the 25–35 age bracket, men are most concentrated, also with almost one-third of their number, in the 35 to 44 age bracket. The character population is structured to provide a relative abundance of younger women for older men, but no such abundance of younger men for older women. Television perpetuates an inequitable and unfair — if conventional — pattern.[52]

Franzwa studied sex roles in magazine serials and stories between 1940 and 1970[53] in *Ladies Home Journal, McCalls,* and *Good Housekeeping.* She reported that women were portrayed in one of four ways: (1) single, looking for a husband; (2) housewife-mother; (3) spinster; (4) widowed or divorced, soon to marry. The common element defining all women in the stories was the presence or absence of a man in their lives. In 1940, 1945, and 1950, six of the sixty-six married women characters had jobs outside the home, and of these six, only two were portrayed as having no role problems. In 1955, 1960, 1965, and 1970, no women with an out-of-home job appeared in the stories sampled.

Roberts, examining fiction in *Ladies Home Journal* from 1960 to 1962 and from 1974 to 1976, found that it remained consistently traditional.[54]

Butler and Paisley[55] and Farley[56] found some evidence that traditional women's magazines are covering more issues of significance to the women's movement. But these researchers were uncertain as to whether this finding was a trend or a fluctuation.

Much research has been generated on sex-role content in child-oriented media — textbooks, comic books, television programs, and films. These data, like the content studies, show shortages of female characters and of positive roles for female characters. For example, Taylor's study examined sex roles in textbooks used in California's state-adopted elementary reading program.[57] In the third-grade reader, Taylor found:

The stories all portray roles of males: of the eight stories in the book, none has a female central character, but they do appear in familiar roles of mother, grandmother and teacher. Males in the reader are shown doing significantly interesting and important things: five of the eight stories feature the relationship of a boy with a male adult, while the others relate the lives of grown men and adventures of a boy alone at the fair.

Many studies have examined the roles of males and females in TV content. Busby[58] and Long and Simon[59] found male and female characters in programs directed toward children to be characterized by traditional male/female stereotypes.

Mayers and Valentine conducted a similar study but used child coders from ages eight to thirteen to evaluate the actions and attitudes of the cartoon characters.[60] These youngsters reported that when compared to males, female characters were less brave, less dominant, less intelligent, less independent, less able to make decisions, had a greater need for security, and had a greater interest in personal appearance.

Welch et al. examined form, as opposed to content, in children's TV programs:[61]

Our purpose . . . was to examine a more subtle level of message that may be conveyed through *forms* used in the medium. Form, as opposed to content, refers to production techniques such as level of action or movement, pacing, camera techniques such as cuts, zooms and animation, and auditory forms such as music, sound effects and narration.

These researchers examined sixty television toy advertisements—twenty directed at girls, twenty directed at boys, and twenty directed at both boys and girls. They found:

The commercials directed at boys contained highly active toys, varied scenes, high rates of camera cuts, and high levels of sound effects and loud music. In the male commercials, the characters were frequently aggressive to each other or to objects, and the narrators were male. Commercials directed at girls had frequent fades, dissolves and background music; the narrators were female. . . . Both neutral and male commercials had predominantly male narrators, and females emerged in relatively little dialogue in the neutral commercials. . . .

The most recent media content studies continue to confirm the sex-role findings reported throughout the 1970s. Signorielli, in a study of marital status in prime-time TV programming on ABC, CBS, and NBC, found that women

and men continue to be presented in stereotypical roles:

The results of all these analyses are remarkably similar and offer little more than a rather stereotypical and traditional portrayal of women and marriage. The picture that emerges is that home and family, marriage and romance are important themes and are usually presented as the domain of the female. Marital status clearly differentiates female characters.[62]

Whipple and Courtney reported that "The overwhelming conclusion of the magazine and television monitoring studies is that advertising still portrays women in traditional roles. One of the most important findings is that women are rarely depicted as authority figures."[63]

Butler and Paisley,[64] Farley,[65] and Skelly[66] found evidence of recent change. Butler and Paisley and Farley report that the traditional women's magazines were more liberal in presenting feminist issues, and Skelly found some lessening of male stereotypes in general interest magazines but reported that change was slight and slow.

In general, sex roles in media content have remained fairly constant over the last ten years. Studies of sex roles in media content completed in the early 1970s will continue to be the point of comparison for future content studies. Busby's study concluded that: "Longitudinal studies of mass media content can be used as indicators of when and in what respects the tenets of the recent women's movement are accepted or rejected by the majority of Americans."[67]

Several observations summarize findings from media content studies:

- Females are underrepresented in comparison to males in almost all media content—television programs, magazine advertising, television advertising, textbooks, children's books, comic books, etc.
- Females appear in limited roles in media content when compared to the roles of males.

- Females are most often associated with domesticity and males with paid employment, entertainment, and leisure activities.
- Females are frequently cast as victims of violence and males as perpetrators of violence.
- Females are identified by their relationships to males—wife, fiancee, mother, girlfriend—much more often than males are identified by their relationship to females.
- Females in media content tend to be younger than their male counterparts. On television, one-third of the women are judged to be between twenty-five and thirty-five years old, and one-third of males on television are judged to be between thirty-five and forty-four years old.
- Females age faster than males in media content. On television, females are frequently cast in roles older than their actual age.
- Older women are especially underrepresented in media content, and the roles of older women are severely limited.
- Television advertising directed at boys uses many camera cuts and sound effects; television advertising directed at girls uses fades, dissolves, and background music.
- Traditional women's magazines are taking a more liberal attitude toward feminist issues.
- Some evidence suggests a slight lessening of traditional male roles in general interest magazines.

One decade may be too short a period to record real changes in media content. Whipple and Courtney[68] note that advertising practitioners have been reluctant to portray women in nontraditional roles because of the uncertainty that the American public would accept the new commercials. They tested the acceptability of commercials showing women in both traditional and progressive sex-roles and reported:

> We found progressive sex-role portrayals in television commercials to be at least equally preferred to, and in some cases more preferred than traditional advertising approaches. . . . The consumers and practitioners in this study concurred that it is possible to create television commercials with progressive portrayals—and to do so effectively—without causing consumer irritation.

With this kind of research and its findings, changes may be on the horizon. Another indication is that most textbook publishers have in-house guidelines to avoid sexist language and materials.

Findings in the early 1970s' content studies are similar to the findings being reported in the 1980s. Some media content studies indicate some changing media roles for males and females, but researchers are uncertain if these findings will be a trend through the 1980s and 1990s.

The Social Impact

The question raised by these content studies of most interest to researchers is: How do these media images affect women in their daily lives? To answer this question, researchers have been concerned about the attitudes associated with being male and female in American society. Researchers found that, historically, negative attitudes have been associated with being female and with female roles. Some early studies of differences in attitudes toward males and females confirmed this negativism.

A 1957 study asked college men and women to list adjectives describing men and adjectives describing women.[69] The students assigned thirty favorable adjectives to males, but only twenty-one favorable adjectives to females; they assigned only eight unfavorable adjectives to men and seventeen unfavorable adjectives to women.

Male positive attributes included witty, thorough, deliberate, industrious, steady, logical, ambitious, aggressive, self-confident, independent, dynamic, and rugged. Female positive adjectives included well-mannered, tactful, pleasant, sociable, gentle, kind, warm, sympathetic, soft-hearted, lovable, dreamy, sensitive, artistic, and religious.

In this same study, male and female college students were asked to list adjectives describing themselves as individuals. The self-descriptions paralleled the descriptions presented for men and women in general. Researchers observed: "Male subjects particularly emphasized men's desirable characteristics; females emphasized women's neuroticism."

Freeman noted that the stereotypical characteristics of females have "some 'nice' qualities, but they are not the ones normally required for the kinds of achievements to which society gives its highest rewards."[70]

A 1970 study of sex-role attitudes held by psychologists, psychiatrists, and social workers shocked the professional health-care community. Broverman et al. reported that the clinicians in the study were:

> . . . more likely to suggest that healthy women differ from healthy men by being more submissive, less independent, less adventuresome, more easily influenced, less aggressive, less competent, more excitable in minor crises, having their feelings more easily hurt, being more emotional, more conceited about their appearance, less objective and disliking math and science.[71]

Survey research of the general American public also found a negativism associated with women. In a 1970 CBS News national survey to determine American attitudes toward men and women,[72] one question asked a national sample of men and women: "Who would you trust more to be your doctor, a man or a woman?" Sixty-eight percent selected a man, and 8 percent selected a woman. To the question: "Who would you trust more to be your lawyer, a man or a woman?" 70 percent selected a man and 9 percent selected a woman.

A 1976 Gallup Poll found similar results. Women as well as men disparaged the abilities of women and indicated a preference to deal with male professionals.[73] The pollsters summarized their findings:

> By a ratio of 6-to-1, women say they would rather have a man than a woman as their boss. Most women would rather deal with male than female doctors, lawyers and bankers. Only in the case of traditionally female

occupations would women prefer to deal with persons of their own sex.

What does 1980s' research reveal?

Some research indicates a negativism still associated with being female. Some early investigations of bias against women have been replicated with similar findings. For example, in 1968, Goldberg found that female college students evaluated a professional article more highly when they thought it had been written by a male rather than a female.[74] In a replication of that study, Paludi and Bauer found similar results.[75] "As was the case in the Goldberg study, women in the present investigation overall valued articles written by John T. McKay more favorably than those written by Joan T. McKay. . . . Men in the present investigation also preferred the male author. . . ."

In a replication of some early research on attitudes about men and women, Ruble asked 128 college males and females to rate typical and desirable attributes of males and females.[76] He found that sex-role stereotypes remained strongly embedded in the minds of this sample of college students, but attitudes about desirable attributes of men/women indicated a less polarized point of view.

In general, most research suggests some lessening of negative attitudes toward women and at the same time that many stereotypes limiting a woman's social mobility are still prevalent.

Zuckerman and Sayre's study demonstrates the ambivalence about changing sex roles.[77] They interviewed children between the ages of four and eight to determine the extent to which recently changing cultural mores have influenced children's sex-role concepts. They reported: "Overall, the data suggest that children's sex-role attitudes are changing, reflecting the changes in society as a whole. . . . Nevertheless, almost all the children report traditional career expectations. . . . The results clearly suggest that society's ambivalence about changing sex roles is reflected in the children' sex-role attitudes."

Margaret Mead observed that gender is regarded as the most important difference between individuals and that only by accepting the role of one's sex can one "attain full membership in the human race."[78] Evidence indicates that at an early age, male and female children learn the attributes and social roles of their sex.

Fagot's 1978 study observed parents and toddlers in their homes and noted the parents' reactions to the children.[79] She found that parents reacted significantly more favorably to the child when the child engaged in same-sex preferred behavior and were likely to respond negatively to a child engaging in opposite-sex preferred behavior.

Fagot found that girls were given more negative responses when engaged in active, large-motor activities. Girls were given more positive responses when they asked for help, engaged in adult-oriented tasks, or engaged in dependent behavior. Boys, on the other hand, were given positive responses when they engaged in large-motor activities but negative responses when they asked for help or engaged in dependent behavior.

Parents indicated that they were not aware of their different responses to male and female children. The reseacher concluded that "Few parents would think of such mundane behavior as 'manipulating objects' as a behavior important to sex-role socialization."

Many reseachers have learned that boys and girls as young as two and three years are aware of sex stereotypes in adult culture and are aware of socially preferred sex role for themselves.[80] Appropriate sex-role behavior is, then, an early acquisition. It is little wonder that sex roles are learned thoroughly and that expectations placed on males and females endure for a lifetime. The point here is that the female's social mobility becomes extremely limited as seen in the facts that both males and females disparage the female's abilities and that parents use strict socialization patterns on toddlers to maintain male/female social roles.

How do the lack of social mobility and restricted social roles lead back to the mass media? Strainchamps provides the answer:

Back in the sixties, as women began to wonder about the validity of their traditional roles, one of the most natural questions to arise was: Where do women get their images of themselves? . . . They found that . . . traditional institutions were indeed guilty of reinforcing stereotyped notions about men vs. women, but they discovered that the most ubiquitous, the most insidious, and therefore possibly the most powerful force dedicated to the maintenance of the status quo was not one of the long established social institutions, but a fairly new one—the mass media.[81]

Gerbner has described the mass media as a "new religion"—a cosmic force or a symbolic environment that one is born into and whose assumptions one accepts almost without question. We are surrounded by every form of the media: they pervade our homes, school rooms, offices, working hours, leisure hours.

Since females have been limited in their social mobility by narrowly and negatively defined concepts of femaleness, the mass media have come under scrutiny for their sex-role content. Throughout the 1980s and 1990s, researchers will continue to investigate the general social attitudes toward the roles of males and females. With careful monitoring of the media and its effects, researchers may be able to document attitudinal changes toward centuries-old sex roles. Sex-role research on the mass media is exciting, since the media are the reflective/projective mirrors of our society and its changes.

Summary

This article explored the roles of the mass media as sex-role socialization forces. Media effects, media content, and the social impact of the media were the primary areas of discussion. An extensive bibliography is provided. The bibliography is divided into three major areas. Media Effects: Sex-role Socialization; Media Content; and Personal and Social Impact of Sex-role Acquisition.

Endnotes

1. See UNESCO reports for media comparisons by country.
2. *Bowker Annual of Library and Book Trade Information*, 28th ed. (New York: R. R. Bowker Co., 1983).
3. Melvin L. DeFleur and Everette E. Dennis, *Understanding Mass Communication* (Boston: Houghton Mifflin, 1981), 78.
4. Warren K. Agee, Philip H. Ault, and Edwin Emery, *Introduction to Mass Communication* (New York: Harper & Row, 1976), 298.
5. *Broadcasting Yearbook*, 1983.
6. *Broadcasting,* April 18, 1977.
7. *Broadcasting*, January 1972.
8. George Gerbner, "The Dynamics of Cultural Resistance," in Gaye Tuchman, A. K. Daniels, and J. Benet, eds., *Hearth and Home: Images of Women in the Mass Media* (New York: Oxford University Press, 1978), 47.
9. Leslie A. Baxter and Stuart J. Kaplan, "Context Factors in Analysis of Prosocial and Antisocial Behavior on Prime Time Television," *Journal of Broadcasting* 27 (1983): 25–36.
10. See, for example: Albert Bandura, "Influence of Models: Reinforcement Contingencies on the Acquisition of Imitative Responses," *Journal of Personality and Social Psychology* 1 (1965): 589–595; Albert Bandura, Dorothea Ross, and Sheila A. Ross, "Imitation of Film-Mediated Aggressive Models," *Journal of Abnormal and Social Psychology* 66 (1963): 3–11; D. J. Hicks, "Imitation and Retention of Film-Mediated Aggressive Peer and Adult Models," *Journal of Personality and Social Psychology* 2 (1965): 97–100.
11. Wilbur Schramm, Jack Lyle, and Edwin B. Parker, *Television in the Lives of Our Children* (Stanford, Calif.: Stanford University Press, 1961).
12. G. A. Hale, L. K. Miller, and H. W. Stevenson, "Incidental Learning of Film Content: A Developmental Study," *Child Development* 39 (1968): 69–77.
13. Jack Lyle and Heidi R. Hoffman, "Exploration in Patterns of Television Viewing by Preschool-Age Children," in *Television and Social Behavior*, Vol. 4 (Washington, D.C.: U.S. Government Printing Office, 1972), 257–273.
14. Eleanor Maccoby, W. C. Wilson, and R. V. Burton, "Differential Movie Viewing Behavior of Male and Female Viewers," *Journal of Personality* 26 (1958): 259–267.
15. Joyce N. Sprafkin and R. M. Liebert, "Sex-Typing and Children's Television Preferences," in Gaye Tuchman, A. K. Daniels, and J. Benet, eds., *Hearth and Home: Images of Women in the Mass Media* (New York: Oxford University Press, 1978).
16. Eleanor Maccoby and W. C. Wilson, "Identification and Observational Learning from Films," *Journal of Abnormal and Social Psychology* 55 (1957): 76–87.
17. Sprafkin and Liebert, op. cit.
18. Researchers found no evidence of selective attention, but they used different methodology. They measured alpha blocking rather than eye contact and eye movement. See J. W. Bryan and Z. Luria, "Sex-Role Learning: A Test of Selective Attention Hypothesis," *Child Development* 49 (1978): 13–23.
19. David H. Goff, Lynda Dysart Goff, and Sara Kay Lehrer, "Sex Role Portrayals of Selected Female Television Characters," *Journal of Broadcasting* 24 (1980): 467–471.
20. Ann Beuf, "Doctor, Lawyer, Household Drudge," *Journal of Communication* 24 (1974): 142–145.
21. M. Morgan, "Television and Adolescents' Sex-Role Stereotypes: A Longitudinal Study," *Journal of Personality and Social Psychology* (1982): 947–955.
22. Mark Miller and Byron Reeves, "Children's Occupational Sex Role Stereotypes: the Linkage Between Television Content and Perception." Paper presented at the International Communication Association Conference, Portland, Oregon, 1976;

published as "A Multidimensional Measure of Children's Identification with Television Characters," *Journal of Broadcasting* 22 (1978): 71–86.

23. Byron Reeves and Bradley S. Greenberg, "Children's Perception of Television Characters," *Human Communication Research* 3 (1977): 113–127.

24. M. Mark Miller, "Factors Affecting Children's Choices of Televised Sex-Role Models," unpublished paper, Department of Communication, Est Lansing, Mich., Michigan State University, 1976

25. Bradley S. Greenberg, Gary Heald, Jacob Wakshlag, and Byron Reeves, "TV Character Attributes, Identification and Children's Modeling Tendencies," paper presented to the International Communication Association Convention, Portland, Oregon, April 1976.

26. Terry Frueh and Paul E. McGhee, "Traditional Sex Role Development and Amount of Time Spent Watching Television," *Developmental Psychology* 11 (1975): 109.

27. Charles Atkin and M. Mark Miller, "Experimental Effects of Television Advertising on Children," paper presented to the International Communication Association Convention, Chicago, April 1975.

28. S. L. O'Bryant and C. R. Corder-Bolz, "The Effects of Television on Children's Stereotyping of Women's Work Roles," *Journal of Vocational Behavior* 12 (1978), 233–244.

29. Emily S. Davidson, Amy Yasuna, and Alan Tower, "The Effect of Television Cartoons on Sex-Role Stereotyping in Young Girls," *Child Development* 50 (1979): 597–600.

30. S. L. O'Bryant and C. R. Corder-Bolz, "Black Children's Learning of Work Roles from Television Commercials," *Psychological Reports* 42 (1978): 227–230.

31. Vicki C. Flerx, Dorothy S. Fidler, and Ronald Rogers, "Sex Role Stereotypes: Developmental Aspects and Early Intervention," *Child Development* 47 (1976): 998–1007.

32. Candice S. Schau, "Evaluating the Use of Sex-Role-Reversed Stories for Changing Children's Stereotypes," ERIC, ED 159 494 (1978).

33. Leslie Z. McArthur and Susan V. Eisen, "Achievement of Male and Female Storybook Characters as Determinants of Achievement Behavior of Boys and Girls," *Journal of Personality and Social Psychology* 33 (1976): 467–473.

34. Jerri J. Kropp and Charles F. Halverson, "Preschool Children's Preferences and Recall for Stereotyped vs. Non-Stereotyped Stories," *Sex Roles* 9 (1983): 261–272.

35. Sally G. Koblinsky, Donna F. Cruse, and Alan I. Sugarawa, "Sex Role Stereotypes and Children's Memory for Story Content," *Child Development* 49 (1978): 452–458.

36. J. W. Bryan and Z. Luria, "Sex-Role Learning: A Test of Selective Attention Hypothesis," *Child Development* 49 (1978): 13–23.

37. Russell A. Barkley, Douglas G. Ullman, Lori Otto, and Jan M. Brecht, "The Effects of Sex Typing and Sex Appropriateness of Modeled Behavior on Children's Imitation," *Child Development* 48 (1977), 721–725.

38. Alexis S. Tan, "TV Beauty Ads and Role Expectations of Adolescent Female Viewers," *Journalism Quarterly* 56 (1979): 283–288.

39. Joyce Jennings, Florence L. Geis, and Virginia Brown, "Influence of Television Commercials on Women's Self-Confidence and Independent Judgment," *Journal of Personality and Social Psychology* 38 (1980): 203–210.

40. Frederick Williams, Robert LaRose, and Frederica Frost, *Children, Television and Sex-Role Stereotyping* (New York: Praeger Publishers, 1981), 146.

41. A. E. Courtney and S. W. Lockeretz, "Women's Place: An Analysis of Roles Portrayed by Women in Magazine Advertisements," *Journal of Marketing Research* 8 (1971): 92–95.

42. Donald E. Sexton and Phyllis Haberman, "Women in Magazine Advertisements,"

Journal of Advertising Research 14 (1974): 41–46.

43. Nancy Roberts, "From Pumps, Pearls and Pleats to Pants, Briefcases and Hardhats: Changes in the Portrayal of Women in Advertising and Fiction in *Ladies Home Journal* 1960–1962 and 1974–1976," ERIC, ED 188 211 (1980).

44. Erving Goffman, *Gender Advertisements* (Cambridge: Harvard University Press, 1979).

45. Thomas J. Whipple and Alice E. Courtney, "How to Portray Women in TV Commercials," *Journal of Advertising* 20 (1980): 53–59.

46. Gerald Skelly and William Lundstrom, "Male Sex Roles in Magazine Advertising, 1959–1979," *Journal of Communication* 31 (1981): 52–57.

47. Judith Hennessee and John Nicholson, "NOW Says: TV Commercials Insult Women," *New York Times Magazine* (May 28, 1972): 12–13 *ff.*

48. Joseph R. Dominick and Gail E. Rauch, "The Image of Women in Network TV Commercials," *Journal of Broadcasting* 16 (1972): 259–265.

49. Nancy Tedesco, "Patterns in Prime Time," *Journal of Communication* 24 (1974): 133–141.

50. Bradley S. Greenberg, Katrina W. Simmons, Linda Hogan, and Charles Atkin, "Three Seasons of Television Characters: A Demographic Analysis," *Journal of Broadcasting* 24 (1980): 49–60.

51. John F. Seggar, Jeffrey K. Hafen, and Helena Hannonen-Gladden, "Television's Portrayal of Minorities and Women in Drama and Comedy Drama 1971–1980," *Journal of Broadcasting* 25 (1981): 277–288.

52. George Gerbner, Larry Gross, Nancy Signorielli, and Michael Morgan, "Aging with Television: Images on Television Drama and Conceptions of Social Reality," *Journal of Communication* 30 (1980): 37–47.

53. Helen Franzwa, "Working Women in Fact and Fiction," *Journal of Communication*

24 (1974): 104–109.

54. Roberts, ERIC ED 188 211, (1980), op. cit.

55. Matilda Butler and William Paisley, "Magazine Coverage of Women's Rights," *Journal of Communication* 28 (1978): 183–186.

56. Jennie Farley, "Women's Magazines and the Equal Rights Amendment: Friend or Foe?" *Journal of Communication* 28 (1978): 187–192.

57. Marjorie E. Taylor, "Sex-Role Stereotypes in Children's Readers," *Elementary English* 50 (1973): 1045–1047.

58. Linda J. Busby, "Defining the Sex-Role Standard in Commercial Network Television Programs Directed toward Children," *Journalism Quarterly* 51 (1974): 690–696.

59. Michele Long and R. J. Simon, "The Roles and Statuses of Women on Children and Family TV Programs," *Journalism Quarterly* 51 (1974): 107–110.

60. Sandra L. Mayers and K. B. Valentine, "Sex Role Stereotyping in Saturday Morning Cartoon Shows," *Journal of Broadcasting* 23 (1979): 41–50.

61. Renate L. Welch, Aletha Huston-Stein, John C. Wright, and Robert Plehal, "Subtle Sex Role Cues in Children's Commercials," *Journal of Communication* 29 (1979): 202–209.

62. Nancy Signorielli, "Marital Status in Television Drama: A Case of Reduced Options," *Journal of Broadcasting* 26 (1982): 585–597.

63. Thomas W. Whipple and Alice E. Courtney, "How to Portray Women in TV Commercials," *Journal of Advertising Research* 20 (1980): 53–59.

64. Ibid.

65. Farley, op. cit.

66. Skelly, op. cit.

67. Linda J. Busby, "Sex-Role Research on the Mass Media," *Journal of Communication* 25 (1975): 107–131.

68. Whipple and Courtney, op. cit.

69. Alex C. Sheriffs and John McKee, "Qualitative Aspects of Beliefs About Men and

Women," *Journal of Personality* 25 (1957): 451–464.

70. Jo Freeman, "Growing Up Girlish," *Trans-Action* (November–December 1970): 37.

71. Inge K. Broverman, Donald M. Broverman, Frank E. Clarkson, Paul S. Rosenkrantz, and Susan R. Vogel, "Sex-Role Stereotypes and Clinical Judgments of Mental Health," *Journal of Consulting and Clinical Psychology* 34 (1970): 1–7.

72. Robert Chandler, ed., *Public Opinion, A CBS News Reference Book* (New York: R. R. Bowker Company, 1972), 47.

73. George Gallup, ed., *The Gallup Poll, 1972–1977*, Vol. 2, 1976–1977 (Dover, Del.: Scholarly Resources, 1978).

74. Paul A. Goldberg, "Are Women Prejudiced against Women?" *Trans-Action* 5 (1968): 28–30.

75. Michele A. Paludi and William D. Bauer, "Goldberg Revisited: What's in an Author's Name?", *Sex Roles: A Journal of Research* 9 (1983): 387–390. Paludi and Bauer's findings were not similar in every respect to those of Goldberg. Paludi and Bauer used some different methodology. They used what they termed masculine, feminine, and neutral articles. (Articles in the fields of politics, psychology of women, and education, respectively.) They found that women did not prefer the "masculine" to the "feminine" article but men did prefer the "masculine" article and the male author.

76. Thomas L. Ruble, "Sex Stereotypes: Issues of Change in the 1970s," *Sex Roles: A Journal of Research* 9 (1983): 397–402.

77. Diana M. Zuckerman and Donald H. Sayre, "Cultural Sex-Role Expectations and Children's Sex-Role Concepts," *Sex Roles: A Journal of Research* 8 (1982): 853–862.

78. Margaret Mead, "Sex and Achievement," *Forum* (November 1935): 301–303.

79. Beverly I. Fagot, "The Influence of Sex of Child on Parental Reaction to Toddler Children," *Child Development* 49 (1978): 459–465.

80. In the bibliography "Personal and Social Impact of Sex-Role Acquisition," see Kuhn, Nash, and Brueken (1978); Flerx, Fidler, and Rogers (1976); Reis and Wright (1983).

81. Ethel Strainchamps, ed., *Rooms With No View* (New York: Harper & Row, 1974), xxv.

Bibliography

Media Effects: Sex-Role Socialization

Abel, John D., and Maureen E. Beninson. "Perceptions of TV Program Violence by Children and Mothers," *Journal of Broadcasting* 20 (1976): 355–364.

Allen, Ruth A. "The Effects of a Non-Sexist Pre-Kindergarten Program on Sex-Role Stereotypes in Young Children," ERIC, ED 174 309 (1979).

Arenstein, Howard L. "The Effect of Television on Children's Stereotyping of Occupational Roles," M.A. Thesis, University of Pennsylvania, 1974.

Ashton, Eleanor. "Measures of Play Behavior: The Influence of Sex-Role Stereotyped Children's Books," *Sex Roles: A Journal of Research* 9 (1983): 43–46.

Atkin, Charles K., and M. Mark Miller. "Experimental Effects of Television Advertising on Children," Paper presented to the International Communication Association Convention, Chicago, April 1975.

Balon, Robert E., Joseph Philport, and Charles F. Beadle. "How Sex and Race Affect Perceptions of Newscasters," *Journalism Quarterly* 55 (1978): 160–164.

Bandura, Albert. "Influence of Models: Reinforcement Contingencies on the Acquisition of Imitative Responses," *Journal of Personality and Social Psychology* 6 (1965): 589–595.

Bandura, Albert, Dorothea Ross, and Sheila A. Ross. "Imitation of Film-Mediated Aggressive Models," *Journal of Abnormal and Social Psychology* 66 (1963): 3–11.

Baran, Stanley J. "How TV and Film Portrayals Affect Sexual Satisfaction in College Students," *Journalism Quarterly* 53 (1976): 468–473.

Baran, Stanley J. "Sex on TV and Adolescent Sexual Self-Image," *Journal of Broadcasting* 20 (1976): 61–68.

Barkley, Russell A., Douglas G. Ullman, Lori Otto, and Jan M. Brecht. "Effects of Sex Typing and Sex Appropriateness of Modeled Behavior on Children's Imitation," *Child Development* 48 (1977): 721–725.

Beuf, Ann. "Doctor, Lawyer, Household Drudge," *Journal of Communication* 24 (1974): 142–145.

Brown, Jane Delano. "Role of Communication in the Development of Sex Role Orientation," M.A. Thesis, University of Wisconsin, Madison, 1974.

Buerkel-Rothfuss, Nancy, with Sandra Mayes. "Soap Opera Viewing: The Cultivation Effect," *Journal of Communication* 31 (1981): 108–115.

Cantor, Joanne R. "What Is Funny to Whom: The Role of Gender," *Journal of Communication* 26 (1976): 164–172.

Chang, Won H. "Characteristics and Self-Perceptions of Women's Page Editors," *Journalism Quarterly* 52 (1975): 61–65.

Cheles-Miller, Pamela. "Reactions to Marital Roles in Commercials," *Journal of Advertising Research* 15 (1975): 45–49.

Child, Irwin L., E. H. Potter, and Estelle M. Levine. "Children's Textbooks and Personality Development," *Psychological Monographs* 60 (1946): 1–7, 45–53.

Collias, W. A. "Temporal Integration and Children's Understanding of Social Information on Television," *American Journal of Orthopsychology* 48 (1978): 198–204.

Comstock, George, Steven Chaffee, Nathan Katzman, Maxwell McCombs, and Donald Roberts. *Television and Human Behavior*, New York: Columbia, 1978.

Davidson, E. S., et al. "Effects of Television Cartoons on Sex-Role Stereotyping in Young Girls," *Child Development* 50 (1979): 597–600.

Dohrmann, Rita M. "Children's Television Programming: A Sex Socialization Agent,"

M.A. Thesis, Drake University, Des Moines, Iowa, 1974.

Donohue, Thomas R. "Black Children's Perceptions of Favorite TV Characters as Models of Antisocial Behavior," *Journal of Broadcasting* 19 (1975): 153–167.

Donohue, Thomas R. "Perception of Violent TV Newsfilm: An Experimental Comparison of Sex and Color Factors," *Journal of Broadcasting* 20 (1976): 185–196.

Elliott, William R., and Dan Slater. "Exposure, Experience and Perceived TV Reality for Adolescents," *Journalism Quarterly* 57 (1980): 409–414.

Fauls, L. B., and W. D. Smith. "Sex-Role Learning of Five-Year-Olds," *Journal of Genetic Psychology* 89 (1956): 105–117.

Feldstein, Jerome H., and Sandra Feldstein. "Sex Differences on Televised Toy Commercials," *Sex Roles: A Journal of Research* 8 (1982): 581–586.

Flerx, Vicki C., Dorothy S. Fidler, and Ronald W. Rogers. "Sex-Role Stereotypes: Developmental Aspects and Early Intervention," *Child Development* 47 (1976): 998–1007.

Frueh, Terry, and Paul E. McGhee. "Traditional Sex Role Development and Amount of Time Spent Watching TV," *Developmental Psychology* 11 (1975): 109.

Gerbner, George, et al. "Cultural Indicators: Violence Profile No. 9," *Journal of Communication* 28 (1978): 176–207.

Gerbner, George, Larry Gross, Michael Morgan, and Nancy Signorielli. "The Mainstreaming of America: Violence Profile No. 11," *Journal of Communication* 30 (1980): 10–29.

Goff, David H., Lynda Dysart Goff, and Sara Kay Lehrer. "Sex Role Portrayals of Selected Female Television Characters," *Journal of Broadcasting* 24 (1980): 467–471.

Greenberg, Bradley S., Gary Heald, Jacob Wakshlag, and Byron Reeves. "TV Character Attributes, Identification and Children's Modeling Tendencies," Paper presented at the International Communication Association Convention, Portland, Oregon, April 1976.

Greenberg, Bradley S., Kimberly Neuendorf,

Nancy Buerkel-Rothfuss, and Laura Henderson. "The Soaps: What's on and Who Cares?" *Journal of Broadcasting* 26 (1982): 519–535.

Hale, G. A., L. K. Miller, and H. W. Stevenson. "Incidental Learning of Film Content: A Developmental Study," *Child Development* 39 (1968): 69–77.

Haugh, S. S., et al. "Eye of the Very Young Beholder: Sex Typing of Infants by Young Children," *Child Development* 51 (1980): 598–600.

Hawkins, Robert, Christine Morelli, Suzanne Pingree, and Donna G. Wilson. "How Children Evaluate Real-Life and Television Women," ERIC, ED 177 574, (1980).

Heneman, H. G. III. "Impact of Text Information and Applicant Sex on Applicant Evaluation in a Selective Simulation," *Journal of Applied Psychology* 62 (1977): 524–526.

Hicks, D. J. "Imitation and Retention of Film-Mediated Aggressive Peer and Adult Models," *Journal of Personality and Social Psychology* 2 (1965): 97–100.

Jackson-Beeck, Marilyn, and Jeff Sobal. "The Social World of Heavy Television Viewers," *Journal of Broadcasting* 24 (1980): 5–13.

Jennings, Joyce, Florence L. Geis, and Virginia Brown. "Influence of Television Commercials on Women's Self-Confidence and Independent Judgment," *Journal of Personality and Social Psychology* 38 (1980): 203–210.

Jennings, Sally A. "Effects of Sex Typing in Children's Stories on Preferences and Recall," *Child Development* 46 (1975): 220–223.

Klapper, H. L. "Childhood Socialization and Television," *Public Opinion Quarterly* 42 (1978): 426–430.

Koblinsky, Sally G., Donna F. Cruse, and Alan I. Sugawara. "Sex Role Stereotypes and Children's Memory for Story Content," *Child Development* 49 (1978): 452–458.

Kropp, Jerri J., and Charles F. Halverson. "Preschool Children's Preferences for Stereotyped vs. Non-Stereotyped Stories," *Sex Roles: A Journal of Research* 9 (1983): 261–272.

LeBouef, Robert A., and Marc Matre. "How Different Readers Perceive Magazine Stories and Characters," *Journalism Quarterly* 54 (1977): 50–57.

Leifer, Aimee D., et al. "Children's Television, More Than Mere Entertainment," *Harvard Educational Review* 44 (1974): 213–245.

Lueptow, L. B. "Social Change and Sex-Role Change in Adolescent Orientation Toward Life, Work, Achievement: 1964–1975," *Social Psychology Quarterly* 43 (1980): 48–59.

Lull, James T., et al. "Recognition of Female Stereotypes in TV Commercials," *Journalism Quarterly* 54 (1977): 153–156.

Lyle, Jack, and Heidi R. Hoffman. "Exploration in Patterns of Television Viewing by Preschool Age Children," in *Television and Social Behavior*, Vol. 4, Washington, D.C.: U.S. Government Printing Office, 1972, 257–273.

McArthur, Leslie Z., and Susan V. Eisen. "Achievements of Male and Female Storybook Characters as Determinants of Achievement Behavior by Boys and Girls," *Journal of Personality and Social Psychology* 33 (1976): 467–473.

Maccoby, Eleanor E., and W. C. Wilson. "Identification and Observational Learning from Films," *Journal of Abnormal and Social Psychology* 55 (1957): 76–87.

Maccoby, Eleanor, W. C. Wilson, and R. V. Burton. "Differential Movie Viewing Behavior of Male and Female Viewers," *Journal of Personality* 26 (1958): 259–267.

McGhee, Paul E. "Television as a Source of Learning Sex Role Stereotypes," ERIC, ED 111 528 (1975).

Meyer, B. "Development of Girls' Sex-Role Attitudes," *Child Development* 51 (1980): 508–514.

Meyer, Timothy P. "Television's Behavioral Models and Children's Perceptions," *Educational Broadcasting Review* 7 (1973): 25–33.

Miller, Mark M. "Factors Affecting Children's Choices of Televised Sex-Role Models," unpublished paper, Department of Communication, Michigan State University, 1976.

Miller, Mark M., and Byron Reeves. "Children's Occupational Sex-Role Stereotype:

The Linkage between Television Content and Perception," Paper presented at the International Communication Association Convention, Portland, Oregon, April 1976.

Miller, Mark M., and Byron Reeves. "Dramatic TV Content and Children's Sex-Role Stereotypes," *Journal of Broadcasting* 20 (1976): 35–50.

Miller, William C., and Thomas Beck. "How Do TV Parents Compare to Real Parents?" *Journalism Quarterly* 53 (1976): 324–328.

Mischel, Walter. "A Social-Learning View of Sex Differences in Behavior," in Eleanor E. Maccoby, *The Development of Sex Differences*, Stanford, Calif.: Stanford University Press, 1966, 56–81.

Mischel, Walter. "Sex Typing and Socialization," in P. H. Mussen, ed., *Carmichael's Manual of Child Psychology*, Vol. 2, New York: Wiley, 1970.

Morgan, M. "Television and Adolescents' Sex-Role Stereotypes: A Longitudinal Study," *Journal of Personality and Social Psychology* 41 (1982): 947–955.

Newcomb, A. F., and W. A. Collins. "Children's Comprehension of Family Role Portrayals in Televised Dramas: Effects of Socioeconomic Status, Ethnicity, and Age," *Developmental Psychology* 15:4 (1979): 417–423.

Newly, T. J., et al. "Preferences of Mexican-American Children for Parents on Television," *Journal of Psychology* 105 (1980): 239–245.

O'Bryant, S. L., and C. R. Corder-Bolz. "Black Children's Learning of Work Roles from Television Commercials," *Psychological Reports* 42 (1978): 227–230.

Olsen, Judith E. "The Relationship between Sex-Role Stereotyping in TV Programming and Children's Autonomy," ERIC, ED 180 040 (1979).

Orwant, Jack E., and Muriel G. Cantor. "How Sex Stereotyping Affects Perception of News Preference," *Journalism Quarterly* 54 (1977): 99–108.

Perry, David G., and Louise C. Perry. "Observational Learning in Children: Effects of Sex of Model and Subjects' Sex Role Behavior," *Journal of Personality and Social Psychology* 31 (1975): 1083–1088.

Pingree, Suzanne. "A Developmental Study of the Attitudinal Effects of Nonsexist Television Commercials under Various Conditions of Perceived Reality," Ph.D. Dissertation, Stanford University, Palo Alto, California, 1975.

Plost, Myrna. "Sex of Career Models Affects Girls' Occupational Choices," M.A. Thesis, California State University, Fullerton, 1973.

Popovich, Paula, and Eliot J. Butter. "Perceptions of the Sex Stereotyped Attributes of Television Characters as a Function of the Sex of the Perceiver," ERIC, ED 189 526 (1980).

Reeves, Byron, and Bradley S. Greenberg. "Children's Perception of Television Characters," *Human Communication Research* 3 (1977): 113–127.

Reeves, Byron, and Guy E. Lometti. "The Dimensional Structure of Children's Perceptions of Television Characters: A Replication," *Human Communication Research* 5 (1979): 247–256.

Reeves, Byron, and M. Mark Miller. "A Multidimensional Measure of Children's Identification with Television Characters," *Journal of Broadcasting* 22 (1978): 71–86.

Reis, Harry T., and Stephanie Wright. "Knowledge of Sex-Role Stereotypes in Children Aged 3 to 5," *Sex Roles: A Journal of Research* 8 (1982): 1049–1056.

Richert, Alphons J. "Behavioral Stability: Sex-Role Stereotyping and Cognition," *Psychological Record* 28 (1978): 627–637.

Rubin, Alan M. "Television Usage, Attitudes and Viewing Behavior of Children and Adolescents," *Journal of Broadcasting* 22 (1977): 355–369.

Rubin, Alan M., and Rebecca Rubin. "Age, Context and Television Use," *Journal of Broadcasting* 25 (1981): 1–14.

Saario, T. N., C. N. Jacklin, and C. K. Tittle. "Sex-Role Stereotyping in the Public Schools," *Harvard Educational Review* 43 (1973): 386–416.

Schau, Candace G. "Evaluating the Use of Sex-Role-Reversed Stories for Changing

Children's Stereotypes," ERIC, ED 159 494 (1979).

Schramm, Wilbur, Jack Lyle, and Edwin B. Parker. *Television in the Lives of Our Children*, Stanford, Calif.: Stanford University Press, 1961.

Schreiber, Elliott. "The Effect of Sex and Age on the Perception of TV Characters: An Inter-Age Comparison," *Journal of Broadcasting* 23 (1979): 81–94.

Scott, Kathryn P. "Effects of Sexist vs. Non-Sexist Reading Materials on Children's Preferences, Sex Role Attitudes and Comprehension," ERIC, ED 169 496 (1979).

Silverman, L. Theresa, and Joyce N. Sprafkin. "The Effects of Sesame Street's Prosocial Spots on Cooperative Play between Young Children," *Journal of Communication* 31 (1981): 34–40.

Sprafkin, Joyce N., and L. Theresa Silverman. "Update: Physically Intimate and Sexual Behavior on Prime Time Television 1978–1979," *Journal of Communication* 31 (1981): 34–40.

Sprafkin, Joyce N., L. Theresa Silverman, and Eli A. Rubinstein. "Reaction to Sex on Television: An Exploratory Study," *Public Opinion Quarterly* 44 (1980): 303–315.

Stein, Aletha H. "Mass Media and Young Children's Development," in *Early Childhood Education,* Chicago: NSSE, 1974, 191–202.

Tan, Alexis S. "TV Beauty Ads and Role Expectations of Adolescent Female Viewers," *Journalism Quarterly* 56 (1979): 283–288.

UNESCO. "Influence of the Mass Media on Attitudes toward the Role of Women and Men in Present-Day Society," E/CN/.6/601 (1976).

Weitzman, L. J., D. Eifler, E. Hokado, and C. Ross. "Sex-Role Socialization in Picture Books for Preschool Children," *American Journal of Sociology* 77 (1972): 1125–1150.

Williams, J. E., S. M. Bennett, and D. L. Best. "Awareness and Expression of Sex Stereotypes in Young Children," *Developmental Psychology* 11 (1975): 635–642.

Williams, Tannis M. "How and What Do Children Learn from Television?" *Human Communication Research* 7 (1981): 180–192.

Zukerman, P., et al. "Children's Viewing of Television and Recognition Memory of Commercials," *Child Development* 49 (1978): 96–104.

Media Content

American Association of University Women, Sacramento, California Branch. "The Image of Women in Television, A Survey and Guide," Sacramento: AAUW, 1974.

Aronoff, Craig. "Old Age in Prime Time," *Journal of Communication* 24 (1974): 86–87.

Aronoff, Craig E. "Sex Roles and Aging on Television," *Journal of Communication* 24 (1974): 124 *ff.*

Bailey, Margaret. "The Women's Magazine Short Story Heroine in 1957 and 1967," *Journalism Quarterly* 46 (1969): 364–366.

Bangs, Lester. "They Won't Get Fooled Again," *Ms.* (August 1972): 23–26.

Bate, Barbara, and Lois S. Self. "The Rhetoric of Career Success Books for Women," *Journal of Communication* 33 (1983): 149–165.

Baxter, Leslie A., and Stuart J. Kaplan. "Context Factors in the Analysis of Prosocial and Antisocial Behavior on Prime Time Television," *Journal of Broadcasting* 27 (1983): 25–36.

Belkaoui, Ahmed, and Jamie Belkaoui. "A Comparative Analysis of the Roles Portrayed by Women in Print Advertisements: 1958, 1970, 1972," *Journal of Marketing Research* 13 (1976): 168–172.

Bereaud, Susan R. "Sex Roles Images in French Children's Books," *Journal of Marriage and the Family* 37 (1975): 194–207.

Bernstein, Joanne. "The Changing Roles of Females in Books for Young Children," *Reading Teacher* 27 (1974): 545–549.

Beuf, Ann. "Doctor, Lawyer, Household Drudge," *Journal of Communication* 24 (1974): 142–145.

Bond, Jean Carey. "The Media Image of Black Women," *Freedomways* 15 (1975): 34–37.

Busby, Linda J. "Defining the Sex-Role Standard in Commercial Network Television Programs Directed toward Children," *Journalism Quarterly* 51 (1974): 690–696.

Busby, Linda J. "Sex-Role Research on the Mass Media," *Journal of Communication* 25 (1975): 107–131.

Butler, Matilda, and William Paisley. *The Flawed Mirror, Sourcebook on Women and the Media,* Washington, D.C.: Communication Press, 1977.

Butler, Matilda, and William Paisley. "Magazine Coverage of Women's Rights," *Journal of Communication* 28 (1978): 183–186.

Cantor, M. "Our Days and Our Nights on TV," *Journal of Communication* 29 (1979): 66–72.

Carlson, Pamela G. "Are Women's Pages Getting Better?" *Editor and Publisher* (May 31, 1975): 108–111.

Cassata, Mary B., Thomas D. Skill, and Samuel Osei Boada. "In Sickness and in Health," *Journal of Communication* 29 (1979): 73–80.

Chapman, Anthony J., and Nicholas J. Garfield. "Is Sexual Humor Sexist?" *Journal of Communication* 26 (1976): 141–153.

Chulay, Cornell, and Sara Francis. "The Image of the Female Child on Saturday Morning Television Commercials," ERIC, ED 095 603 (1974).

Clarke, Peter, and Virginia Esposito. "A Study of Occupational Advice for Women in Magazines," *Journalism Quarterly* 43 (1966): 477–485.

Courtney, A. E., and S. W. Lockeretz. "Women's Place: An Analysis of the Roles Portrayed by Women in Magazine Advertisements," *Journal of Marketing Research* 8 (1971): 92–95.

Courtney, A. E., and T. W. Whipple. "Women in TV Commercials," *Journal of Communication* 24 (1974): 110–118.

Culley, James D., and Rex Bennett. "Selling Women, Selling Blacks," *Journal of Communication* 26 (1976): 160–174.

Defleur, Melvin. "Occupational Roles as Portrayed on Television," *Public Opinion Quarterly* 25 (1964): 54–74.

Despenza, Joseph E. *Advertising the American Women,* Dayton, Ohio: Pflaum, 1975.

Dohrmann, Rita M. "A Gender Profile of Children's Educational TV," *Journal of Communication* 25 (1975): 56–65.

Dominick, Joseph R., and Gail E. Rauch. "The Image of Women in Network TV Commercials," *Journal of Broadcasting* 16 (1972): 259–265.

Donagher, Patricia G., et al. "Race, Sex and Social Example: An Analysis of Character Portrayal on Inter-Racial Television Entertainment," *Psychological Reports* 37 (1975), 1023–1034.

Doolittle, John, and Robert Pepper. "Children's TV Ad Content: 1974," *Journal of Broadcasting* 19 (1975): 131–142.

Downing, Mildred, "Heroine of the Daytime Serial," *Journal of Communication* 24 (1974): 130–139.

Drew, Dan G., and Susan H. Miller. "Sex Stereotyping and Reporting," *Journalism Quarterly* 54 (1977): 142–145.

Erlich, Carol. "The Male Sociologist's Burden: The Place of Women in Marriage and Family Texts," *Journal of Marriage and Family* 33 (1971): 421–430.

Farley, Jennie. "Women's Magazines and the Equal Rights Amendment: Friend or Foe?" *Journal of Communication* 28 (1978): 187–192.

"A Feminist Looks at Children's Books," *School Library Journal* (January 15, 1971): 19–24.

Feminists on Children's Media. "Sexism in Children's Literature," *The United Teacher Magazine* (February 1972): M–1.

Flora, Cornelia B. "The Passive Female: Her Comparative Image by Class and Culture in Women's Magazine Fiction," *Journal of Marriage and the Family* 33 (1971): 435–444.

Fraad, Harriet. "Sex Role Stereotyping and Male-Female Character Distribution in Popular, Prestigious and Sex Role Defining Children's Literature from 1959–1972," Ed.D. Dissertation, Columbia University, New York, 1975.

Franzblau, S., J. Sprafkin, and E. Rubinstein. "Sex on TV: A Content Analysis," *Journal of Communication* 27 (1977): 164–170.

Franzwa, Helen H. "Working Women in Fact and Fiction," *Journal of Communication* 24 (1974): 104–109.

Friedman, Leslie J. *Sex Role Stereotyping in the Mass Media: An Annotated Bibliography,* New York: Garland Press, 1977.

Frisof, Jamie K. "Textbooks and Channeling," *Women: A Journal of Liberation* 1 (1969): 26–28.

Gantz, Walter, Howard Gartenberg, and Cindy Rainbow. "Approaching Invisibility: The Portrayal of the Elderly in Magazine Advertisements," *Journal of Communication* 30 (1980): 56–60.

Gany, O. "Pornography and Respect for Women," *Social Theory and Practice* 4 (1978): 395–421.

Gardner, Jo Ann. "Sesame Street and Sex-Role Stereotypes," *Women: A Journal of Liberation* 1 (1970): 42.

Gerbner, George, Larry Gross, Nancy Signorielli, and Michael Morgan. "Aging with Television: Images on Television Drama and Conceptions of Social Reality," *Journal of Communication* 30 (1980): 37–47.

Goff, David H., Lynda Dysart Goff, and Sara K. Lehrer. "Sex-Role Portrayals of Selected Female Television Characters," *Journal of Broadcasting* 24 (1980): 467–471.

Goffman, Erving. *Gender Advertisements,* New York: Harper & Row, 1979.

Graeber, Dianne B. "A Decade of Sexism in Readers," *Reading Teacher* 26 (1972): 52–58.

Greenberg, Bradley S., Robert Abelman, and Kimberly Neuendorf. "Sex on the Soap Opera: Afternoon Delight," *Journal of Communication* 31 (1981): 83–89.

Greenberg, Bradley S., D. Graef, C. Fernandez-Collado, F. Korzenny, and C. K. Atkin. "Sexual Intimacy on Commercial Television during Prime-Time," *Journal of Broadcasting* 57 (1980): 30–37.

Greenberg, Bradley S., Kimberly Neuendorf, Nancy Buerkel-Rothfuss, and Laura Henderson. "The Soaps: What's on and Who Cares?" *Journal of Broadcasting* 26 (1982): 519–535.

Greenberg, Bradley S., Katrina W. Simmons,

Linda Hogan, and Charles Atkin. "Three Seasons of Television Characters: A Demographic Analysis," *Journal of Broadcasting* 24 (1980): 49–60.

Guenin, Zena B. "Women's Pages in American Newspapers: Missing out on Contemporary Content," *Journalism Quarterly* 52 (1975): 66–69.

Haskell, Deborah. "The Depiction of Women in Leading Roles in Prime Time Television," *Journal of Broadcasting* 23 (1979): 191–196.

Haskell, Molly. *From Reverence to Rape: The Treatment of Women in the Movies,* New York: Holt, Rinehart and Winston, 1974.

Hatch, Mary G., and David L. Hatch. "Problems of Married and Working Women as Presented by Three Popular Working Women's Magazines," *Social Forces* 37 (1958): 148–153.

Hellman, Judith S. "Occupational Roles in Children's Literature," *Elementary School Journal* 77 (1976): 1–4.

Hennesee, Judith, and Joan Nicholson. "NOW Says: TV Commercials Insult Women," *New York Times Magazine* (May 28, 1972): 12–13 *ff.*

Hoerger, Shelly. "Models of Success in Women's Magazines: An Analysis of Biographies Directed at Different Target Audiences," M.A. Thesis, University of Pennsylvania, Philadelphia, 1975.

Houseman, Jerry P. "A Study of Selected Walt Disney Screenplays and Films and the Stereotyping of the Role of the Female," Ph.D. Dissertation, University of the Pacific, Stockton, Calif., 1973.

Howe, Florence. "Feminism and Literature," In Susan K. Cornellon. *Images of Women in Fiction*, Bowling Green, Ky.: Bowling Green Popular Press, 1972, 253–277.

Israel, Lee. "Women in Film: Saving an Endangered Species," *Ms.* 3:8 (1975): 51–57.

Jederman, Jean E. "The Sexual Stereotype of Women in Children's Literature," Ph.D. Dissertation, Northern Illinois University, DeKalb, Ill., 1974.

Journal of Communication, "Daytime Serial Drama: The Continuing Story," a four-article series 31 (3:1981): 83–115.

Kallan, Richard A., and Robert D. Brooks. "Playmate of the Month: Naked but Nice," *Journal of Popular Culture* 8 (1974): 328–336.

Kaplan, Ann. "The Feminist Perspective in Film Studies," *University Film Association Journal* 26 (1974): 5 *ff*.

Kaplan, Milton. "Women in Advertising," *The Quarterly Journal of the Library of Congress* 32 (1975): 366–369.

Katzman, Natan. "Television Soap Operas: What's Been Going on Anyway?" *Public Opinion Quarterly* 35 (1972): 200–212.

Key, Mary Ritchie. "The Role of Male and Female in Children's Books—Dispelling All Doubt," *Wilson Library Bulletin* 46 (1971): 167–176.

Kirschner, Betty Frankle. "Introducing Students to Women's Place in Society," *American Journal of Sociology* 78 (1973): 1051–1054.

Kraft, Linda. "Lost Herstory: The Treatment of Women in Children's Encyclopedias," *Library Journal* 98 (1973): 218–227.

LaDow, Stephanie. "A Content Analysis of Selected Picture Books Examining the Portrayal of Sex Roles and Representation of Males and Females," ERIC, ED 123 165, (1976).

Levine, Joan B. "The Feminine Routine," *Journal of Communication* 26 (1976): 173–175.

Levinson, Richard M. "From Olive Oyl to Sweet Polly Purebred: Sex-Role Stereotypes and Televised Cartoons," *Journal of Popular Culture* 9 (1975): 561–572.

Long, Michele, and R. J. Simon. "The Roles and Statuses of Women on Children and Family TV Programs," *Journalism Quarterly* 51 (1974): 107–110.

Lowry, Gail L., and Malcolm Kirby. "Sex on the Soap Operas: Patterns of Intimacy," *Journal of Communication* 31 (1981): 90–96.

Lukenbill, W. Bernard. "Fathers in Adolescent Novels: Some Implications for Sex Role Reinterpretation," *School Library Journal* 20 (1974): 26–30.

McArthur, Leslie Z., and Beth G. Resho. "The Portrayal of Men and Women in American TV Commercials," *Journal of Social Psychology* 97 (1975): 209–220.

McNeil, Jean C. "Feminism, Femininity and the Television Series: A Content Analysis," *Journal of Broadcasting* 19 (1975): 259–271.

McNeil, Jean C. "Imagery of Women in TV Drama," *Journal of Broadcasting* 19 (1975): 283–288.

Manes, Audrey, and Paula Melnyk. "Televised Models of Female Achievement," *Journal of Applied and Social Psychology* 4 (1974): 365–374.

Maronde, Doreen N. "What Is She Like? A Study of Feminine Roles on Saturday Morning Children's Television," M.S. Thesis, Iowa State University, Ames, Ia., 1974.

Matkov, Rebecca R. "Ladies Home Journal and McCall's in 1960 and 1970: A Content Analysis," M.A. Thesis, University of North Carolina, Chapel Hill, 1972.

Mayers, Sandra L., and K. B. Valentine. "Sex-Role Stereotyping in Saturday Morning Cartoon Shows," *Journal of Broadcasting* 23 (1979): 41–50.

Meade, Marion. "Women and Rock: Sexism Set to Music," *Women: A Journal of Liberation* 2 (1970): 24–26.

Mellen, Joan. *Women and Their Sexuality in the New Film*, New York: Horizon Press, 1974.

Merritt, Sharyne, and Harriet Gross. "Women's Page/Lifestyle Editors: Does Sex Make a Difference?" *Journalism Quarterly*, 55 (1978), 508–514.

Miller, Susan H. "Changes in Women's/Lifestyle Sections," *Journalism Quarterly* 53 (1976): 641–647.

Miller, Susan H. "The Content of News Photos: Women's and Men's Roles," *Journalism Quarterly* 52 (1975): 70–75.

Morris, Monica. "Newspapers and the New Feminists: Black Out As Social Control?" *Journalism Quarterly* 49 (1972): 37–42.

Newkirk, Carole R. "Female Roles in Non-Fiction of Three Women's Magazines," *Journalism Quarterly* 54 (1977): 779–782.

Nietzke, A. "Hostility on the Laugh Track," *Human Behavior* 3 (1974): 64–70.

Nilsen, Alleen P. "Women in Children's Literature," *College English* (May 1971): 918–926.

Nolan, J. D., et al. "Sex Bias on Children's Television Programs," *Journal of Psychology* 96 (1977): 197–204.

Northcott, Herbert, John F. Seggar, and James L. Hinton. "Trends in TV Portrayals of Blacks and Women," *Journalism Quarterly* 52 (1975): 741–744.

O'Kelly, Charlotte G. "Sexism in Children's Television," *Journalism Quarterly* 51 (1974): 722–723.

O'Kelly, Charlotte G., and L. E. Bloomquist. "Women and Blacks on TV," *Journal of Communication* 26 (1976): 179–184.

Palmore, Erdman. "Attitudes toward Aging As Shown by Humor," *Gerontologist* 11 (1971): 181–186.

Petersen, M. "The Visibility and Image of Old People in Television," *Journalism Quarterly* 50 (1973): 569–573.

Poe, Alison. "Active Women in Ads," *Journal of Communication* 26 (1976): 185–192.

Rachlin, Susan K., and Glenda L. Vogt. "Sex Roles as Presented to Children by Coloring Books," *Journal of Popular Culture* 8 (1975): 549–556.

Richards, Carol R. "Stylebooks vs. IWY: The Right to Choose Ms., Miss or Mrs.," *American Society of Newspaper Editors Bulletin* (September 16, 1976): 6–8.

Roberts, Nancy L. "From Pumps, Pearls and Pleats to Pants, Briefcases and Hardhats: Changes in the Portrayal of Women in Advertising and Fiction in *Ladies Home Journal*, 1960–1962 and 1974–1976," ERIC, ED 188 211 (1980).

Roberts, Patricia, and Dewey Chambers. "Sugar and Spice and Almost Always Nice: A Content Analysis of the Caldecotts, 1976," ERIC, ED 127 556 (1980).

Rockman, Ilene F. "Sex Role Stereotyping in Children's Literature: A Selective Bibliography," ERIC, ED 1780920 (1980).

Rosen, Marjorie. *Popcorn Venus: Women, Movies and the American Dream*, New York: Coward McCann and Geoghegan, 1973.

Rossi, Lee. "Whore vs. the Girl-Next-Door: Stereotypes of Women in *Playboy, Penthouse* and *Oui*," *Journal of Popular Culture* 9 (1975): 90–94.

Scheibe, Cyndy. "Sex Roles in Television Commercials," *Journal of Advertising Research* 19 (1979): 23–28.

Schneider, Kenneth, and Sharon B. Schneider. "Trends in Sex Roles in Television Commercials," *Journal of Marketing* 43 (1979): 79–84.

Seggar, John F. "Imagery as Reflected through TV's Cracked Mirror," *Journal of Broadcasting* 19 (1975): 297–299.

Seggar, John F. "Imagery of Women in Television Drama: 1974," *Journal of Broadcasting* 19 (1975): 273–282.

Seggar, John F. "Television's Portrayal of Minorities and Women: 1971–1975," *Journal of Broadcasting* 21 (1977): 436–447.

Seggar, John F. "Women's Imagery on TV: Feminist, Fair Maiden, or Maid?" *Journal of Broadcasting* 19 (1975): 289–294.

Seggar, John F., Jeffrey K. Hafen, and Helena Hannonen-Gladden. "Television's Portrayal of Minorities and Women in Drama and Comedy Drama: 1971–1980," *Journal of Broadcasting* 25 (1981): 277–288.

Seggar, John F., and Penny Wheeler. "World of Work on TV: Ethnic and Sex Representations in TV Drama," *Journal of Broadcasting* 17 (1973): 201–214.

Sexton, Donald, and Phyllis Haberman. "Women in Magazine Advertisements," *Journal of Advertising Research* 14 (1974): 41–46.

Shechtman, Stephen A. "Occupational Portrayal of Men and Women in the Most Frequently Mentioned Television Shows of Preschool Children," ERIC, ED 174 356, (1979).

Sheikh, Anees, et al. "Children's TV Commercials: A Review of Research," *Journal of Communication* 24 (1974): 126–136.

Signorielli, Nancy. "Marital Status in Television Drama: A Case of Reduced Options," *Journal of Broadcasting* 26 (1982): 585–597.

Silverman, L. T., J. N. Sprafkin, and E. A. Rubinstein. "Physical Contact and Sexual Behavior on Prime-Time TV," *Journal of*

Communication 29 (1979): 33–43.

Skelly, Gerald, and William J. Lundstrom. "Male Sex Roles in Magazine Advertising, 1959–1979," *Journal of Communication* 31 (1981): 52–57.

Smith, Don D. "The Social Content of Pornography," *Journal of Communication* 26 (1976): 16–24.

Smith, M. Dwayne, and Marc Matre. "Social Norms and Sex Roles in Romance and Adventure Magazines," *Journalism Quarterly* 52 (1975): 309–315.

Smith, Terry, and Jack Levin. "Social Changes in Sex Roles: An Analysis of Advice Columns," *Journalism Quarterly* 51 (1974): 525–527.

Smythe, Dallas W. "Reality as Presented by Television," *Public Opinion Quarterly* 18 (1954): 143–156.

Sommers, Tish. "The Compounding Impact of Age and Sex, Another Dimension of the Double Standard," *Civil Rights Digest* 7:1 (1974): 2–9.

Spiegleman, Marvin, Carl Terwilliger, and Franklin Fearing. "The Content of Comics: Goals and Means to Goals of Comic Strip Characters," *Journal of Social Psychology* 37 (1953): 189–203.

Sprafkin, Joyce N., and L. Theresa Silverman. "Update: Physically Intimate and Sexual Behavior on Prime Time Television 1978–1979," *Journal of Communication* 31 (1981): 34–40.

Stemple, Diane, and Jane E. Tyler. "Sexism in Advertising," *American Journal of Psychoanalysis* 34 (1974): 271–273.

Sternglanz, Sarah, and Lisa A. Serbin. "Sex Role Stereotyping in Children's TV Programs," *Developmental Psychology* 10 (1974): 710–715.

Stocking, Holly S., et al. "Sex Discrimination in Prime Time Humor," *Journal of Broadcasting* 21 (1977): 448–459.

Taylor, Marjorie. "Sex-Role Stereotypes in Children's Readers," *Elementary English* 50 (1973): 1045–1047.

Tedesco, Nancy. "Patterns in Prime Time," *Journal of Communication* 24 (1974): 119–124.

Tilghman, Romalyn A. "A Content Analysis of Goals and Occupations of Heroines in Three Women's Magazines: 1944–1972," M.S. Thesis, University of Kansas, Lawrence, 1974.

Truby, J. David. "Women's Lib vs. Madison Avenue," *Sexual Behavior* 2 (1972): 44–48.

Tuchman, Gaye. "Women's Depiction by the Mass Media," *Signs* 4 (1979): 528–542.

Tuchman, Gaye, A. K. Daniels, and J. Benet, eds. *Hearth and Home: Images of Women in the Mass Media*, New York: Oxford University Press, 1978.

Venkatesan, M., and Jean P. Loseo. "Women in Magazine Ads: 1959–1971," *Journal of Advertising Research* 15 (1975): 49–58.

Verna, Mary E. "The Female Image in Children's TV Commercials," *Journal of Broadcasting* 19 (1975): 301–309.

Von Hoffman, Nicholas. "Women's Pages: An Irreverent View," *Columbia Journalism Revue* 10:2 (1971): 52–54.

Wagner, Louis C., and James B. Banos. "A Woman's Place: A Follow-Up Analysis of the Roles Portrayed by Women's Magazine Advertisements," *Journal of Marketing Research* 10 (1973): 213–214.

Ward, Francis. "Black Male Images in Film," *Freedomways* 14 (1974): 223–229.

Weitzman, Lenore, et al. "Sex Role Socialization in Picture Books for Preschool Children," *American Journal of Sociology* 77 (1972): 1125–1150.

Welch, Renate L., Aletha Huston-Stein, John C. Wright, and Robert Plehal. "Subtle Sex-Role Cues in Children's Commercials," *Journal of Communication* 29 (1979): 202–209.

Whipple, Thomas W., and Alice E. Courtney. "How to Portray Women in TV Commercials," *Journal of Advertising Research* 20 (1980): 53–59.

"Women: Nine Reports on Role, Image and Message," *Journal of Communication* 24 (1974): 103–155.

Wortzel, Lawrence H., and John M. Frisbe. "Women's Role Portrayal Preferences in Advertisements: An Empirical Study," *Journal of Marketing* 38 (1974): 41–46.

Zillman, Dolf, and Holly Stocking. "Putdown Humor," *Journal of Communication* 26 (1976): 154–163.

Personal and Social Impact of Sex-Role Acquisition

Bem, Sandra, and E. Lenney. "Sex-Typing and the Avoidance of Cross-Sex Behavior," *Journal of Personality and Social Psychology* 33 (1976): 48–54.

Block, J. H. "Another Look at the Sex Differentiation in the Socialization Behaviors of Mothers and Fathers." In F. Denmark and J. Sherman, eds., *Psychology of Women: Future Directions of Research*, New York: Psychological Dimensions, 1978.

Block, J. H. "Assessing Sex Differences: Issues, Problems and Pitfalls," *Merrill-Palmer Quarterly* 22 (1976): 283–308.

Broverman, Inge K., Donald M. Broverman, Frank E. Clarkson, Paul S. Rosencrantz, and Susan R. Vogel. "Sex-Role Stereotypes and Clinical Judgments of Mental Health," *Journal of Consulting Psychology* 34 (1970): 1–7.

Burns, B. "The Emergence and Socialization of Sex Differences in the Earliest Years," *Merrill-Palmer Quarterly* 22 (1976): 229–254.

Clark, S., and M. K. Lane. "Women's Behavioral Manifestations of Traditional and Liberated Role Concepts," *Journal of Psychology* 98 (1978): 81–89.

Cosentino, F., and A. B. Heilbrun. "Anxiety Correlates of Sex-Role Identity in College Students," *Psychological Reports* 14 (1964): 729–730.

Deaux, K., and T. Emswiller. "Explorations of Successful Performance on Sex-Linked Tasks: What Is Skill for the Male Is Luck for the Female," *Journal of Personality and Social Psychology* 29 (1974): 80–85.

Deutsch, Francine M., and Frederick T. L. Leong. "Male Responses to Female Competence," *Sex Roles* 9:1 (1983): 79–90.

Ellis, L. J., and P. M. Bentler. "Traditional Sex-Determined Role Standards and Sex Stereotypes," *Journal of Personality and*

Social Psychology 25 (1973): 28–39.

Erkut, Sumru. "Exploring Sex Differences in Expectancy, Attribution, and Academic Achievement," *Sex Roles: A Journal of Research* 9 (1983): 217–231.

Erskine, Helen. "The Polls: Women's Role," *Public Opinion Quarterly* 35 (1971): 275–290.

Fagot, Beverly. "The Influences of Sex of Child on Parental Reactions to Toddler Children," *Child Development* 49 (1978): 459–465.

Flerx, Vicki C., Dorothy S. Fidler, and Ronald W. Rogers. "Sex Role Stereotypes: Developmental Aspects and Early Intervention," *Child Development* 47 (1976): 998–1007.

Garrett, C. S., et al. "Development of Gender Stereotyping of Adult Occupations in Elementary School Children," *Child Development* 48 (1977): 507–512.

Gerdes, Eugenia P., and Douglas M. Garber. "Sex Bias in Hiring: Effects of Job Demands and Applicant Competence," *Sex Roles: A Journal of Research* 9 (1983): 307–317.

Gilbert, Lucia A., June M. Gallessich, and Sherri L. Evans. "Sex of Faculty Role Model and Students' Self-Perceptions of Competency," *Sex Roles: A Journal of Research* 9 (1983): 597–605.

Goldberg, P. A. "Are Women Prejudiced against Women?" *Trans-Action* 5 (1968): 28–30.

Greenberg, R. P., and P. B. Zeldow. "Effects of Attitudes toward Women on Sex Attribution," *Psychological Reports*: 39 (1976): 807–813.

Hartley, R. E. "A Developmental View of Female Sex-Role Definition and Identification," *Merrill-Palmer Quarterly* 10 (1964): 3–16.

Hartley, R. E., and R. P. Hardesty. "Children's Perceptions of Sex-Roles in Childhood," *Journal of Genetic Psychology* 105 (1964): 43–51.

Hartley, R. E., and Armin Klein. "Sex-Role Concepts among Elementary School Age Girls," *Marriage and Family Living* 21 (1959): 59–64.

Hartley, Ruth E. "Sex-Role Pressures and the

Socialization of the Male Child," in Joseph H. Pleck and Jack Sawyer, eds., *Men and Masculinity*, Englewood Cliffs, N.J.: Prentice-Hall, 1974.

Heilbrun, A. B. "Sex-Role Identity and Achievement Motivation," *Psychological Reports* 12 (1963): 483–490.

Horner, M. "Toward an Understanding of Achievement-Related Conflicts in Women," *Journal of Social Issues* 28 (1972): 157–175.

Kitay, P. M. "A Comparison of the Sexes in Their Attitudes and Beliefs about Women," *Sociometry* 34 (1940): 399–407.

Kohlberg, L. A. "A Cognitive-Developmental Analysis of Children's Sex-Role Concepts and Attitudes," In E. Maccoby, ed. *The Development of Sex Differences*, Stanford, Calif.: Stanford University Press, 1966.

Komarovsky, M. "Functional Analysis of Sex Roles," *American Sociological Review* 15 (1950): 508–516.

Konstam, V., and H. B. Gilbert. "Fear of Success, Sex-Role Orientation and Performance in Differing Experimental Conditions," *Psychological Reports* 42 (1978): 519–528.

Kuhn, D., S. Nash, and L. Brucken. "Sex Role Concepts of Two- and Three-Year-Olds," *Child Development* 49 (1978): 445–451.

Looft, W. R. "Vocational Aspirations of Second Grade Girls," *Psychological Reports* 28 (1971): 241–242.

Lunneborg, P. "Stereotypic Aspects in Masculinity-Femininity Measurement," *Journal of Consulting and Clinical Psychology* 34 (1970): 113–118.

Maccoby, Eleanor E., and C. N. Jacklin. *The Psychology of Sex Differences*, Stanford, Calif.: Stanford University Press, 1974.

Makros, J. R., and E. Koff. "Sex Stereotyping of Children's Success in Mathematics and Reading," *Psychological Reports* 42 (1978): 1287–1293.

McKee, J. P., and A. C. Sheriffs. "The Differential Evaluation of Males and Females," *Journal of Personality* 25 (1957): 356–371.

McKee, J. P., and A. C. Sheriffs. "Men's and Women's Beliefs, Ideals and Self Concepts," *American Journal of Sociology* 64 (1959): 356–363.

Mischel, W. "Sex-Typing and Socialization." In P. H. Mussen, ed. *Carmichael's Manual of Child Psychology*, New York: Wiley, 1970.

Nadelman, L. "Sex Identity in American Culture: Memory, Knowledge and Preference Tests," *Developmental Psychology* 10 (1974): 413–417.

Paludi, Michele A., and William D. Bauer. "Goldberg Revisited: What's in an Author's Name?" *Sex Roles: A Journal of Research* 9 (1983): 387–390.

Pomerantz, S., and W. C. House. "Liberated Versus Traditional Women's Performance Satisfaction and Perception of Ability," *Journal of Psychology* 95 (1977): 205–211.

Price, G. E., and S. B. Borgers. "Evaluation of Sex Stereotyping Effect as Related to Counselor Perceptions of Courses Appropriate for High School Students," *Journal of Counseling Psychology* 24 (1977): 240–243.

Rosen, B. C., and C. S. Aneshensel. "Sex Differences in the Educational-Occupational Expectation Process," *Social Forces* 57 (1978): 164–186.

Rosenkrantz, P. S., et al. "Sex-Role Stereotypes and Self Concepts in College Students," *Journal of Consulting and Clinical Psychology* 32 (1968): 287–295.

Ruble, Thomas L. "Sex Stereotypes: Issues of Change in the 1970s," *Sex Roles: A Journal of Research* 9 (1983): 397–400.

Saario, T. N., C. H. Jacklin, and C. K. Tittle. "Sex-Role Stereotypes in the Public Schools," *Harvard Educational Review* 43 (1973): 386–416.

Schiff, E., and E. J. Koopman. "Relationship of Women's Sex-Role Identity to Self-Esteem and Ego Development," *Journal of Psychology* 98 (1978): 299–305.

Sheriffs, A. C., and R. F. Jarrett. "Sex Differences in Attitudes about Sex Differences," *Journal of Psychology* 35 (1953): 161–168.

Sheriffs, A. C., and John McKee. "Qualitative Aspects of Beliefs about Men and Women," *Journal of Personality* 25 (1957): 451–464.

Siegal, C. L. "Sex Differences in the Occupational Choices of Second Graders," *Journal of Vocational Behavior* 3 (1973): 15–19.

Slevin, Kathleen, and C. Ray Wingrove. "Similarities and Differences among Three Generations of Women in Attitudes toward the Female Role in Contemporary Society," *Sex Roles: A Journal of Research* 9 (1983): 609–623.

Spaeth, J. L. "Differences in the Occupational Achievement Process between Male and Female College Students," *Social Education* 50 (1977): 206–217.

Spence, J. T., R. Helmrich, and J. Stapp. "Ratings of Self and Peers on Sex-Role Attributes and Their Relation of Self-Esteem and Conceptions of Masculinity and Femininity," *Journal of Personality and Social Psychology* 31 (1975): 29–39.

Thompson, S. K. "Gender Labels and Early Sex Role Development," *Child Development* 46 (1975): 339–347.

Tomeh, A. K. "Sex Role Orientation: An Analysis of Structural and Attitudinal Predictors," *Marriage and Family* 40 (1978): 341–354.

Torrance, E. Paul. "Thinking in the Early School Years: Changing Reactions of Girls in Grades Four through Six to Tasks Requiring Creative Scientific Thinking," Minnesota: Bureau of Educational Research Minneapolis, (1960).

Vanier, D. J., and N. M. Hardison. "Age as a Determinant of Sex-Role Stereotyping," *Psychological Reports* 42 (1978): 35–38.

Vener, A. M., and C. A. Snyder. "The Preschool Child's Awareness and Anticipation of Adult Sex-Roles," *Sociometry* 29 (1966): 159–168.

Williams, J. E., S. M. Bennett, and D. L. Best. "Awareness and Expression of Sex Stereotypes in Young Children," *Developmental Psychology* 11 (1977): 635–642.

Williams, John, and Deborah L. Best. *Measuring Sex Stereotypes: A Thirty-Nation Study*, Beverly Hills, Calif.: Sage Publications, 1982.

Wolf, W. C., and R. Rosenfeld. "Sex Structures of Occupations and Job Mobility," *Social Forces* 56 (1978): 823–844.

Zimet, S. G., and C. N. Zimet. "Teachers View People: Sex Role Stereotyping," *Psychological Reports* 41 (1977): 583–591.

Zuckerman, Diana M., and Donald H. Sayre. "Cultural Sex-Role Expectations and Children's Sex-Role Concepts," *Sex Roles: A Journal of Research* 8 (1982): 853–862.

This essay reviews the present status of empirical investigation into television composition, enumerates the major variables involved in studying the structure of television pictures, and summarizes the available quantitative research studies of television's major compositional elements.

Empirical investigation of television's compositional principles has had a slow start. Academic study of the factors involved in the medium's structure—lighting, color, staging, editing, and sound—has only recently begun to emerge. Qualitative research on the nature and effects of television compositional elements is especially rare.

A brief review of the reasons for this scarcity shows that certain compositional elements have been singled out repeatedly, while others have been almost completely ignored. The three most important reasons for the relative shortage of quantitative research studies on television composition are (1) misconceptions about the differences and similarities of the visual communication media, (2) the complexity of visual composition as an object of study, and (3) the general lack of understanding of biometric research procedures.

A failure to recognize key differences between the media of film and television is one reason for the lack of empirical research in television composition.[1] Television scholars have relied on principles borrowed from studies of film, not recognizing the inherent differences between the two media. The time has come to recognize television as a unique medium. Several scholars of television composition, including Tarroni,[2] Millerson,[3] Zettl,[4] and Davis,[5] have underlined these differences. According to Tarroni:

> In television, we have, without any possible doubt, an instrument (the camera and other technical equipment), a material (for after all, sound waves and light waves are themselves a *material*), and a technique (the artist must carry out a series of operations which are by no means identical with those carried out by a film director or the producer of a play).[6]

The lighting materials, instruments, and techniques used by television differ from those used in film, and thus the effects produced by

19
Empirical Studies of Television Composition

Nikos Metallinos

the images of the two media also differ. Zettl warns that the aesthetic potential of such compositional elements of television lighting as "outer orientation," "inner orientation," "external lighting," "internal lighting,"[7] which are unique to the TV medium, have not been fully explored.

Visual images created by the film cameras and projected onto the large film screen differ from images produced and seen on the small TV screen. Picture quality, screen size, and image size are obviously different. The effects of such variables on viewer perception and responses are not so obvious and have not been empirically measured. Some structural similarities exist among the visual communication media of painting, photography, film, and television—primarily in such compositional elements as screen direction; object and area proportions; and perception of colors, balance, shape, scale, dimension, and form, among others.[8, 9] Several empirical studies of these factors have been conducted, particularly in connection with the field forces theory, which covers most of these variables.[10]

Field forces theory holds that the composition of a screen image is a mathematical composite of the strength and direction of influence (vectors) of each compositional element comprising it.

In the composition of television and film images, the elements of time, motion, and editing are crucial, applied differently in each medium. Such timing and editing techniques as fades, dissolves, cuts, and superimpositions mechanically and aesthetically differ in the two media.[11] Empirical studies of the effects of these elements on viewers are yet to be done.[12]

Confusion over television's nature and its social purpose has contributed to the absence of studies on TV sound. It was once common to consider television as equivalent to radio with visuals. This false notion has been a stumbling block in exploring the best ways of matching pictures with sounds.[13]

The study of the syntax of visual messages is a complex endeavor.[14] It is not easy to achieve necessary experimental control and isolation of compositional elements to test their effects on perceived pictorial composition. Recognizing the complexities and the difficulties that such studies present, some researchers have suggested using advanced, more precise, nonlinear measuring methods and techniques.[15]

Most past communication researchers lacked a sufficient understanding of relevant research in other disciplines. They tended to adopt the research approaches and techniques of data collection and analysis common among some behavioral scientists, including speech behaviorists who did not have enough knowledge of studies in perceptual psychology (visual and auditory), neurology (studies of eye fixation and brain functioning in visual and auditory information processing) and physiology, which, if not essential, are useful in understanding the structure of visual message perception.[16]

The principal compositional elements referred to have been explored in the pioneering studies of Kepes,[17] Moholy-Nagy,[18] Taylor,[19] Millerson,[20] Arnheim,[21, 22] Dondis,[23] and Zettl,[24] who have provided theoretical bases for future studies and singled out additional compositional elements requiring exploration and scientific delineation. Among the older film studies, which were either extended to television or borrowed by television researchers, are those on the impact of such elements as color, motion, shot content, camera angle, and speaker credibility.[25] These studies examine visual communication variables common to both media. Although it would be false to conclude that the effects of these compositional elements are the same for both television and film, the contributions of these studies have been significant.[26, 27]

The following section reviews the empirical studies of television composition, which are grouped under the headings lighting and color, staging, editing, sound.

Research Studies of TV Lighting and Color

Lighting and color as aesthetic agents in the media of still photography, film, and television have been discussed by Faber,[28] who speculated on the role of light and color in revealing environment; Arnheim,[29] who focused mainly on light in color paintings, still photography, and film; Millerson,[30] who considered the role of light and color in the structure of TV pictures; Dondis,[31] who outlined the role of light and color as prime elements of the visual message, including paintings, photographs, and moving images; and Zettl,[32] who dealt specifically with light and color as compositional elements (aesthetic agents) of television pictures.

Quantitative studies in which some aspect of lighting and/or color for film and television was the principal or secondary variable can be divided into those (1) dealing with the effects of lighting angles, (2) discussing the differences, similarities, and effects of color vs. black-and-white pictures, and (3) examining color as an effective element of instructional materials.

Lighting angle refers to the angle at which an object being televised (or filmed) is struck by the light from a designated lighting instrument(s). Figure 19-1 illustrates that two angular measures are required to place a lighting instrument in three-dimensional space—a horizontal angle and a vertical angle. In most cases, the lighting instrument in these studies is the key light, typically defined as the instrument establishing the scene's principal apparent lighting source.

In support of Millerson's[33] and Zettl's[34] speculations, a Tannenbaum and Fosdick study on lighting angles[35] showed that manipulating the angle of the key light source affected viewer perceptions. Low-angle or high-angle lighting of subjects can create either a negative (low key) or a positive (high key) viewer response.

The perceived differences between black-and-white and color images as well as color preferences, color associations, and color attributes have been explored by researchers in audiovisual communication media. Vandemere's study of the differences between color and black and white in instructional films[36] bridges film and video studies of the subject. Scanlon's experimental study of viewer perceptions of color and black-and-white television

was the first attempt to measure such differences.[37] Additional representative studies include Winn and Everett on the effectiveness of rating color and black-and-white pictures;[38] Katzman and Nyenhuis on color and black and white as perceptual stimuli;[39] Booth and Miller[40] and Spangenberg[41] on the differences between learning from black-and-white and learning from color stimuli; and Winn on the structure of multiple free associations to words, to black-and-white pictures, and to color pictures.[42] These studies identified areas of communication in which color pictures appear to be preferable to black and white when used to (1) provide information, (2) attract viewer attention to specific objects or situations, (3) facilitate learning, and (4) enhance and/or elicit viewer aesthetic responses.

Empirical studies dealing with the use of color as a contributing element in enhancing viewer ability to receive instruction include Dwyer[43] and Kanner,[44] studies dealing with color stimuli as instructional variables, and Huntley's study of color as an emotional factor in television.[45] Snowberg[46] found that the best background colors for graphics legibility are (in order of legibility) white, yellow, green, red, and blue. Franzwa, studying picture familiarity and retention of visual detail, found that color pictures of familiar animals were retained better than their black-and-white counterparts.[47] Research studies on the use of colors in art, design, and advertising, in terms of color preferences,[48, 49] color associations,[50] and color attributes[51, 52] reveal some interesting findings. However, considering that color preferences, associations, and attributes change according to age, locality, education, income, sex, nationality, etc., these findings tend to be inconsistent, highly specialized, and thus ungeneralizable. Chu and Schramm[53] review studies on television in education. Schramm also has pointed to the need for formative research:

I fear the preceding pages have proved that whereas one can derive stimulating general ideas from theoretical research in television, when a producer wants to translate these into

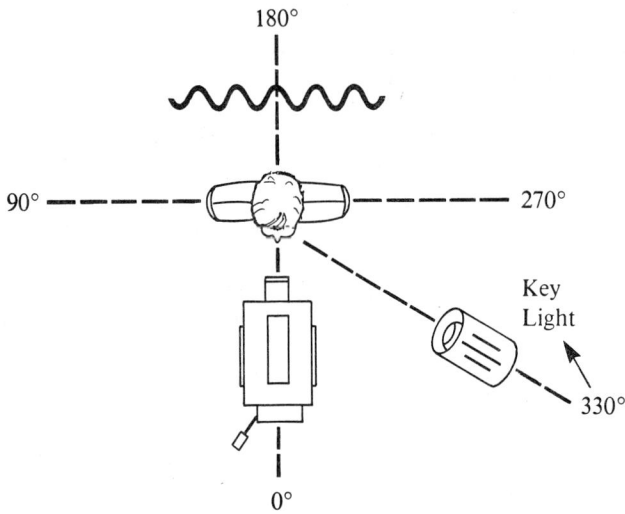

a. Horizontal Lighting Angle of a Key Light

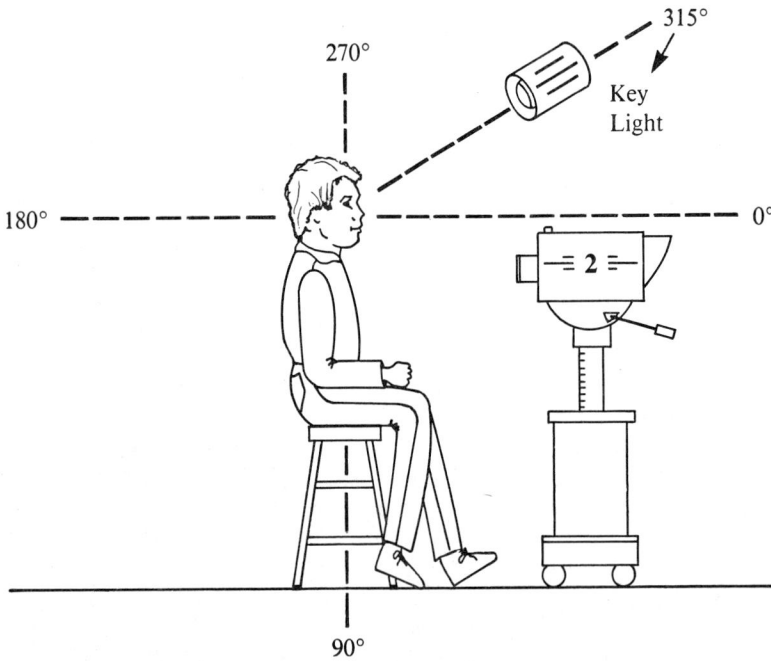

b. Vertical Lighting Angle of a Key Light

Figure 19-1 Angular location of a lighting source.

specific guidance, he must rely either on his own creative instincts or on formative research. And without in the least underestimating the value of creativity, I would say that I have seldom seen an activity that has greater need than ETV for formative research.[54]

Formative research, the subject of an essay by Bittner and Carroll in this volume, consists of research during the development and production of a program aimed at improving the program's effectiveness.

Research Studies on TV Staging

Studies of TV staging include empirical studies dealing with placement and interaction of visual elements within the concentrated space of the television screen. These studies typically attempt to verify existing theories of effective composition of moving images. TV staging involves such compositional elements as (1) size of image; (2) camera angle; (3) shape, form, proportion, or direction of action; (4) perception of space, object size, and depth cues; (5) field forces; and (6) multiscreen presentations.

Studies of image size are concerned with the relationship between screen size and viewer perception and the relative dominance of some object or objects within the screen. Studies of screen size versus viewer perception include studies of human factors in engineering designs of electronic screens. Using methods from psychophysical scaling, Hatada, Sakata, and Kusaka[55] explored the lower limit of screen size and position associated with viewer sensation of reality. Figure 19-2 illustrates their conclusions as to the ideal real screen.

Tiemens's study of the visual composition of the 1976 Ford-Carter Presidential debate is a careful study of dominance within the screen.[56] Each shot of each debate was examined on a screen divided into ruled squares in order to estimate the relative area of the screen occupied by each candidate. Other image size studies include investigations of image size as visual language,[57] of image size changes as perceived by children,[58] of image size versus speaker credibility,[59] of the possible value of varying television shots,[60] and the psychological effect of image size variation.[61] An interesting study by Wurtzel and Dominick compared the use of closeup and medium shots in televising various acting styles.[62]

Camera angle as a variable of visual composition has been studied by researchers in photography, film, and lately in television. Tiemens's[63] study on the relationship between camera angle and credibility of speaker, along with Mandell and Shaw's[64] study on the effects of camera angle and body movements and Baggeley and Duck's[65] experiments on the effects of camera angle in educational TV programs, are among the pioneering efforts. The McCain et al. study on the effects of camera angle on source credibility and attraction is one of the most recent on the subject.[66] Extended from previous research on photography and film and expanded into television, these studies provide valuable insight into general principles of television composition. They are positive contributions toward the building of a theory of television aesthetics.

Research on viewer preference for certain shapes and viewer perception of the orientation of objects within the visual field has been conducted by Dwyer,[67] who attempted to measure the relative effectiveness of visual illustrations of different shapes. French manipulated the complexity of various pictorial patterns to affect children's perception.[68] Myatt and Carter[69] systematically varied pictorial variables of color, shape, proportion, and picture detail to estimate their combined effect on children. Viewers' relative preferences for such simple figures as triangles, circles, squares, and rectangles have long been studied by perceptual psychologists.[70, 71, 72] More research extending these perceptual studies to the familiar images of television is warranted.

A number of studies have dealt with picture elements affecting perceptions of image depth. Mangan has studied the iconic (pictorial) literacy and education of people of different cultures.[73] Evans and Seddon investigated the perception of depth cues among Nigerian stu-

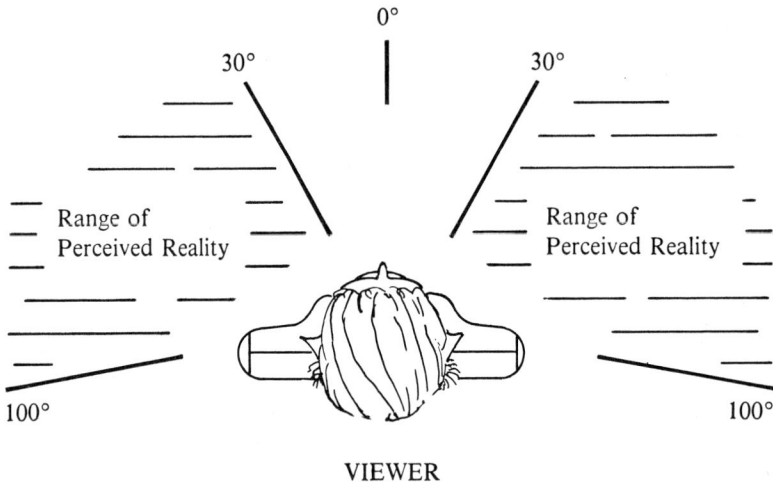

a. Horizontal Viewing Angle Required
for Perception of Reality

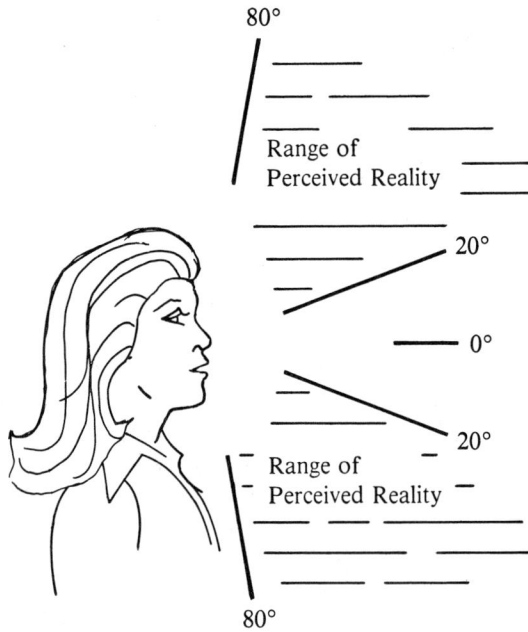

b. Vertical Viewing Angle Required
for Perception of Reality

Figure 19-2   Range of screen viewing angles yielding perception of reality.

dents.[74] Deregowski studied both depth cues and pictorial perception of people from different cultures.[75, 76] Miller also studied the perception of pictorial materials by people of different cultures.[77] Nicholson and Sedden examined the perception of pictorial spatial relationships by Nigerian students.[78] The rapid development of satellite communication has increased the need for a global understanding of visual communication signals among all cultures.[79]

Field force theories of composition have been discussed by Arnheim,[80] Millerson,[81] Dondis,[82] and Zettl.[83] Screen field forces interact and energize the field for the audience. Field forces include asymmetry of the screen, main direction, magnetism of the frame, attraction of mass, figure-ground relationships, psychological closure, and vectors. Empirical investigations derived from field forces theory will be important to future understanding of television composition.[84]

The principles of visual composition — movement, direction, balance, shape, form, growth, space, tension, expression[85] — along with the principles of visual perception — constancy, space, depth, distance, motion[86] — and the neurological principles governing the processing and the cognition of visual stimuli by the two hemispheres of the human brain,[87] will all be considered by systematic study of the field force theory.[88]

A detailed review of existing research on field forces has been provided by the author elsewhere.[89] It is worth reviewing selected quantitative studies on the asymmetry of the screen, magnetism of the frame, and figure-ground interrelations that have contributed to the study of television composition. An Avery and Tiemens study on the syntax of visual messages concluded that the semantic differential as a technique of measuring aesthetic dimension (the asymmetric placement of visual elements within the field) is more accurate than the Likert scale technique,[90] which was adopted by Metallinos in an early study on the subject.[91] Fletcher's study of asymmetry, using magnitude estimation scaling,[92] asked a sample of Blacks and a sample of Caucasians to rate

the attractiveness of asymmetric landscapes. He concluded that, if location of mass rather than direction of index vector is considered the appropriate index to asymmetry, Blacks may prefer left over right asymmetry.

The only extant studies on figure-ground relationships as a field force are those by Baggeley and Duck[93] and Coldevin[94, 95] on the effects of adding background elements behind the newscaster. On magnetism of the frame as a field force, the exploratory study by Herbener et al.[96] emphasizes the importance of the frame in visual composition. Unfortunately, empirical investigations have not been conducted on the field forces of attraction of mass, main direction, psychological closure, and vectors.

In the many studies on multi-image presentations, practitioners, theorists, and researchers cover both the perception and the effects of such presentations.[97, 98] Zettl extended such research to the specific study of multiscreen television.[99] He investigated (1) difference between divided screen and multiscreens; (2) number of screens and screen configuration; (3) screen gestalt; (4) screen emphasis and vector structure; (5) montage; and (6) technical considerations. Explaining his approach, Zettl states:

> Rather than dividing a single screen into smaller units and thereby reducing each spatial field in size, we expand the field of the television screen into several self-contained, yet interdependent, space-time entities. Very much like the tiles of a mosaic, the multiple screens combine and expand into a complex, yet clarified and intensified screen Gestalt.[100]

Zettl emphasizes that additional investigation and research are "essential if we are to develop a valid and useful multi-screen aesthetic."[101]

It is evident from this review that empirical studies on television staging are preliminary at best. Only a few elements of television screen images have been studied formally. As Herbener states: "The possibilities are extensive, and as graphic communication becomes increasingly influential in our lives, the empirical exploration of these possibilities becomes increasingly important."[102]

Research Studies on TV Editing

Time, motion, and editing collectively constitute the third major area of inquiry in television composition. To arrive at the television editing techniques he considers unique to television, Zettl extensively discusses the factors of time and timing in making the TV picture.[103] Malik also emphasizes the importance of movements (electronic beam, camera, inner movement) in the construction of the moving image.[104] Time and motion, as compositional factors, are considered the synthetic catalysts of television editing, which Zettl calls "*tertium quid,*" the third thing.[105] The significance of timing, movement, and editing or montage as aesthetic energizers that stimulate viewer response has also been underlined by Millerson, who suggests various specific television editing techniques.[106]

Film montage theories, developed by Eisenstein,[107] Pudovkin,[108] Arnheim,[109] Goldberg,[110] and Gregory,[111] provide the stimulus for empirical research on such film editing topics as "The Effect of Motion and Cutting-Rate in Motion Pictures,"[112] "Film Movement and Affective Response and Effect on Learning and Attitude Formation,"[113] "The Bilateral Effect of Film Context,"[114] and "Cognitive Aspects of Sequence in Visual Communication."[115] Millerson[116] and Zettl[117] provide theoretical concepts on which more TV editing research could be based.

The effects of such TV editing elements as cutaways or cutting on action and editing for a three-person interview or ABC cutting, were studied by Baggeley and Duck.[118, 119] Qualitative research and verification of TV editing factors observed by Zettl[120] (such as continuing or converging index and motion vectors, analytical or sequential editing) and idea-associative montage techniques, such as comparison and collision, are needed.

It has been speculated that the small size, low quality television picture requires fast pace to attract and keep viewer attention. This fast pace may, in turn, cause viewer hyperactivity—what Berger calls "hyperkinesis."[121] According to Berger:

The more we react to signals rather than symbols (though the relationship between the two is complicated, I admit), the more impulsive we become, the more we approach hyperkinesis. The programming on television also contributes to our excitability. In some commercials, for example, there may be as many as 70 or 80 quick cuts in a 60 second advertisement, which means that we become terribly "speeded-up" as we watch the images flickering before us.[122]

On the other hand, Anderson et al.,[123] examining hyperactivity, impulsivity, disorganized behavior, and shortened attention spans in preschool children watching *Sesame Street,* found no evidence to support the notion that "rapid television pacing has an immediately negative impact on preschool children's behavior."[124] This finding coincides with that of an early study by Schlater on the effects of television's fast pace.[125]

Undoubtedly, more systematic research is needed on these and other compositional factors pertinent to TV editing. The rules for selecting shots and the laws dictating their juxtaposition could become critical in television composition. As Millerson states:

We may not know why we are influenced in particular ways by certain visual arrangements, but their effects are regular enough to provide us with rational working principles, so we no longer need to distribute subjects around tentatively, hoping that they will produce the effect we want. We develop a background of understanding that helps us to arrange, correct and improve camera shots in an organized fashion.[126]

Research Studies on TV Sound

The conventional TV picture, and consequently the conventional TV program, consist of both sights and sounds. The aesthetic impact of a program depends on the harmonic interaction of both elements. Some observers suggest that "the ears may be more vital than the eyes in getting the most of television."[127] Critics of educational television productions claim that "historically the producers and re-producers of educational broadcast materials have concentrated on the video to the detriment of the audio."[128]

The audio component of the ordinary television receiver has always been of relatively low quality, partly because of misunderstandings as to what can be broadcast and of the economics involved in corrrecting it. In explaining the reasons for such low quality television sound components, Schubin states:

> Why don't set manufacturers improve their sound systems? They say it's because television stations don't transmit programming that requires good sound. The television stations say they don't transmit such programs, because their networks don't feed them. Their networks don't feed them, because network audio lines are incapable of high fidelity transmission. And the common carrier in charge of the audio lines? They claim there is no need to upgrade the lines — witness the fact that the set manufacturers have not improved their sets.[129]

Empirical research on any aspect of television sound is rare. Only a few scholars such as Zettl[130] and Millerson[131] have stressed the significance of TV sound as an aesthetic agent as important as visuals. Zettl, for example, observes that television "demands close-up [clear, distinct and supportive] sounds, small sounds brought close to the ears of the perceivers, very much like the visual close-up that can elevate a simple gesture to an intense art."[132] Millerson theorizes that television's aural-visual relationships are due to: (1) the picture's impact on the sound $S \leftarrow P$, (2) the sound's impact on the picture $P \leftarrow S$, (3) the cumulative effect of sound and pictures $S + P = E$, and (4) some further idea carried by picture and sound combined $S + P = X$.[133]

Most quantitative research on the nature of sound (its perception and its effects on listeners) has been conducted by physicists,[134] perceptual psychologists,[135] and musicologists.[136] The bulk of studies on sound in the media of film and television (1) deal with the impact of audio in preparing instructional materials in education, (2) compare audio-recorded messages to live instruction, and (3) compare the effectiveness of multiple audio channel recordings of instructional materials for educational purposes.

Among the studies exploring the impact of audio in preparing instructional materials in education are Dworkin and Holden's[137] pioneering study comparing filmstrip sounds with those of the classroom lecture. Hempstead studied the influence of media-message components on student recall and attitude toward the learning experience.[138] Audio-recorded messages are compared to live instruction in the study by Morrel et al.[139] of the cognitive and affective effects of audio-programmed electronic feedback and oral-teacher feedback; Main and Griffiths[140] report a similar study. Hartman's[141] study of recognition learning under multiple channel presentations and Nasser and McEwen's[142] study on the impact of the alternative media channels in learning are among the most important in this area. A comprehensive review and evaluation of the results of research on the use of audiovisual media for teaching adults is provided by Campeau,[143] although it is slightly out of date.

No empirical research studies have been done on (1) the nature of television sounds, (2) the functions of TV sounds, (3) the characteristics of television sound as opposed to film sound, and (4) the criteria for combining TV sound harmonically and compatibly with the corresponding pictures. As Zettl suggested some time ago:

> A careful analysis of the relationship of pictures and sounds, their rhythmic and structural similarities and differences, their harmonic and contrapuntal combinations, can, of course, lead to significant insights into the aesthetic potentials of the television medium.[144]

Summary

The slow development of empirical research on television composition is due to (1) the inability of early media theorists to separate the scope and nature of television from those of the film, (2) the complexity inherent in the control and measurement of television compositional factors, and (3) a lack of understanding of biometric research procedures (mostly in the areas of perception, neurology, and physiology).

Existing empirical studies of television composition can be grouped into four main areas—lighting and color, staging, editing, and sound.

1. Studies of TV lighting and color include compositional variables that (a) deal with the effects of lighting angles; (b) discuss the differences, the similarities, and the effects of color versus black-and-white pictures; and (c) examine color as an effective factor in instructional materials.
2. Studies on TV staging discuss (a) size of images; (b) camera angle; (c) shape, form, proportion, direction of action; (d) perception of space, object size, and depth cues; and (e) field forces and multiscreen presentations.
3. Studies on TV editing include such compositional factors as (a) television timing, (b) continuity editing, and (c) rapid pace.
4. No research studies have been done on TV sound (as a compositional factor). Only a few studies on the use of sound in preparing instructional materials could be cited.

The limited empirical research on television composition should encourage scholars to pursue this area. Television is a new and rapidly expanding medium. The technological developments in such areas as TV production automation, computerized editing, digital television, and color synthesizers underscore the importance of studying television composition and viewer response to visual messages. The structure of the visual message is a complex phenomenon for study. As Dondis points out:

> To understand visual media, to express ideas in visual terminology, it will be necessary to study the components of visual intelligence,

the basic elements, the syntactical structures, the perceptual mechanisms, the techniques, the styles and systems. By studying them, we can control them as man has learned to understand, control and use language. Then, and only then, will we achieve visual literacy.[145]

Endnotes

1. M. Murray, *The Video-tape Book: A Basic Guide to Portable TV Production* (New York: Taplinger Publishing, 1975), 24–32.
2. E. Tarroni, "The Aesthetics of Television," *Television: The Critical View*, H. Newcomb, ed. (New York: Oxford University Press, 1979), 437–461.
3. G. Millerson, *The Technique of Television Production*, 9th ed. (New York: Hasting House Publishers, 1972), 328–353.
4. H. Zettl, *Sight, Sound, Motion: Applied Media Aesthetics* (Belmont, Calif.: Wadsworth Publishing, 1973), 100–147.
5. D. Davis, "Television and Art: The Circle and the Triangle," *TV and the Visual Arts*, Prix Italia, ed. (Milano: ERI/Editioni RAI Radio-Televisione-Italiano, 1979), 27.
6. Tarroni, op. cit., 440.
7. H. Zettl, "The Rare Case of Television Aesthetics," *Journal of the University Film Association* 30 (1978): 3–8.
8. R. Arnheim, *Art and Visual Perception* (Berkeley: University of California Press, 1974), 32–359.
9. D. Dondis, *A Primer of Visual Literacy* (Cambridge, Mass.: MIT Press, 1973), 39–66.
10. N. Metallinos and R. K. Tiemens, "Asymmetry of the Screen: The Effect of Left Versus Right Placement of Television Images," *Journal of Broadcasting* 21 (1977): 21–33.
11. Zettl, "The Rare Case of Television Aes-

thetics," 6–8.

12. Metallinos, "Looking to New Areas for Research in Broadcasting," *Feedback* 21 (1979): 18–22.

13. Zettl, *Sight, Sound, Motion: Applied Media Aesthetics*, 367–371.

14. R. K. Avery and R. K. Tiemens, "The Syntax of Visual Messages: An Empirical Investigation of the Asymmetry of the Frame Theory," paper presented to the Speech Communication Association, Washington, D.C., December 19, 1975, 1.

15. J. E. Fletcher, "Empirical Studies on Visual Communication: Some Methodological Considerations," paper presented to the Speech Communication Association, Minneapolis, Minn., November 3, 1978, 2.

16. M. F. Malik, "Video Psychology," *Journal of the University Film Association* 30 (1978): 9–13.

17. G. Kepes, *Language in Vision* (Chicago: Paul Theobold and Co., 1944).

18. L. Moholy-Nagy, *Vision In Motion* (Chicago: Paul Theobold and Co., 1947).

19. J. A. Taylor, *Design and Expression in the Visual Arts* (New York: Dover Publications, 1964).

20. Millerson, *The Technique of Television Production*.

21. R. Arnheim, *Film As Art* (Chicago: University of Chicago Press, 1953).

22. Arnheim, *Art and Visual Perception*.

23. Dondis, op. cit.

24. Zettl, *Sight, Sound, Motion: Applied Media Aesthetics*.

25. R. K. Avery and R. K. Tiemens, "Visual Communication Research: A Point of View," *Feedback* 17 (1976): 3–6.

26. R. W. Wagner, "Film Research: The Need for a New Breed," *Educational Communication and Technology Journal* 26 (1978): 65–78.

27. G. Coldevin, "Experimental Research in Television Production Techniques and Presentation Strategies: Current Directions," *Journal of Educational TV and Other Media* 6 (1980): 92–98.

28. B. Faber, *Light, Color and Environment* (New York: Van Nostrand Reinhold, 1972).

29. Arnheim, *Art and Visual Perception*, 292–323.

30. Millerson, op. cit., 61–92, 411–433.

31. Dondis, op. cit., 50–56, 85–103.

32. Zettl, *Sight, Sound, Motion: Applied Media Aesthetics*, 15–97.

33. Millerson, op. cit., 59.

34. Zettl, op. cit., 30.

35. P. H. Tannenbaum and J. A. Fosdick, "The Effect of Light Angle on the Judgement of Photographed Subject," *AV Communication Review* 8 (1970): 253–262.

36. A. W. Vandermere, "Color vs. Black and White in Instructional Film," *AV Communication Review* 2 (1953): 121–134.

37. T. J. Scanlon, "Viewer's Perception of Color, Black-and-White TV: An Experiment," *Journalism Quarterly* 47 (1970): 366–368.

38. W. D. Winn and R. J. Everett, "Affective Rating of Color and Black and White Pictures," *Educational Communication and Technology Journal* 27 (1979): 148–156.

39. N. Katzman and J. Nyenhuis, "Color vs. Black and White Effects on Learning, Opinion, and Attention," *AV Communication Review* 20 (1972): 16–28.

40. G. D. Booth and H. R. Miller, "Effectiveness of Monochrome and Color Presentations in Facilitating Different Learning," *AV Communication Review* 22 (1976): 403–422.

41. R. Spangenberg, "What Is Better for Learning? Color or Black and White?" *Audio-Visual Instruction* 21 (1976): 80.

42. W. D. Winn, "The Structure of Multiple Free Associations to Words, Black and White Pictures and Color Pictures," *AV Communication Review* 24 (1976): 273–293.

43. F. M. Dwyer, "Color as an Instructional Variable," *AV Communication Review* 19 (1971): 399–416.

44. J. H. Kanner, *The Instructional Effec-*

tiveness of Color in Television: A Review of the Evidence (Stanford, Calif.: ERIC Clearinghouse on Educational Media and Technology, 1968).

45. S. L. Huntley, "Color as an Emotional Factor in Television," *Journal of Broadcasting* 2 (1958): 259–262.

46. R. L. Snowberg, "Bases for the Selection of Background Colors for Transparencies," *AV Communication Review* 21 (1973): 191–207.

47. D. Franzwa, "Influence of Meaningfulness, Picture Details, and Presentation Mode of Visual Perception," *AV Communication Review* 21 (1973): 209–223.

48. T. Nelson, D. Allan, and J. Nelson, "Cultural Differences in the Use of Colors in Northwest Canada," *International Journal of Psychology* 6 (1971): 283–392.

49. K. Gotz and K. Gotz, "Color Preference of Art Students: Surface Colors I," *Perceptual and Motor Skills* 35 (1975): 1103–1109.

50. R. Cimbalo, K. Beck, and D. Sendziak, "Emotionally Toned Pictures and Color Selection for Children and College Students," *The Journal of Genetic Psychology* 133 (1978): 303–304.

51. H. Johnson, "Love is Red, and Power is Blue, Sex is Pink . . . What Colour Are You?" *Marketing Communications* 296 (1968): 103.

52. R. Nelson, *The Design of Advertising* (Dubuque, Iowa: Wm. C. Brown Publishing, 1973).

53. G. L. Chu and W. Schramm, *Learning From Television: What the Research Says* (Washington, D.C.: National Association of Educational Broadcasters, 1967).

54. W. Schramm, "The Researcher and the Producer in ETV," *Public Telecommunications Review* 5 (1977): 21.

55. Toyohiko Hatada, Haruo Sakata, and Hideo Kusaka, "Psychophysical Analysis of the Sensation of Reality Induced by a Visual Wide-Field Display," *SMPTE Journal* 89 (1980): 560–569.

56. R. K. Tiemens, "A Visual Analysis of the 1976 Presidential Debates," *Speech Monographs* (1978).

57. S. R. Acker and R. K. Tiemens, "Image Size as an Element of Visual Language," paper presented to the Speech Communication Association, Washington, D.C., December 1976.

58. R. Tiemens and S. Acker, "Children's Perception in Size of Televised Images," *Human Communication Research* 7 (1981): 340–346.

59. S. C. Wood, "The Relationship between Image Size and Speaker Credibility in Televised Mass Communication," paper presented to the Speech Communication Association, San Antonio, Texas, November 1979.

60. T. McCain and G. Repensky, "The Effect of Camera Shot on Interpersonal Attractiveness for Comedy Performances," paper presented to the Speech Communication Association, Chicago, December 1972.

61. J. P. Baggeley and S. W. Duck, "Psychological Effects of Image Variations," *Video and Film Communication* 8 (1975): 11–17.

62. A. H. Wurtzel and J. R. Dominick, "Evaluation of Television Drama: Interaction of Acting Styles and Shot Selection," *Journal of Broadcasting* 16 (1972): 103–110.

63. R. K. Tiemens, "Some Relationships of Camera Angle to Communication Credibility, *Journal of Broadcasting* 14 (1970): 483–490.

64. L. M. Mandell and D. L. Shaw, "Judging People in the News Unconsciously: Effects of Camera Angle and Bodily Activity," *Journal of Broadcasting* 17 (1973): 353–362.

65. J. P. Baggeley and S. W. Duck, "Experiments in ETV: Further Effects on Camera Angle," *Educational Broadcasting International* 8 (1975): 183–184.

66. T. A. McCain, J. Chilberg, and J. Wakshlag, "The Effect of Camera Angle on Source Credibility and Attraction,"

Journal of Broadcasting 21 (1977): 35–46.

67. F. J. Dwyer, "Exploratory Studies in the Effectiveness of Visual Illustrations," *AV Communication Review* 18 (1970): 235–249.

68. J. E. French, "Children's Preference for Pictures of Varied Complexity Pictorial Pattern," *Elementary School Journal* 53 (1952): 90–95.

69. B. Myatt and J. M. Carter, "Picture Preference of Children and Young Adults," *Educational Communication and Technology Journal* 27 (1979): 45–53.

70. G. Murch, *Visual and Auditory Perception* (New York: Bobbs-Merrill, 1973), 122–126.

71. Taylor, *Design and Expression in the Visual Arts*, 10–25.

72. N. Metallinos, "Children's Perception, Retention and Preference of Asymmetrical Composition in Pictures," in R. Braden and A. Walker, eds., *Television and Visual Literacy: Readings From the 13th Annual Conference of I.V.L.A.* (Bloomington, Ind.: Indiana University Press, 1982), 33–34.

73. J. Mangan, "Cultural Conventions of Pictorial Representation: Iconic Literacy and Education," *Educational Communication and Technology Journal* 26 (1978): 245–267.

74. G. S. Evans and G. M. Seddon, "Responsiveness of Nigerian Students to Pictorial Depth Cues," *Educational Communication and Technology Journal* 26 (1978): 303–320.

75. J. B. Deregowski, "Orientation and Perception of Pictorial Depth," *International Journal of Pychology* 6 (1971): 111–114.

76. J. B. Deregowski, "Pictorial Perception and Culture," *Scientific American* 227 (1972): 82–88.

77. R. J. Miller, "Cross-Cultural Research in the Perception of Pictorial Materials," *Psychological Bulletin* 80 (1973): 335–350.

78. J. R. Nicholson and G. M. Seddon, "The Understanding of Pictorial Special Relationships by Nigerian Secondary School Students," *Journal of Cross-Cultural Psychology* 8 (1977): 381–400.

79. L. Briggs, "Visual Literacy: A Current Problem of Needs and Resources," *Vision and Hindsight: The Future of Communications* (London: International Institute of Communications, 1976), 5.

80. Arnheim, *Art and Visual Perception*, 1–31.

81. Millerson, op. cit., 249–295.

82. Dondis, op. cit., 20–28.

83. Zettl, *Sight, Sound, Motion: Applied Media Aesthetics*, 116–147.

84. N. Metallinos, "Composition of the TV Picture: Some Hypotheses to Test the Forces Operating within the Television Screen," *Educational Communication and Technology Journal* 27 (1979): 203–214.

85. Arnheim, *Art and Visual Perception,* 1–425.

86. J. Boddy, *Brain Systems and Psychological Concerts* (New York: John Wiley, 1978).

87. C. Bloomer, *Principles of Visual Perception* (New York: Van Nostrand Reinhold, 1976).

88. N. Metallinos, "Biometric Research in Neurology and Perception Related to the Study of Visual Communication," paper presented to the Broadcast Educators Association, Dallas, Texas, March 23, 1979.

89. N. Metallinos, "Composition of the TV Picture: Some Hypotheses to Test the Forces Operating Within the Television Screen."

90. R. K. Avery and R. K. Tiemens, "The Syntax of Visual Messages: An Empirical Investigation of the Asymmetry of the Frame Theory," paper presented to the Speech Communication Association, Washington, D.C., December 29, 1975.

91. N. Metallinos, "Asymmetry of the Screen: The Effect of Left vs. Right Ori-

entation in Television Images," Ph.D. Dissertation, University of Utah, Salt Lake City, 1975.

92. J. E. Fletcher, "Right and Left Asymmetry Assessment by Magnitude Estimation," paper presented to the Speech Communication Association, Washington, D.C., December 4, 1977.

93. J. P. Baggeley and S. W. Duck, "Experiments in ETV: Effects of Adding Background," *Educational Broadcasting International* 7 (1976): 208–209.

94. G. O. Coldevin, "Comparative Effectiveness of TV Production Variables," *Journal of Educational Television* 2 (1976): 21–24.

95. G. O. Coldevin, "Experiments in TV Presentation Strategies: Effectiveness of Full Screen vs. Corner Screen Location Establishment Background Visuals," *Educational Broadcasting International* 11 (1978): 17–18.

96. G. F. Herbener, G. N. Van Tubergen, and S. S. Withlow, "Dynamics of the Frame in Visual Communication," *Educational Communication and Technology Journal* 27 (1979): 83–88.

97. D. G. Perrin, "A Theory of Multi-Image Communication," *AV Communication Review* 17 (1969): 368–381.

98. E. B. Golstein, "The Perception of Multiple-Images," *AV Communication Review* 23 (1975): 34–68.

99. H. Zettl, "Towards a Multi-Screen Television Aesthetic: Some Structural Considerations," *Journal of Broadcasting* 21 (1977): 5–19.

100. Zettl, "Towards a Multi-Screen Television Aesthetic: Some Structural Considerations," 6.

101. Ibid., 18.

102. Herbener et al., "Dynamics of the Frame in Visual Communications," 83.

103. Zettl, *Sight, Sound, Motion: Applied Media Aesthetics*, 295–325.

104. Malik, "Video Psychology," 11.

105. Zettl, *Sight, Sound, Motion: Applied Media Aesthetics,* 314.

106. Millerson, *The Technique of Television Production*, 236–318.

107. S. M. Eisenstein, *Film Form*, Jay Leyda, ed. and trans. (New York: Harcourt Brace, 1957).

108. V. I. Pudovkin, *Film Technique and Film Acting* (London: Vision Press, 1958).

109. R. Arnheim, *Film As Art* (Berkeley: University of California Press, 1966).

110. H. D. Goldberg, "The Role of Cutting in the Perception of the Motion Picture," *Journal of Applied Psychology* 35 (1951): 70–71.

111. J. R. Gregory, "Some Psychological Aspects of Motion Picture Montage," Ph.D. Dissertation, Urbana, University of Illinois, 1961.

112. R. Penn, "The Effect of Motion and Cutting-Rate in Motion Pictures," *AV Communication Review* 19 (1971): 29–50.

113. W. C. Miller, "Film Movement and Affective Response and Effect on Learning and Attitude Formation," *AV Communication Review* 17 (1969): 172–181.

114. J. M. Foley, "The Bilateral Effect of Film Context," Master's Thesis, University of Iowa, Iowa City, 1966.

115. S. Worth, "Cognitive Aspects of Sequence in Visual Communication," *AV Communication Review* 16 (1968): 121–145.

116. Millerson, *The Technique of Television Production*.

117. Zettl, *Sight, Sound, Motion: Applied Media Aesthetics*.

118. J. P. Baggeley and S. W. Duck, "Experiments in ETV: Effects on Edited Cutaways," *Educational Broadcasting International* 8 (1975): 36–37.

119. J. P. Baggeley and S. W. Duck, "Experiments in ETV: Interviews and Edited Structure," *Educational Broadcasting International* 8 (1975): 93–94.

120. Zettl, *Sight, Sound, Motion: Applied Media Aesthetics*, 238–325.

121. A. A. Berger, "The Hidden Compulsion in Television," *Journal of the University Film Association* 30 (1978): 4–46.

122. Ibid., 46.

123. D. R. Anderson, S. R. Levin, and E. P. Lorch, "The Effects of TV Program Pacing on the Behavior of Pre-School Chil-

dren," *AV Communication Review* 25 (1977): 159–166.

124. Ibid., 164–165.

125. R. Schlater, "Effects of Speed of Presentation on Recall of Television Messages," *Journal of Broadcasting* 14 (1970): 207–214.

126. Millerson, *The Technique of Television Production*, 248.

127. T. Schwartz, "Listen," *TV Guide* 27 (1979): 1.

128. B. Skalnik, "The Ears Have It," *Educational Broadcasting* 9 (1976): 49.

129. M. Schubin, "TV Sound: The Bastard Gets Around," *Videography* 1 (1976): 41.

130. Zettl, *Sight, Sound, Motion: Applied Media Aesthetics,* 328–379.

131. Millerson, *The Technique of Television Production*, 319–327.

132. Zettl, "The Rare Case of Television Aesthetics," 5.

133. Millerson, *The Technique of Television Production*, 327.

134. F. A. Saunders, "Physics & Music," *Readings from Scientific American: The Physics of Music* (San Francisco: W. H. Freeman, 1978), 7–15.

135. G. Murch, *Visual and Auditory Perception*, 159–213.

136. B. J. Morgan and O. R. Lindsley, "Operant Preference for Stereophonic over Monophonic Music," *Journal of Music Therapy* 3 (1966): 135–143.

137. S. Dworkin and A. Holden, "An Experimental Evaluation of Sound Filmstrips vs. Classroom Lectures," *Journal of the Society of Motion Engineers* 68 (1959): 383–385.

138. J. O. Hempstead, "Media and the Learner: The Influence of Media Message Components on Students' Recall and Attitudes toward the Learning Experiment," Ph.D. Dissertation, University of Wisconsin, Madisoin, 1973.

139. J. E. Morrell, C. R. Walker, C. Loughery, J. Funk, G. Ruoff, and B. B. Proger, "Cognitive and Affective Effects of Audio-Programmed Electronic Feedback and Oral Teacher Feedback," *AV Communication Review* 22 (1974): 303–315.

140. R. E. Main and B. Griffiths, "Evaluation of Audio and Pictorial Instructional Supplements," *AV Communication Review* 25 (1977): 167–179.

141. R. F. Hartman, "Recognition Learning under Multiple Channels Presentation and Testing Conditions," *AV Communication Review* 9 (1961): 24–93.

142. D. L. Nasser and W. J. McEwen, "The Impact of Alternative Media Channels: Recall and Involvement with Messages," *AV Communication Review* 29 (1976): 263–272.

143. R. L. Campeau, "Selective Review of the Results of Research on the Use of Audio-Visual Media to Teach Adults," *AV Communication Review* 22 (1974): 5–39.

144. H. Zettl, "The Study of Television Aesthetics," *Educational Broadcasting Review* 2 (1968): 40.

145. Dondis, op. cit., 181.

20
Program Development Research

John R. Bittner
James K. Carroll

Program development research has its greatest application in producing instructional television (ITV) programming. A stage-by-stage process combining different research methods, program development research is defined as identifying, constructing, implementing, and evaluating an ITV program based on predetermined instructional goals and the needs of a target audience.[1] Applying this definition, we might produce an ITV program to teach sailing to high school students or narrow the goals and the audience to produce an ITV program on television lighting for college TV production classes.

The increased importance of ITV programming and the prospects for its expanded use make program development research an important part of broadcast communication. Since the 1960s, the academic community has placed increased emphasis on accountable ITV programming—programming that can be proven to satisfy certain needs or accomplish specific predetermined goals. Another area of rapid growth is the use of ITV in business and industry; more major corporations now use television for in-house training and information than there are commercial television stations in the United States. In addition, new technologies such as fiber optics and satellite communication are dramatically increasing available communication channels, many of which will carry ITV programming. The Annenberg University of the Air and the Corporation for Public Broadcasting's commissioned study of ITV in colleges and universities indicate that ITV is a continuing area of interest and expansion.[2]

Despite activity in ITV, educators and administrators are realizing that to be an acceptable educational tool, ITV must be cost effective, especially when compared to other instructional strategies. Emphasis thus has been placed on applying and evaluating ITV through systems models where cost benefits must be viewed in comparison to program effectiveness.[3] This stress on producing accountable ITV involves a stage-by-stage process we have labeled program development research.[4] This essay examines this process stage by stage, knowing that the reader may become involved in producing accountable ITV programming. Understanding this process stage by stage will enable the reader to be a more responsible practitioner and consumer of ITV programming.

Stage 1: Program Planning

Stage 1 of program development research involves the planning and initial research functions associated with launching the production process. The first consideration is precisely determining the identified population with an identified need.

Researching the Target Audience

Developing an accountable ITV program requires researching the characteristics of the target audience and understanding what learning capacities or deficiencies may exist. A good way to begin studying these characteristics is to examine other teaching and learning materials used successfully with the same audience. For example, if we decide to produce an ITV program about television lighting techniques for junior high school students, we would employ a different strategy than that used with the same subject for college students. The language level and thus the script would differ. The attention span would also be different. The range of abilities would vary to a greater degree in junior high school, since the college curriculum can eliminate some slow learners. Such basic considerations become important in the program planning stage of program development research.

Identifying Need and Selecting a Medium

Equally important to understanding the population is identifying the need. Too many education and media proponents give scant attention to whether an ITV program is needed or whether another mode of presentation would be more efficient, more effective, and even less costly. Some subjects and learning atmospheres lend themselves better to media other than ITV.

Dale aptly demonstrates the different learning conditions of various media when he dis-cusses information as being presented at different levels of abstraction.[5] The highest level of abstraction, Dale posits, is that of verbal symbols — written or spoken words. At the lowest level of abstraction is direct, purposeful experience. About midway between these two extremes is instructional television. Trying to use ITV to teach something that demands direct, purposeful experience will not work. For example, in spite of all the ITV teaching techniques we might employ, teaching someone to knit a sweater demands that the person work with knitting needles and yarn — a direct, purposeful experience. Similarly, spending thousands of dollars to produce an ITV program to teach policy and coverage plans to insurance agents would be a waste of money when a booklet would do the job as well.

In addition, do not overlook the possibility that someone else may have produced the ITV program being planned. Major libraries of ITV programs have evolved, some associated with individual schools and colleges, some aligned with state systems of education, and some privately supported depositories. If a program meeting the needs of the target audience is available and we can use it, producing another is a waste of time.

Reviewing the Literature and Consulting Experts

No one is an expert in everything, and people involved in developing ITV programs realize this more than most. An accountable program demands consulting what others have written and what the experts know.

Assume we have decided to produce a short ITV program teaching some basic elements of television lighting to college students in a television production course. Our ITV program will be used as an insert in a lecture and placed on library reserve so students can review the program. As a start, we will review some key literature about television lighting. Books related to the subject would be the most readily available source; general television production texts and works on television lighting may suffice. More complex ITV programs will demand more detailed research. A ten-part series on key Civil War battles would require more research than our example of television lighting.

Consulting experts, both content and instructional, is next. In developing any ITV program, experts can add insights that might not appear in the literature and can also point out new developments. The teacher planning to use the program should be consulted at every stage of program development. He or she must feel positive about the program and can add important input on how the program can be adapted to fit particular course needs.

Consulting with an engineer is also vital. Every medium has its limitations, and television is no exception. Knowing what the medium cannot do is as important as knowing what it can do. Perhaps special hookups or circuits are needed, or perhaps existing facilities need modification for a special production problem. Keeping the engineer apprised of the program's goals and the production schedule is critical to avoid technical pitfalls that could jeopardize the production.

Stage 2: Identifying Objectives

Once we have made the decision to move ahead with the ITV program, the second stage in the developmental research process is to identify the program's objectives.

General Objectives

Refer again to our hypothetical program teaching TV lighting. We first list important concepts we want to communicate, such as (1) the functions of the key, back, and fill lights; (2) positioning of these lights; and (3) lighting intensity adjustments. These preliminary statements of important concepts or goals, the general objectives, precede the more specific behavioral objectives.

Second, these concepts or general objectives should be arranged in a logical sequence. For instance, we have listed as 1, 2, and 3 the basic concepts we want our ITV program to teach. If we rearrange these objectives and produce our

program accordingly, we might confuse the student. To understand the correct positioning of the lights, we first must know their functions. To understand intensity, we must know about both functions and positions of the lights. That is why we arranged our objectives — functions, positioning, and intensity — in this order.[6] In doing so, we are identifying specific en route behaviors, which consider building antecedent abilities — every objective logically prepares the student for the next one. We may also want to specify entry behaviors — prerequisite skills the student should possess before viewing the program. The student preparing to view our proposed ITV program on television lighting should first be able to read a light meter. Thus, the ability to read the light meter is an entry behavior.

Behavioral Objectives

Now that general objectives have been developed, we can move on to behavioral objectives: precise statements that systematically describe a given set of measurable behaviors a learner is to demonstrate after viewing the ITV program.

Behavioral objectives, when written properly, consist of three distinct parts: conditions, terminal behavior, and criterion. The conditions describe what the learner will have available while attempting to demonstrate success in achieving the objective. For our ITV program on television lighting, the conditions portion of a behavioral objective for positioning the lights could read:

> Given a series of pencil-and-paper examination questions describing functions of the key, back, and fill lights, the student will. . . .

Terminal behavior refers to the end product, or learner behavior desired after viewing the ITV program. Using this example, the objective could be expanded to include the terminal behavior enclosed here by parentheses:

> Given a series of pencil-and-paper examination questions describing the functions of

key, back, and fill lights, the student will (correctly identify the functions of each light . . .).

The final portion of a well-written behavioral objective includes the criterion—the minimum level of acceptable performance the learner should demonstrate after viewing the ITV program.[7] We would expand our sample objective to include the criterion (enclosed in parentheses):

Given a series of pencil-and-paper examination questions describing the functions of key, back, and fill lights, the student will correctly identify the functions of each light (with 75 percent accuracy).

When the minimum level of acceptable performance is not specified in a given objective, we may assume that 100 percent accuracy is expected. Criteria will be discussed in more detail in Stage 4 of program development research.

Now that we have completed a sample behavioral objective for the functions of the lights, we write a behavioral objective for the positions of the lights and another for the intensity adjustment. For positions of the lights, the behavioral objective will read:

Given a series of pencil-and-paper examination questions describing positioning of the key, back, and fill lights, the student will correctly identify the positioning of each light with 75 percent accuracy.

For the intensity adjustments, the objective will read:

Given a series of pencil-and-paper examination questions describing intensity adjustments of the key, back, and fill lights, the student will correctly identify the correct intensity of each light with 75 percent accuracy.

The Action Verb in Behavioral Objectives

Notice that the sample objective uses the action verb *identify,* an important part of a be-

havioral objective. Below are two partial lists of verbs, one with verbs that are vague, the other with verbs open to fewer interpretations.

Vague

be aware of	appreciate
learn	know
study	believe
understand	assume
enjoy	value
apply	perform
contribute	succeed
consider	realize
teach	grasp

Less Vague

describe	solve
locate	write
list	recite
contrast	differentiate
identify	state
draw	select
diagram	discuss
collect	add
compare	multiply

Terminal behavior should be described only by the verbs open to the fewest possible interpretations. Behavioral objectives attempt to clarify the end product of an instructional sequence; ambiguous verbs defeat the objective. In the case of our television lighting program where highly specific information is being taught, verbs located under the heading "Less Vague" clarify exactly what students must do in order to demonstrate success in achieving the objective.

Reviewing briefly, remember some common characteristics of well-written behavioral objectives. First, the behavioral objective should communicate a given instructional intent, or what the learner can do once he or she has viewed the ITV program. Second, a behavioral objective should exclude all possible alternatives; each objective should contain only one main concept. As the number of concepts increase, so should the number of behavioral ob-

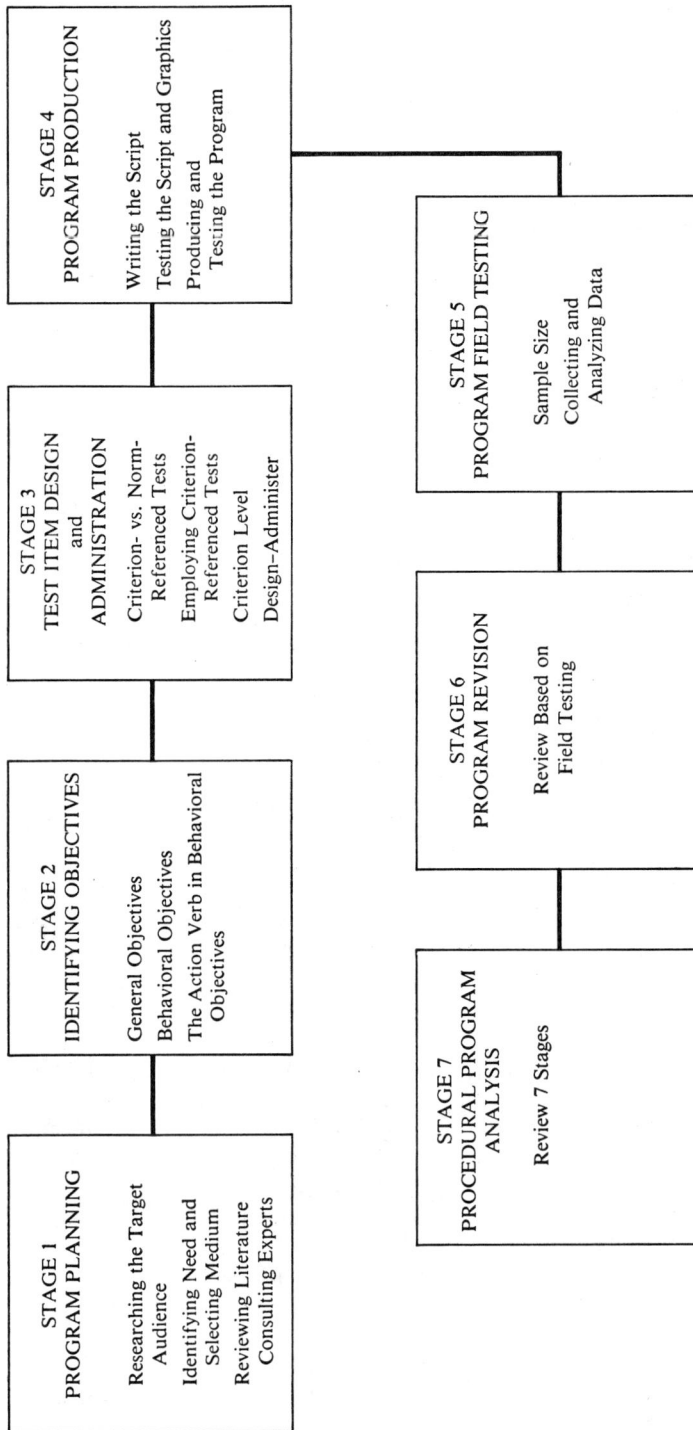

STAGE 1
PROGRAM PLANNING

Researching the Target
Audience
Identifying Need and
Selecting Medium
Reviewing Literature
Consulting Experts

STAGE 2
IDENTIFYING OBJECTIVES

General Objectives
Behavioral Objectives
The Action Verb in Behavioral
Objectives

STAGE 3
TEST ITEM DESIGN
and
ADMINISTRATION

Criterion- vs. Norm-
Referenced Tests
Employing Criterion-
Referenced Tests
Criterion Level
Design–Administer

STAGE 4
PROGRAM PRODUCTION

Writing the Script
Testing the Script and Graphics
Producing and
Testing the Program

STAGE 5
PROGRAM FIELD TESTING

Sample Size
Collecting and
Analyzing Data

STAGE 6
PROGRAM REVISION

Review Based on
Field Testing

STAGE 7
PROCEDURAL PROGRAM
ANALYSIS

Review 7 Stages

Figure 20-1   The formative research process.

jectives. Third, achievement can be measured. Finally, an objective should use an appropriate action verb.

Stage 3: Test Item Design and Administration

In Stage 3 of program development research, test items to measure the performance stated in the behavioral objectives are designed and pilot tested. Specifically, we want to measure en route and terminal behaviors. In an actual classroom situation, we want to be sure we can test entry behaviors—in our ITV program, reading a light meter.

Testing for en route behaviors is important for two reasons. First, since we are presenting an ITV program with sequential learning, we need to make sure students achieve successful performance on the objective presented first before going on to later ones. Second, in more elaborate ITV programs where an entire series is produced, measuring en route behaviors before showing the program can indicate advanced students who know what is taught in one part of the ITV series and thus can bypass this part and move on to subsequent parts. Where ITV programs are stored in information retrieval systems and self-paced individual viewing exists, measuring entry and en route behaviors becomes more critical.

Criterion-Referenced Tests versus Norm-Referenced Tests

Tests measuring student behavior can be classified into two categories: criterion-referenced and norm-referenced tests. Criterion-referenced tests assess an individual's competence in relation to a predetermined standard and performance level. They grow directly out of behavioral objectives. The predetermined standard represents the terminal behavior specified in the behavioral objective, and the performance level represents the minimum level of performance needed for mastery of the objective. In our hypothetical ITV program, the terminal behavior is concerned with gaining knowledge about television lighting and

the minimum level of performance is 75 percent accuracy.

Norm-referenced tests compare an individual's performance in relation to others on the same test. Assessment of individual change is not a primary concern of norm-referenced tests and, as a result, the use of such tests gives little indication of the degree of learning that takes place. Rather, the tests point out that one individual is more proficient than another. Behavioral objectives are seldom used in conjunction with norm-referenced tests. Thus our discussion deals with criterion-referenced tests to measure student performance based on our behavioral objectives.

Employing Criterion-Referenced Tests

Criterion-referenced testing is an integral part of the teaching-learning process. Objectives are written, teaching based on these objectives is initiated, learning occurs, and the degree of learning is measured. Results of criterion-referenced tests can be used to determine which objectives have been achieved by a particular student, and which objectives need further work. In elaborate ITV programs where pre-tests are administered, students can be directed to more relevant objectives or other parts of the ITV series as indicated by their entry-level achievement. Learning is measured independently of any reference to the performance of others. Because an individual's performance on a criterion-referenced test is measured in relation to some performance standard, this standard, as stated in the behavioral objective, must be determined before constructing the tests. Once this standard has been determined, test results are used to locate a student's progress toward achieving the criterion reference.

The criterion-referenced test must be complete before the ITV program can be finished. Although this process may appear to be in reverse of logical program development, the procedure is valid. Preparing good and appropriate test items once the program has been produced is impossible and nullifies the progressive stage-by-stage process of program development research. Designing the criterion-referenced test first provides an opportunity to determine the precise kinds of terminal and en route behaviors desired throughout the program. Caution should also be taken to avoid the pitfall of throwing in test items whose reflected behaviors are absent from the stated objectives. An item-by-item check of each behavioral objective should occur as the criterion-referenced test is designed.

Minimum Designated Criterion

To achieve mastery of the predetermined behavioral objective, the student must meet a minimum designated criterion. To determine a realistic criterion figure, most often expressed in percentages (70 percent, 80 percent, 90 percent, etc.), a few guidelines exist. Selecting an appropriate criterion level may originate as intuition based on our experience with the subject matter. This criterion decision, using intuitive thinking, may change over time and after a re-evaluation of the behaviors expressed. Another aid in selecting an appropriate test criterion is the performance of previous learners in the same or similar kinds of content areas. Finally, assistance from teaching colleagues proficient in the subject may be invaluable in selecting appropriate criterion levels. The maximum realistic figure for establishing a criterion measure is 85 percent.[8] Any figure above this is likely to cause undue frustration on the part of both student and teacher.

Designing the Test Instrument

Applying our discussion to our hypothetical ITV program on television lighting, we would first construct sample examination questions to test each behavioral objective. We might construct four multiple-choice questions to test each objective—a total of twelve questions. Content validity would be important—making sure the test accurately reflected the information we wanted to test. Checking with experts in test design would be beneficial. Appropriate reliability checks would also be necessary. Under no circumstances should we include questions not reflected in the behavioral objectives; they tell nothing about the effectiveness of the production.

If we decide to develop both a pre- and post-test, two test forms with parallel questions will be necessary. The pretest will be almost identical to the posttest, but with slightly different phrasing. Students thus will not learn the posttest answers by taking the pretest. A pretest measure helps determine whether some students already know about the functions, positioning, and intensity adjustments of lights and can therefore bypass the ITV program and go on to other material. As noted, pretests are especially valuable when multipart programs are used or self-paced learning is administered.

Test Administration

We want to administer the tests on a sample population to determine whether the tests are parallel and where test revision might be necessary.[9] For example, if results show most students are answering certain questions, then these questions may be too easy. Perhaps the multiple-choice questions lack variety, or perhaps we inadvertently referred to the correct answer in writing the question. Or, perhaps students do not understand certain words in a question. This is a common mistake when dealing with beginning students. Content experts are involved with their own jargon; they forget that students unfamiliar with the discipline do not understand many of the terms. Good test design and administration eliminate these pitfalls before the final test instrument is reproduced.

Checking that questions are parallel is important. Suppose we designed question one on both the pretest and posttest to be parallel and then test this information. If most students miss the question on the posttest, but answer it correctly on the pretest, we would want to determine what caused the problem and rectify it.

Different philosophies abound on how the sample instrument should be administered. Some prefer to administer the testing instruments to a target audience but not provide any instruction in the subject matter with which the ITV program deals. Others prefer to administer a pretest, lecture the audience on the subject matter, then administer the posttest. The lead author of this essay, in working with ITV at the college level, prefers a combination of methods. He assembles a group of approximately ten people who understand the subject matter (advanced students) and gives each a copy of the tests and answers. Then an open discussion of the test instruments' wording takes place. Although administering the tests to a target population is still important, minimal revision has been necessary when a frank discussion of the tests has been conducted.

Clearly, however, no shortcuts can be taken at this stage of program development research. The test instruments must accurately measure attainment of the goal stated in the behavioral objective. The inconvenience of repeating a test adminstration, checking on content or wording, or checking with colleagues or target audience members is a small price to pay for the assurance that the tests are valid. A large sample is not necessary, but the tests must be administered to a target audience identical or as close as possible to the audience for which the ITV program is intended.[10] Even one grade level can cause serious problems and render a program useless. The purpose of administering the test at this stage is to improve on its construction, not test what the student knows.

Stage 4: Program Production

In Stage 4, the actual production of our ITV program takes place. Here, the results of the previous stages of program development research come to bear on the final instructional product.

Writing the Script

Just as we worked closely with the behavioral objectives when preparing tests to measure student performance, we work closely with the behavioral objectives when preparing the script. If professional help from an experienced writer is available, use it. If not, make sure the script undergoes revision until it is as succinct as possible. Although good production and artistic presentation are important and help hold student interest, the final program test is how well it teaches the objectives. A creative masterpiece is useless unless it gets the job done. Of course, the goal should be to integrate both results and artistic expression into the final product, keeping in mind that the true test will be how well students score on the examination questions.

Another important consideration will be program length. Since our program is relatively short, we do not need to be concerned with viewer fatigue. But research and practice indicate that twenty to thirty minutes pushes the attention span to its limit. Shorter programs properly integrated into lectures are more effective. Thus, when planning an ITV production, remember the time element. An evening prime-time documentary that can be watched by the casual viewer differs from an in-school production on which the viewers will be tested on what they have learned directly from the program.

Learner practice built into the script is also important, especially when trying to teach difficult concepts. Review questions followed by the correct answers can be written into the script to self-test the viewer. Repetition is another good device. Appropriate review and reinforcement can also be obtained through graphics or characters superimposed over the visual.

Testing the Script and Graphics

Now that we have written the script and designed the basic graphics, it is time to try out the program. Notice we try it out before it is actually produced. It is easier and less costly to test the script and graphics now than to produce a complete program and have to revise it.

Select a target audience that mirrors the audience for whom the ITV program will be produced. By reading the script aloud, displaying the graphics or enlarged storyboard, and then testing the target audience, we can immediately see where the script and graphics need work. Notice we said script and graphics, not the objectives or the test. The revision is in the program, not in the goals or the method of measuring the successful attainment of those goals. Following an analysis of the test results, including audience comments about the program, we revise the script and graphics. Another test of the script and graphics may be necessary. If everything appears satisfactory and we are meeting our criterion (75 percent accuracy on the set of four questions corresponding to each behavioral objective), we can produce the program.

Producing and Testing the Program

During production, we need to remember the program's specific purpose and not be distracted by new artistic opportunities that might destroy the program's effectiveness. Changing camera shots, altering the set, and other changes when production begins must be monitored for their effect on the finished product. After the program is produced, it is time to try it out on a larger population.

Stage 5: Program Field Testing

The program is now presented to many students under actual field testing conditions. Again, a number of principles should be considered.

Sample Size

The sample population should be large enough to produce an acceptable minimum sample error based on the size of the audience that will eventually view the program. An appropriate experimental design must also be selected.

Avoid testing students who will not be part of the population exposed to the program. Decisions about revising an ITV program would have a shaky foundation if based on data obtained from Iowa farmers when the subject is ice fishing and is to be aired in Alaska high schools.

Collecting and Analyzing Data

To revise in a logical and constructive manner, data must be carefully collected and analyzed. Avoid immediate inferences based on field data. Where a separate field testing staff is employed, guidelines should be strictly enforced concerning premature inferences based on casual observation. If funds are available, the problem can be alleviated by hiring an independent consulting firm without a vested interest in the program's success.

With a general idea of the program field-testing stage in mind, let us turn again to our hypothetical television lighting program. Assume that the target audience of fifty students will come from multiple sections of a college-level introductory television production course and that they enter the course with no background in television lighting skills. To verify this assumption, we interview each student, selecting only students with no experience. The enrollment may be diminished slightly, given the results of our preinterview session and the possibility of a few students dropping the course.

When our student groups have been randomly assembled and the pretests, ITV program, and posttests administered, appropriate statistical comparisons can take place. Gain scores between pretest and posttest can be compiled. Depending on the sophistication of the experimental design, checks on sampling and test effect can be made.[11] Further checks on parallel questions between the pretest and posttest forms can also be built into the design. A means of collecting student opinions about the program and tests also should be included.

The simplest and most effective method is to permit each student to write an opinion on the back of the test. This method permits the greatest latitude for expression. Specific questions are not advised because they can narrow the possible responses and eliminate an important comment or reaction. A perusal or content analysis of these written opinions will suggest possible changes in the program or test. Some student opinions may be peripheral to the program's subject. For example, a student might state that a particular scene is "silly and trite." Or a student might note that a certain dialogue is "condescending and sexist." These comments do not deal directly with the program's subject, yet they do alert the producer to certain program conditions that could interfere with learning process.

Stage 6: Program Revision

When the results of field testing have been analyzed, the instructional program is revised, if needed. Given the luxury of time and finances, many field testings may occur with subsequent revisions. These field tests may entail all or part of the instructional program, depending on how elaborate the program is, how many parts are involved, and the initial results.

Some important principles must be considered when revising the program. Because of a tendency to protect one's interests, the person responsible for the program should not lead the revision. It is easy to overlook negative results and assume success when a program is actually deficient. The primary consideration is for the student to achieve the predetermined behavioral objectives. If this does not occur, revising those portions of the program responsible for the failure must be undertaken. This could include additional and more relevant practice, better sequential arrangement of material, and a more concerted effort in promoting interest in the program.

Stage 7: Procedural Program Analysis

In this final stage in program development research, an examination is made of all procedures used in completing the preceding stages. For instance, the rules and guidelines making up each stage of the production process are scrutinized. In addition, revision procedures are screened with alternate methods considered. When faulty measures are discovered, they are revised.

In the case of our TV lighting program, a careful analysis might be made of such items as the type of test questions used, the statistical methods used in analyzing field data, the type and amount of practice afforded each student while viewing the program, and the nature and applicability of each revision. Stage 7 is a general review stage, a check and recheck before the ITV program is released for distribution.

Summary

This essay defines program development research as: Identifying, constructing, implementing, and evaluating an ITV program based on predetermined instructional needs of a goal and the target audience. The practical application of the definition to the design and execution of a developmental research project entails a series of progressive steps.

In Stage 1, Program Planning, planning decisions are made, the target audience analyzed, subject matter researched, and experts consulted. Stage 2 is Identifying Objectives. Behavioral objectives are precise written statements systematically describing a given set of observable behaviors a learner is to demonstrate after viewing the ITV program. Behavioral objectives consist of three distinct parts: conditions, terminal behavior, and a criterion. Stage 3, Test Item Design and Administration, examines the expected behaviors in the target audience and then designs and pilot tests instruments to test those behaviors. Stage 4 is Program Production, where the ITV program is actually produced. Stage 5 in program development research consists of Program Field Testing. Design strategy is selected, and the program is administered to many members of the target audience under field testing conditions. Following results of the field testing, Stage 6, Program Revision, occurs. In the final stage, Procedural Program Analysis, a complete review is made of all procedures used in the previous six stages.

With the increased use of ITV in all levels of education and industry, program development research is becoming an increasingly important strategy.

Endnotes

1. Adapted from James K. Carroll and John R. Bittner, "A Developmental Model for Validating Instructional Programming," *International Journal of Instructional Media* 2 (1975): 211–215.

2. "Annenberg May Give $150 Million for a 'National University of the Air,'" *The Chronicle of Higher Education* 18 (1979): 2; "CPB Documents Use of ITV at Colleges," *Broadcasting* 48 (1979): 68, 70.

3. Some recent examples of these concerns can be found in P. O. Marsh, "The Instructional Message: A Theoretical Perspective," *ECTJ* 27 (1979): 303–318; R. Kaufman, "From HOW to WHAT to WHY: The Search for Educational Utility," *ECTJ* 26 (1978): 107–121; S. Thiagarajan, "Instructional Product Verification and Revision: 20 Questions and 200 Speculations," *ECTJ* 26 (1978): 133–141.

4. W. J. Popham and E. L. Baker, *Rules for the Development of Instructional Products* (New York: American Book Company, 1971). The authors are indebted to Popham and Baker for their pioneering work in developmental processes from which many ideas originated and are presented here as they relate to ITV programming.

5. E. Dale, *Audio Visual Methods in Teaching*, 3rd ed. (Hinsdale; Ill.: Dryden Press, 1969), 180–134.

6. Objectives can also be arranged in order of importance when sequential learning is not required.

7. On some occasions, behavioral objectives can be stated without a specific criterion, usually when the information deals with difficult to measure or even nonmeasurable behavior and uses such vague concepts as *application* or *support*. For example, a behavioral objective could read: *Given twenty scaled items dealing with the uses of television for instructional purposes, the student will indicate his or her appreciation of the medium as a tool for education.* Notice the measuring instrument is a scaled item where no right or wrong answer is possible. A nonmeasurable objective could read: *Having viewed an ITV program on television lighting, the student will develop a greater appreciation for the role television lighting plays in the production process.* Each of these objectives could be said to deal with behavioral objectives commonly associated with the affective domain—values, opinions, likes, dislikes, beliefs—in comparison to behavioral objectives associated with the cognitive domain—knowledge acquisition, skill development, and other behaviors that are easily identified, observable, and measurable.

8. C. C. Ross and J. C. Stanley, *Measurement in Today's Schools* (Englewood Cliffs, N.J.: Prentice-Hall, 1969), 101.

9. This is ideally accomplished through an item analysis, where we can determine how many students selected each possible choice on each multiple-choice question. To examine the importance of an item analysis, let us assume we have produced an ITV program dealing with the effects of sugar on our bodies. The program is designed for eighth graders. To hold their attention, we have included animation. In a segment explaining how too much sugar can overload the pancreas and force it to work hard to produce insulin, we show a cartoon character holding its stomach as the narrator explains the function of the pancreas. In the test of this program, we include the following question:

> Eating too many sweets can cause your pancreas to:
>   A. stop functioning.
>   B. work hard to produce insulin.
>   C. transform sucrose into waste.
>   D. inflict severe stomach cramps.

When we run an item analysis of the multiple-choice questions, we find that out of thirty children taking the test, the answers were apportioned among the four choices as follows:
A. 0 selected answer A.
B. 20 selected answer B (the correct answer).
C. 1 selected answer C.
D. 9 selected answer D.

Based on our test, we see that our program did not meet its objective since only 67 percent of the group selected the correct answer (20 is 67 percent of 30). What went wrong? Perhaps the script needs rewriting. A closer examination of the item analysis, however, reveals that students translated our cartoon character holding his stomach to mean that eating too many sweets can cause stomach cramps. Thus, the key to revising the program is not to change the script but to change the visual example. Yet, without the item analysis, we might not have known what went wrong.

10. An appropriate method of administering the exam is to split a class of thirty into two groups of fifteen students each. Group One takes the pretest while Group Two takes the posttest. When the testing is completed, Group One takes the posttest while Group Two takes the pretest. In this manner, all thirty students take both forms. The reason for breaking the exam down into two forms and administering it in two parts is to disguise the parallel questions. Students will never have more than one form in front of them at a time. This procedure used in our hypothetical example represents alternative-form reliability.

11. See especially D. T. Campbell and J. C. Stanley, *Experimental and Quasi-Experimental Designs for Research* (Chicago: Rand McNally, 1966), 13–22.

Additional References

Bunyan, J. A., and M. C. Crimmins. *Television and Management: The Manager's Guide to Video,* White Plains, N.Y.: Knowledge Industry Publications, 1977.

Cronback, L. J. *Essentials of Testing,* 3rd ed., New York: Harper & Row, 1970.

Gagne, R., and L. J. Briggs. *Principles of Instructional Design,* New York: Holt, Rinehart and Winston, 1974.

Kibler, R. J., D. J. Cegala, L. L. Barker, and D. T. Miles. *Objectives for Instruction and Evaluation,* Boston: Allyn and Bacon, 1974.

Wood, D. N., an D. G. Wylie. *Educational Telecommunications,* Belmont, Calif.: Wadsworth Publishing, 1977.

Name Index

Subject Index